# CHILD DEVELOPMENT

**The Dorsey Series in Psychology**

**Advisory Editor**
**Wendell E. Jeffrey**
*University of California, Los Angeles*

# CHILD DEVELOPMENT

## Psychological, Sociocultural, and Biological Factors

**Carol Tomlinson-Keasey**

University of California, Riverside

**1985**

**THE DORSEY PRESS**
Homewood, Illinois 60430

ISBN 0-256-03104-5

Library of Congress Catalog Card No. 84–72286

*Printed in the United States of America*

1 2 3 4 5 6 7 8 9 0 D 2 1 0 9 8 7 6 5

*To Blake, Kai and Amber*

# Preface

In the last decade, our understanding of how children develop has undergone unprecedented growth. This growth results in part from the sheer volume of research in a variety of new areas. But the change in the field reflects more than just additions to our knowledge. What we are seeing is a new way of looking at this knowledge. Psychologists are no longer content to present differing views and let the proponents of those views argue their cases. Instead, we recognize the legitimacy of a variety of approaches to understanding child development. Further, developmental psychologists are attempting to integrate these differing points of view into a more complete and coherent view of the child.

This text furthers that integration process by presenting psychological, social, and biological factors that intertwine in the life of a child. This text covers the traditional topics of a child development text, but it does so with a view toward interrelating these various influences. As such, it offers a balanced picture of the various forces that guide a child.

Although psychologists have always acknowledged a role for biological factors, the mention of these factors has been largely confined to chapters on genetics. After that, biological factors seemed to fade from the scene. The biological background of the child is seen as a continuing influence in this text. In discussions of language acquisition, competence, and attachment, the biological heritage of the child is integrated with the psychological and sociological forces that are operating.

Social factors that influence development have often received fleeting mention in textbooks. New information from children who overcome early, stressful environments indicates that social factors are often as important as psychological factors in determining the path the child will take. Hence, discussions of sex differences, schooling, and parent-child relationships pay heed to the importance of sociological factors.

Even when covering the standard psychological influences on child development, this text takes a somewhat different approach. The attempt is to blend the contributions of several views of the child into a multifaceted and flexible understanding of the forces that create the individuality we prize.

The integration and organization that are hallmarks of this text necessitate a topical, rather than a chronological, approach. A topical approach has several advantages. First, students are presented with the complete discussion of a topic in a single chapter. This encourages a coherent understanding of the area. It also enables professors to present issues and differing theoretical positions. Finally, a topical approach encourages a discussion of methodological issues. The methods used become critical if students are to understand that different approaches all contribute something novel to our understanding of children.

The field of child development has become so large that no text can cover all of the important experiments. Authors must choose which experiments merit detailed discussion and which experiments are mentioned in passing. My strategy in selecting experiments was to discuss a representative or pivotal experiment in enough detail so that students could understand how the researchers reached their conclusions. Then other similar experiments were mentioned to reinforce or extend the findings of the "example." This strategy makes the book organized, readable, and interesting to students. When combined with a topical approach, this strategy means that students can get into the heart of a field for a brief moment and then step back again for more general discussion.

A book that is well organized and presents material in an integrated way is inherently more interesting to students than one which lacks a coherent story line. In this text, I have tried within each chapter to tell a story about the research in that area. Often, the story is embellished with case histories that make the point in a way that experiments never could. The case histories are not appended or isolated. They are embedded in the story and present an interesting character for the student to use as a reference.

Another example of the integrative approach of this text is the way adolescence is treated. The development of adolescents is often discussed in a chapter or two at the end of child-development texts. In keeping with my stress on an organized, coherent approach to a topic, I have presented information on adolescence within each topic. When cognitive development is discussed, the cognitive operations of adolescents are described. When peer relationships are the topic, the changing influence of peers is traced from infancy through adolescence. Whether the topic is divorce or brain development, the meaningful literature on adolescence is woven into the chapter.

As a professor, I feel a continuing responsibility to prepare my students for the demanding, yet rewarding task of raising children. Hence, this text includes research on contemporary problems that parents face. Genetic counseling, the effects of divorce on children, and maternal employment are just a sample of topics that are relevant to contemporary parents.

Understanding human behavior is an adventure. In this text, I have tried to capture some of the spirit and wisdom which developmental psychologists have brought to their research. My hope is that students will enjoy this book, learn from it, and become involved in the adventure of understanding development.

During the long months of writing this book, I incurred many debts to people who encouraged me by discussing, criticizing, and praising each chapter. The first line of review was my husband, Blake Keasey, whose thoughtful and repeated readings of the manuscript were coupled with continuing discussions of the material. His effort helped turn wandering descriptions into a more vivid story about development. Furthermore, he even acted like he enjoyed it. To give me time, he made dozens of sacrifices. Undoubtedly, the biggest was taking the children to Europe for six weeks so that my writing would not be disturbed!

Reviewers from all areas of developmental psychology spent long hours correcting both substantive and expository lapses. It pleases me to be able to thank Wendell Jeffrey; David Brodzinsky, Rutgers University; Dave Moshman, University of Nebraska-Lincoln; Joseph C. LaVoie, University of Nebraska-Omaha; Edith D. Neimark, Rutgers University; John Ireland, University of Evansville; Jeanette Reuter, Kent College; Robert Plomin, University of Colorado; Anita M. Sostek, Georgetown University Hospital; Nancy A. Busch-Rossnagel, Colorado State University; and Joyce Jones, Cornell University for their contribution to the text. The staff from the Dorsey Press were honest, humorous, and helpful as they guided me through the publishing process. The finished text owes a great deal to their counsel. The final product, of course, represents the end result of a thousand decisions to include some material and exclude other. These decisions are the lonely province of the author.

Writing a book on human development sounds so easy, especially when you have taught the course for so many years and think you have such a clear idea of what would really help a book be exciting and meaningful to students. The completion of the project, however, places an untold and unexpected burden on family and friends. My running partner, Lynda Warren, was subjected to chronic egocentric ramblings as the book slowly took shape. Her only defense was to fun faster so I would have to end my ramblings. Family members are equally helpless. They are expected to be tolerant, to help readily when asked, and to slight their own projects in the interest of "the book." My children, Kai and Amber, helped initially by being understanding and taking over various household responsibilities. They also participated in more active ways by checking bibliographic references, typing tables of contents, and writing programs that changed references from "old" APA style to "new" APA style. Like Blake, they gave unselfishly so that my goal could be realized. Dedicating this book to the three of them is a token acknowledgement of their unfailing support.

**Carol Tomlinson-Keasey**

# Contents

## Part 2
## Infancy

## Part 3
## The mind's eye

# PART 1

## The roots of child development

# C H A P T E R    1

# Introduction to developmental psychology

## INTRODUCTION

Once upon a time there was a young prince, who believed in all things but three. He did not believe in princesses, he did not believe in islands, he did not believe in God. His father, the king, told him that such things did not exist. As there were no princesses or islands in his father's domaines, and no sign of God, the young prince believed his father.

But then, one day, the prince ran away from his palace. He came to the next land. There, to his astonishment, from every coast he saw islands, and on these islands, strange and troubling creatures whom he dared not name. As he was searching for a boat, a man in full evening dress approached him along the shore.

"Are those real islands?" asked the young prince.

"Of course they are real islands," said the man in evening dress.

"And those strange and troubling creatures?"

"They are all genuine and authentic princesses."

"Then God also must exist!" cried the prince.

"I am God," replied the man in full evening dress, with a bow.

The young prince returned home as quickly as he could.

"So you are back," said his father, the king.

"I have seen islands, I have seen princesses, I have seen God," said the prince reproachfully.

The king was unmoved.

"Neither real islands, nor real princesses, nor a real God, exist."

"I saw them!"

"Tell me how God was dressed."

"God was in full evening dress."

"Were the sleeves of his coat rolled back?"

The prince remembered that they had been. The king smiled.

"That is the uniform of a magician. You have been deceived."

At this, the prince returned to the next land, and went to the same shore, where once again he came upon the man in full evening dress.

"My father the king has told me who you are," said the young prince indignantly. "You deceived me last time, but not again. Now I know that those are not real islands and real princesses, because you are a magician."

The man on the shore smiled.

"It is you who are deceived, my boy. In your father's kingdom there are many islands and many princesses. But you are under your father's spell, so you cannot see them."

The prince returned pensively home. When he saw his father, he looked him in the eyes.

"Father, is it true that you are not a real king, but only a magician?"

The king smiled, and rolled back his sleeves.

"Yes, my son, I am only a magician."

"Then the man on the shore was God."

"The man on the shore was another magician."

"I must know the real truth, the truth beyond magic."

"There is no truth beyond magic," said the king.

The prince was full of sadness.

He said, "I will kill myself."

The king by magic caused death to appear. Death stood in the door and beckoned to the prince. The prince shuddered. He remembered the beautiful but unreal islands and the unreal but beautiful princesses.

"Very well," he said. "I can bear it."

"You see, my son," said the king, "you too now begin to be a magician."

Fowles, J. *The Magus: A Revised Version*, pp. 550–552. Copyright © 1965, 1977 by J. R. Fowles Ltd. By permission of Little, Brown & Company.

John Fowles' fable highlights some of the stumbling blocks that hinder the search for truth. Because any science is essentially a search for the truth, the prince's experiences can be extrapolated to the science of developmental psychology. Students embarking on a new course of study resemble the prince. These students usually have little background in the subject area, and therefore do not have the information to assess the truth of everything they hear and read. They are forced to believe their professors, just as the prince was forced to believe his father. But professors and authors, like the king in the fable cannot dispense "real" truth. When the king tells the prince that there is no truth, the prince vacillates between alternatives. As students become acquainted with developmental psychology, they too will realize that there is no real truth. Facts abound and several magicians compete for the students' attention, but absolute truth is elusive.

The domain of developmental psychology is similar to the prince's domain in other ways. The prince was concerned with islands, princesses, and gods. Developmental psychologists are concerned with factors that foster development—biological variables, childhood experiences, and a child's social climate. The prince's land lacked islands and princesses; the neighboring fiefdom had both. So it is in developmental psychology. In the search for truth, some researchers and theorists slight biological variables, while others tend to minimize the impact of the culture on the child.

Researchers and theorists who search for truth are the magicians in the fable. They examine a small realm of the total field of developmental psychology, and then establish current truths. These truths, however, are subject to the same frailties as the prince's truths. Developmental psychologists do not intentionally disregard information, but researchers with particular beliefs ask different questions and use different methods to answer their questions.

The following example illustrates how researchers' views might influence their interpretation of experiments. Psychologists who do not believe in stages of development are likely to look for quantitative differences between the way a preschooler and an adolescent remember information. They might demonstrate that a preschooler can remember 7 items from a list of meats, fruits, and vegetables, while an adolescent can remember 25. These psychologists believe that the memory skill is present in both preschoolers and adolescents, but is more developed in adolescents. From their point of view the change occurs in the quantity a child remembers.

Psychologists who believe children pass from one stage to another are interested in the differences between preschoolers' and adolescents' memories. In an identical experiment, they might notice that the preschoolers recalled items at random, while the adolescents first remembered the fruits, then the vegetables. For these psychologists, the important difference is a qualitative one—preschoolers do not classify the items in the list. These psychologists would conclude that adolescents have a quality to their memory skills that preschoolers lack.

This example demonstrates that psychological theorists and researchers sometimes take such different stances on the major issues in developmental psychology that it seems as if, like the prince, they are under the spell of a particular magician. In this chapter, the different magicians of developmental psychology are introduced. By looking at magicians who have once reigned and whose truths have been superseded by new truths, students are given an immediate advantage over the prince. They know that yesterday's truth has yielded to today's truth, and that tomorrow's truth will likewise change. Even though they may fall under the spell of a particular magician, they will know that other lands exist where the local magicians believe in the impossible.

## MAGICIANS FROM THE PAST

In medieval societies a special period for childhood, distinct from adulthood, was unknown. Life spans were short and the majority of children died before they were five. At the age of six or seven children began working, often for 14 to 16 hours a day (Kessen, 1965). Children, however, were not considered neglected; they simply belonged to a culture and time when human life had little value. Life for everyone was a struggle and no special concern or understanding extended to the childhood years (Aries, 1962).

The awareness that the childhood years deserved some special attention and consideration came during the 18th and 19th centuries. Jean Jacques Rousseau and John Locke were primarily interested in philosophical questions about the nature of humans, but they broached the idea, for the first time in Western culture, that the skills and deficiencies of adults might be traced to the experiences of the child. Each of these men saw the childhood years in a somewhat different way. John Locke argued forcefully that children were blank tablets waiting to be etched by their experiences. It was the responsibility of society and parents to train children and mold their characters for the betterment of the society.

Rousseau thought children were noble and untainted. Children, he argued, have their own ways of seeing, thinking, and feeling, and should be given as free a rein as possible to explore the wonders of life. Rousseau felt that children who were given freedom during the early years would realize their full potential as adults and would be able to make substantial contributions to the social order. For society's sake, then, parents and educators should let children follow their own inclinations. It is obvious from these statements that Rousseau recognized and valued innate differences in children. While Locke urged parents to mold their children's attitudes and values, Rousseau tried to dissuade those who would force every child into a single mold.

Rousseau and Locke disagreed vehemently about why childhood was important and how these years should be spent. They did agree, however, that the period of childhood merited special attention, and they alerted the educated public to the special status of children. Still, a century passed before Charles Darwin legitimized the scientific investigation of children.

The controversy that swirled around Darwin after he published *The Origin of Species* extended to every corner of the scientific community. Scientists of all persuasions were called to take sides, to offer their opinions, and to defend their views. The heated debates and emotionally charged atmosphere that characterized this period created a base of thought, excitement, and motivation that inspired further ideas. If species evolved into other species, then it was only a small step to the belief that children evolved or developed into adults. Darwin stimulated interest in the study of children by arguing that humans would not be understood by a rational and logical analysis of adults. If we really want to understand adults, we must look to their origins—in nature and in the child (Kessen, 1965).

In addition to launching the scientific study of children, Darwin wrote one of the first baby biographies. His theory of evolution resulted from the detailed observations he made while on the famous voyage of the Beagle. Once back in England, Darwin applied the same observational skills to his firstborn child. His diary about Doddy Darwin was one of the first scientific records of a child's development. Darwin recorded the reflexes of infancy, the slow accumulation of visual skills during the first month of life, and the gradual coordination of the infant's eyes and hands (Darwin, 1877). Darwin briefly discussed many of the directions that investigations of child development have since taken.

Another century has passed and the field of developmental psychology retains vestiges of these early theoreticians, but they would hardly recognize the variety and sophistication of the theoreticians who have followed them. Today the field of developmental psychology is characterized by many different realms, each headed by scores of theoreticians, and each providing a particular slant on the way children develop. As an introduction to the field of developmental psychology, we will devote this chapter to an examination of several of the most prominent realms: the biological, the ethological, the structural, the experiential, and the social.

## THE BIOLOGICAL REALM

The biological nature of the human organism can hardly be denied. Any attempt to explain behavior which does not recognize our evolutionary past and our biological characteristics is obviously incomplete (Eaves, Last, Young, & Marten, 1978). We develop from the union of two cells, and as will be explained in the next chapter, the chromosomes contained in these two cells maintain a continuing influence over our lives. The extent and complexity of that influence is a recurrent theme in developmental psychology, known as the *nature-nurture controversy*.

**Preformationism**

In the biological realm of developmental psychology, researchers are interested in the contributions of heredity in a person's development. Some of the early thoughts about these contributions seem almost laughable today. Before scientists discovered chromosomes, the preformationists believed that a tiny, fully formed human existed at conception and was nurtured in the womb until it was large enough to survive (see Figure 1–1). This "truth" dominated scientific embryology from the 5th century until the 18th century (Crain, 1980). It was finally laid aside when scientists used better microscopic lenses in the study of embryos.

The notion that the organism changed and developed in the womb brought other changes to the biological bases of development. Even though the idea of genes as the agents of development had not even been conceived, philosophers realized that the contributions of heredity did not cease at conception. Rousseau (1762) believed that nature functioned as a hidden tutor, prompting the child to develop different capacities at different times. Scientists have since noted that genetic influences continue throughout the life span, orchestrating puberty, baldness, disease, and many other functions and behaviors.

**Maturation**

Arnold Gesell, a 20th-century psychologist wooed by the biological kingdom, documented the continuing effects of heredity. After earning a doctorate in psychology, Gesell decided to attend medical school because he was entranced by the "seasons and sequences" he had observed in children (Gesell & Ilg, 1943). Throughout a 50 year career, he documented the continuing influence of genes on motor behavior. This process, labeled *maturation*, was governed by a genetic timetable.

In an often quoted experiment designed to examine the role of maturation,

**Figure 1—1**          **Preformationism**

*Historical Pictures Service, Chicago*

The preformationists believed that the sperm contained a fully formed human. This idea reigned from before Christ until the 18th century.

Gesell and his colleague Helen Thompson (1929) spent six weeks training one twin to climb stairs. The first twin became an expert stair climber. The untrained twin could not climb stairs, even with assistance. After one week of practice, however, the second twin could also climb stairs. After two weeks of training she was as proficient as her twin. The early training accelerated the first twin's stair climbing, but the untrained twin caught up rapidly. Moreover, the second twin required much less time to reach the same state of proficiency. These experiments stressed the importance of the inner timetable and introduced generations of parents and psychologists to the concept of *readiness*. Before embarking on toilet training or reading instruction, we now evaluate the child's readiness to learn such skills.

Gesell's commitment to the maturational timetable prompted him to develop careful norms for the ages at which most children learn to sit, creep, and skip (Gesell & Ilg, 1943). Even though these norms were introduced in the 1940s, they are still widely used and quoted. Their continued usefulness is a testament to the power of the biological factors that determine motor development. These norms also demonstrate that developmental psychologists can establish certain facts as truths.

The criticisms against Gesell's maturational theory mushroomed during the

1950s and 1960s. Developmental psychology began an impassioned swing to the view that experiences and environmental variables were critical factors in development. If intelligence, school achievement, and success were controlled by environmental factors, then environments could be adjusted so that all children had equal opportunities to learn. Psychologists, motivated by these social ideals, hoped that interventions during the infant and preschool years might be translated into successful school careers for disadvantaged children. Although the goals were laudable, the zeal of the period had some unfortunate by-products. The entire culture, eager to rectify the discrimination of the past, fell unwittingly into the error of thinking that biological individuality was not compatible with the democratic belief in equal opportunity (Cattell, 1982).

**Behavioral genetics**

During the period of intense environmentalism, researchers from the biological domain were often shunned and sometimes harassed (Cattell, 1982; Herrnstein, 1982). This climate began to change in the 1970s. Perhaps it was the greater precision and clarity of their experiments that won researchers in the biological realm more support. Perhaps it was the advances in allied fields such as genetics and biology that prodded psychologists to look again at biological variables. Whatever the reasons, the field of behavioral genetics has blossomed and is currently a source of exciting and important research.

Genetic engineering is no longer a fantasy of the future. It is a useful tool in contemporary medicine (Davis, 1983). Furthermore, the benefits of genetic engineering are just beginning to be realized (Cattell, 1982). Genetic engineering may be responsible for vast improvements in human life in the next two centuries.

These new views depart radically from the maturational view of Gesell. Acknowledging a biological aspect to health, personality, or intelligence is no longer synonymous with ignoring environmental variables. In fact, behavioral genetics has alerted us to the sensitive and ongoing interchange between genes and environments. The playing out of the inner timetable suggested by Gesell is not immutable. People prone to diabetes who control their diet may never have the disease. Those at risk for heart attacks can decrease that risk by adjusting their lifestyles. In a similar vein, it has been suggested that children with schizophrenic parents may be insulated from the disease if they have stable home situations and if their mothers are involved instead of withdrawn or negative (Sameroff, Seifer, & Zax, 1982). Even the controversies about intelligence that permeated earlier decades have been tempered. Social programs with the single goal of increasing intelligence are no longer promoted. Instead, programs strive to provide a variety of benefits to mothers and children which will enhance the quality of the child's life, improve school attendance, and improve the child's attitudes toward school (Lazar & Darlington, 1982; Maccoby, Kahn, & Everett, 1983).

In short, we have moved beyond the simple question about the relative contributions of heredity and environment to intelligence and personality (Anastasi, 1958). We are asking, instead, about the kinds of environments that optimize development and the kinds of environments that trigger negative outcomes in people who are biologically vulnerable (Garmezy, 1982). The contemporary approach to behavioral genetics, while focusing on biological factors, recognizes that this is just one of many threads that must be evaluated while studying development.

**Teasing apart nature and nurture**

Researchers from the biological realm are interested in isolating and studying the influence of genes upon behavior. This is relatively easy when the genes have dramatic effects on behavior. Children with Down's syndrome, sickle cell disease, and cystic fibrosis all carry a gene that has unmistakable effects on behavior. Looking for the more subtle ways that genes influence personality and intelligence is much more difficult. To isolate these subtle genetic effects, researchers have devised several unique methods. In one of these methods, individuals who are closely related and thus share the same genes are compared with individuals who are not related. Identical twins, for example, have exactly the same genes. Fraternal twins and siblings share about half their genes. Half siblings and cousins have fewer genes in common, and so on. If genes have an effect on intelligence, it will be apparent when we compare these groups.

Comparisons between groups of individuals often rely on correlational techniques. Calculating a correlation coefficient allows us to assess the relationship between two variables. The correlation coefficient that is obtained can range from 1.00 to −1.00. A positive correlation indicates that as one variable increases, so does the second variable. A perfect positive correlation (1.00) indicates that an increase in one variable is paralleled by a fixed increase in the second variable. A negative correlation indicates that as one variable increases, the second decreases. A correlation coefficient of zero indicates no relationship between the two variables.

Looking at different patterns of correlations has helped answer important questions asked by psychologists in the biological realm. For example, the correlation between the IQs of identical twins who are raised together is .85. If they are raised in different homes, the correlation decreases to .67. The correlation between siblings who are raised together is .45. If they are raised in separate homes, the correlation falls to .24 (Bouchard & McGue, 1981). This series of correlations helps define the relationship between intelligence and genetics.

Correlation coefficients tell us about the degree of the relationship between two variables. They don't tell us what causes that relationship. The relationship described by a correlation coefficient could be due to a third variable that is not even measured. For example, the correlation between height and weight is quite high. But being tall does not cause children to weigh more. Instead, both variables—height and weight—are a function of genetic and nutritional variables.

Correlational techniques are also used in adoption studies to separate the effects of heredity and environment. When twins or siblings are adopted by different families, their inborn skills and abilities are nourished by different environments. If, as adults, they have little in common, researchers can conclude that the environments were primarily responsible for directing development. If, on the other hand, their mannerisms, interests, and skills are very similar, then genetic factors governed development. Of course, psychologists cannot separate children at birth and place them in different environments. We must capitalize on chance occurrences and all the uncontrolled factors that such chance occurrences bring with them. Despite these problems, adoption studies have been very useful to researchers in the biological realm.

In this book, evidence from the biological realm will be included as one orientation to the understanding of development. The chapter on genetics will introduce students to the biological foundations of behavior. But the biological foundations of development will continue after the chapter on genetics is concluded. In discussions of cognitive skills, personality aberrations, and sex differences, evidence from the biological realm will be considered. Even aggression and evading disabilities are areas where biology ought to be considered if we are to have a complete picture of development. Recently, sociobiologists have extended the search for biological threads to cultural practices. How we select our mates, how we prepare food, and whether or not we encourage tattooing or scarring are cultural practices that may influence the gene pool (Lumsden & Wilson, 1981). Examining this orientation helps alert students to the different views held by psychologists within the biological realm.

Although all contemporary developmental psychologists understand that biological factors are important to development, the nature-nurture controversy continues to ebb and flow. In the 1980s this controversy is not the simplistic either-or argument that reigned in earlier decades. Tracing development from the chromosomes to the expression of a behavior some 10, 20, or 50 years later requires psychologists to examine the continuing and subtle interchanges between the environment and the genes. Although the interchange is complex, the intricacy is often lost in popular versions of the nature-nurture controversy (see Figure 1-2).

## THE ETHOLOGICAL REALM

Psychologists from the biological realm are concerned with the hereditary aspects of behavior. Their colleagues in the ethological realm study the evolutionary significance of behavior. Typically they investigate courtship, mating, nesting, parenting, and dominance behaviors that are important for the survival of a species. Such an orientation for developmental psychologists is somewhat unexpected. Perhaps that is why this viewpoint has often been ignored. Recently, however, developmental psychologists have become convinced that an ethological orientation can contribute to our understanding of the behavior of children and to our understanding of development.

**Figure 1—2**     **The continuing nature-nurture controversy**

## Confucian Work Ethic
## Asian-born students head for the head of the class

When the Westinghouse Science Talent Search named its top achievers this month, the announcement was yet another instance of a growing national trend. Grand Winner Paul Ning, 16, is not a native-born American. The son of a Taiwanese diplomat, Ning came to the United States at the age of three. By 11, he was constructing a simple wind tunnel to study the relationship between velocity and pressure. Now a senior at the elite Bronx High School of Science in New York City, Ning feels, "You have to be aggressive in your studies to really understand what you're doing." Adds his mother: "He always tries to prove to us and to himself that he is the best."

Paul Ning is part of a phenomenon obvious to any American who has not been glued to his Sony for the past decade: Asian Americans are only about 1.5 percent of the U.S. population, but what they lack in numbers they make up for in achievement. Out of 40 Westinghouse finalists, nine were born in Asia and three others were of Asian descent. Some 10 percent of Harvard's freshman class is Asian American. While no more than 15 percent of California high school graduates are eligible for admission to the University of California system, about 40 percent of Asian Americans qualify.

Experts are uncertain about the reasons for high Asian performance. William Dean, who directs special programs in Fort Collins, Colorado, where there are 150 Asian-born students, observes that whatever the students' verbal skills, "there is a universal language available in mathematics." The Asians speak it fluently. The national norm for math on the Scholastic Aptitude Test is 467 out of a possible 800. In 1981, Asian Americans averaged 513. In California, a remarkable 68 percent of Japanese-born students scored over 600, as did 66 percent of students born in Korea.

Some attribute the academic success of Asians to a genetic superiority. In his controversial study, British Psychologist Richard Lynn claimed that the Japanese score 11 points higher on the Wechsler IQ test than the American average. Their superior performance on tests of block designs, mazes, and picture arrangement, however, may be related to the early study of the complex ideograms that compose their alphabet.

Most educators believe that Asian scholastic achievement has more to do with nurture than nature. They argue that Asian immigrants are accustomed to a more rigorous schedule; the Japanese, for instance, attend school 225 days instead of a typical U.S. schedule of 180. Many Asian-American children have well-educated parents. James Blackwell, a sociology professor at the University of Massachusetts in Boston, believes that high Asian income levels may account for above-average math performance, since parents are able to send their children to better schools and give them such home aids as learning toys and computers. Most Asians regard education as the best avenue to recognition and success. Bronx Science Principal Milton Kopelman is reminded of "the youngsters who came out of the homes of East European immigrants several decades ago. There is pressure to work, and there is also great respect for education." Sociologist William Liu, who directs the Asian-American mental health center at the University of Illinois' Chicago campus, stresses the importance of cultural conditioning. "In the Confucian ethic, which permeates the cultures of China, Japan, Viet Nam, and Korea, scholastic achievement is the only way of repaying the infinite debt to parents, of showing filial piety."

Is academic excellence the product of genetics or the environment? This issue receives a great deal of attention in the popular press. The complexity of the issue, however, is seldom addressed.

Ethologists trace their roots to Charles Darwin and his insight that species adapt to a particular ecological niche. Two finches may have very different beaks; two iguanas may have entirely different coloration. These differences represent adaptations to environmental circumstances that influence survival. Darwin's observations were largely confined to physical differences rather than behaviors. He convinced the scientific community that physical adaptations were important to survival.

It was left to Konrad Lorenz (1965) and Niko Tinbergen (1951) to consider whether particular behaviors might be important to survival. They began their investigations by observing geese, starlings, beetles, fighting cocks, and a fish called the stickleback. In every case their observations were turned into a catalog of the animal's behavior in its natural setting. From this catalog they extrapolated the adaptive characteristics of the hopping of birds, the red belly of a stickleback, and the imprinting of geese and ducks. Their classic studies were the beginning of an era in which ethological analyses were conducted on hundreds of species.

An ethological approach has become standard for research with other species. Psychologists, however, have been slower to see the value of such studies with humans. Part of psychology's reluctance stems from the interests of developmental psychologists. For years researchers in the field focused somewhat narrowly on questions about intelligence, learning, school achievement, and cognitive skills. These behaviors are less amenable to an ethological approach than parenting and mating. We now recognize that developmental psychology

**Ethologists studying natural behavior**

*Herman Kacher*

Konrad Lorenz was one of the fathers of ethology. In this picture, he is also mistaken as the geese's mother.

should strive to understand all aspects of development. Acceptance of these broader goals opened the door to ethological analyses.

Another reason for the delay in applying ethological concepts to the study of children is the wide range of human behavior. In humans, behaviors that are adaptive for the species, like nesting, mating, territorial defense, and parenting, account for only a small portion of all human behavior. Furthermore, even when psychologists focus on these behaviors, so many layers of learning may have covered the basic response that it is often impossible to link specific behaviors with an evolutionary base. The rough-and-tumble play of young primates, including children, poses this kind of problem.

Of what significance is a sandlot soccer game, a neighborhood wrestling match, or an afternoon spent swinging in the park with a friend? Ethologists believe that play must be important to survival. Otherwise children would conserve their energy, use their time more profitably, and avoid possible injury and exposure to danger (Symons, 1978). Perhaps play serves as a training ground where children can develop and practice complex motor skills that adults need (Beckoff & Byers, 1981). Alternatively, play may be a way to establish relationships with peers. Through play, children learn to communicate, to control aggression, and to develop social bonds (Beckoff & Byers, 1981). Play may even provide children with cognitive skills (Bruner, 1976). All of these suggestions seem reasonable, but proving that child's play serves a loftier purpose requires getting beneath the cultural veneer of humans (Beckoff & Byers, 1981).

Despite the difficulty in assessing the adaptive value of human behaviors Eckhard Hess (1970) has argued convincingly for the inclusion of ethological studies in developmental psychology. His belief in the power of ethology is based on two points: (a) innate behavior is the necessary and sufficient condition for the survival of most organisms; and (b) learned behavior, alone, is the necessary and sufficient condition for the survival of none. Although he recognizes that developmental psychologists are most interested in humans and that humans are heavily influenced by learning, this does not change his insistence on these two points.

Hess's first point is an important one and has prompted developmental psychologists and pediatricians to study the reactions between mothers and fathers and their infants in the first hours and days of life. The bond that parents form with their newborn infants may have an evolutionary base and could be designed to insure that all children have at least one person committed to caring for them. An evolutionary mechanism like bonding exists in many other species (Klaus & Kennell, 1982) and certainly increases the chances that helpless newborns will survive. Hess's second point, that learning by itself will not insure survival, is also applicable to humans. Learning does not occur quickly enough in the human infant to insure survival. Therefore, Hess challenged psychologists to look for behaviors that must be present for the infant to survive.

John Bowlby has responded to this challenge. Even though infants are not capable of taking care of themselves, they are not passive. Bowlby (1969) believes that they can signal adults quite effectively through crying and smiling

**Figure 1—3**          **Attachment**

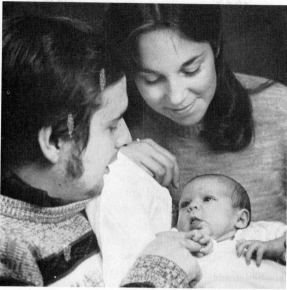

*Paul Damien: CLICK/Chicago*

To ethologists imprinting is not limited to a few species of birds. The attachment that develops between parent and child is similar in many ways to imprinting.

(see Figure 1–3). Starting from this ethological foundation, Bowlby (1980) has built a theory describing human attachment. He believes that the development of a secure attachment during the first year of life is an important step in social development.

Both the literature on bonding and attachment demonstrate the viability of an ethological approach to particular issues in developmental psychology. But the influence of the ethological realm is not limited to studies in these areas. Like researchers from the biological realm, ethologists have developed methods to analyze behaviors they believe important and have contributed concepts somewhat unique to their orientation.

**Naturalistic observation**

From the outset, ethologists have emphasized the importance of observing the natural behavior of animals in their own habitats. It is only in these natural settings that scientists can see how a particular behavior helps the species adapt. Scientists would never understand the elaborate camouflage of insects, the tail slapping behavior of beavers, the ritualized mating dances of birds, or the social interaction of bees if single animals were removed to a laboratory and never examined in their natural settings. But applying this same concept to humans has met with more resistance.

Naturalistic observation has always been listed as a method for studying human development. In textbooks of the 1960s and 1970s, it was presented as a preliminary strategy for collecting information. Its flaws as a research strategy were noted quickly, and the discussion moved to experimental strategies. Ethologists take exception to this cursory treatment (Tinbergen, 1963) and have been winning more and more converts in developmental psychology. Observing in a natural setting does have its drawbacks, but so do most methods of collecting data. However, many of the disadvantages of naturalistic observation can be overcome.

One of the first drawbacks is that observations can be very subjective. A quick glance at baby biographies and diaries reveals that the observations of mothers and fathers are often clouded by their involvement with the baby. If observations cannot be repeated by other investigators, they are of no value to understanding development. This problem, however, can be overcome if investigators define clearly the behaviors they are observing and if several investigators can agree on their observations. Under these circumstances, observation is as objective as any other method of collecting information.

A second drawback of observations in the natural setting is that they cannot be controlled. Ethologists might list this as a plus rather than a minus, especially in the early stages of investigating a behavior. But after a behavior has been carefully catalogued, even ethologists will intervene to check the accuracy of their conclusions (Hess, 1972).

A more important drawback to observations is the fact that some important behaviors occur very infrequently in the natural environment. Aggression, for example, may be important to survival, but it may only occur on rare occasions. It's easy to picture a frustrated psychologist sitting with pen poised above paper, waiting months for an instance of aggression to occur. Designing situations that provoke aggression would certainly be more efficient.

Despite these drawbacks, ethologists have marshalled compelling evidence that descriptions of behavior in a natural setting should be the basis for understanding development. To underscore this point, Hess looks briefly at the way unnatural environments, like zoos, affect behavior. Mating, a behavior clearly necessary if species are to survive, is often disrupted in captivity. Every spring, international attention is drawn to the giant pandas as zoologists try to encourage them to mate. Parenting, another behavior essential to the survival of all species, is also easily disturbed in captive populations. Mothers raised in zoos sometimes seem strangely inefficient in their caretaking and are much more likely to abandon their offspring than mothers who have grown up in the wild. Although zoo administrators can intervene and save the infants, the problem is perpetuated if, as adults, these animals become unwilling mates or uncaring mothers (Ruppenthal, Arling, Harlow, Sackett, & Suomi, 1976). Artificial environments promote artificial behaviors and hinder our attempts to understand how specific behaviors contribute to the survival of a species.

The ethological influence in developmental psychology has made observation a popular research strategy. Children are likely to be videotaped or followed with a tape recorder so observers do not have to rely on their memories.

### Captivity and behavior

*Jesse Cohen, National Zoological Park*

Living in captivity sometimes interferes with the development of behaviors basic to survival. Mating successfully is necessary to preserve the species, yet giant pandas, raised in captivity, often have problems mating.

Such observations have had a marked effect on our understanding of how children acquire language (Greenfield & Smith, 1976; Bloom, 1973). Discussions of language acquisition prior to 1970 seem awkward and remote and little is said about the process that takes place as a child learns to speak. Taped recordings of children's early language revamped the entire field of psycholinguistics. An ethological approach has been used with similar success to investigate attachment (Ainsworth, Blehar, & Waters, 1978), dominance (McGrew, 1972), the importance of fathers (Pedersen, 1981), the role of peers (Bronson, 1981), and mother-infant interaction (Stern, 1977).

Ethologists consider every aspect of the environment worthy of mention, from the length of the grass where a bird builds its nest, to the head movements a bird makes when courting. A similar concern for completeness is found in contemporary developmental studies that advocate a systems approach. Frank Pedersen (1980, 1981), whose research has focused on the importance of the father, chides psychologists for studying fathers in isolation. He and Clarke-Stewart (1978) favor naturalistic studies that will uncover the interdependencies between the mother, the father, and the child. The family functions as a system, not as a group of individuals acting independently. Therefore, the family must be studied as a system. Michael Lewis (1982) goes a step further in advocating a systems approach. A complete picture of social development will require investigations that include peers and siblings in addition to the mother, father, and child.

**Learning and ethology**

Ethologists have recognized that even behaviors like mating and parenting are not immune to environmental influences. After all, if these behaviors were based entirely on evolutionary givens, whether animals were in a zoo or not would be of no importance. Ethologists concede that learning is important, but are quick to point out that the most effective learning reflects evolutionary givens.

Learning is best understood as a layer built over biological predispositions. Animal trainers would be the first to agree that successful training builds on naturally occurring behaviors. Breland and Breland (1961) describe some of their training efforts that obviated instinctive behaviors. In one example of the misbehavior of organisms, they trained pigs to pick up coins and place them in a "piggy bank" several feet away. For each successful deposit, the pigs were rewarded with food. Their huge appetites meant that the training proceeded

**Operant conditioning**

*Courtesy of Animal Behavior Enterprises, Inc.*

This pig was trained using instrumental conditioning to push a market basket. Breland and Breland were able to reinforce this behavior without the intrusion of misbehavior.

quickly. But after several weeks, the learned responses began to deteriorate. The pigs would pick up the coin, but instead of heading straight to the bank, they would drop the coin, root for it, drop it again, root it along the way, pick it up, toss it in the air, and so on. Their instinctive food-getting behaviors actually began to interfere with their ability to obtain food rewards in the training situation. Breland and Breland call this *instinctive drift* and, in many instances, it is more powerful than the learned behavior.

The lesson for developmental psychologists is that learning should build on evolutionary givens, not conflict with them. For this to happen, we need to know what the evolutionary givens are. We cannot, for example, blot out the millions of years that the earth has been rotating, subjecting all its inhabitants to the highly predictable cycle of night and day. Our sleeping habits, our temperatures, the levels of hormones in our bodies, and other more subtle behaviors are all affected. Acknowledging this heritage is actually the first step toward learning how to function most efficiently within its limits. Thanks to researchers from the biological realm, we know that one can adapt to the night shift, that moving the biological clock forward is easier than moving it backward, and that demanding continuing changes of our biological clocks is more difficult than adjusting to one change and remaining in that cycle for a considerable length of time (Czeisler, Moore-Ede, & Coleman, 1982). We can now add our recent cultural invention, the night shift, to our evolutionary heritage in an intelligent way. Perhaps other recent cultural inventions, like reading, could be meshed with our perceptual skills in a more efficient way.

## Critical periods and sign stimuli

Like the biological realm, the ethological realm has contributed some unique concepts to developmental psychology. One of these is the concept of *critical periods*. As used initially by ethologists, this term referred to a very short period of time during which an immature organism was especially sensitive to a particular experience. Mallard ducks, for example, are sensitive to other objects at about 16 hours of age and will normally form an attachment to their mothers during this period. After 32 to 45 hours, the sensitivity is replaced by fear (Hess, 1970). For Mallard ducks the short interval between 16 and 32 to 45 hours is indeed critical. In other animals and in humans, the time period for a particular experience is not nearly as limited, so it is designated a *sensitive period* or a sensitive phase of development (Immelmann & Suomi, 1981). A sensitive period for establishing social behavior in humans may last for a year or two instead of a few hours (Bowlby, 1969).

Sensitive periods in humans are not as absolute as they are in other animals (Colombo, 1982). A sensitive period signals a time when stable behaviors can be established with ease. Language acquisition in humans fits into this category. Children learn language readily from birth to five years of age (Krashen, 1975). Their brains seem predisposed to untangle the barrage of words they hear (Chomsky, 1978). Of course, language learning is not limited to this period. Many people acquire a second language as adults. But the way they learn the new language seems to differ from the way they learned language as a child (McLaughlin, 1980).

A sensitive period implies that early experiences have lasting consequences. Ethologists studying a variety of mammals have shown that sexual behavior, maternal behavior, and socialization require specific experiences to develop normally (Immelmann & Suomi, 1981). Rhesus monkeys who had differing social experiences as infants are a good example. Some monkeys were reared as isolates for either 6 or 12 months. During this time, their only experience with humans or monkeys was to be fed through portholes. A second group of monkeys was fed by a human caretaker. Every four hours these monkeys were cradled in the arms of the nursery workers and fed from a baby's bottle. Their only contact for 25 days was with humans. After they were weaned they were housed individually in a cage. A third group was also raised in the nursery, but after weaning was housed with another monkey. A fourth group was raised by their mothers. As infants they had daily contact with their peers.

Two years after these initial experiences, the monkeys were tested to see if they preferred to be near humans or monkeys. The monkeys were allowed to leave the center compartment of an enclosure and go into a compartment occupied by a monkey or one occupied by a human. The monkeys who had been hand fed spent 600 percent more time near the human than they spent near the monkey. Monkeys who had been isolated during the first months of their lives spent most of their time in the neutral, central compartment, shunning both humans and monkeys. The other groups overwhelmingly preferred to be near the monkey. These preferences existed even though all of the monkeys had played with their peers during the second year (Sackett, Porter, & Holmes, 1965). The experiences these monkeys had as infants had a lasting effect on their social preferences.

Aggression in mammals may be another behavior that is susceptible to particular social experiences during development (Agren & Meyerson, 1979). Whether or not rhesus monkeys are aggressive as adults is influenced by their access to playmates during infancy (Suomi & Harlow, 1977). If monkeys have no opportunity to play with their peers during the first nine months of life, they have great difficulty forming stable relationships later. As adults, they are excessively aggressive toward their peers (Harlow & Harlow, 1969).

Of course, information from other species cannot be generalized directly to humans. These studies can, however, serve as the foundation for investigations of aggression in humans (Blurton-Jones, Ferriera, Farquhar-Brown, & McDonald, 1979). Child abuse is one example of unnatural aggression. It often occurs among adults whose own childhood was marked by isolation or abuse (Parke & Lewis, 1981). The ethological intimation is that parental behavior, which should have been organized in the early years, was not sustained by the harsh environment. It should be noted that only a small portion of the parents who were isolated or abused as children abuse their own children. Still, the parent's history is usually the best predictor of abuse (Starr, 1970; Vietze, Falsey, Sandler, O'Connor & Altemier, 1980).

The existence of sensitive periods in human development remains a legitimate area of research (Clarke & Clarke, 1976; Leiderman, 1981). Whether or not sociability, aggression, sexual behavior, or other social behaviors in humans are influenced by experiences during a sensitive phase is a tantalizing question that remains to be answered. Ethologists hope that the continuing debate will spur research efforts.

The concept of *sign stimuli* is also derived directly from ethology. In the animal kingdom, certain colors or displays will trigger mating behavior. The iridescent blue and green tail of the male peacock interferes with movement, but it attracts females. The red belly of the male stickleback means that a particular territory is taken. This sign is so specific it could easily read "intruders will be attacked."

Similar sign stimuli may operate in human behavior (see Figure 1–4). Lorenz (1943) has suggested that babyishness could be such a sign. The particular configuration of eyes, face, and head size that characterize immature animals has a special appeal (Cann, 1953). Ethologists suggest that this immature configuration of facial features is a sign that facilitates caretaking (Hess, 1970).

**Figure 1–4**      **Sign stimuli**

*Campbell Soup Company*

Babyishness or cuteness may attract adults. Lorenz suggested that the particular configuration of the infant's face attracted parents and encouraged caretaking. The adult faces he includes do not produce the same reaction. Advertisers have often capitalized on this reaction by using figures that are cherubic.

The smile is another sign that has been studied in humans (Eibl-Eibesfeldt, 1979). Using careful observations of mothers playing with their infants, Stern (1977) has shown that infants' smiles provoke immediate affection and prolonged attention from their mothers. In the language of ethology the child's smile "releases" the mother's attention and affection and leads, in turn, to more and broader smiles from the infant. A biologically governed sign, the smile the child produces, becomes the first step in a cycle of mother-infant interaction that gradually develops into a mutual, long-term attachment.

Children who are both deaf and blind begin to smile at the same time as sighted children—around six weeks of age. Initially, their smiles are as broad as the smiles of their sighted peers. But after several months, their faces become less expressive and their smiles less captivating (Eibl-Eibesfeldt, 1979). Stimulation from the environment does not penetrate the deaf and blind child's limited sensory system. As a result, the child's responsiveness decreases. Studying the development of the smile in blind and sighted children illustrates the interaction between biological givens and environmental stimulation.

The contribution of the ethological realm to the study of child development is still being realized. As we examine bonding, attachment, parenting, language acquisition, and social development, we will continue to encounter the ethological perspective. Such a perspective has proven its value in understanding aspects of normal social development. In years to come, it may allow us to trace the detours that produce nonadaptive behaviors (Zabel & Zabel, 1982).

**The smile as a sign**

*Anna Kaufman Moon: Stock, Boston*

One of the sign stimuli thought to affect human behavior is the smile. Parents are invariably attracted to a smiling child, and a smile is interpreted as a signal that the child is ready to play. Over a period of months, the smile helps strengthen the attachment bond between parent and child.

## THE STRUCTURAL REALM

Psychologists from the biological and ethological realms devoted their efforts to dissecting biological aspects of development. An appreciation of biology's role in development is also present in the structural realm. It serves as a starting point for the main event—the child constructing new and more complex ways of functioning. The child is the central character in the structural realm, and biological bases of behavior and the continuing environmental stimulation are only supporting roles. Children draw from their evolutionary past, their genetic makeup, their environmental circumstances, and their culture to fashion a coherent view of the world. Psychologists from the structural realm follow the children's activities and chart their progressively more mature views of the world.

**Active organism**

Structuralists celebrate the active nature of the child. Like Rousseau, they insist that children guide their own development and master their environments in small incremental steps. The child's role in constructing knowledge and the structures that characterize each new advance in knowledge follow from this basic view of the child.

The infant is born with primitive action systems rooted in biology. Slow, deliberate, and sometimes tedious efforts gradually transform these action systems into more useful strategies for exploring the environment. Consider grasping. At birth, grasping is a reflex that the child cannot control (Zelazo, 1976). Any small object put into the infant's hand is automatically grasped (see Figure 1–5). Nine months later, this primitive reflex has been transformed into a very efficient pincer grasp (Bayley, 1969). Using this grasp the child can explore buttons, marbles, bottle caps and other small objects. Their own activity is the force that prods infants to move from reflexes to the pincer grasp. Their goal is to act on the environment. The result is a picture of the world that is constantly being revised.

**Constructivism**

Structuralists also believe that children construct their own knowledge. Children combine their previous knowledge with each new piece of information so that their concepts are constantly being reorganized. Each reorganization represents a higher, more stable level of cognitive functioning.

Constructivism also implies that children regulate their own conceptual development. When childrens' minds are stuffed with knowledge they don't understand, their thinking becomes chaotic (Kamii & DeVries, 1978). A group of kindergarten children learned that "if an object floats, it floats because it is lighter than a piece of water the same size." The children were able to repeat this rule. They were even able to pass tests which required them to recall this information. This knowledge is useless from a structuralist point of view unless it is integrated into the child's overall understanding of the earth. After a class

**Figure 1—5**                    **Exploring small objects by grasping**

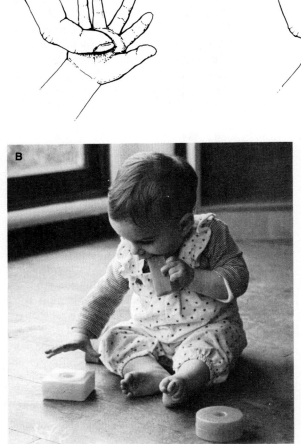

*Elizabeth Crews: Stock, Boston*

(A) At birth, the child's behavior consists primarily of reflexes, like grasping, that the child cannot control. (B) A few months later, after interacting with the environment and modifying those reflexes, grasping has become a highly controlled, specific behavior.

had learned this fact, Kamii let the children experiment with a large bar of ivory soap and several small pieces of soap. Their explanations of the results were full of contradictions. One child observed that a small piece of soap would float because it was lighter. She then argued that another small piece sank because it was heavier. A structuralist interprets this common occurrence as evidence that children have not integrated new facts with other knowledge they have obtained (Furth & Wachs, 1974). They have learned a rule about floating objects, but this rule exists in a separate, somewhat isolated compartment.

**Figure 1—6**     **Constructing the world**

*Susan Lapides: Design Conceptions*

Constructivists view the child as an active organism who avidly explores the environment and solves problems as they arise.

We have all experienced the "aha" phenomenon—a moment when a solution to a problem suddenly clicks. Such moments of enlightenment are evidence that we have forged another link between new knowledge and old knowledge: we are constructing new understandings.

**Structures and stages**

Children who actively explore their environments accumulate knowledge in steps (see Figure 1–6). At 6 months, 10 years, and 19 years, their knowledge about a phenomenon will be different. Each new integration will be more complete, and each new integration will be more like the adult's view of the world. To get a feeling for *structures* and *stages*, let us consider how children might understand gravity at different ages.

At birth, the infant does not realize that when objects are no longer supported they fall to the ground. After the first few months of life, infants are able to construct this knowledge. By eight months, infants avidly explore the effects of gravity by dropping and throwing most objects they grasp. Their understanding of gravity is based on the action of objects.

A third grader's understanding of gravity is much more sophisticated. Students at this age might hear the story of Galileo's experiments with falling objects. According to the story, Galileo dropped a 10-pound ball and a one-pound ball from the Tower of Pisa. Galileo's students observed that both balls hit the ground at the same instant. Contemporary third graders might have weighed themselves on a scale that tells their weight on Mars or Jupiter. They might have also learned that a person's center of gravity influences how well they can jump. They might know that astronauts lose calcium from their bones, fluid from their legs, and may even grow an inch or more while they are in the weightless environment of space (Bodde, 1982). At this age, the child's understanding of gravity involves a loose integration of various facts under the general heading "gravity."

In college, physics majors encounter gravity at still a different level. The known facts concerning gravity are integrated and aligned with related facts from other areas of astronomy and physics. These students can likewise follow the theoretical revisions of Galileo's work proposed by Newton and Einstein. They use the facts about gravity to form abstractions and theories about weightless environments.

The different levels of knowledge that the infant, school child, and college student demonstrate about gravity represent different stages or structures. The infant's knowledge is based on actions. The school-age child collects facts. The college student attends to theoretical possibilities. Each organization or stage builds on the knowledge accumulated in the previous stage, but each stage represents a reorganization of the earlier knowledge at a higher level.

**Structural theories**

The principles of structuralism were first applied to the development of children by James Mark Baldwin (1915). Since then structuralist tenets have been used to explore a wide range of topics in developmental psychology.

Heinz Werner characterized the process of development as a systematic progression from a global, undifferentiated understanding of the world to an organized, finely differentiated view in which children integrated all of their information. The child's views were characterized as concrete and somewhat rigid. By adolescence, consciousness expanded and became more flexible (Werner, 1948). Werner's theory was very global and almost any sequence of behavior could be interpreted within his framework of increasing differentiation. He did not define a particular sequence of stages, nor did he tell us what characterized mature thought. Nevertheless, his notion of increasing differentiation has been generally accepted in developmental psychology.

The most prominent structuralist position in developmental psychology is Jean Piaget's theory of cognitive development. In fact, his theory is cited widely as one of the few true models of structuralism. Other theorists use stages to describe how a child changes, but their stages don't necessarily reflect higher levels of organization. These hierarchical, progressive levels of understanding are essential to the structuralist position.

A child's understanding of moral issues is another area that has been analyzed using a structural explanation. Lawrence Kohlberg, building on Piaget's early work, has suggested that moral development involves a series of stages in which knowledge about morality is accumulated and integrated. In the earliest stages, moral decisions are determined by what an authority figure decrees. After listening to a story about a man stealing a drug for his dying wife, a 10 year old might argue that, "It's not right to steal: It's against the law." In the

### Development as differentiation

Heinz Werner characterized development as a process of increasing differentiation. Even the child's drawings become progressively more differentiated over a period of years.

Source: Kamii, C. (1981). Application of Piaget's theory of education: The preoperational level. In I. E. Sigel, D. M. Brodzinsky, and R. M. Golinkoff (Eds.), *New direction in Piagetian theory and practice.* Hillsdale, NJ: Lawrence Erlbaum.

later stages, moral issues are resolved on the basis of justice and principles (Colby, Kohlberg, Gibbs, & Lieberman, 1983; Kohlberg, 1981). College students often respond to moral dilemmas that involve breaking the law by saying, "If there is no legal alternative, then he's morally obligated to steal the drug because a human life is more important than money. He'd probably have to go to jail though, because it's against the law." The progression in moral development that Kohlberg outlines parallels the shift from concrete to abstract levels of cognitive functioning that Piaget outlines.

Some aspects of personality development may also move through a series of hierarchical stages. Jane Loevinger (1976) has presented a structural view of ego development. Loevinger states that infants do not have egos. Toddlers, however, begin to develop a sense of identity when they insist upon dressing themselves and resist suggestions with an emphatic, "No!" As children learn to anticipate rewards and punishments, the ego emerges. From that point, children pass through stages of conformity, conscientiousness, and autonomy. A small percentage of children reach a final integrated stage.

Structuralism does not fit every area of development. Autism or schizophrenia in children as well as many aspects of social development do not readily fit into a structuralist model. Structuralist tenets are usually reserved for areas in which knowledge accumulates.

**The methods of structuralism**

How do you recognize a structure? One has to define a structure from the child's behavior. As in the other realms presented, the structuralists have developed unique methods that address the issues of structures and stages.

The *longitudinal* study, a standard method in developmental psychology, is very useful to structuralists (Wohlwill, 1973). This method charts the progress of the same individuals over a period of time (see Figure 1–7). The classic longitudinal studies of the 1930s, known collectively as the Berkeley Growth Studies, charted intelligence, physical growth, and personality development from birth to adulthood (Bayley, 1968; Block, 1971; Mussen, Honzik, & Eichorn, 1982). If psychologists are interested in charting individual progress and in showing how structures change, then longitudinal studies would seem to be the best method.

Studying a subject over many years is difficult. Subjects in longitudinal studies often move or drop out of the study. If you are studying intellectual growth

**Figure 1—7**  **Cross-sectional and longitudinal studies**

Cross sectional

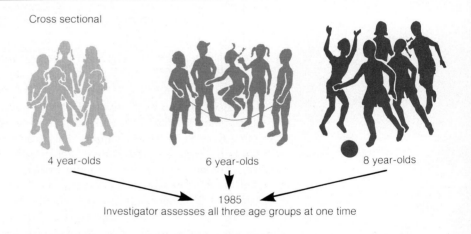

Longitudinal

In cross-sectional studies, children from different age groups are tested to determine how a particular ability changes. Longitudinal studies follow the same children, testing them several times.

over a five-year period and lose 20 percent of your subjects, your results may be altered. Your attrition may not be random. Perhaps the 20 percent who dropped out were the most uncomfortable being asked questions they couldn't answer. When the number of subjects in a sample declines, the investigators must determine whether the remaining subjects differ from the initial group.

Longitudinal studies have other disadvantages. They are expensive because they take years to complete. Furthermore, the results of repeated testing may be invalid (Wohlwill, 1973). If the subjects take the same IQ test eight times and get progressively higher scores, does this indicate an increase in intelligence or is it a result of practice?

Because longitudinal studies have these disadvantages, most psychologists use *cross-sectional* studies. Experimenters compare a cross section of subjects in a particular age group with a cross section of subjects at another age. In this type of study you are measuring individuals of different age groups at the same time (see Figure 1–7). Investigators assume that the differences they observe between age groups would be the same as in a longitudinal study.

Many investigators, seeing that they have neither the time nor the money to conduct longitudinal investigations, decide to use cross-sectional studies. If they are interested in structural change, they may include some longitudinal features in their study. For example, investigators may select a cross section of subjects who are in a pivotal period of cognitive development and then follow cognitive progress for a few months, hoping to see critical changes take place in the individuals (Kuhn, 1976).

A research strategy that combines a longitudinal and cross-sectional approach is called a *cross-sequential* study. In this strategy, psychologists follow several groups of children of different ages (Holtzman, Diaz-Guerro, & Swartz, 1975; Nesselroade & Baltes, 1974). For example, children aged four, six, and eight might be selected for a study in cognitive development. All of the children are then followed for two years. At the end of two years, the investigators will have seen how children between the ages of 4 and 10 handle cognitive tasks. By combining features of both the longitudinal and cross-sectional approach, they have traced cognitive development over a six-year period in two years.

Structuralists are interested in how children approach the world and how they think about problems. Simply asking a child a question that requires a yes or no answer is not enough. Structuralists want to know why children think the way they do. They want to know if children will change their answer when presented with disconfirming evidence and if they will generalize from information they have. Information like this requires a different interviewing technique. Piaget, in an effort to chart the child's thinking, developed the *clinical method* (Piaget, 1969). The clinical method tries to combine the standardized questioning of the researcher with the individual approach of a clinical psychologist.

The clinical method is often roundly criticized by psychologists who are not sympathetic to the goals of structuralism (Brainerd, 1978). They argue that such an interview lacks standardization. Furthermore, once the interview is completed, the experimenter decides how the child approached the problem by determining whether the answer was an example of concrete reasoning or more abstract reasoning. This decision introduces an element of subjectivity that many psychologists question. To structuralists, these criticisms merely indicate that the critics do not understand their goals. Because of their complexity, cognitive structures are not amenable to the rigid, standardized techniques of experimentally oriented research. Piaget argues that such methods constrict children's behavior and are more likely to produce erroneous conclusions than the clinical method (Ginsburg & Opper, 1979).

Despite these criticisms, many of the tenets of structuralism have permeated developmental psychology. Few psychologists view the organism as the passive recipient of environmental training proposed by Locke. Instead, they believe children organize the information they encounter as they explore the environment. The notion of stages and the seemingly ephemeral structures, however, make some psychologists uneasy (Brainerd, 1978).

As the topics of this book are introduced, students will repeatedly encounter the structuralist perspective. Research on cognitive development (Piaget, 1970), language development (Brown, 1973), moral development (Kohlberg, 1981), imagery (Piaget & Inhelder 1972), and memory (Piaget & Inhelder, 1973) frequently have structuralist components. In fact, whenever the child's knowledge of an area accumulates and becomes more organized, the reader is likely to be introduced to stages in the acquisition of that knowledge.

## THE EXPERIMENTAL REALM

Experiences shape our development. Our potential as humans can be hindered or fulfilled depending on our environment, our stimulation, and the choices we make. Psychologists in this realm, aware that it is easier to modify a child's experiences than the genetic or evolutionary components of development, are committed to examining the effects that external events have on the child's development.

**Behaviorism**

The *behaviorists* felt that Freud's emphasis on mentalistic concepts, like the unconscious, was unscientific and misdirected. Such processes defied the objective observations that should form the foundation of scientific inquiry. To make psychology more scientific, behaviorists limited their investigations to the study of observable events.

John Locke set the tone for this behaviorism with his conviction that infants passively record the stimulation from their environments. This view was carried to an extreme in the early part of the 20th century when John Watson, one of the founders of the behavioral school of psychology, proclaimed that infants were infinitely malleable. Watson offered to mold any 12 infants into doctors, lawyers, or indian chiefs by controlling their environments (Watson, 1924). Watson and other behaviorists believed that they could predict and control children's behavior by judiciously manipulating the environment in which they were raised (Bijou & Baer, 1961).

One of Watson's most famous demonstrations involved a child nicknamed Little Albert (Watson & Rayner, 1920). Albert was shown a tame white rat when he was 11 months old. Albert showed no initial fear of the rat and reached out to pet it. Every time he touched the rat, the experimenters struck a steel bar with a hammer. Startled and frightened by the loud noise, Albert began to cry. After only seven pairings of the frightening noise and the rat, Albert began to cry at the sight of the rat. Furthermore, his fear generalized to a white rabbit, a large ball of cotton, and even a Santa Claus mask. Objects that were not similar, like blocks, were not affected by his new fear (see Figure 1–8).

Although this demonstration has been questioned (Harris, 1979; Samuelson, 1980), it illustrates how the early behaviorists viewed learning. Albert's fear was built on an association. Pavlov demonstrated similar learning in dogs when he paired food with a bell. Such arbitrary pairings lead to a form of learning called *classical conditioning*.

The accidental pairing of two stimuli can hardly account for all behavior. A much more common mode of learning is called *instrumental conditioning*. It depends on the consequences children experience when they behave in particular ways. A word of praise, an affectionate hug, a five dollar bill, a coveted toy, or a piece of candy are some of the positive reinforcements that parents and teachers use to strengthen or increase the frequency of a behavior (response). Ignoring a behavior has the opposite effect. The frequency of the behavior will decrease if it is not reinforced.

Punishment can also decrease the frequency of a response (Parke, 1977). Lectures, spankings, the witholding of affection, or sending children to their rooms are punishments (negative consequences) that parents use to change their child's behavior. Decreasing the frequency of a response—how often David taunts his sister—and weakening that response are different. Punishment suppresses the behavior, but it does not necessarily weaken the response. As soon as the children are in a new situation, David may begin teasing his sister again. Punishments that are consistent, are accompanied by an explanation, and are administered by an affectionate parent are likely to weaken the undesirable behavior (Parke, 1977).

In the 1940s and 1950s, researchers from the experiential realm were convinced that they could control large segments of a child's behavior by using the right combination of reinforcement, lack of reinforcement, and punishment. In his classic book *Walden II*, B. F. Skinner (1948) went so far as to outline a utopian community in which behavioral principles were used to promote honesty, achievement, and cooperation, and to eliminate the baser human emotions like anger, jealousy, and fear (see Figure 1–9).

Sounding a similar note of optimism, Keller and Schoenfeld proclaimed that environmental events control an individual's behavior. The environment "teaches the individual what he may and may not do, giving him norms and

**Figure 1—8**          **Little Albert**

*His first view of a rat*

A great many people believe that children fear furry animals. This eight-month-old youngster is seeing a live, furry animal for the first time. He reaches for the rat as boldly as he reaches for his toys. Nor does he shudder and draw back when his hands touch the animal.

*After conditioning*

A loud bang is sounded every time the rat is presented. After only seven pairings of the noise and the rat, Albert begins to fear the rat.

*He now fears his furry friend*

We see here a man-made, built-in fear. This is the same infant. This fear was experimentally built in by the process of conditioning. Now the moment the child sees the rabbit he cries.

*Now he fears even Santa Claus*

After conditioning, even the *sight* of the long whiskers of a Santa Claus mask sends the youngster scuttling away, crying, and shaking his head from side to side. He had never seen a Santa Claus before. This reaction is also a direct result of our setting up in him conditioned fear of the rabbit.

John Watson's experiment in which 11-month-old Albert was taught to fear furry objects has been used for decades as an example of how fears may be learned from random pairings of events in the environment.

Source: Watson, J. B. (1928) *Psychological care of infant and child* (pp. 23, 25, 28). New York: W. W. Norton.

**Figure 1—9**     **Walden II**

In the following selection from Walden II, T. E. Frazier is conducting a tour of the children's quarters at Walden II. He and Mrs. Nash are explaining how children are reared without anger and jealousy. Professor Burris, the narrator, and Mr. Castle are listening to an explanation of how emotions are encouraged or eliminated at Walden II.

"Sorrow and hate—and the high-voltage excitements of anger, fear, and rage—are out of proportion with the needs of modern life, and they're wasteful and dangerous. Mr. Castle has mentioned jealousy—a minor form of anger, I think we may call it. Naturally we avoid it. It has served no purpose in the evolution of man; we've no further use for it. If we allowed it to persist, it would only sap the life out of us. In a cooperative society there's no jealousy because there's no need for jealousy."

". . . How do you make sure that jealousy isn't needed in Walden II?" I said.

"In Walden II problems can't be solved by attacking others," said Frazier with marked finality.

"That's not the same as eliminating jealousy, though," I said.

"Of course, it's not. But when a particular emotion is no longer a useful part of a behavioral repertoire, we proceed to eliminate it."

"Yes, but how?"

". . . Take this case.

"A group of children arrive home after a long walk tired and hungry. They're expecting supper; they find, instead, that it's time for a lesson in self-control: they must stand for five minutes in front of steaming bowls of soup.

"The assignment is accepted like a problem in arithmetic. Any groaning or complaining is a wrong answer. Instead, the children begin at once to work upon themselves to avoid any unhappiness during the delay. One of them may make a joke of it. We encourage a sense of humor as a good way of not taking an annoyance seriously. The joke won't be much, according to adult standards—perhaps the child will simply pretend to empty the bowl of soup into his upturned mouth. Another may start a song with many verses. The rest join in at once, for they've learned that it's a good way to make time pass."

Frazier glanced uneasily at Castle, who was not to be appeased.

"That also strikes you as a form of torture, Mr. Castle?" he asked.

"I'd rather be put on the rack," said Castle.

"Then you have by no means had the thorough training I supposed. You can't imagine how lightly the children take such an experience. It's a rather severe biological frustration, for the children are tired and hungry and they must stand and look at food; but it's passed off as lightly as a five-minute delay at curtain time. We regard it as a fairly elementary test. Much more difficult problems follow."

"I suspected as much," muttered Castle.

"In a later stage we forbid all social devices. No songs, no jokes—merely silence. Each child is forced back upon his own resources—a very important step.

"I should think so," I said. "And how do you know it's successful? You might produce a lot of silently resentful children. It's certainly a dangerous stage."

"It is, and we follow each child carefully. If he hasn't picked up the necessary techniques, we start back a little. A still more advanced stage"—Frazier glanced again at Castle, who stirred uneasily—"brings me to my point. When it's time to sit down to the soup, the children count off—heads and tails. Then a coin is tossed and if it comes up heads, the 'heads' sit down and eat. The 'tails' remain standing for another five minutes."

Castle groaned.

"And you call that envy?" I said.

"Perhaps not exactly," said Frazier. "At least there's seldom any aggression against the lucky ones."

"May you not inadvertently teach your children some of the very emotions you're trying to eliminate?" I said. "What's the effect, for example, of finding the

**Figure 1–9  Concluded**

anticipation of a warm supper suddenly thwarted? Doesn't that eventually lead to feelings of uncertainty, or even anxiety?"

"It might. We had to discover how often our lessons could be safely administered.

All our schedules are worked out experimentally. We watch for undesired consequences just as any scientist watches for disrupting factors in his experiments."

Source: Skinner, B. F. (1948). Walden II (p. 82–94). New York: Macmillan. Reprinted with permission of Macmillan Publishing Company from Walden Two by B. F. Skinner. Copyright 1948, renewed 1976 by B. F. Skinner.

ranges of social behavior that are permissive or prescriptive or prohibitive. It teaches him the language he is to speak; it gives him his standards of beauty and art, of good and bad conduct; it sets before him a picture of the ideal personality that he is to imitate and strive to be. In all this, the fundamental laws of behavior are to be found" (Keller & Schoenfeld, 1950, p. 366).

In learning laboratories throughout the United States, psychologists tried to discover the fundamental laws of behavior by conducting elaborate studies of how rats, monkeys, and children learn (Stevenson, 1970; Schwartz & Lacey, 1982). Researchers asked what types of reinforcers are most effective, how long it takes to build or extinguish a response, and what factors cause a newly learned behavior to generalize. In these investigations, which were the mainstay of developmental psychology for two decades, the experimental method was the preferred technique and the majority of studies were conducted in laboratory settings.

**The experimental strategy**

The experimental strategy is often favored over other techniques because the researcher can control other variables that might affect the behavior. In a simple experiment, for example, a psychologist might compare how quickly children learn when they are rewarded for every response with how quickly they learn when they are rewarded for every other response. If, at the end of the experiment, the group that was reinforced for each response has learned faster, the experimenter might conclude that reinforcing each response is the best way to promote rapid learning (Bijou & Baer, 1961). But even in this simple study, experimenters need to draw valid conclusions. The experimenter must be sure that the groups have the same level of expertise. The number of boys and girls should be the same because one sex may learn more rapidly than the other. The reinforcer needs to be equally attractive to all children. The experimenter might want to see both groups at the same time of day. In short, researchers using the experimental technique try to establish that the groups of subjects they are comparing are similar except for the treatment they receive. If the groups differ after the treatment, then it is reasonable to conclude that the treatment caused the difference.

Although it is still a prominent research method in developmental psychology, the laboratory experiment does not hold the revered spot it once did.

Bronfenbrenner (1977) is especially critical of the artificial nature of laboratory experiments. He has accused developmental psychology of being a science that explores "the strange behavior of a child in a strange situation with a strange adult" (p. 277–278). He questions whether these findings help us understand how children behave in the real environment.

## Behavioral modification

In response to these criticisms, psychologists from the experiential realm began to apply laboratory techniques in more natural settings. Case reports began to document changes in a child's behavior through the use of reinforcements. A 21-month-old child who had tantrums at bedtime was a case in point. Instead of responding to the child's tantrums, the parents ignored them. Within 10 days, the child fell asleep without a whimper (Williams, 1959). Sidney Bijou and Donald Baer (1967) compiled dozens of similar success stories (see Figure 1–10). Aggressive children were subdued (Lovaas, 1961), children with school phobias began to attend school without any anxiety (Lazarus, 1971), shy children hesitantly approached their peers (Harris, Wolf, & Baer, 1964), and hyperactive children attended to their schoolwork (O'Leary & Pelham, 1977).

Even more astounding was the success of these procedures with mentally retarded and autistic children. By dividing each task into small components and reinforcing mentally retarded children for successfully performing each component, children in institutions were taught to dress themselves, take care of their personal needs, wash their hands before eating, and even answer simple arithmetic problems and read simple words (Bijou, Birnbrauer, Kidder & Tague, 1966).

Autistic children who had engaged in years of self-destructive behavior also profited from *behavioral modification* techniques. One child, a nine year-old schizophrenic, had been self-destructive since she was three. She banged her head and arms, pinched and slapped herself, and set her hair on fire by using an electric heater. Her behavior was changed using behavioral modification techniques (Lovaas, Freitag, Gold, & Kassorla, 1965).

With their success in modifying behaviors, researchers in this realm might have been convinced that the control of all human behavior was simply a matter of controlling an individual's reinforcements. More time and research tempered this optimism. Areas where behavioral principles could be applied effectively were pinpointed, but the limitations were also discovered.

The early versions of behaviorism were as extreme in their promotion of environmental factors as Gesell's view was in its promotion of biological factors. Just as Gesell's theory was superseded by a more complex view of biological factors, the early behavioral view yielded to more complex views of environmental factors. The new views retain the emphasis on objectivity and the experimental flavor, but they have a broader and more elaborated understanding of the relationship between the environment (the stimulus) and behavior (the response).

In contemporary developmental psychology, both information processing

**Figure 1—10**                    **Behavioral modification**

Jimmy, 10, was referred to the child guidance clinic because he was unable to go to school. A month prior to the referral he had suffered a bronchial infection, following which the Christmas holiday season occurred. After that, the youngster refused to return to school, in spite of efforts by the parents, the teacher and the principal. The patient stated that when he thought about going to school in the morning he became frightened and often vomited. His previous school attendance record was excellent, as was his school-work performance.

The patient described many arguments at home involving everyone in the family. He indicated that he would not be overly concerned if his father moved out of the house, but if his mother left, it would be quite different. "If she goes, the whole family would fade away. We would have to go to another home . . ." This concern about losing his mother was evidenced at other times; for example, the patient also stated that if his mother went to the store, he often imagined that she might get hit by a car. Other factors that seemed related to his concerns were: (1) Jimmy got lost as a small child and remembered how terribly frightened he was; (2) five years previously when his mother was working he had worried a good deal about her; (3) his mother often used the phrase: "Some day I'll be dead, and you'll wish you had me. You'll want help, and I won't be there." And in referring to school, she often said, "One of these days when you get home, I won't be here."

After six months of therapy, shortly before school was to start, the patient indicated that he was nervous about trying to go back to school but indicated that he felt better than he had six months previously. He also stated that he felt he knew himself better and felt more confident. There appeared to be a good relationship between Jimmy and the therapist. On the day he was to return to school, the patient could not take the step out of the home, and again he panicked.

At this point, a behavioral modification procedure called "desensitization" was started. Jimmy was told that each day the therapist would accompany him to school and that together they would approach the school gradually. Since it was known that he could tolerate going by the school in a car, the first step consisted of Jimmy and the therapist sitting in the car in front of the school. The other steps were as follows: (2) getting out of the car and approaching the curb; (3) going to the sidewalk; (4) going to the bottom of the steps of the school; (5) going to the top of the steps; (6) going to the door; (7) entering the school; (8) approaching the classroom a certain distance each day; (9) entering the classroom; (10) being present in the classroom with the teacher; (11) being present in the classroom with the teacher and one or two classmates; (12) being present in the classroom with a full class. This procedure was carried out over 20 consecutive days, including Saturdays and Sundays.

The therapist and Jimmy began by coming to school early in the morning when no one else was present. Jimmy was told to report any uncomfortable feelings he was experiencing, and when he reported that he was feeling afraid, the therapist immediately indicated that it was time to return to the car and generously praised Jimmy for what he had accomplished.

After the 20-day desensitization period, Jimmy was able to attend school.

Source: Garvey, W. P. & Hegrenes, J. R. (1966). Desensitization techniques in the treatment of school phobia. *American Journal of Orthopsychiatry, 36, 147–152.*

and social learning theory acknowledge a debt to the early behaviorists. After considering information processing, we will turn to the social realm and a discussion of social learning theory.

**Information processing**

Attempts to apply the principles of behaviorism to all human actions proved impossible. Many of the behaviors we would like to encourage in humans are not overt. Cognitive skills, for example, include many processes that are of interest, but are not readily observable (Estes, 1978). Children reading silently may move their eyes and some children may partially mouth the words, but these behaviors really tell us nothing about the cognitive processes involved in reading. The same is true of solving a complex puzzle. To understand these cognitive activities, we need to know the process children use between the time the puzzle is presented and their solution. In short, we need to know what is happening in the child's mind between the stimulus and the response.

Asking subjects how they solved a problem, a technique called *introspection*, is too subjective for scientists. Such responses as, "I guess my l'il ole brain told me," (Furth & Wachs, 1974) are not very helpful in understanding problem solving techniques. Another technique is to question children about the material they have read or the items they have memorized. This technique tells us about the child's reading or remembering skills, but does not tell about the method they used.

**Figure 1–11**     **Information processing**

Problem: Add 4 + 8

Process:

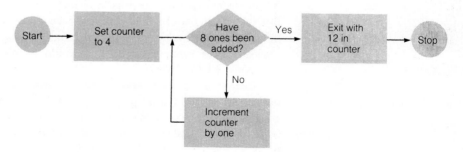

Information processing borrows concepts and terminology from the field of computer science. This chart diagrams the processes a child goes through when adding two numbers. Flowcharts of cognitive processes that children use are becoming more common in developmental psychology.

Source: Resnick, L. B. (1980). The role of invention in the development of mathematical competence. In R. H. Kluwe & H. Spada (Eds.), *Developmental models of thinking* (p. 215). New York: Academic Press.

Because these techniques neglect cognitive strategies, information processing theorists have been forced to develop their own approach. They began by borrowing the vocabulary of computer science. Computers process, transform, store, and retrieve information. The cognitive skills of a child might also be called coding, transforming, storing, and retrieving information. A computer programmer tries to construct a sequence of processes that the computer will perform to solve a particular problem (see Figure 1–11). Information processing theorists have extended these flowcharts and tree diagrams to children's reasoning (Klahr, 1980). Computers solving problems require a specific amount of memory space and take so many seconds or minutes to perform the calculations. Similar concepts such as M-space (Pascual-Leone, 1980) and reaction times (Jensen, 1981) have found their way into developmental psychology.

**Memory and information processing.** How children remember is one area that *information processing* theorists have investigated extensively. When children memorize a list of words, the processes occur in a sequence of layers. First, the list is processed by the senses. If children are reading the list, the first layer of processing occurs in the eyes and the related perceptual organs. The initial processing of each item takes only a fraction of a second. The word is then transferred to a memory area that is specifically reserved for visual information. This second level of processing takes somewhat longer, maybe a second. Once the information is stored in the visual memory, it can be processed further by more complex systems that are at the core of thinking.

At the deeper levels of processing, the child puts information into a *short-term memory buffer* where it is attended to for 5 to 10 seconds before it is transferred to a longer-term storage level. *Long-term memory* in adults seems to be unlimited and is organized as a network of associated concepts. Once information is in long-term memory, it can be transferred to other levels or it can become the base for a search of all layers of memory (Klahr, 1980).

A child's long-term memory is not as efficient as an adult's. Children are slower, they make more errors, and they do not remember as well as adults. But this doesn't mean that children have a different system of remembering information. Instead, it means that children lack some essential facts, some procedures, or some strategies that would enable them to use their system efficiently (Klahr, 1980).

**Cognitive processes viewed from several realms.** This brief outline of an information processing approach to memory introduces us to the concepts of the realm. We notice immediately that this position differs from both the behavioral view and the structural view. Information processing theorists adhere to several of the principles endorsed by the early behaviorists. The computer analogy retains a vestige of the view that the organism is passive. We also see an emphasis on the role of the environment as promoted by the early behaviorists.

Although some information processing theorists work within the confines of the computer analogy, others have gone beyond those boundaries and have incorporated structural ideas. By including organizational concepts like structures and hierarchies of information, the information processing theorists have broadened their ability to explain cognitive processes (Estes, 1978).

Two essential differences between the structural and the information processing views remain. The first is the tenet that children's cognitive skills change. Information processing theorists believe that after age five, and maybe earlier, the information processing system of the child is a miniature of the adult system (Klahr, 1980). A second difference focuses on the initiation of cognitive activity. To researchers in the structural realm, the child is the source of activity. For information processing theorists, the initiation of processing in a child depends, to a great extent, on the input from the environment. Even though information processing theorists do not emphasize the child's role in initiating action, they do recognize that the child's thought processes are modified by new information (Klahr, 1980). Their concept of self-modification is similar to the principle of self-regulation espoused by the structural theorists.

Information processing and behavioral modification are only two of the fields

## Computer-assisted instruction

*Rhoda Baer: Folio Inc.*

Computer-assisted instruction depends on several principles from the early behaviorists. The skill to be learned, such as multiplication or division, is divided into small steps. As children practice each step, they are reinforced for correct answers. At the end of the program, they will have mastered the skill in its most complex form.

that have evolved from the experiential realm. Programmed instruction, behavior therapy, computer-assisted instruction, classroom management, and curriculum innovations are other areas of developmental psychology that are currently concerned with arranging the environment to facilitate certain behaviors.

The experiential realm is one of the largest realms in developmental psychology and includes a diverse group of psychologists. This diversity fosters differences in opinions. In time, these differences lead to the formation of other realms. The final realm we will consider, the social realm, is a branch of the experiential realm that emphasizes the importance of social experiences.

## THE SOCIAL REALM

Psychologists in the social realm come from a variety of backgrounds. Many of them are interested in how children learn to behave in socially acceptable ways, and their research concentrates on the socialization process. Some, called social learning theorists, chart the development of aggression, empathy, cooperation, competition, and sex roles. Others are interested in personality development. They ask questions such as what determines whether an infant will be well adjusted or maladjusted as an adult. Erik Erikson's theory of psychosocial development describes the steps a child might take in becoming a productive adult. Even though Erikson's interests are very different from the social learning theorists, they both share the opinion that a child's development is orchestrated by social agents—parents, teachers, peers, and the culture. These two theoretical positions will introduce us to the social realm.

**Social learning theory**

Social learning theory draws heavily from two different approaches to development—the psychoanalytic view, made famous by Freud, and the behavioral views espoused by Watson and Skinner. Social learning theorists share Freud's emphasis on the importance of social experiences, but they are methodologically more in tune with the scientific approach of learning theorists.

Sigmund Freud demonstrated to the Victorian community the powerful effect that society could have on the development of children. In case after case, the adults he saw in private practice were burdened by early emotional conflicts that had not been resolved (see Figure 1–12). Trying to catalogue these experiences led Freud to his theory of psychosexual development.

Human development, Freud decided, was a series of conflicts between the unbridled impulses of the *unconscious* (the id) and society's civilizing influences (the *superego*). The mediator between these two forces was the *ego*, which stood for reason and good sense (Freud, 1965). The ego, like the rider of a horse, must control the *id* and keep its powerful impulses headed down a path of socially acceptable behavior. With the ego at the reins, we submit to toilet training, we learn to leave the comfort of our mothers to attend school, and we adhere to a variety of social customs that regulate sexual conduct, aggression, and emotional outbursts.

**Figure 1—12**     **The Wolf-Man**

The Wolf-Man became ill at 18 years of age after a bout with gonorrhea. He was entirely incapacitated and completely dependent upon other people when he began his psychoanalysis several years later. He could not dress himself, he could not study, he was not prepared for any livelihood, and he had no satisfactory relationships (Gardiner, 1971).

His illness, reconstructed from Freud's account, actually dates from a severe neurotic disturbance, which began immediately before his fourth birthday. His parents who were wealthy Russians had been on a summer holiday. When they returned, they found their complacent four-year-old transformed. "He had become discontented, irritable and violent, took offense on every possible occasion, and then flew into a rage and screamed like a savage" (Freud, 1971, p. 160). An Englishwoman who seemed to be the cause of the problem was dismissed, but the odd behavior did not disappear.

Through analysis, Freud learned that the patient's older sister had started sexual play with the boy just before his behavior changed. The sexual play had included masturbation and the boy had been caught by his nanny. The woman explained that masturbation "wasn't good; children who did that, she added, got a 'wound' in the place" (Freud, 1971, p. 169). The boy became convinced that his sister had suffered that wound since she did not have a penis. He developed an unconscious fear of castration.

At about the same time a consuming fear of wolves appeared. This fear came from a particular picture-book, in which a wolf was represented, standing upright and striding along. Whenever the boy caught sight of this picture he began to scream like a lunatic that he was afraid of the wolf coming and eating him up. His sister loved to show him this picture to terrorize him.

During analysis, the Wolf-Man remembered a terrifying dream that occurred at this same period. In the dream six or seven white wolves appeared in a tree. The child was terrified again of being eaten. After this dream, the boy developed a religious obsession. Before bed, he would say extensive prayers, kiss all the holy pictures in the room, and make innumerable signs of the cross upon himself and his bed (Freud, 1971). This new obsession reduced his anxiety about wolves. As a result, some of his wild behavior disappeared. As a child the boy had some atypical eating behaviors and occasionally lost control of his bowels. All of these symptoms are significant in the analysis.

After four years of analysis, Freud uncovered the roots of the original neurosis. The fear of being eaten by a wolf actually represented the child's fear of a sexual relationship with his father. It seems the child had seen his parents making love and this scene heightened such fears. At times the boy loses his appetite, another indication of his fear of being eaten up. The sexual development of the Wolf-Man goes awry at this point, as his sexual preferences become somewhat ambivalent. At puberty, he does engage in sexual relationships with women, but complains that he cannot bear women. When at age 18 he contracts gonorrhea, his earlier unresolved sexual ambivalence and anxieties resurface. His mental state slowly declines until he is helpless and dependent.

After his analysis with Freud, the Wolf-Man completed his studies within a short time, got a degree from law school, and a license to practice law. With the outbreak of World War I, he left Russia and worked in an insurance company for 30 years. He married and cared for his wife for 23 years. He was also able to build several lasting friendships. After his analysis, then, he was successful at work, in forming relationships, and at marriage. Because his case received such wide attention, it has been followed by several other psychoanalysts. Except for a brief reanalysis as an adult, the Wolf-Man seems to have led a normal adult life. Muriel Gardiner, who knew him for over 40 years, concludes, "There can be no doubt that Freud's analysis saved the Wolf-Man from a crippled existence" (Gardiner, 1971, p. 366).

The Wolf-Man is one of Freud's most famous cases. It illustrates how the unresolved fears and anxieties of childhood can plague mental health in adulthood.

Source: Gardiner, M. (1971). *The Wolf-Man*. New York: Basic Books.

Freud's writings, and especially his focus on the sexual nature of the child, pushed the young field of psychology into unexpected prominence. As it had with Darwin, the prominence and controversy that surrounded Freud's views facilitated comment, exchange, and new views from other scientists.

Psychologists of an experimental persuasion reacted against mentalistic concepts like the id and superego. Concepts that could not be observed were regarded as untrustworthy, epiphenomena, or simply fictional (Bandura, 1977). Behaviorists preferred to substitute terms that described observable actions. Dollard and Miller (1950) talked about *basic drives* instead of the id, and about *social reinforcements* instead of a superego. Drives and reinforcers could be measured and studied experimentally while the id and the superego resisted such quantification.

Social learning theory was inspired by some of Freud's hypotheses (Sears, Alpert, & Rau, 1965). Like Freud, the social learning theorists felt that social agents played a central role in the child's development. They also accepted Freud's notion that the experiences of the child influenced later behavior. But they specifically excluded some of Freud's mentalistic tenets because they could not be studied objectively. For methodological expertise they looked not to Freud, but to the behaviorists.

In the early years, then, social learning theory was an eclectic field that adapted concepts from one theory and methods from another. Under the guidance of Albert Bandura, social learning theory matured and began to take a shape and direction that set it distinctly apart from either the psychoanalytic view or the behaviorists (Bandura & Walters, 1963; Bandura, 1977; Bandura, 1982).

Bandura (1977) acknowledged the contribution that behaviorists had made to the field of psychology, but criticized their mechanistic models. He suggested that these models were no longer appropriate because they required a direct connection between environmental stimuli and an individual's responses. He argued instead that the events and the individual's responses are not directly connected, but are indirectly linked by (*a*) vicarious experiences, (*b*) symbolic skills, and (*c*) self-regulatory processes.

**Vicarious experiences.** Children learn through vicarious experiences. This was a novel idea to theorists who felt that behavior had to be followed by specific consequences if the child was to learn. But to psychologists who watched children play house, discipline dolls, or swear like their parents, this seemed to be stating the obvious. Children learn by observing and imitating when there are no environmental consequences for either (see Figure 1–13).

Bandura points out that in the case of children it would be inefficient and time consuming to reinforce each behavior, especially when children learn quickly through observation and imitation. Learning by observation allows children to acquire large, integrated patterns of behavior without having to go through the tedious process of trial-and-error learning (Bandura, 1977). Girls in Guatemala learn to weave by observing a teacher. When the girls feel they

**Figure 1—13**          **Imitation**

James Holland: Stock, Boston.

Children learn by observing and imitating.

are ready, they take over. To the strict behaviorist, such learning would be impossible because the girls received no reinforcement. In behavioral terms, they demonstrate *no-trial learning* (Bandura, 1965).

Learning by observation is not only faster than learning by reinforcement, it is necessary for both development and survival. In trial-and-error learning, the errors can produce costly or even fatal consequences. "For this reason, one does not teach children to swim, adolescents to drive automobiles, or novice medical students to perform surgery by having them discover the appropriate behavior through the consequences of their success or failures" (Bandura, 1977, p. 12). When mistakes are hazardous and costly, we rely on observational learning. Our prospects for survival as a species would dwindle rapidly if we could learn only by suffering the consequences of trial and error.

It is also difficult for social learning to occur entirely through reinforcement. Do children learn about aggression, sex roles, cooperation, empathy, and stealing through reinforcement? Children do not have to steal and be punished before they can understand that stealing is inappropriate. Bandura suggests that children learn about social taboos by observation. Research concerning the effects of television on children provides a good example. "Mr. Roger's Neighborhood," a television program built around social lessons, increases cooperation and other prosocial behaviors like sharing and helping (Freidrich & Stein, 1975). Aggressive, violent shows, on the other hand, have promoted aggressive behavior in some children (Leibert, Sprafkin, & Davidson, 1982). In both cases, the observational component of the learning is obvious.

To learn by observation, children must attend to a model and sort out the important features of the modeled behavior. They must also remember what they have seen by using images or verbal symbols. In experiments involving observational learning, the highest level of learning is achieved when the observer organizes and rehearses the behavior before it is repeated (Jeffery, 1976). The final component of observational learning involves using these memories to imitate a model.

**Symbolic skills.**  The suggestion that children can learn through observation puts cognitive processes back into the learning equation. The social learning theorists included not only observation, attention, and memory, but also symbolic skills (Bandura, 1977). The use of language and symbols enables humans to think about their experience, analyze it, and tell others. Human symbols also have the power to extend behavior into the future. We can plan, create, and imagine due to our ability to manipulate symbols. Symbols allow us to anticipate the probable consequences of different actions and, having understood those consequences, to change our behavior. Given that symbols have such a dramatic effect on behavior, a theory of human behavior cannot afford to neglect symbolic activities. Including thought processes between the stimulus and the response added another dimension to early behavioristic paradigms.

To some theoreticians, thought paves the way for language (Piaget, 1962). In this view, infants learn language after they have explored objects and understand the relationship between people, actions, and objects (Brown, 1973). Lev Vygotsky, a Russian psychologist, takes a different view. He argues that thought and language are initially separate aspects of development that gradually become intertwined. In this view, language can influence a child's thought. When a two-year-old admonishes herself that an object is a "no-no," we are seeing the force of language.

**Self-regulation.**  Bandura (1977) also insists that a theory of human behavior must include self-regulation. Children do not simply react to external influences. They select, organize, and transform the stimulation the environment provides. By recognizing that children regulate their environments, we are admitting that children not only have control over their environments, they often initiate change. Infants tired of playing signal their fatigue by fretting or crying. The mother usually responds by lowering the level of stimulation and putting the infant to bed. Notice that infants' interpretation of the same environmental event, playing with mother, changes depending on how tired they are. When they no longer enjoy the playing, their crying effectively regulates the environment.

Bandura's view of learning does not completely ignore reinforcement. He separates the process of learning a behavior from actually performing that behavior. Few of the children who watched Evil Kneivel jump the Snake River Canyon imitated his behavior. However, if they were stranded in a dangerous situation, children might build a ramp and try to execute a small jump to reach safety. The behavior is available to them should they need to perform it. Once children have learned a particular behavior, whether or not they perform it may be influenced by reinforcements. People learn many behaviors through observing, but they are most likely to demonstrate what they have learned if they think that others will approve.

"In the social learning view, people are neither driven by inner forces or buffeted by environmental stimuli" (Bandura, 1977, p. 11). Instead, children use their cognitive skills to observe, interpret, and remember the environment. They mesh this information with previous knowledge and their own goals to direct their behavior. In an earlier section, we examined the views of information processing theorists. They reject a stimulus-response model as too restrictive for the understanding of cognitive development. To them the gap between the stimulus and the response is actually filled with information processing concepts. Social learning theorists also reject the stimulus-response model as inappropriate for understanding socialization, and they fill the gap with symbolic and cognitive skills that enable children to interpret their society (Bandura, 1982).

## Psychosocial development

Even though Erik Erikson's theory of psychosocial development is based on Freud's theories, Erikson extended the concepts of his mentor. As a young artist, Erikson accepted an invitation from Freud's daughter, Anna, to teach school children in Vienna. Erikson studied Freud's psychoanalytic views and saw how Anna Freud had extended those views to include children. In the 1930s, his studies were interrupted by Hitler's rise to power. Erikson and his family fled to the United States and settled in Boston.

In the new environment, Erikson's own ideas began to take shape. As Boston's first child analyst, he encountered many children with emotional difficulties. He juxtaposed his experience in the clinical setting with information from other sources. He lived among the Sioux Indians and observed the Yurok Indians so that he could study children in different cultures. He also took time to investigate the development of normal children. His theory of psychosocial development reflects his broad experience with individuals of all ages who lived in a variety of cultures and circumstances.

Whereas Freud had seen the child's emotional development as a series of sexual conflicts, Erikson saw these same changes as a series of social conflicts. For example, Freud's anal stage highlighted the conflict that raged between children and their parents when toilet training began. Erikson viewed this conflict from a broader perspective. It was not toilet training, per se, that was important, but the larger issue of how a child maintains some autonomy in the face of a variety of social pressures. A mother who begins placing her infant on the potty at nine months is likely to have similar uncompromising notions of how the child must dress, eat, sleep, and obey. The child's struggle to maintain some autonomy will be very difficult in the face of so many demands.

The period of adolescence offers another example of how Erikson recast Freud's sexual conflict into a larger social framework. In Erikson's opinion, adolescents are not just struggling to master their genital impulses, they are trying to find an identity for themselves in the larger social world. Erikson's own adolescence was initially characterized by uncertainty as he wandered around Europe "trying to come to grips with himself" (Coles, 1970).

In addition to recasting Freud's theory in social terms, Erikson extended Freud's views. Freud had concentrated on the conflicts that originated early in life and were completed by adolescence. Erikson saw development as continuing throughout the life cycle. The eight social crises he outlines include three that occur after adolescence. During these years, adults struggle with developing intimacy, being productive, and accepting their lives.

Freud was often criticized for building a theory of emotional development based on neurotic patients from Vienna's upper classes. Erikson's theory has a much broader cultural base and is not restricted to aberrant development. Erikson begins by describing the path normal development takes, and the eight crises that individuals will have to resolve. If individuals negotiate these crises successfully, they will be well-adjusted individuals.

Critics of Erikson suggest that his concepts are intriguing, but untestable (Crain, 1980). In response, Erikson notes, "I came to psychology from art, which may explain, if not justify, the fact that the reader will find me painting contexts and backgrounds where he would rather have me point to facts and concepts" (Erikson, 1950, p. 17). In actuality, many of Erikson's concepts explored new horizons in psychology. Such exploration typically begins with broad brush strokes. As we will see in our discussions of personality development, Erikson is one of the few theorists to describe personality development from birth to old age.

## THE FIELD OF DEVELOPMENTAL PSYCHOLOGY

This brief journey through some of the realms of developmental psychology indicates the diversity of ideas and questions that occupy the local magicians. In addition, it exposes the student to the range of methods that are used and adapted to answer the questions of each realm. If, after reading all five realms, you feel that each of the magicians has discovered a kernel of truth, then I have been successful in introducing the field. Other authors may well have divided the realms differently or included magicians that I have neglected. Nevertheless, all of us have the same task—to prepare you for the range of opinions and the myriad research stances that prevail in the field of developmental psychology.

If, like the prince in the fable, you are searching for a single answer to the question, "How do children develop?" you will not find it. The study of child development is actually the study of the influence biological, ethological, structural, experiential, and social factors have on children. A comprehensive understanding of child development must include all of these factors.

Accepting the fact that development is the synthesis of many variables does not mean, however, that all viewpoints are equally valid. Magicians from each realm focus on behaviors that seem particularly appropriate to their perspective. The truths they discover may open up an entirely new way of approaching one topic in development, yet not be applicable to others.

Ethologists are less interested in achievement in school than they are in mating and parenting. School achievement is a recent addition to the culture, and the species will probably survive even if every child does not receive a college education. Mating and parenting, however, are essential to survival. We would expect ethologists to concentrate on these areas, and we would expect the truths derived from ethological investigations to be more applicable to these areas than to scholastic achievement.

Gesell, a magician from the biological realm, demonstrated the power of maturation, but his experiments focused on motor skills. When Watson isolated the importance of experience, he studied fears. Perhaps, each of these early magicians offered us some truth. Motor development is undoubtedly more heavily influenced by biological factors than are most fears.

Piaget believed that cognitive progress is facilitated by exploring and experiencing contradictions. Notice, however, that Piaget focused on the understanding of natural occurrences such as the force of gravity. Social knowledge is conventional and arbitrary (Kamii, 1981). Christians celebrate Christmas on the 25th of December; history texts tell us that Balboa discovered the Pacific Ocean. Knowledge like this may require substantial reinforcement from the environment before it becomes part of a stable, functional conceptual system. Exploration may lead to a stable understanding of information based on physical laws or logic, but social knowledge is less likely to be mastered during exploration.

The point is that understanding the child may require several kinds of explanations, and explanations that fit one area of development may not be applicable to other areas. Also, methods of inquiry that have served one realm may not address the issues that serve another realm. Laboratory experiments ignore variables that could be important in the natural setting (Bronfenbrenner, 1980). Short-term studies of cognitive skills are not likely to indicate how individuals change. Ethological studies are not very useful for studying memory skills.

On a broader level, the realms we have looked at do have points of convergence. All of them are trying to identify the salient processes in human development and to understand the "how" and "why" of development. Even though the social learning theorists, the information processing theorists, and the structuralists approach the topic of cognitive development from very different perspectives, they all agree that children organize information. Such convergence, even on a few concepts, might convince us that it is just a matter of time before the truth about development is clear.

My own suspicion is that an introductory chapter for a child development text written a hundred years from now will still be struggling with the truth about development. Some of the realms we have discussed in this chapter will have fallen into disfavor. Others will be included only for historical purposes and will have been supplanted by newer, more differentiated versions. Without doubt, some will be entirely new and almost unrecognizable to us.

Although human development may never be translated into a few laws that apply to everyone, we currently know enough to describe many aspects of development and to make limited predictions about behavior. These accomplishments are impressive when the subject is as challenging as the transformation of a single cell into an infant, a child, and, ultimately, an adult.

**Chromosomes and genes**

Karyotypes
Chromosomal deviations

**Learning to band chromosomes**

Minor chromosomal deviations
Genetic engineering

**Metabolic errors in genes**
Tay-Sachs disease
Cystic fibrosis
Sickle cell disease
Phenylketonuria
Sex-linked characteristics

**Developmental genetics**

**Separating hereditary and environmental influences**

Pedigree studies, twin studies, and adoption studies
Sociobiology

**Summary**

# CHAPTER 2

# Human behavioral genetics

The modern awakening of genetics dates from 1953 when a race was being run on both sides of the Atlantic to see who could be the first to decipher the structure of the *DNA* molecule. In the United States, Linus Pauling and his colleagues at Cal Tech were armed with bits and pieces of the chemical puzzle that would reveal the structure of DNA. But it was Francis Crick in England and a young American, James Watson, who combined information from chemistry, physics, and biology and finally succeeded in formulating a hypothetical model of DNA—the double helix (Watson, 1968). By arranging chemical elements as stairsteps in a double winding staircase, it was possible to show how an organism's biological beginnings could be coded on a single strand of DNA. Armed with the chemical understanding of DNA, the science of genetics exploded. In 30 years, the structure of DNA was ascertained, regulator genes were found, banding techniques were developed, karyotypes of fetal chromosomes were prepared, DNA was constructed in a test tube, and a human genetic defect was corrected with a gene created in the laboratory (see Figure 2–1). Because unraveling the secrets of the genes promises a better understanding of how we develop, the science of human development was deeply affected. In this chapter, we will trace the discoveries in the field of genetics and examine their effect on human development.

Increasing knowledge about the biological aspects of the organism has renewed our interest in the investigation of the biological factors that underpin human behavior. No serious scientists have ever denied the role of biology in human development. When that role was more obscure, it was easy to focus on the observable, environmental determinants of behavior and to ignore or pay lip service to the biological side.

Today, however, the role of biology in the development of human behavior is no longer obscure. It is widely recognized that all behaviors have a biological basis and that each individual begins with a particular complement of genetic material.

## CHROMOSOMES AND GENES

The essential "you" is determined by the 46 *chromosomes* that are a part of the nucleus of every cell in your body. These seemingly small bits of protein and *nucleic acid* orchestrate every aspect of the development of a human being.

**Figure 2—1**                    **Genetic milestones**

| | | |
|---|---|---|
| Gregor Mendel | Principles of genetic transmission | 1866 |
| Walter Sutton Theodore Boveri | Suggested chromosomes were involved in genetic transmission | 1903 |
| Thomas Morgan | Discovered that genes were arranged in sequences along the chromosomes | 1910 |
| Oswald Avery Colin MacLeod Maclyn McCarty | Demonstrated that DNA was the genetic material | 1943 |
| Jim Watson Francis Crick | Identified the double helix structure of DNA | 1953 |
| Joe-hin Tjio Albert Levan | Documented 46 chromosomes in humans | 1956 |
| Francis Jacob Jacques Monod | Suggested the role of regulator genes | 1961 |
| Mark Steele Roy Berg | Determined fetal karyotype from cultured amniotic fluid | 1966 |
| C. Valenti E. F. Shutta T. Kehaty | Diagnosed Down's syndrome prenatally | 1968 |
| Torbjorn Caspersson L. Zech C. Johansson | Developed techniques for banding chromosomes | 1970 |
| Paris Conference | Agreed on International Classification for human chromosomes | 1971 |
| Stanley Cohen Annie Chang | Created recombinant DNA in a test tube | 1972 |
| John Morrow Stanley Cohen Annie Chang Herbert Boyer Howard Goodman Robert Helling | Inserted DNA from a toad into a bacteria, paving the way for altering DNA | 1974 |
| Yuet Wai Kan | Successfully corrected a human genetic defect with an artifically constructed gene | 1982 |

In order to understand the profound impact that chromosomal material has on development, we need to examine chromosomes in some detail.

For years, scientists suspected, but were unable to prove, that the nucleus of the cell was critical in transmitting genetic information. In an attempt to clarify the structures of the nucleus, scientists began adding a purplish stain to the cell preparation. These stains were absorbed better by certain parts of the nucleus, named chromosomes (from the Greek "chromos" which means color and "somo" which means body). Once chromosomes could be identified, their central role in transmitting genetic information began to unfold.

At the turn of the century, chromosomes were identified as the chemical material crucial to genetic transmission. But this discovery reflected only a surface awareness of the complexities of genes. What chromosomes are made of and how the information contained on the chromosomes is used by the body were questions that took many more years to answer. We now know that chromosomes are composed of tightly coiled threads of the molecule *deoxyribonucleic acid* (DNA). The double helix of the DNA molecule is depicted in Figure 2–2. It resembles a winding staircase and can have as many as 30,000 steps. A *gene* is a section of this staircase having approximately 1,000 steps. Each gene begins and ends with a special series of steps—a sort of road map that says Gene A starts here and ends there. Between these two points on the DNA molecule there is a specific arrangement of chemical bases—the stairsteps of the molecule. When this arrangement of stairs is copied or transmitted, a protein is produced. The function of genes, then, is to supply the code for a particular protein. Proteins serve as the major building material of living organisms, and, in the form of *enzymes*, they govern all the biochemical activities of our bodies. Proteins can vary tremendously in structure and usually have a specific chemical activity. The differences between individuals and species are essentially differences between proteins. When someone comments that you must have a gene for curly hair, what they mean is that a section of DNA on one of your chromosomes codes for a particular protein. This protein determines whether you have straight or curly hair. Knowing that chromosomes are composed of DNA and that a gene is a particular section of DNA will make it easier to understand the role of chromosomes in development.

**Figure 2–2**     **The structure of DNA**

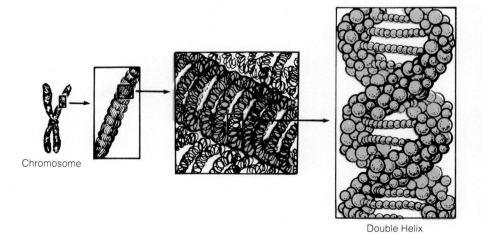

Chromosome

Double Helix

Chromosomes are composed of coiled strands of DNA. Genes are sections of this DNA, indicated by a particular sequence of bases (steps of the staircase).

Chromosomes are only seen clearly while the cell is actually dividing. So researchers discovered how the nucleus of a cell divides while looking for chromosomes. They watched with fascination as the chromosomes doubled, the membrane separating the nucleus from the cell body disappeared, the chromosomes lined up along a spindle in the cell, and then migrated to the cell's poles. This process of cell division was labeled *mitosis* (from the Greek "Mitos" meaning thread) because of the threadlike appearance of the chromosomes. The end result of mitosis is two cells that are duplicates of the original (see Figure 2–3).

Mitosis explains how our cells obtain all the genetic information that was in the original egg and sperm. This process does not explain how the egg and sperm cells end up with only 23 chromosomes each. If mitosis were the only

**Figure 2–3**                    **Mitosis**

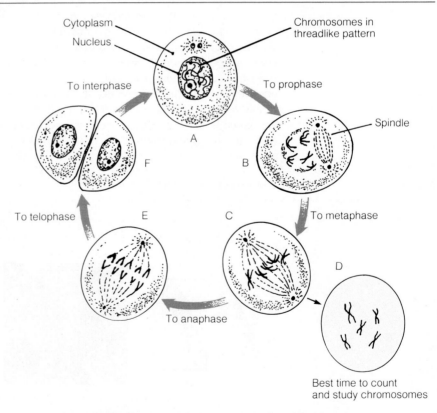

Mitotic cycle. A. Chromosomes in resting state; B. Chromosomes are duplicated and condensed; C. Chromosomes are arranged on a spindle; D. Best time to count and study chromosomes; E. Chromosomes move toward poles; F. Chromosomes uncoil; cycle complete.

Source: Levine, L. (1980). *The biology of the gene* (p. 78). St. Louis: C. V. Mosby.

**Figure 2—4**    **Genetic roulette**

During meosis, half of the parents' chromosomes are randomly selected for the egg or sperm cell.

The process of meosis reduces the number of chromosomes by one half through two successive duplication sequences.

Source: Nagle, J. J. (1979). *Heredity and human affairs.* St. Louis: C. V. Mosby.

mode of cell division, then each egg and sperm should have 46 chromosomes and the combination of the two would have 92 chromosomes. Since a species is characterized by a stable number of chromosomes, there has to be another method of cell division that reduces the number of chromosomes.

Meosis is a process of cell division designed especially for egg and sperm cells. Normal humans have 46 chromosomes—23 from their mother's egg cell and 23 from their father's sperm cell. Which of the mother's and father's chromosomes become part of the next generation is determined by a form of genetic roulette called *meosis* (from the Greek meaning to diminish). In this process, the cell divides, but instead of the two chromosomes duplicating, as in mitosis, only *one* member of each pair of chromosomes goes into the new cell. This simple process allows for an astronomical number of possible combinations of chromosomes. Imagine, for example, throwing 23 two-sided dice for the mother, then throwing a different set of 23 two-sided dice for the father (see Figure 2–4). The two sets of dice, representing the mother's and father's chromosomes, are then merged into a new human. The probability of throwing exactly the same set of 23 maternal chromosomes and exactly the same set of paternal chromosomes is infinitesimal—about 1 in 70 trillion. Given that the current world population is about 4½ billion and the total number of human beings that have ever lived on this planet is less than 7 billion, it is safe to say that every human that is not an identical twin is genetically unique. It is possible that your sibling could have the flip side of all of your mother's and father's chromosomes and that the two of you would have nothing, chromosomally, in common. However, it is far more likely that you and your sibling would share about half of your mother's and half of your father's chromosomes.

Each species has a constant number of chromosomes. Most humans have 46; our nearest relatives—chimpanzees, gorillas, and orangutans have 48 (Yunis & Prakash, 1981). Roundworms have two chromosomes. Other species with more than 46 chromosomes are the horse with 64, the dog, 78, the pigeon, 80, and the carp, 104 (LaBarba, 1981). The number of chromosomes has no evolutionary significance. What is important is that the number of chromosomes within each species remains constant. Extra chromosomes, as well as any deletions of chromosomal material, are typically associated with some abnormality within the species.

## Karyotypes

To find out more about an individual's chromosomes, a *karyotype* can be prepared. The first step involves drawing a sample of blood (see Figure 2–5). The cells from the blood sample are grown in a culture and stained. Finally, a photograph of the chromosomes is taken. The chromosomes can then be counted and ordered according to size and shape. A normal male karyotype is 46, XY, and a normal female karyotype is 46, XX. The number refers to the chromosome count and the XY specifies the two sex chromosomes.

## Chromosomal deviations

Any deviation from the normal pattern of 46 chromosomes can affect the organism. If in the process of cell division an entire chromosome is deleted, a spontaneous abortion will occur (Emery, 1979). The only exception to this rule is Turner's syndrome (45, XO). Even with this syndrome, 95 percent of the conceptions are spontaneously aborted during the early months of pregnancy (Hamerton, Canning, & Smith, 1975).

**Turner's syndrome.** Girls with Turner's syndrome have a karyotype of 45, XO; the O reflecting the lack of another X or Y chromosome. The primary characteristic of these girls is their short stature; most are below the third percentile for height. Girls with this syndrome do not develop the secondary sex characteristics associated with puberty. Hormonal therapy is used to induce puberty, but the girls remain sterile (Money, Klein, Beck, 1979).

The development of verbal skills in girls with Turner's syndrome is normal. Any deficits in intellectual skill usually occur in spatial skills, visual form discrimination, and visual memory (Garron, 1977; Rovet & Netley, 1981).

A case history prepared by the psychohormonal unit at Johns Hopkins University illustrates the psychological difficulties of these young women. Cindy S., 10 years old, was referred to the clinic because of severe psychological

**Figure 2—5**      **Preparing a karyotype**

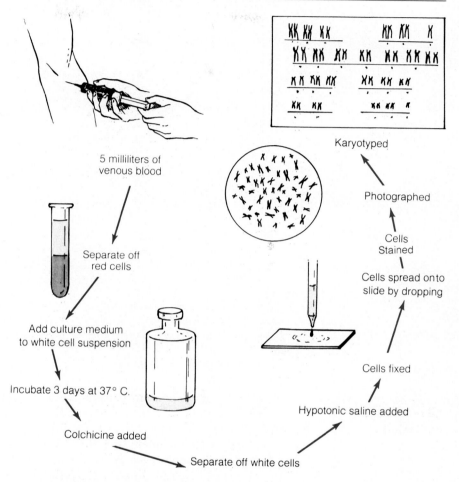

5 milliliters of
venous blood

Separate off
red cells

Add culture medium
to white cell suspension

Incubate 3 days at 37° C.

Colchicine added

Separate off white cells

Hypotonic saline added

Cells fixed

Cells spread onto
slide by dropping

Cells
Stained

Photographed

Karyotyped

Preparing a Karyotype of an individual's chromosomes.

Source: Emery, A. E. (1979). *Elements of medical genetics* (5th ed., p. 55). Edinburgh: Churchill Livingstone.

difficulties due to her shortness. She has been studied for eight years. During her early teens, the patient was suicidal because her friends learned about her medical condition. Males teased her excessively, suggesting that she would be an ideal partner for sexual experimentation, because pregnancy would be impossible. To counteract the teasing, Cindy created an alternate identity, pretending to be her cousin. This ruse simply added to her burden since she was now regarded as crazy. With the onset of estrogen treatment, her problems decreased. Gradually, the suicidal thoughts subsided. After high school, Cindy attended a large state university and did very well. She was considering gradu-

**Figure 2–6**            **The effects of extra chromosomal material on intelligence**

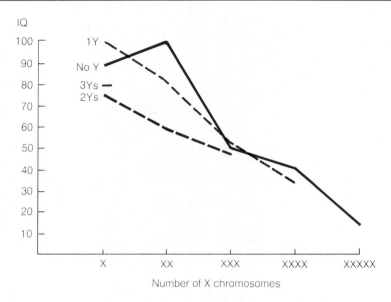

Chromosomal abnormalities have a negative effect on intelligence. Children who have two or three extra chromosomes are likely to be profoundly retarded.

Source: Ehrman, L., & Parsons, A. (1981). *Behavior genetics and evolution* (p. 67). New York, McGraw-Hill.

ate school, but was concerned about her scores on the entrance exams because of her difficulties with math and spatial problems (Money, Klein, & Beck, 1979).

Turner's syndrome results from the lack of a chromosome. The more typical genetic mishap results from an extra chromosome. As shown in Figure 2–6, the more extra genetic material, the greater the retardation (Ehrman & Parsons, 1981). Mental retardation is often present even when there are few physical differences resulting from the extra chromosome. This is the case in females with a karyotype of 47, XXX. Cases involving three, four, and five X chromosomes with one Y chromosome have been reported and the atypical chromosomal pattern is associated with intellectual impairment. Likewise, individuals with three, four, and five Ys have been reported, and they too suffer intellectually (Townes, Ziegler, & Lenhard, 1965).

**Down's syndrome.** The most widely known deviation caused by an extra chromosome is Down's syndrome, also called trisomy (three chromosomes) 21 because afflicted individuals have an extra 21st chromosome. This extra chromosomal material produces the characteristic physical features of Down's syndrome—the almond-shaped eyes caused by epicanthal folds on the eyelids, a flat nose, and a protruding tongue. Intellectually, these children can be mildly to profoundly retarded.

**Figure 2—7**                    **Down's syndrome**

*Courtesy W. B. Saunders Co.*

A Down's syndrome child.

Down's syndrome children are placid and good natured. Their friendly personalities make home care possible. The stimulation offered by home care combined with the educational programs provided by school districts has contributed to some increase in the intellectual functioning of these children. In Seattle, Washington, for example, an experimental program was offered to Down's infants. The program continued until the children were six years old. Thirty-one children from this program were then compared with 26 other Down's children who did not participate in the program. The children in the program had a mean IQ of 60 with some individuals scoring as high as 92. The children who had not been in the program had a mean IQ of 40. The highest score achieved by a child not in the program was 64 (Bennett, Sills, & Brand, 1979). Whether the advantage given by this program will be maintained remains to be seen. It seems unlikely because Down's children have difficulty with language and reasoning. The mean IQ of 50 at five years of age usually decreases to approximately 38 when the child is 13 (Melyn & White, 1973). Still, programs that begin in infancy may have a more permanent effect on intellectual skills than programs started in later years (Connolly & Russell, 1976).

The incidence of Down's syndrome is about 1 in every 700 births (Smith & Berg, 1976). Older mothers, however, have an increased risk of having a Down's child (see Figure 2–8). The standard reason given for this increased risk is that the reproductive system is not functioning as smoothly in older women and mishaps in cell division are more common. This explanation has been questioned recently because more younger mothers are having children with Down's syndrome (Mikkelsen, Fischer, Stene, Stene, & Petersen, 1976). In 1966 and 1970, women over 35 gave birth to 50 percent of all Down's children. By 1975, women over 35 produced only 28.5 percent of all Down's infants (Milunsky, 1979). Because it is hard to argue that the reproductive system is not functioning smoothly with the younger mothers, other explanations have been sought. Perhaps the change is due to better maternal care for all mothers. Between 65 percent and 80 percent of fetuses with Down's syndrome are spontaneously aborted (Creasy & Crolla, 1974). Better care could be reducing the number of spontaneous abortions. It is also possible that women over 35 have had genetic counseling and have chosen to abort any affected fetuses (Hansen, 1978). A more ominous explanation focuses on the increase in environmental radiation, pharmacological agents, and thyroid antibodies and suggests that these environmental hazards are increasing the number of genetic mistakes (Berg, 1979).

The age of the mother is so widely publicized as a critical factor in Down's syndrome that few people have thought about the father's role. Until the 1970s it was impossible to tell whether the mother or the father had contributed the extra chromosome. However, new ways to stain chromosomes make the specific light and dark bands on chromosomes visible. It is now possible to identify which chromosome comes from the father and which comes from the mother. These techniques have shown that the mother is not always the one who contributes the extra chromosome. In 20 to 40 percent of the cases of Down's syndrome, the father contributed the third chromosome (Magenis, Overton, Chamberlain, Brady, & Lovrien, 1977). In Figure 2–9, we can identify two of the 21st chromosomes (c) in the child's karyotype as coming from the father. Only one (a) comes from the mother.

As might be expected, the age of the father is a factor. The incidence of fathers contributing to a Down's syndrome child increases slowly up to age 49,

**Figure 2–8**      **Relationship between maternal age and Down's syndrome**

| Mother's age | Incidence of Down's children |
|---|---|
| 15–19 | 17.5 |
| 20–24 | 20.2 |
| 25–29 | 29.5 |
| 30–34 | 46.6 |
| 35–39 | 159.5 |
| 40–49 | 670.5 |

This graph depicts the number of children born with Down's syndrome per 100,000 births. As the mother becomes older, the number of affected infants increases dramatically.

Source: Health Education and Welfare Statistics, 1974.

**Figure 2—9**              **Tracing a chromosome through generations**

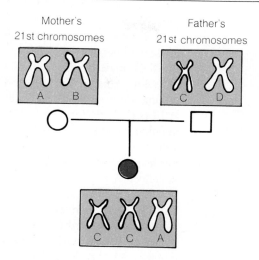

Inheritance of an extra chromosome 21 (Down's syndrome) from the father. The mother's chromosomes are labeled AB, and the father's chromosomes are labeled CD. The child received the mother's B chromosome and two C chromosomes from the father.

Source: Magenis, R. E., Overton, K. N., Chamberlin, J., Brady, T., & Lovrien, E. (1977). Parental origin of the extra chromosome in Down's syndrome. *Human Genetics, 37,* p. 11.

then rises sharply for fathers 55 and older (Stene, Fischer, Stene, Mikkelsen, & Petersen, 1977).

**Klinefelter's syndrome.** Males with Klinefelter's syndrome have an extra X chromosome, 47, XXY. Like the Turner's females, Klinefelter's males are not identified until puberty when they fail to develop body and facial hair and other secondary sex characteristics. These males are usually sterile, and like Turner's girls, there are varying reports about whether afflicted individuals are mentally retarded. IQs below 50 are rare and the mean IQ in one study was 85 with some individuals scoring as high as 115 (Zellweger & Simpson, 1977).

The intellectual problems that Klinefelter's males experience are often due to a language deficit. As toddlers, they often have difficulty forming sentences. Instead of saying, "I want some milk" they might say, "I want some white stuff." As they grow older, this deficit becomes more obvious. In a Boston study, five Klinefelter's boys were identified at birth and have been studied for some years. All five were referred for remedial reading by their first grade teacher, who had no knowledge of their chromosomal status. These boys, however, often had spatial IQ scores of 120 or higher (McBroom, 1980).

Males with Klinefelter's syndrome also seem to have personality and emotional problems. As infants, Klinefelter's males tend to be less active and less rebellious than normal boys. During the childhood years, they seem more compliant and often have difficulty concentrating. As adults they are more prone to a variety of behavioral problems—being depressed, obsessive, or anxious (Money, Klein, & Beck, 1979).

**The XYY connection.** The karyotype 47, XYY has received a great deal of media attention. Sometimes labeled as a supermale because of his height, the XYY male has been characterized as predisposed to violent and aggressive behavior. This picture of the XYY male came from chromosomal screening among prison populations. The incidence of XYY among criminal populations is 19 per 1,000; but there are only 1.3 per 1,000 XYY males in the total male population (Jarvik, Klodin, & Matsuyama, 1973). This means the XYY individual commits crimes 15 times as often as the typical male. It is, however, a big leap to conclude that these individuals are predisposed to aggression and violence. A closer analysis of the XYY criminals reveals that, for the most part, they are not incarcerated for violent or aggressive crimes against individuals. Instead, their crimes are usually minor crimes involving property. In some cases, the crimes seem impulsive and poorly planned. One XYY male had been caught trying to rob several homes while the families were present. Another XYY male falsely reported a stolen automobile, then waited for the police to arrive (Witkin et al., 1976).

Limiting studies of XYY males to samples of men who are in prison has some obvious drawbacks. If our information about all women came from studies of female inmates, our picture of women's behavior might be very distorted. Generalizing from XYY males in prison to all XYY males is also likely to lead to a distorted picture. An accurate picture of the behavior of XYY men can only be obtained by studying a random sample of these males. Such a survey was undertaken in Denmark during the 1970s.

Over 4,000 adult males who had been born in Copenhagen, Denmark between 1944 and 1947 were screened for chromosomal abnormalities. As a result 16 Klinefelter's males and 12 XYY males were located. Using a battery of tests, these two groups were compared with a group of normal men. The authors found that XYY males were not any more aggressive than the other two groups of men. As in studies done in the United States, a higher proportion of XYY men had criminal records, but their crimes were not any more violent than the normal males or the Klinefelter's males. It seems, instead, that their troubles with law enforcement agencies stem from their inferior intellectual skills and their impulsiveness. Both the Klinefelter's men and the XYY men scored lower than normal on an intelligence test, and both atypical groups had attended school for shorter periods of time (Witkin et al., 1976). Since the completion of this massive study, most psychologists have argued that the reduced intellectual capacity of XYY men leads to more arrests and more difficulties with the law. In any case, there is no reason to screen all men over 6′1″ to see if they are XYY; nor is it appropriate to screen newborn males for this disorder. The great majority of XYY individuals do not get into trouble with the law, and those that do are usually not violent.

Doing karyotypes on a large, random sample of the population is expensive and time consuming; but the results often provide valuable new information about chromosomal abnormalities. In a screening of all males born in Boston from 1970 through 1974, 11 Klinefelter's and 13 XYY males were found. But the birth of the atypical karyotypes did not occur evenly over the four years of the study. For as long as 14 months, no XYY or XXY males would be born. Then, inexplicably, three or four would be born within a couple of months. This pattern suggests that a virus or some other external environmental factor is involved (McBroom, 1980). If the environmental factor could be identified, it might be possible to reduce the number of men with these chromosomal abnormalities.

Large-scale screenings of newborns also pose ethical and moral questions. Should doctors tell parents if their child is an XYY male? It is possible that parents would be unduly alarmed by this information and would overreact to normal aggression. In addition, professionals have to be very conservative about labeling any child at an early age. The label might be interpreted by parents or teachers in a way that would interfere with the normal development of the child.

On the other hand, early identification of an XYY male might help professionals alleviate some of the problems that the parent and child face during development. Bruce, an XYY male, was first seen by a school counselor when he was six. His mother explained that he had violent temper tantrums, but that he was not particularly aggressive. Before a karyotype was done, his parents were often blamed for the boy's lack of self-control. Knowledge of the boy's chromosomal status took some of the pressure off the parents and helped them work with professional counselors. If your child was an XYY male, would you want to know?

## LEARNING TO BAND CHROMOSOMES

The bulk of our information about chromosomal abnormalities is from studies that simply counted the number of chromosomes. However, by the late 1960s these counts were no longer providing any new information. Only five chromosomes could be readily identified and further understanding of chromosomes seemed to be at a standstill (Hsu, 1979). Then, in 1970, Caspersson and his colleagues successfully stained chromosomes with a fluorescence substance. Photographs of human chromosomes now showed differing patterns of fluorescence, from very bright areas to dimly fluorescent zones (Caspersson, Zech, & Johanson, 1970). A second and less complex technique called Giemsa-Trypsin banding was also perfected (Seabright, 1971). Using these techniques, researchers could positively identify each of the 46 human chromosomes. Figure 2–10 presents the classification system used for chromosomes. The areas of each chromosome that are darkly banded contain more densely packed genes than the lighter areas. The first three chromosomes (Group A) are the largest, and the *centromere*, or juncture of the chromosome, is located toward the middle of the chromosome. The next two chro-

**Figure 2–10**          **International classification system for human chromosomes**

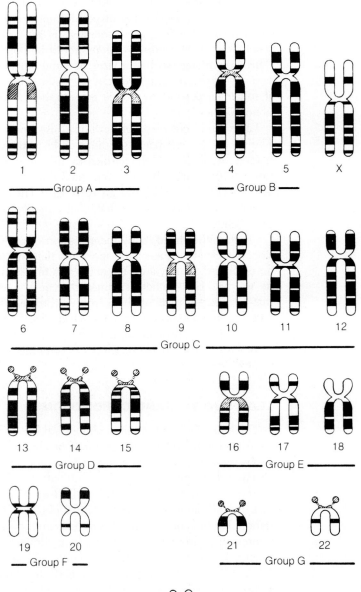

A diagrammatic representation of the human chromosomes, showing the banding patterns and numbering scheme adopted at the Paris Conference in 1971.

Sources: Thompson, J. S., & Thompson, M. W. (1980). *Genetics in medicine* (p. 25). Philadelphia: W. B. Saunders.

mosomes (Group B) are also large, but the centromere is not located in the middle of the chromosome. These two groups of chromosomes contain a great many genes; hence any abnormalities in them are likely to affect the fetus. These fetuses will be spontaneously aborted very early in the pregnancy. Chromosomes 6–12 (Group C) are smaller and also have the centromere slightly off center. In chromosomes 13–15 (Group D), the centromere is so far off center that the upper areas of the chromosomes are hardly visible. The same is true of chromosomes 21–22 (Group G). The tiny arms of these chromosomes are especially vulnerable and are likely to break off during cell division. It is very easy for the top arms of chromosome 15 to be exchanged for an arm of chromosome 21. Such an exchange is called a *translocation*. Groups E and F (chromosomes 16–20) are also short chromosomes, but their centromeres are more centrally located; hence translocations are not as common.

The 23d pair of chromosomes consists of the sex chromosomes. The male sex chromosome, designated by the letter "Y," is markedly different from the female sex chromosome, designated by the letter "X." As shown in Figure 2–10, the X chromosome is twice the size of the Y chromosome. The lack of any darkly banded areas on the Y chromosome indicates that the Y chromosome does not carry as much genetic information as the X chromosome. Females have two X chromosomes, while males have one X and one Y. In terms of the international identification system, the X is often grouped with chromosomes 6–12 and the Y is grouped with the 21st and 22d chromosome.

Once chromosomes could be individually identified, trisomies of chromosomes 13, 14, 15, 16, 17, 18, 19, and 22 were found in human infants. These infants were often born alive but usually survived for only a few weeks or months (Trunca, 1980). Trisomies of the first 12 chromosomes (groups A, B, and C) undoubtedly occur during cell division, but the fetus is aborted very early in development. The folklore that spontaneous abortions are nature's way of fixing its mistakes has been documented repeatedly. In one careful study, karyotypes were made of 1,500 fetuses that were spontaneously aborted. These karyotypes revealed that over 60 percent of the fetuses that had been aborted prior to 12 weeks of gestation had chromosomal abnormalities (Boue, Boue, & Lazar, 1975). A common statistic is that 15 percent of all conceptions are spontaneously aborted (Emery, 1979). This is likely to be an underestimate since some abortions occur before the woman even realizes she is pregnant. Typically these fetuses are the ones that would be the most severely affected if they were to survive (Therman, 1980).

**Minor chromosomal deviations**

The banding techniques developed in the 1970s did more than help us identify individual chromosomes. These techniques have made it possible to look closely at the specific sequence of genetic material on each chromosome. With these banding techniques, we can isolate small areas on the chromosome that have been deleted, areas that have been repeated or duplicated, inversions of a section of DNA, and translocations of chromosomal material. Geneticists

**Figure 2–11**                    **Chromosomal breakage**

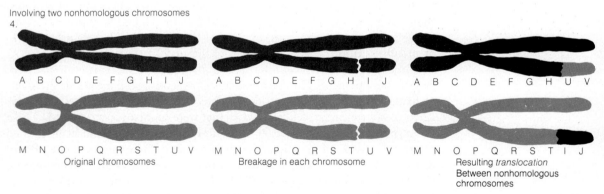

Involving one homologous pair of chromosomes

1.

A B C D E F G H I J
Original chromosome

A B C D E F G H I J
Breakage and elimination of H gives a *deletion*

A B C D E F G I J

2.

A B C D E F G H I J

A B C D E F G G H I J
Repetition of segment G gives a *duplication*
(this may occur in various ways)

3.

A B C D E F G H I J

A B C D H G F E I J
Breakage in two places and incorporation of segment
EFGH in reverse order, HGFE, produces an *inversion*

Involving two nonhomologous chromosomes

4.

A B C D E F G H I J

M N O P Q R S T U V
Original chromosomes

A B C D E F G H I J

M N O P Q R S T U V
Breakage in each chromosome

A B C D E F G H U V

M N O P Q R S T I J
Resulting *translocation*
Between nonhomologous
chromosomes

When chromosomes are duplicated, sections of chromosomes can be deleted, duplicated, inverted, or translocated. These four processes may have an effect on the child's
behavior.

Source: Ehrman, L. & Parsons, P. A. (1981) *Behavior genetics and evolution* (p. 54). New York:
McGraw-Hill.

have even been able to locate *fragile sites* on chromosomes—areas on the chromosomes that are likely to break when a cell divides (Sutherland & Hinton,
1981; Jacky, Beek, & Sutherland, 1983). If a section of the chromosome
breaks off, it may become reattached again in the correct way, it may move
to another site, or it may attach again upside down. Sometimes the broken

area is lost altogether. Figure 2–11 demonstrates the sequence of events during each of these processes.

Deletions of chromosomal material often lead to behavioral abnormalities. The *cri du chat* syndrome is characterized by the loss of a section of the short arm of the fifth chromosome. Children born with this deletion have a cry that sounds like the mewing of a cat; hence the name. In addition, the *cri du chat* infant often has cardiac defects, does not grow normally, and is mentally retarded.

Duplications of material on the chromosomes have also been found. One patient had a duplication of a single-banded area on the 10th chromosome. The symptoms he presented—moderate mental retardation, delayed psychomotor development, and retarded language development—have also been found in other children who had abnormalities of the 10th chromosome (Kovisto, Herva, & Linna, 1981).

*Inversions* of chromosomal material occur during cell division. The chromosome breaks in two places and a segment of chromosomal material is turned around. This means that the normal sequence of genes is changed. Notice that in this case no genetic material is added or lost; yet because the sequence is altered, behavior is affected.

When one section of a chromosome is small and off center, it is easy for translocation of chromosomal material to occur. A balanced translocation means that the arm of one chromosome has been exchanged for the arm of another chromosome during cell division. Such balanced translocations may have no adverse effect on the person because no chromosomal material has been gained or lost. However, translocations may affect that person's ability to reproduce (Stoll, 1981).

Banding techniques have only been in use for a short time. As these techniques are improved and are applied to wider samples, a great deal will be learned about the effects of minor alterations of human chromosomes. In 1981, for example, researchers in India did a genetic screening of 74 mentally retarded patients. Giemsa-trypsin staining showed that almost 20 percent of these patients had chromosomal abnormalities that had not been previously detected (Moghe, Patel, Peter, & Ambani, 1981).

Some diseases may be associated with an atypical set of chromosomes. Identical twin girls developed acute leukemia 19 months apart. The first twin was diagnosed at 17 months after a two-week history of pallor, bruising, and bleeding from a tooth socket. Despite aggressive treatment, she died a few months later. The second twin was brought to the clinic a year and a half later, with a similar history of bruising and fretfulness. Tests revealed that she, too, had acute undifferentiated leukemia. A chromosomal analysis indicated that both twins had an extra 19th chromosome (Hartley & Sainsbury, 1981).

New areas on chromosomes that indirectly affect complex behaviors are constantly being discovered. A spelling disability particular to some families seems to be related to an area (or locus) on the 5th chromosome (Smith, Kimberling, Pennington, & Lubs, 1983). A mild form of mental retardation is associated with an alteration of the 16th chromosome (Weatherall, et al., 1981), and a locus on the 6th chromosome may make some people susceptible to depression (Weitkamp, Stancer, Persad, Glood, & Guttorms, 1981). These loci are often found by accident and no one knows how the gene causes the behavior. In essence, the investigators in these studies have worked backward, finding a disorder and then examining the chromosomes of the affected individuals to see if the chromosome differs from a normal karyotype. There are many intermediate steps between the chromosomal differences and the behavior that are not understood.

Attempts to map the genes take the opposite approach. By splicing selected sections of DNA from a human into a frog or a mouse, new artificial genes can be created. When these new genes begin to function, they produce a protein that the old gene did not produce. We know then that the additional protein is the result of the human gene. This procedure allows scientists to link a human gene with the production of a particular protein. Using this procedure, over 200 genes have been located on the chromosomes, and the number of genes that are identified or "mapped" increases daily (Siniscallo, 1978). In most cases, however, knowing what protein is produced does not tell us much about the traits and behaviors that might be influenced by that protein. Nevertheless, finding out what protein a gene manufactures paves the way for genetic engineering.

**Genetic engineering**

Genetic intervention refers to any conscious manipulation that affects the frequency or expression of genes. Improved nutrition and adequate prenatal care can enhance a child's development and increase the likelihood of that child producing healthy children. This is a form of genetic intervention. Genetic interventions also try to reduce the detrimental effects of a gene. Providing insulin to a diabetic or reducing phenylalanine in a PKU patient's diet are examples. In these interventions, the gene pool is not altered.

Actually altering the gene pool is often termed *genetic engineering*. Prenatal screening to detect defective fetuses in combination with therapeutic abortions actually reduces the number of children born with genetic defects. The opposite of aborting defective fetuses is creating healthy fetuses. Lesley Brown and her husband John had not been able to conceive a child. Gynecologists determined that Mrs. Brown's oviducts were blocked and eggs could not pass into the uterus. To bypass the blockage, Dr. Steptoe, a reproductive physiologist, extracted one of the mother's eggs, fertilized it in a laboratory dish with the father's sperm, and implanted the developing embryo into Mrs. Brown's uterus. When Louise Brown was delivered nine months later, the attending gynecologist, Dr. Edwards, noted "the last time I saw her she was a beautiful 8 celled embryo" (Test-tube Baby, 1978, p. 68).

These examples of genetic engineering are only the beginning of our attempts to control our genetic destiny. It is entirely possible we will soon be able to select genetic characteristics as well as to screen others. Such engineering will be able to counteract incapacitating genetic defects. However, these skills could be misused or abused to satisfy a frivolous whim.

## METABOLIC ERRORS IN GENES

The biochemical basis of human functioning is especially evident when there is a dysfunction of one of the metabolic processes. Not being able to metabolize carbohydrates, sugars, or fats can have serious consequences for the developing human being. A single gene that does not produce the correct protein or enzyme can cause a toxic chemical to build up in the child's system. This single gene effect is seen in Tay-Sachs disease, cystic fibrosis, sickle cell disease, and PKU. All of these diseases are recessive. In other words, in order to have the disease, you must receive the defective gene from both your mother and your father (see Figure 2–12). A person who has only one gene will be a carrier, but will not express the disease. If two carriers marry, the probability of them passing the disease to their child is one in four or 25

**Figure 2–12**                    **Genetic transmission of recessive traits**

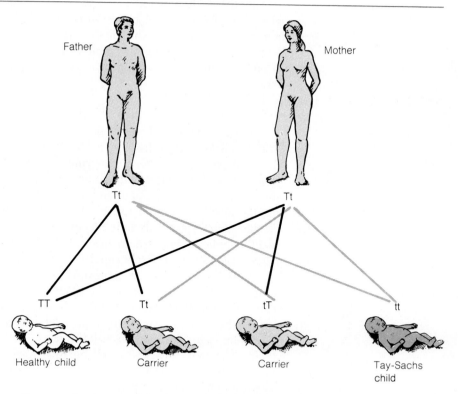

Two parents who carry the gene for Tay-Sachs marry. Their children may inherit either the healthy gene or the Tay-Sachs gene from each parent. The first combination is a healthy child who is not a carrier. That child received the normal gene from both parents. The second and third possibilities are a child who is healthy but who carries the Tay-Sachs gene. The fourth possibility is a child who has Tay-Sachs. This child received a Tay-Sachs gene from both the mother and the father.

percent. Seventy-five percent of the time, the parents can expect a healthy child.

**Tay-Sachs disease**

Tay-Sachs disease is one of the recessive genetic diseases that has severe consequences for the child. It results from the body's inability to break down fatty compounds. These compounds circulate in the bodies of normal individuals, but they are broken down by an enzyme that Tay-Sachs children lack. The gene that should produce this enzyme is defective; so instead of being flushed from the bloodstream in the normal fashion, these fatty compounds begin to accumulate. Over a period of months, their toxic effects begin to appear. A child who appeared normal and healthy at birth begins to change as the fatty compounds build up in the bloodstream. Rapid, irregular eye movements and paralysis develop during the first year. By the age of two or three, motor and neurological deterioration is advanced, and by the age of five the child typically dies.

Although there is no effective treatment for the disease, parents who might give birth to a Tay-Sachs child can be identified. Tay-Sachs is most common among Ashkenazi Jews who are descendants of central and eastern European Jews. Mass screening of these ethnic groups has identified thousands of carriers. If both parents are carriers, genetic counseling and prenatal screening of the fetus are in order (Kaback, 1977).

**Cystic fibrosis**

Unfortunately not all metabolic errors are as easily detected as Tay-Sachs disease. Cystic fibrosis, like Tay-Sachs, occurs when a defective or absent gene does not produce a necessary enzyme. Without this enzyme, a thick, sticky mucus clogs the passages of the lungs and leads to serious infections. The thick mucus also clogs other glands and ultimately causes their destruction. Managing the disease requires a special diet, administration of antibiotics and pancreatic extracts, and daily lung therapy. With this kind of aggressive management, children who used to die early in childhood are living for 30, and occasionally 40 years (Fischman, 1979).

Cystic fibrosis occurs in approximately 1 of every 2,000 births among the white populations and is carried by about 5 percent of white adults (Fischman, 1979). It is much less frequent among nonwhites. There is currently no screening test for parents. Nor is there prenatal screening to determine whether a developing fetus will be affected (Epstein, Breslow, Fitzimmons, & Vayo, 1980). The only way adults find out that they are carriers is by having an affected child. Having had an affected child once, the probability of parents having another one is 25 percent.

Whether to have more children is a difficult decision for the parents. One unusual family chose to continue having children. They had eight children. Given the odds, only two should have had cystic fibrosis. Instead, five of their eight children were affected. The parents still felt that the children had happy,

# CASE HISTORY OF TAY-SACHS
## The hopeful legacy of a child's passing
*By Ursula Vils*

Mara Leilani was born to Richard and Barbara Gould, an alert, lively, lovely baby girl. They lived in the gentle climate of Hawaii, and the proud parents took Mara with them everywhere. She was the kind of baby people could not resist.

"We'd take her out to a restaurant and people would pick her up, play with her. We wouldn't see her the whole time," recalls her mother.

At 8 months, Mara still was not sitting up. Barbara Gould wondered about that, but it didn't worry her. "I just figured she was a lazy kid. I've never been athletic and I just figured, like mother, like daughter."

During a regular checkup, Mara's pediatrician said, yes, she should be sitting up by now. He suggested the Goulds take her to a neurologist.

So began "a horrible month taking her around for different tests." Richard Gould, an MD, consulted his medical books to try to learn what might be wrong with his daughter. Among the childhood maladies listed was Tay-Sachs disease, a little-known genetic malady, that destroys the nervous system, causing rapid physical deterioration, blindness, total mental retardation—and death between three and five.

One of the indications of Tay-Sachs, Dr. Gould read, is a cherry red spot in the eye. A doctor had said Mara's eyes were normal, so the Goulds dismissed the possibility of Tay-Sachs.

The Goulds decided to take Mara to New York, where Rick's parents lived, for additional testing. Just before they were to leave, an Army pediatrician examined Mara and commented on a cherry red spot in her eyes.

"He didn't seem to know what it meant," Mrs. Gould said, "but it was a terrible moment for us because we knew everything. And she was so beautiful."

"Yes" said Dr. Gould quietly, the awful memory obviously still vivid, "at that moment she was perfect."

Mara Leilani Gould died Thanksgiving Day, aged 4.

Richard Gould and his wife are both New Yorkers. Originally Barbara lived across the street and it took three years to meet her. They have been married 10 years, "a good marriage" says Barbara, "but this—Mara—made us closer."

After graduating from the University of Texas,

Rick spent three years in Hawaii as an intern. It was there that the Goulds delightedly awaited the arrival of their first-born child, an event that turned to heartbreak within months.

However, Mara was not the last baby for the Goulds. When the Goulds trotted Mara from doctor to doctor, it was known that when both parents carry the fatal gene, there is one chance in four with each pregnancy that the baby will have the disease. The Goulds decided to adopt another baby. Maile, their adopted daughter, turned out to be a robust, energetic baby.

Then, through a friend, the Goulds learned that parents could successfully have babies tested in the womb for Tay-Sachs. They decided to have another baby.

"At this point, knowing that a fetus could be tested, we got pregnant again," said Dr. Gould. "Barbara flew from Hawaii to San Diego to be tested. We were told we would have a second Tay-Sachs baby. The first one was still at home dying."

Mrs. Gould flew to San Diego a second time for testing, a precaution against error. Again, the test indicated a Tay-Sachs baby. She returned to San Diego a third time, this time for an abortion.

Despite the tragedy of two Tay-Sachs pregnancies, the Goulds decided to try again. This time the tests were negative, and Tammy, a sturdy, dimpled little girl was born.

Dr. Michael Kaback, Director of the Tay-Sachs Disease Prevention Program in Los Angeles reports that in more than 200 pregnancies tested, almost exactly one fourth turned out to be Tay-Sachs babies, and almost every one of those was aborted. That is one side of the picture. The other is that 150 healthy children have been born who would not have been conceived if these tests were not available.

Rick and Barbara Gould and their daughters, Maile and Tammy now live in Ojai, California. Soon there will be another baby. Barbara is pregnant again. "This baby is OK," Dr. Gould said. "No Tay-Sachs. And one of the fringe benefits is that in testing the amniotic fluid, we could also know the sex of the child."

"A boy," said Barbara Gould delightedly.

"David," said her husband.

useful lives (Fischman, 1979). More often, parents who have one affected child elect to adopt children or to limit their family.

**Sickle cell disease**

Sickle cell disease is another familiar genetic disease. Although sickle cell affects the blood cells, the disease at the genetic level is the result of a change in one amino acid. Remember that genes code for proteins and proteins are composed of amino acids. Approximately 574 amino acids make up the protein in hemoglobin. The change in one of these amino acids leads to sickle cell disease (Winchester, 1971).

In the United States, approximately 1 out of every 10 black Americans is a carrier for sickle cell (Maugh, 1981a). The high incidence occurs because the sickle cell trait offers some protection against malaria. In regions of the world where malaria constituted a threat to the population, individuals with sickle cell trait were more likely to survive and reproduce. The sickle cell trait gave individuals an adaptive advantage. It's not surprising then that in some regions of Africa, as many as 30 percent of the population carry the sickle cell trait (Emery, 1979).

**Normal blood cells and blood cells in sickle-cell disease**

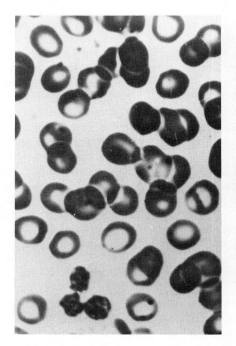 

*The Sickle Cell Disease Foundation of Greater New York*

Normal, donut-shaped blood cells are contrasted with irregular blood cells characteristic of sickle-cell disease.

# A DAY AT A TIME: LIVING WITH SICKLE CELL

I can't remember a time when I didn't know that I was a sickler, a victim of sickle-cell anemia. My parents explained it to me when I was about four years old. My older sister has the disease too. When she was born, the doctors informed my parents that she would not live to be six. The doctors did not tell them, however, that any other children they had might also inherit the disease. When I was born almost five years later, doctors tested me for the disease; the reports came back negative. Nine months later, I became very ill and had to be hospitalized. This time the doctors discovered that I too had sickle-cell anemia, and I was given the same prognosis as my sister. My sister is now 31; I am 26.

My worst crisis—the term given to the breaking down of red blood cells and the accompanying pain—occurred my last year of college. Against my doctor's recommendation, I'd gone away to school to become a teacher and was living on campus. Six weeks before the end of the first semester, I awoke from a sound sleep in intense pain. My whole body felt like one gigantic toothache—the closest I can come to describing a sickle cell crisis. I tried to move my arms but every movement intensified the pain. I felt as though the air was being suctioned out of the room; everything went black.

My next memory was of waking up in the hospital in severe pain, begging to be given more pain medication. I floated in and out of consciousness, paralyzed from the shoulders down for five days and totally blind for several hours. While conscious I heard my doctors tell my mother I had suffered a "sickle cell stroke," had contracted pneumonia and pleurisy and would not survive the night. I heard my mother crying and wanted to comfort her—to tell her that the doctors were wrong and that I would live through this crisis as I had the dozens before. That crisis lasted six weeks. I lost 20 pounds and had to learn to walk, dress and feed myself again.

My first and only teaching position was at the junior high school in my hometown. I was a replacement for a language arts instructor who had taken maternity leave. I loved the kids, and they seemed to like and respect me, but I dreaded the day when my three months would end. Then I got lucky. The other language arts and social studies teacher had to resign. I hated to see her go, but I was glad to be able to continue teaching.

Everything was going smoothly until two weeks before the end of school, when I had a crisis and had to be hospitalized. Needless to say, I was not rehired for the following school year.

Let it be understood that I have not given up—I will never do that. My sister is now happily married and employed by an insurance company. She and I are fighters—thanks to our parents. Like most women, I would like to marry someday and have a family. But the man I marry must be willing to adopt children. I know that I am not physically strong enough to have a baby. It has been painful for me to face this truth because I truly love children. Besides my own personal safety, I can't take the risk of bringing a child into the world when there is a chance that he or she may inherit this disease. I can't endure that emotionally.

I realize that there will always be certain restrictions and rules that I will have to adhere to. But whenever I am really depressed—and it is easy to become so—I remember that I am not alone. There are literally millions of people with this disease and more research is being done every day. I can't give up. I have things to do, places to go. I plan to live a long, full life.

Sickle cell disease occurs when both parents transmit the sickle cell trait to their child. If both parents are carriers, the chance of the child having sickle cell disease is 25 percent. A simple blood test will detect whether or not an adult is a carrier. Until recently, knowing whether both parents were carriers was not particularly helpful because there was no way to determine whether the unborn child had the disease. In 1976, however, a prenatal screening test for sickle cell disease was devised (Kan, Golbus, & Trecartin, 1976). Now parents who are carriers can request prenatal screening in much the same way that Tay-Sachs parents do.

Sickle cell disease is marked by periodic crises. When the cells receive enough oxygen, they retain the normal donut shape. When the cells are deprived of oxygen, their shape resembles a sickle. These sickle-shaped cells are not as flexible as the normal donut-shaped cells and literally get stuck in the body's narrow capillaries. Once the blood flow is obstructed, the surrounding muscle does not receive oxygen. Patients experience severe pain in their joints, abdomen, and chest. These crises sometimes cause heart and liver damage. Sickle cell patients often develop an enlarged heart as the body tries to facilitate the transport of oxygen to the organs (Cerami & Washington, 1974).

Until the 1980s, treatment of sickle cell disease was directed primarily toward relieving the pain associated with crises and trying to prevent damage to the major organs. Now there are several scientists trying to find treatments that will prevent cells from becoming sickle-shaped (Takashima & Asakura, 1983). Within the next 10 years, scientists hope to prevent the recurrent crises that are responsible for the most debilitating effects of sickle cell disease (Maugh, 1981b).

The quality of life for patients with sickle cell disease has improved during the last decade. Still, there are many misconceptions about sickle cell disease. These stem from confusing the person who carries the trait with the person who has the disease. Sickle cell trait means that individuals are carriers. Like Tay-Sachs and cystic fibrosis carriers, they do not have the disease. Nevertheless, individuals with sickle cell trait have been refused employment as airline stewardesses, given increased life insurance rates (Headings, 1979), and been refused entrance to the Air Force Academy (Severo, 1981). Even though such misguided decisions have been reversed, they have made the black population reluctant to participate in screening programs for fear of negative repercussions.

**Phenylketonuria**

Phenylketonuria (PKU) is another recessive metabolic disorder carried by approximately 1 out of every 20 people. Children with this disease lack the enzyme to break down phenylalanine. Phenylalanine is one of the 20 essential amino acids our bodies need to function properly. However, PKU children are not able to metabolize this amino acid, and an abnormal buildup occurs. The accumulation of this amino acid prevents the central nervous system from developing normally. The result is a child with arrested brain development and brain tissue damage. Untreated children have IQs ranging from below 20 to 85 (Matarazzo, 1972).

Fortunately, there is a very effective treatment for PKU—changing the child's diet so that an optimum amount of phenylalanine is eaten. By eliminating meats and dairy products and substituting protein sources low in phenylalanine, the amount of phenylalanine in the bloodstream can be controlled. Because the amino acid does not accumulate, the child's central nervous system can develop normally and mental retardation can be reduced or eliminated (Hsia, 1970). The success of this regime depends on detecting affected children early. Hence, almost all states have PKU screening for newborns. Affected children are started on the diet within the first weeks of life. Until the 1980s it was thought that children could gradually be taken off the diet when the growth of the brain was nearly complete, between four and six years of age. There are now indications that maintaining the diet until adolescence or later may be beneficial. In Poland, a study showed that children who remained on the diet had higher IQs than those who began eating normal amounts of phenylalanine (Cabalsha, Duczynska, Borzymowska, Zorsha, Koslaca-Folga, & Bozkowa, 1977). In 1982, the Collaborative Study of PKU Children in the United States reported a decrease in school achievement among children who discontinued the diet. They immediately circulated a resolution to all pediatricians recommending that children with PKU remain on the diet (Koch, Azen, Friedman, & Williamson, 1982).

Given the success of the diet, we now have many PKU children growing into adulthood and assuming normal roles in our society. For most, this includes marriage and a family. A PKU woman is no longer adversely affected by the phenylalanine in her system. But if she becomes pregnant and continues to have excess phenylalanine in her bloodstream, her unborn child will be affected. Hence, to date very few PKU mothers have given birth to normal infants (Komrower, Sardharwalla, Coutts, & Ingham, 1979). It seems that not only must PKU women return to the diet during pregnancy, they must be on the diet before conceiving (Levy, Kaplan, & Erickson, 1982). Otherwise, the high levels of the protein in the maternal bloodstream impede the development of the brain during the early weeks of pregnancy.

A father with PKU will pass the PKU gene to his child. If his spouse is not a carrier, the child will not be affected; but the child will carry the gene for PKU. If the spouse is a carrier, there is still a 50–50 chance that the child will not be affected.

PKU illustrates a metabolic error in humans that has been controlled by normalizing the body chemistry. One of the goals of future research is to find agents for many metabolic disorders that mimic the natural functioning of the body.

**Sex-linked characteristics**

Males have an X and a Y chromosome; females have 2 Xs. This variation has allowed geneticists to map the X chromosome more completely than any other chromosome. Since the Y chromosome is small and contains a limited amount of genetic material, the one X chromosome that males have becomes very important. Any gene on the male's X chromosome will be expressed regardless of whether it is normally dominant or recessive. Over 100 X-linked recessive traits, including color blindness, hemophilia, and several types of muscular dystrophy, have been located on the X chromosome. Hemophilia will be used to illustrate the genetic transmission of X-linked recessive diseases.

Hemophilia results from the absence of a protein that promotes the clotting of the blood. Since the lack of the protein is recessive, females who have a normal X will not have hemophilia. Instead, they will be carriers. Males, however, have no other X chromosome to counteract the recessive gene and will have the disease.

Queen Victoria of England was a carrier of hemophilia. One of her sons was afflicted and died of complications caused by the disease at the age of 31. At least two of Queen Victoria's daughters, and several of her granddaughters, carried the gene. As these daughters married into the royal families of Europe, some of the male heirs were afflicted. One of Victoria's granddaughters, Alexandra, married the Czar of Russia. Their son, Alexis, born in 1904, was a hemophiliac. The anguish and desperation of his parents during Alexis' repeated episodes of internal bleeding are often cited as factors in the Czar's inability to govern effectively (Massie & Massie, 1975).

Now victims of hemophilia do not have to lead highly restricted lives or suffer the same pain as Alexis. A concentrated and purified form of the clotting factor that hemophiliacs lack can be made from normal blood plasma. By adding this clotting factor to the blood, a hemophiliac can lead a relatively normal life.

During the 1970s, there was no prenatal screening test for hemophilia, but parents who knew they were at risk could determine the sex of the child. If the fetus was female, she would not be affected, even though she might be a carrier. If the fetus was male, parents could consider a therapeutic abortion. This choice was not a very satisfactory one because parents might abort a healthy fetus. Now prospective parents have another option. If prenatal screening indicates a male fetus, a sample of fetal blood can be obtained from the placenta. Analyzing the sample will indicate whether or not the fetus has the disease. Since a female fetus would not be affected and since a male fetus has a 50–50 chance of not having the disease, the odds are 75 percent that a healthy baby will be born.

Hemophilia illustrates the increased risk for recessive disorders that males can expect because of their single X chromosome. The lack of a second X chromosome may also contribute to the biological advantage that women enjoy throughout life. Although 135 males are conceived for every 100 females, more males are miscarried so that there are 106 males born for every 100 females. This imbalance equalizes quickly because males are more susceptible to childhood diseases. By middle age, women outnumber men. In old age, women are less susceptible to a variety of chronic diseases and disabilities and outlive males by an average of eight years.

The list of chromosomal and metabolic errors that have been discussed in this chapter is a very abbreviated one. They were selected to familiarize students with genetic disorders that occur frequently and to provide information about solutions for genetic problems. Of more importance to developmental psychologists is the continuing role that genes play throughout the life span.

## DEVELOPMENTAL GENETICS

So far the discussion has focused on the chromosomes contributed to the fertilized egg (zygote) by the father and mother. As indicated by the genetic errors that can take place in this process and by the effect these errors can have on the organism, the contribution of each parent is vitally important for normal development. However, this microscopic amount of genetic material is only the beginning of a lifetime of interaction between the chromosomes and the environment (Plomin, 1983). During this interaction, genetic instructions carried on the chromosomes are translated into traits and behaviors. In individuals with the correct chromosomal makeup, the interaction between the genes and the environment is the major force shaping development.

Gregor Mendel was the first to examine the way genes from parent plants determined the outcome of the next generation of plants. Working in a small monastery garden he discovered some of the basic principles of genetic transmission (Mendel, 1866). When we study Mendel's early experiments with peas, it is easy to believe that human genes are transmitted as directly as in Mendel's experiments. However, the link between genes and human behavior is not that straightforward. Instead, there are several ways in which genes might affect behavior (Plomin, 1981). These are depicted by the models in Figure 2–13. In all of these models, the person's genetic makeup or *genotype* is represented on the left. The *phenotype* on the right represents the behavior or trait that results.

The first model depicts genetic transmission as described by Mendel. In his classic experiment, the genetic characteristics or genotype lead irrevocably to the trait of interest, either a tall or a short pea plant (see Figure 2–14). Mendel was also able to demonstrate the *dominant* character of some traits and the *recessive* character of others. Since short peas resulted about 25 percent of the time, Mendel concluded that tall peas were dominant and short peas were recessive. As we have seen, several metabolic disorders in humans adhere to this dominant and recessive model.

The transmission of the great majority of human traits is much more complex than the dominant-recessive notion outlined in Model 1. Even with a trait as simple as eye color, the route from genotype to phenotype has complexities. There is no single gene for blue eyes or brown eyes. There are approximately 20 genes that code for differing proteins, all of which play a part in determining the color of your eyes (Nagle, 1979). The genetic input for complex aspects of behavior such as intelligence or personality can involve hundreds of genes. In other words, intelligence and personality are *polygenic* traits. The existence of traits that are determined by many genes begins to demonstrate how the transmission of human genetics differs from Mendel's experiments with peas.

**Figure 2—13**    **Pathways from the genotype to the phenotype**

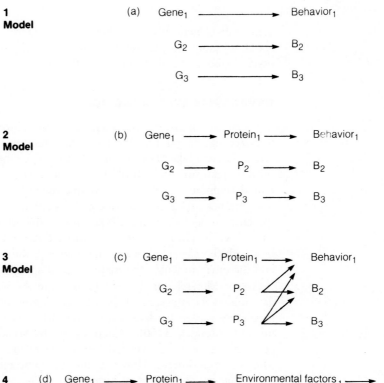

**1**
**Model**    (a)    Gene₁ ⟶ Behavior₁

G₂ ⟶ B₂

G₃ ⟶ B₃

**2**
**Model**    (b)    Gene₁ ⟶ Protein₁ ⟶ Behavior₁

G₂ ⟶ P₂ ⟶ B₂

G₃ ⟶ P₃ ⟶ B₃

**3**
**Model**    (c)    Gene₁ ⟶ Protein₁ ⟶ Behavior₁

G₂ ⟶ P₂ ⟶ B₂

G₃ ⟶ P₃ ⟶ B₃

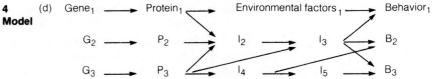

**4**    (d)    Gene₁ ⟶ Protein₁ ⟶ Environmental factors₁ ⟶ Behavior₁
**Model**

G₂ ⟶ P₂ ⟶ I₂ ⟶ I₃ ⟶ B₂

G₃ ⟶ P₃ ⟶ I₄ ⟶ I₅ ⟶ B₃

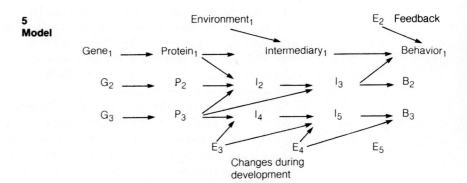

**5**
**Model**    Environment₁    E₂ Feedback

Gene₁ ⟶ Protein₁ ⟶ Intermediary₁ ⟶ Behavior₁

G₂ ⟶ P₂ ⟶ I₂ ⟶ I₃ ⟶ B₂

G₃ ⟶ P₃ ⟶ I₄ ⟶ I₅ ⟶ B₃

E₃    E₄    E₅

Changes during
development

Models of genetic transmission showing increasingly complex routes from the genotype to the phenotype.

Source: Plomin, R. (1981). Ethological behavioral genetics and development. In K. Immelmann, G. W. Barlow, L. Petrinovich, & M. Main (Eds.), *Behavioral development: The Bielefeld interdisciplinary project* (p. 261). New York: Cambridge University Press.

**Figure 2–14**          **Mendel's tall and short peas**

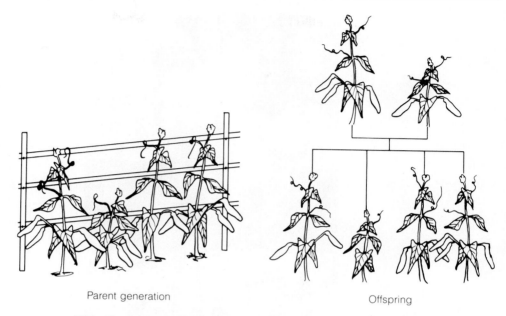

Parent generation                                    Offspring

When Mendel crossed tall and short peas, he found that the offspring were not medium height. Three fourths of them were tall, and one fourth were short.

Mendel's experiments accurately detailed the influence of plants on the next generation. However, Mendel did not know how this genetic information was transmitted. We know now that the genes Mendel referred to are sections of DNA on a chromosome and that each section codes for a specific protein. Model 2 shows genes coding for proteins which in turn affect behavior. Model 2 adds the fact that proteins and enzymes carry the genetic information. This is an advance over Mendel's views because the model shows the intermediate steps between the genes and behavior. Model 2, however, still misrepresents the complex series of events that occur between a particular human gene and a specific trait or behavior.

The third model shows genes coding for proteins that influence several behaviors. Each gene has only one primary effect—directing the synthesis of a protein. This primary effect, like a stone thrown in a pond, can produce ripples or secondary effects. In PKU children, for example, the primary effect is the lack of an enzyme. But PKU children are usually blond and fair—a secondary effect of the gene. Unless their diet is modified during the early weeks of life, PKU children will be mentally retarded (Thompson & Thompson, 1980). As would be expected if both effects are determined by the same gene, correcting the diet also means that these children develop more pigment in their skin and hair. This illustration adds the important principle, *pleiotropy*,

**Pleiotropy and PKU**

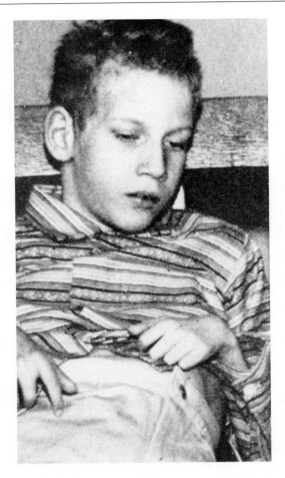

The enzyme deficiency that causes mental retardation in PKU also causes fair coloring and blond hair. These secondary effects of one gene illustrate the principle of pleiotropy.
Source: From Frank L. Lyman, *Phenylketonuria* (Springfield, Ill.: Charles C Thomas, 1963), p. 174.

to developmental genetics. Pleiotropy means that a particular protein can have an effect on several traits or behaviors. The third model, then, indicates that once a protein is produced by a gene, that protein can have a branching effect. A single protein can affect the creases in our hands, our intellectual development, and aspects of our personality.

The fourth model is a more accurate view of behavioral genetics of humans because it includes environmental factors. Genes do code for proteins, and proteins have an effect on many traits; but the effects that proteins have on behavior can be influenced by the environment. Consider the incidence of schizophrenia. It occurs much more frequently in the lower social classes (Hammer, 1972). Being in the lower socioeconomic strata, however, seems far removed from the hallucinations and broken thought patterns of schizophrenia. How might such an external situation be relevant to the incidence of schizophrenia? Suppose that schizophrenia is a result of a buildup of the chemical dopamine in the brain (Friedhoff, 1972). Suppose also that the person's diet contributes to this chemical buildup. Finally, suppose that a chaotic home environment was very stressful to an adult. The stress could also contribute to the toxic buildup of dopamine. In the lower socioeconomic classes, the likelihood of a poor diet and a chaotic home environment may be very high and these external events could aggravate a predisposition toward schizophrenia. This scenario is admittedly speculative, but it illustrates the potential influence that environmental factors can have on the expression of the gene.

The fifth model considers all of the factors outlined in the first four models. In addition, it takes into account the changes that infants undergo as they become children, adolescents, adults, and senior citizens. This model includes the feedback that occurs within the whole system and demonstrates that genes are active at different times during development. Recall that every time cells divide, the new cells have exactly the same chromosomes as the original. Although every cell has the complete set of genetic blueprints, only a small portion, about 10 percent, of that genetic material is active at any point in time (Davidson, 1976). A cell in the heart does not need to manufacture liver enzymes. Hence, the DNA that would code for liver enzymes does not function. All of the DNA in all of the cells in the body cannot be active or turned on in a highly specialized and complex organism like a human being. We also know that changes in an organism are activated at different times during development. A girl does not reach menopause at the same time she reaches puberty. There is a necessary order to the development of an adult. If cells are to produce only the correct kinds of enzymes and if people are to develop in the normal fashion, some kind of regulatory mechanism has to turn genes on and off.

Coded on the chromosomes are not only the genes, but instructions to turn genes on or off. These instructions may be activated by *jumping genes, split genes,* or several other dynamic mechanisms that trigger genetic expression (Hunkapiller, Huang, Hood, & Campbell, 1982). The timed expression of a gene occurs during sexual maturation. For years, the child remains sexually immature. At some point determined by the genes, the food supply, the child's weight, and exercise, the genes that code for the development of secondary sexual characteristics begin to function. Hormonal changes begin, and the child becomes an adult. Many genes, whose effects are entirely normal, have this type of delayed onset. Delaying the expression of genes until the appropriate time in the life span is a part of normal gene function.

The genes are "like notes on an instrument played through time by an epigenetic hand" (Barlow, 1981, p. 196). When a woman becomes pregnant, a host of new notes are played, preparing her body for the changes that accompany pregnancy. When the child is born, the song changes to provide for nursing the child. As the child is weaned, the tune changes again. Throughout life, changes are mediated by the expression and repression of DNA in concert with the environment that surrounds the child.

Turning on specific genes at the correct moment in development can be illustrated by the nursing of infants. In order to digest their mother's milk, babies need a particular enzyme, lactase, in their digestive system. This enzyme appears in the baby's system at birth and in many mammals, including some humans, disappears when the child is weaned (Barlow, 1981). In essence, the gene for the enzyme is turned on when it is needed and turned off when it is no longer necessary. In most Caucasians, this enzyme never turns off and adults can also enjoy milk (Gottesman, 1975). In non-Caucasian populations, 60–80 percent of the adults lack this enzyme. Milk gives them indigestion and diarrhea. In these people, the necessary enzyme is no longer present. In still another segment of the population, the presence of the enzyme depends on cues from the environment. The gene for producing lactase will be active past infancy as long as the person continues to drink milk (Ehrman & Parsons, 1981). When the person stops drinking milk, the gene will turn off. This example illustrates the variety of ways that genes can function to influence the development of the child.

When genes turn on later in life, the effect on the organism can be negative. One of the clearest examples of a negative genetic influence is Huntington's disease. This disease is named after George Huntington, a Long Island physician who lived during the late 19th century. He and his father studied several generations of a single family that suffered from the disease and kept detailed records on the members who became ill. This disease is of special interest to geneticists and developmental psychologists because the average age of onset is 35–45 years (Stern, 1973). Once symptoms begin, victims of Huntington's disease experience a slow degeneration of the nervous system that is invariably fatal.

The most famous victim of Huntington's disease is folk singer Woody Guthrie. In his early 40s, he began to experience difficulty walking and was occasionally arrested for being drunk. He died 15 years later. During his last years, he was confined to his bed and could only communicate by blinking his eyes. As often happens with Huntington's disease, Woody had fathered three children—Arlo, Joady, and Nora—before he knew that he carried the Huntington's gene (Hendin & Marks, 1978).

Unlike many of the recessive metabolic disorders that have been discussed, the gene for Huntington's disease is dominant. The children of Huntington's victims have a 50–50 chance of having the disease. Living with this threat becomes increasingly difficult as the children become adults and watch their affected parent deteriorate. Recently, scientists discovered a marker for Huntington's disease which is located on chromosome number 4. This discovery is giving new hope to adults who would like to have children but know that one of their parents has Huntington's disease. A prenatal test to determine whether

**Pedigree of family at risk for Huntington's disease**

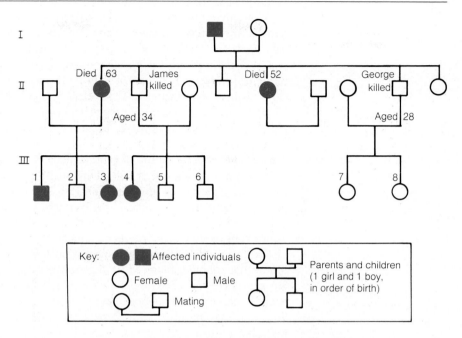

Huntington's disease traced through three generations. The mother and father in generation I had five children. Two of the boys were killed before middle age, but each had already fathered children. Two of the girls in the second generation had Huntington's disease and died at 63 and 52 years of age. Since one of James's daughters in the third generation is affected, James would have had the disease had he lived. George's children are not old enough yet to determine whether they have the gene.

Source: Ehrman, L., & Parsons, P. A. (1981, p. 49). *Behavioral genetics and evolution.* New York: McGraw-Hill.

a fetus carries the gene is a reasonable possibility within the next few years (Kolata, 1983).

Huntington's disease is an example of a single dominant gene being expressed during middle age. Many other diseases—diabetes, heart disease, cancer, schizophrenia, and depression—that are not expressed until late in life also have a genetic component. Most of these diseases are not determined by a single gene and most of them are influenced dramatically by the environment. Hence, the genetic factors are not as clear as in Huntington's disease.

Diabetes, for example, is hereditary; but many people who carry the genotype will not express the defect if their weight and diet are controlled. Even after people have been diagnosed as diabetic, they can often be returned clinically to a prediabetic or nondiabetic status if they lose weight. Nutrition, then, is one environmental factor that affects the clinical manifestation of diabetes. By monitoring the amount of sugar ingested, an individual can help keep the gene for diabetes turned off.

Other environmental agents that might alter the expression of a trait include temperature, stress, radiation, drugs, diseases, and chemical agents. Chemical agents in the form of industrial chemicals, pesticides, cosmetics, dyes, and food additives are a relatively new part of human society. Their mutagenic influence on genes is often not known. In recent years, more and more concern has been expressed about the effect of these chemicals on humans (Berg, 1979). The use of several popular chemicals—like saccharin and DDT—has either been banned or restricted because these chemicals pose a danger to humans.

Once the intricate nature of gene regulation is unraveled, it may be possible to turn genes on and off at will. This might provide humans with the ability to control a variety of diseases. The gene for Huntington's disease might be permanently repressed. Diabetic adults might have the insulin production process turned on again. The correct instructions might stop the proliferation of tumor cells or slow down the aging process.

The five models of genetic transmission that have been discussed show the routes that are often followed from genotype to phenotype. Some human traits are expressed efficiently and directly, like Mendel's peas (Models 1 and 2). More often, the route is not direct (Models 3, 4, and 5). For complex traits, the route may be filled with detours and side streets, all of which affect the traits and behaviors that are expressed.

Even Models 4 and 5 do not tell the whole story of development. There are still several other factors that can affect the expression of a gene. For example, modifier genes exist. As the name suggests, the presence or absence of these genes can modify, inhibit, or facilitate the expression of another gene. When this happens, there are differences in the degree of *penetrance* and expressivity of a gene.

Reduced penetrance occurs when an individual carries the genotype for some particular trait, but that trait is not evident. Modifier genes and the genetic background act to prevent the trait from being expressed. So, for example, the genetically determined condition polydactyly, which results in extra fingers and toes, exhibits about 90 percent penetrance (Nagle, 1979). In other words, only 90 percent of the individuals who carry the gene will have extra fingers and toes.

*Expressivity* is another example of how an individual's genetic makeup can be modified. Some children with sickle cell disease have crises frequently and are hospitalized several times a year. Other children, with the same genetic background, are seldom hospitalized and seem to experience few crises. The difference hinges on the degree to which sickle cell disease is expressed.

Variations in penetrance and expressivity are most commonly attributed to gene modifiers, although external environmental factors can also have an effect. The variation in expression serves as a constant reminder that human genes do not exist in isolation. Each gene is a segment of DNA among other segments, located on a chromosome, and this whole genetic complement exists within a particular environment.

We see, then, the complex ways in which the genetic bases of the organism become expressed during the development of the organism. Waddington (1962) tried to capture this interaction in all its complexity when he suggested an "epigenetic landscape." To understand this concept, visualize a hiker. At some point during the hike, a narrow canyon or sheer cliff dictates that only one path can be followed. At another point, walking in an open plain or valley, any number of paths can be selected. In this example, the general shape of the landscape represents the genotype of an individual. The path selected by the hiker represents the end product or phenotype. For some traits, in which the path between genes and behavior is quite direct, this landscape will be rather narrow and the path will be limited. For other traits, the landscape might be almost flat, meaning that the hiker was not constrained by genetic considerations.

## SEPARATING HEREDITARY AND ENVIRONMENTAL INFLUENCES

Developmental genetics emphasizes the lifelong influence of the genes, and the various processes that intervene between the genes and the expression of behavior. But this viewpoint tends to sidestep an intriguing question: Is there a strong genetic component to a particular behavior? Although not particularly popular, this question is not a frivolous one. Knowing whether schizophrenia is due primarily to a chemical error or to an aberrant mother-child interaction will help the search for cures. As we have seen with PKU and diabetes, a genetic component does not eliminate the possibility for intervention. Instead, it points the way to interventions that might be effective (Scarr & Weinberg, 1983).

How can we examine the contribution of the genes and separate it from the effects of the environment? With animals it is easily done because we can breed them for specific traits and alter their environment. Psychologists, however, cannot breed humans or place one child in an impoverished environment and one in a stimulating one. There are, however, several methods of teasing apart the contribution of the genes and the environment.

**Pedigree studies, twin studies, and adoption studies**

By examining related individuals for the same traits, we can get an overview of the genetic contribution. Francis Galton, Charles Darwin's cousin, took a keen interest in such *pedigrees*. He gave prizes to strangers who would send in family pedigrees through which a trait could be traced (McClearn & DeFries, 1973). In 1869 he published *Hereditary Genius*, a pedigree analysis of poets, scientists, military commanders, musicians, statesmen, and judges. Given that Galton's studies took place long before the method of genetic transmission was discovered, his methods and findings were very sophisticated.

Today, pedigrees are used primarily for tracing family traits caused by a single dominant or recessive gene, such as Huntington's disease or hemophilia. When pedigree studies for traits like musical skill are presented, critics immediately and rightly ask whether the musical gift of a son, like Johann Strauss, resulted from the genes the senior Strauss gave him or the enriched musical environment he enjoyed as a child. The answer, undoubtedly, is both; and the pedigree has not helped separate the role that Strauss's heredity played. One solution would be to study several Strauss clones that were raised in a variety of musical and nonmusical environments.

Studies of twins come close to this scientific ideal. The rationale behind these studies is that the degree of genetic similarity can be varied while the environmental similarity stays the same. Identical or *monozygotic* twins develop from a single egg, hence they carry exactly the same set of chromosomes. If they are raised in the same home, they experience very similar environments. Fraternal or dizygotic twins result from two separate eggs. Like siblings, they share approximately 50 percent of their genes. If a trait is influenced extensively by the genes, we would expect monozygotic twins to be very similar on that trait, much more similar than dizygotic twins or siblings. As the relationship between people becomes more distant, their genetic similarity is reduced and their similarity on any trait should decrease if that trait is genetically determined. By looking at how similar monozygotic and dizygotic twins are on a particular trait, we can begin to see if that trait has a large genetic component.

Ronald Wilson (1983) has used the twin method to trace the intelligence of monozygotic and dizygotic twin pairs. He first tested the twins when they were three months old. At that time, both monozygotic and dizygotic twin pairs received similar scores on the intelligence tests. As the children grew up, however, their scores diverged. Monozygotic twins became more like each other, while dizygotic twins became less similar (see Figure 2–15). Wilson's 15-year study not only allows us to look at the genetic component of intelligence, it allows us to see how the genetic template is expressed over a 15-year period.

Dyslexia, the inability to read with understanding, is another trait that has been studied using the twin method. In four separate studies involving 36 monozygotic twins, both twins were found to have the trait (Herschel, 1978). When dizygotic twins were examined, less than a third of the pairs were both dyslexic.

Results from studies done on schizophrenia, depression, criminality, alcoholism, and introversion-extroversion are presented in Figure 2–16 as examples of the twin method. On all of these complex behavioral traits, monozygotic twins were more similar than dizygotic twins.

These studies used many sets of twins. On occasion, an event is so rare that a case study approach is used. This was the case with the Genain quadruplets. Identical girls, given pseudonyms of Nora, Iris, Myra, and Hester, were born to an alcoholic, paranoid father whose family had a history of psychiatric disorders. The father fenced the children in, eliminated any social activities, and patrolled the house with a gun (Rosenthal, 1963). All the girls were very shy,

**Figure 2–15**          **Intelligence of monozygotic and dizygotic twins**

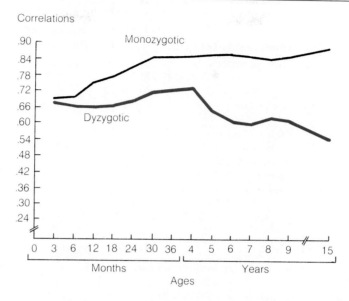

Monozygotic twins become more similar in intelligence as they get older. Dizygotic twins become less similar.

Source: Wilson, R. S. (1983). The Louisville twin study: Developmental synchronies in behavior. *Child Development, 54,* p. 311.

a common finding among children who later develop schizophrenia. The investigators who studied this family for 20 years, felt that Nora, the firstborn and the natural leader of the girls, would be the one most likely to avoid a schizophrenic breakdown. Yet she was hospitalized while in her early 20s. As her father's favorite, she was constantly harangued by him. Myra, the only sister not hospitalized, dodged her father successfully. Despite a schizophrenic breakdown and some severe problems as an adult, she was able to lead a reasonably normal adult life (Segal & Yahraes, 1979). Would the girls have become schizophrenic if they had been raised in a more positive environment?

This question could be answered by an adoption study, another invaluable method for separating the relative influence of heredity and the environment. What is the likelihood that the children of schizophrenic mothers will develop schizophrenia even if they are raised by adoptive parents? If the influence of a normal home environment is paramount, then few of these children should become schizophrenic. If the genes are very influential, many of these children would be expected to become schizophrenic despite their normal environment. In one of the first attempts to answer this question, Heston (1970) studied 47 children of schizophrenic mothers who were adopted during the first three days of life. For a control group, he studied another set of adopted chil-

**Figure 2–16**  **Similarity between identical twins and fraternal twins on personality measures**

| Personality trait | Monozygotic twins (identical) | Dizygotic twins (fraternal) |
|---|---|---|
| Schizophrenia | | |
|   Gottesman & Shields (1972) | 50% | 9% |
|   Kringlen (1967) | 38 | 14 |
| Alcoholism | | |
|   Kaij (1957) | 49 | 27 |
| Manic-depression | | |
|   Kringlen (1967) | 33 | 0 |
| Harvald & Hauge (1965) | 60 | 50 |
| Mendels (1974) | 74 | 19 |
| Personality | | |
|   Nichols (1966) | 51 | 25 |
|   Horn, Plomin, & Rosenhan (1976) | 44 | 19 |
|   Floderus-Myhed, Pedersen, & Rasmuson (1980) | 39–62 | 16–29 |
|   Carey, Goldsmith, Tellegren, & Gottesman (1978) | 46–61 | 23–46 |
|   Loehlin & Nichols (1976) | 50 | 3 |
| Criminality | | |
|   Crowe (1974) | 36–100 | 0–54 |

dren who did not have schizophrenic mothers. By middle age, 16 percent of the children of schizophrenics were also schizophrenic, but none of the children in the control group were. Given that schizophrenia is a complex set of behaviors and is likely to be influenced by many genes, it is interesting that the children of schizophrenics were more often mentally retarded and were more likely to have a sociopathic or a neurotic personality. In all, 66 percent of the children of schizophrenic mothers were affected in some way, while only 18 percent of the adopted children whose mothers were not schizophrenic had any of these problems (Heston, 1970).

Adoption studies have also been used to study complex behaviors such as alcoholism. A common belief is that alcoholism is caused primarily by frustrations on the job, unemployment, or a variety of other environmental factors. To investigate the possibility of a genetic component, 55 adopted males whose biological parents were alcoholic were studied into adulthood. All of the children were adopted before they reached six weeks of age, and they had no further contact with their biological parents. When these men were studied at 30 years of age, 18 percent had already become alcoholic. Their difficulties with alcohol were serious enough to involve legal, social, employment, or marital problems. In a similar group that had also been adopted but did not have an alcoholic biological parent, the rate of alcoholism was 5 percent

**Figure 2–17**                 **An adoption study**

| | | Biological parents | |
| --- | --- | --- | --- |
| | | Alcoholic | Nonalcoholic |
| **Adoptive parents** | Alcoholic | 46% | 14% |
| | Nonalcoholic | 50% | 8% |

If the biological parent was an alcoholic, the child, even when adopted into another family, had problems with alcohol about 50 percent of the time. Whether or not the adoptive parents were alcoholic was not as significant.

Source: Schukit, M. D., Goodwin, W., & Winokur, G. A. (1972). A study of alcoholism in half-siblings. *American Journal of Psychiatry, 128*, 1132–1136.

(Goodwin, Schulsinger, Harmanson, Guze, & Winokur, 1973). These surprising findings led investigators to ask whether being raised in an alcoholic home would increase the incidence of alcoholism. To answer this question, Schuckit, Goodwin, and Winokur (1972) interviewed some 200 alcoholics. They found that the biological background was more important than the home environment in determining whether or not an adopted child became an alcoholic adult (see Figure 2–17).

These findings demonstrate that even behaviors like alcoholism that seem to be environmentally controlled can have a genetic component. Obviously, having a biological parent who was alcoholic does not lead inevitably to alcoholism, since half of those who had alcoholism in their biological background did not become alcoholics.

Pedigrees, twin studies, and adoption studies indicate the existence of a particular trait or behavior that has a genetic component. These studies do not tell us how particular genes, coding for a protein, might contribute to the complex behaviors we see in schizophrenics or alcoholics. However, clues to this process are being sought by biochemists who are looking at the neurotransmitters in the brain. A lower level of an enzyme or several enzymes may cause a buildup of neurotransmitters that is accompanied by the hallucinations and paranoia so common in schizophrenia.

Intelligence involves another complex set of skills that clearly has a substantial genetic component. Writing in the 1960s, Arthur Jensen was dismayed by the lack of any mention of genetic factors in individual differences in intelligence. His articles, arguing that about 80 percent of the variability in intelligence is attributable to genetic factors, provoked a storm of controversy (Jensen, 1972). Other investigators scoffed at Jensen's views, suggesting that his evidence was inadequate and his conclusions were illogical (Kagan, 1969). Twin studies and adoption studies conducted since 1970 have helped document the genetic component (Bouchard & McGue, 1981; Scarr & Weinberg,

1983). In a recent, comprehensive review of these studies, Bouchard and McGue present data from over 90,000 pairs of individuals representing degrees of relationship from identical twins to unrelated children raised in the same home. The results of their review are presented in Figure 2–18. For the 4,672 monozygotic twins, the correlation between their IQs was surprisingly high (.86). Monozygotic twins reared apart also had very similar IQ scores (.72). For dizygotic twins reared together, the correlation fell (.60); but it was somewhat higher than the score for siblings reared together (.47). Unrelated children raised in the same home showed the smallest relationship (.30).

As in earlier studies, the intellectual similarity between two people was remarkably consistent with what would be expected given their genetic similarity. The closer the genetic relationship, the more similar the IQ scores. This does not discount the importance of environmental factors. There is a difference between the monozygotic twins raised in the same home and those who spent their childhoods in different environments. Similarly, the dizygotic twins were more similar than siblings. These results must be attributed to the environments that the children experienced (Bouchard & McGue, 1981).

Perhaps the most fascinating experiments of the relative influence of heredity and environment come from identical twins who have been separated early in life and raised in different environments. These studies allow us to assess the impact of different environments on the same genetic makeup. Because identical twins are a rare occurrence and are usually raised by their biological parents, the number of subjects available for this kind of study is limited. Despite this drawback, several investigators have traced identical twins raised by different parents (Bouchard & McGue, 1981, Farber, 1980; Shields, 1962).

The most extensive study of identical twins who have been raised apart is an ongoing project at the University of Minnesota. To date, over 50 sets of identical twins have been found. The majority of these twins were separated early in life and spent their critical childhood years in different homes. Many had not seen each other prior to becoming subjects in the study. Once they arrived in Minnesota, the twins took a complete battery of psychological tests, including tests of intelligence, information processing, memory, mechanical ability, and spatial processing. They were given a thorough medical evaluation and were fingerprinted, videotaped, interviewed, wired to electrodes, and questioned about their tastes, fears, and fantasies (Bartlett, 1981).

The results showed striking similarities among the twins. Their IQ scores were often so close that they could be the scores of the same person taking the test for a second time. A pair of British twins came from very different social classes. "You could tell the difference in their backgrounds as soon as they spoke. . . . The one from London had a cockney accent, and the one from Dorchester had an accent somewhere between BBC and the queen." Despite their different backgrounds and education, their IQs were "practically identical, in fact, one point apart in favor of the cockney" (Barlett, 1981, p. 7).

In other cases, dramatic differences in the environments were associated with discrepant IQ scores. One twin, raised in Florida by a fisherman in a

**Figure 2—18**   **Genetic factors in intelligence**

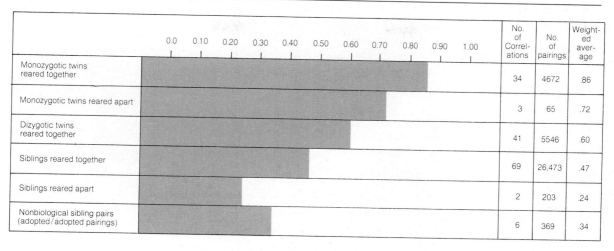

| | 0.0 0.10 0.20 0.30 0.40 0.50 0.60 0.70 0.80 0.90 1.00 | No. of Correlations | No. of pairings | Weighted average |
|---|---|---|---|---|
| Monozygotic twins reared together | | 34 | 4672 | .86 |
| Monozygotic twins reared apart | | 3 | 65 | .72 |
| Dizygotic twins reared together | | 41 | 5546 | .60 |
| Siblings reared together | | 69 | 26,473 | .47 |
| Siblings reared apart | | 2 | 203 | .24 |
| Nonbiological sibling pairs (adopted/adopted pairings) | | 6 | 369 | .34 |

The relationship between intelligence scores of pairs of twins and siblings. The average correlation across studies is indicated by the vertical bar. Monozygotic twins receive very similar scores, dizygotic twins are less alike than monozygotic twins but more alike than siblings.

Source: Bouchard, T. J., & McGue, M. (1981). Familial studies of intelligence: A review. *Science, 212,* p. 1056.

home with few books, left school after 10th grade. His brother, adopted by a more cosmopolitan family, became an electronics expert with the CIA and lived all over the world. His IQ was 20 points higher than his twin's. These results have prompted the investigators to suggest that environments must differ radically if they are to produce children with different IQs.

Dramatic differences in environments might have an effect on IQ, but they do not necessarily produce dramatic differences in personality. The Stohr and Yufe twins grew up in radically different environments. Oskar Stohr was raised in Germany as a catholic and a Nazi. His twin, Jack Yufe, was raised in the Caribbean as a Jew. Oskar was raised by his mother and grandmother. Jack was raised by his father. When they met at Minnesota they shared many mannerisms and habits, but more objectively, their profiles on the Minnesota Multiphasic Personality Inventory were very similar. Professor Brouchard cites these twins and their similarities to demonstrate that the sex of the parent does not necessarily mold personalities in different ways (Holden, 1980).

Other surprising similarities appeared in the data. In one set of twins, both boys stuttered, both had a fear of heights, and, at the age of 23 when they first met, both were actively homosexual. Phobias are often described as the product of environmental learning, yet sets of twins would independently report being afraid of water, of heights, or of being confined (Eckert, Heston, & Bouchard, 1981).

**Identical twins through the life span**

Frances Gill left; Kathryn Abbe right.
Age six months.

Kathryn Abbe left; Frances Gill right.
Age five years.

Frances Gill left; Kathryn Abbe right.
Age 10 years.

Frances Gill left; Kathryn Abbe right.
Age 16 years.

Kathryn Abbe left; Frances Gill right.
Holding twin cousins. Age 48 years.

Frances Gill left; Kathryn Abbe right.
Age 60 years.

*Photographs by Margaretta Mitchell*

Identical twins at 6 months, 5 years, 10 years, 16 years, 48 years, and 60 years.

Studies of twins who have been raised apart provide evidence for genetic propensities that are expressed in a variety of environments; but there are criticisms that can be leveled at these studies. For example, in earlier studies of twins reared apart, the twins were often raised by relatives or friends who shared a similar lifestyle. Adoption agencies try to place all children with parents who will provide a reasonable environment. The point is that the environments in which twins are raised may not be radically different. Hence, the finding that twins are very similar does not justify the conclusion that the genes are the critical factor. These kinds of criticisms are difficult to respond to because psychologists cannot randomly assign one twin to a detrimental environment just to see if that environment will exert an influence on the child's personality. But when twins raised apart have very similar scores on measures of tolerance, conformity, flexibility, self-control, and sociability, the influence of genetics seems undeniable.

## Sociobiology

The profound influence of a person's genetic makeup on physical traits such as hair and eye color has been understood and accepted for decades. The genetic foundation for more complex traits and behaviors, such as intelligence and schizophrenia, is still a source of some contention. There are few who would deny that a genetic component exists, but the force of that component remains a debated issue. Still, schizophrenia and intelligence are traits that characterize a particular individual. Is there a genetic component to behaviors that characterize a culture?

It is part of the conventional wisdom that culture originates from environmental variables and that there are few, if any, biological bases to culture. Dobzhansky (1963) argued that culture is not inherited through genes, but learned from other human beings. He suggested that genes are no longer the primary force they were; instead, we have an entirely new, nonbiological or superorganic agent that determines change—culture. The fact that our culture changes so readily is used to support the argument that there can be no genetic input into culture. Evolutionary change, it is argued, would be accomplished much more slowly.

Now the field of sociobiology is challenging this view. In 1975, Edward Wilson suggested that human evolution depended on the selection of certain social characteristics and that social behaviors such as altruism, choosing a spouse, aggression, and parental behavior may have a genetic foundation. Sociobiology emphasizes an evolutionary view of the human being, suggesting that social behaviors, such as aggression and cooperation, are represented in the genes because they influenced our survival in earlier epochs. Wilson cites many examples of social behaviors in other species—altruism in bee colonies, social organization in ant colonies—that are biologically based. He then applies the same principles to human societies, arguing that early humans cooperated in finding food and in fending off predators. "Cooperation during hunting was perfected, providing a new impetus for the evolution of intelligence, which in turn permitted still more sophistication in tool using, and so on through cycles of causation" (Wilson, 1975, p. 568). This cycle—cooperation, increasing intelligence, and increasing success as a species—constitutes the base for culture.

To sociobiologists, genes are linked to culture in a deep and subtle manner which they label gene-culture coevolution (Lumsden & Wilson, 1981). Demonstrating this coevolution requires three steps. In the first step, different cultural practices are identified. The second verifies the link between cultural practice and genetic fitness. One cultural practice that Wilson cites as altering genetic fitness is tattooing. Tattooing actually punctures the skin, and depending on the culture, pigments might be put into the wounds. In cultures like the Marquesas, the lack of sterilization combined with the practice of body tattooing meant that members of the tribe who were tattooed were subjected to a variety of infections and diseases. In some tribes, where decorating the entire body with tattoos was fashionable, as many as 60 to 70 percent of the members died (Blumberg & Hesser, 1975). There is no doubt that this cultural practice affected the genetic fitness of the tribe in an adverse way (see Figure 2–19).

Another example of a link between culture and genetic fitness can be drawn from the foods we eat. Humans need to eat lysine—an essential protein. Maize, which was the only cereal grown in the new world, contained large quantities of lysine; but it was in an indigestible form. Special cooking methods were required to unlock this essential protein. Cultures that discovered and used the special cooking techniques thrived, other cultures did not. Consequently, the cultural practice of cooking maize a particular way enhanced the genetic fitness of a group of people.

These two examples illustrate how cultural practices affect the survival of a group. Do practices that increase the genetic fitness or survival of a group become represented in the genes? Not directly; we certainly do not have a gene that directs the way we cook corn. But the sociobiologists suggest an indirect route. In successful groups, the cultural practices and the gene pool will evolve together. After many generations, perceptual, sensory, and cognitive systems that are mediated by the genes might facilitate that particular cultural practice.

The first steps in the sociobiologist's argument have been well documented. There are different cultural practices and these practices do affect the genetic fitness or survival of a group. It is certainly reasonable that cultural practices and the gene pool evolve together. The more tenuous part of the theory is the link between the culture and the gene. Even the sociobiologists admit that the link is very indirect (Lumsden & Wilson, 1981). Critics of sociobiology argue that it is entirely theoretical.

One of the purposes of theory is to stimulate debate and experimentation. Certainly, sociobiology has accomplished that. Psychologists, sociologists, and anthropologists are at least arguing about whether some aspects of our culture could be represented in some form in our genes. Did earlier Homo sapiens select their mates for their hunting prowess, leadership, and skill at tool making, assuring their survival and the survival of their children? Were these skills

**Figure 2—19**                    **Body tattooing on the Marquesas**

*Historical Pictures Service, Chicago*

Body tattooing among the Marquesas spread infection and disease. This is an example of a cultural practice that affected the survival of a group of people.

reflected in physical attributes like a healthy appearance and well developed muscles? Hence, do we now have a propensity to select mates who have these physical attributes? Some sociobiologists suggest that we do (Freedman, 1979), but such propositions are extremely difficult to prove or to disprove; so much of the debate is rhetorical. One certainty exists—any paths that might wind from gene to culture would be much more indirect than any of the five models that were considered to link genes and behaviors.

## SUMMARY

Deciphering the structure of the DNA molecule was the catalyst for the recent explosion of information in the field of genetics. Once the structure of

DNA was clear, biologists turned their attention to the molecular basis of genetic transmission. As a result, we now have a much clearer understanding of the relationship between chromosomes, genes, and proteins. Too many chromosomes can cause the mental retardation that is characteristic of Down's children, or the language problems of a Klinefelter's boy. Too few chromosomes result in the short stature of a Turner's girl. Even when the number of chromosomes is correct, sections may be duplicated, deleted, inverted, or translocated. All of these minor changes in the chromosomes can have decided effects on development.

Metabolic errors on particular genes are often passed from parent to child. Tay-Sachs, sickle cell disease, PKU, hemophilia, and cystic fibrosis are all due to a defective gene that does not produce a necessary protein or enzyme. Methods of defusing the effects of these abnormalities have been found, and new methods are being tried daily to help people who have genetic deficits live more normal lives. Genetic engineering may someday rectify minor chromosomal abnormalities and metabolic disorders by splicing a new gene into a person's chromosomal material to replace the defective one. Although such a possibility was treated like science fiction a few years ago, it is now an attainable goal.

Understanding the biological basis of human development requires more than a familiarity with genetic abnormalities and defects. Genetic transmission of human traits is much more complex than the genetic transmission of peas. The concepts of polygenetic inheritance, pleiotropy, penetrance, and expressivity are part and parcel of understanding genetic transmission in humans. When and how a particular gene is expressed can also be influenced by environmental variables, regulator genes, and the aging process.

Following the lead of biologists, psychologists have become interested in the genetic factors that affect complex and extreme behaviors like alcoholism, schizophrenia, and dyslexia. Since animals cannot read and seldom become alcoholic or schizophrenic, and because experiments cannot be conducted on human children, we have used twin studies, adoption studies, and pedigree studies to examine the role biology plays in the development of these behaviors. Although these studies seldom provide definitive answers by themselves, the body of literature, taken as a whole, indicates that biology is an important factor in a host of complex behaviors.

Some theorists are no longer limiting the search for biological influences to individual traits. Sociobiologists argue that our culture, our interpersonal skills, and our behavior in groups all have some biological foundation. Even the fact that we are searching in these directions indicates that biology is regarded as a potent and continuing force in the development of human behavior.

# CHAPTER 3

# Nine months in utero

During the nine months from conception to birth, the fertilized egg winds its way down the fallopian tubes, buries itself in the wall of the uterus, and is systematically transformed, first into a developing fetus, and then into a squalling newborn. The transformations that take place in the organism during these months are unparalleled during the rest of development. In the short period from conception until birth, a child's size increases 2 million times. In the next 18 years, the child's weight will only increase 25 times and the child's height will only increase 3.5 times. Just from the standpoint of growth, then, the *intrauterine* period is extraordinarily important for the rest of development. But growth is just one aspect of intrauterine development. The central nervous system, the physical structures of the body, and the internal organs are also formed during this period. Trauma to the developing embryo or fetus in the form of drugs, diseases, environmental chemicals, and radiation can have permanent and irreversible effects on the formation of these systems. Perhaps the ancient Chinese were correct in figuring age from the moment of conception. To leave out the development of the fetus during the first nine months would be to miss a vitally important and fascinating part of the story of human development.

## A KALEIDOSCOPE OF CHANGES

**From ovum to embryo**    The fertilized egg or *zygote* reaches the wall of the uterus in 7 to 10 days. There it sinks into the spongy tissue until it is totally submerged and surrounded by maternal tissues that are rich in blood. The exchange of nutrients and waste between the mother's blood and the fertilized egg begins. At this point, the fertilized egg becomes an *embryo*. The embryonic period extends from two weeks to two months after conception. It is a critical phase because all of the major structures and systems of the body are formed during this period.

Development of the embryo proceeds at such a rapid rate that by the third week after fertilization, the embryo can no longer satisfy its nutritional needs by simply letting nutrients diffuse to the various cells of the embryo. To support the development of the embryo, the nutrients from the mother have to be distributed rapidly and equitably throughout the organism. A blood transport system is nature's answer to the problem. By the 23d day after conception, the heart of the embryo begins beating to facilitate the pumping of nutrient-laden blood to all parts of the body, thereby insuring that all the systems of the embryo are receiving the necessary building materials.

**Placenta.**    The placenta is also critical to the development of the embryo. The placenta is a membrane much thinner than one of the hairs on your head (.002 millimeters). It keeps the maternal and fetal blood systems entirely separate— yet allows for nutrients to pass to the fetus. The mother's blood actually forms pools right next to the placenta. From these pools of blood, materials

**Figure 3—1**                    **Placenta**

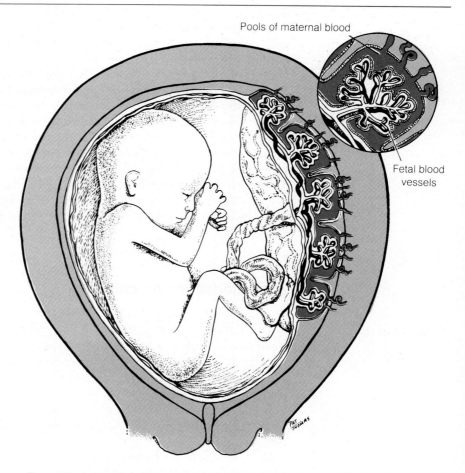

The mother's blood, laden with nutrients, forms pools next to the placenta. Nutrients cross the placenta and are transported to the fetus.

Source: Dryden, R. (1978). *Before birth* (p. 96). London: Heinemann Educational Books.

pass through the placental membrane (see Figure 3–1). Here the nutrients are picked up by the fetus's developing circulatory system and transported to areas where they are needed.

The thin placental membrane allows small molecules such as amino acids, sugars, hormones, and vitamins to pass to the fetus. Certain drugs—antibiotics, nicotine, alcohol, and general anesthetics—also diffuse freely across the membrane. These substances need no help in crossing the placenta because their molecules are so small. Larger molecules such as vitamin C and some proteins need help to cross the placenta. Because they are actively conveyed across the placenta, the concentration of these substances is often higher in the fetal bloodstream than in the maternal bloodstream.

The placenta supplies oxygen to the fetus, provides nutritional material, and flushes waste products from the fetal system. The protective function of the placenta is more subtle. The placenta screens out some potentially harmful materials, especially bacteria. This protective function led to the term placental barrier. We know now, however, that barrier is an inappropriate image to have of the placenta. Many kinds of dangerous chemicals can cross the placenta and harm the fetus.

**Embryonic vulnerability.** During the embryonic period, the developing organism is extremely vulnerable to such harmful substances because they can damage the many systems forming in the body. The drug, thalidomide, provides an illustration. Thalidomide helped mothers relax, but if taken during the embryonic period, it was likely to interfere with the formation of the fetal limbs. A mother taking the drug on the 35th day of pregnancy would have a normal infant. A mother taking the drug on the 25th day was likely to have a child with deformed arms (Stern, 1981). Other agents can harm the fetus if taken during the embryonic period. Unfortunately, many women are not even aware that they are pregnant until the embryonic period is over. Accordingly, they do not monitor their intake of food and drugs as carefully as they would if they knew a child was forming in their womb.

**Six-week-old embryo**

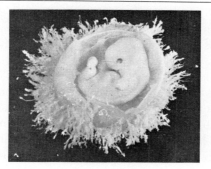

*Dr. Landrum B. Shettle*

A six-week old embryo that is approximately one inch long. Notice that the head accounts for a large portion of the embryo.

Nature does its own monitoring of the embryo during the first two months of gestation. Embryos that have chromosomal errors are usually aborted during this period. In fact, embryos aborted during the first three months, or first trimester of pregnancy, are very likely to be seriously defective and therefore unable to survive.

**The fetal period**

The structures formed during the embryonic period are extended during the fetal period. By the fourth month of pregnancy, the fetus resembles the newborn even though it is only 4½ inches long. The arms, legs, and head begin to function somewhat independently. The face, formed during the embryonic period, is now easily recognized as a human.

Systems of behavior that are evident in the newborn are organized during the fetal period. Basic reflexes appear and many of the sensory systems become functional. By six months of gestation, the eyes have developed and can be opened and closed. The hearing of the fetus is functional from seven months in utero. Whether or not these sensory systems convey information to the fetus is less clear. The eyes have never been exposed to light and the sounds that penetrate the womb tend to be loud and undifferentiated.

**Brain development.** The brain undergoes dramatic changes during the fetal period. At the end of the embryonic stage, the brain was a prominent feature. As shown in Figure 3–2, the head of the two-month-old embryo accounts for half of the organism. But if we could examine the outer layer of the brain, the *cerebral cortex*, we would see that it is practically smooth during the embryonic period. During the fetal period, the number of cells in the brain increases rapidly (Cheek, 1979). The cortex becomes wrinkled or convoluted and will begin to look like the shell of a walnut (see Figure 3–2). At about the seventh month of gestation, the connections between the neurons of the brain are extensive enough to promote simple behaviors. The fetus will react when the mother is exposed to harsh light or loud noises. Most of the reflexes of the newborn are present in rudimentary form. The rapid growth of the brain during the fetal period means that it is especially susceptible to environmental insults.

Unlike many other animals, newborn humans are completely helpless and dependent. If humans had a longer gestation period, the infant might not be born in such a helpless state. Of course, you also have to consider the size of the infant's head. If it became any larger in utero, the child would have difficulty passing through the birth canal. Some theorists feel that the size of the female pelvis limited brain growth in utero and led to an evolutionary change in the development of the brain. At birth, the brain of the gorilla and the brain of the human are about the same size. But the gorilla's brain expands very little, and the human child's grows rapidly for several years (Chai, 1976). Our gestation period seems to be an evolutionary compromise that takes into account the size of the birth canal, the size of the child's head, and the ability of the child to survive outside the uterus. The helplessness and immaturity of

**Figure 3–2**                    **The development of the brain**

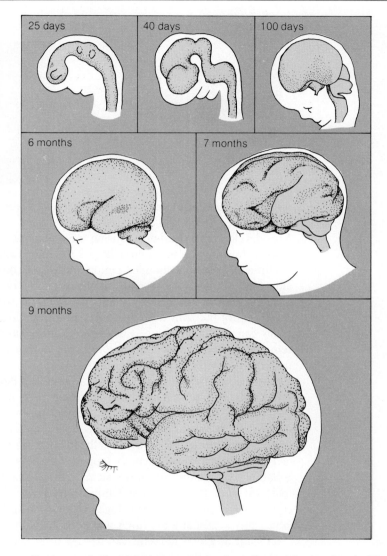

The human brain originates as prominent swellings at the head end of the neural tube. The convolutions and fissures of the brain's surface do not begin to appear until about the middle of pregnancy.

Source: Cowan, W. M. (1979). The development of the brain. *Scientific American, 241*, 112–133.

the human newborn reflects the fact that the brain is still at a very immature stage (Dryden, 1978).

**The respiratory system.**  Like the brain, the respiratory system undergoes dramatic changes during the fetal period. When infants take their first breath, their immediate well-being hinges on their lungs. The lungs of the

## Intrauterine development

 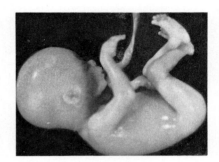

*Dr. Landrum B. Shettle*

Photos of the embryo and fetus at various stages of development.

fetus develop from two buds. During the embryonic phase these buds begin to branch, forming the main bronchi and the lobes of the lungs. This branching continues throughout the fetal period and is not completed until several years after birth. Prior to the seventh month in utero, the surface area of the lungs is so limited that premature infants are likely to suffer respiratory problems. The lungs of the fetus have been likened to waterlogged sponges. Before newborns can begin breathing, the amniotic fluid saturating the lungs must be removed. Some of this fluid is forced out during the birth process. The remainder is absorbed rapidly after birth.

The maturity of the respiratory system at birth often determines a premature infant's chances for survival. Babies born before 24 weeks of gestation or weighing less than 21 ounces (699 grams) seldom survive. Although all of the fetal organs and systems are quite well developed by 24 to 26 weeks of gestation, fetuses born during this period usually die of respiratory difficulties.

The lungs are more likely to support infants born after 26 to 33 weeks of gestation. The central nervous system in these infants is developed enough to maintain respiration and body temperature. However, respiratory illnesses are common and mortality is still high. During 34 to 38 weeks of gestation, the fetus gains weight and the lungs mature sufficiently to insure survival.

The age at which the fetus can survive in the outside world has been dropping steadily in the wake of improvements in the medical care of premature infants. One of the tiniest premature infants to survive to date is Ernestine Hudgins. She was born at 22 weeks of gestation and weighed less than a pound. At two months of age, doctors felt she had a good chance for a normal life (Associated Press, 1983).

The premature infant has commanded a great deal of attention. Infants on the other end of the continuum are also at risk. Postmaturity is dangerous because the placenta becomes inadequate and even begins to deteriorate as term approaches. If the birth is delayed, the infant may suffer from lack of oxygen.

**Sexual development.** During the first six weeks of gestation, male and female fetuses do not differ sexually. Between the sixth and eighth week, a surge of hormones (androgen) causes the XY fetus to develop into a male. If there is no androgen present, the fetus continues to develop as a female. Rather than Eve being formed from Adam's rib, Adam was formed by a surge of androgen.

The importance of these hormones can be seen in cases where the fetus, genetically a female, is exposed to androgens during pregnancy. At birth, the child might have both ovaries and a penis. The genital anomalies can often be corrected surgically. But the hormone's effects are not restricted to the sex organs. The brains of males and females are also influenced by the types and quantity of hormones circulating in the fetus. Girls who were "masculinized" in utero grew up as tomboys, showed little or no interest in handling and caring for babies, and preferred active games and competitive sports (Money & Ehrhardt, 1972). It should be pointed out that the androgens did not affect how the women perceived themselves. They were typically happy and successful as wives and mothers.

Money and Ehrhardt argue that the girls have been "psychologically" masculinized. There may be a similar cognitive masculinization. Two physicians at a Chicago hospital recently noted that men who had low levels of androgen during adolescence were not as good at spatial tasks as men with normal levels of this hormone; yet all of the men had similar verbal skills (Hier & Crowley 1982). These authors present animal results, results from other humans, and their own data to support the viewpoint that the presence of androgen influences the way the brain is organized, and that, in turn, is linked to spatial skills.

The multifaceted roles that hormones play in the body are just beginning to be appreciated. Their influence on sexual development has been obvious for years, but their influence on psychological aspects of behavior, on cognitive functioning, and on the development of diseases in later life is only beginning to be explored. The exposure of the fetus to selected hormones could significantly alter a host of developmental processes.

The fetal period is a time of remarkable growth and organization. Structures formed during the embryonic period become mature enough to sustain life outside the womb. The brain grows at the rate of millions of cells each day (Cowan, 1979). The neural connections that will eventually direct behavior are begun. Any events that alter this development or the organization of the brain may have long-term effects on the child.

## MATERNAL FACTORS

The mother, as host for the developing fetus, provides an environment that can optimize or inhibit development. The nutritional environment is crucial to the developing fetus. Other factors, such as the mother's age and her emotional state, may also affect the fetus. In this section, we will describe the maternal factors that impinge on the fetus.

**Nutrition**

Whether or not the mother is well nourished has an immediate and visible effect on her ability to reproduce. In the most extreme cases of malnutrition—starvation and famine—women stop menstruating and hence do not even conceive children. This is followed by a precipitous drop in the birthrate. If the mother does not have a certain amount of body fat, the reproductive system does not function. A decrease in birthrate occurred during 1916 and 1917 in Germany when the allied blockade caused widespread starvation and again in Holland during World War II. The famine in Holland was eight months long, and its effects on the population were studied in some detail. Only one third of the expected number of births occurred during this period. The children who were born were not immune to the effects of the famine. Miscarriages, abortions, stillbirths, neonatal deaths, and malformations all increased in children conceived during the famine (see Figure 3–3). Those children who survived had little vitality and very low resistance to disease (Hurley, 1980).

Famine is an extreme condition and it would be remarkable if the children conceived and born during such privation escaped untouched. Malnutrition or poor nutrition are much less extreme. Indeed, much of the world's population suffers from malnutrition. Not long ago, the fetus was regarded as a parasite that would be nutritionally protected at the expense of the mother. This viewpoint has been revised. The fetus is not well nourished unless the mother's diet is adequate (Hurley, 1980).

A study of mothers in rural Iowa provides an example. The diets of 400 pregnant women were evaluated and related to the condition of the infants at birth. The newborns with the lowest birth weights, the lowest vitality, and the largest number of deaths were born to the mothers with the poorest diets. Almost 10 percent of their infants were premature. In contrast, the women who were well nourished had few premature births (Jeans, Smith, & Stearns, 1955).

Studies that have varied the diets of female animals lead to the same conclusion—the nutritional status of the pregnant female affects the growth, vitality,

**Figure 3–3**

**The effects of famine on the fetus**

| Condition | Incidence (percent of births) | |
| --- | --- | --- |
| | **Prewar** | **Conceived in hunger** |
| Abortion and miscarriage | 1.67 | 8.3 |
| Prematurity | 5.27 | 8.4 |
| Stillbirth | 3.5 | 4.0 |
| Neonatal death | 1.55 | 5.1 |
| Malformed | 1.36 | 2.4 |

The outcome of pregnancies in Rotterdam during World War II demonstrates that during a famine, unborn children suffer too.

Source: Smith, C. A. (1947). The effect of wartime starvation in Holland upon pregnancy and its product. *American Journal of Obstetrics and Gynecology, 53,* 599–606.

and survival of the fetus (Winick, 1979). These studies do not tell us whether the nutritional environment in utero has long-term effects on the developing child. Of primary concern is the effect, if any, that malnutrition has on the brain.

**Nutrition and brain growth**

The graph in Figure 3–4 shows the rate of brain development in the human. The total brain weight and total DNA increase enormously during the last half of pregnancy, and they continue to increase at a rapid rate during the first two years of life. Dobbing and Sands (1973) have argued that the brain is especially vulnerable during this period. Since we cannot experiment on the brains of children, much of the research on nutrition and brain growth has been conducted on animals. Rats have a period of rapid brain growth shortly after birth. Even relatively mild restriction of food during this period can affect the number of cells and the amount of DNA in their brains (Rozovski & Winick, 1979). A substandard diet during this entire period has a permanent effect on the development of the brain. The absolute number of cells remains low no matter how the diet improves. If, however, malnutrition takes place after the brain is

**Figure 3–4**   **Brain growth**

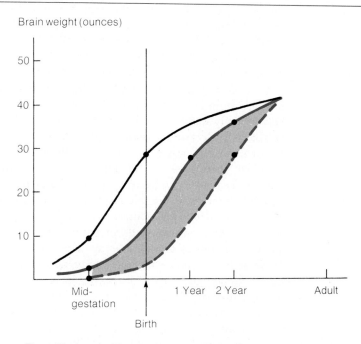

The critical period for brain growth in humans is from the 20th week of gestation until two years after birth.

formed, the brain cells shrink. With adequate food, the cells will return to normal size. In other words, the full range of brain function can be recovered.

The studies on the growth of the human brain indicate a similar pattern. Winick and Rosso (1975) examined the brains of infants who died of malnutrition during the first year of life and found fewer cells than in a normal brain. Children who recovered and had good diets still had smaller head sizes five years later.

The intellectual development of children who were severely malnourished during the period of peak brain growth has been assessed by dozens of studies. The results generally demonstrate that children who eat well are taller, score higher on IQ tests, and perform better in school (Winick, 1979). Unfortunately, malnutrition seldom occurs in isolation. When you test a five- or ten-year-old who was malnourished in utero, has also grown up in an unstimulating environment, has a history of disease, and is surrounded by poverty, it is impossible to attribute the low IQ score solely to malnutrition. We need to examine situations where the child was malnourished during the period of rapid brain growth, but was well nourished later.

The most optimistic results come from the children malnourished during the Holland Famine. Prior to and after the famine, the women were well fed. During the eight months of famine, the adults received 750 or fewer calories per day and lost 25 percent or more of their original body weight. When the boys who were born during this period were old enough to be inducted into the armed forces, they were given rigorous mental and physical examinations. They did not differ from children conceived and born during periods of plenty. This study suggests that the damage from malnutrition can be overcome if the malnutrition exists for a limited period of time.

A similar experiment of nature occurred when children born in Korea were adopted into middle-class American homes. Almost one third of these children were severely malnourished, falling below the third percentile for height and weight on their first birthday. Another third had suffered some malnutrition. And a final third was well nourished. By the time these children were seven years old, there were no differences in weight. The malnourished group was still shorter than the other two groups. All of the groups performed normally on tests of intellectual development. The malnourished group had a mean IQ of 102, the marginally nourished children had an IQ of 105, and the well-nourished children had an IQ of 111. Even children who had suffered severe malnutrition during the intrauterine period and the first year of life experienced an amazing recovery when they were raised in an environment where they were no longer deprived (Winick, Meyer, & Harris, 1975).

When Korean children were not adopted until three years of age, their recoveries were not as remarkable. Those who had experienced severe malnutrition, for three years instead of two, had lower than normal IQs and performed poorly in school. Apparently, the ability of the human brain to recover from severe malnutrition is limited. If malnutrition continues throughout the fetal period and the first three years of life, when the major cell divisions are taking place, recovery will not be complete (Winick, 1979).

**Maternal age**

When should women have their families? Child development texts written during the 1960s recommended the years from 20 to 35. The authors argued that before 20 the reproductive system was immature and risks to the fetus were high. Between 20 and 35, the woman's body was mature and functioned efficiently. After 35, however, the reproductive system began performing less efficiently, and the risk of fetal defects again increased. Fifteen years is not a very long period in which to have children, and several changes in society have meant that these limits have been extended.

**Teenage pregnancies.** More and more teenagers are sexually active. Approximately 60 percent of the female population have sexual experiences before they are 19; almost 20 percent before they are 15 (Blum & Goldhagen, 1981). Of these sexually active teenagers, 50 percent report that they do not use contraceptives on a regular basis (Zelnik, 1981). It is not surprising then, that the number of teenage pregnancies has skyrocketed (Stickle, 1981). In recent years, one out of every five births in the United States was to a teenager. In urban centers, one of every two babies was born to a teenager (Graham, 1981).

The disadvantages of a teenage pregnancy are legion. Teenagers have many problems during labor and delivery. Infants born to teenage mothers are often premature. Their mortality rate is twice that of infants born to mothers over 20 (Graham, 1981). These problems do not necessarily reflect an immature reproductive system; they could be due to poor nutrition, lack of prenatal care, or the lower socioeconomic status of many teenage mothers. Teenage mothers are the least likely of all age groups to obtain prenatal care from early in their pregnancy. If they obtain prenatal care, they are less likely to experience problems during labor and delivery (Blum & Goldhagen, 1981). Teenagers in general are renowned for their poor diets. Pregnant teenagers eat the same empty calories and often do not eat enough (Jacobsen, 1981).

The physical problems that teenage mothers have could be overcome by proper prenatal care, improved diets, and prenatal screening. It is more difficult to overcome the sociological disadvantages. Because 80 percent of the teenagers who become pregnant do not complete high school, they start out at the lowest rung of the socioeconomic ladder (Card & Wise, 1978). Marriages that do occur in this age group are often forced and seldom last. Teenagers between 14 and 17 years of age have the highest divorce rate of any age group (McCarthy, 1981). Even the second marriages of these women are likely to end in divorce. Once the father leaves, the mother must seek employment. Some teenagers manage to break out of this vicious cycle, complete their education, and secure reasonable jobs. Many do not.

Trying to reverse teenage sexual activity is like trying to reverse the tide. A more reasonable goal might be to convince teenagers that sexual activity must be accompanied by sexual responsibility. Programs that provide information about conception and contraception are available, and these programs seem to be having some effect. Between 1973 and 1978, the birth rate among 18- and 19-year-olds declined for the first time in 25 years (Stickle, 1981).

**Pregnancies past 30.** Currently, about 10 percent of America's first time mothers are 30 or older. Although this used to be a cause for concern, the chances today are very high that a woman in this age group will have an uneventful pregnancy. Women in their 30s and 40s have better diets, get more exercise, and are in better physical condition than they were 20 years ago. They may be 30 to 40 years old chronologically, but are 20 and 30 years of age physiologically. Many new medical techniques are available to help assess the health of both the mother and the fetus on a continuing basis. The physical risks to the mother and child must be counted in the disadvantages column, but many of these can be surmounted.

Sociological factors should also be considered. Older women are often in the best position to raise a child in a healthy environment. They are likely to be financially secure. Increasingly, women spend their 20s launching their careers. Then, with their husbands, they make a deliberate decision to have a child. The couple is mature and committed to the responsibilities that a child entails. The fathers tend to become involved and contribute enthusiastically to raising the child. These children are born into a loving, secure, and emotionally stable environment.

Women who delay having families may have trouble conceiving. Doctors have always thought that women retained a high fertility rate until over 35 years of age. In 1982, a French fertility clinic reported that women over 30 did not become pregnant at the same rates as women under 30. The clients at this clinic all had sterile husbands. In order to have a child, they had artificial insemination every month for a year. Therefore, all of the women had 12 chances to conceive a child. During the year, 75 percent of the women in their 20s became pregnant. In the 31 to 35 age group, 62 percent became pregnant, and in the women over 35, the rate dropped to 54 percent (Schwartz & Mayaux, 1982).

The age of the mother is an important influence on the fetus, but not necessarily because of the reproductive system. The sociological advantages of mothers over 35 tend to balance or even outweigh the physiological disadvantages of motherhood. With teenage mothers, the sociological factors can become a distinct disadvantage.

**Emotional states of the mother**

Old wives' tales about the effects of stress on a pregnant woman abound. Women were often told that living through a frightening experience, like a flood or thunderstorm, would leave its mark on the fetus, as would a divorce, death in the family, or other emotionally draining experience. Although such extreme statements are probably not true, it does make sense to ask if the emotional state of the mother affects the fetus. We know that hormones affect the fetus, and we know that stress can alter hormonal levels. We also know that maternal stress in animals can produce overreactive offspring. But we do not know whether stress in pregnant women affects the fetus. High levels of anxiety in women have been related to miscarriages, premature births, and a variety of delivery problems. But perhaps these women had good reason to be anxious. In many cases, they had already miscarried once or had some problem earlier in the pregnancy. The miscarriages, abortions, and delivery problems might be caused by some very real physical problems (Carlson & La-Barba, 1979). Stott (1971) examined anxiety in European women who were pregnant during WWII. He concludes that the stress of war increased the number of birth defects. He also argues that the problems of teenage mothers stem from the stress of being pregnant, not from an immature reproductive system. Stott may be right, but in both of these groups of mothers, there are other factors, like poor diet, that could be responsible for defects in the children. Numerous authors have described effects on the pregnancy or the child that they have then attributed to the mother's emotional state. In most studies, however, other explanations could be invoked. Suffice it to say, that it is certainly possible for a fetus to be influenced by a mother who is overwrought and anxious. Yet the studies that have been done are not very convincing (Carlson & LaBarba, 1979).

## PATERNAL INFLUENCES ON THE FETUS

In many discussions of intrauterine development, the possibility that the father might have some effect on the fetus is studiously ignored. The general explanation for this oversight is that men produce sperm on a continuing basis. As a result, drugs and radiation that might damage one batch of sperm disappear rapidly from the system and a new, untainted batch of sperm is produced. This explanation turns out to be a bit misleading.

At the height of the thalidomide tragedy, there were two reports of a child born with the characteristic thalidomide deformities whose mothers never used thalidomide. The fathers, however, had taken the drug (Editorial, 1964). These reports suggested that fathers might transmit some drugs and the teratogenic effects through their semen. This process of transmission has now been documented in nine different species (Joffe, 1979). Males have transmitted adverse effects to their offspring after they were exposed to thalidomide, methadone, and ethanol (Soyka & Joffe, 1980). The same process seems to apply to humans.

At the turn of the century, there were several studies of men continuously exposed to high levels of industrial lead. Their wives were prone to spontaneous abortions and newborn mortality was high. More recent surveys have indicated that the wives of dentists and anesthetists have more spontaneous abortions and give birth to more infants with congenital anomalies than the rest of the population (Joffe, 1979). Being exposed to industrial lead and anesthetics on a continuing basis could affect the sperm that are produced. Sperm production takes about two months (Reinisch, 1984). During this period, continual exposure to teratogens could certainly cause defective sperm. Given that men often work around hazardous chemicals, gases, and metals, it is important to find out whether these occupational hazards can be transmitted to the fetus via the sperm. The few studies available indicate that the father will be part of continuing research on birth defects.

## TERATOGENIC AGENTS

The embryo and fetus face numerous hazards while they are still enjoying the protection of the mother's womb. For some years, scientists thought that the womb offered complete protection for the fetus. Since 1941 when Gregg demonstrated the effect of German measles (rubella) on the fetus, physicians have taken an increased interest in the study of *teratogens*, which translated literally means monster-producing agents.

Almost any environmental agent could be a teratogen. Viruses and diseases that affect the mother may have a negative effect on the child. Rubella is the classic example. Chemicals ingested by the mother may cross the placenta and damage the child. Nicotine, alcohol, and heroin are a few examples of drugs mothers ingest willingly. Prescription drugs, such as thalidomide, diethylstilbestrol (DES), barbiturates, and antibiotics have been taken by unsuspecting mothers and have had profound effects on the fetus. These verified teratogens are only a few of the chemical agents to which the fetus is exposed. The environment that surrounds us contains many agents that have teratogenic effects—some we know about, many we do not.

The women of Minamata Bay in Japan had no idea why, suddenly, so many of their infants were retarded and severely deformed at birth. Investigations revealed that a nearby industry was discharging mercury into the water. The women were eating the fish that had sustained their seaside community for hundreds of years. Tragically, the fish now contained teratogenic doses of mercury (Tsubaki & Irukayama, 1976).

Chemicals such as mercury that subtly find their way into our systems pose a very real threat to the unborn child. The Environmental Protection Agency lists over 32,000 sites that contain hazardous wastes and estimates that over 35 million metric tons of hazardous industrial waste are produced each year. This waste is then disposed of in lagoons, landfills, or ponds. Hazardous chemicals from these waste sites can enter the water table, the soil, and the air (Sloan, Shapiro, & Mitchell, 1980). Pregnant women who think they are taking every reasonable precaution to protect their unborn child from teratogenic agents may never suspect that the water they drink, the air they breathe, or the fresh vegetables they buy could contain teratogenic chemicals.

To further underscore the magnitude of the chemical problem, consider that there are 60,000 chemicals used in the United States and Canada today and only 3,500 have been tested to see if they are teratogens. Each year, between

1,500 and 2,000 new chemicals are introduced into our environments. Only a few are put through the lengthy and costly testing procedures required to assure their safety. Unfortunately, the effects of many chemicals may be very subtle or may take years to appear. In some ways, it is easier to ferret out the chemical cause for extensive, obvious deformities, like the truncated limbs of the thalidomide child or the Minamata disease caused by mercury poisoning. Tracing more complex behaviors like hyperactivity or attention problems to a single chemical or a particular combination of chemicals is much more difficult. Even the government agencies that have been established to protect the people typically monitor only newborns that show visible and serious deformities (Sloan, Shapiro, & Mitchell, 1980).

Not all the women who took thalidomide and not all the women in Minamata Bay had deformed children. Why are certain children affected while others are spared, and what determines how seriously children will be affected? The answers to these questions lie in a general understanding of how toxic agents affect the fetus.

The most critical information to have is when the mother was exposed to

**Teratogenic agents**

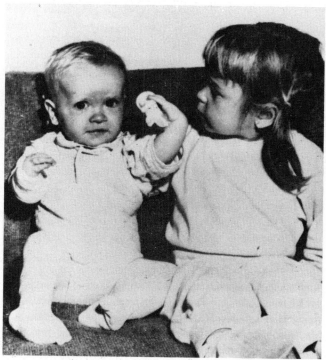

*The Associated Press*

Children exposed to thalidomide in utero have a distinct set of birth defects.

**Figure 3–5**                     **Timing of insults**

### Timing of embryotoxicity

| Oogenesis | Spermatogenesis | | | | Embryo | Fetus | Neonate | Lactation |
|---|---|---|---|---|---|---|---|---|
| | –8 | –4 | 0 Fertili- zation | 1 5 Implantation | 10 | 20 30 | 40 Birth | |
| | | | | Gestation (weeks) | | | | |
| **Drugs** | Hormones LSD | Phenytoin Thalidomide Methadone Estrogen | Hormones Contraceptives Abortifacients | Methylmercury Diethylstibestrol Thalidomide Phenytoin Alcohol Aminopterin Estrogen Androgen Progestin | Tetracyclines Quinine Chloroquine Goitrogens Thiouracil Teridax Salicylates Heavy metals Antibiotics Smoking | IV fluid Salicylates Vitamin K Naphthalene Blockers Reserpine Morphine Sedatives Analgesics Chloride Cardiovascular drugs | Biazepan Lithium Methylmercury Atropine Anticoagulants Antithyroids Antimetabolites Cathartics Iodides Narcotics Tetracyclines | |
| **Micro- organisms** | | | | Rubella Toxoplasmosis Varicella Syphilis Cytomegalovirus Herpes | Rubella Toxoplasmosis Varicella Syphilis Cytomegalovirus Herpes | | Herpes Cytomegalovirus | |
| **Radiation** | X-radiation | | | Atomic radiation | | | | |
| **Possible effects** | Chromosomal damage Death | Death Abortion Malformation Prematurity | Prematurity Abortion | Prematurity Abortion Death Malformation | Prematurity Abortion Organ damage Fetal morbidity | Neonatal morbidity | Infant morbidity | |
| **Maternal factors** | Age Season Metabolism Emotions | | Neural endocrine state | Nutrition Maternal disease Crowding Social class Geography Season | Maternal disease | | Maternal disease | |

Drugs and diseases are most likely to affect the structure of the fetus if taken during the first two months of pregnancy.

Source: Schwarz, R. H., & Yaffe, S. J. (1980). *Drug and chemical risks to the fetus and newborn.* New York: Alan R. Liss.

the toxic substance. Figure 3–5 is a time line showing the effects of toxic agents from before conception through lactation. Chemicals, drugs, and radiation can be a potential danger to the child even before the child is conceived. A mother whose system is depleted and abused by heroin is not a particularly good host for a fetus. Drugs and radiation may affect how well the mother's reproductive system functions and thereby influence whether the child will have the normal complement of chromosomes.

According to Figure 3–5, there are not many agents that have an effect on the fertilized egg during the first three weeks. This is misleading because spontaneous abortions are the most typical result of insults during this period. The embryonic period is a period of heightened vulnerability. During the last trimester of pregnancy, the brain and central nervous system are very vulnerable.

Figure 3–5 illustrates several principles of teratogenic agents.

1.  The timing of a teratogenic agent is critical. Teratogens may disrupt the development of an organ during one period of development, but have no effect later.
2.  A teratogen taken prior to conception may affect the embryo.
3.  If the fetus is exposed to a teratogen early in the formation of a structure, the damage to that structure will be greater than if the fetus is exposed later.
4.  Teratogens that have no effect on the mother may have devastating effects on the fetus.
5.  A teratogen may produce defects that are not apparent at birth (Goldman, 1980).

**Drugs**

Drugs are intended to save lives, not harm them. We would be wise, however, to remember the following caution from an anonymous writer, "All drugs have two effects—the ones we know about and the ones we do not know about." The effects we do not know about often include teratogenic influences on the embryo and fetus.

Some drugs affect the fetus in the same way they do the mother, but because the fetus is so small, the effect is magnified. A two-month-old fetus weighs less than an ounce; the average mother weighs 130 pounds. Any drugs that the mother takes are formulated for her weight. Depending on how easily the drug crosses the placenta, the fetus may be getting a dose hundreds of times stronger than the dose the mother is taking. Aspirin taken by adults causes a minute amount of bleeding into the stomach. For the fetus, the same aspirin may cause more severe hemorrhaging (Rumack, Guggenheim, Rumack, Peterson, Johnston, & Braitwaite, 1981).

Drugs taken during the embryonic period may have an entirely different and unexpected effect on the fetus. There is no way to predict these kinds of effects. Only systematic research will indicate whether or not a particular drug is a teratogen. Before drugs are marketed, they are tested for teratogenic effects on at least two other species. But the test is often limited to examining the offspring for structural defects. Such testing is not likely to reveal subtle behavioral differences, or effects that are hidden for 20 years, or effects that are likely to be specific to humans (Stern, 1981). Some of the drugs that are considered in this section have been used for hundreds of years, but their effects on the fetus have only been ascertained in the last 10. One aim of this chapter is to dem-

## A PARTIAL LIST OF KNOWN TERATOGENIC AGENTS

| Drug | Effect |
|------|--------|
| Thalidomide | Missing limbs, deformed limbs, ears deformed. Occasionally eyes and internal organs affected. |
| Hormones | Alter genitalia; females sometimes |
| Androgens | labeled as males at birth; Males have small penises. |
| Diethylstilbestrol | Females are more likely to have cancer of the vagina, males produce deficient sperm. |
| Estrogen | In some males, behavior and personality are affected. |
| Folic acid antagonists | Cleft palates, facial deformities. |
| Alcohol | Mental retardation, growth retardation, small head size. |
| Anticonvulsants | Facial deformities, cleft palate, masculinization of female infants. |
| Alkylating agents | Kidney defects, deformities in fingers, cleft palate. |
| Iodides | Neonatal deaths, deformities of thyroid. |
| Salicylates (aspirin) | Decreased birth weight, higher infant mortality, cleft palate. |
| Tranquilizers | Cleft palate, heart defects. |
| Amphetamines | Heart defects. |
| Antibiotics | Deafness, cleft palate. |
| Dioxin | Miscarriages, heart defects. |
| Nicotine | Miscarriages, low birth weight, Sudden Infant Death Syndrome. |

Some of the drugs known to affect the fetus. Adapted from Shwarz, R. H., & Yaffe, S. J. (1980). *Drug and chemical risks to the fetus and newborn* (p. 15). New York: Allen R. Liss.

onstrate the effects that many kinds of chemicals can have on the developing human in the hope that women will avoid as many drugs as possible during their own pregnancies. The first group of drugs to be considered are those that are widely available, sanctioned by society, and sought out by the mother.

**Fetal alcohol syndrome.** Over 2,300 years ago, Aristotle alerted us to the dangers of drinking alcohol during pregnancy—"foolish and drunken and harebrained women most often bring forth children like unto themselves, morose and languid" (Streissguth, Landesman-Dwyer, Martin, & Smith, 1980). Drinking alcohol during pregnancy was regarded as a potentially dangerous practice throughout the 18th and 19th centuries (Warner & Rosett, 1975). Despite these repeated warnings, the effects of alcohol were dismissed during the majority of the 20th century. Researchers who did find retarded children born to alcoholic mothers attributed the retardation to poor nutrition or other confounding conditions. As recently as 1965, when almost every drug was being scrutinized for effects on the fetus, alcohol was still regarded as generally harmless.

The controlled study of alcohol as a potential teratogen began in France, where a group of French doctors investigated 127 infants born to alcoholic mothers. To their surprise, these children had flattened noses, widely separated eyes, tiny heads, low birth weights, and lowered intelligence (Lemoine, Harrousseau, Borteyru, & Menuet, 1968). Two doctors in the United States soon concurred with these conclusions, and the investigation of the effects of alcohol during pregnancy began in earnest (Jones & Smith, 1973). Consuming alcohol during pregnancy is now recognized as the "most frequent known teratogenic cause of mental retardation in the Western World" (Clarren & Smith, 1978, p. 1066).

The characteristics of infants with fetal alcohol syndrome have been widely publicized in recent years because it is an entirely preventable syndrome. Growth retardation and mental retardation are the most common characteristics; they occur in over 80 percent of the children. Mothers who abuse alcohol have infants who are short and have very small heads. Unlike premature infants, who begin to catch up on their growth after birth, fetal alcohol syndrome infants do not have a growth spurt. They typically remain below the third percentile in length and weight (Streissguth et al., 1980).

The retardation of children diagnosed as having fetal alcohol syndrome can

**Figure 3—6**  **Physical characteristics of child with fetal alcohol syndrome**

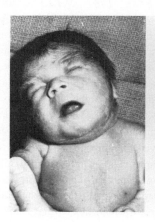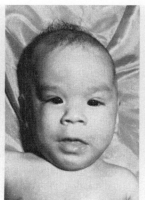

*Dr. Ann P. Streissguth, University of Washington*

Fetal alcohol syndrome. Physical characteristics include short nose, thin upper lip, low-set ears, widely spaced eyes. This child was photographed at birth, eight months, and four and a half years; the child's IQ was 40—45 at each evaluation from eight months on.

vary from slight to severe. The average IQ reported in a series of studies from France, Germany, Sweden, and the United States is 68 (Streissguth et al., 1980). In one Seattle study of children between 9 months of age and 21 years, the average IQ was 64 with a range from 16 to 105 (Streissguth, Herman, & Smith, 1978a). Children with fetal alcohol syndrome can also be identified by a characteristic set of facial features. They have narrow eye slits and eyes that are widely spaced (see Figure 3–6). They have flattened noses like Down's syndrome children. In some cases, the palmar crease of the hand is abnormal, and the connecting tissue of the brain, called the corpus callosum, is absent.

The mental retardation that accompanies fetal alcohol syndrome is not reversible. Despite a stimulating environment, nutritious food, and caring parents, children with fetal alcohol syndrome may never recover their mental skills (Streissguth, Herman, & Smith, 1978b; Iosub, Fuchs, Bingol, Stone & Gromisch, 1981). Furthermore, a child may lack these physical symptoms, but still be mentally retarded. A group of researchers in Seattle studied 23 children who had been born to alcoholic mothers. When these children were seven years old, they were matched on age, race, geographic region, and mother's education with children whose mothers did not abuse alcohol during pregnancy. Even though the two groups of children did not differ in physical appearance, 44 percent of the children born to the alcoholic mothers had IQs below 79. Only 11 percent of the comparison group had IQs that low (Jones, Smith, Streissguth & Myrianthopoulous, 1974).

The intellectual deficits these children suffer appear to be caused by injury to the brain in utero (see Figure 3–7). Autopsies performed on the brains of children who were stillborn or died during the neonatal period indicate that the brains of children whose mothers drank heavily during pregnancy are not organized normally (Clarren, Alvord, Sumi, Streissguth, & Smith, 1978).

Exactly how alcohol impedes the development of the brain is now being investigated (Borges & Lewis, 1981). When an adult drinks an alcoholic beverage, the alcohol is converted into *acetaldehyde*. Acetaldehyde is a poison and could be the villain in fetal alcohol syndrome. The accumulation of acetaldehyde is what makes adults feel sick after they have had too much to drink. Because alcohol is one of the substances that passes freely across the placenta, concentrations of alcohol in the fetal bloodstream are as high as concentrations in the maternal bloodstream. The fetal liver may not be able to metabolize alcohol as efficiently as the mother's liver (Abel, 1980), and the accumulating poison may interfere with the development of the fetal brain.

Most women, however, are not alcoholics and do not have 6 to 12 drinks a day. What are the effects of moderate social drinking, or an occasional fling, or even a minimal amount of alcohol on an unborn child?

To examine the effects of binge drinking, we need to consider what organs are being formed during the mother's binges. Dobbing (1976) has identified two periods when the developing brain is very vulnerable to teratogenic agents. The first occurs during the 12th to 18th week of gestation when the basic structures of the brain are forming. The second occurs during the last three

**Figure 3—7**                    **Brain of child with fetal alcohol syndrome**

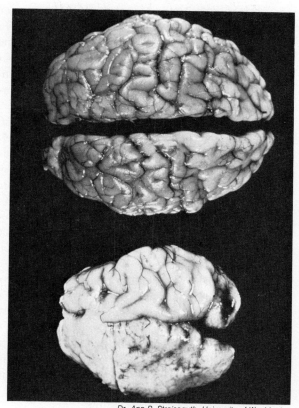

*Dr. Ann P. Streissguth, University of Washington*

A comparison of the brain of a normal newborn with the brain of an infant with Fetal Alcohol Syndrome who died five days after birth.

months of pregnancy when the crucial connections between different areas of the brain are being made. All of the symptoms of fetal alcohol syndrome are not likely to appear unless the woman has been drinking rather heavily throughout pregnancy. But some of the symptoms can occur in women who have gone on a drinking binge during these critical periods. If a woman has been drinking heavily during the last three months of pregnancy but has abstained before that, the physical characteristics normally associated with fetal alcohol syndrome are likely to be absent, but the child's brain could be affected (Clarren et al., 1978). Or, if the mother goes on a binge when the fetal eyes are developing, the child may develop *epicanthal folds* or *ptosis*, two common eye problems of fetal alcohol syndrome children (Mulvihill, Klimas, Stokes, & Risemberg, 1976). These results indicate that binge drinkers are at risk for having a child with some of the effects of fetal alcohol syndrome.

What about mothers who are moderate drinkers or social drinkers? Do they risk having a child who is small and mentally retarded? Hanson, Streissguth, and Smith (1978) reported on mothers who had more than four drinks a day, mothers who had 2 to 4 drinks a day, and mothers who had fewer than two drinks a day while they were pregnant. Figure 3–8 indicates that 19 percent of the children born to the heavy drinkers had some of the abnormal features associated with fetal alcohol syndrome, while 11 percent of the infants of moderate drinkers also had some symptoms. Women who had fewer than two drinks a day did not have an increased risk for symptoms of fetal alcohol syndrome (Hanson, Streissguth, & Smith, 1978).

Given the results of this study, the National Institute of Alcohol Abuse and Alcoholism began to talk about children who had fetal alcohol effects. Some of these, that occur in the absence of the full syndrome, are low birth weight, hyperactivity, sleep disturbances in the newborn, stillbirths, poor sucking ability, and attention problems during preschool (Rosette et al., 1979; Shaywitz, Cohen, & Shaywitz, 1980; Thompson, 1979). In 1981, the Surgeon General's office reviewed the literature on alcohol and found that women who drink as little as one ounce of alcohol a day tend to have infants who are smaller than normal. Women who drink an ounce of alcohol twice a week have more miscarriages (Food and Drug Administration, 1981). This information prompted the recommendation that pregnant women abstain from alcohol completely during pregnancy.

Alcohol is such a commonly used drug in Western societies that complete abstinence is often regarded as nonsense; hence, educating women about its dangers is a difficult task. The National Institute of Alcohol Abuse and Alcoholism is actively publicizing the dangers of alcohol to women of childbearing age and has even attempted, unsuccessfully, to put a warning label on bottles of alcohol.

**Figure 3–8**                          **How much is too much?**

| Maternal alcohol consumption | | | Abnormal newborns with some features of FAS | |
|---|---|---|---|---|
| **AA*** | **Drinks per day** | **N** | **Percentage** | **N** |
| ≥ 2.0 | (≥ 4 drinks per day) | 16 | 19 | 3† |
| 1.0 to 2.0 | (2 to 4 drinks per day) | 54 | 11 | 6 |
| < 1.0 | (≤ 2 drinks per day) | 93 | 2 | 2 |

Alcoholic women often give birth to children with fetal alcohol syndrome. Even moderate drinkers have infants with some characteristics of fetal alcohol syndrome.

*AA = Average ounces of absolute alcohol consumed per day, in month preceding recognition of pregnancy, according to self-report.

†Two of these three newborns had enough FAS characteristics to receive an FAS diagnosis; their mothers also had a clinical diagnosis of alcoholism.

Source: Streissguth, A. P., Landesman-Dwyer, S., Martin, J. C., & Smith, D. W. (1980). Teratogenic effects of alcohol in humans and laboratory animals. *Science, 209,* 353–361.

**Nicotine.** The harmful effects of nicotine are so widely accepted that in the last 10 years, thousands of smokers from every walk of life have quit smoking. Unfortunately, almost 30 percent of the women in the United States still smoke (Surgeon General, 1981), and their smoking can affect the fetus (Witter & King, 1980). The most consistent and obvious effect of smoking is on the newborn's birth weight. Consider these statistics:

1. Women who smoke give birth to infants who weigh approximately a half pound (200 grams) less than the newborns of nonsmokers.
2. Infants who weigh less than 5 pounds (about 2500 grams) are 20 times as likely to die within the first year of life.
3. Smoking contributes to 20 to 40 percent of these underweight infants born in the United States and Canada (Kessler & Newberger, 1981).

These statistics underline how smoking, by itself, plays a major role in infant mortality. Since birth weight is the single most important factor in whether the infant lives or dies, mothers who smoke are clearly jeopardizing their infant's survival.

As with alcohol, the dose is important. Mothers who smoke two packs of cigarettes a day are more likely to have small babies and stillborn babies than light smokers. Heavy smoking is also associated with bleeding during pregnancy, more infections of the amniotic fluid, premature delivery, and with the placenta detaching from the womb prematurely (Surgeon General, 1981).

The child who is exposed to nicotine in utero may continue to be affected. A longitudinal study of 11,000 British schoolchildren indicated that children of smokers were shorter and had lower reading comprehension and mathematical ability at ages 7 and 11 (Butler & Goldstein, 1973). But two other studies have found no differences in maternal smoking and later intelligence (Lefkowitz, 1981; Hardy & Mellits, 1972). Smokers' children require more hospitalizations, more visits to the doctor, and more use of specialized services than children whose parents do not smoke (Rantakallio, 1978). Some long-range deficits in neurological functioning have been linked to maternal smoking. Children of smokers are more likely to evidence minimal brain dysfunction, abnormal electroencephalograms, and hyperkinetic behavior patterns (Dunn, McBurney, Ingram, & Hunter, 1977).

In the United States, hospitals and universities often collaborate on important questions. One such project studied the offspring of 50,000 women during an eight-year period (1958– 1966). The study found an alarming link between mothers who smoked and children who died of sudden infant death syndrome. Subsequent studies have shown that smoking appears to injure the fetal brain stem and thereby increases the risk of sudden infant death syndrome (Krous, Campbell, Fowler, & Catron, 1981). Sudden infant death syndrome is the second leading cause of death for infants between one month and one year of age. As more studies confirm the relationship between maternal smoking during pregnancy and sudden infant death syndrome (Fribourg, 1982), the case against smoking during pregnancy becomes even more compelling.

The effects of smoking during pregnancy are often confounded with the effects of other substances. Women who smoke are more likely to use other drugs, including alcohol, than women who do not smoke. This makes the effects of smoking more difficult to isolate. Women who smoke while they are pregnant are very likely to continue smoking while the child is growing up. The passive exposure to nicotine that children experience as they grow up may be related to respiratory difficulties such as pneumonia and bronchitis (Colley, Holland, & Corkhill, 1974). Such exposure makes it hard to tell whether the child's difficulties are due to nicotine exposure in utero or passive inhalation of cigarette smoke as the child grows.

Recently, cigarettes that are lower in tar and nicotine have been introduced. Initially, it was hoped that these cigarettes would reduce the health risks for smokers. This hope has not been realized. Investigations that have compared low tar and nicotine cigarettes to other kinds of cigarettes have found that smoking any type of cigarette has similar effects on the fetus and newborn (Surgeon General's Report, 1981).

Periodically the Surgeon General reviews the literature about cigarette smoking. Here are the conclusions from the 1981 report.

1. Cigarette smoking during pregnancy has adverse effects on the mother, the fetus, the placenta, the newborn infant, and the child in later years. There is no evidence that low tar and nicotine cigarettes decrease or increase these health risks.
2. Problems that have been linked to smoking during pregnancy include placenta previa (the placenta precedes the baby out of the uterus), abruptio placenta (the placenta detaches from the wall of the uterus too early), vaginal bleeding, and reduced average birth weight of the newborn.
3. Smoking by pregnant women increases the risk of spontaneous abortion, premature delivery, fetal death, and prenatal death. Parental smoking is associated with the sudden infant death syndrome.
4. Children of smoking mothers show a greater susceptibility to some adverse health effects, such as bronchitis, pneumonia, and respiratory disease, during early childhood (Surgeon General, 1981, p. 170).

The complications and grief caused by these problems could be reduced significantly if women were to stop smoking during their pregnancies.

**Caffeine.** Drinking coffee is a simple pleasure for much of the world's adult population. The caffeine in coffee provides the early morning lift that gets many people to work and the after lunch lift that gets them through the afternoon. It is common in our culture to drink three to four cups of coffee a day, and many coffee drinkers report downing more than 7 cups a day. Does this amount of caffeine pose any risk to the developing fetus? Four cups of coffee may contain up to 700 mg of caffeine (Vaughan, 1981). This amount of caffeine has been shown to be a teratogenic agent in animals (Weathersbee, Olsen, & Lodge, 1977). Based on the animal research, the United States Food and Drug Administration has proposed removing caffeine from its list of substances that are generally recognized as safe and has issued a press release cautioning pregnant women to limit their caffeine intake.

Studies of pregnant women who drink coffee have not been very useful. Drinking coffee and smoking often go together, and the low birth weights, premature births, stillbirths, and spontaneous abortions sometimes attributed to caffeine may actually have been due to nicotine (van den Berg, 1977). In studies that have attempted to separate the effects of smoking and drinking coffee, there is the hint that some of the low birth weight is not accounted for by smoking (Hooke, 1981). Whether or not caffeine affects birth weight, drinking four or fewer cups of coffee a day does not seem to be systematically related to the most common birth defects (Rosenberg, Mitchell, Shapiro, & Slone, 1982).

**Heroin.** Alcohol, nicotine, and caffeine are all common, widely used substances. Illicit drugs that are used by a smaller percentage of women may also affect the fetus. Mothers who use heroin carry their unborn child in an intrauterine environment that is vastly different from the norm. Like many other teratogenic agents, heroin causes pregnant women to have small, premature infants. As many as half of the infants born to addicted mothers weigh less than 2,500 grams (5½ pounds). Their prematurity and low birth weight make them more vulnerable at birth. In one clinic, 59 children were born to mothers who were heroin users; six were stillborn or died within a few hours (Naeye, Blanc, Leblanc, & Khatamee, 1973).

When adults use heroin frequently, they often contract hepatitis. If a pregnant woman becomes infected, her newborn will probably catch the disease. This infection also decreases the child's chances for survival. Heroin addicts seldom have adequate diets. Their eating habits are probably partly responsible for their tiny infants.

Despite all of these complications and the fact that these children have lived their first nine months in an environment laced with heroin, they have few structural defects or abnormalities. When the newborns who died were examined, there were no signs of degeneration or inflammation of the brain or any other organs (Naeye, Blanc, Leblanc, & Khatamee, 1973).

Using these examinations as a guideline, one might suppose that if the infant lives through the withdrawal period, avoids infection, and gains weight, development will proceed normally. This is not the case. Infants who are withdrawn from heroin in the nursery continue to display some withdrawal symptoms for three to six months. They are restless, agitated, sleep for only brief periods, and seem abnormally irritable. By four to six months of age, these initial symptoms have subsided (Wilson, Desmond, & Verniaud, 1973).

Wilson and his colleagues were able to follow 14 children for over a year to see if there were lingering symptoms. Between one and two years of age, half of these children developed heightened activity levels, short attention spans, sleep disturbances, and temper tantrums. In earlier reports, these problems have been attributed to the mother's erratic lifestyle. But in Wilson's study, all of the children were raised in stable foster homes (Wilson, Demond, & Verniaud, 1973). Hence, the authors suggest that the heroin exposure in utero is responsible for the behavioral problems. It is interesting that these 14 children performed normally on tests of development, except where hyperactivity or a short attention span interfered with adaptive performance.

Heroin abuse by the mother is not associated with any obvious structural deformities or with any long-term cognitive deficits. However, the state of the infant is clearly impaired during the newborn period, and behavioral disturbances begin to show up between a year and two years of age.

**Prescription drugs**

Prior to the 1960s, the impact that prescription drugs might have on the developing fetus was largely ignored. The thalidomide tragedy changed that.

**Thalidomide.** In the late 1950s, thalidomide, a tranquilizing agent, was introduced in Europe. It was effective and seemed to be safe, even in large doses. The drug was marketed and targeted for pregnant women. Shortly after women began using thalidomide, a number of infants were born with shortened arms and legs. The University Pediatric Clinic in Hamburg, Germany, observed a sudden rise in this almost unheard-of deformity. There had been no cases of shortened limbs reported between 1949 and 1959. One case was reported in 1959, 30 cases in 1960, and 154 cases in 1961. The previous rarity of the defect, as well as the sudden, dramatic increase in the number of cases, meant that something was causing the change. The search led to the drug thalidomide. In virtually every case of shortened limbs, the mother had taken thalidomide between the third and eighth week of pregnancy. Although the drug had been successfully tested on animals, it was discovered that the teratogenic effects of thalidomide are specific to humans (Stern, 1981).

**Diethylstilbestrol (DES).** Prior to 1967, only 68 cases of vaginal cancer had been reported in the medical literature. It was a rare disease, seen only in older women. In 1966, a doctor diagnosed vaginal cancer in a 15-year-old girl. Within the next three years, six more cases were diagnosed, all in women under 20 (Herbst, 1981). The appearance of seven cases in three years prompted physicians to search for a cause. Three physicians—Herbst, Ulfelder, and Poskanzer (1971)—studied the medical histories of these girls. There was nothing that would suggest a cause for the cancer. Finally, they checked the prenatal history of the mother. All of the mothers had taken DES while they were pregnant. The drug had been prescribed in the late 1940s to mothers who suffered habitual abortions. One mother joked that her children were DESperate children. The use of DES increased during the 1950s until its efficacy was questioned. But it was another 15 years before the long-term effects of the drug were apparent. During this time, DES was prescribed for between one and three million women (Yoonessi, Mariniello, Wieckowska, Angtuaco, & Diesfeld, 1981).

Since 1966, 400 cases of vaginal cancer have been found among the daughters of mothers who took DES while they were pregnant. The mothers of these cancer patients usually began taking DES before the 12th week of pregnancy

(Herbst, 1981). Luckily, vaginal cancer affects a relatively small number of DES daughters, but there are other effects of being exposed to DES. Changes in the genital tract have been reported in about 25 percent of these women. Infertility is another problem. Many of these women lose their babies prematurely because their uterus is small or their cervix does not function normally (Veridiano, Delke, Rogers, & Tancer, 1981).

Initially, doctors thought that male children of DES mothers suffered no ill effects. However, follow-up studies have shown that a third of the men exposed to DES have some genital tract abnormalities. Further, their sperm is not as concentrated and there are changes in the sperm's structure and mobility (Gill, Schumacher, Bibbo, Straus, & Schoenbe, 1979). Whether or not these changes will be linked with fertility problems is not yet known. Also, the possibility of an increased cancer rate in males has not been completely ruled out. Testicular cancer was once among the rarest of diseases. The incidence has tripled since 1972. Is it just a coincidence? Some physicians think the increase is linked to DES (Parachini, 1980). Had doctors not been alerted by the increased occurrence of vaginal cancer, DES would probably never have been linked to the less serious problems that males have experienced (Stern, 1981).

DES is not the only hormone that has been administered to mothers. Steroids are often prescribed for pregnant women. Some of them are chemically related to androgen and can masculinize a female fetus. Progestin is similar to androgen and was used during the 1950s to prevent miscarriages. The daughters who were in utero suffered varying degrees of masculinization.

Medications that are prescribed by physicians are usually considered safe. Unfortunately, a physician's information is limited by the extent of research on a new drug. Results of animal tests are not always a reliable predictor of what will happen when humans take the drug. If drugs have not been tested for long-term effects, then no matter how conscientious physicians are, they do not know what to expect. The teratogenic effects of diethylstilbestrol (DES) did not appear for almost a generation.

The tragic effects of thalidomide and DES have now been recognized. They were only discovered because each produced an effect that was rare in the species. The fetal alcohol syndrome became apparent because of the atypical appearance of the children, not because of the mental retardation. Some researchers still question the diagnosis of fetal alcohol syndrome if the physical anomalies are absent. It is very difficult to prove that a drug causes cleft palate, because this is a relatively common birth defect. If a drug causes even more subtle nervous system disorders, like hyperactivity or attention problems, the likelihood of that link being discovered is very small (Stern, 1981).

Large-scale studies suggest that what we know about the effects of drugs on the fetus may represent the proverbial tip of the iceberg. One study in Connecticut identified 1,100 infants who had some congenital malformation. The investigators then interviewed the mothers concerning any medications they had taken during pregnancy. Mothers whose infants had no birth defects were also interviewed. Of all the mothers interviewed, 44.5 percent used one or

## THE DOCTORS I CAN'T FORGIVE
*By Judith Turiel*

"Better late than never," I might have said, with a sign of relief when my first period began. I was 15 years old, and all my friends had started menstruating during the previous several years. "Be patient," my doctor had counseled. "Some girls just start later. The range of normal is wide."

So when my period came, I could finally reap the excitement that hovers around junior-high-school girls about those things. I proudly exercised the special prerogative of not changing into my gym suit that first day. My mother smiled too when I told her that afternoon. "Now you're really a woman," she said.

Then months went by, and there was no second period. "That's not unusual," the pediatrician reassured me, and I read the same thing in books. But after about a year, when I still had not had another period, I went with my mother to an obstetrician/gynecologist. The gynecologist prescribed hormones. "Sometimes we try to mimic the normal cycle with these hormones. Then when we stop them, the body takes over. It imitates."

So we tried several rounds of hormones. Unfortunately, though, my body would not be coaxed into imitation. I went away to college without having had another period.

I saw an impressive procession of gynecologists during that time. Once, I inquired whether, since I never had had a period after the first one, I needed to use any contraceptives. "Absolutely," the doctor told me as he wrote out a prescription for the Pill. "There's no guarantee you won't become pregnant. And birth control pills will be very good for you. They'll regulate your period."

I took the Pill for seven months and greatly enjoyed painful cramps and heavy periods. I did not learn until years later that taking the Pill was not at all a good idea—that it might only have further suppressed my own hormonal system and that, for reasons I did not yet know, I should have avoided taking hormones altogether.

I was told other things too during those years. Once as I lay on my back, my feet in the too-familiar stirrups, a sheet draped over the lower half of my body, the doctor remarked that I had an "infantile uterus." These words, so casually spoken, struck me to the quick. They were another blow to someone struggling to think of herself as a woman, to deal with sexuality and perhaps soon, marriage. He neglected to explain that these words mean "very small," and that many doctors do not accept that clinical term.

In 1969 I went to my mother's gynecologist to take care of a vaginal infection. He did a routine Pap test. A few days later, his nurse called us "The doctor would like to repeat Judith's Pap test." The results had been abnormal. The second test and a biopsy showed malignant or premalignant cells in my cervix. The doctor expressed surprise at seeing cells like these in a woman my age. The abnormal cells were surgically removed. The surgery would not affect my ability to have children, the doctor said.

In 1972, my mother and I heard about DES. Daughters exposed in utero to DES were now found to have higher than normal rates of cervical and vaginal cancer, as well as other abnormal but nonmalignant cellular changes in the reproductive tract. My mother, who had had two miscarriages, checked with her doctor. Yes, she had been given DES. Those "suspicious cells" in my cervix were now at least less mysterious. I was to continue Pap tests and, like all DES daughters, to undergo a procedure called colposcopy (viewing the cervix and vagina through a special instrument) every six months.

In 1972 I had been married for a year. If I wanted to become pregnant, there was a fairly good chance that a drug called "Clomid" would "fool my body." My husband and I talked. He was certain he would like to have children. I was afraid I never could. We decided to plunge ahead. In 1978 I learned I was pregnant. No one could be more surprised than I, and no one more ecstatic.

After five and a half months of what appeared to be a routine pregnancy, my husband and I found ourselves in a hospital labor room, with my obstetrician hurrying to connect me to intrave-

**THE DOCTORS I CAN'T FORGIVE** *Concluded*

nous medication that perhaps would stop the contractions of premature labor. The attempt to stop the labor failed, and our son was born the next day. He was rushed into intensive care, where he died after a few horrible hours.

The obstetrician concluded that my cervix had started dilating days before the delivery. He said I had an "incompetent cervix" caused most likely by my exposure to DES.

After those first dead months following the birth, I tried to learn what I could about DES, the menstrual cycle, the dangers of premature births. I read medical journals. Research was beginning to reveal alarming rates of miscarriages and premature births in DES daughters. I learned that recent medical research has suggested higher-than-normal rates of infertility, tubal pregnancy, and menstrual irregularity among DES daughters, including in some, an absence of ovulation.

At my most recent monthly checkup, my "fertility doctor" told me for the first time that he thinks I am having difficulty becoming pregnant again, even on the Clomid, because of abnormalities in my cervix and uterus caused by the DES my mother was given during her pregnancy. I asked him whether he thought DES might be the cause of my lack of ovulation as well. He said he didn't know.

DES, which has caused me so much pain, has at least allowed me new and needed understandings. I know to keep myself informed. I know that there must be continued pressure for more research about DES. I know that doctors have not always read the latest medical journals. I know they cannot care about the outcome of my case nearly as much as I do.

Source: Turiel, J. (1981, February). The doctors I can't forgive. *Redbook, 156,* 44–50.

more prescribed drugs during part of their pregnancy. The most common drugs were those prescribed for nausea, and they were not associated with any increased risk to the offspring. However, women who took other prescription drugs during pregnancy had a 30 percent higher risk of delivering a congenitally malformed infant. Antidepressants, antibiotics, tranquilizers, codeine, and other narcotic analgesics were used more often by mothers who had affected offspring. If mothers smoked and used drugs, their infants were much more likely to have some congenital defect (Bracken & Holford, 1981).

We can't conclude from this study that drugs are always responsible for the newborn's problems. Perhaps the mother's medical problem affected the fetus, not the drug. It is also important to remember that some women require medication. Diabetic or epileptic women must maintain their medication during pregnancy. Making an intelligent decision about the use of drugs means weighing the consequences of the drug against the benefits. If a mother has become severely dehydrated from vomiting, a medication to alleviate nausea is warranted.

**Diseases**

Diseases that the mother contracts can also affect the fetus. Bacterial infections like syphilis or gonorrhea can have long-term and catastrophic effects on the fetus. Viral infections such as rubella sometimes infect the placenta as well as the fetus. Metabolic disorders such as diabetes can make the fetus's environment less hospitable. The optimistic note about most diseases is that obstetricians have learned how to manage them so that the effects on the fetus have been minimized or eliminated.

**Rubella.**  Rubella was one of the most feared diseases of pregnancy. During the periodic epidemics of German measles that swept the country, thousands of unborn children were affected. The only way to prevent these effects was to expose young girls to the disease. This one exposure assured lifelong immunity.

The rubella virus infects the fetus in utero and may also infect the placenta. Unlike the mother's infection, which only lasts three days, the fetal infection persists over a long period of time. If the mother has rubella during the first eight weeks of pregnancy, the ears, eyes, and heart of the fetus are likely to be damaged. Spontaneous abortions are common if the infection occurs during the early weeks. If the fetus does not abort, a variety of birth defects ranging from mental retardation to hearing defects are possible. If the mother has rubella after eight weeks, the fetus is less likely to be affected. Deafness, however, may still result (Stevenson, 1977).

Fortunately, a vaccine for rubella has been developed. The female will acquire a lifelong immunity to rubella if she is vaccinated or if she has the disease. Measles vaccinations are now required by many states before the child can attend school. If every schoolchild could be vaccinated, the deafness and mental retardation caused by rubella would disappear.

Many women of childbearing age do not know if they have had rubella or been vaccinated. A simple blood test will indicate whether the protective antibodies are present in the bloodstream. If a woman finds out that she is not protected against rubella, she sometimes seeks vaccination. Doctors are understandably reluctant to vaccinate a woman of childbearing age. If she should already be pregnant, the results could be disastrous. If a pregnant woman is infected, a therapeutic abortion is possible.

**Herpes.**  There are two types of herpes simplex virus. Type 1 generally affects the face, producing the common cold sore. Type 2 involves the genitals and poses a serious hazard for the unborn child. Premature births occur in over 50 percent of mothers who have active infections. After birth, the infant develops skin lesions, and the infection progresses, sometimes affecting the brain and other organs. Mortality rates are as high as 80 percent when the disease spreads throughout the newborn's system (Whitley, Nahmias, Soong, Galasso, Fleming, & Alford, 1980).

If the mother has an active case of genital herpes, the infant becomes infected while traveling down the birth canal. One way to keep a fetus from being infected is to deliver the child by *Cesarean section*. This is a common treatment when mothers have had little prenatal care and arrive for delivery with an active case of genital herpes. Unfortunately, 70 percent of the women who have infants with herpes have no symptoms of the disease during the weeks prior to delivery. This makes it very difficult to diagnose and treat the infant.

**Syphilis.** Syphilis in newborns can be prevented, yet 1,000 new cases are reported every year. Prior to the discovery of penicillin, syphilis accounted for one quarter of all stillbirths and neonatal deaths (Stevenson, 1977). Since many women may be exposed to syphilis and not be aware of it, pregnant women are routinely tested for syphilis. If syphilis is detected and treated during the first four months of pregnancy, the child will not be infected. Syphilis only affects a newborn if (a) the mother receives no prenatal care, (b) she receives no treatment once she is diagnosed, or (c) she becomes reinfected after the testing.

**Rh negative blood.** Most people carry a blood factor labeled Rh *positive*. Approximately 15 percent, however, carry a negative Rh factor. If an Rh negative woman marries a man whose blood is Rh positive, the fetus will be Rh positive. Under normal circumstances, the mother's body would recognize an Rh positive factor as being a foreign substance. But during pregnancy, the placenta keeps the two blood systems separate. During delivery, however, there is a chance that some of the baby's blood will mingle with the mother's. Once this happens, the mother begins to build up antibodies to the foreign blood factors and, in subsequent pregnancies, her body may actually recognize the fetus as a foreign body and try to destroy it. Fortunately, medical advances can now keep the mother from building up antibodies to be used against her own infant. Mothers who are Rh negative and give birth to an Rh positive infant should receive a shot of *Rhogam* after any delivery or abortion. This shot prevents the mother from building up antibodies. Subsequent pregnancies can proceed without any peril to the fetus. The two provisos to add to the Rh story are that the Rhogam must be administered within 72 hours after delivery, and the shot must be administered whenever there is a possibility that the bloodstreams of the fetus and mother might have mixed.

Pregnant women with diabetes, epilepsy, heart disease, and high blood pressure require special attention during pregnancy. The medications used to control these diseases and the added burden that a pregnancy places on the mother's body means that these women need to be especially diligent about their prenatal care.

**Environmental hazards**

**Radiation.** Radiation is a natural as well as a man-made hazard. Each person receives approximately 120 millirads of natural radiation each year. Since man's discovery of X-rays in 1895, however, our exposure to radiation has doubled. X-rays, background radiation, and atomic and nuclear bombs all release ionizing radiation that has the potential for producing fetal death, genetic defects, birth defects, and cancer. Radiation is such a potent teratogen that a single dose of over 300 rads has been used to induce abortion (Mayer, Harris, & Wimplfheimer, 1936).

The Hiroshima and Nagasaki tragedies demonstrated convincingly that radiation affected the embryo and fetus. Infants born to mothers in these cities often had serious malformations. Deaths during the neonatal period were common.

In addition, there were many abortions and stillbirths, and weight at birth was well below the norm.

Since 1946, scientists have studied the sad legacy of atomic radiation on the fetus. The children who survived are now adults, and their experience in utero continues to affect their lives. Their head and body size remain small, and many of the adults with small heads are mentally retarded (Miller & Blot, 1972).

Despite the power of these findings, they do not provide definitive answers to questions about radiation. The end of the war was a chaotic period in Japan, and a variety of other environmental factors—infection, poor nutrition, and stress— might have influenced the fetuses. Teasing out the effects of radiation has required many other studies.

During pregnancy, it is sometimes necessary to X-ray the mother's abdomen. Children who have been exposed to such diagnostic levels of X-rays in utero are more likely to develop leukemia and tumors of the nervous system than a comparison group of children (Holford, 1975). As a group, they are twice as likely to die during the first 10 years of life (Diamond, Schmerler, & Lilienfeld, 1973). These effects occur with very low doses of radiation, measured not in rads, but millirads. The reason for the increase in tumors is not immediately obvious. Perhaps X-rays interfere with the function of controlling genes. The effect of these altered genes only becomes apparent as the child grows (Steward & Kneale, 1970).

The Japanese studies indicated another consequence of low exposures to radiation—premature aging. Kato (1971) studied children who had been exposed to radiation during the last three months of pregnancy. These children had a higher death rate than children who were not exposed, and the children who received the largest dose were the most likely to die. The causes of death were not specific, suggesting that low doses of radiation during the last part of pregnancy might prematurely age the children.

Long-term studies of premature aging are rare, primarily because of the time and effort required to conduct them. In one such study, over 1,400 females who had been exposed to diagnostic X-rays during the last months of pregnancy were compared to a matched sample. As 20-year-olds, there were no differences between the two groups in terms of mortality or cancer. However, whereas the control group typically reported that their health was "excellent," the exposed group often reported that their health was "fair" or "good." Perhaps this small difference at 20 years of age is an indication of premature aging that will become more prominent in another 30 years (Meyer & Tonascia, 1981).

We know that diagnostic X-rays affect a fetus. Do diagnostic X-rays administered to adults damage their reproductive systems and reduce their chance of having a healthy child? The appearance of chromosomal abnormalities in children born to younger parents has led researchers to suspect that increased radiation is the cause. Uchida and Curtis (1961) first suggested that repeated abdominal X-rays before conception could increase the frequency of Down's syndrome children. Their alarming results prompted other investigators to study women who had diagnostic X-rays. One sample of 972 women who received diagnostic X-rays gave birth to 10 children with an extra chromosome. Prior to the radiation exposure, these women had given birth to 972 other children. Only one of them had an extra chromosome (Uchida, 1979). Of course, the women were older when they gave birth to the affected child. Hence, the chromosomal abnormality could have been due to maternal age.

This study addresses the influence of diagnostic X-rays on the mother. The father contributes half of the genetic material. Do diagnostic X-rays affect the male reproductive system? At least one study suggests that they do. Boue and his colleagues interviewed the fathers of 1,500 fetuses that were spontaneously aborted. These fathers had been exposed to more occupational radiation than normal (Boue, Boue, & Lazar, 1975). This study from France raises the issue of background radiation—that radiation which is a normal part of our environment. Is it possible that background radiation affects the fetus? Kerala, India, is an area famous for its high level of background radiation. A high percentage of Down's syndrome children as well as children with other chromosomal abnormalities are born in this area (Kochupillai, Verma, Grewal, & Ramalingaswami, 1976).

There is a positive note in the radiation literature. Being exposed to radiation once does not mean that the reproductive system is irreparably damaged. Japanese women who were exposed to the A-bomb conceived and delivered many children in the years after the blast. These children did not suffer an increased number of birth defects (Schull, Otake, & Neel, 1981). Perhaps exposure to radiation has an effect on the reproductive system for a few days or a few months. Over a period of time, the mechanism that leads to chromosomal abnormalities may be repaired (Uchida, 1979).

The conclusions we can draw from this information are somewhat tenuous. Certainly we know that radiation can harm the fetus. Prenatal exposures of 20 to 50 rads can affect how easily a rat learns and can produce permanent changes in the nerve cells of the brain (Hicks & D'Amato, 1980). The effects of background radiation on a fetus probably depend on dose and frequency of exposure. The possibility that the body can repair damage due to radiation is a hopeful sign.

**Chemicals.** Chemicals in the environment pose an unknown and unresearched threat to pregnant women. Love Canal, Niagara Falls, New York, is anything but picturesque. Much of the community was built on a landfill that had been used for disposing of toxic industrial chemicals. After several years of heavy rains, the chemicals began to percolate to the surface, forming pools in the backyards and basements of residents. The human toll has been heavy— almost 30 percent of the recent pregnancies among the women have ended in miscarriages and over 20 percent of the children born have had birth defects (McHeil, 1978). Based on these figures, the New York Health Commissioner recommended that pregnant women leave the area immediately so as not to endanger their unborn children. Ultimately, the 700 families living there were all moved.

Chemical waste dumps are hazardous sites; but the influence of toxic chemicals has been felt in communities that are not used as waste dumps. Alsea, a logging community in Oregon, discovered that the herbicide used to promote early growth of Douglas Firs was interfering with the early growth of humans. A spray containing Dioxin was used each year to kill deciduous trees so that the Douglas Fir, a pine tree, would prosper. In June of 1978, shortly after the forest service finished its annual spraying, eight women in the area suffered miscarriages. The women alerted the Environmental Protection Agency. The EPA agreed that the miscarriages were not coincidental and placed an emergency ban on two widely used herbicides containing Dioxin (McFadden, 1979). Dioxin was known to cause birth defects, tumors, and miscarriages in animals. The unsuspecting women of Alsea supplied the human evidence. During the month of June, from 1972 to 1978, the women of Alsea suffered 130 miscarriages per 1,000 births. In two areas of Oregon where no spraying occurred, the comparable figures were 44.9 and 46 miscarriages per 1,000 births (Turner, 1979).

During the war in Vietnam, many military personnel were exposed to agent orange, a chemical relative of Dioxin. Recent reports indicate that children born to these men have more birth defects than would normally be expected. A recent Air Force survey indicated that 14 infants whose fathers had been exposed to agent orange died during the first month of life. In a comparable group of men who had not been exposed to agent orange, only four infants died (Tumulty, 1984). Veterans groups argue that these findings document the anecdotal evidence of Vietnam veterans and Vietnamese parents that exposure to agent orange affects the reproductive system.

This brief description of hazardous chemicals should serve to alert us to the teratogenic effects of many substances. Increased vigilance will help parents, physicians, and researchers protect the unborn child.

## CHANGING THE COURSE OF FETAL DEVELOPMENT

**Genetic counseling**

All parents want a normal, healthy child. In fact, a common answer to the question, "Do you want a boy or a girl?" has become, "I don't care, as long as it's healthy." Genetic counseling is a health-related profession that tries to fulfill this wish. The growth of genetic counseling has been fueled by three factors: the increase in our understanding of genetics and genetic diseases, the development of techniques that allow genetic errors to be detected prenatally, and the changes in legal and social attitudes toward contraception and abortion. These factors only speak to the medical aspects of genetic counseling. The counseling aspect is just as important. Prior to the 1980s, the primary users of genetic counseling were couples who had a child suffering from some genetic disease. Imagine the feelings of recrimination, fear, anxiety, and depression a young couple feel when they are told their child has Down's syndrome or Tay-Sachs or sickle cell disease. The field of genetic counseling was actually a response to these parents and their need for help, information, support, and understanding during a difficult period of adjustment.

Genetic counselors have a several pronged goal. They must help an individual or family comprehend the medical facts. This includes the diagnosis, the probable course of the disorder, and the available techniques for managing the disorder. They must help parents appreciate the way that heredity contributes to the disorder and the risk for recurrence. They must help the family choose a course of action that is appropriate in view of their risk and the family goals. Finally, they must help the family adjust to the disorder in any affected family member (Kessler, 1979). Genetic disorders occur among nearly 5 percent of newborn infants (Kessler, 1979). The relatives of these infants may at some point in their lives see a genetic counselor.

The techniques available for helping such clients increase daily. Prenatal testing for over 100 metabolic errors and dozens of chromosomal abnormalities is now available (see Figure 3–9). In addition, the fetus can be probed using the noninvasive method of ultrasound, fetal cells can be analyzed, fetal blood can be tested, or the fetus can be examined directly. The discovery of a new method of prenatal testing may revolutionize the field of genetic counseling. Called *chorion biopsy*, it can be used to detect birth defects as early as the seventh week of pregnancy. The chorion is the precursor of the placenta and it contains the same genetic information in its cells as the fetal cells. Taking a sample of the chorion is simpler than waiting 16 weeks to obtain a sample of

**Figure 3–9**          **Partial list of genetic disorders that can be diagnosed in utero**

Chromosomal disorders
  Down's syndrome
  Cri du chat syndrome
  Sex chromosome anomalies (Klinefelter's syndrome, 47 XXY, 47 XYY, Turner's syndrome, 45 XO, etc.)
  Translocations of chromosomes
  Deletion of chromosomes
Metabolic disorders
  Tay-Sachs
  Sickle-cell anemia
  Galactosemia
  Spina bifida
  Maple syrup urine disease
  Hurler syndrome
Structural defects
  Facial abnormalities
  Spina bifida
  Neural tube defects
  Microcephaly
  Cleft palate
  Skeletal abnormalities

Selected genetic disorders that can be detected in utero using amniocentesis, fetoscopy, metabolic assays, ultrasound, or radiography.

Source: Milunsky, A. (1979). *Genetic disorders and the fetus.* New York: Plenum Publishing.

amniotic fluid. Should a defect be found, women can have an abortion during the first trimester of pregnancy, when abortions are safer and simpler. Knowing about a defect during the embryonic or early fetal period may also allow doctors to treat the fetus in utero (Rodeck & Morsman, 1983).

**Examining the fetus**

There are three ways of examining the fetus in utero. The first, X-ray, is used only in emergencies because of the danger to the fetus. The second, ultrasound, is used frequently because it has few known risks, can be used early in pregnancy, and permits both external and internal structures to be visualized. The third, fetoscopy, allows the doctor to directly examine the fetus in utero. This procedure is still used sparingly because of the risk to the fetus.

**Ultrasound.** Ultrasound uses sound pulses that travel into the patient. As different maternal and fetal tissues are encountered, part of the sound wave is reflected and transformed into a visual image. Because ultrasound is not an invasive technique, it is one of the most popular tools in prenatal diagnosis.

Ultrasound is used to determine fetal age accurately. Exact fetal age is needed for an amniocentesis. If amniocentesis is performed too early, there might not be enough amniotic fluid to assess the status of the fetus. Ultrasound is also used routinely during the actual amniocentesis. Having a picture of the fetus and the placenta makes the process of obtaining amniotic fluid much safer. Ultrasound is commonly used to diagnose multiple pregnancies. In some cases, when carrying the child endangers the mother, ultrasound helps indicate when the fetus is sufficiently mature to survive independently.

In genetic counseling, ultrasound is used to diagnose structural abnormalities. The quality of the image that is produced with ultrasound has improved greatly in the last few years and has led to widespread use of ultrasound and increased confidence in the results. Ultrasound can diagnose cases in which the head is abnormally small or the growth of the brain is retarded. Spina bifida, heart and kidney abnormalities, and limb malformations can also be detected.

**Fetoscopy.** Fetoscopy involves puncturing the uterine wall to actually view the fetus. It is regarded as a high-risk procedure, and one that is only used when the increased risk to the fetus is warranted. Fetoscopy has been used to obtain skin and scalp tissue for the purpose of biopsies. It has also been used to detect subtle malformations that cannot be detected with ultrasound.

**Amniocentesis.** Chromosomal errors as well as metabolic errors that affect a fetus can be detected by amniocentesis. During this procedure, doctors take a sample of the amniotic fluid surrounding the developing fetus. Fetal cells suspended in the fluid can be examined for biochemical and chromosomal defects (see Figure 3–10).

Once fetal cells are obtained, they can be karyotyped in the same manner as adult blood cells. With a karyotype in hand, doctors can make very accurate assessments about the chromosomal status of the fetus. Amniocentesis is easy

**Figure 3–10**          **Amniocentesis**

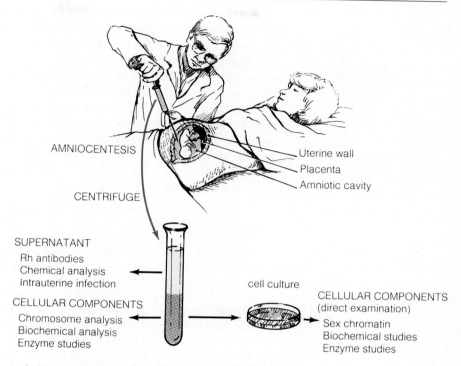

AMNIOCENTESIS

Uterine wall
Placenta
Amniotic cavity

CENTRIFUGE

SUPERNATANT
Rh antibodies
Chemical analysis
Intrauterine infection

cell culture

CELLULAR COMPONENTS
Chromosome analysis
Biochemical analysis
Enzyme studies

CELLULAR COMPONENTS
(direct examination)
Sex chromatin
Biochemical studies
Enzyme studies

A doctor performs amniocentesis to check fetal health.
Source: Nagle, J. J. (1979). *Heredity and human affairs* (p. 120). St. Louis: C. V. Mosby.

to perform and is almost 100 percent safe. Ultrasound is used to locate a pool of amniotic fluid and to help the doctor find a route to that pool that avoids the fetus and the placenta (Campbell, 1979). Using ultrasound with amniocentesis has another advantage. Both the mother and doctor can see the fetal movements and heart beat before, during, and after amniocentesis. Actually seeing the fetus move after the procedure relieves mothers who are worried that amniocentesis might harm the fetus. Although amniocentesis can be emotionally draining, the vast majority of parents are told that their child will be normal and healthy. In the small percentage of cases in which the fetus is defective, therapeutic abortions are possible. For those parents who do not want to consider an abortion, the information about the status of their child at least gives them some months to learn how to care for their child.

In the future, all couples might visit a genetic counselor, just as they now visit an obstetrician. For now, prospective parents are urged to seek genetic counseling for any of the following reasons: They have an affected child; they have sisters, brothers, aunts, uncles, or grandparents who have some genetic or metabolic error; the mother has had several spontaneous abortions; the mother is 35 or older.

Genetic counselors are trained in both genetics and counseling. They often have to deal with the despair, anger, frustration, and depression that parents feel when they face the trauma of a defective fetus or the birth of a defective child. Genetic counselors do more than issue statistical probabilities. They help parents understand the medical facts and how heredity contributes to a particular disorder. If couples have an affected child, genetic counselors help with the initial adjustment and the management of the child. If such parents would like to have more children, the alternatives and choices will be explained. If couples have not had any children but are "at risk" for a particular disease, any prenatal tests that are available will be explained, complete with advantages and limitations. Finally, should a therapeutic abortion be elected, the counselor will support the parents.

> Mr. and Mrs. S., ages 38 and 36, had been married for 10 years. They had postponed childbearing until their business was successful. Both looked upon the recommended amniocentesis as a routine procedure, much as one would view a premarital examination. The amniocentesis, however, revealed that Mrs. S. was carrying a Down's child. The first postamniocentesis session was extremely difficult for everyone, with both members of the couple crying. The decision to have an abortion was made, and everything went well. However, the fact of the translocation had really not been absorbed. The third session was held after the individual chromosomes of the couple had been studied. The results showed that Mrs. S. was carrying a balanced translocation. This information came as a great shock to both, but, as one might expect, particularly to Mrs. S. She called herself "damaged" and felt that she could never have a child. The husband tried to comfort her, but she was devastated. (Grobstein, 1979, p. 112)

As indicated by Mrs. S.'s case, amniocentesis has been recommended as a standard part of the obstetrical care of women over 35. For most of these women, the amniocentesis will promise a healthy, normal baby.

The decisions that must be made by parents are very difficult and involve moral and ethical issues. To understand the human side of genetic counseling, some of the genetic diseases that were introduced in Chapter 2 are discussed here in terms of parental decisions. Perhaps the easiest decision to make involves a Tay-Sachs fetus because there is no way of preventing the deadly course of the disease. Furthermore, a normal child can be expected in 75 percent of subsequent pregnancies. A more difficult decision is posed by cystic fibrosis. Your first child, now two years old, has cystic fibrosis. Hence, both you and your spouse are carriers. Your chance of having a normal child is 75 percent, but there is no prenatal screening test. Once a child is conceived, you have to wait until it is born to know if it has the disease. Do you elect to have another child? What about parents who are at risk for having a child with sickle cell disease? The fetus is diagnosed in utero as having sickle cell disease. Is an abortion warranted given the medical advances for this disease? Suppose you are over 35 and have a routine amniocentesis done. The results indicate that the fetus has an abnormality compatible with a long life span, such as Klinefelter's syndrome (XXY). Would you abort this child? These decisions are ones that most professionals feel should be made by the parents. In making such difficult decisions, parents are often guided by their religious views, the severity of the genetic anomaly, financial considerations, and their own family.

Genetic counseling allows parents who are at risk for some genetic disorders to have a healthy, normal child. Of course, genetic counseling could be used for whimsical selection, too. Parents might have five boys and want a girl. Should genetic counseling be available to them? Providing parents with information seems relatively harmless. But prenatal screening for this purpose would use resources and talent that are limited and would subject the mother and fetus to procedures that do carry some risk. No one is anxious to abuse genetic counseling in this fashion. Currently, genetic counseling offers great promise for reducing human suffering. That promise can be best realized if people are educated about genetic diseases, their financial and emotional toll, and possible interventions.

## Surgical interventions

Prior to the 1980s, parents of an abnormal fetus had a choice to abort or to carry the child to term. Now, some parents have the option of trying to repair the defect while the fetus is still in the womb.

One of the first cases of surgery in utero involved a 40-year-old woman who had no children and was carrying fraternal twins. A routine amniocentesis revealed that one of the twins had Down's syndrome; the other was normal. The mother wanted to have the normal twin, but could not face the burden of raising the handicapped twin. The mother sought help from the medical profession. After explaining the risks to the mother, the physicians inserted a needle into the heart of the defective fetus. That fetus died. The healthy twin was delivered 20 weeks later (Karenyi & Chitkara, 1981).

Another set of fraternal twins presented a different problem to doctors in San Francisco. The male twin's bladder was blocked. As the twins grew, there was a potentially fatal buildup of fluid in his bladder. To relieve the problem, doctors inserted a drainage tube. Through the rest of the pregnancy, the fetal bladder drained harmlessly into the amniotic fluid. Both twins were born at eight months gestation, and both were healthy (Golbus, Harrison, Filly, Callen, & Katz, 1982).

Tubes have also been used to drain excess fluid from the fetal brain on two separate occasions. Several months after delivery, the authors describe one infant's appearance as normal. The development of the brain was more normal than it would have been without the intrauterine treatment (Clewell et al., 1982).

These operations were performed while the fetus was in the womb. Dr. Harrison of the University of California at San Francisco has since had a case where there was no alternative but to open the womb, correct the problem, and put the fetus back in the womb until delivery. The fetus had a urinary obstruction and was slowly dying of kidney damage. The April operation to correct the obstruction was successful, and the child was born in July. However, the infant's lungs had been damaged by the obstruction, and he died nine hours after birth (Harrison, Golbus, Filly, Callen, Katz, Lorimier, Rosen, & Jonsen, 1982).

These cases illustrate the new skills and technology that can be used to enhance a fetus's chances of survival. The physicians involved are quick to add that these procedures involve unsolved problems. Surgery in utero may save a life but lead to a lifelong handicap. Premature labor is always a risk, and the health of the mother is a factor to consider. Still, these cases are the first steps down a new road—modifying the fetus while it is still in the intrauterine environment.

## SUMMARY

The fetus is not shielded from the environment while in the womb. From conception through the embryonic phase, insults from the environment can cause structural damage that will never be repaired. From the third month of gestation until the baby is delivered, a teratogenic agent may slow the growth of the fetus. Because of its rapid growth, the brain is especially susceptible to environmental agents during the fetal period.

Since the mother actually carries the fetus, she provides the environment in which the fetus is nurtured. The mother's diet, her emotional state, and her age may have positive or negative effects on fetal development. The father has been treated like an innocent bystander for many years. Now we suspect that he, too, can influence the fetus.

Teratogenic agents are plentiful. Drugs, like alcohol, nicotine, and heroin, may cause immediate physical effects, as well as behavioral effects that are not apparent for years. Prescription drugs are another source of concern. The DES and thalidomide tragedies are a sad testament to the lack of sufficient research before drugs are prescribed for pregnant women. Hormones seem to have the potential to alter physical structures, psychological traits, and cognitive skills. Even antidepressants, antibiotics, and tranquilizers—common drugs in our society—have been associated with birth defects.

Diseases used to be a major concern for pregnant women. Now many of these diseases have been brought under control. Current preventive measures mean that syphilis and rubella no longer threaten the unborn child. Rh blood incompatibility, diabetes, and heart problems used to pose problems for pregnant women. With proper prenatal care, these problems do not need to interfere with the delivery of a healthy child.

Environmental teratogens pose a growing concern. Chemicals, radiation, and environmental contaminants may all harm the fetus. Because so many of these agents are new, our knowledge of their danger is limited.

The knowledge we have about the development of the fetus has made it possible to intervene during the intrauterine period. Fetal cells are examined, their blood is analyzed, and images of their bodies are displayed. When defects are found, parents may choose to end the pregnancy, to continue the pregnancy, or to try to repair the problem before the child is born. Genetic counseling and intervention during the fetal period are two new approaches to help the unborn child.

Nine months in utero seems like a very brief period compared to the 70-odd years that we live after birth. But this brief period provides the foundation for those years. By maximizing the health and development of the fetus, we assure the child the best possible start in life.

**The birth**

First stage of labor
Second stage of labor
Third stage of labor

**The psychological impact of medical advances**

Medication during labor and delivery
Electronic fetal monitoring

**The psychological experience of birth**

Psychological aspects of labor
Natural childbirth

**Becoming a family**

The process of bonding
The transition of parenthood

**The newborn infant**

Apgar scores
Neurological evaluations
The Kauai study
Premature infants

**Summary**

# CHAPTER 4
# Birth

About 5000 BC, the Egyptians began using hieroglyphics to tell the story of their civilization. In a fresco on the walls of the Mammeisi temple are the first records of childbirth (see Figure 4–1). The fresco tells us that women had supportive attendants during birth. Women delivered their babies while in a squatting position. Notice that one of the attendants carries both a symbol for life and the symbol of protection. These symbols suggest that childbirth, like most aspects of Egyptian life, was shrouded in mysticism and guided by the supernatural.

Relying on the supernatural during childbirth is a common feature of most cultures. Through the ages, an amazing array of birthing customs have been practiced. In ancient cultures, men opened doors and took lids off pots to ease the coming of the child. Women sometimes dressed in their husband's clothes to deceive the spirits that might harm the child.

We now know that some of these customs protected the woman from infection. Eskimo women, once pregnant, no longer shared food from the family pot, but only ate food that was prepared separately. Birth huts, used by many cultures, were set apart from the rest of the village. Women were sometimes isolated in these huts for as long as a month. During this time, food was given to the mother on the end of a stick so that no other hands would touch hers. At the end of her "confinement," there was usually a ritual of cleansing.

**Figure 4–1**          **Egyptian depiction of birth 7,000 years ago**

Delivery of the Egyptian goddess Ritho. Notice that all of the attendants are female and that the mother delivers in a squatting position.

During labor, some Indian tribes wrapped the woman in a blanket and shook her. This practice would make sure the child was in the correct position. During labor, several cultures suspended the woman from a tree or provided her with a post to grab. To ease back pain, the Loango had an attendant stand on the mother's back (Findley, 1933).

While these practices seem bizarre and humorous, some of them are making a comeback. Many contemporary books recommend that the mother assume a standing or squatting position during labor. These positions use gravity more effectively than lying in a bed. The birth stool used in the 17th and 18th century is again available. The 1980s version is made of plastic rather than wood, but the purpose is the same.

This glimpse of some of the practices used by other cultures during childbirth is presented as a framework for studying our customs. Undoubtedly, a text from the 2080s will refer to some of our customs as bizarre and primitive. Despite the differences in the rituals that surround birth, the actual process of birth has not changed.

## THE BIRTH PROCESS

After nine months of sheltering the fetus, the uterus begins to make subtle changes. The base of the uterus, an area called the cervix, begins to soften in preparation for birth. When the *amniotic fluid* or "bag of waters" breaks, labor has begun or is about to begin.

**First stage of labor**

In order for the fetus to pass through the birth canal, the cervix must expand. This is caused by contractions of the uterus. When the fetus's head is pushed down by a contraction, the tissues of the cervix are drawn apart. Slowly, the cervix becomes dilated or widened to 10 centimeters or 4 inches (see Figure 4–2). At this point, the fetus can begin to travel the 9-inch path to the outside world.

**Second stage of labor**

When the cervix is dilated, mothers are instructed to push. Typically, such instructions are not necessary because the mother has an overwhelming urge to push. As a contraction comes, the mother holds her breath and presses down for five to six seconds. This pushing helps the baby wind its way down the birth canal. Before birth, the wet layered hair on the top of the baby's head can be seen in the birth canal. As the head crowns or pushes against the vaginal tissue, the mother relaxes and the baby's head eases out. When the baby's head emerges, it often looks violet or purple and is covered with a white film that looks like cottage cheese. As the baby begins to breathe, oxygen is transferred from the infant's lungs to the bloodstream, and the violet color changes to pink. After the head is delivered, the rest of the body seems to slip out easily. Any mucus that might hinder the child's breathing is quickly removed, and the small, wet, slippery bundle begins to cry lustily.

**Figure 4—2**          **Dilation of the cervix**

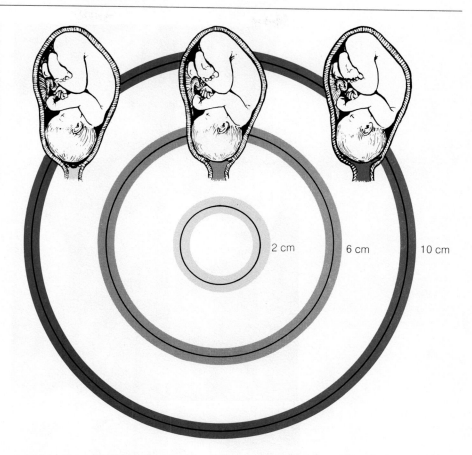

2 cm          6 cm          10 cm

The cervix has to widen or dilate to 10 centimeters before the uterus can press the baby out. The dilation of the cervix is called the first stage of labor.

Source: Kitzinger, S. (1981). *The complete book of pregnancy and childbirth* (p. 208). New York: Alfred A. Knopf.

**Third stage of labor**

The uterus continues to contract after the baby is born. These contractions help the placenta separate naturally from the uterine wall. The placenta is usually delivered in 10 to 15 minutes, completing the birth.

## THE PSYCHOLOGICAL IMPACT OF MEDICAL ADVANCES

Fifty years ago, the process of birth was left to nature. With advances in medicine, obstetricians can now control many aspects of the process. If a mother goes into labor prematurely, physicians can sometimes stop labor. If labor is progressing slowly, they can speed it up. If necessary, physicians can induce labor. With an injection, physicians can also ease the pain of the

### Panel on human birth

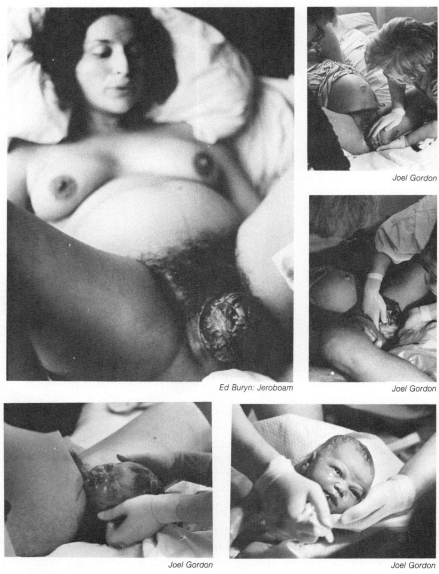

Ed Buryn: Jeroboam

Joel Gordon

Joel Gordon

Joel Gordon

Joel Gordon

A human birth.

mother. Throughout the delivery, physicians can monitor the condition of the fetus. If the fetus appears to be distressed, they can opt for a Caesarean delivery. These medical procedures have saved the lives of countless infants and mothers. In 1915, approximately 100 infants died for every 1,000 born. By 1960, the infant mortality rate had dropped to 25 infants in every 1,000 born (Shapiro, Schlesinger, & Nesbitt, 1968). Currently, fewer than 14 infants die

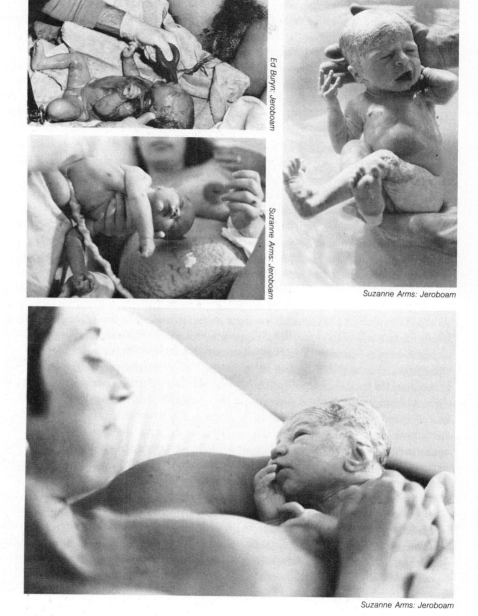

Ed Buryn: Jeroboam

Suzanne Arms: Jeroboam

Suzanne Arms: Jeroboam

Suzanne Arms: Jeroboam

for every 1,000 born (McQuarrie, 1980). The declining infant mortality rate is one of the success stories of contemporary medicine. A footnote to that story is the psychological impact that medical procedures have on the mother or the child. It is this psychological component that currently interests developmental psychologists and which will be explored in this chapter.

**Medication during
labor and delivery**

Relief of pain during childbirth is, like most obstetrical procedures, of recent origin. During much of modern history, taking any medication for the relief of labor pains was regarded as sinful and morally reprehensible. In the 16th century, Agnes Sampson was tried for heresy before King James. Her crime was taking a concoction rumored to relieve the pains of childbirth. The king ruled that she was a witch, and she was burned at the stake on the Castle Hill of Edinburgh (Findley, 1933). Queen Victoria changed these beliefs when she received chloroform during two of her births. Receiving anesthesia during delivery suddenly became very popular. No one was concerned about its effect on the baby even though Queen Victoria's physician noted that infants born to chloroformed mothers did not "kick and scream in the violent way and grasp the bedclothes with the force, during the first minute after birth, that is observed under other circumstances" (Snow, 1853).

From Queen Victoria's time until the 1960s, the array of medications that could be used during delivery grew rapidly, and a new favorite appeared about every five years. The caudal, the spinal, the saddle block, and the paracervical block were, like hit records and diets, each popular for a period. Initially, each was heralded as an effective pain reliever that had few side effects. The slow process of investigating each drug scientifically soon proved that all of the medications had side effects—some more worrisome than others. The side effects could be classified according to the effects on the mother, effects on labor, and effects on the baby. Since our concern is with the development of the child, we will focus on the effects that medication during delivery have on development during the first month.

The fetal brain or central nervous system (CNS) is still very immature at birth. Hence, medications taken during labor have the potential for altering or preventing the complete development of the brain (Guth & Clements, 1975). In adults, there is a barrier that helps separate the brain from any toxic substances in the blood. This blood brain barrier is incomplete in newborns. Hence, medication given to the mother has easy access to the central nervous system of the fetus. The liver and kidneys of the full-term fetus are also very immature. In an adult, these organs help clear toxic drugs from the system. But these organs are not as efficient in the nine-month-old fetus. Demerol, a medication used commonly in labor, has a half life of three hours in an adult. In the newborn the drug's half life is 22.7 hours (Perriss, 1981). This means that medications given to the mother during labor and delivery can continue to affect the fetus long after they have been cleared from the mother's system.

Although there are dozens of drugs that can be used during labor and delivery, they fall into a small number of categories. As these drugs are reviewed, remember their effect on adults will vary. Remember also that the dosage is very important in determining the consequences for the fetus; smaller doses are associated with milder effects. Finally, the time of administration is important. If the drug is administered six hours before birth and is effective for two to three hours, the infant is not likely to be greatly depressed at birth. A drug administered just a few minutes before birth might have its maximum effect on the fetus at the moment of birth.

**Analgesics.** Physicians generally regard narcotic *analgesics* such as demerol and nisentil to be the most effective drugs to relieve pain. As a result, these are the most frequently administered obstetrical pain killers (Brackbill, 1979). Small doses are helpful to the mother who has difficulty coping with her labor contractions. The drug typically reaches a peak of effectiveness in 60 to 90 minutes and lasts for two-three hours. Like all obstetric medications, the analgesics cross the placenta and depress the central nervous system of the fetus. When analgesics are administered, it is very common for labor to slow down appreciably.

When analgesics are used, the newborn's respiration is depressed for at least 48 hours (Weiner, Hogg, & Rosen, 1979). The child's sucking responses may be weak, various reflexes may be sporadic, and the child's responses to external stimulation may be affected (Weiner, Hogg, & Rosen, 1977). Recently, obstetricians have been trying to combat the infant's respiratory depression by giving the infant a second drug to counteract the effect of the analgesic (Perriss, 1981). Although the newborn is affected by analgesics, there seem to be no long-term effects with this obstetrical medication. As the drug is removed from the system, these babies cannot be distinguished from the babies of mothers who received no medication during delivery (Brackbill, 1979).

**Anesthesia.** Anesthesia means "loss of sensation." A general anesthetic means that the patient loses sensation throughout the body. In contrast, a local or regional anesthetic affects only a specific area. General anesthetics cross the placenta rapidly and depress the central nervous system of the fetus. The use of general anesthesia for delivery is not recommended because it increases the risk to the mother. Even in Caesarean births, doctors are likely to choose a local anesthetic. General anesthetics depress the functioning of infants more than any other type of medication, and they are associated with the longest lasting effects on the infant (Bowes, Brackbill, Conway, & Steinschneider, 1970; Brackbill, 1979).

Local anesthetics are also known as regional blocks. During childbirth, they are designed to block pain from the navel to the knees. These medications are very effective at blocking the pain of first- and second-stage labor and, hence, they have been widely used. Regional anesthetics do not depress the fetus as much as general anesthetics. However, they still cross the placenta and do affect the fetus. The once-popular paracervical block slows the infant's heart rate (Perriss, 1981). Many of these regional blocks also prolong labor. Because there is no sensation in the pelvic floor muscles, mothers cannot tell whether they are bearing down. As a result, obstetricians are often forced to use forceps, an instrument that looks like salad tongs, to deliver the baby (Perriss, 1981). Another side effect of regional blocks is to lower the mother's blood pressure. This can reduce the amount of oxygen the fetus receives. Babies born to these mothers can be nervous and jittery. Other regional anesthetics produce drowsy infants. During the first two days after delivery, infants are not as alert, their limbs sometimes flop like rag dolls, and they do not respond as well as unmedicated infants (Kitzinger, 1981). Even the currently popular epidural block slows labor, increases the use of forceps, and affects the newborn's behavior (Murray, Dolby, Nation, & Thomas, 1981).

**Long-term effects of anesthetics.**  Although many investigators have studied the effects of drugs on the fetus and newborn, very few have been concerned with any long-term effects of anesthetics given during labor and delivery. The tacit assumption seems to be that the effect of the anesthetic is transient. If this assumption is correct, then obstetricians and pediatricians must remain vigilant only during delivery and while the infant is in the hospital. If, however, there are long-term effects, obstetricians, pediatricians, and parents might all redouble their efforts to reduce medication during delivery.

Yvonne Brackbill has been at the forefront of the research to determine whether anesthetics used during delivery have any long-term effects. She has tested infants at birth and at 1, 4, 8, and 12 months. During all of these periods, she finds that infants whose mothers received anesthesia during labor differed from infants whose mothers did not (Brackbill, 1976; Brackbill, 1979). Further, she notes that in some cases the effects of medication increase rather than decrease after birth. Alexandrowicz and Alexandrowicz (1974) agree and further report that the amount of trembling and smiling among infants is not different four days after delivery. At the end of a month, however, the medicated infants smiled less and trembled more. Since it is highly unlikely that the infant is still under the influence of the medication, other explanations have been offered for these results. The most popular one is that a drowsy infant and a medicated mother take longer to establish a close, warm relationship. If this is true, then less smiling would be predicted in infants who had been medicated during delivery.

You might think that anesthesia would have its biggest effect on physical measures of infants. The biggest differences however are found on tests of the infant's behavior. In one test, called a habituation test, the infant sees the same toy repeatedly. Normally, the infant gets bored and no longer responds. Infants whose mothers were heavily medicated take much longer to habituate. These kinds of cognitive tasks are influenced by the mother's medication. Blood gas values, skin discoloration, and other physical indices are less likely to be affected. Brackbill argues that medication affects tasks that "demand from the infant intensive efforts, strenuous exertion, high-energy output, continued coping with environmentally imposed stimuli, or sustained attention" (Brackbill, 1979, p. 110).

Differences in intelligence scores among infants that are found several months after birth have been attributed to the medication the mother received during delivery (Brackbill, 1979). A large-scale study that looked at the birth histories of one-year-olds found that the infants' intelligence scores were related to the use of anesthesia during labor and delivery (Goldstein, Caputo, & Taub, 1976). When these same children were examined at nine years of age, anesthesia was no longer a factor (Caputo, Goldstein, & Taub, 1981). By then the mother's intelligence and social class were the best predictors. The results suggest that anesthesia during delivery has, at most, a temporary effect on intellectual skills (Caputo et al., 1981).

**Electronic fetal monitoring**

Throughout the birth, doctors monitor the fetal heartbeat. This used to be accomplished with a simple stethoscope. Now there are more sophisticated ways of monitoring the fetus. Sometimes a transducer is placed over the mother's abdomen to monitor the heartbeat externally. In some hospitals, an electrode is inserted into the vagina and attached to the baby's head. The fetal heartbeat is then registered electronically on a monitor. If the heartbeat increases or decreases rapidly, an alarm is sounded. Monitoring the fetus in this way is credited with saving many infants. Amato (1977), for example, observed a mortality rate of 23/1,000 in unmonitored infants; but only 3/1,000 in monitored infants. Tipton and Lewis (1975) observed a drop from 10 deaths per 1,000 births to 3 deaths per 1,000 in the two year-period following the institution of fetal monitoring. Baumgarten (1981) surveyed 18 hospitals and found that fetal monitoring had reduced the infant death rate by 50 to 75 percent.

Despite these statistics, psychologists have some doubts about fetal monitoring. Their doubts spring from the psychological effects that such monitoring has on the mother. The mother can no longer move around during labor. This may make her more anxious and decrease the control she has over the pain. To attach an internal monitor to the fetus, the sack containing the amniotic fluid must be ruptured. Doing this artificially may make labor progress more rapidly. When contractions come very rapidly, mothers have more difficulty continuing the patterned breathing they have practiced. As a result, mothers may require more medication.

Fetal monitoring sometimes produces rather than reduces fetal distress. Mothers who feel caged and frightened release a chemical called epinephrine. Large quantities of epineprine may interfere with labor and decrease the supply of oxygen to the fetus (Morishima, Yeh, & Jane, 1979). In such cases fetal monitoring becomes detrimental to labor and delivery (Sokol, Zabor, & Rosen, 1976). Monitoring the fetus using radio signals is a recent innovation that does not require the mother to be connected to a machine. Women seem to prefer this method, and it does not seem to slow labor (Kitzinger, 1981). Because the mother is able to be in an upright position, she can cope with pain better and the uterus can work more efficiently.

Fetal surveillance seems to be accepted in the field of obstetrics. One of the newer techniques involves taking a blood sample from the baby's head as it comes down the birth canal. Blood samples can be a more accurate indicator of distress than electronic fetal monitoring (Willcourt & Queenan, 1981). Its proper use, however, depends on a laboratory staff that is experienced with the technique. In the next few years, new techniques that assess the fetus and monitor the oxygen supply will undoubtedly be tried. Since lack of oxygen is a major cause of brain damage, handicapping conditions, and fetal death, surveillance of the fetus could be very valuable. This advance, however, like many medical procedures, will have to be integrated with the psychological needs of the parents.

To summarize, medications given to the mother during delivery undoubtedly have an effect on the infant during the neonatal period. The extent of this effect varies depending on the particular medication, the dose the mother received, and when she received it. Whether or not anesthesia has any long-term effect is not clear. It is possible that medication given to the mother could disrupt the central nervous system of the infant or it could inhibit mother-infant interaction. These kinds of effects can be very subtle and difficult to detect. It is also possible that the long-term effects that have been documented are really due to differences in the mothers. It is very possible that educated mothers seek doctors, hospitals, and birth settings that minimize medication (Caputo et al., 1981). These same mothers are also likely to provide loving, stimulating environments. At one year of age, their babies may score better than infants who were medicated, but the environment, not the medication, is responsible.

The procedures that are used during labor and delivery are selected for medical reasons. These procedures can often have subtle psychological effects. In the past, the psychological aspects of labor and delivery have been ignored or belittled. In the last decade, they have been recognized as central factors in the birth. To understand the psychological factors that operate during labor and birth, we need to shift the perspective from the technical aspects of the birth to the actual experience of birth.

## THE PSYCHOLOGICAL EXPERIENCE OF BIRTH

The cycle of life, from birth to death, used to take place within the confines of a person's home. Loved ones provided support and shared the joy or grief of the event. During the last half century, the rapid changes in medical expertise have mandated that these critical life events be shifted from the home to the hospital. During the shift, human needs and the emotional involvement of loved ones began to take a back seat. The heroic procedures of modern medicine assumed center stage. The medical strides made during this period have reduced the hazards of childbirth by two thirds and have increased the life span substantially (HEW, 1979). But the lack of concern for the human aspects of birth and death sometimes tarnished the marvels that doctors could accomplish and prompted those who wanted to die or give birth in a more family-oriented atmosphere to rebel.

In the rebellion that enveloped childbirth, the psychological and sociological concerns of parents have resurfaced as important aspects of delivery. Furthermore, these nonmedical aspects of childbirth have gained new respectability from studies which demonstrate that emotional factors may influence the course of labor and delivery. The involvement of the entire family in the birth may help cement the unit that will offer love and support for the child in the future. Hence, a contemporary approach to the birth of a child should integrate the emotional needs of the parents with medical concerns for both the mother and child.

## The psychological aspects of labor

Before physicians knew how to speed up a sluggish labor, one woman might have spent 18 hours in labor giving birth to her first child, while the woman next to her spent 4 hours. Today, women delivering their first child can expect to be in labor between 6 and 12 hours. In successive pregnancies, children arrive in five to eight hours (Russell, 1980). Some of this reduction in the length of labor is attributed to better medical management of labor. The fact that pregnant women get more exercise and eat healthier food is also credited with reducing the length of labor. Another part of the reduction can be attributed to psychological variables.

Thanks to prenatal classes, mothers understand what will be happening to their bodies. They also learn some very effective strategies for coping with labor contractions. After attending these classes, couples report that they feel "prepared" and "ready" to deal with labor. Women who lack this kind of preparation are more likely to be frightened by the strange environment and less able to cope with labor pains.

Having a companion present speeds up labor so dramatically that most obstetricians are committed to the slogan "no woman shall labor alone." One obstetrician in Dublin, Ireland, guarantees a personal nurse for every mother throughout labor. This policy has proved a source of great encouragement to patients and has contributed to much shorter labor for women delivering their first child (O'Driscoll & Stronge, 1975).

Prolonged labor is not good for either the mother or the child. The longer the labor, the more likely the fetus is to suffer a lack of oxygen (anoxia). A long labor also affects the mother. Unfortunately, fear and anxiety can be translated directly into physiological factors that slow labor. Given this knowledge, it becomes obvious that the mother's feelings and needs should be an important factor in labor. Circumstances that can lower her apprehension should be incorporated into the delivery process whenever possible. Activities that would increase her fears should be avoided. The many forms of natural childbirth are all designed to accomplish these goals.

## Natural childbirth

The natural childbirth movement was a reaction to the unbridled use of drugs in the delivery room. Physicians began to realize that the drugs that were easing the pain of the mother during labor and delivery posed a danger to the child. A physician describes the practice of obstetrics in the 1960s. Mothers were still heavily medicated and passive. Babies were often depressed and in need of resuscitation (Sumner & Phillips, 1981, p. 17). Newborns sometimes took over five minutes to begin breathing, and it was seven minutes before some cried (Muller et al., 1971).

The natural childbirth movement initiated by Grantly Dick-Read (1944) and extended by Lamaze (1958) and Leboyer (1975) let mothers replace drugs with psychological techniques that decreased the pain without affecting the infant. These techniques capitalized on three psychological principles that help the mother during childbirth. First, educate the mother about the process. Second, provide support for the mother. Third, give the mother an active role in the process. These psychological boosts can reduce or eliminate the need for drugs during delivery.

**Educating the parents.** Education has a powerful influence over a person's ability to understand and deal with pain. Patients who are given information about their impending operations and instructions for coping with surgery require less medication and are sent home earlier than patients who receive no information (Weisenberg, 1977). The same effect occurs in childbirth (Chertok, 1972).

Dick-Read was the first to argue that mothers should be educated about the birth process. He showed that other animals gave birth in cozy, secluded, familiar places where the mother felt safe. He contrasted this with the sterile, unfamiliar hospital environment where strangers monitored human births. Dick-Read also observed the relaxation that animals achieved naturally and the breathing patterns that seemed to help them bring forth their young. Why, he asked, didn't humans relax and allow the child to be born? He reasoned that mothers found it impossible to relax because they were frightened and did not know what was happening. Hence, mothers needed to understand what their bodies were doing and what they could do to help. The natural childbirth movement in westernized countries built on Dick-Read's advice. Prepared childbirth classes, Lamaze classes, Leboyer classes, and tours of the maternity ward and birthing rooms are all designed to educate parents about the birth process and to familiarize them with the environment.

Understanding the birth process can relieve anxiety and reduce the mother's need for pain relievers during labor and birth. But education for childbirth encompasses more than understanding the process. It includes preparing the mind and the body for birth. It means learning relaxation techniques and using a mental set to trigger the relaxation response. It means learning breathing patterns that help the mother over contractions and enable her to push the baby during the second stage of labor. The doctors and nurses behind the natural childbirth movement did something that the rest of the medical profession did not do. They educated the mother about the process of birth and showed her how to prepare for it. The result, a delivery that required a minimum of drugs, was welcomed by everyone.

**Supporting the parents.** The mothers who first read Dick-Read and Lamaze and were trying to forego drugs for the safety of their children had little support. Nurses were ready to administer drugs, and the fathers had been banished to a waiting room. The mothers needed someone who could provide some emotional support for them during labor. The father was the logical person; he was interested, willing, and, best of all, free. When medical personnel realized that having the husband present helped reduce the mother's need for drugs, they encouraged the husband to stay with his wife, to reassure her, to massage her back, to help her breathe, and to time contractions. Now most hospitals allow the father, a family member, or a friend to be present during labor.

**Giving the parents an active role.** The term natural childbirth means more than delivery without drugs. It has come to mean that the entire birth process is natural and intervention is usually not necessary. It also means that the woman is an active participant in a normal process rather than a passive recipient of medical care. During the 1970s, many couples decided not to have their babies in a hospital so that they could maintain control over the birth. In some communities, home deliveries soared. When alternative birth centers were established or a doctor who encouraged natural childbirth was available, the number of births in that hospital often increased fourfold (Sumner & Philips, 1981). These dramatic fluctuations in the number of babies born in hospitals proved that many couples wanted to play an active role in the birth of their child.

These three psychological factors, educating and preparing a woman for birth, supporting her during labor, and giving her an active role in the birth are incorporated into all of the methods of natural childbirth that are currently in vogue. Are they really effective in reducing the mother's pain and ensuring a rapid, uncomplicated delivery?

Providing companionship for a mother during labor has a marked effect on the length of labor. In a study done in Guatemala, women without any companion had an average labor of 19.3 hours. Another group of women were met in the labor room by a supportive companion who rubbed their backs and held their hands. These women averaged 8.7 hours in labor. Furthermore, 79 percent of those mothers who did not have a companion experienced other problems during labor that lead to Caesarean births, forceps deliveries, or more medication. Only 37 percent of the women with companions developed these problems (Sosa, Kennell, Klaus, Robertson, & Urrutia, 1980).

This study is particularly significant because whether or not a mother had a companion was not determined until she arrived at the hospital to give birth. Note also that the companions used in the study were all strangers to the women. The authors suggest that a husband or friend could be an even greater comfort (Sosa et al., 1980). Exactly why a companion had such a marked effect on the length of labor was suggested earlier. Women without companions were more anxious (Sosa et al., 1980).

This study documents the role of a supporting companion. What about the preparation that women get in Lamaze classes? Is this effective in reducing pain? This simple question turns out to be a very difficult one to answer. Women who choose Lamaze training may differ in important ways from women who adopt a wake-me-when-it's-over attitude. Worthington and Martin (1980) decided that the best approach to the question was to simulate the cyclic nature of labor contractions. Women immersed their hands in ice water for a period—then withdrew them—and immersed them again. Women who had been trained in Lamaze breathing techniques could tolerate the ice water for longer periods than women who used long, slow breathing (Worthington & Martin, 1980). This study removes all of the variables of the actual labor and delivery situation and, like the Guatemalan study, assigned women to groups randomly. Hence, it provides documentation of the effectiveness of Lamaze techniques in increasing tolerance for pain.

Finally, there is the issue of control. People can tolerate pain and other kinds of aversive stimulation if they feel that they have some control (Cohen, 1980). Obviously women cannot control when their contractions begin and end. But having a way to cope with the pain, such as a breathing pattern, makes it seem as if they have some control. There are other cognitive strategies that help a person control pain. In childbirth, rather than thinking about the contraction, women concentrate on a rose, a favorite piece of music, or a happy memory.

The body has its own system for dealing with pain. *Endorphins*, chemicals in the brain that are related to morphine, are released if a person is in pain. Stories of men who were severely wounded and still performed incredible physical feats are a tribute to the endorphins that their system released. During pregnancy, the body's level of endorphins increases gradually until it reaches a peak approximately two days before birth (Gintzler, 1980). These natural pain relievers are nature's attempt to help the mother.

The three points emphasized in natural childbirth—education and preparation, support, and control—all have an impact on some aspect of the childbirth process. Education and preparation can reduce anxiety and increase tolerance for pain. Support from husbands, family members, or friends can reduce the time in labor and the number of complications that may occur. Being an active participant in the delivery and having some control over the situation increases the mother's ability to deal with the pain.

**Home deliveries.** During the 1970s, many young couples made the decision to have their child at home. In California, for example, out-of-hospital births accounted for between 5 percent and 20 percent of all babies born (Patterson & Peterson, 1980; Shy, Frost, & Ullom, 1980). To physicians who have watched proudly as the infant mortality rate in the United States dropped, this trend was regarded as a giant step backward. The medical literature was filled with alarms about the dangers of deliveries at home (DeVries, 1980).

When some of the fervor about this issue subsided and information was finally examined, it was found that the dangers of at-home deliveries were often exaggerated by the method of reporting statistics. Home deliveries vary widely. Some are planned, screened by obstetricians as being low-risk deliveries, and are attended by an experienced nurse or midwife. Others are unplanned, sudden, and often disastrous. The common practice of reporting births as either in-hospital or out-of-hospital does not separate these two categories. To get a fair accounting of the dangers of at-home births, they have to be divided into planned and unplanned births. This has been done in North Carolina. The results are important for those trying to assess the risks and merits of having babies at home.

In North Carolina, lay midwives are legally allowed to attend the home deliveries of women who have been designated as low risk. Between 1974 and 1976, the infant mortality rate at these low-risk, at-home births was 4 deaths per 1,000. Actually, the three deaths that occurred in 768 deliveries were associated with congenital abnormalities and may not have been preventable. Hospital deliveries for the same period had an infant death rate of 7 per 1,000 births. Remember, though, that hospital deliveries included all of the high-risk pregnancies (Burnett, Jones, Rooks, Chen, Tyler, & Miller, 1980). Unplanned deliveries that occurred at home had an infant death rate of 120 per 1,000 births. Although this study indicates that at-home deliveries are fairly safe for women who have a good prenatal history and a trained attendant, obstetricians are quick to point out that some of the complications of delivery cannot be predicted (Thornton, 1981). The resources available at a hospital mean that the hospital is still the safest place to have a baby. Having the emergency equipment of the hospital available is not incompatible with letting parents enjoy the birth of their child. The birth center, a feature of many contemporary hospitals, provides for emergencies and encourages the parents' participation.

**Birth centers.** The Alternative Birthing Center (ABC) began in the United States in 1969, after Philip Sumner visited France. Sumner was astounded at the atmosphere of tranquility and exultation that accompanied several Lamaze births. Despite his enthusiasm, the concept of a birth center did not initially enjoy widespread acceptance in the United States. Since 1970, however, several factors have spurred the medical community to develop alternatives to the traditional hospital delivery. First, the feminist movement championed a greater role for women in obstetric settings. Second, obstetricians became concerned about the lack of flexibility in hospital standards and procedures. Third, hospital births became so expensive that young couples sought other alternatives (Barton, Rovner, Puls, & Read, 1980).

Birth centers offer a compromise between the highly managed hospital delivery and the relaxed familiar delivery that can be accomplished at home. At birth centers, the environment is carefully constructed to make the hospital room look like a home. Rocking chairs, queen-size beds, bean-bag chairs, stereos, relaxing murals, and other comfortable furnishings are standard. Mothers and fathers are the stars of the show. The physician, nurse, or midwife assumes the role of facilitator.

Birth centers offer the peaceful surroundings, lack of anxiety, and security that characterize home deliveries. They also offer medical expertise if compli-

**The celebration of birth**

*Jeroboam*

The birth of a child is currently regarded as a sensitive, beautiful event that is to be cherished and celebrated.

cations arise during birth. In most birth centers, the emphasis is on a family celebration. The birth of a child is regarded as a sensitive, beautiful event that is to be cherished and savored by the whole family.

Birth centers also offer prenatal education, nutritional advice, classes to prepare the couple for childbirth, and education about infant care. In addition, birth centers encourage the father's participation in labor, birth, and baby care. They emphasize noninvasive support techniques in lieu of drugs and anesthetics. Birth centers allow the couple to settle into one room and do not transfer the mother to the brightly lit delivery room when the birth is imminent. In some birth centers, rheostated lights can be dimmed as the baby emerges, the mother can lift her own baby to her breast, determine its sex, and nurse the baby. Birth centers recognize the importance of the mother and father having time with their new baby. They provide an opportunity for quiet family interaction before the baby is examined. The focus on the whole family is obvious throughout the hospital stay. Separations between the mother and infant are minimized, siblings are allowed to visit, and fathers are involved in infant care (Sumner & Phillips, 1981).

Birth centers have reduced the expense of having a baby at the hospital. The birth center is both a labor and delivery room where there is typically little need for anesthesia. The mother's hospital stay is often less than 24 hours, and while the mother is in the hospital, her infant is with her. All of these changes have made having a baby at the hospital more affordable, as well as more enjoyable (Allgaier, 1978).

**The role of the father.**   In most westernized countries, fathers are now welcome in both the labor and delivery rooms. Their presence is consistent with the principles of providing support and giving both parents an active role.

### Family-centered birth

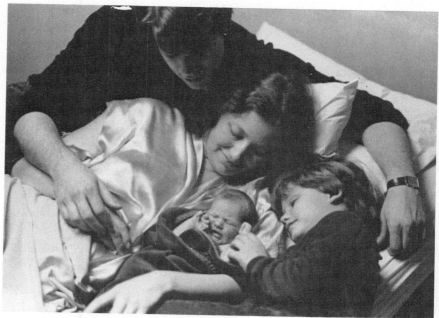

Joel Gordon

In birth centers, the entire family is allowed to visit the new baby.

Throughout history, however, men have played a relatively minor role in the actual birth of the child. Before 1800 men, for modesty's sake, were not involved in childbirth. Even doctors were barred from the delivery if they were male. In the 1500s, a Hamburg physician who was curious about childbirth dressed as a midwife and sneaked into the delivery room to see a child born. Unfortunately, he was caught and, as was customary during that period, was burned at the stake (Lieberman, 1976). Louis XIV of France used his title to get his court physician into the delivery room. Since then, the presence of doctors and surgeons in delivery rooms has been accepted, but other males have been excluded.

*The Expectant Father,* published in 1964 as a guide for fathers-to-be, suggests that fathers might want to be with their wives during the early stages of labor. The book warns that "the great majority of physicians and nurses doubt that any purpose is served by permitting a father to watch the actual delivery" (Schaefer & Zisowitz, 1964, p. 77). In the 20 years since that book appeared, the delivery of a child has changed from a somewhat worrisome medical problem to a joyous celebration of one of life's peak experiences. The father's presence and participation in childbirth is consistent with this idea.

When fathers were first allowed in the delivery room, they had little to do. They reported feeling awkward and a little unwanted. Fathers soon proved their value in the labor room. They served as coach, chief back rubber, head cheer-leader, and timer. Soon, they had jobs in the delivery room, too. They supported the mother as she pushed, they cut the umbilical cord, they held and bathed the baby. In short, they became a member of the delivery team. One father reports that his wife was having trouble maintaining her breathing pattern during the second stage of labor. The doctor left the father and mother alone until they were able to reestablish their breathing pattern, thereby acknowledging the father's importance in the delivery room (Grad, Bash, Guyer, Acevedo, Trause, & Reukauf, 1981).

The father's role in helping the mother during delivery seems to be well established. The father typically derives a great deal of pleasure from being present at the birth. After the birth, fathers report that they experience an incredible elation. Although each father describes the experience differently, the following impression is representative. "Do you know, I never expected this to be so beautiful. It is such a miracle. I felt as though I was floating on a cloud. Nothing prepared me for the exhilaration of the actual birth" (Grad, Bash, Guyer, Acevedo, Trause, & Reukauf, 1981, p. 136).

Family-centered births that include the father and other members of the family are now common, and fathers no longer feel isolated. The birth and the celebration of the new life confirm the father's role and provide a solid foundation for a close relationship with the child. Rather than being timid around their newborns, fathers are interested and competent. Greenberg and

---

### FATHERS IN THE DELIVERY ROOM

Fathers report feelings of awe at watching their child being born and holding their infants in the first minutes of life.

Lyn Svoboda always knew he wanted to be in on the delivery of his children. He and his wife, Jill, took childbirth classes in preparation for their first child.

At one point the labor pain became so intense, Svoboda recalls his wife saying, "I've had it. I'm perfectly rational, I just don't want to do this anymore, get me out of here."

"Of course that really wasn't an option. A couple of minutes later, when the baby was born, there was such a change, my wife just glowed," Svoboda says. He glows talking about the experience.

"The miracle of it, that my wife and I had produced something like this was exhilarating.

The Durans opted to have their son, Nicholas, born at a Birthing Center, an alternative to hospital delivery that provides a homelike atmosphere in a medical setting.

Bud was with Carol through the whole delivery. Looking back, he recalls it as "the fastest five hours of my life." Friends stopped by after the birth and drank the wine and cheese the Durans had brought with them.

After Nicholas was born, it was his dad who cleaned him and gave him his first bath.

"I washed his head, his feet, his hands. I took my time. Then I dressed him—and I had never dressed a baby in my life. Everyone else was in a panic that I'd drop him or something. But I just held him and the tears dropped down my face."

John Greene Jr. remembers tears at each of his three children's birth. He says, "They come to your eyes—you feel real proud. It's just a magic moment."

Jim Calkins watched his children being born and then held them. "Holding Kimberly and Nicholas after they were born was a feeling like I've never felt in my life before. It's the best feeling I've ever had. It's incredible."

Source: Tetzlaff, J. M. (1982, June 20). An album of proud fathers. *Press Enterprise*, Section 3, p. 1.

Morris (1974) report that fathers begin developing a bond with their infant during the first three days of life and that fathers experience a feeling of *engrossment* or preoccupation with the newborn. Parke and his colleagues have also watched fathers, mothers, and their new infants interact (Parke & O'-Leary, 1976; Parke & Sawin, 1976). The fathers they studied did not shy away from playing with their infants. Fathers actually held and rocked the infants more than the mothers. When confronted with their newborns, men were neither stoic nor passive. They looked, touched, talked to, and kissed their infants in exactly the same way as mothers (Parke, 1979).

Fathers, even in this age of equality, do not engage in as much caretaking as the mother. This does not mean that they cannot. When asked to feed their infants, fathers were very responsive to the infant's cues. The fathers altered the feeding, burped the infant if necessary, or just waited if the baby sneezed. Their success at feeding was indicated by the fact that infants drank as much when fed by the father as they did when fed by the mother. The caricature of the uninvolved father welcoming his infant into the world with a formal handshake and a brisk hello is not accurate. Fathers are more than involved, they are exuberant; and their feelings are expressed in a variety of tender, nurturant responses toward their infants.

**Leboyer's gentle birth.** The main characters in the drama of birth are the mother, the father, the attending medical personnel, and the baby. Frederick Leboyer, a French obstetrician, became convinced that the other characters in the drama had gradually stolen the limelight. Medical personnel had assumed a larger and larger role. The father, denied even a bit part for years, was vying for a part as a supporting character. The mother had been given an expanded role since Frederick Lamaze demonstrated the advantages of natural childbirth; but no one had spoken for the baby. Leboyer became that spokesman. In his version of "Birth," the baby would be restored to center stage. The baby's needs would be first and foremost. The environment would be adjusted to meet these needs. To this end, LeBoyer argued that the harshness of the environment upset infants and that they deserved to be brought into the world in a gentle, caring way. Most babies cry at the moment of birth, and these first cries guarantee a flow of oxygen into the lungs. But a newborn's crying should not persist. If babies are treated with respect and gentleness, their eyes will open, they will become alert and calm, and the stage will be set for them to meet their mother and father.

Leboyer argued that mothers must be treated with respect and dignity during labor, not as the container for the baby. He believed that the environment should be geared to softness rather than high technology. Lights should be dimmed, noise levels should be lowered, and the delivery room should be a quiet place that facilitates the relaxation mothers need to perform their jobs. The baby is handled gently and slowly. He or she is massaged until crying stops. A warm bath should be part of the period of getting acquainted.

Leboyer's suggestions were often greeted enthusiastically by parents, but were questioned by physicians. As research accumulated on various aspects of

### The Leboyer bath

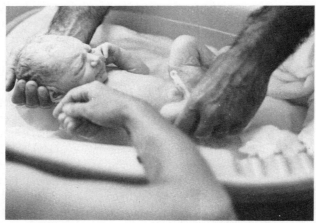

*Suzanne Arms: Jeroboam*
A father gives his infant a bath immediately after delivery.

the gentle birth, it became clear that LeBoyer's methods were safe for mothers and newborns (Crystle, Kegel, France, Brady, & Olds, 1980). Indeed, the quiet delivery room, immediate mother-infant contact, and the father's participation were described as advantages.

Physicians who have tried the gentle birth have observed the quiet, alert state Leboyer says is the right of every infant. In a clinical study, 40 low-risk mothers were assigned randomly to either a Leboyer delivery or a conventional delivery. At first, the infants from both groups cried. Then they calmed down and spent the majority of their first hour in a quiet, alert state. Infants delivered by the Leboyer method spent 41.5 minutes in this state while the infants delivered in a more conventional fashion spent 35 (Saigal, Nelson, Bennett, & Enkin, 1981). Leboyer discusses the relaxed atmosphere that infants can experience in a gentle birth. This, too, has recently been noted in the medical literature. Infants delivered by the Leboyer method were relaxed and did not tremble and shudder as much as infants delivered by conventional methods (Oliver & Oliver, 1978). In addition, infants delivered by the Leboyer method "tended to have better motor processes, better responses to stress on the first day of life, and better state control at 72 hours" (Nelson, Enkin, Saigal, Bennett, Milner, & Sackett, 1980). Leboyer suggests that this relaxed atmosphere carries over into the infant's first years. However, at eight months there were no discernible differences between infants delivered by the Leboyer method and a more conventional delivery. In short, the Leboyer method of delivery poses no additional risks for the infant or the mother. It offers the advantage of having an alert, relaxed infant to begin responding to the father and mother.

In the future, some of Leboyer's respect for the infant will probably be found in nurseries for premature babies. Intensive care units for premature infants offer extraneous stimulation that is probably aversive to the infant. Sound levels are comparable to the sound of a starting bus, and lights are very bright and always on. At least one investigation has suggested that the steady exposure to these noise levels can damage a premature infant's hearing (Gottfried, Wallace, Sherman, King, Coen, & Hodgman, 1981). Allen Gottfried is recommending that the endless noise, buzzers, and alarms in the nursery be reduced, that colorful wallpaper be added, and that the lights be lowered, at least at night. All of these changes could be accomplished without compromising medical standards, and the infants might benefit.

A successful birth does not depend on whether the father was able to bathe the baby or whether the baby was monitored. The critical aspects are whether the mother is relaxed, in control, and has support. If these are present, the chances that she will be able to have a healthy infant with a minimum amount of medication are excellent. When this kind of atmosphere can be fostered by small changes that make the environment more familiar or by having a friend present, then these requests should be met. However, what is pleasant and familiar for one mother may be unpleasant and immodest for another. Flexibility to meet each mother's needs will result in the best outcomes for the most mothers.

## BECOMING A FAMILY

How do parents come to love their children? Where do they get the interest and stamina to tolerate, indeed enjoy, the incessant demands made by an infant, to nurture the child through illness, and to protect and care for the child? In their landmark books, *Maternal-Infant Bonding* and *Parent-Infant Bonding*, Klaus and Kennell, two pediatricians from Case Western Reserve University, trace the development of the bond that is forged between parents and their newborn infant. They characterize this bond as the strongest of all human ties. They define it as a unique relationship between two people that is specific and endures through time. In research spanning two decades, they have documented the events that trigger, foster, or disturb the parents' bond to the child (Klaus & Kennell, 1976, 1982).

**The process of bonding**

There is no magical point during the pregnancy that most mothers or fathers can identify as being critical to their developing attachment for their child. Instead, they identify a series of events that foster an attachment. Planning the pregnancy, having the pregnancy confirmed, and accepting the pregnancy seem to be events that help the mother become attached to the fetus. Feeling the first movements of the fetus is another milestone. Many mothers comment that at this point they really begin to feel that the fetus has an identity. Mothers and fathers often speak humorously and affectionately about how the fetus is behaving. "Bozo seems to be a budding place kicker for the Miami Dolphins" or "Two-Ton Tess has decided that it's time for her daily dozen." Such comments mark the early stages in the formation of an attachment. We know that parents are attached to their infants at birth because of their need to grieve if the infant is stillborn or dies shortly after delivery.

Even before the child is born, then, there are hints of the affectionate bond that the parents are forming. The events surrounding birth serve to cement that bond. During this period, fathers and mothers are predisposed to becoming bonded to their infants. It is not the only time that parents can form a bond, but it is an optimal time.

When they first hold their infants in the delivery room, mothers and fathers do not just examine their babies from afar. They engage in a very specific series of events that facilitate their attachment. They align their faces with the infant's so that they are eye-to-eye. This particular positioning, called *en face*, is a hallmark of a parent's curious approach to the newborn baby (see Figure 4–3).

Mothers and fathers are very involved in looking at the infant's eyes. One

**Figure 4–3**                    **En face**

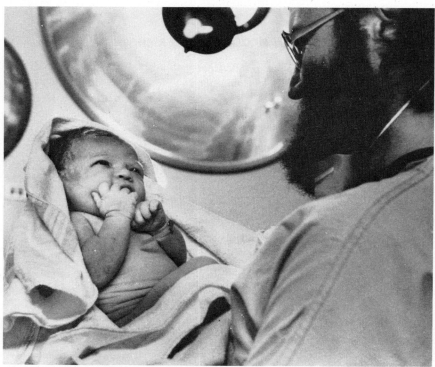

*Suzanne Arms: Jeroboam*

A father holding his infant in the *en face* position.

mother in Klaus's study conveyed what many mothers have felt when she pleaded with her newborn, "Open your eyes. Oh, come on, open your eyes. If you open your eyes, I'll know you're alive" (Klaus and Kennell, 1976, p. 70). As Leboyer noted, infants do open their eyes (see Figure 4–4). The long alert, awake period that occurs during this first hour is not repeated again until the seventh day after birth (Packer & Rosenblatt, 1979). The mother's desire to see the infant's eyes and the newborn's alert, awake period work together to facilitate bonding. To capitalize on this eye contact between parents and child, physicians now delay the silver nitrate drops that are routinely put in infants' eyes until the parents and infant have had some time together.

Touching plays an important role in bonding. After observing many mothers interact with their newborns, Klaus and Kennell described the touching sequence that mothers use as they become familiar with their infants. When mothers are given their nude infants shortly after birth, they progress very quickly from hesitant touching, to counting the fingers and toes, to massaging and stroking their infants with their whole hand. This sequence is followed quickly and naturally. Mothers of premature infants take much longer to feel comfortable massaging their infant. When they first meet their tiny offspring, they are likely to poke at the infants or just touch the baby with their fingertips rather than massaging or stroking their tiny bodies (see Figure 4–5). Fathers go through a similar process when they first meet their premature sons or daughters. Almost a third of the fathers did not touch their newborns during the first visit to the nursery. Those who did were as hesitant as the mother in establishing contact, and most of the fathers only touched the infants' arms or legs (Gaiter & Johnson, 1981).

Both mothers and fathers alter their voices when speaking to their newborns

**Figure 4—4**

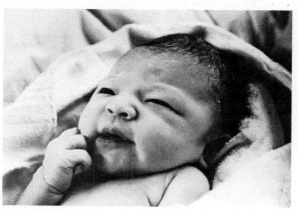

Suzanne Arms: Jeroboam

At birth, most infants cry, but within a few minutes they settle down and assume a quiet, alert state that is perfect for bonding. A six-minute-old infant in the quiet, alert state.

**Figure 4—5**          **Becoming attached**

Suzanne Arms: Jeroboam

Parents go through a series of steps in cuddling their newborns. First they touch, then caress, then stroke and massage the baby. Parents of premature infants have more difficulty feeling close to their infants and hesitantly touch their infants using only their fingertips.

in the delivery room. They speak slowly and gently in a voice that is pitched higher than their normal speaking voice (Klaus & Kennell, 1982). This type of speech helps alert newborns and directs their gaze to the parent's face.

Breast-feeding seems to help all of the pieces of the bonding process fit together. Skin-to-skin contact is mandated. The mother can establish eye contact easily, and she can massage, stroke, and talk to the infant while she nurses. By using all of these cues, the mother rapidly develops a special feeling or bond for this specific baby.

**Bonding in other mammals.** Many mammals form lasting bonds at birth. Separations of the mother and infant during this period disrupt that bond. Sheep often reject their infants if the infants are taken from them at birth and returned several hours later. However, if the mothers are with their newborns for a few days and then the infants are separated, all of the ewes will accept their lambs when they are returned (Poindron & Le Neindre, 1980). Apparently, in the period following birth, the infants are licked and marked by the mother. This marking helps her recognize and accept her infant. Goats provide a similar example. If newborn goats are removed for more than two hours at birth, the mothers will not accept them when they are returned. But

## MOTHER'S ATTACHMENTS ARE FOR SPECIFIC BABIES

The attachment of the mother is not an indiscriminant love of infants. It is a particular feeling for a particular infant. Several stories of mix-ups in the newborn nursery of hospitals underline the individual nature of the attachment. In Israel, a mix-up of two infants created a national furor. The infants were initially given to the wrong mother by some hospital workers who could not read the Hebrew name tags. When the infants were switched, one mother was concerned that her infant did not seem to have the proper birth markings. The doctor agreed and a third switch was made. With all the uncertainty surrounding who belonged with whom, blood tests were ordered. They confirmed the mix-up. But, by the time the blood tests were done, the infants had been with their mothers for six weeks. The mothers demanded more proof and a tissue-typing expert was called. His elaborate tests also documented the mix-up. After hearing his explanation, one distraught mother commented, "I know you are logically right, but if I talk to you from the bottom of my heart, it's difficult for me to accept what you say." The other mother agreed, "It sounds so easy, going through a change, but only a mother knows the meaning of such a thing."

Klaus and Kennell would be able to sympathize with the mothers' plight. Such a change after several weeks disrupts the attachment for a specific infant that has been forming. In addition to feeling considerable loss when the babies were switched for the final time, these mothers had to begin the attachment process all over again.

if they are allowed even five minutes of contact, the mothers will accept them after a longer, three-hour separation.

Rosenblatt and his colleagues have studied the bond that mother rats develop for their newborn pups. The studies have shown that at birth a mother rat's actions toward her newborn are dictated by hormones. To demonstrate this, they gave a young female rat who had never been pregnant a blood transfusion from a mother who was due to deliver momentarily. The young rat immediately behaved maternally toward a litter of newborn pups. Without such a transfusion, it takes days for a young female to show any maternal interest in newborn pups. From this, Rosenblatt concluded that hormones play a role in maternal behavior. However, as the days pass and hormone levels fall or stabilize, cues from the environment must be strong enough to trigger maternal responses. The usual cue is the presence of the newborn pups (Rosenblatt & Siegel, 1981).

These animal studies prompted Klaus and Kennell to draw four conclusions about the importance of separations during the formation of the maternal-infant bond. First, separations can have a negative effect on maternal behavior. Second, separations that occur immediately after birth have the strongest effects. Third, each species seems to have a specific length of time that a separation can be endured. Finally, if the separation extends beyond this period, the effects on mothering behavior are drastic and irreversible (Klaus & Kennell, 1982, p. 138). The sweeping conclusions that Klaus and Kennell drew have prompted a great deal of research on the bond that forms between mothers and their newborns.

**Evidence for human bonding.** Perhaps the first step in evaluating the effect of separations between mothers and their infants is to describe situations that involve a separation. When the infant is born at home, there is no separation. At the other extreme, premature infants are sometimes taken to an entirely different hospital where more specialized personnel and services are available. The separation between the mother and infant in these situations is complete until the infant is released. These long separations do seem to disrupt the mother's feelings toward her infant. Mothers say that they feel as if they do not even have a child.

If a separation at birth has an effect on humans, then mothers of premature infants would be the most likely group to experience a disruption of the mother-infant bond (Barnett, Leiderman, Grobstein, & Klaus, 1970). This prediction goes against our intuitive feeling that mothers of premature infants would be the most tender and caring. Yet, dozens of studies have now documented the disproportionate number of premature infants who leave the hospital in good health with a prognosis for normal development. Within a few months, they often return as abused children or children who have failed to thrive (Hunter, Kilstrom, Kraybill, & Luda, 1978; Frodi & Lamb, 1980). Although as a group, premature infants are more likely to be abused than full-term infants, it is important to point out that most premature infants are not abused. Even though mothers and infants experience a separation at birth, the majority of them form a strong, healthy bond. Women who have older children and have to be separated from their premature infants seem to weather the separation better and quickly develop a strong bond to their infant.

The number of premature infants who are abused certainly suggests that removing the infant from the mother at birth can affect maternal bonding. There are other factors that might explain the mother's behavior toward her premature infant. Premature infants are not as responsive to their mothers. This may make it difficult for the mother to become involved. Premature infants tend to have shriller cries than full-term infants (Frodi & Lamb, 1978), again making them less lovable. Their small size means that premature infants require more care, need to eat more often, sleep less, and cry more than full-term infants. These difficulties associated with prematurity may be responsible for the high incidence of abuse and neglect—not the separation at birth that occurred between the mother and child.

Since the evidence from studying premature infants can be interpreted in several ways, Klaus and Kennell tried to assess the effect of separations in a different way. They looked at the circumstances surrounding the births of infants who were later rejected, abused, or failed to thrive. A sizable proportion of these children (between 13 and 41 percent) had experienced a separation at birth (Klaus & Kennell, 1982). These results reinforce the view that the circumstances surrounding the birth are an important factor in the mother-infant bond, and that separations are a factor in some abuse and neglect.

These studies suggested to Klaus and Kennell that parents and infants should not be separated at birth. Instead, everything possible should be done during the birth to foster the bond between parents and their newborns. With this in mind, Klaus and Kennell decided to let mothers spend a little extra time with their infants in the delivery room. When they were observed 12 hours later, mothers who were allowed to hold their infants shortly after birth spent more time kissing their babies, looking at them, and playing intimate touching games (Klaus & Kennell, 1976). Presumably, the bonding experience right after delivery hastened the mothers' ability to interact lovingly with their infants.

This somewhat surprising result has now been replicated by dozens of investigators all asking the same questions. Does additional time for close contact during the first minutes, hours, and days of life alter the quality of the mother-infant bond? Mothers given more contact have been found to nurse their babies for longer periods of time (Sosa, Klaus, Kennell, & Urrutia, 1976; Thomson, Hartsock, & Larson, 1979), soothe their infants more, hold their babies *en face* more, kiss them, look at them, and maintain more physical contact than mothers who experienced the regular hospital routine (Klaus & Kennell, 1982). Not every study has found these kinds of effects. Marilyn Svejda and her co-workers videotaped mothers interacting with their infants 36 hours after the birth. They found no differences between mothers who were given extra contact and mothers who were not (Svejda, Campos, & Emde, 1980). Klaus and Kennell point out, however, that all of the mothers in this study were given at least five minutes with their infant immediately after delivery.

Extra contact certainly may make an immediate difference in how mothers interact with their infants, but does this minor alteration have any influence after the neonatal period? Long-term follow-up studies report that small differences persist between mothers who were given more contact and those who were not. Four months after the birth, Siegel and his associates visited the homes of mothers who had early contact with their infants at birth and mothers who did not. The early contact mothers were more accepting of their infants and consoled their infants more than control mothers (Siegel, Bauman, Schaefer, Saunders, & Ingram, 1980). Even two years after the birth, early contact mothers conversed with their children more, and their children had better language skills than mothers who did not have the special contact (Ringler, Trause, Klaus, & Kennell, 1978). These findings add credence to the belief that there is a period in the first days of life that is optimal for fostering a bond between mother and child. The bond meshes with other parenting behaviors and hence can continue to influence the child.

The bond formed at birth might alter some destructive patterns of parenting. O'Connor and his associates examined the effect that extended contact at birth had on the parenting of 277 lower class mothers who were delivering their first child. After 17 months, 10 of the women who had not been allowed extra contact with their infants had abused or neglected their children. Only two of the mothers with more contact had similar disruptions in their parenting behavior (O'Connor, Vietze, Sherrod, Sandler, & Altemeier, 1980).

Not everyone shares Klaus and Kennell's enthusiasm. Michael Lamb (1982c) believes that giving the parents an opportunity to be with their newborn adds a humanizing element to the birth. But he finds no support for long-term effects of bonding. Other investigators acknowledge a minor role for early contact in maternal attachment, but emphasize the importance of social variables such as economic status, race, education, and age (Leiderman, 1981). Klaus and Kennell concur that these social variables are important. They point out, however, that you cannot change the age or race of the mother. You can change whether or not a mother and her infant are allowed time at birth to form a bond.

At the beginning of this discussion, four conclusions about the importance of bonding at birth were listed. After reviewing the evidence concerned with humans, we can conclude that extra contact at birth enhances maternal behavior toward the child, and separation at birth is associated with more difficulties in the mother-child relationship. We can also conclude that separations occurring immediately after birth have the strongest effects. Whether or not there is a specific length of time that a human can endure a separation is not clear from the information that we have. Many mothers are separated from their infants for weeks but forge a strong bond once their infants come home. Finally, Klaus and Kennell argue that if the separation extends beyond the sensitive period, the effects on mothering behavior are drastic and irreversible. The information we have suggests that this is generally not true for the human species (Lamb, 1982c). Adopting parents have had no contact with their children at birth. In most cases, these parents become very attached and committed to their children.

Although the conclusions drawn by Klaus and Kennell have been qualified, their studies helped focus attention on the effects of minor procedural changes in the delivery process. Isolation used to be a standard part of the hospital birth. Infants were regarded as especially vulnerable to infection and were practically barricaded in the newborn nursery. Rooming-in, the practice of having the mother and infant together, was absolutely forbidden. Parents and families were the source of germs, and hence only short peeks at their infant through a glass window were allowed.

We now know that rather than being the source of infection, contact with mothers helps infants resist infection (see Figure 4–6). In Guatamala prior to 1976, all premature and *Caesarean section* babies were kept in a central nursery. The infant mortality rate hovered around 17 deaths per 1,000 births. Most of these deaths were the result of infection. A major earthquake destroyed some of the health facilities, and the overcrowding that resulted led to a change in the hospital's policy—babies were kept with their mothers. Even though the mothers' beds were crowded closely together, the infant mortality

**Figure 4—6**                     **Incidence of infection**

| | 1975* | 1976 | 1977 | 1978 |
|---|---|---|---|---|
| Live births | 8,456 | 12,500 | 14,094 | 14,302 |
| Infection rate† | 17 | 3 | 2 | 3 |

Rooming-in

The incidence of infection in full-term infants before rooming-in was allowed and after rooming in was allowed.

*From Urrutia, J. J., Sosa, R., Kennell, J. H., & Klaus, M. H. (1980). Ciba Foundation Symposium, 77, Excerpta Medica, 171–186.
†Per thousand.

rate due to infection dropped to 2 to 3 per 1,000 births (Urrutia, Sosa, Kennell, & Klaus, 1980). Contact with the mother decreased the infants' susceptibility to infection.

In a poor Guatemalan Indian village, the home births were monitored for eight years. During this period, there was not a single case of a serious skin infection even though the hygienic conditions were poor. In Guatemala City, many newborns discharged from sterile hospitals contracted serious skin infections. All of them had been separated from their mothers for the first 12 hours. Allowing the mother and child to be together seems to infuse the child with the mother's harmless bacteria and protects the baby from the more dangerous hospital bacteria.

Despite these studies, hospitals were reluctant to allow mothers in the nursery for premature babies. In the 1970s, when it was shown that isolating these infants might actually decrease their chances of surviving, the barricades began to fall. Premature nurseries now encourage mothers and fathers to come in and care for their child. When premature infants are touched, rocked, fondled, or cuddled daily, they have fewer respiratory problems, gain weight faster, and show cognitive advances that last months after they are discharged from the hospital (Barnard, 1975; Leib, Benfield, & Guidubaldi, 1980; Scarr-Salapatek & Williams, 1973). Mothers and fathers can take over these aspects of their child's care and at the same time begin the process of attaching to their infant.

**The transition to parenthood.** Becoming parents for the first time constitutes a major transition in the lives of adults. As with any major change, there is a feeling of insecurity and a period of searching before the mother, father, and baby establish a comfortable relationship as a family.

Assuming the role of father or mother adds a new dimension to the adult's identity. Women grappling with their new role report feeling unprepared for the role of mother. They express anxiety about their ability to hold a wriggling baby or comfort a crying one. Fathers express concern about their ability to provide for the baby. They also report being worried about their wives during delivery. In addition to these concerns about their ability to function in their

### Parents in the modern premature nursery

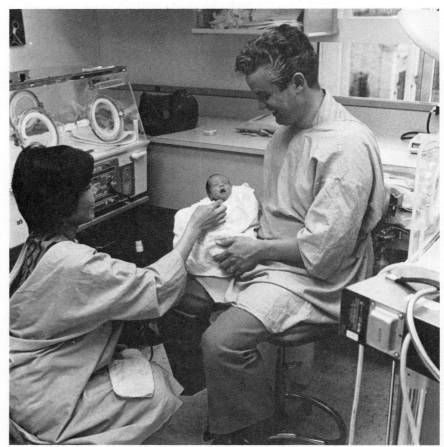

Fredrick D. Bodin: Stock, Boston

Mothers and fathers are encouraged to come to the premature nursery to care for their infants. Within a few days, parents can take over some of the care of the infant and begin to build an attachment.

new role, adults must deal with a host of new issues when they become parents for the first time. They must take a stance on a variety of child-rearing questions. They must make decisions about who will care for the child. Many of these decisions have a financial impact on the family. What happens if the wife quits her job? If both parents continue to work, who will care for the child? These kinds of decisions as well as the actual arrival of the baby alter the lifestyle of the couple.

The role of parent has to mesh with the role of spouse and with the career roles that each parent has. Psychologists studying the impact that the first child has on a couple's relationship report that parenthood can precipitate a crisis in the couple's relationship (Feldman, 1981). Carolyn Cowan and her colleagues found that the arrival of the first child alters the couple's sex life, changes their patterns of communication, and decreases the amount of time that they spend together (Cowan, Cowan, Coie, & Coie, 1978). The attention that is showered on the child can make either the husband or wife feel jealous or abandoned. Many of these changes result directly from the inordinate amount of time spent caring for a child during the first weeks of life. Adding both the husband's and wife's hours, Cowan et al. (1978) found that new parents spent between 70 and 174 hours a week caring for their new baby.

Parenthood also pushes the couple toward more traditional roles. Despite plans to divide the parenting chores equitably, most couples report that within a few weeks women are doing the majority of the child care and men are becoming more dominant in tasks outside the home. Giving up their equalitarian ideals can cause conflict and feelings of betrayal.

Women often make an obvious adjustment in their careers. Going from full-time employment to part-time employment is very common. Many women take off a few months and then decide that they do not want to return to their jobs on a full-time basis. The adjustments women make can be seen in their assessments of their lives. The role of mother assumes more and more importance during the first months of a child's life. Ancillary roles like consumer and friend tend to decrease in importance.

The impact of the child on the couple is not entirely negative. Surviving the early months often strengthens the bond between the couple. Seeing their spouse succeed in the parent role kindles new admiration and respect for their mate. The responsibility of being parents sometimes helps adults mature.

Whether the transition to parenthood is a time of crisis or growth seems to depend on the factors that surround each couple. Becoming parents for the first time certainly increases physical and psychological vulnerability. There is little doubt that several aspects of the transition are experienced as stressful. Cowan et al. suggest that the need for support is as important in this transition as it is at other major life transitions, such as divorce or retirement. She and her colleagues also argue that more preparation for the stressful aspects of parenthood would help couples cope.

## THE NEWBORN INFANT

**Apgar scores**

At one minute and five minutes after birth, the baby receives its first evaluation—the Apgar score. Developed by Virginia Apgar (1953), this scale was designed to help physicians communicate about a newborn's condition in a uniform way. The Apgar score is derived from five different measures (see Figure 4–7). On each measure the baby can receive a score of 0, 1, or 2. A total of 9 or over is considered a normal score, and there are many perfect 10s in the delivery room. A score of 7 or below causes concern, because it means that the baby is depressed on several indices. Often a baby's one-minute Apgar score will be lower than the five-minute score. During the four minutes be-

**Figure 4—7**    **The Apgar score**

| What is tested | Points given | | |
|---|---|---|---|
| | **0** | **1** | **2** |
| Heart rate | Absent | Below 100 beats per minute | 100 beats per minute or more |
| Breathing | Absent | Slow or irregular | Regular |
| Skin color | Blue | Body pink, extremities blue | Pink all over |
| Muscle tone | Limp | Some movements | Active movements |
| Reflex response | Absent | Grimace only | Cry |

The Apgar score is an evaluation of the infant on five measures. These measures are assessed immediately after birth and again five minutes after birth.

Source: Kitzinger, S. (1981). *The complete book of pregnancy and childbirth* (p. 280). New York: Alfred A. Knopf.

tween scores, many babies turn pink and their breathing becomes more regular. Apgar scores make the doctor's assessments of the baby more specific. It's the difference between saying, "it's really hot" and saying, "it's 105." Having specific scores also enables investigators to do follow-ups and compare infants.

For example, in 1981 a report was issued about the effects of smoking habits on the pregnancies of 43,000 women. If mothers smoked, their infants were likely to have lower Apgar scores. This effect was especially marked in infants of black mothers. Fifty percent of black women who smoked more than two packs of cigarettes a day had infants with Apgar scores of 7 or below (Garn, Johnston, Ridella, & Petzold, 1981). Fortunately for their infants, black women smoke less than white women. In any case, this large-scale study demonstrates how Apgar scores can be used to determine the effects of nicotine, alcohol, medication, or fetal monitoring on the newborn.

Apgar scores also provide some information about future development. Infants with scores between 0 and 3 are not very likely to survive. Those who do survive have a higher incidence of *cerebral palsy* and often suffer hearing and speech difficulties. However, low Apgar scores are not always associated with developmental problems. Eighty percent of the infants who survived were neurologically normal at seven years of age (Nelson & Ellenberg, 1981). Apgar scores have also been used to predict intelligence later in life. As expected, children with low Apgar scores had lower intelligence scores at eight months of age (Serunian & Broman, 1975). Apgar scores, however, did not predict intelligence at three or four years of age (Shipe, Vandenberg & Williams, 1968; Broman, Nichols, & Kennedy, 1975). Apgar scores are probably a good predictor of a child's functioning for a few months, but several years later, the nutrition, stimulation, and the emotional support that the child receives override the Apgar score.

## Neurological evaluations

The Apgar score is just one evaluation that infants have early in life. During the first hour, newborns will also be weighed, their head circumference measured, and their total length recorded. Often with the baby still at the mother's side, the doctor will begin a more complete examination—checking the genitals, listening to the baby's heart, feeling the abdomen for size and placement of major organs, rotating the legs, checking the mouth to make sure the palate is formed correctly, and feeling the skull bones on the infant's head. This examination is really just an inspection and is designed to alert physicians to any problems that might require medical attention.

A day or two after birth, a more complete and systematic neurological examination is usually performed. Sensory systems like hearing and vision are checked, and the neurological functioning of the neonate is assessed. Certain reflexes are expected to be present at birth. The *moro reflex* is tested by making infants feel that they are being dropped or by startling the infant. In Figure 4–8, the infant's head is lifted just a bit, then the support is relaxed. The infant responds by flinging both arms apart and then bringing them back together. After the first few months, this reflex should gradually disappear. If it does not, there may be some neurological problem.

Newborns form tight little fists around anything that is put into their hands. This "grasping reflex" or "palmar reflex" is often maintained for short periods if the infant is lifted.

The strength of the sucking reflex is also checked. By two months of age, this reflex is considerably modified. Weak sucking at birth may indicate neurological abnormalities. Many reflexes may be somewhat weaker than normal if the mother received medication during the delivery.

Often mothers will show off their newborns by having them demonstrate their ability to "walk." When held in a standing position and moved slowly forward, an infant will alternately lift and place both feet. This is the "walking reflex."

The tonic neck reflex is more easily shown than described (see Figure 4–8). Infants turn their heads to one side and then extend the arm and leg on that same side of the body. The other arm and leg remain flexed. The pose is sometimes described as the fencing position.

The assessment of reflexes is really only meaningful if reflexes are abnormal or weak. By definition, reflexes do not require cognitive control. However, reflexes probably form the foundation for motor skills that the child does not yet control (Zelazo, 1976). The tonic neck reflex, for example, turns the head in the direction of the outstretched hand. This reflex biases the development of eye-hand coordination. Thus, the tonic neck reflex can be used to predict handedness in infants. The fact that the tonic neck reflex can predict handedness is one example of how reflexes become coordinated into more purposive patterns of reaching and grasping.

It would be helpful if assessments of the newborn included some higher level functioning or neurological organization. Terry Brazelton, a pediatrician from

**Figure 4—8**                    **The newborn's reflexes**

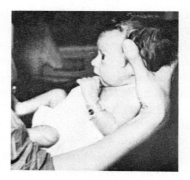 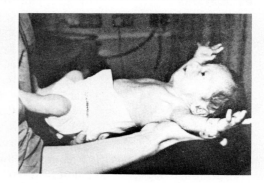
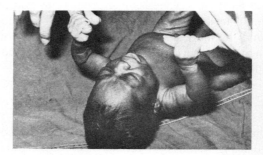 

The infant comes equipped with a set of reflexes that are routinely evaluated during the first few days of life.

Source: Dubowitz, L. & Dubowitz, V. (1981). *The neurological assessment of the preterm and full-term infant* (pp. 35, 38). Philadelphia: J. B. Lippincott.

From Burton L. White, *Human infants: Experience and psychological development* (1971). Used with the permission of the author and Prentice-Hall, Inc.

Harvard, has tried to accomplish this in his Brazelton Neonatal Behavioral Scale by including items that require some cognitive responses by the infant. Can the infant turn his head toward a shaking rattle or a ringing bell? Can the infant focus on and follow a large, colorful ball or toy? When a light or a sound is presented repeatedly, does the infant show alert attention initially and less attention after several repetitions? The infant's responses to items like these are more indicative of higher level functioning than are reflexes. Even so, the correlation of Brazelton scores with later functioning is far from perfect.

After screening thousands of infants, doctors found 53 that were called "neurologically suspect" at three days of age. These infants had been given the

Brazelton twice during the first week of life. When they were seven years old, these children were reexamined for neurological abnormalities. At that time, 38 of the children were pronounced normal and 15 were confirmed as neurologically handicapped. How well did the Brazelton scale succeed in finding the 15 children who were neurologically impaired? The Brazelton identified 12 as abnormal when they were only two to six days old. Unfortunately the scale identified nine other normal children as abnormal, and it did not identify three who were impaired. Even though Brazelton's measure identified many of the impaired children, the false alarm rate of 24 percent is worrisome (Als, Tronick, Lester, & Brazelton, 1979).

The problem of predicting neurological traits using infant assessments is a common one and cannot be easily solved. How do you measure something that is present only in a rudimentary way? One professor suggested that measuring cognitive skills in a newborn is like trying to predict how heavy a man's beard will be when he is only four days old. The intellectual processes that you want to measure are not present.

There is still another problem. Physicians are more interested in physical outcomes and symptoms. Psychologists are more interested in behavioral functions and cognitive performance. Neonatal assessments of functioning may not correlate with later physical symptoms, but they may predict poor school achievement or problems in attention. Both psychologists and physicians will continue to look for ways to predict later functioning. Identifying the problem early would help solve the problem or alleviate the condition. Yet the search may continue to be a frustrating one. As the child grows, many of the physical variables that you would expect to relate to later behavior are overshadowed by social variables. The increasing importance of the social milieu has been documented in the Kauai study.

**Kauai study**

In 1955, all the families of children born on the island of Kauai were asked to participate in a study that began during pregnancy and continued until the children were 18 years old. Approximately 700 families were studied. The children consisted of Japanese, Filipinos, Hawaiians, and many families of mixed heritage. Half of the fathers were skilled or semiskilled laborers. Many of the mothers had less than eight years of education.

The study followed children who had some breathing problems during their delivery, a time that is also referred to as the *perinatal period*. Investigators divided their subjects into groups according to perinatal stress. At birth 31 percent of the children had some minor complications, 10 percent had more involved problems, and 3 percent experienced serious stress during labor and delivery. These three groups of children were evaluated extensively at 1, 2, 10, and 18 years of age (Werner & Smith, 1979).

By 10 years of age, the children who experienced minor complications could not be differentiated from those whose pregnancy, labor, and birth were routine. Those with moderate birth complications, and especially the group with serious birth problems, still differed on some measures of adjustment and intelligence.

What happened to the infants during birth was not as important as what happened to them at home. The highest proportion of children with adjustment problems at age 10 came from unstable homes that did not provide the child with emotional support during the first two years of life. In other words, if the only information you had was information about the child's home environment, you would do a better job of predicting the child's intelligence and adjustment at age 10 than if you knew whether the child had suffered perinatal stress.

The same pattern was reported when the children turned 18 (see Figure 4–9). Seventy-nine percent of the children who suffered severe perinatal stress still had a host of problems. The incidence of mental retardation was 10 times greater than for the rest of the group. Twenty percent of the children had been in trouble with the authorities, and many continued to be handicapped by physical problems. The majority of those subjected to moderate perinatal stress were free of serious physical, learning, or behavioral problems by 18. The mildly stressed group had no more problems than the control group (Werner & Smith, 1977).

This study documents the ability of most children to overcome birth complications and develop normally. Through two decades of studying this sample, the authors find that if children had a stable home life they were less likely to have adjustment problems regardless of whether they experienced perinatal stress. Unstable and chaotic family life combined with perinatal stress to produce the largest deficits. Except for those infants who had serious complications

**Figure 4–9**  **The Kauai study**

| Problems | Total 1955 cohort (N = 698) | Youths with moderate perinatal stress (N = 69) | Youths with severe perinatal stress (n = 14) |
|---|---|---|---|
| All significant problems | 36.0% | 33.0% | 79.0% |
| Mental retardation | 3.0 | 6.0 | 29.0 |
| Significant physical handicaps | 6.0 | 6.0 | 14.5 |
| Significant mental health problems (schizoid, paranoid, obsessive-compulsive) | 3.0 | 9.0 | 14.5 |
| Delinquency | 15.0 | 17.0 | 21.5 |
| Teenage pregnancies | 6.0 (of females) | 14.0 (of females) | 0 |

The Kauai study followed children with moderate and severe perinatal stress for 18 years. The investigators traced the effects of birth stress, home stability, emotional support, and the temperaments of the children on later adjustment.

Source: Werner, E. E., & Smith, R. S. (1979). An epidemiologic perspective on some antecedents and consequences of childhood mental health problems and learning disabilities. *Journal of the American Academy of Child Psychiatry, 18,* p. 296.

at birth, the short- and long-term impact of the home environment appears to be more powerful than the residual effects of the birth complications.

A low standard of living was associated with both biological stress and family instability. The instability and stress, rather than the poverty, led to persistent behavioral and learning problems. Poverty alone did not create problems. The overwhelming majority of the children who were poor "coped very effectively in the second decade of their lives; few committed any delinquent acts, or presented achievement or discipline problems in school, or were in need of mental health services by the time they reached the threshold of adulthood" (Werner & Smith, 1979, p. 304).

The conclusions in the Kauai study are that mild insults at birth are overcome rather rapidly; moderate insults can usually be overcome by a stable home environment and emotional support from the parents. Severe insults are likely to take their toll regardless of social factors or psychological support.

**Premature infants**

Another group that experiences difficulty during birth is the premature child. The follow-ups on these children are extensive (Friedman & Sigman, 1981). Physicians, parents, and psychologists are interested in the long-term effects of being born too soon or too small. Like the Kauai study, one has to differentiate between groups. All children weighing less than 2,500 grams (about 5½ pounds) and born three weeks before term are considered premature. There is, however, a substantial difference between a 2,500-gram baby born at 37 weeks and a 1,000-gram baby (about 2.2 pounds) born at 27 weeks.

Very premature infants, those weighing less than 1,500 grams (3.3 pounds), did not survive until recently. At major medical centers, about 80 percent of these children now survive (Hunt, 1981). Are these children irreparably damaged, or do they have some hope for a normal life? Jane Hunt has followed some of these babies with very low birth weights for eight years. At four years of age, about two thirds of the children were in the normal or superior range of intellectual functioning, and about one third were below normal. The four children with the lowest IQs were born before 1969. Since then, better medical care has not only helped these infants survive, but has helped them retain their intellectual capacities.

At eight years of age, these children with very low birth weights were tested again using a different test. In the new test, there were some problems that required the coordination and integration of visual information. The children had to arrange cartoon-like pictures so that they told a story. They also had to arrange red and white blocks into a particular pattern. Many of the children had difficulty with these new tasks and hence scored lower overall than they had when they were four. Hunt (1981) concludes that approximately 4 out of 10 infants with birth weights below 1,500 grams will experience significant developmental problems in childhood. But she also comments that since her follow-up of premature infants, medical care has improved and that future studies might find a larger percentage of these infants performing normally.

## THE CHILD SAVERS
*By Robin Marantz Henig*

One thousand grams is about the weight of three good-sized grapefruits, a typical Sunday newspaper or two dense loaves of bread. And it's about the weight of the human being that was presented to Roni Handler last Halloween as her first baby, a boy.

"The doctors and nurses didn't think the baby would come out in one piece," says Mrs. Handler, 25, who went into labor in the 26th week of her first pregnancy—more than three months before her due date. But he came out pink, breathing and weighing 2 pounds 1 ounce. And he was a boy. All I had wanted was a boy. We were ecstatic.

The months to follow were grueling ones for Roni and Scott Handler and their new son, Zachary. During 12 weeks in the intensive-care nursery of Children's Hospital National Medical Center in Washington, Zachary rode the roller coaster of prognoses that plagues so many of the babies born too early or too small. He had a little bit of everything, lung problems, a few days on a mechanical ventilator, a suspected hemorrhage in his brain, a bout with an intestinal disorder and episodes of dangerously depressed breathing. But he survived each crisis and he grew. By January he weighed nearly five pounds, and the hospital sent him home.

Zachary is a miracle baby. His survival represents one of the proudest advances in neonatology, the subspecialty of newborn care formally recognized by the American Academy of Pediatrics. But it also represents neonatology's Achilles' heel: As ever younger babies with ever-more-fragile organ systems are saved, more are leaving the intensive care nursery with medical and psychological problems left in part by the very technology that saved them.

As recently as the mid 1970s most babies of Zachary's size died and 15 percent of those who lived suffered handicaps. But today the odds of survival—and intact survival—have shifted to Zachary's side. The best neonatology units in the country can save 80 to 85 percent of the infants born weighing 1,000 to 1,500 grams (2.2–3.2 pounds). Even more remarkable, 50 to 60 percent of the babies weighing 750 to 1,000 grams at birth (1.6–2.2 pounds) survive, too.

Of the 39,000 infants born each year weighing less than 1,500 grams, roughly 13,000 die, and 3,000 are seriously damaged. Another 4,000 are moderately impaired. Is this too high a price to pay for the 19,000 normal healthy babies?

Her prediction was confirmed in 1982 when a group from USC reported that 69 percent of their very premature infants were developing normally (Teberg, Wu, Hodgman, Mich, Garfinkle, Azen, & Wingert, 1982).

Another study followed children who weighed between 1,500 and 2,500 grams at birth. On verbal tasks, their IQ scores at nine years of age did not differ from children of normal weight. However, these children showed the same deficit in visual tasks as the infants with very low birth weights. Contrary to expectations, the most important predictor of overall intelligence at nine years of age was not the birth weight of the child, but the mother's IQ and social class (Caputo, Goldstein, & Taub, 1981).

In the Kauai study of perinatal stress, we saw that severe stress was still evident in behavior at 10 and 18 years of age. Moderate stress tended to be overshadowed by the stability of the family and whether or not they were supportive. The same conclusions apply to premature infants. Infants with very low birth weights have developmental problems that continue into middle childhood. In children in an intermediate category, the mother's intelligence and social class begin to assume more importance than whether or not the infant was premature. Mild and moderate insults during labor and delivery cause justifiable concern. However, by the time the child is of school age, the problems of labor and delivery are just one factor that can contribute to a child's personal and social adjustment and his or her success in school (Sameroff, 1981).

## SUMMARY

The process of birth, from the beginning hormonal triggers to the delivery of the placenta, has been studied in great detail. Many of the physiological aspects of birth are understood and can even be imitated by physicians. The physical process is only one part of the wonder of birth. The psychological and social factors that were not considered important a few years ago are receiving much more attention today. This attention is due, in part, to the success of natural childbirth.

Proponents of natural childbirth demonstrated convincingly that educating the mother about the birth, supporting her during labor, and giving her the means to control the discomfort of contractions had a positive effect on everyone. Now labors are shortened. Hence, birth complications are reduced. The mother's recovery is measured in hours rather than days. Infants are alert from the first breath and are able to begin forming bonds with their parents. Fathers have also benefited. When mothers were given a role in the birth, fathers were enlisted to help. Now births are a celebration of the renewal of life, and the family unit is the center of that life.

The formation of a loving family unit has its beginning during birth. The bond that develops between the mother and her specific infant is cemented during the period immediately following birth. Hence, contact between the mother and infant should be encouraged. In the case of premature infants, the effects of a separation can be minimized by encouraging the parents to visit the infant and become involved in its care. Parenthood is a major transition for adults. It can be a time of crisis or a time of growth. Support systems and preparation for their new role would help parents make the transition.

Psychologists who study children are concerned with how life's events shape the continuing development of the child. In the case of birth, we want to know if prematurity, medication, perinatal stress, and other problems will continue to play a major role in the child's life. Although it is difficult to summarize the many aspects of birth that could affect later development, it seems that the events of birth are only important for the short-term unless they either affect the basic systems of the child or become intertwined with new phases of development.

Severe trauma during birth has a continuing effect on the child because of the damage to the organism. Less severe effects can influence development especially if they combine with other negative factors like an unstable home or lack of emotional support. If the home is stable and the parents are supportive, the effects of many birth complications are overcome by middle childhood.

# P A R T   2

Infancy

**The brain**

Parts of the brain
Development of the brain
Organization of the brain

**Processes modifying the brain**

Plasticity of the brain
Stimulation of the brain
Restricting sensory experiences
Humans who experience deprivation
Brain development and behavior
Hormones
Nutrition

**The organization of the brain prejudices behavior**

States—the basic rest-activity cycle
Hemispheric specialization
Sudden infant death syndrome
Biologically based sex differences
Ethnic differences

**Infant feeding practices**

Breast-feeding
Obesity

**Physical development**

Human growth
Motor skills

**Summary**

# CHAPTER 5
# The organization of behavior

John Locke characterized the human infant at birth as a *tabula rasa*, a blank slate, ready to record the experiences of life. This concept was challenged even in the 17th century by those who believed that children's development progressed in a similar and orderly fashion despite very different experiences. In this debate, the arguments between Locke and his detractors were largely philosophical. The biological evidence to refute Locke's concept of the newborn was not available. That evidence is now available, and it indicates that infants have a complex, if immature, cerebral organization that guides their interaction with the environment.

Trying to understand development without some understanding of this organization is an indirect endorsement of the view that biology is of no consequence in development. Psychologists are committed to deciphering behavior, and this includes understanding the biological underpinnings of behavior. Knowing how the brain develops, what the important systems are, and how structures vary from one individual to another should provide us with important information. We need this information to help children learn efficiently, to devise the most appropriate materials and methods of instruction, and to optimize total development (Jeffrey, 1980).

Developmental psychologists have come to realize that we have much in common with colleagues in the neurosciences (Wittrock, 1980). By helping each other, we may find out what causes stuttering, why Johnny cannot read, whether stimulation alters a child's brain, and why one child excels at spatial tasks and another becomes a master violinist. We may even be able to prevent some of the fundamental problems of childhood—mental retardation, abnormal patterns of development, and degeneration of the nervous system (Lund, 1978).

In this chapter, then, the physical or biological aspects of the infant's behavior will be detailed. Special attention will be paid to describing how the brain is organized and how it guides, records, and is modified by the infant's everyday interchanges with the environment.

## THE BRAIN

At birth, the brain weighs about 350 grams (12 ounces) in a normal full-term infant. During the next two years, the period of infancy, the brain's

**Figure 5—1**                          **Cortex of the brain**

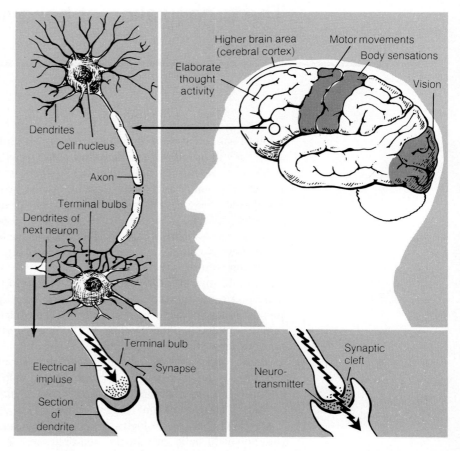

The brain with a section of the cerebral cortex enlarged to show the neurons. The main parts of the neuron are the dendrites, the axon, and the synapses. This system permits rapid, accurate communication to all parts of the human body.

Source: McMahon, F. B., & McMahon, J. L. (1982). *Psychology: The hybrid science.* (p. 38). Homewood, IL: Dorsey Press.

weight triples (Conel, 1939–1967). Since the behavioral changes of infancy and the changes in the child's brain go hand in hand, we need to begin our study of infancy with a description of the brain and its major components (see Figure 5–1).

**Parts of the brain**          The *cortex*, from the Greek word meaning bark, is the outer covering of the brain and in evolutionary terms, it is the newest part of the brain. Although less than one eighth of an inch thick (2.5 millimeters), the cortex contains billions of *neurons*. These neurons are essentially the grand control center for human behavior.

Communication is the basic mission of the central nervous system. In complex organisms, such as humans, there must be a command center that filters input from all of the senses, makes decisions about appropriate actions, and carries out those decisions. Our eyes absorb the information that there is a car coming at us. Our brain decides where we should jump. Our legs carry out the decision. The neuron is the intermediary that relays the information from our eyes to the cortex of the brain, and then relays the decision from the cortex to our legs (Kimble, 1977). The speed and accuracy of the relays are essential for our survival. If our neural pathways were not coordinated, we might hear something and not know where to look to see it. The neural communication system must be very flexible in addition to being fast and accurate.

Neurons have three major parts—axons, *dendrites*, and synaptic endings (see Figure 5–1). The dendrites are the sentries for the neurons. They pick up information from other neurons. When the stimulation or information that the sentry receives reaches a certain level, it tells the neuron, and the neuron is activated. That is, it fires. An impulse then travels along the *axon* to the other end of the neuron where the impulse is transmitted to other neurons via a *synapse*. This pattern of communication is repeated over thousands of neurons until the appropriate action has been taken or until the stimulation stops. This quick and oversimplified description of how neurons transmit information will serve as a foundation for our discussion of brain development.

## Development of the brain

All living things change during development, and the brain is no exception. The changes in the brain are accomplished by three basic processes—cell division, cell migration and specification, and cell death.

**Cell division.** The human brain requires a minimum of 10 billion cells to perform its communication and control functions. Forming that many cells cannot be accomplished overnight. One estimate is that neurons in the human brain must be generated at the rate of 250,000 per minute during the last months of pregnancy (Cowan, 1979). In most mammals, the growth spurt of the brain lasts a few days. But in humans, cell division continues from about 20 weeks of gestation to approximately one year of age (Hofer, 1981). Within this period, the most accelerated growth takes place immediately before and after birth (Dobbing & Sands, 1979). This long period of maturation and growth after birth accounts for our large and complex brains. It also explains why there is so much plasticity in the human. At birth, the brain still has a lot of growing to do. If birth complications have not seriously damaged the brain, there is a good chance that the brain can repair and modify itself during the postnatal growth period. The fact that our brains grow so much is a tremendous advantage in some respects. But it also poses a few problems. The skull cannot be fused at birth or the brain's growth would be limited. Nature has accommodated the brain's needs by leaving spaces between our skull bones.

In humans, these bones are not completely fused until adulthood (Hofer, 1981).

**Cell migration and specification.**   The formation of the brain has been compared to the process of colonizing a new territory by a tribe of settlers (Hofer, 1981). Each neuron or settler has a journey to make which is called, appropriately enough, cell migration. As the neurons begin to migrate, they stay in contact with other "settlers" and head for a certain spot. It is important to note that more neurons are made than there are homesteads, and only those neurons that successfully establish a territory survive.

Staking out a territory for each neuron is part of the process of cell specification. Each cell has a particular job to perform, and groups of cells become organized into hierarchical systems in the brain so they can communicate quickly and perform their collective jobs efficiently (Hofer, 1981). After each neuron has established its territory, it begins to mature, developing an axon and dendrites (see Figure 5–1). Dendrites and the dendritic spines that form on each branch of the neuron are an indication of the settler's ability to communicate with others. Mature neurons with well developed dendritic systems can be in touch with hundreds of other neurons (see Figure 5–2).

**Cell death.**   Even before cell division and cell migration are completed in the brain, the number of nerve cells begins to decline (Hofer, 1981). Cell death is actually a positive process early in the development of the brain. The

**Figure 5–2**                    **Synapses of the brain**

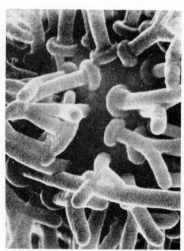

*United Press International Photo*

The dendritic network is so complex that a single neuron can receive messages from literally hundreds of other cells. The illustration shows several synapses of a tiny area of the brain.

development of many structures and tissues in the brain is sculptured by selective cell death. Depending on the area of the brain, between 15 percent and 50 percent of the original neurons are weeded out by cell death (Cowan, 1979). Cell death also selectively destroys neurons that have migrated to the wrong place. This decline in neurons does not necessarily reduce the brain's communication system. Each established neuron sends out dozens of dendrites, and these dendrites produce hundreds of spines. The difference that dendrites and dendritic spines make in the communication of neurons is depicted in three views of the child's brain at different ages (see Figure 5–3). Three-month-olds have a lot of space between each neuron, and the dendrites linking them are limited. By 15 months of age, the interconnecting of the neurons through dendritic contacts is more developed. Few of the cells seem isolated. By two years of age, the number of neurons has decreased, but the intercommunication is enhanced by the vast network of dendrites and dendritic spines (Conel, 1939–1967).

**Figure 5–3**          **The development of neuronal networks in the brain**

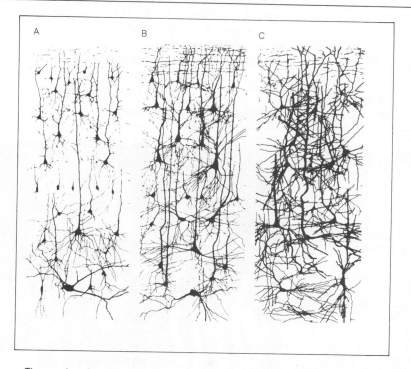

The newborn's neurons are isolated and interconnections are few. As the child developes, the neuronal networks become more extensive and behavior becomes more integrated: (a) three-month-old; (b) 15-month-old; (c) two-year-old.

Source: Conel, J. L. (1939–1967). *The postnatal development of the human cortex* (Vols. 1–8). Cambridge, MA: Harvard Univ. Press.

**Organization of the brain**

As neurons are established and their dendritic networks developed, impulses are carried from one neuron to another via chemical *neurotransmitters*. Neurotransmitters can simultaneously activate whole systems of the brain and inhibit others. Being able to inhibit parts of the brain is crucial to development. In the case of a two-month-old infant we will call Simone, the presentation of a familiar stuffed animal leads Simone to kick both legs, bat both arms alternately, open and close her mouth, and move her tongue in and out of her mouth. All the while the child's eyes are wild with excitement. By six months, Simone focuses on the toy, reaches one hand smoothly up, grabs the toy, and in the same motion, stuffs it into her mouth and begins sucking. One of the major differences between the two-month-old and the six-month-old is that at six months, the nervous system is more organized. Hence, the brain can identify the systems that are needed to perform the activity and inhibit those that are not. Another difference is that at six months, all of Simone's behaviors mesh smoothly. Seeing, grasping, and sucking are different, loosely connected systems in the two-month-old. By six months, the systems are integrated, and the action proceeds in one fluid motion.

At birth, the human infant's behavioral repertoire consists largely of reflexes and a few patterned behaviors like turning the head toward sound. During the first months of life, these reflexes become part of more complete brain circuits. If, in adulthood, the brain is injured, these infantile reflexes can reappear. The injury has damaged the communication between systems and disrupted the organization of the brain leaving the isolated reflex (Hofer, 1981).

**Figure 5—4**                     **The organization of the brain**

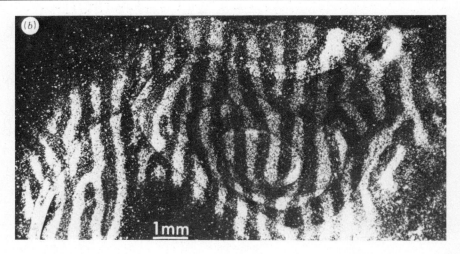

The visual cortex is organized into columns of cells that have related functions. The columns are indicated in this picture by the light and dark patterns.

Source: D. H. Hubel and T. N. Wiesel (1977) "Functional architecture of macaque monkey visual cortex," *In Proceedings of the Royal Society of London* B, Vol. 198 (pp. 1–59).

Throughout childhood, the nervous system forms more and more interconnections between neurons. As each network is formed and integrated with other networks, we can talk about the organization of behavior. Hubel and Weisel found an obvious organization in the brain. In their pioneering research, they actually showed how the cells in the visual cortex were organized into columns (see Figure 5–4). Further, they demonstrated that each column or arrangement of cells had a particular job to perform in the brain (Hubel & Weisel, 1979).

## PROCESSES MODIFYING THE BRAIN

**Plasticity of the brain**

The procedures that operate in forming and organizing the brain may seem rigid and predetermined, and some aspects of them are. There is, however, a great deal of flexibility or plasticity in the system. The ultimate organization of the brain is a function of the continuing transactions between these biological processes and external events. Nutrition, hormones, diseases, injuries, and the presence or lack of stimulation can potentially alter the organization of the brain. These events can influence the brain in three ways. They can simply *maintain* the biological processes that are typical of development, they can *facilitate* those processes, or they may actually *induce* neural development (Gottlieb, 1976). In subsequent sections, we will see that light is needed to just maintain the development of the visual system. Supernutrition during pregnancy not only maintains the normal level of cell division but facilitates the formation of cells. Providing a playground for rats actually induces new neural structures. Because of their ability to maintain, facilitate, or induce development of the brain, the external events that influence the organization of the brain deserve close scrutiny.

**Stimulation of the brain**

Rosenzweig, Krech, Bennett, and Diamond (1962) were the first to document the effects that a stimulating environment had on a rat's brain. Working at the University of California at Berkeley, these psychologists put one group, the isolates, into a standard laboratory cage. Another group, the social butterflies, had two playmates. A third group, the playground set, were placed in a 2 × 3 foot cage overflowing with playmates. Each day a new set of toys was put in the playground so the rats had ropes, ladders, steps, and inclined planes to play on. After just a few weeks, the rats in this complex cage had heavier brains with a thicker cortex, and their dendrites had more branches than either of the other groups of rats. These physical differences are only part of the story. The behavior of the playground set also changed. They solved mazes and complex learning problems better than rats who did not have a playground. These results were obtained quickly with young rats, but even middle-aged rats profited. After being in the playground, their brains showed more dendrites and dendritic spines. (Rosenzweig & Bennett, 1978).

These studies were the first to show that everyday experiences can be translated into physical structures in the brain. Since then, this line of research has been extended to include different animals and experiences. To see if the effects on the rats' brains could be enhanced even further by a more stimulating environment, Rosenzweig and his colleagues constructed a 30-foot square area with natural vegetation in which the animals could tunnel and behave like rats in the wild. This environment had an even more dramatic effect on the structure of the brain than the playground (Rosenzweig & Bennett, 1978).

Monkeys' brains are also susceptible to this kind of enrichment. Are humans'? It is very probable that the same processes operate. We do not know what constitutes an enriched environment and a deprived one for a human child. Probably the terms deprived and enriched are too global. We have to specify the experiences a child has in terms of the areas of the brain that are stimulated. Then we need to ask whether this area of the brain has enough stimulation to maintain its development, to facilitate its development, or to induce development. This is the case in Rosenzweig's work. Most of the effects of his playground and natural environments occur in a specific area of the brain and could probably be called inducing effects. As we shall see in ensuing chapters, there have been a great many attempts to systematically enrich the environments of humans. However, for obvious reasons, none of these have included any structural assessments of the children's brains.

Stimulation is seen as a factor that facilitates and even induces neural development. Stimulation can be carried too far. If animals are constantly in a lighted environment, their visual system will not develop normally (Riesen, 1982). Other experiences such as constant sound or rocking might also have a negative effect on the organization of the brain. The effects of overstimulation are just beginning to be studied. The effects of a lack of stimulation, however, are well known.

**Restricting sensory experiences**

Kittens who are raised in the dark and then brought into the light have difficulty seeing. They collide with chairs, walk over edges, and cannot touch toys that they see (Hein, Vital-Durand, Salinger, & Diamond, 1979). Similarly, raising monkeys in the dark sharply and permanently reduces their ability to see clearly (Riesen, 1982). When animals are raised in the dark, their neurons are deprived of all stimulation. Hence, instead of growing dendrites and dendritic spines, the cells atrophy and die. The lack of stimulation from light not only causes cells to degenerate, but affects the whole organization of the visual system (LeVay, Wiesel, & Hubel, 1980). We can see these effects most clearly by looking at experiments in which just one eye was kept closed for a few weeks. Neurons that would normally be stimulated by the closed eye died. The neurons receiving stimulation from the one open eye took over more space. However, the blindness that results from closing one eye can be reversed. To accomplish this, you have to close the experienced eye and let the neurons in the other eye establish some territory (Hofer, 1981). Children who wear eye patches to correct visual deficits are hoping for the same results. The eye patch is supposed to eliminate the strong eye as a competitor and give the weak eye time to strengthen its neural connections.

The same principles that apply to kittens raised in the dark also apply to humans who have congenital cataracts and have their sight restored surgically. When their bandages are first removed, they cannot see the difference between an orange and a banana even though their vision is fine from an optical stand-point. They know the differences by touch; but their experiences with touching have not been integrated with vision. Like the kittens raised in the dark, they remain blind until they are able to integrate what they see with their other senses (von Senden, 1960).

von Senden reports on a 10-year-old girl who had some vision until age seven, when she became completely blind. When her cataracts were removed three years later, this was her reaction:

> She behaved exactly as before the operation, and so could still be regarded as blind. One could pass large, bright objects before her eyes without pro-ducing the slightest effort to focus them. She behaved as though completely blind, bumped into everything, would only move forward groping cautiously with outstretched hands and dragging her feet on the floor. Left to herself, she sat listlessly in her chair for hours at a time, face expressionless, head bent slightly forward and looking directly to the ground; even working with her hands produced no change in the direction of her gaze. (von Senden, 1960, p. 239)

Results like these have led psychologists to suggest that these patients are cortically blind. Their vision is normal, but some changes at higher cortical levels have taken place that render the visual cues uninterpretable (Allik & Valsiner, 1980).

To summarize, sensory experiences and events in the external world help organize the brain in four different ways. First, simple sensory events such as the presence of light maintain the normal development of that area of the brain. Second, sensory experience is necessary to establish each cell's territory and to encourage the growth of dendrites. Third, experience helps determine which nerve networks will function efficiently. The old adage practice makes perfect applies to neural pathways, because repeatedly activating one neural pathway means that information is transmitted more efficiently. Finally, the pathways that are established tend to inhibit other pathways from operating (Hofer, 1981). The development of the brain is not a rigid, lockstep process that proceeds independently of experience. Both simple and complex experi-ences play a central role in defining the ultimate organization of the brain.

**Humans who experience deprivation**

Pecos Bill, Disney's legendary character, fell out of his parents' covered wagon and was raised by coyotes. In the legend, Pecos grows up to be the "roughest, toughest critter" around. He does not suffer any ill effects because of his unusual parents. In cases not conceived in Disney's imagination, the results are quite different. The Wild Boy of Aveyron is one of several wild *feral* children discovered in previous centuries who lived and foraged in the woods, isolated from humans.

When the Wild Boy of Aveyron was first befriended by a psychologist, he could not communicate even with signs or gestures. He was given to bursts of laughter followed immediately by profound depression. He walked and ran on all fours. The child seemed to have an extraordinary sense of smell that he used to recognize people or to explore unfamiliar objects. He also seemed to be impervious to changes in temperature and was not bothered by pain. Sexual behavior and normal emotional responses were missing. In short, his whole existence could not be differentiated from an animal (Humphrey & Humphrey, 1932; Lane, 1976). Despite years of patient instruction, Professor Itard never succeeded in getting the boy to speak.

Similar accounts of children growing up in the wild were initially regarded as evidence that early isolation and deprivation caused irreversible damage to the brain. Such conclusions were premature. There really is not enough information to know what happened to these children. We do not know how long the children lived in isolation. It could have been a few months or many years. A more serious problem is that we do not know whether these children were normal at birth. If they were normal, why were they abandoned? It seems likely that there was something wrong with the children that led to their being abandoned in the first place. Since none of the children ever learned to communicate and since there was no one to provide a more detailed history, questions about who these children were and where they came from were never answered satisfactorily. As a result, most psychologists regard these accounts as interesting descriptions, nothing more.

In 1970, however, a child who had been severely isolated and deprived was discovered in California. Her case—the story of Genie—was studied extensively by psychologists, linguists, and physicians (Curtiss, 1977). Unlike the feral children, birth records were available and indicated a normal labor and delivery and a normal infancy through six months. Her father, however, did not like children, and when at 14 months a pediatrician suggested that Genie might show signs of mild retardation, he began his reign of terror. By 20 months, Genie was imprisoned in a small bedroom. She was harnessed to an infant's potty seat during the day, unable to move anything except her fingers and hands, feet and toes. At night, she was restrained in a contraption similar to a strait jacket. If Genie made any noises she was beaten by her father. No one was allowed to speak to her. Her mother, rapidly going blind, was also beaten and felt powerless to change the situation. Finally when Genie was 13, she and her mother escaped. Soon afterward, Genie came to the attention of the authorities.

When Genie was admitted to the hospital, she was like the feral children. She had no bladder or bowel control, had never worn clothes, was unable to vocalize, and had bizarre emotional tantrums. For several years, psychologists and psycholinguists worked with Genie trying to rehabilitate her. From the beginning, they wondered how much of the 12 years of deprivation could be undone.

When Genie was found, she was about the size of an eight-year-old. Since she had never eaten solid food, she did not know how to chew or swallow. She could not stand erect or straighten her limbs. Her walk was really a shuffle. Although Genie never had any physical therapy, a lot of her most obvious physical problems and some of her most distasteful habits just seemed to disappear. Within a few months she gained weight, grew taller, and developed sexually. Her walk became steadier, her carriage more erect (Curtiss, 1977).

Although they took longer, the changes in Genie's social and emotional behavior were quite astounding. After five years, Genie looked and behaved much more like a human being. She was capable of expressing affection and sharing. She occasionally initiated some play sequences with others. She showed more depth of feeling—crying when it was appropriate and even blushing. She still had tantrums, but they were less frequent. Although she had not mastered all of the social graces, she now exercised much more control over her body.

Language posed the most difficulties. Genie learned language and used it to communicate; but her language was inflexible and childlike. It seemed that she was not capable of mastering many of the grammatical conventions of the English language, although she did understand them. While her vocabulary may continue to increase, there is reason to believe that her grasp of syntax and grammar will not. Although many attempts have been made to teach her to read, they have not succeeded. Conceptually, Genie appears to be much brighter than her language skills suggest. Communication problems and emotional outbreaks make it difficult to assess her intelligence. Seven years after she was found, her verbal scores indicated that she functioned at about the level of a six-year-old. When she was asked to perform tasks that did not require verbal skills, she reacted more like a 12-year-old (Curtiss, 1982).

Psychologists are more comfortable suggesting that Genie's brain has been permanently altered as a function of her deprivation than they were with the feral children. The tests that were administered to Genie included assessments of how her brain functioned and which parts of her brain were reacting to the environment. These tests indicated that, unlike the majority of people, Genie was relying on the right hemisphere of her brain for producing language. Would her brain have developed normally if she had not been deprived? No one knows for sure, but Curtiss points out that even retarded children do not have the patterns of brain functioning that Genie has (Curtiss, 1982).

In terms of the model we have been using for this chapter, it is tempting to conclude that Genie's language environment was not stimulating enough to maintain the normal development of the language centers in the left hemisphere of her brain. Her visual experiences, while definitely limited, were more varied. Perhaps they were sufficient to maintain much of the functioning of the right hemisphere. It is interesting to note that Genie needed glasses to correct her nearsightedness. She could not see farther than 10 feet. Is it a coincidence that the distance from her potty chair to the door was 10 feet, or is this another example of how the environment did not provide enough stimulation to maintain Genie's vision beyond 10 feet?

Children in institutions provide a less extreme view of what happens with social isolation and maternal deprivation. Investigators that have traced the development of orphans invariably find that their progress is slower than normal infants (Paraskevopoulos & Hunt, 1971). One of the first delays that is seen in institutionalized children is in language development (Provence & Lipton, 1962). It is impossible to say whether this level of deprivation actually affects the child's brain. Perhaps most orphanages provide enough stimulation to maintain the development of the brain, but not enough to facilitate or enhance that development. We do know that moving these children from an orphanage to a warm, stimulating home can transform them from thin, shy recluses to healthy, active, and curious children in a matter of months (Winick, Meyer, & Harris, 1975).

Sensory deprivation and isolation have an obvious impact on development. These effects are most dramatic when the isolation or deprivation occurs early in life, is severe, and is prolonged. Whether or not the effects are permanent depends on when the deprivation occurred, how long it persisted, and what behaviors one is investigating (Gollin, 1981). Humans seem to show remarkable resiliency. Having learned about the development of the brain, we can speculate about the source of this resiliency. First, humans have a long period during which the basic neurons are being formed. Hence, even malnutrition or deprivation that continues for months is not as serious as it might be in a rhesus monkey, whose brain spurt lasts four days (Dobbing & Sands, 1979). Suppose children are malnourished for several months during pregnancy. Granted, they have fewer cells at birth. But the process of cell division is not complete. Suppose further that they are put into a very stimulating environment. The cells they have will form complex networks of neurons, interconnected by dendrites and dendritic spines. After a few years, it would be hard to tell that they started with fewer cells. Remember also that the initial process of cell division produces many more cells than are necessary. This kind of redundancy is typical of nature when an important system is being developed. Women have thousands more eggs than they can ever use, and men have literally millions of sperm when one will do the job.

**Brain development and behavior**

In all of the data on humans, there is the nagging question of the relationship between brain structure and behavior. What evidence is there that the two are related? Reports in the 1950s and 1960s emphasized how meaningless the size of the brain was. Einstein's brain, it was reported, did not differ from average, run-of-the-mill brains. These pronouncements came before Rosenzweig and his colleagues told us where to look for differences. Gross indices like the weight and size of the brain are not likely to reveal big differences. Rosenzweig's work suggested that we needed to look at the cortex and to examine the number of dendrites and dendritic spines that existed.

More recent studies, based on Rosenzweig's animal work, have suggested that there are structural differences in the human nervous system that are re-

**Figure 5—5**      **The organization of the brain and behavior**

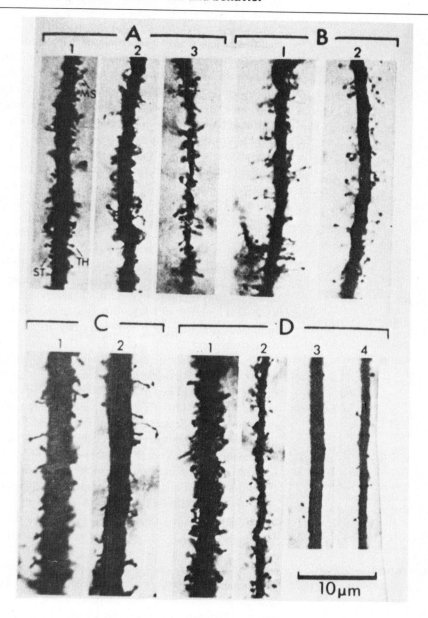

How does the organization of the brain affect behavior? Here are samples of the dendrites of children. Section A shows the dendrites of a normal six-month-old baby. Section B shows the cortex of a retarded 10-month-old. The dendritic spines of this baby are longer and thinner. Some appear to be tangled. Section C shows the dendrites of a three-year-old retardate. He has fewer dendritic spines than the six-month-old. Section D shows a 12-year-old profoundly mentally retarded child. Notice that he has virtually no dendritic spines.

Source: Purpura, D. P. (1974). Dendritic spine "dysgenesis" and mental retardation. *Science, 186,* 1126–1128.

lated to behavioral difficulties. Purpura (1974), for example, examined the brains of six severely mentally retarded children who died. A profoundly retarded 12-year-old had virtually no dendritic spines. A retarded 10-month-old had spines that seemed to be entangled. A similar lack of dendritic spines may be a common feature in mentally retarded children (see Figure 5–5).

The case history of a dyslexic boy suggests a relationship between the structure of the brain and behavior. The patient, a left-handed boy, had a normal birth, and his development during the first two years was uneventful, although he was reported to be clumsier than his siblings. His speech, however, was delayed and when he went to school, he had difficulties reading and spelling. He was diagnosed as dyslexic—unable to read. A neurological evaluation indicated nothing abnormal and, like many children with reading problems, his IQ was normal. Despite intensive tutoring, his reading scores at age 19 were equivalent to a third grader. When he was 20, he died unexpectedly in an accident. His parents agreed to let neuroscientists examine his brain. No gross abnormalities were present, but a microscopic examination revealed that the section of his cortex which should have supported language and reading was quite disorganized. The cell layers were scrambled and primitive cells were sprinkled through the cortex (Galaburda & Kemper, 1979). This case history and the report by Purpura indicate that some behavioral disturbances may have a physical counterpart in the structure of the brain. They also tell us that when such structural differences do exist, they are likely to be small and not immediately obvious.

What does it take to maintain, facilitate, or induce the growth of the human brain? Enriching experiences and stimulation probably facilitate the organization of the brain. They may even induce further development. In extreme cases such as the feral children, Genie, and children who are blind or deaf, sensory restrictions may be so severe that normal development of specific areas of the brain is not maintained. In less extreme cases, such as infants in institutions, the sensory stimulation is probably sufficient to maintain the minimal development of the brain. For unexplained reasons, the organization of the brain occasionally goes awry even with adequate stimulation from the environment. This would seem to be the explanation for the structural differences in Purpura's mentally retarded children and the dyslexic boy.

## Hormones

Hormones are often left out when factors that modify the brain are discussed. Hormones, however, are intricately involved in the development of the brain. The word *hormone* is derived from the Greek verb meaning to urge on or excite. Hormones are normally viewed as playing that kind of role in sexual behavior. But their importance to human behavior extends beyond the obvious sexual differences. Hormones can alter the tissue and hence the structure of the body. These *organizational* effects, seen most clearly in the differing sexual equipment of men and women, are permanent. Hormones can also modify behaviors by affecting the chemical balance in the body. The monthly cycle in women depends on differing hormones being released into the bloodstream at specific times. These effects are termed *activational* and will be reversed if the hormone is not present.

Thanks to some careful animal research and to our increasing ability to locate and identify hormones, we now know that at least two hormones, testosterone and estrogen, have both organizational and activational effects on the human brain. Testosterone, the major male hormone, exerts some action on virtually every tissue in the male's body (Bardin & Catterall, 1981) including the brain. The testosterone that is released by the male fetus begins to alter the structure of the fetal brain in utero. One of the areas in the brain that is permanently affected is a small area in the middle of the brain called the hypothalamus (Jacobson & Gorski, 1981). The hypothalamus is facetiously known as the brain's arcade because it controls many of life's pleasures—eating, drinking, and sexual behavior. The hypothalamus also directs aggressive behavior and the release of other hormones.

Because the hypothalamus of the brain is structurally different in males and females, and because the two sexes have differing hormonal levels, there is a biological basis for differences between the sexes (MacLusky & Naftolin, 1981). However, relating structural differences in certain cells of the brain to differences in behavior requires scientists to make a logical leap. Many differences in structure, such as the shape of a person's hands or nose, are of little importance to behavior. Given the current climate emphasizing equality between the sexes, suggesting that sex differences may have a biological base is not particularly popular. Hence, researchers are understandably reluctant to make the leap from a small structural difference to behavioral differences without evidence that indicates how a structural difference influences behavior.

The evidence concerning circulating hormones is much less tenuous. Researchers agree that the levels of hormones in the body affect both the brain and behavior. In the case of aggression, these hormonal differences have been linked to behavioral differences (Reinisch, 1981).

## Nutrition

The importance of nutrition to the organization of the brain cannot be overemphasized. The cellular growth of the brain depends on an adequate supply of nutrients. The number of cells as well as the size and complexity of the mature neurons can be adversely affected by poor nutrition. A small reduction in cells from a short period of malnutrition does not seem very important. If cell numbers were greatly reduced, however, the organization of the brain could be permanently changed. In 1969, scientists were able to determine how many brain cells were actually lost due to severe malnutrition. They examined the cortex of three Chilean children who had died from malnutrition. The cortex of their brains had half as many cells as a normal brain (Winick & Rosso, 1969). Since these children were severely malnourished, scientists now estimate that malnutrition may cause a child to lose as few as 10 percent or as many as 50 percent of the cells that would become neurons. A loss of 50 percent would mean that normal development of the brain was not being maintained (Dickerson, 1981).

Psychologists have always assumed that there was an optimum number of cells and malnutrition reduced that number. Now they are wondering if supernutrition might induce cell division that otherwise would not have occurred. Providing supernutrition for animals has resulted in a larger number of brain cells being formed (Zamenhof & Van Marthens, 1978). To date, however, there has been no evidence to indicate that supernutrition is accompanied by superior performance on particular tasks. On the one hand, a greater number of cells may only mean that there is more competition during cell migration. We know that more brain cells are created than will survive. On the other hand, it is possible that future research will indicate that larger numbers of cells are translated into behavioral effects.

The generalization that an adequate diet facilitates development of the brain is certainly true. But what is meant by an adequate diet? The studies of malnutrition have typically been concerned with the amount of food available to the child. They have seldom considered the quality of the food. Eating 2,500 calories of junk food does not provide the same nutrients for the brain as eating 2,500 calories of fruits, vegetables, grains, dairy products, and meats. Although the kind of food eaten after the first year or two probably has a minor effect on the structure of the brain, the chemistry of the brain can still be influenced (Blusztajn & Wurtman, 1983). An inadequate diet can upset the delicate balance of neurotransmitters that keep the brain functioning smoothly. Sleepiness, hyperactivity, or learning problems are possible if there are excesses or shortages of particular nutrients (Cohen & Wurtman, 1979; Wurtman & Wurtman, 1977). These behavioral effects are much more subtle than the effects of malnutrition. If they are recognized, they can be reversed by restoring the chemical balance of the brain.

Much of the research about the effect of nutrients on the brain is very recent. We are coming closer to understanding the requirements of the brain and how the body supplies them. The brain is separated from the bloodstream by a membrane called the blood brain barrier. Because of this membrane, scientists assumed the brain was protected from the vagaries of diets. But it is not. The brain is dependent for its nutrients on the bloodstream. These nutrients have to be transported across the membrane to get into the brain's supply system. Once there, the nutrients are transformed into neurotransmitters.

As we learn more about the relationships between nutrients, the brain, and behavior, the spectre of junk food becomes more ominous. Visualize a train with a limited number of seats transporting nutrients from the blood stream across the blood brain barrier. If a particular nutrient is not on that train, the brain must await the next transport, and if the diet is poor, the next and the next. Over a long period of time, the loss of particular nutrients can interfere with the formation of chemical neurotransmitters in the brain. We are now realizing that, rather than the brain being immune to the effects of diet, the diet has acute control over the brain's chemistry (Cohen & Wurtman, 1979).

The real challenge ahead will be to understand how changes in the brain's chemistry are translated into behavioral effects.

## THE ORGANIZATION OF THE BRAIN PREJUDICES BEHAVIOR

Probably nothing is as vital to a child's development as the optimal growth and development of the brain. Hence, the discussion so far has focused on how the brain is formed and organized, and what factors maintain, facilitate, or induce the development of the brain. But this is only the beginning. At birth, contrary to the *tabula rasa* view, the organization of the brain prejudices or biases development in certain directions. Despite its immaturity, the brain exerts an amazing amount of control over the infant's behavior. The chemistry of the brain causes infants to awaken for the infamous 2 AM feeding and encourages a deep slumber just when grandma arrives to see her first grandchild. The organization of the brain may partially dictate differences between males and females, and somehow the brain is responsible for the incredible differences that exist between infants.

**States—the basic rest-activity cycle**

It is no secret that an alert infant will turn toward a squeaking toy. The same squeak will be met with studied indifference if the infant is sleepy and might elicit a startle reaction if the baby is in *slow-wave sleep*. These different reactions, called states, are attributed to changes in the body's internal conditions. Sleeping and waking states wax and wane throughout each day. Whether infants feel alert or drowsy is often relatively independent of the stimulation they are receiving from the environment. These states are better understood in terms of the chemical processes that are taking place in the brain (Parmelee & Sigman, 1976).

A few examples of how states affect adults should make the discussion clearer. Although college students often blame their professors for their propensity to sleep in class, in many cases, it is the chemical state of the sleep-deprived student that encourages the behavior, not the professors. Likewise, to study successfully at 3 AM , students have to battle the body's chemical changes that are urging them to sleep. Jet lag, the awful feeling of awakening bright eyed in California at 3 AM because you just flew in from London, is due to your body's chemistry switching normally from its sleeping to its waking state. To document these states in adults, scientists have lived in caves for long periods of time without any knowledge of when it is daytime or nighttime. They find that their bodies dictate a set rhythm that is reasonably close to the normal cycle of humans (Carlson, 1980). This *circadian* or daily rhythm is just one of the cycles that is dictated by the chemistry of our bodies. Another is the *basic rest-activity cycle.*

All mammals have a basic rest-activity cycle. In adults, this cycle is 90 minutes long and can be seen most clearly during sleep. In infants, the cycle is between 40 to 60 minutes long. This cycle is first seen during the fetal stage about five months after conception when the brain begins to develop rapidly (Sterman, 1972). Every 40 minutes or so, the fetus seems to move and kick actively. This is followed by a period of quiet sleep. The infant's rest-activity cycle remains about 40 minutes long throughout infancy, then it gradually lengthens to the 90-minute adult cycle (Sterman, 1979). This cycle is controlled by the lower areas of the brain, and it represents the infant's first efforts at efficiently organizing a variety of behaviors and functions.

The 40 to 60 minute cycle is the basic pattern of infant states, but it is soon shuttled to the background. As the brain matures, the day-night cycle that we are all familiar with is superimposed on this pattern. The day-night pattern is not evident at birth or even at two weeks. Figure 5–6 shows that infants sleep

**Figure 5–6**                    **Infant behavioral states**

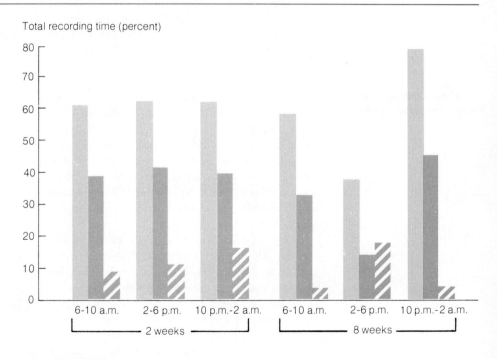

Total recording time (percent)

Total sleep
Active sleep
Fussy-crying

At birth, infants do not follow any day-night routine. They cry as much at night as during the day. After a few weeks, their behavior has been modified. Now, much less of their crying occurs in the late evening.

Source: Sostek, A. M. & Anders, T. F. (1981). The biosocial importance and environmental sensitivity of infant sleep-wake behaviors. In K. Bloom (Ed.), *Prospective issues in infancy research* (p. 108). Hillsdale, NJ: Lawrence Erlbaum.

or cry almost equally during the morning, afternoon, and late evening when they are two weeks old. By eight weeks, however, they are sleeping more and crying less during the late night hours (Sostek & Anders, 1981).

The states of the newborn infant that are defined by the basic rest-activity cycle can be divided into (*a*) quiet sleep, (*b*) active sleep, (*c*) awake—quiet and inactive, (*d*) waking—active, and (*e*) crying. Sleep is one of the most interesting infant states. Newborns sleep approximately 16 hours a day, and half of that time is spent in a state called active sleep. Active sleep or *rapid eye movement (REM)* sleep, as it is called in adults, is so named because if you watch sleeping adults their eyes begin to move rapidly under their closed lids about every 90 minutes. Premature infants spend 70 to 80 percent of their lives in active sleep. Full-term infants spend 50 percent of their lives in active sleep and the other 50 percent is equally divided between quiet sleep and wakefulness. By adulthood, less than one quarter of our night is spent in REM sleep (see Figure 5–7).

**Figure 5–7**   **REM sleep during the life span**

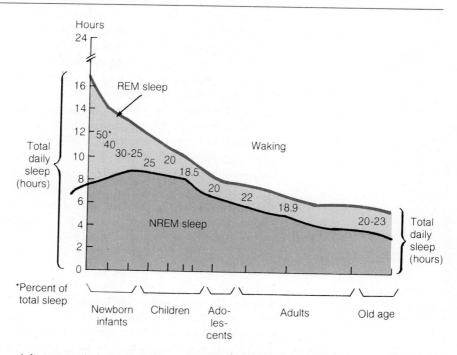

Infants spend almost 50 percent of their sleeping time in rapid eye movement (REM) sleep. Adults spend only about 20 percent of their time in REM sleep.

Source: Roffwarg, H. P., Muzio, J. N., & Dement, W. C. (1966). Ontogenetic development of the human sleep-dream cycle. *Science, 152,* 604–619. Revised since publication by Dr. Roffwarg.

Why should infants spend so much time in active sleep? The truth is, no one knows. Psychologists agree that the frequency of active sleep makes it an important state. They also agree that it must have some evolutionary significance, but that is where the agreement ends. Although we have no explanations for the dominant rhythms of infancy, we can describe them. Active and quiet sleep represent two separate states that are accompanied by differing patterns of respiration, heart rate, and muscle tone. These different states are ample evidence of patterns in the infant's behavior that, in modified form, continue throughout the life span. They also demonstrate how the brain exercises control over some basic behavioral states.

## Hemispheric specialization

The human brain is divided into two lobes—the left and right hemispheres. Until recently, it was thought that these hemispheres were identical at birth and gradually became specialized so that each performed somewhat different functions. In fact before the 1950s, having two hemispheres was regarded as another example of nature's redundancy. This view was fueled by the finding that you could remove an entire hemisphere from young children who suffered from a brain tumor and the remaining hemisphere would take over all of the functions of the brain. If this operation was done before two years of age, the child seemed to suffer few effects (Basser, 1962).

Further research has tempered this optimism and demonstrated that the newborn's two hemispheres are not identical. Anatomical studies of the infant's brain have documented structural differences between the two hemispheres. The planum temporale, an area of the brain that is associated with language skills, is significantly larger in the left hemisphere than the right (Wada, Clarke, & Hamm, 1975). In most people, there are also differences in the cerebral arteries of the two hemispheres and the front sections of the brain (Geschwind, 1979). This structural difference is translated into both preferences and behaviors. As these preferences are described, keep in mind that the left hemisphere controls the right side of the body, and in most adults, the left hemisphere controls language. The right hemisphere controls the left side of the body and seems to be more attuned to spatial problems.

Once we observed infants closely, the asymmetry of the brain seemed to be quite general. The tonic neck reflex is one indication that the infants prefer one side of the body. When lying on their backs, close to 90 percent of newborns turn their heads to the right (Turkewitz, 1977). The asymmetry of the brain is obvious from other behaviors. When they turn their head to the right, they usually see an outstretched arm. Liederman and Coryell (1981) argue that this is how the tonic neck reflex biases handedness and accentuates the brain's preference. When a rattle is placed in each hand, it is held longer by the right hand (Caplan & Kinsbourne, 1976). If you put electrodes on an infant's head and record how the brain reacts to different kinds of stimulation, you will find that when syllables are presented to the infant, the brain patterns from the left hemisphere change. When a musical chord is presented, the brain patterns from the right hemisphere change (Molfese, 1977).

All of these results point to an asymmetry in the organization of the brain. This asymmetry is clearest in language and language-related tasks. The left hemisphere is predisposed to attend when someone is speaking. As the child develops, many behaviors such as language acquisition and learning to read, write, and spell may be influenced by this early organization of the brain.

## Sudden infant death syndrome (SIDS)

Sudden infant death syndrome, also known as crib death, may be an example of the brain not being sufficiently organized to maintain the vital function of breathing. Sudden infant death syndrome kills 10,000 infants each year before they celebrate their first birthday. As the name implies, death is sudden and unexpected. After the first month, more infants die from SIDS than from any other cause. In the last few years, we have learned a great deal about the victims of SIDS. They are often boys who have a mild cold. Their mothers are more likely to be young and, in many cases, they smoke. The risk of having a child die from SIDS is greater among women in the lower socioeconomic classes, among women who have used narcotics during pregnancy, and among women who have not had prenatal care or were ill during their pregnancy. Asian Americans have the fewest number of children die from SIDS while American Indians, Eskimos, and Afro-Americans have the highest incidence. Twins are more likely to die of SIDS, and in three cases both twins were found dead together. More infants die during the winter months, and deaths occur most frequently during the first four months of life (Shannon & Kelly, 1982a).

Although we do not know exactly why infants stop breathing, there are currently some good guesses. One guess is that the brain stem, the section of the brain that maintains breathing, is not mature enough to control breathing properly. Any mild obstruction of the air passages, as might occur in an infant with a cold or even when the infant shifts in sleep, may be sufficient to stop the breathing (Shannon & Kelly, 1982b).

Despite the fact that the causes of SIDS are obscure, some infants have been saved by parents who learned to use electronic monitors in the home (see Figure 5–8). Infants who have stopped breathing once and have been revived are candidates for this home monitoring. Results with the monitor are usually excellent. Out of 400 children whose parents had been monitoring them at home, only four died. Three of these deaths occurred because the parents did not hear the alarm. In one case, the infant could not be revived. Infants do not have to be monitored indefinitely. Whatever is wrong is usually cleared up before the first birthday.

## Biologically based sex differences

When considering how the organization of the brain biases behaviors, the issue of sex differences always comes up. Are the differences between males and females built into the brain in any systematic fashion? This issue must be faced even though it always sparks heated controversy. It would be foolish to argue that there are not any differences between the sexes. There are obvious physical differences, and we know that these are due to hormonal surges dur-

**Figure 5—8**    **The fight against sudden infant death syndrome**

Barbara Durney rolled over in bed about 1 AM and sensed something was wrong with the baby in the crib next to her. "I got up and she looked, well, cloudy," Barbara remembers. "I shook her and she seemed okay, so I went back to bed."

But the next day was different. Kerri-Lynn was snoozing in her baby seat when she suddenly stopped breathing. She turned blue and limp. Barbara shook and shook and shook her baby. Finally, the color returned to Kerri-Lynn's body.

Barbara Durney, 24, and her husband, Charlie, 30, confused and frightened, took Kerri-Lynn to a hospital near their home in suburban Boston. The medical staff decided there was really no big problem; maybe the baby was just reacting to some stomach surgery she had had a few days before. But they agreed to admit Kerri-Lynn for observation.

It didn't take long to prove Barbara right. She stayed close while Kerri-Lynn was hospitalized. At one point a nurse had propped up the four-month-old baby in a high chair, and suddenly, once again, the little body went limp and turned blue. Barbara screamed for help.

Barbara had caught her baby having an attack of *apnea*—a word that means, simply, a cessation of breathing. Apnea is critical to the lives of many babies because it may be a cause of "crib death."

Crib death, also known as sudden infant death syndrome or by the acronym SIDS, is often called "the silent killer," and it is perhaps the single biggest cause of death for babies between a month and a year of age. Each year up to 10,000 infants in America may succumb to this mysterious phenomenon, which usually hits when a baby is sleeping. Often, healthy infants are put to bed or to nap and just don't wake up. For no apparent reason, they just stop breathing and die.

The cause or causes of SIDS are not yet known, and there is no cure. All that we know is that if the spells of apnea are caught, and the baby can be revived before the oxygen deprivation is fatal, chances for survival are good; in such

cases, the infant will outgrow the condition, usually by the time he or she is a year old.

Barbara Durney's persistence may have saved her baby's life. Within hours after Barbara had caught the apnea attack in the hospital, Kerri-Lynn was transported to a nearby hospital, which pioneered a program designed to catch and treat these apnea spells.

The first step in this program is to give an infant tests that indicate the presence of apnea and rule out other conditions. The baby is also put on an electronic monitor that measures her respiration rate and heart rate at all times. This entails strapping a little band with electrodes around her belly and plugging wire leads from the electrodes into a machine about the size of a tape deck. When this is completed, the baby is "on the monitor" and two green lights blink away contentedly when all is well. But if her breathing (or heart) rate falls below the prescribed level, the green lights disappear and red warning lights flash instead while a loud beeper beeps an audible warning.

Help should come within 10 seconds. Someone must either shake the baby or choose one of the more severe methods of resuscitation to bring the infant out of the spell.

This is what was done to Kerri-Lynn and her mother and father were initiated into the uniquely difficult world of monitor-baby parents. Life for the Durneys has not been the same since. They had to be trained to use the equipment and become experts in revival techniques, but they have also had to make radical changes in their lifestyle. Since the response to the warnings must be quick, having a baby on a monitor means never being more than 10 seconds away.

"You live with this monitor that attaches you to that baby 24 hours a day. It's almost like an umbilical cord," comments Georgette Olsen, a 30-year-old registered nurse whose fourth baby has been on a monitor since he was eight weeks old. "It got so bad I had to have somebody in so I

**Figure 5—8**     *Concluded*

could go to the bathroom." At one time Georgette said she couldn't get the mail, run the vacuum or even go into the kitchen and turn on the blender.

The monitoring concept has met with some resistance in the medical field. But to mothers like Mary Jo Kleinhenz who lost her first baby to SIDS and then monitored her two subsequent children, there is no question about whether the stress is worth it. "Consider the alternative to living with a monitor. Consider living with the fear of death every time you put the baby to sleep. At least with a monitor we felt we were doing something, not just standing by watching our baby die."

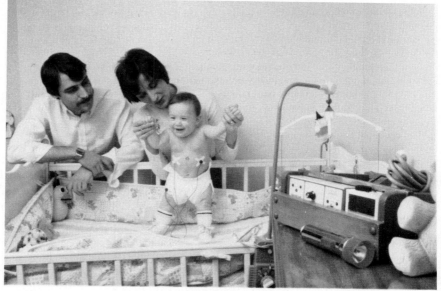

*Courtesy* Parents Magazine

Source: Goldstein, M. (1982, May). *Parents Magazine*, pp. 83–86. Picture from *Parents Magazine* (1981, October). Reprinted by permission of Marilyn Goldstein.

ing the prenatal and adolescent periods. It is also foolish to argue that there are no differences in the brain. There are clear differences between males and females in the hypothalamus of the brain. The monthly cycles of females depend on hormonal stimulation that originates in the hypothalamus (Gray & Drewett, 1977). The argument begins to get heated when the significance of these differences is discussed. Those who would like to believe that males and females are equal in every respect, save the obvious physical ones, argue that the differences in the brain are associated only with sexual functioning. Others believe that the differences in the brain and the accompanying hormonal differences are associated with a variety of behavioral and cognitive differences. Neither side denies the pervasive influence of the culture, and both can cite a long list of socialization practices that promote sex differences (Maccoby & Jacklin, 1974).

To examine how the brain might influence different behavior in the two sexes, we need to look at the differences between male and female infants that appear with a great deal of regularity during development. It is also helpful to know whether the differences exist in a variety of other cultures. If a sex difference exists in all cultures and in most other species, then it is likely that development is being channeled along that particular pathway by some biological force.

There are several physical differences between the sexes in infancy. At birth, females are shorter and weigh less than males (Wolff, 1981). At birth, girls have a more advanced skeletal age which is maintained throughout childhood (Wolff, 1981). At birth, selected regions of the cerebral cortex are more mature in females (Conel, 1939). During infancy, the brains of females develop more rapidly (Waber, 1979). In addition, females are more likely to survive. This is true in infancy and in every other age period. Even in studies of males and females in a religious order, where food, habits, and stress were similar, women outlived men (Madigan, 1957). Although 106 males are born for every 100 females, by adolescence the numbers are equal (Barfield, 1976). These physical differences exist in practically every culture studied.

Infant girls have greater organizational stability. This means they do not fluctuate as much as boys on many behavioral measures. One example is intelligence test scores. We have already discussed the difficulty in using infant scores to predict intelligence later in life. In fact, such predictions for boys consistently fail. Girls' scores, however, seem to be more stable. The rate at which girls vocalize during infancy is related to intelligence scores years later (Moore, 1968; Cameron, Livson, & Bayley, 1967; Kagan, 1971). This does not necessarily mean that vocalizing is a precursor of intelligence. Rather, it means that a girl who talks early is also likely to learn other skills easily. The behavior of boys at an early age is much more erratic and depends more on their environment. Mothers seem to have a greater impact on the intelligence of their sons. In a longitudinal study conducted at the University of California at Berkeley, the relationship between the mother and her son was an important factor in how well he performed on IQ tests. One group of mothers was affectionate and allowed their sons to explore their environment. Often their sons' scores were below average in the first year, but they made rapid progress in later years. Other mothers were hostile and punitive. Although their sons often did well on the IQ tests given during the first year, they tended to have low IQs after four years of age. The mother's behavior did not have the same effect on girls (Bayley & Schaefer, 1964). The stability of the girls' behavior during infancy is attributed to their biological maturity (Freedman, 1974) and hence is included here as a physical sex difference.

Psychological, emotional, and social differences that exist during infancy are less obvious. One that most investigators agree on is the degree of rough-and-tumble play. Boisterous wrestling and running are favorite pastimes of young males regardless of their species (Archer, 1981). Most ethologists regard rough-and-tumble play as a safe way for males to practice behaviors and skills that they will need as adults. This sex difference may be tied to the prenatal hormones that mediate the physical differences between the sexes. The link between rough-and-tumble play and hormones has been tested in monkeys. If female monkeys are exposed to androgens during pregnancy, they will spend much more time in rough-and-tumble play. Human females whose mothers are given androgens during pregnancy react similarly. These girls engage in more active play and are often labeled tomboys (Money & Ehrhardt, 1972). Rough-and-tumble play meets the criteria we have established for biologically based sex differences. It occurs widely in humans, can be found in our nearest relatives, and has been linked to prenatal hormones (Ehrhardt & Meyer-Bahlburg, 1981). This does not mean that culture has no effect. Fathers encourage such play in their sons from the early weeks of life (Parke, 1981).

Consensus is also achieved on activity level (Block, 1976; Seward & Seward, 1980). Generally, boys are more active than girls, and this difference is noticeable during the first months of life. Activity level is one of many variables, however, that gives psychologists headaches. In one study, activity level is measured by the number of hours the infant is awake during the day. In another study, it is measured by how quickly and vigorously infants object when you take their bottle away. In a third, it is measured by how many squares on the floor of a room an infant covers in a set period of time. Do these measure the same thing? The basic problem is that even though we all seem to have an intuitive understanding of activity level, it is difficult to measure.

Another problem that is true of activity level and most other variables on which there are sex differences is that the distributions of male and female scores overlap. In the hypothetical example given in Figure 5–9, there are 100 boys and 100 girls. You measure their activity level by counting how many

**Figure 5–9**  **Overlapping distributions***

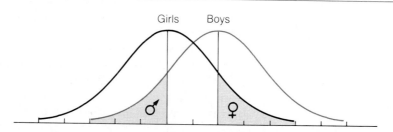

Girls    Boys

Activity levels of males and females overlap a great deal. There are many males who are less active than most girls, and there are many females who are more active than 50 percent of the males. Even though there is a statistically significant difference between the sexes in activity level, it would be difficult to predict where a particular girl or boy would fall.

*Shaded areas show girls who are more active than half of the boys and boys who are less active than half of the girls.

steps they take in a two-hour period of free play. The results show that some girls' scores equaled the highest scores of boys, while some boys were not active at all. Overall, however, there were more boys receiving high activity scores than girls. This small difference means that statistically boys are more active than girls. If we try to predict whether a particular girl will be less active than a particular boy, we will often be wrong. This phenomenon, described as overlapping distributions, is a caveat to keep in mind when sex differences or any other individual differences are being discussed. If there is a great deal of overlap in the scores of males and females, then a statistical difference is not meaningful for any particular individual.

A final problem with variables such as activity level is that there are huge differences between children regardless of their sex. The number of hours a newborn sleeps can range from 10 to 18, and children at each end of this range are considered normal. Despite all of these provisos, the bulk of the information we have suggests that boys are more active than girls.

Language behavior is another area where there are clear sex differences. Girls learn to talk sooner, use longer sentences, have larger vocabularies (Clarke-Stewart, 1973), have fewer speech problems, and have fewer reading problems (Barfield, 1976). This difference seems to be present early in infancy and has been attributed to the maturational advantage that girls have. Cultural variables are not excluded in the research on language acquisition. Studies show that mothers talk to their daughters more than their sons (Korner, 1974). This cultural difference may account for some of the sex differences that we see in language skills. It probably does not explain all of the difference.

Aggression is the trait on which there is the most agreement. Males are more aggressive in every culture for which evidence is available. Males of most non-human primates are more aggressive than females. Aggression has also been firmly linked with prenatal hormones (Reinisch, 1981a; Reinisch & Haskett, 1981).

What about more subtle personality traits? Some authors say that fear and anxiety are peculiarly female traits and appear at early ages. The best data we have from studying infants suggest that if there is a sex difference in these traits, it does not appear during infancy (Seward & Seward, 1980). Of course, all the problems discussed in the section on activity level are applicable here. If 18-month-old girls cry more than boys when their mothers leave (Kagan, 1971), is that fear, anxiety, or is it attachment? Is that the same trait that is measured when an infant cries after being startled?

Areas where clear sex differences exist in infancy include aggression, language skills, activity level, rough-and-tumble play, and physical maturity. Evidence on several others, such as fear, anxiety, and exploratory behavior, is not clear. Cognitive differences with the exception of language skills are not evident during the first two years. But remember that measuring cognitive skills during this period is a tenuous undertaking.

Sex differences in infants are not as common as one might expect, and they are not as common as they will be in later years. This adds fuel to the view that socialization practices promote sex differences. Unfortunately, such a conclusion oversimplifies the issue. There are at least two sound reasons why biologically based sex differences might not appear until later in life. The first is the difficulty of measuring traits and behaviors during infancy. There are not many studies on spatial skills in infants, yet this is one of the areas in which sex differences are most obvious in adults. Likewise, our attempts to measure anxiety in infants may not be tapping the same behaviors that we see at age 12. The second reason that biologically based sex differences might not appear until adolescence is the effect of hormones. Prenatal hormones begin to influence the fetus early in gestation. It is not, however, until puberty that the full effects of these hormones are felt by the organism. Since Jeanne Block's lucid review of sex differences (1976), much more attention has been paid to sex differences in adolescents and to populations that for one reason or another are deficient in hormones or have an excessive level of hormones. These studies indicate that the onset of puberty and the hormonal changes that influence puberty may have effects that were not obvious in infancy. Deborah Waber suggests that the hormonal surge at adolescence may reorganize brain functions at puberty in the same way they reorganize physiology. But she, too, cautions that the behavioral differences that result are small and that a great deal of overlap exists between the sexes (Waber, 1979).

## Ethnic differences

Since there are sex differences and individual differences in the structure and hormone levels of the brain, differences between relatively isolated cultures might exist. Physical differences exist in cultures around the world, and some of these differences are seen in the build of an adult's body. The long limbs characteristic of Africans provide larger surface areas for evaporation and cooling. The shorter limbs of the Eskimos help conserve heat (Tanner, 1978). Some biologically based differences also seem to appear in motor development. Babies born in Africa start life with a more mature motor organization than babies born in Europe or the United States (Geber & Dean, 1967; Warren, 1972). During the first week, African children can control their heads when pulled to a sitting position and they can lift their heads when they are lying on their stomachs (Freedman, 1974).

Freedman was one of the first investigators to study personality differences in babies from different ethnic groups. He compared the temperament of Caucasian and Oriental-American infants. He limited his study to newborns and tested them when they were a little over 30 hours old. Although the two groups were similar in motor development, social development, and the development of their central nervous systems, he found differences in temperament. Chinese-American newborns were more placid. If aroused or upset they could quiet themselves. When crying infants were picked up, they stopped crying almost immediately. European-American infants were more difficult to comfort. Freedman (1974) does emphasize that there was considerable overlap in the scores of the two groups. He concludes that Chinese-Americans and

European-Americans have biologically based differences in temperament and that these differences bias the behavior of children and influence the entire culture. Perhaps he is right. On the other hand, two groups of 24 infants who were tested on a set of somewhat subjective items seems like a tenuous base for predicting cultural differences. We certainly need more evidence from larger groups of infants before accepting Freedman's conclusions. Chen-Chin Hsu from Taiwan has tried to supply this evidence. His assessment of 300 four- to eight-month-old Chinese infants also indicated that they differed from American infants (Hsu, Soong, Stigler, Hong, & Liang, 1981). Chinese infants were found to be more intense, less active and less adaptable. Still, the differences reported are not very large and could be explained by cultural factors rather than biological ones.

From this brief review, we can see that the brain's organization can direct the behavior of the infant. A newborn's states are determined largely by the brain. These states are soon modified by feeding schedules and sleeping schedules, but the basic rest-activity cycle remains. The organization of the brain does not always have such a direct influence. In the case of temperament, sex differences, and hemispheric specialization, the organization of the brain tends to bias, rather than direct, the child's behavior.

## INFANT FEEDING PRACTICES

Because nutrition plays such an important role in the development of the child's brain, we should examine some of the practical aspects of food and feeding. What are the advantages and disadvantages of breast feeding an infant? How are newborns provided the most nutritious start? Can infants be overfed? Malnutrition is a worldwide and very visible problem, but there are children who suffer from the reverse problem—obesity. We need to look at both of these problems.

**Breast-feeding**

Texts on child development have typically emphasized the psychological aspects of feeding an infant. Feeling close to the infant, stopping to play and talk to the infant, making feedings an important time for mother-infant interaction; these are the critical psychological components. From this point of view, it does not matter if mothers breast-feed or bottle-feed their infants. Both types of feedings can facilitate the attachment behaviors that help the mother-infant relationship. But proponents of breast-feeding point to the skin-to-skin contact and the lack of propped bottles as important pluses for breast-feeding (Jelliffe & Jelliffe, 1979).

Breast-feeding confers other advantages on both the mother and infant. These advantages are important enough that the American Academy of Pediatrics has resolved to urge all mothers to breast-feed their children. Let us examine the reasons for their resolution. First, the mother benefits. The whole reproductive system is geared for women to nurse. To prepare for nursing, women accumulate about 10 pounds of fat during pregnancy that is really a storehouse for the nursing infant. Women who nurse use up many more calories per day than women who do not. They will soon use up their stored supply of fat and return to their normal weight (Winick, 1980). In contrast, the mother who is not nursing has no use for the stored weight and must lose it by dieting.

Another benefit for the mother who nurses her child is the rapid return of the uterus to its original size. During the first week after birth, the mother might feel mild cramps in the uterus each time the baby nurses. This is a sure sign that the uterus is being tugged back to its original shape.

The convenience of breast-feeding cannot be ignored. The milk is always ready in a sterile container and heated precisely to body temperature. The 2 AM feeding merely means taking the infant into your bed and relaxing. There is nothing to mix, heat, or test.

The infant who is nursed gets the best possible start in life. All mammals breast-feed, but the milk provided for a newborn whale is very different from the milk provided for a goat. In other words, mother's milk is individualized for each species. There are several important differences between human breast milk and the cow's milk that is often substituted for it—differences in the amount and form of protein, carbohydrates, and vitamin C (Winick, 1980). Although infant formulas try to duplicate the nutritional qualities of breast milk, they are not completely successful.

Breast milk also protects the infant against a variety of infections and increases the infant's resistance to disease (Ogra & Greene, 1982). Intestinal disorders and ear infections are much less common in breast-fed babies. Because breast milk is easier for the infant to digest than cow's milk, there are fewer instances of diarrhea and the dangerous dehydration that can accompany diarrhea (Chaney, Ross, & Witschi, 1979).

Breast-feeding does have disadvantages. A breast-fed baby may get hungry faster than a bottle-fed baby because the protein content of breast milk is lower than cow's milk (Ogra & Greene, 1982). Hence, every three to four hours, the mother has to be with her infant. Nursing mothers who are aware of this simply plan to feed the child on demand. Mothers who work have more difficulty. Determined mothers have devised ingenious ways to continue nursing even if they cannot be present all of the time. Some mothers freeze their breast milk for use at times when they cannot be home. Others use a formula at noon and breast-feed the rest of the time. Some have even received permission to have their infants at the office while they are nursing. Another disadvantage is that mothers have to control their diet because alcohol, drugs, or pesticides will be transferred to the infant in the breast milk.

Although there are many advantages to nursing, women raise healthy, happy babies using bottled formulas. This is especially true in westernized cultures where water is pure and can be boiled readily. In other areas of the world, bottle-feeding is not accomplished so readily. In fact, in many third-world countries, American corporations are being taken to task for discouraging mothers from breast-feeding. To understand the issue, a little background information is necessary.

In some countries, as many as 50 percent of the children suffer from a form of malnutrition called protein calorie deficiency. Winick (1980) calls it the single-greatest health hazard to the world's children. This protein-calorie deficiency is the cause of two diseases—marasmus and Kwashiokor. Both of these diseases are linked to bottle-feeding.

Marasmus, an infection characterized by dehydration, diarrhea, and vomiting, usually occurs in infants younger than 18 months who are bottle fed. Bottle-feeding can become a problem if there is no refrigeration, if the water is contaminated, or if sterilization procedures are lax. Even with the best hygiene, the bottle-fed child is more susceptible to infection than the breast fed child. If you add unsterilized equipment or contaminated water, infection is practically guaranteed. Then an insidious cycle begins. Infection leads to diarrhea, and the infant becomes dehydrated. The dehydration means that milk is not tolerated well, so diarrhea and dehydration continue. Even with good care, as many as 20 percent of the infants can die (Winick, 1980). On a recent trip to Africa, I spoke with medical missionaries from England who admitted that they sometimes encouraged mothers who were not breast-feeding to feed their child Coca-Cola. They argued that Coca-Cola is tolerated much better than formulas. It is not mixed with contaminated water, will keep the infant from becoming dehydrated, and will provide the child with glucose. While admitting that this solution was far from satisfactory, they acknowledged that if the mother was not breast-feeding, they really did not have many alternatives once a child became sick and could not tolerate formulas.

This situation has outraged people who are authorities on nutrition. Here are parts of Michael Latham's remarks to a convention on world nutrition.

> The rapid spread of bottle-feeding, replacing breast-feeding, for young babies is having disastrous consequences, both in terms of health and also in terms of economics. The baby bottle has been termed "the baby killer," and that is just what it is in many places. The artificial formula or powdered milk is so expensive that the mixture gets overdiluted, leading to serious malnutrition. Contamination of the water and inherent difficulties in preparing a relatively sterile mixture result in infection and diarrhea. Yet bottle-feeding is spreading because of Western influence, because of advertising, because of profits to be made by manufacturers, because of unfortunate medical influence, and for a host of other socioeconomic reasons.
>
> In addition to affecting the health of babies and causing many deaths, reduction in breast-feeding increases fertility, leading to a narrower spacing between children. It has recently been postulated that breast-feeding may be having more effect in many countries in controlling fertility than all the birth-control methods put together in those countries. Breast-feeding definitely delays ovulation.
>
> Breast-feeding has very important economic consequences. Bottle-feeding is extremely expensive for the family. The cost is over half the minimum wage or more in countries where, often, more than 60 percent of the popu-

## Marasmus

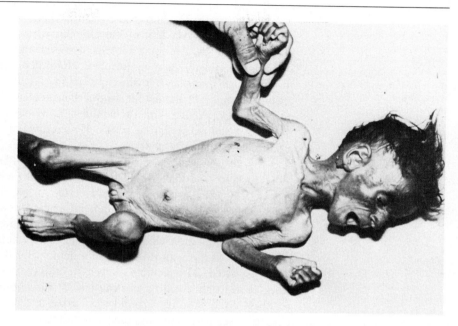

Malnutrition leads to a cycle of infection, diarrhea, and dehydration called Marasmus that is often fatal. Marasmus is not nearly as common in mothers who breast-feed their infants.

Source: From Myron Winick, *Malnutrition and Brain Development* (New York Oxford University Press, 1976) by permission of the author and the publisher.

lation earns less than the minimum wage. The economic implications for a nation as a whole are also tremendous if one considers the amount of milk that would have to be imported if all breast-feeding were to cease. (Latham, 1978, p. 426–427)

Since 1978, some countries have taken steps to decrease the marketing of breast-milk substitutes. In these countries, the number of mothers who nurse has increased substantially, the incidence of infection has decreased, and infant mortality has decreased (Ambulatory Pediatric Association, 1981). Another benefit is that the next pregnancy is delayed. If a child is completely breast fed, that is, there are no formula supplements, then the mother secretes a hormone which inhibits ovulation. In Central Africa, medical records were kept on mothers who were nursing their infants and mothers who were not. Nine months after delivery 74 percent of the women who were not nursing were already pregnant. Only 7 percent of the mothers who were nursing were pregnant. It was two years after delivery before 74 percent of the nursing women were pregnant (Brown, 1982).

**Obesity**

Obesity in infancy is not an immediate concern to the child's health. If maintained into adulthood, it may shorten the individual's life. Unfortunately, obesity that begins in childhood is often a signal of a lifelong weight problem (Grinker, 1981). Over half of the children who are obese at age 10 will be obese in their 30s. An obese adolescent is even more likely to have a continuing weight problem. As a group, obese children and adolescents are at risk for the problems that plague overweight adults. As the degree of overweight increases in children, the likelihood that the problem will persist past childhood also increases. Despite these probabilities, some obese children lose weight and maintain a normal weight as adults. Hence, predicting what will happen with a particular child is difficult.

Being an obese child is a source of concern. Obese children have higher blood pressure and higher cholesterol levels than their peers (Coates & Thoresen, 1980). They also have a negative view of themselves and spontaneously make remarks such as, "I know that I'll be fat forever" (Sallade, 1973). This negative self-concept is not helped by the tormenting they receive from their peers. When children were asked to rate the likeability of five boys and girls depicted in pictures, they consistently demonstrated negative attitudes toward the obese child. The pictures showed a child wearing a leg brace, a child in a wheelchair, a child with a missing hand, one whose face was disfigured, and an obese child. The obese child was ranked as least likeable, perhaps because obesity is seen as a self-imposed handicap (Richardson, Goodman, Hastorf, & Dornbusch, 1961).

Obese children and adolescents encounter similar negative attitudes from adults and the society as a whole. Discrimination from schools, colleges, and some occupations has been documented (Grinker, 1981). It is little wonder that obese children develop a poor self-image and tend to isolate themselves. Sometimes even family interactions seem to go awry for these children. Given the psychological consequences of obesity in childhood, we need to know what causes obesity and how we can prevent it.

The fundamental cause of obesity is an excess of food that is stored as fat. This makes it sound very simple—get rid of the excess food and the fat disappears. Millions of chronic dieters will confirm that it is not that simple. There is more to obesity than number of calories consumed. At least three different theories have been proposed to explain the physiological basis of obesity.

One theory suggests that obese children have an excess number of fat cells that make it difficult to lose weight, especially after adolescence. According to this view, dieting merely shrinks the size of the fat cell, but the number remains the same (Coates & Thoresen, 1980).

A second theory argues that obesity is due to an increase in the size of fat cells. There is no doubt that obese individuals have larger fat cells than other adults. The question that needs to be answered is what triggers these differences. Joel Grinker from Rockefeller University believes that the answer lies in the changes in cellular tissue that take place from birth to 10 years of age. Fat cells, like most cells, grow during the first year of life and reach an adult stage around the first birthday. Once these cells reach adult size, if more food is eaten than the body can use, the body makes more fat cells (Sjöström, 1980). This happens with obese children. Between the ages of 2 and 10, their fat cells get larger and larger, finally forcing the production of more fat cells (Grinker, 1981).

A third theory argues that a *set point* exists in the brain that functions like a thermostat to regulate eating behavior. When specific indicators fall below a particular point, the brain mobilizes the body to eat. Such a set point explains why when most adults step on the scales, the needle hovers around a single point. In obese individuals, this set point maintains an obese state. Obese adults with a large number of fat cells can actually experience starvation when they try to lose weight. Their cells, deprived of essential fluids, signal the brain to eat, and thus drive people to regain the pounds they have struggled to lose. The chronic dieter has typically lost the same 10 to 15 pounds on numerous occasions, but has seen them reappear over a short period of time. Regaining lost weight is attributed to this set point. Although this is an intriguing hypothesis, and although it does explain the difficulty that obese individuals have in keeping weight off, many questions remain unanswered. Hence, the set-point theory must be viewed as just that—a theory.

These three theories represent some of the old and new ideas about the physiological basis of childhood obesity. With more research, we may discover that all three theories have some validity (Roche, 1981). We may also learn what triggers cells to behave the way they do. Genetics, feeding practices, and exercise are all potential candidates.

Genetic factors are universally recognized as important determinants of obesity. If both parents are obese, the child's chances of avoiding obesity are small—approximately 70 percent will become obese. When only one parent is obese, the child stands a much better chance of staying slim throughout adulthood—only 40 percent become obese. If neither parent is obese, less than 10 percent of their children will have a weight problem as adults (Collip, 1980). This, of course, is hardly a convincing argument for genetics because obese parents may just feed their children too much. However, such a cultural explanation does not fit the data either. Look at Jack Spratt couples—the lean male and obese female. Their children might be expected to be more obese than the children of slim women with fat husbands. As it turns out, whether it is the husband or the wife that is fat—40 percent of the children are obese (Foch & McClearn, 1980). Remember, too, that 60 percent of the children that are eating the same food in the same household do not become overweight as adults.

Information from twin studies and animal studies also points to a genetic factor in obesity. If one of a pair of identical twins is obese, the other is very likely to be obese; but this is not true for fraternal twins (Börjeson, 1976). In addition, adopted children do not mirror the weight patterns of their adoptive parents. There is literally a zero relationship between how much adopted chil-

**Figure 5—10**  **The genetics of obesity**

| Relationship | Weight | Weight/Height |
|---|---|---|
| Parents | | |
|    Biological | .31 | .26 |
|    Foster | .00 | .00 |
| Siblings | | |
|    Biological | .39 | .37 |
|    Foster | .01 | .03 |

The correlations from this table indicate that adopted children are likely to be obese only if their biological parents are obese. If their adoptive parents are obese, even though the children live in that environment and eat the same food as the parents, they are likely to remain at a normal weight.

Source: Börjeson, M. (1976). The etiology of obesity in children. *Acta Paediatrica Scandinavia, 65,* 279–287.

dren weigh and the weight of their adoptive parents (see Figure 5–10). The children are more like their biological parents and siblings (Börjeson, 1976).

While no one denies the influence of genetics, what we eat, how we eat, and how often we eat also affects our weight. Two examples of how environmental pressures can affect weight come from Japan and Hawaii. In Japan, sumo wrestling is a national sport. Eighteen-year-olds who are interested in becoming wrestlers are encouraged to eat up to 6,000 calories a day. Even with their vigorous training, these wrestlers soon become quite obese (Fujiwara, 1978). Obesity was also encouraged in Hawaiian royal families. If the Alii Nui (the queen) did not weigh over 300 pounds, her power was more likely to be questioned. According to legend, her five or six meals a day meant that the common people could see that she was a great woman from a distance (Michener, 1959).

In contemporary Western cultures, adults go to great lengths to stay slender, but they take pride in showing off their plump babies. Knowing this, pediatricians examined the effect that early feeding patterns had on childhood obesity. Eighty infants were placed on a "prudent diet" which emphasized fruit without sugar, vegetables, milk, meats and cheeses, yoghurt, and gelatin. Three years later these children were compared with 50 children who had not been on any special diet. Only 2 percent of the prudent diet infants were overweight, but 25 percent of the control children were overweight (Pisacano, Lichter, Ritter, & Siegel, 1978). Given these results, pediatricians are encouraging mothers not to overfeed their infants. In addition to watching their child's diet, mothers are advised not to interpret every cry as indicating that the baby is hungry and to avoid a tendency to have the baby finish the bottle or have one more bite (Collip, 1980).

Exercise is often a forgotten factor in the energy equation. Active children require more calories than sedentary children. Hence, increasing activity leads to weight loss (Brownell & Stunkard, 1980). This approach is currently being

## The environment and obesity

Consulate General of Japan, Chicago

Some cultures encourage obesity in segments of the population. The sumo wrestlers in Japan must be heavy to be successful.

recommended as an alternative to dieting, especially with children. The basis for this recommendation is a series of studies examining the activity levels of obese children. In a summer camp attended by both obese girls and girls who maintained a normal weight, motion pictures were taken of the girls playing tennis, volleyball, and swimming. During a volleyball game, the obese girls were standing or sitting during 90 percent of the observations. The other girls were more likely to be running, jumping, or trying to hit the ball (Bullen, Redd, & Mayer, 1964).

Obesity limits activity and seems to start a cycle that maintains obesity (James & Sahakian, 1981). Fat children cannot run as fast or as long as their friends. Consequently when playing a game, the obese child is given the position that requires the least effort or is asked to keep score. The obese child moves to the sidelines, becomes less active, and gains more weight. To interrupt this cycle of inactivity, obese children need to be involved in an exercise program or an activity that requires a lot of energy. Even if the additional exercise does not cause the child to lose weight, it may keep the child from gaining more weight.

Obesity affects millions of children. Despite our lack of understanding of the physiological factors that control obesity, we do know that genetics, exercise, and eating habits all play a part. Until we understand obesity better, the best advice we can give parents is to establish an exercise program for their children and monitor their diet.

### PHYSICAL DEVELOPMENT

**Human growth**

The earliest longitudinal record is one that depicts human growth. In 1796, Count Philibert Gueneau de Montbeillard began to chart the height of his son. The figures are reproduced here because they provide an example of an individual's growth for 18 years (Tanner, 1978). The graph at the top of Figure 5–11 shows the increase in height from birth to 18 years of age. By studying this curve, you can see that growth is more rapid during some periods than others. The graph at the bottom of Figure 5–11 identifies these growth spurts by depicting the height gained each year. Notice that rapid growth occurs during the first two years and levels off from ages four to eight. At age 11, the Count's son only grew about an inch and a half. He began his adolescent growth spurt at 12 and grew almost five inches (12.5 centimeters).

Figure 5–12 shows the growth velocity at different ages for boys and girls. The girls' curve is practically identical to the boys' until nine years of age. Then the girls' adolescent growth spurt begins. This growth spurt is followed by a slowing of growth after the age of 13 and accounts for most of the difference between the final height of males and females.

Current height and weight charts for boys and girls from 2 to 18 years of age are given in Figure 5–13. The mean height of an 18-year-old girl in the United States is nearly 5 feet, 5 inches (164 centimeters) and the mean weight is 125 pounds. The mean height of an 18-year-old boy is nearly 5 feet, 10 inches (177 centimeters) and the mean weight is 152 pounds (U.S. Health Statistics, 1977). What are the factors that determine whether you are at this mean, at the 10th percentile, or at the 90th percentile?

A person's height depends on nutrition, genetics, growth hormones, and when the adolescent growth spurt occurs. Nutrition has been discussed. Improved nutrition is partially responsible for the height increase that has occurred in the last century. An 18-year-old today is six inches (15 centimeters) taller than his great-great grandfather was at 18 (Tanner, 1978). Since the 1960s, this trend for children to be taller than their parents has slowed, especially in the industrialized nations of the world.

Growth hormone, produced by the pituitary gland, is also necessary for normal growth. Children who do not secrete any of this hormone rarely grow taller than 4 feet, 8 inches (130 centimeters). Growth hormone can now be extracted from the pituitary glands of humans. The extract is given to children who do not produce any growth hormone. These children grow more rapidly than normal and even catch up with some of their peers. Until recently, growth hormone was synthesized from human brains. Hence, it was very dif-

**Figure 5–11**  **Human growth**

Height (centimeters)

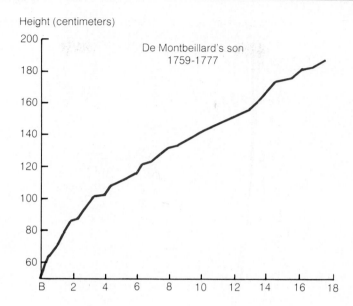

Height gain (centimeters per year)

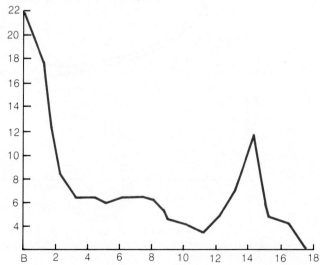

An individual record of de Montbeillard's son's growth in the 19th century. The first section shows the gradual increase in height from birth to age 18. The second section indicates how much growth occurred each year. Growth is most rapid during infancy and adolescence.

Source: Tanner, J. M. (1978). *Fetus into man: Physical growth from conception to maturity*. Cambridge, MA: Harvard Univ. Press.

**Figure 5—12**        **Growth curves for males and females**

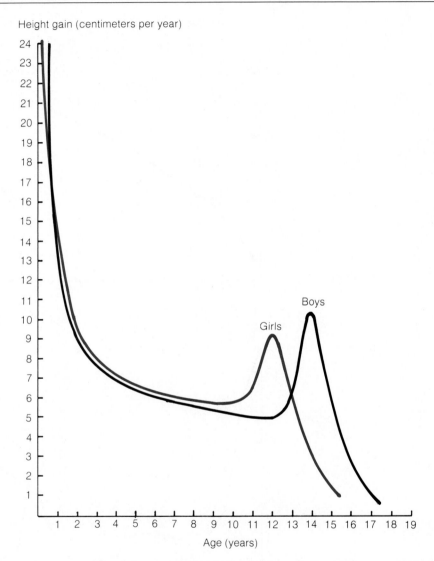

Height gain (centimeters per year)

Age (years)

Growth curves for height in boys and girls. These curves indicate the periods of rapid and slow growth. As shown, girls reach their adolescent growth spurt approximately two years before boys.

Source: Tanner, J. M. (1978). *Fetus into man: Physical growth from conception to maturity*. Cambridge, MA: Harvard Univ. Press.

**Figure 5–13**   **Height and weight charts**

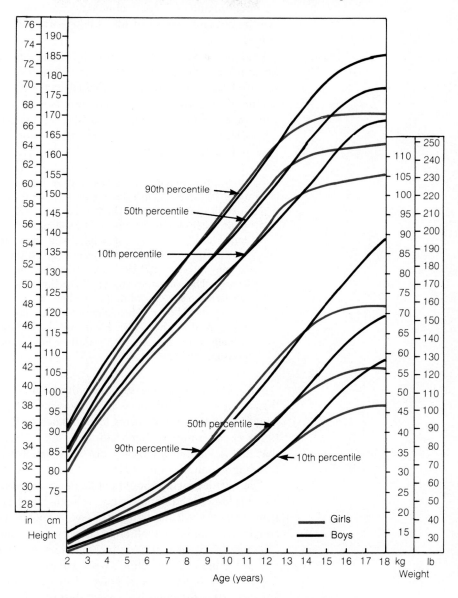

Current height and weight charts for children in the United States

Source: Foreyt, J. P., & Goodrick, G. K. (1981). Childhood obesity. In E. J. Mash & L. G. Terdal (Eds.), *Behavioral assessment of childhood disorders*. New York: Guilford Press.

ficult to obtain. A small vial could cost $10,000. Because treatments were expensive, they were limited to children who were producing no growth hormone. Thanks to genetic engineering, growth hormone can now be produced in large quantities. This technological advance means that growth hormone will be available for all of the children who need it and it will be reasonably priced.

Children who are in very stressful situations often fail to grow normally. Stress inhibits the production of growth hormone. When the source of stress is removed, growth hormone is released and the children resume growth. This condition, known as deprivation dwarfism or failure-to-thrive, may explain why some children who have adequate diets do not grow as they should (Gardner, 1962). The following example from World War II underlines the role that stress plays in growth.

> A British nutritionist, Elsie Widdowson, studied the growth of 50 children in two small municipal orphanages in postwar Germany. For the first six months of the study, the children in both orphanages ate only official rations. After six months, the children living in The Bird's Nest received additional bread, jam, and orange juice while those at The Bee Hive remained on the same diet. Mrs. Widdowson expected the children at The Bird's Nest to grow more rapidly. Her expectations did not consider the matrons in charge. The woman in charge of The Bird's Nest was a stern disciplinarian. The tension she created in the children meant that they didn't grow as much as they should have. The children in The Bee Hive who had a kinder matron gained weight rapidly. Six months later, the children at The Bee Hive actually weighed more, even with their limited diet (Gardner, 1972; Widdowson, 1951).

Folk wisdom has long suggested that children grow more in the summer than at other times of the year. This is definitely true among European and American children and seems to be related to the longer number of daylight hours in the summer. Light falling on the eye somehow signals the organism that this is a growing season—just as it signals some animals that this is the breeding season (Tanner, 1978).

The role of genetics should not be underplayed in predicting a child's height. The likelihood of a couple who are both 5 feet tall having a basketball star is negligible. Even if the father is 6 feet, 4 inches and the mother is 5 feet, the couple may not have a tall child. Each parent contributes to the child's height (Tanner, 1978). It is sometimes important to know a child's growth rate. X-rays of the bones in the child's wrist will predict future growth very accurately. Figure 5–14 shows the wrist bones of two 14-year-old boys. The X-ray on the left shows that the child has a great deal of space left between the bones in his wrist. Notice too, that the *growth plates* at the end of the arm bones look like separate pieces of bone. This X-ray tells us that this boy has a bone age of 12 years and he will continue to grow for several years. The growth plates in the X-ray on the right are almost indistinguishable from the arm bones, and there

**Figure 5—14**                    **Wrist X-rays reveal growth**

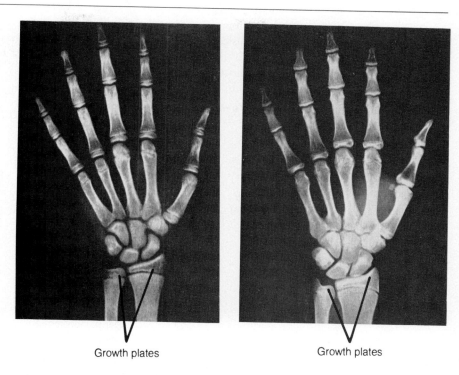

Growth plates                                   Growth plates

Wrist X-rays are used to indicate how much more growing a particular child will do. The wrist of the 14-year-old boy on the left indicates that he has much more growing to do. The 14-year-old on the right has completed his growth.

Source: Tanner, J. M. (1978). *Fetus into man: Physical growth from conception to maturity* (p. 80). Cambridge, MA: Harvard Univ. Press.

is little space left between bones. This child has a bone age of 16, and growth is virtually complete.

Wrist X-rays are normally used to assess the future growth of children who are either very tall or very short. These tests help physicians decide whether or not to intervene in the child's normal growth. Sometimes wrist X-rays are used to determine the growth of an athlete or dancer. The Royal Ballet often suggests that children seeking entry into the elite Corps de Ballet have wrist X-rays taken. Ballet dancers must conform to a fairly narrow range of heights; hence, children who could be outside that range might want to reconsider embarking on years of rigorous, specialized training (Tanner, 1978).

**Motor skills**

The landmarks of infancy are most obvious in the child's motor development. An infant lifts its head, rolls over, creeps, sits up, crawls, stands, and finally walks. Each success is proudly recorded by the parents. The age of attaining each of these milestones is some indication of the infant's development. Nancy Bayley has designed a test of infant motor development that shows how many steps the child has mastered. The average age of mastering a task is listed in Figure 5–15, as well as the range of ages when babies master the skill. These ranges, often months apart, attest to the individual differences in acquiring simple motor skills (Bayley, 1969).

**Figure 5–15**        **Bayley's motor development scale**

| Walking | Mean age for mastery (months) | Range of ages for mastery (months) | Fine motor grasping | Mean age for mastery (months) | Range of ages for mastery (months) |
|---|---|---|---|---|---|
| Crawling movements | .4 | .1–3 | Holds onto red ring | .8 | .3–3 |
| Sits with support | 2.3 | 1–5 | Arm thrusts in play | .8 | .3–2 |
| Pulls self to sitting | 5.3 | 4.–8 | Opens hands | 2.7 | .7–6 |
| Prewalking progression | 7.1 | 5.–11 | Grasps with palm | 3.7 | 2–7 |
| Pulls to standing position | 8.1 | 5.–12 | Partially opposes thumb | 4.9 | 4–8 |
| Walks with help | 9.6 | 7–12 | Reaches with one hand | 5.4 | 4–8 |
| Stands alone | 11.0 | 9–16 | Reaches for pellet | 5.6 | 4–8 |
| Walks alone | 11.7 | 9–17 | Thumb opposed to finger | 6.9 | 5–9 |
| | | | Finger prehension | 7.4 | 6–10 |
| | | | Pincer prehension | 8.9 | 7–12 |

Grasp of a Cube

Precarious grasp        Palmar grasp        Finger grasp        Forefinger grasp

Grasp of a Raisin

Whole hand contact        Scissors grasp        Index finger approach        Neat pincer grasp

Nancy Bayley developed a scale of motor tasks that are completed in infancy. The different skills that precede walking and grasping are indicated. The average age for mastering the task is indicated as well as the range of the children's ages when they mastered the task.

**Figure 5—15**     *Concluded*

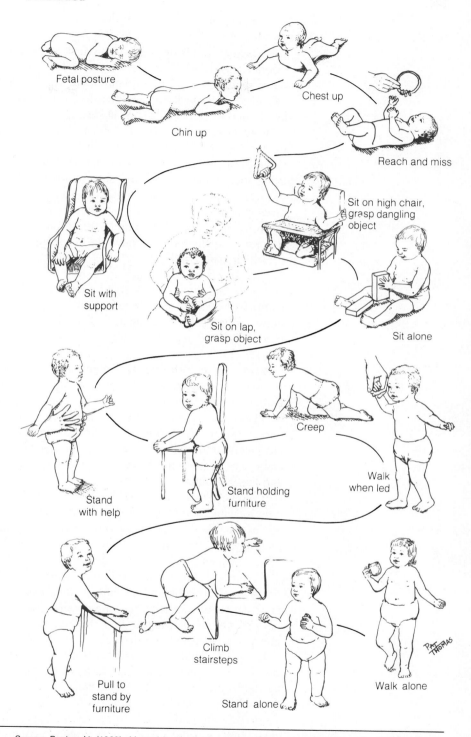

Fetal posture

Chin up

Chest up

Reach and miss

Sit with support

Sit on lap, grasp object

Sit on high chair, grasp dangling object

Sit alone

Stand with help

Stand holding furniture

Creep

Walk when led

Pull to stand by furniture

Climb stairsteps

Stand alone

Walk alone

Source: Bayley, N. (1969). *Manual for the Bayley scales of infant development.* New York: Psychological Corporation.

**Walking.** Walking is one of the first motor skills that was studied in detail (Shirley, 1931; McGraw & Breeze, 1941). In the 1930s, children usually raised their heads at 1 month and began creeping at 10 months and walking at 15 months. In the 1980s, children follow the same sequence, but are walking by 12 months (Frankenberg & Dodds, 1967).

**Reaching and holding.** Infants also go through a series of steps as they master the use of their hands and fingers. Newborns use their hands to bat or swipe in the general direction of toys. By kindergarten, children are capable of using their fingers to perform fine motor skills such as stringing beads and coloring within the lines of a picture. This progression is less familiar than the development of walking, so it will be presented in more detail.

To reach an object, the infant bats at the object with closed fists and swinging arms. At this point, infants do not seem to have a great deal of control over their hands and arms (Huff & Halton, 1978). By four months however, the eye and hand work together. Rather than swiping, infants open their fists and grab the object. Even at this stage, the child grabs the object with his palm. In two more months, children will pick up objects with their fingers, not with their palms (see Figure 5–15). The opposition of the thumb and index finger, another step in development, appears at approximately nine months (Bayley, 1969).

**Rhythmical behaviors.** Motor skills also include the kicking, rocking, waving, and bouncing that infants engage in for hours. Recent research by Esther Thelen (1981) has helped us understand the function of rhythmical behaviors during the first year of life. Rhythmical behaviors are a transition stage between behaviors that are reflexive and uncoordinated and behaviors that are precise and controlled. For example, rhythmical kicking movements become very frequent just before the child begins to creep. Rocking on the hands and knees is noted prior to crawling.

If mothers rock, carry, and bounce their children, the children do not engage in as many rhythmical movements. When infants do not receive enough of this stimulation, they may compensate by producing these movements by themselves. Infants in institutions often rock themselves (Provence & Lipton, 1962). Isolated monkeys also engage in rocking (Harlow & Harlow, 1962).

Rhythmical motor behavior is another way the infant can signal the mother. At about six months of age, any exciting event—the mother appearing, the presentation of a favorite toy, or even dinnertime—will trigger rhythmical behaviors. Dr. Thelen argues that children respond to changes in the environment by producing these simple patterned movements.

Using Dr. Thalen's research, a scenario of how brain development, rhythmic behavior, and motor skills fit together can be written. Remember that in newborns the neurons of the cortex are relatively isolated. The motor behavior that newborns use consists primarily of reflexes. As the cortical neurons develop more dendrites and form integrated patterns, the behaviors become more rhythmical and the infant can activate a particular part of the body. When neuronal networks are mature, motor coordination is smooth, precise, and controlled by the infant. This scenario fits well with the hierarchical organization of the nervous system that was presented earlier in the chapter. Rhythmical behaviors seem to be patterns of activity generated by the brain. Their existence shows that the infant's cortex is maturing and that finer, more precise movements will soon follow (Connolly, 1981).

Another aspect of motor development that correlates with the development of the brain is the order in which motor control takes place. Motor development starts from the head and spreads to the legs—a pattern called *cephalocaudal* development. Infants gain control over their heads, eyes, and mouth before they gain control over their hands. The lower half of the body and the legs are the last to be controlled by the infant.

**Factors influencing motor development.** The genetic component in motor development has been documented by studies of twins. If one identical

**Figure 5–16**             **Experience and motor development**

*Ray Rairall: The Associated Press*

Experience can influence motor development. This eight-month-old is getting an early start at a difficult motor skill.

twin girl is walking, her twin is likely to be walking also. Fraternal twins are less likely to reach the motor stages at the same time (Wilson, 1976).

Nutritional deficiencies that affect the growth of the brain also affect the mastery of various motor skills. Given the scenario of neurological development and motor development that was outlined above, we would expect infants with poor diets to begin rhythmical behaviors later. Extending rhythmical behaviors into controlled sequences will also take longer if poor nutrition delays the development of the brain.

The experiences that an infant has during the first months of life can also influence motor development. First-born children tend to walk earlier, presumably because of the extra stimulation and attention they receive (Bayley, 1965). Newborns who receive extra practice of the walking reflex for the first two months walked earlier than a group who did not receive that kind of stimulation (Zelaso, Zelaso, & Kolb, 1972). A variety of culturally determined child-rearing practices seem to affect motor development. Mothers from Zambia carry their children everywhere until they can sit upright without falling over. Once children have mastered this position, their mothers encourage them to practice a variety of motor skills. These children are likely to walk early (Goldberg, 1972). In the Yucatan, infants master fine motor skills earlier than in the United States, but they walk later. The authors note that the children are never allowed to play on the floor and hence have little chance to practice the skills they need to walk (Solomons & Solomons, 1975). Early experience can also facilitate specialized skills that otherwise might not appear for years. The water skiing sensation in Figure 5–16 is eight months old.

## SUMMARY

Understanding brain development is becoming increasingly important in the study of the physical development of the child. Hence, this chapter began with a short description of the communication center of the brain—the cerebral cortex. The neuron, the messenger in the brain, receives information from the environment and relays it to decision-making areas of the brain. The development of this communication system is achieved through the processes of cell division, cell migration and specification, and cell death. Since the brain does not develop in a void, the child's environment can affect all three of these processes. Some environments are so lacking in stimulation that the brain's development is not even maintained at a normal level. Fortunately, humans have a long period of brain development that makes it possible to recover from mild deprivation. More severe deprivation, like that experienced by Genie, may well have a permanent effect on the brain. Her years of isolation and deprivation were accompanied by a pattern of brain functioning that is not normal, even in children who are mildly retarded. Most environments facilitate the development of the brain; and Rosenzweig demonstrated that with stimulation from the environment, it is possible to induce development which otherwise would not have occurred.

Hormones, food, and disease can also modify the development of the brain. Hormones can alter the structure of the brain permanently or they can activate changes such as puberty. Good nutrition will increase the number of brain cells, will encourage dendritic branching and the growth of dendritic spines, and will supply the brain with the right nutrients for optimal performance. The opposite case, severe malnutrition, means that an infant begins life with fewer brain cells, has fewer nutrients to promote dendritic branching, and may have sleeping or learning problems because the brain is not receiving the needed nutrients.

The brain controls an infant's states and biases other aspects of the infant's behavior. The biasing is seen in hemispheric specialization and some sex differences. Even if the brain biases the child toward being a left hander, a determined parent or an accident that leads to amputation can change that bias. The same is true of sex differences between males and females. The socialization of the child can modify or exaggerate the built-in biases of the brain.

Physical development during the first year depends on feeding practices. The severely malnourished and the obese infant represent the two extremes of underfeeding and overfeeding. Two of the most severe consequences of underfeeding are marasmus and Kwashiokor. Although relatively rare in westernized countries, these diseases are very common in Africa and can often be linked to the feeding practices of the mother. Breast-feeding, in addition to providing a food specially formulated for human growth, protects a child from infection. In third-world countries, it also affords a measure of birth control and is much less expensive than formulas. Obesity is more common in westernized countries. Genetic factors play an important role in obesity, but it may be that encouraging the infant to finish the last bite also causes obesity.

As with weight, a child's height is a function of genetics and nutrition. Height can also be affected by growth hormones and stress. Interestingly, if the stress a child is experiencing is removed, catch-up growth will occur.

The mastery of motor skills—turning over, crawling, sitting up, and walking—is an area of development that is watched proudly by parents. Although the sequence of behaviors that precedes walking has been known for years, the link between brain development, rhythmical behavior that the infant controls, and the acquisition of motor skills is a recent one.

# CHAPTER 6
## Cognitive development in infancy

To perceive, to know, to learn, to remember, to understand—these activities are considered the essence of being human. Studying how children acquire these high-level cognitive skills occupies a prominent place in developmental psychology. Beginning at birth we want to know what infants look at and what they see. We want to know how they learn that water spills, whether they remember what happened yesterday, and how they remember it. In short, we want to chart the workings of an infant's mind, from the first uncontrolled reflexes to the first word.

In this chapter, we will follow infants as they learn about their environments. This goal will take us on a fascinating tour through infant laboratories around the world. In these university laboratories infants, sometimes only a few hours old, are photographed when they open their eyes and are monitored while human faces appear and disappear. In some laboratories, infants can turn their heads and make a mobile spin. They can kick their feet and see brightly colored plastic butterflies swoop and dive above them. In other labs, psychologists spend hours playing a version of hide-and-seek with nine-month-olds. All of these experiments are designed to help us understand how the infant acquires knowledge about the world.

### METHODS

Before we begin this excursion into infant cognition, we need to consider the limitations that surround research with infants. You cannot ask a simple question and get a straight answer. Infants are notorious for falling asleep the minute that all the equipment is set up and running properly. Furthermore, young infants do not have a great deal of control over their bodies. In the past, this lack of control has been like the adolescent experimenting with the flea. After removing all the flea's legs, the young scientist commanded the flea to jump. The flea remained still. Two more commands were ignored and the adolescent recorded, "Flea is deaf." For many years, psychologists underestimated the skills and abilities of infants because it was so difficult to get the infant to respond. Recently, psychologists have devised ingenious ways to find out what is going on in the child's head. As we consider these methods, remember that the first rule of infant research is to know the state of the infant.

Testing an active-alert infant yields very different results than testing an infant who is on the verge of sleep. If an infant is in an active, alert state, how do we proceed?

**Observation**

Some of the best studies of infants have come from observation. Jean Piaget developed this simple skill into an art. His classic book on the origins of intelligence is based on careful, scientific observations of three infants in different situations (Piaget, 1952). Esther Thelen's (1981) research on rhythmical behavior in infants also involved close and continued observation of one type of behavior. These observations of infants have provided detailed descriptions of the behavioral changes that occur during the first two years of life.

**Direct assessments of infants**

Despite their value, observations are often subjective. For this reason, it is useful to circumvent the observer and measure the infant's behavior directly. Some of the behaviors of infants that have been used in experimental studies include the infant's sucking response, heart rate, and electrical potential of the infant's brain.

**Sucking.** Sucking is often used to measure attention. The baby sucks a nipple that is hooked to a polygraph (see Figure 6–1). As the infant sucks, the psychologist presents different pictures or sounds to the infant. With each presentation, the infant stops sucking momentarily. If the same sound is presented 10 or 12 times, infants interrupt their sucking less and less. By monitoring infants' sucking, we can assess their attention.

**Heart rate.** An infant's heart rate is another measure psychologists use to understand the infant's experiences (Campos, 1976). When a new toy or sound

**Figure 6–1**     **Recording an infant's respiration, heart rate, and sucking**

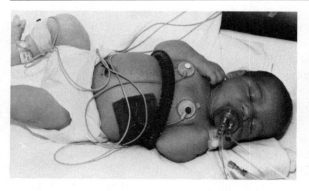 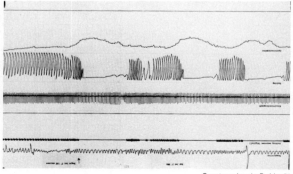

*Courtesy Lewis P. Lipsitt*

This newborn infant is prepared for simultaneous recording of respiration, heart rate, and sucking.

is presented to an infant, the heart rate slows down (Kagan & Lewis, 1965). This response is very reliable. If infants are placed in a situation that the experimenter thinks is stimulating, but the infant's heart rate does not change, the experimenter revises his assessment of the situation.

The classic visual cliff experiment provides an example of how heart rate is used to study an infant's behavior (see Figure 6–2). As soon as infants can crawl, they will avoid the deep side of the cliff—where it looks as if they might fall (Gibson & Walk, 1960). What about infants who cannot crawl. Are they aware of the deep side of the visual cliff? Joseph Campos (1976) has shown that two and three-month-old infants "notice" the deep side. That is, their heart rate slows down. Infants only a month old show no change in heart rate (Campos, 1976).

**Figure 6–2**          **Visual cliff experiment**

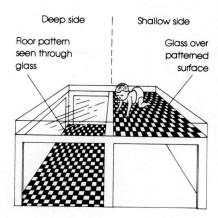

*William Vandivert*

A trusting infant is coaxed across the optical illusion of a cliff. Infants avoid the visual "cliff" as early as six months of age. Their reluctance to cross it indicates that they can perceive depth and realize that they might fall.

Source: What do babies know? (1983, August 15). *Time, 122*, p. 55. Copyright 1983 Time Inc. All rights reserved. Reprinted by permission from Time.

A decrease in heart rate typically means that you have the infant's attention. What about an increase in heart rate? Fear-provoking and distressing situations seem to increase the infant's heart rate. Placing a six-month-old on the deep side of the visual cliff will increase the heart rate (Campos, 1976). Not only do these infants notice, they are frightened.

**Measurements of electrical activity in the brain.** Recordings from the surface of the brain, called *event related brain potentials*, are a third technique used to study infants' cognitive processes (Hofmann, Salapatek, & Kuskowski, 1981). This technique involves placing electrodes on the infant's scalp and recording the brain's response to a stimulating event. Event related brain potentials require no response from infants, yet they provide a reliable measure of central nervous system activity (Courchesne, 1977).

Dennis Molfese is one investigator who is using event related brain potentials to study infant behavior. He places electrodes on the left and right sides of the infant's head. Then the words "dog" or "boy" are spoken or a C major chord is played on the piano (see Figure 6–3). The electrical activity on the two sides of the brain indicates that, even in infants, the two hemispheres process these stimuli in very different ways (Molfese, 1979).

**Figure 6—3**                          **Auditory evoked potentials**

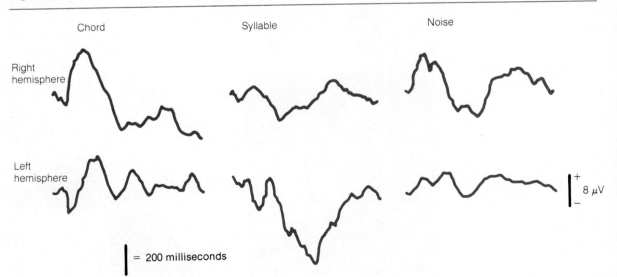

Auditory evoked potentials recorded from the left and right hemispheres of an infant. When the infant hears a chord, the right hemisphere registers the event more clearly than the left. However, when a syllable is presented, the left hemisphere registers the event more clearly. During the first months of life, the left hemisphere is already especially sensitive to speech sounds.

Source: Molfese, D. L. (1977). Infant cerebral asymmetry. In S. J. Segalowitz & F. A. Gruber (Eds.), *Language development and neurological theory* (p. 24). New York: Academic Press.

Similar measures have been used to assess how the brain reacts when a picture of a toy is presented (Cohen, DeLoache, & Strauss, 1979). The infant's reactions to pictures of faces is especially interesting. Based on the electrical activity of their brains, we can conclude that four- to seven-month-old infants are able to remember a face that is presented frequently. They can also discriminate the first face from a second one that is presented occasionally (Courchesne, Ganz, & Norcia, 1981).

Although newborns cannot talk and have limited control over their bodies, we have learned that they have sophisticated skills for learning about their environment. The cognitive development of infants builds on these initial skills.

## THE NEWBORN'S REPERTOIRE OF SKILLS

### Vision

At birth, an infant's eyes are still very immature. The cells at the center of the retina are short and thick instead of long and slender as they will be in a few months (Abramov, Gordon, Hendrickson, Hainline, Dobson, & La-Bossiere, 1982). In addition, the infant's ability to focus is not as automatic as it is in adults (Banks, 1980). This physiological immaturity limits how well the infant can see. Large objects and contrasts can be seen, but the infant's image contains few details. When objects are close to newborns, specifically between seven and nine inches, they can see more clearly.

Presenting infants with different pictures and recording the time they spend looking at each tells us about the infant's visual preferences. The favorite is the human face, and this preference seems to be built into the infant's visual equipment. Infants just 9 minutes old prefer the human face to other visual targets (Goren, Sarty, & Wu, 1975). It is unlikely that they have learned this preference. Infants prefer patterns that are somewhat complex and patterns that incorporate a contrast. The eye of a human incorporates this kind of sharp contrast. Perhaps it is this feature that attracts infants to the human face.

The fact that a newborn sees best at seven to nine inches means that whenever the child is being held for feedings, there is an enticing target in his visual field—the mother's face. More than one ethologist has suggested that this is a way of insuring that the infant will become familiar with its mother's face. At two weeks of age when infants are presented with pictures of their mother and a stranger's picture, they spend a longer time looking at their mother. They look away, even turning their heads, when the stranger's picture is presented (Carpenter, 1974).

### Hearing

Newborns hear very well. They react to sounds by turning their heads and eyes toward the sound. This sense is also well developed *in utero* (Birnholz & Benacerraf, 1983). One can imagine the sounds a fetus hears—the sloshing of the mother's stomach, the heartbeat, and the mother's muted voice. It has been suggested that the fetus develops some familiarity with the mother's voice *in utero*. From filming the mother-infant interaction and analyzing each frame, we know that the mother's voice is very effective in arousing infants who are only 12 to 20 hours old. When infants hear their mothers speak, they become alert and begin to move in a way that is coordinated with their mother's sing-song narrative (Condon & Sander, 1974).

By three days of age, infants recognize their mother's voice. This was determined by having infants suck on a nipple that would activate a recording. While they sucked, infants heard either their mother or a stranger reading Dr. Seuss's book, *And To Think That I Saw It On Mulberry Street*. These newborns recognized their mother's voice and would start sucking to turn on the recording of their mother's voice. The stranger's voice was not nearly as appealing. These infants lived in a group nursery and were taken to their mothers four times a day for feeding. Hence, no child could have had more than 12 hours of exposure to the mother's voice. Perhaps the infants learned to recognize their mother's voice in those 12 hours, or perhaps they learned *in utero* (DeCasper & Fifer, 1980).

As with vision, infants prefer patterned or complex sounds rather than pure tones. The most effective sound for alerting the neonate is a complex one—the human voice. The higher frequencies that both mothers and fathers adopt when talking with infants are very effective attention getters.

## Smell and taste

The sense of smell in humans is often regarded as unimportant, but it probably plays a role in mother-infant interaction. Each of us has an odor that is as unique as our fingerprints (MacFarlane, 1977). Such odors are most likely to be noticeable when people are in close contact. A mother and her infant maintain this kind of contact. Olfactory cues may help the infant and mother recognize each other. Newborns have a well developed sense of smell and can distinguish the particular fragrance of their own mothers as early as the 10th day after birth (MacFarlane, 1977).

The fetus can and does experience different tastes. On rare occasions, it is necessary to X-ray the fetus. To make the X-rays as useful as possible, an opaque substance that shows up on the X-ray is injected into the amniotic fluid. The fetus often quits drinking the fluid the minute the injection is complete, primarily because the substance has an unpleasant taste. When the amniotic fluid is sweetened, however, the fetus will drink more of it than usual. The fetus prefers sweet tastes even *in utero*.

Steiner (1979) has photographs of newborns who participated in a taste experiment before their first postnatal feeding (see Figure 6–4). The three infants in the photographs were not given anything in the first stimulus condition. They received distilled water in the second condition, and a sweet liquid in the third condition. The fourth substance was sour, and the fifth was bitter. Steiner reports that the facial expressions of the babies are similar to the facial expressions of adults when given the same substances. The

**Figure 6—4**                    **Can infants taste the difference?**

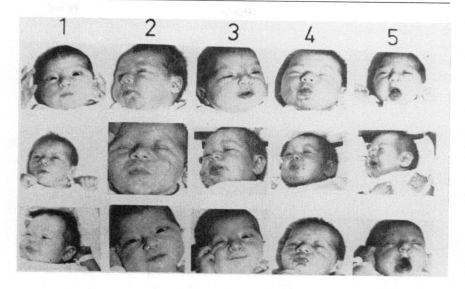

Newborn infants as they appear (1) when awake, (2) when tasting distilled water, (3) when given a sweet solution, (4) when given a sour solution, and (5) when given a bitter solution. These expressions, much like adults' responses to the same substances, indicate that newborns can taste the difference.

Source: From Steiner, J. E. (1979). Human facial expressions in response to taste and smell stimulation. In H. W. Reese & L. P. Lipsitt (Eds.), *Advances in child development and behavior* (Vol. 13). New York: Academic Press. Reprinted by permission.

sour taste elicited a puckering of the lips, while the bitter taste evoked a spitting reaction.

**Touch**

Infants from many species are sensitive to touch and seem to prefer warm skin. The animal's preference for this kind of contact comfort was shown in a classic study by Harry Harlow (1958). Infants were fed by mother substitutes constructed of wire. They preferred the softer, cuddlier terry cloth mothers even though they did not provide food. One of the arguments given to persuade human mothers to breast-feed is that it maximizes this kind of skin-to-skin contact between the mother and infant. A sensitivity to pain is also evident in newborns. Being circumcised and having the heel pricked to test for PKU provoke immediate, lusty cries of pain in the neonate.

Newborns can see, hear, feel, taste, and smell. In addition, they have a variety of reflexes and loosely patterned behaviors. These basic skills and behaviors form the foundation for the child's rapid cognitive development. With this catalog of beginning skills in mind, we can turn to the cognitive changes that occur during the first two years.

**Contact comfort**

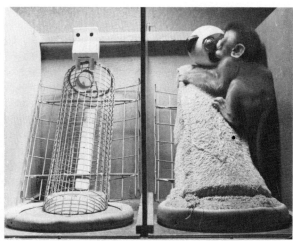

*University of Wisconsin Primate Laboratory*

Although the wire mother provided these infant monkeys with milk, they preferred the softness of the terry cloth mothers and stayed with them except when they had to feed.

## SENSORY MOTOR DEVELOPMENT

For over 50 years, Jean Piaget, a Swiss psychologist, conducted research on children's thoughts. Piaget began his studies in the 1930s when there were no computers to average brain potentials or motion picture projectors to view and code each frame of an infant's behavior. Armed with a pencil and a notebook, he recorded the changes in the behavior of his three children—Laurent, Lucienne, and Jacqueline—and made inferences about the cognitive capacities that had to accompany these changes. In a rich and detailed set of descriptions, he charted how infants developed during the first two years—a period he named the sensory motor period. From the 1930s until the 1980s, he extended his study of cognition, ultimately presenting a theory that described the acquisition of knowledge from birth through adolescence.

**Constructing the environment**

Piaget's view of cognitive development veered sharply from the most popular view at that time. He regarded infants as actively involved in the construction of their experiences. The notion that children construct their knowledge permeates Piaget's writings (Furth, 1969). Children do not passively wait for the environment to have an impact. Instead, they use the information or organization that they already have to order, catalog, and process the people and objects they encounter. An example of how a person's organization might shape the environment will help clarify Piaget's views. Suppose you are shown the following 20 numbers for five seconds and are asked to reproduce them:

4 9 1 6 2 5 3 6 4 9 6 4 8 1 1 0 0 1 2 1.

The array is too long for most people to remember in five seconds. However, if you have an organization or structure for these numbers, you might be able to reproduce them after only five seconds. The numbers listed are actually the squares of the numbers 2 to 11. With this information, you can easily construct the array. In Piaget's terms, your organization of numbers, which includes information about squares, helps you remember that array.

All humans possess internal organizations or structures that they use to help them understand their environment. The process of interpreting the environment in terms of your internal structures is called *assimilation*. You assimilated the array of numbers presented earlier to your internal structure about squares. Preschoolers and infants have no understanding of the squares of numbers. Hence, even the additional clue would not help them remember the array of numbers. Still, preschoolers and infants have organized a lot of information about their world. This information often determines how they assimilate their environment. Preschoolers may assimilate all large four-legged animals to a single concept—cows. Infants also assimilate the environment to their organization. Once infants learn how to throw objects, they throw all sorts of objects. They assimilate or understand these objects in terms of the action of throwing.

These three examples illustrate how adults, preschoolers, and infants all assimilate information into their internal organization and structure. The process of assimilation begins at birth, and the initial organization or structure consists of the newborn's reflexes and basic sensory skills.

A person's internal organization is not static but undergoes many changes through the life span. Elementary schoolchildren do not confuse cows and horses because their understanding of animals includes horses, goats, and elephants. These changes in the child's structures are accomplished by a process called *accommodation*. Although the child engages the environment with a given organization, if there is something new and different in the environment that does not fit that organization neatly, the child alters the organization. Through accommodation, the toddler expands his organization of four-legged animals to include horses, hippos, goats, and elephants. The infant expands his understanding of objects to include those that are thrown and those that are squeezed or banged.

These two processes, assimilation and accommodation, explain how the child constructs the environment. At any point, there is an internal organization guiding interaction. That organization changes when children experiment, learn, or encounter information that does not fit the way they have been organizing their environment.

This brief introduction to Piaget's theory suggests that the child's interactions with the environment are fluid and dynamic. They are also directed by the child. Information cannot be delivered to children with the expectation that they will master it. Some information fits with what they already know and is assimilated easily. Some information is new, but children can incorporate it into their organization by expanding their internal structures. Some information, however, is very foreign, and children are not likely to be able to use it at all. One has only to compare what three college students remember from the same lecture to see that the organization and understanding students bring to the lecture influences what they learn.

Once we understand assimilation and accommodation we can draw another conclusion—changes in a child's internal organization are made gradually. It would be impossible to teach infants about the squares of numbers if they have no understanding of numbers. A persistent psychologist could undoubtedly get a toddler to parrot "the square of 3 is 9." A meaningful understanding can only occur after the child understands quantities and the relationships between numbers.

Finally, we can conclude that the same processes operate throughout life. Infants, children, college students, and adults are all constantly revising their

**Figure 6—5**                                          **Piaget's theory**

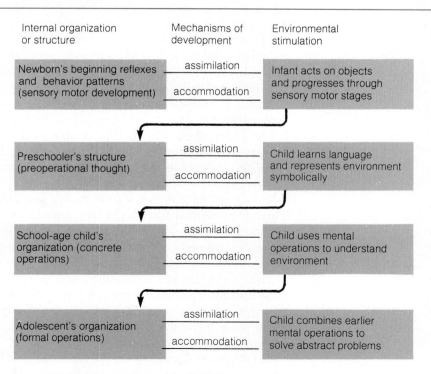

Assimilation and accommodation are two processes that continue throughout the life span. As children learn and change through these two processes, they acquire differing skills. These abilities define the stages Piaget has made famous.

understanding of the world through the dual processes of assimilation and accommodation. But at each age, the resulting organizations look quite different (see Figure 6–5).

**Stages**

After outlining the processes that infants use to acquire knowledge, Piaget began to describe the differences in the ways infants, preschoolers, school-age children, and adolescents understand their environments. At each of these ages, different internal structures are operating. The internal organizations that infants exhibit are limited. Unlike adults, infants are not constantly thinking about their environment. Their knowledge is based on actions. These actions become organized into patterns of behaviors called *schemes*. Cognitive growth is the result of the infant actively exploring the environment and developing more organized schemes. During the first two years, Piaget outlines six different milestones based on the child's rapidly changing schemes.

**Stage 1—exercising reflexes and built-in patterns of behavior— birth to 1 month.** The newborn's beginning equipment, as we have seen, is primarily a set of reflexes and some loosely patterned behaviors. These reflexes and beginning sensory skills constitute the initial organization of the child. During the first month, through the dual processes of assimilation and accommodation, these initial skills become more stable, more useful, and more organized. After perfecting the sucking reflex, the infant may suck fingers, blankets, stuffed animals, and his parents' shoulders. The same is true of the "looking" reflex. In the first week, the infant's eyes are not always coordinated. By exercising the eyes, the pattern of behavior that is called "looking" becomes well established. During active alert states, the infant does a great deal of looking. Even the grasping reflex changes during the first month of life and is gradually transformed into a grasping scheme. All of these initial behaviors—sucking, looking, and grasping—are part of the infant's initial equipment. As these skills become more organized, they provide the infant with a way to explore. The looking scheme, the grasping scheme, and the sucking scheme are actually the organizations that guide the infant's transactions with the environment. More sophisticated structures evolve from these rudimentary schemes.

Notice that there is very little intentional behavior during this period. Infants do not decide to suck a pacifier. When a pacifier accidentally touches the lips, the infant begins sucking. The automatic character of the infant's response is a hallmark of Stage 1.

**Stage 2—extending reflexes—1 to 4 months.** Before infants can really understand the world, they must coordinate the information that is being gathered through the schemes of looking, grasping, or sucking. Although this coordination takes time, the beginning steps are seen during the second stage of the sensory motor period. At the beginning of this stage, the infant notices the association between some action and a consequence. For example, Laurent's hand somehow gets into his mouth. When he loses contact with his hand, he tries again to get his hand into his mouth.

His arms, instead of gesticulating aimlessly, constantly move toward his mouth. Thirteen times in succession I have been able to observe the hand go back into the mouth. There is no longer any doubt that coordination exists. His right hand may be seen approaching his mouth. But as only the index finger was grasped, the hand fell out again. Shortly after, it returned. This time the thumb was in the mouth. I then remove the hand and place it near his waist. After a few minutes, the lips move and the hand approaches them again. (Piaget, 1952, p. 52–53)

The importance of the second stage of sensory motor development is that the schemes we saw in the first stage no longer exist in isolation. The infant

---

**Figure 6—6**                    **Coordinating the eyes and hands**

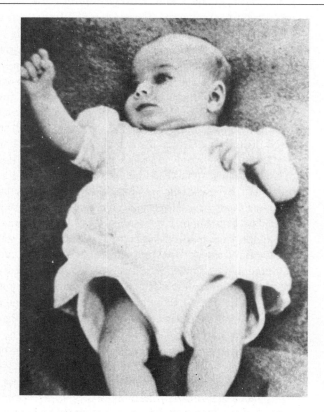

The simple act of looking at what you are holding requires that the child's eyes and hands work together. The process of coordinating the schemes of grasping and looking involves the following states: (1) swipes at object, (2) unilateral hand raising, (3) both hands raised, (4) hand regard, (5) alternating glance between hand and object, and (6) clasping hands together.

Source: From White, B. L., Castle, P., & Held, R. (1964). Observations on the development of visually directed reaching. *Child Development, 35,* 349–364. Reprinted by permission of the Society for Research in Child Development.

begins to relate these behaviors. Laurent's struggle to get his hand into his mouth illustrates the gradual changes that take place in the sucking and grasping schemes so that ultimately infants can direct their hand to their mouth quickly and effectively. Laurent is practicing two schemes—sucking with his mouth and swiping with his hands. Initially, these two actions are isolated. As he achieves hand-mouth coordination, a new higher level behavioral scheme is established (see Figure 6–6). Now he can maneuver his hands into his mouth. This new action reflects the infant's revised organization or structure.

In addition to coordination, we see that the infant takes a more directive role in exploring. Looking is one scheme that demonstrates this increased control. When looking was merely an exercise, it was not particularly directed. Now Laurent explores by looking. This is a subtle change but an extremely important one. When reflexes were the primary way of responding, the infant had much less control. Now the infant is influencing the exploration, the looking, and the grasping.

In the second stage of the sensory motor period, there is a definite change from the reflexive behavior of the first stage. The skills that the child had at birth have been practiced and organized into higher level schemes that involve two senses. More importantly, infants have much more control over these behaviors.

**Stage 3—integrating senses—4 to 10 months.** Each stage builds on the one before, and comparing behaviors in two adjacent stages makes the limits of the earlier stage and the progress of the later stage clear. In this period, all the senses become fully coordinated. Not only can infants get their thumbs into their mouths, they can see or hear an object, direct their arm to it, grab it, and put it in their mouths. Jacqueline hears a rattle shake. She cannot see it, but she reaches in the direction of the sound and turns her head to see if she can see the rattle. When her hands touch it, she grabs it and pulls it into view. She finishes this whole coordinated sequence by sucking on the object she obtains. The coordination of earlier, isolated schemes (i.e., seeing, grasping, sucking) is complete. The child now has a more flexible and more sophisticated organization to guide the exploration of the environment.

In this stage, the intentions and goals that were missing before become more evident. The child observes an action, then tries to reproduce it. For example, rhythmical kicking causes some toys attached to Jacqueline's bassinet to shake. This display motivates her to try to make them shake again. The initial occurrence is, as in the second stage, accidental. But once it happens, the child can willfully reproduce it.

The combination of fully coordinated schemes and the ability to carry out simple goals helps the child explore everyday objects. Toward the end of this stage, infants understand that objects exist independently of them. This realization, fittingly called the *object concept*, is really a monumental accomplishment because it signals the beginning of symbolic processes. To understand that an object is permanent and still exists when it cannot be seen or heard or felt means that the infant has developed some way to imagine or remember the object. Acquiring an object concept signifies a transition from relying on actions and simple schemes to representing the world in the mind. Hence, we need to examine the object concept in some detail. To form an object concept, infants must first understand that an object is the sum of their impressions. Mother is no longer an isolated voice, a particular face, or a pleasant odor as she was in Stage 1. Now that these schemes are integrated, the child forms a multifaceted representation of mother. It takes many hours of contact with an object and a lot of active exploration to understand all of its facets. Infants have this kind of contact with their mothers. Hence, it is not surprising that the first object that infants seem to understand as a collection of different pieces of information is their mother.

At the University of Edinburgh, Bower devised a mirror illusion to show the change in the way infants perceived their mothers. Bower arranged mirrors so that several replicas of the mother appeared in the baby's view. Before five months of age, the children were not upset by these multiple images. After about five months, seeing several images upset the infants. Bower (1982) concludes that having laboriously decided that they have only one mother, infants five months and older are disturbed by the appearance of several mothers.

Earlier we noted that infants could recognize their mother's face, voice, and odor during the first month of life. In the first month, the mother's face and voice were isolated because the schemes of looking and hearing were not coordinated. The essence of the infant's task during the third stage of sensory motor development is to coordinate the senses. Hence, what was known before as a familiar voice now becomes linked with information about odor and face so that together these coordinated schemes define a new concept—mother. The object concept is first evident when infants realize that their mother exists independently of them. But the object concept continues to evolve during stage four and encompasses much more than the child's parents.

**Stage 4—coordination of schemes—10 to 12 months.** During this stage, infants begin to understand other objects in the same way they understand their parents' permanence. Prior to developing an object concept, an infant seems to think that any change in the object makes it a different object. Keith Moore has a compelling video tape of a six-month-old girl reaching for a Kewpie doll. As she reaches, the experimenter slowly turns the doll upside down. The child immediately withdraws her hand and stares. Apparently, the view of the doll upside down is so different that the infant responds to the object as if it is a strange new object (Moore, 1979).

Another experiment called the disappearing toy illustrates the child's tenuous understanding of objects. This is an easy experiment to conduct with infants in the 6- to 11-month age range: Use one of the child's favorite toys and a kitchen towel. Once you have the infant's attention, slowly put the toy under the towel. This involves no sleight-of-hand or tricks. The infant is supposed to watch. Now see if the infant can find the toy. Many younger children will reach for the towel but in a moment or two will abandon the search. A 10-

month-old will quickly pull the towel away and grab the toy. The two infants have very different reactions to the disappearing toy. Once the toy disappears, the younger acts as if it never existed. Out-of-sight, out-of-mind seems to explain the behavior. Older children seem to be able to hold an image of the toy in memory long enough to conduct a search. They have developed a concept of an object that endures even when the object disappears.

There might be another interpretation for this change in behavior. It could be that the six-month-old does not have the ability to remove the towel. If this is the case, it is a replay of the flea experiment mentioned earlier. Psychologists are concluding that the infant cannot hold an object in memory, but that is not really the problem. It might be that the towel is too big for the infant to manage. To check this possibility, Gratch covered the toy with a see-through cover. Now the six-month-old infants had no trouble removing the cloth and grabbing the toy (Gratch, 1972). As long as infants could see the object, they reached for it. But when they lost visual contact with it, the object, in effect, disappeared. This experiment demonstrated that six-month-old infants cannot find the object because they have trouble remembering it, not because they cannot remove the towel.

The hide-and-seek technique has been used to explore other facets of the child's memory. Some researchers have tried to fool the children. They hide a set of keys while the children watch. When the children pull the cloth off, they find a toy car. If the infants are searching for the keys, they should register surprise and keep searching. At nine months, infants do seem confused by this trick, but they do not continue searching. By 18 months, they not only seem perplexed, they continue to search. These children know what went under the cloth and they also know that it still exists somewhere (Gratch, 1979).

The development of an object concept is a landmark in the development of memory. As infants develop more experience with objects, they can represent objects in their minds. This representation is the basis of later symbolic behavior.

Once infants understand that objects and people exist independently, they can engage in much more thoughtful behavior. An infant can plan actions to accomplish more complex goals. Laurent demonstrates his ability to coordinate different schemes in the following vignette:

> At six months I present Laurent with a matchbox, extending my hand laterally to make an obstacle. Laurent tries to pass over my hand, or to the side, but he does not attempt to displace it. Finally, at seven months Laurent reacts quite differently almost from the beginning of the experiment. I present a box of matches above my hand, but behind it, so that he cannot reach it without setting the obstacle aside. But Laurent, after trying to take no notice of it, suddenly tries to hit my hand as though to remove it. I let him do it and he grasps the box. (Ginsburg & Opper, 1979, p. 51)

As in Stage 3, the child is behaving intentionally and has a clear goal in mind. But the coordination of schemes that is required in Stage 4 is quite different. The behaviors Laurent must combine now are much more involved than coordinating the eyes and hands. He must learn how to use his coordinated schemes to get beyond obstacles. This takes thought.

**Stage 5—search for novelty—12 to 18 months.** Infants who have a concept of an object and can remember objects, who can plan a course of action, and who are mobile are well prepared to investigate their world. They begin their exploration in earnest during the fifth stage. Using their full repertoire of coordinated schemes such as throwing, dropping, rubbing, and banging, toddlers scrutinize every facet of their environment. Infant explorers like to watch tissues come out of the box, one at a time. They like to flush objects down the toilet, unroll toilet paper, and pour water on the floor. Through these investigations, children discover new information about their environment and new means of accomplishing their goals. When an unfamiliar situation is encountered, as it often is, the child adapts strategies that have worked before.

> Jacqueline intentionally let objects she was holding fall to the ground. During her meal, while she is seated, she moves a wooden horse to the edge of her table until she lets it fall. She watches it. An hour later she is given a postcard. Jacqueline throws it to the ground many times and looks for it. She systematically pushes a thimble to the edge of the box on which it is placed and watches it fall. (Piaget, 1952, p. 270)

Those who are familiar with small children will recognize this behavior as an exceedingly trying one. However, if you recognize the motivation for the infant's behavior, the "throw it" or "drop it" game becomes more tolerable. Jacqueline is learning that you do not have to push objects to the ground. They will fall if you simply let go of them. She is using her coordinated schemes to investigate her universe.

Jonas Langer, a Piagetian scholar, believes that the action sequences produced during Stage 5 are the roots of abstract logic. He points out that people sort the world into categories on an abstract level. Objects are identified by color, mass, weight, density, volume, and function. The logic that underlies these categories can be seen in action sequences similar to Jacqueline's (Langer, 1980). Infants learn that when they drop different objects, some float downward, others bounce, while still others break. Their action sequences help them form rudimentary classes that will later be transformed into a symbolic classification system.

Infants 9–12 months old will select similar objects to manipulate. When given a tray containing four small plastic human figures and four small red "broom handles," infants begin to separate the two groups of objects (Starkey, 1981). This is another example of a rudimentary classification system based on the action schemes of the sensory motor period.

**Stage 6—beginning of thought—18 to 24 months.** The emphasis through the fifth stage of sensory motor development is on action. Although we can see the beginnings of representation in the child's memory of ob-

**Exploring**

Larry Robins

Children are ready to explore their environments when they have mastered the object concept and have attained some degree of mobility.

jects, the child still relies on manipulation. However, during the sixth stage, the role of action begins to recede and we see thoughtful assessments assume more importance. The ability to remember something that was not present was first acknowledged with the object concept. At that point, the child's ability to reconstruct objects was very limited. Now infants not only reconstruct images of people and objects that are absent, they can manipulate these images in their mind. As a result, they can think about problems. The experimenter of Stage 5 gives way to the philosopher of Stage 6. During this final period of sensory motor development, infants, who now know a great deal about the environment, begin to use their information to solve problems.

Laurent is seated before a table and I place a bread crust in front of him, out of reach. Also, to the right of the child I place a stick about 25 centimeters long. At first Laurent tries to grasp the bread without paying attention to the instrument, and then he gives up. I then put the stick between him and the bread. Laurent again looks at the bread, without moving, looks very briefly at the stick, then suddenly grasps it and directs it toward the bread.

But he grasped it toward the middle and not at one of its ends so that it is too short to attain the objective. Laurent then puts it down and resumes stretching out his hand toward the bread. Then without spending much time on this movement, he takes up the stick again, this time at one of its ends, and draws the bread to him. He begins by simply touching it, as though contact of the stick with the objective were sufficient to set the latter in motion, but after one or two seconds at most, he pushes the crust with real intention. He displaces it gently to the right, then draws it to him without difficulty. Two successive attempts yield the same result. (Piaget, 1952, p. 335)

Laurent's attempts to reach the bread with his hand did not work so he devised an alternate plan. Remember that when the environment does not fit neatly into a child's structure, the child can alter that structure. Laurent does this and his second plan, using the stick, suggests that he can visualize the stick reaching the bread and bringing it close enough to grab. It is the thoughtful use of the stick that is unique to this stage. Laurent not only visualizes the stick, he imagines how it will help him solve the problem. Being able to transform an image like this gives infants untold flexibility and power. Once children can imagine an object being changed, thoughts can direct the child's actions. Prior to Stage 6, the actions of the child helped the child form images. At this point, a revolution occurs and the images and thoughts of the child begin to direct the actions (Ginsburg & Opper, 1979).

To review the changes in the child's conception of the world, let us look again at newborns. They exercise their reflexes and built-in patterns of behavior until they gradually gain control over their eyes, hands, and mouth. With a few more weeks of effort, these isolated patterns become coordinated into action schemes. Exploring objects—by seeing them, touching them, and sucking on them—helps infants realize that the people and objects in the environment have an independent existence.

Once children understand that objects have a permanence of their own, they can begin to represent these objects. Now hide-and-seek games reveal the child's conceptual understanding of the world. Equipped with integrated senses and the ability to remember—at least for short periods of time—the infant investigates the environment with gusto. At the culmination of the sensory motor period, the infant is able to devise new approaches to problems by manipulating the world symbolically rather than physically.

This quick review of two years of concentrated effort on the part of the infant seems to gloss over the incredible changes that take place (see Figure 6–7). At Stage 1, the newborn has little anticipation, intentionality, no words, and no conceptual understanding of how the world functions. A short 18 to 24 months later, infants anticipate, imitate, initiate, have a firm grasp of their immediate environment, can think about different ways to solve a problem, and have a limited vocabulary.

Piaget's observations, first published in 1936, have stood the test of time.

**Figure 6—7**      The sensory motor period*

| | Stage 1— exercising reflexes (birth–1 month) | Stage 2— extending reflexes (1–4 months) | Stage 3— integrating senses (4–10 months) | Stage 4— coordination of schemes (10–12 months) | Stage 5— search for novelty (12–18 months) | Stage 6— beginning of thought (18–24 months) |
|---|---|---|---|---|---|---|
| Milestones of each stage | Practices reflexes until they function smoothly. | Extends reflexes to new objects. | Fluid coordination of all the senses is achieved. | Child can represent objects in the mind. | Child searches for novelty in the environment. | Child thinks about the problem before acting. |
| | Practices built-in patterns of behavior. | Coordinates simple schemes like grasping and looking. | The "object concept" is attained in the last months of this stage. | Child demonstrates the beginning of symbolic behavior and memory. | Child can use several interchangeable schemes to achieve goals. | Thought begins to dominate action. |
| Intentionality | Child has no intentionality. | Infant can repeat behaviors that cause specific events. | Child can anticipate events and results of actions. | Child decides on goal, then acts to achieve goal. | Child conducts experiments to see what will happen. | Child can mentally manipulate objects to reach goals. |
| The "object concept" | Child has no understanding of an object. | Child looks where object disappears for a few moments. | Child can find object that is partially hidden. | Child can find an object that is completely hidden. | Child can find objects hidden under one of several covers. | Children can find objects that are put in a container and then hidden. |
| Control | The infant has minimum control over the external environment. | Child directs and controls simple schemes. | Child directs and controls complex schemes. | Child has control over complex actions and can use them to discover new facets of objects. | Child combines actions and representations to control environment. | Child has symbolic as well as physical control. |

Each stage of the sensory motor period signifies the attainment of new skills.

*The ages listed should be considered guidelines. Many children will achieve these milestones earlier; some will achieve them later.

Almost 50 years later, this description still provides an accurate overview of the changes in the infant's thought patterns. The coordination of schemes, the formation of early memories, the development of the object concept, and the relationship between language and thought are all new areas of research that have grown out of Piaget's descriptions of the sensory motor period. In addition, extensions of Piaget's work with infants have been conducted in the areas of vision, memory, learning, and concept development. With these extensions of Piaget's ideas, our understanding of an infant's cognitive development has become much more elaborate and detailed. Let us consider some of these recent findings.

## THE DEVELOPMENT OF VISUAL PERCEPTION

Piaget's views have prompted detailed investigations into the infant's visual skills. At the University of Denver, Marshall Haith used an infrared camera to photograph infants in the dark. Not only did these very young infants (24 to 96 hours old) open their eyes in the dark, they opened them more than in the light. Once the infants' eyes were open, they searched diligently for something to look at (Haith & Goodman, 1982). Why should infants scan the darkness? Haith suggests that it is the nature of their visual system to search the environment and then to scan anything they find in that environment. Further, the infants he studied were anything but passive. They opened their eyes to the point of strain and changed their fixation every half-second (Haith, 1980).

In the next experiment, Haith presented simple contrasts or "edges" to infants in normally lighted surroundings. The infants employed two visual strategies—searching and scanning. When the infants opened their eyes, they would search the area with broad jerky sweeps of their visual field. If an edge was found, infants stopped their broad search pattern and confined their looking to the general vicinity of that edge. They then began to scan horizontally back and forth across the edge.

Why do newborns search the area and then focus on edges? Haith suggests that these behaviors maximize the development of the visual cortex and provide experience that is essential to the further development, modification, and integration of the brain. By scanning the edges, newborns fire neurons in the visual system that facilitate the system's development. The newborn's visual system is organized so that the sharpest images are seen at seven to nine inches. Scanning these sharp images provides the experience that will gradually enable infants to see clearly at much greater distances.

Haith's description is a thought-provoking account of the perceptual strategies and skills of neonates. Do the same principles guide the attention of infants after the first month? In the second stage of sensory motor development, the rules for looking change. Now infants prefer to look at patterns that are discrepant or novel.

**Novelty**

In 1964, Robert Fantz demonstrated that novel stimuli catch the eye of infants between two and six months of age (Fantz, 1964). If infants are shown the same picture over and over, they look at it less and less. They become habituated to it, hence the procedure is called *habituation*. If you then show them something new, they will look at the new picture for a longer time than they will look at the familiar picture. This general technique of familiarizing an infant with one picture and then substituting a new one has become one of our most reliable ways of studying attention, visual development, and memory. It should be noted, however, that infants do not prefer a novel picture until they are quite familiar with the initial picture. If you present the second picture before infants understand the first one, you may not see the habituation (Rose, Gottfried, Melloy-Carminar, & Bridger, 1982).

Fantz's early experiments established an important principle of infant attention—namely, that infants prefer novel patterns to very familiar ones. It also provided a method to investigate the infant's other visual capacities. Suppose we wanted to know if infants could distinguish between blue and green. We might first habituate infants to a blue circle. When the infant no longer looked at the blue circle, we would substitute a green one. If the infants now studied the green circle, it would mean that they perceived it as new and different. Hence, we could conclude that infants could tell the difference between the two colors. If the infants were not interested in the green circle, we would conclude that they could not distinguish between blue and green. Experiments like these have established that infants can perceive colors, simple forms, lines, angles, and contrasts during the first weeks of life (Cohen, 1979).

**Moderate discrepancy**

Piaget argued that newborns extend their capacity to understand the world gradually through the dual processes of assimilation and accommodation. A picture that is unlike anything they have ever seen is likely to be so discrepant that they cannot assimilate it. A picture that is very familiar is not likely to be interesting. Hence, infants are most likely to look at a picture that is different in a limited number of ways (Kagan, 1970). McCall and his colleagues have tested this notion by presenting 2½-month-old infants with brightly colored arrows that pointed in different directions (see Figure 6–8). Infants were shown one arrow until they were familiar with it. Then a second arrow was presented. If infants were initially shown the vertical arrow, they were most attentive to the diagonal arrow and least attentive when the horizontal arrow was presented (McCall, Kennedy, & Appelbaum, 1977). These results suggest that some discrepancy helps maintain attention, but pictures that are too discrepant are ignored. Similar results supporting the moderate discrepancy hypothesis have been found with infants as young as 28 hours and as old as 7½ months (McCall & McGhee, 1977).

To summarize, visual development changes rapidly during the first months of life (McCall & Kennedy, 1980). Newborns prefer high-contrast edges that

**Figure 6—8**                    **Moderate discrepancy**

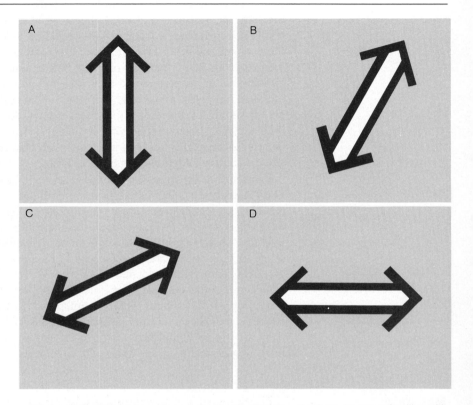

Three-month-old infants prefer moderate discrepancy. If infants become familiar with Arrow A, they will prefer Arrow B and will be less interested in Arrow D.

Source: McCall R. B., Kennedy, C. B., & Appelbaum, M. I. (1977). Magnitude of discrepancy and the distribution of attention in infants. *Child Development, 42,* 772–786.

exercise their searching and scanning skills. As infants gain proficiency and control over these skills, they begin to search for novel or moderately discrepant objects to explore visually (Werner & Perlmutter, 1979). One of the most interesting objects to explore is the human face. A description of how the infant learns to understand the human face should tell us more about the development of the visual system.

**Faces**

The newborn prefers looking at human faces, but as mentioned earlier, this represents a preference for contrasts and edges rather than the whole pattern that we call a face. The way the infant processes a face follows the same developmental course as any other visual stimulus (Cohen, DeLoache, & Strauss, 1979). Initially, the infant looks at one or two edges or high-contrast features. Then attention is focused on the external parts of the face (see Figure 6–9). By two months of age, infants spend more of their time looking at the internal features such as the eyes and mouth (Maurer & Salapatek, 1975). This explains why one-month-olds do not react to pictures of faces that have the eyes and mouth in the wrong places. When pictures of a face with the scrambled features are presented to these infants, they do not seem to notice that anything is awry. They are too busy scanning the outside edges of the face. Two-month-old infants notice that the face is not as it should be, and they prefer the face in its normal arrangement (Maurer & Barrera, 1981). Older infants are also very interested in the human face. They are attracted by the animation and complexity of the human face (Sherrod, 1979). Looking at the internal features of a face, such as the eyes and mouth, helps infants distinguish emotions and expressions. By three months of age, infants can tell the difference between a smiling face and a frowning face (Barrera & Maurer, 1981).

At four months, infants respond to the whole face and scan it in a thorough and systematic way. This flexible and systematic scanning promotes recognition and allows the five-month-old to begin abstracting concepts from the many different faces they have scanned. Now they can tell whether a face is that of a man or woman. They can also look at two poses of the same person and tell each pose apart. These fine discriminations mean that the infant is reacting to the whole face and not just isolated features like the eyes or mouth. Notice that the infant does not seem to integrate various parts of faces and figures until

**Figure 6–9**          **Scanning Strategies**

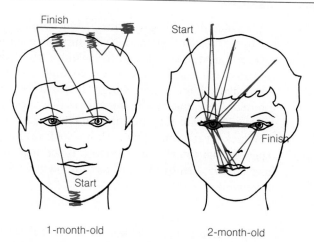

Infants who are only one month old concentrate on the edges of a face. A month later, infants focus more on the internal features.

Source: Maurer, D., & Salapatek, P. (1976). Developmental changes in the scanning of faces by young infants. *Child Development, 47,* 523–527.

four to five months of age (Cohen et al., 1979). This is exactly what Piaget would predict. In his view, the integration of information cannot begin until the skill of looking is well developed and flexible.

**Constructing abstractions**

The fact that five-month-olds can differentiate male and female faces indicates that they are beginning to develop two prototypes of the faces they see—one male and one female. This is one of the earliest examples of infants abstracting the essentials from their experience and forming a general concept. Because concept formation is such a critical aspect of cognitive development, these first abstractions deserve to be examined closely. Experiments tracing concept development begin by familiarizing infants with several pictures representing a single concept—like female faces or stuffed animals (Cohen & Strauss, 1979). The infants are then shown a woman or animal they have not seen before. If they react to it as a novel picture and stare at it for a long time, they have not acquired the concept. If, however, they look briefly and do not study the picture, it suggests that they have assimilated this new picture into their concept of female faces or stuffed animals. After six months, infants readily develop abstract concepts from visual information (Cohen et al., 1979; Rovee-Collier & Sullivan, 1980). These concepts become part of the infant's organization or structure. As infants encounter new faces, they will be able to assimilate them. In addition, their concept of faces will become more complex as they accommodate old faces, young faces, happy faces, and sad faces to their concept of face.

## MEMORY

It is difficult to imagine humans functioning without being able to remember the familiar people and events in their environment. Without memories, each task would be new and the infant would have to repeat the same familiarization and learning processes every time a person or event was encountered. Fortunately, human infants begin to remember familiar aspects of their environments very quickly. By three days, they recognize their mother's voice. By 10 days, they can recognize their mother's particular fragrance. At two weeks, they look away from a stranger, but look readily at their mother's face. Recognizing that something is familiar is the first step in the recall process. We have already seen this kind of recognition at work in the development of visual perception.

**Recognition memory**

When Robert Fantz (1964) first presented two different pictures to infants, his purpose was to find out what infants liked to look at. It soon became apparent that we could also investigate what the infant remembered by using the habituation technique. Because infants prefer novelty and visual materials that are moderately discrepant, we know that the infant has some recognition memory. If infants prefer novel faces, it means that they at least recognize one as being a face they have seen before. The same is true for moderate discrepancy. In order for infants to react to arrows that differ, they must recognize that the arrow they are now seeing differs from the initial arrow.

These experiments on visual memory do not require infants to remember information for a long period of time. The arrow or familiar face is presented repeatedly so that the infant can develop an understanding of that object. The novel face or discrepant arrow is presented immediately after the familiar picture. Nor do these experiments require the infant to recall an object. Like multiple choice tests for college students, these experiments only require infants to have enough information to recognize the object when it appears.

How long are visual presentations remembered? That depends on the age of the infant and how long the infant is allowed to look at the visual presentations (Rose, 1981). In general, infants have a remarkable recognition memory for visually presented information. To look at the stability of recognition memory, researchers have familiarized an infant with a face, then retested the child after several days. Surprisingly, five-month-old infants still retained some information about the face they had seen after a two-week delay (Fagan, 1973). Recognition memory is also remarkably immune to minor disruptions (Fagan, 1977b). Even if you present several other pictures between the familiarization phase and the test phase, infants are likely to remember the picture that they initially studied (Cohen, 1979). Pictures of faces seem to be retained the longest. If you substitute pictures of geometric forms, six-month-olds are likely to forget readily (Rose, 1981). The fact that infants recognize faces earlier and can remember them longer is not surprising. They have more experience with faces and, in Piaget's terms, have a more complex organization for faces.

When the habituation technique is used, a picture is typically presented for several short time periods. When infants are no longer interested in looking, it is assumed that they are familiar with the picture. Can infants recognize a picture after just 10 to 15 seconds of looking? The answer seems to be that they can. The recognition is not as clear-cut as when infants control their looking, but the results of several experiments now suggest that four- and five-month-old infants can recognize an object after presentations lasting only a few seconds (Fagan, 1977a; Olson, 1979). It seems that an infant's recognition memory is very durable and that some recognition can be established in a very short time. Still, recognition must be considered an immature way to remember the world since the infant must see the person or object before recognition occurs.

**Reconstructing events**

The ability to reconstruct the events of the past signals a higher level of cognitive processing. It is difficult to know when infants begin to reconstruct memories because it is a mental process that takes place without anyone else being aware of it. John Watson (1982) has suggested that when we see a child searching for hidden objects and imitating, we can be confident that reconstructive memory is present.

The hide-and-seek test of object permanence is perhaps the best clue to the infant's developing memory (Piaget, 1954). Remember that in these tasks the infant watches an object disappear and must hold an image of that object in memory long enough to guide a search. This memory process requires more than recognition. The infant has to reconstruct the missing object in the mind's eye. Typically, such complex reconstruction does not occur until 8 to 10 months of age (Sophian, 1980).

The infant's ability to reconstruct a memory is far from perfect at eight months. Nathan Fox has demonstrated how fragile the infant's memory is in an object permanence task. Infants were familiarized with a toy. Then while they watched, the toy was hidden (see Figure 6–10). If the infants were allowed to search immediately, they usually found the toy. But if infants were prevented from searching for the toy for even three seconds, they were likely to forget about the object. By 10 months, they were much better at remembering. Even with a seven-second delay, all of the infants found the toy (Fox, Kagan, & Weiskopf, 1979).

**Figure 6–10**            **The object concept**

Baby sees toy.

As baby starts to reach for the toy it is covered by a cup.

Baby is baffled and makes no attempt to retrieve the toy by removing the cup.

An object-permanence test. In such tests young babies (around six months) fail to search for the hidden object, acting as if it no longer existed. Learning that objects continue to exist signals the beginning of the child's ability to reconstruct experiences. This ability is used to study memory and higher level cognitive skills.

**Imitation**

The object permanence tests suggest that infants begin to reconstruct memories at about eight months of age. Do the studies of imitation suggest a similar age for reconstructive memory? There have been several reports of young infants imitating simple adult gestures like sticking out the tongue (Gardner & Gardner, 1970; Meltzoff & Moore, 1977) or matching an adult's sad, happy, or surprised expression (see Figure 6–11). If such imitation occurs, one might argue that an infant is able to reconstruct events earlier than eight months. The imitative gestures we see at this young age are loosely organized patterns of behavior, and the child's control over them is far from exact (Anisfeld-Moshe, 1979). In Tiffany Field's study, for example, it took a while for the infants to organize a surprised face, and sometimes the infant gave a surprised face when they had seen a sad face (Field, Woodson, Greenberg, & Coren,

**Figure 6–11**        **Infant imitation**

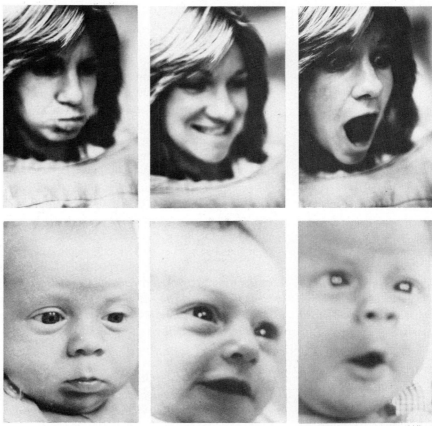

*Dr. Tiffany Field, University of Miami*

Infants seem to imitate adults very early in life, but the imitation is unstable and difficult to document.

1982). Hence, these instances of early imitation are often viewed as isolated and immature. Sometimes what looks like imitation in the early weeks is a game initiated by the infant and continued by the adult (Piaget, 1962). Other instances of imitation in the early weeks of life seem to be explained by the fact that infants who are alert use their entire repertoire of behaviors (Hayes & Watson, 1981). This often means that they open and close their mouths and stick out their tongues. In her dissertation, Jacobson (1979) found that infants stuck out their tongues just as often when they saw a felt-tip pen as when the behavior was modeled. Early instances of imitation are evidence that the infant is trying to match events that occur. As we have seen, even this matching is quite difficult.

The more sophisticated imitation that appears toward the end of the first year requires the infant to reconstruct something that has happened and then consciously attempt to imitate it. In a fascinating study of the development of imitation, Kenneth Kaye and Janet Marcus followed infants from six months to a year hoping to see this reconstructive imitation develop. Their report indicates that infants of this age have to struggle to reconstruct the model they have seen. At first, the infants might imitate one part of what the model did. If they were supposed to shake a bell until it rang twice and then put it down, they might just shake it. If they were supposed to touch their ear, they sometimes clapped and sometimes touched their face. Throughout, the infants marched to their own drummer. During the time when they were supposed to be imitating opening the mouth, they might touch their ear (Kaye & Marcus, 1981).

Reconstructing events is clearly a difficult thing for infants to do. To succeed they must be able to remember the event and reconstruct a recognizable copy. This assumes good motor control and it also assumes that the various systems for processing information, like the eyes and the mouth, are well coordinated. Even the development of schemes accomplished in Stage 2 and the coordination of schemes accomplished in Stages 3 and 4 do not guarantee an accurate imitation. Children can imitate normal events like driving a car and brushing their hair before they can imitate atypical events like drinking from the car and driving a cup (Killen & Uzgiris, 1981). Both sets of events require the same motor development and coordination of senses. Driving a car taps into the familiar schemes or organization that infants have about cars. Driving a cup does not. Here we see how the organization that a child is developing facilitates imitation. This is the same process as using your information about numbers to remember a long array of squares. Both tasks require an underlying organization that guides behavior.

Imitation continues to develop into the second year and forms the basis for the imaginative play of toddlers. Piaget managed to capture Jacqueline in a vignette that illustrates deferred imitation. Jacqueline is 16 months old.

> Jacqueline had a visit from a little boy whom she used to see from time to time, and who, in the course of the afternoon got into a terrible temper. He screamed as he tried to get out of a play-pen and pushed it backwards,

stamping his feet. Jacqueline stood watching him in amazement, never having witnessed such a scene before. The next day, she herself screamed in her play-pen and tried to move it, stamping her foot lightly several times in succession. (Piaget, 1962, p. 63)

Jacqueline's imitation is notable because it is reconstructed the next day. Further, we know it is an imitation because she does not really seem irritated. Imitation, especially in toddlers and preschoolers, can be deferred for long periods of time. Yet, the influence of a model is very apparent as the preschooler puts on the same apron as her parents, uses the same pans, and uses the same words as her parents when she scolds her dolls.

When infants are asked to search for hidden objects or to imitate behaviors, we are able to examine their ability to reconstruct events no longer present. The cognitive skills that this requires are more complex than recognizing a picture. Hence, it is not surprising that these skills do not appear until well after recognition memories.

**Associative memory**

A third type of memory that we see in infants is associative memory. In these situations, infants learn to expect two events to occur together. If infants are fed a sweet solution from a rubber tube, they soon learn to suck when that tube is presented, even if the sweet solution is missing (Lipsitt & Werner, 1981). In this case, the infants learn to associate the rubber tube with the sweet solution. This simple kind of association has been reported in neonates. However, it is unstable and difficult to establish (Sameroff & Cavanagh, 1979).

Infants can also remember an association between their actions—sucking, head turning, and kicking—and the consequences of those actions (see Figure 6–12). For example, when infants in John Watson's laboratory at Berkeley turn their heads, a mobile turns (Watson & Ramey, 1972). When infants in Carolyn Rovee-Collier's lab kick their feet, wooden cubes attached to a mobile "dance" (Rovee-Collier & Capatides, 1979). As they see that their actions cause the mobile to move, the infants turn their heads frequently and kick their feet vigorously. They clearly remember the association between their actions and the mobile's movement.

The story of associative memory does not end with infants mastering the association. Not only do infants engage in much more head turning and foot kicking when they are controlling these events, but they become very involved in the process. They begin to coo, smile, and become more excited each time they successfully make the mobiles move (Watson, 1972). Why are they so pleased at being able to make a mobile move? John Watson suggests they are learning that they can control their environment. He goes on to suggest that learning you have some control might be one of the most powerful lessons of infancy. To support this conclusion, Watson reports on three different groups of eight-week-old infants. The first group could make a mobile turn by moving their heads. A second group of infants watched passively as their electronically controlled mobiles turned. In a third group, the mobile never moved.

**Figure 6—12**          **Associative memory**

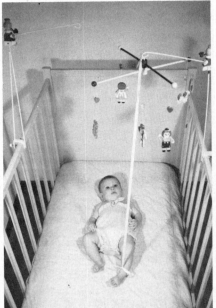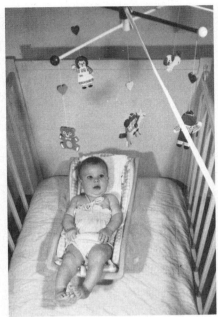

*Photograph by Breck P. Kent, courtesy of Carolyn Rovee-Collier*

Infants learn associations as young as six weeks. This three-month-old has learned that kicking his foot while the ribbon is attached to his ankle makes the mobile move.

After these infants had been exposed to the mobile in their homes, they were brought to the laboratory. Here they had another chance to learn that they could turn the mobile by moving their heads. The group that had been able to control the mobiles at home quickly learned that the mobile in the laboratory reacted in the same way. The group whose mobile at home did not turn learned that this mobile was different. Soon they could make this mobile turn. The infants who watched passively as the mobile at home turned never learned to control the mobile in the laboratory (Watson, 1971). Watson suggests that even eight-week-old infants can learn whether or not their actions affect what happens to them. When infants see that they have some power, they coo and smile. Further, they exercise their control to help them figure out their world. They are the essence of the active organism that Piaget described. On the other hand, infants who never see direct links between their actions and what happens may be learning that they are helpless and that nothing they do matters (Finkelstein & Ramey, 1977). These children may wait passively for the environment to affect them. If Watson is right, learning that they are in control is much more important to infants than being able to remember any single association.

## Forgetting

Infants forget quickly. Infants less then eight or nine months of age have trouble remembering the location of a light that flashed three seconds earlier. They do remember the light for a second. By one year, infants' memories are more durable and they will be able to remember where the light flashed, even after a delay of nine seconds (Brody, 1981). Remembering where a light flashed requires reconstructive memory. Recognition occurs earlier, and infants can recognize pictures even after a delay of several days.

Piaget noted that an infant's associations must be repeatedly confirmed lest the infant forget. Within a week, even the excited, cooing, kicking infant in Carolyn Rovee-Collier's study will forget that kicking made the mobile move. This forgetting would be discouraging if it meant that infants had to learn the response all over again. The memories of an infant as young as three months of age can be confirmed or reactivated. After learning that kicking could make a mobile move, infants did not repeat this activity for two weeks. Normally, they would have forgotten the association between kicking and the mobile. However, the day before the test, the infants were reminded of the association by seeing the mobile dance. The next day, at their testing session, these infants remembered that kicking caused the mobile to move (Rovee-Collier, Sullivan, Enright, Lucas, & Fagan, 1980). These results suggest that although infants do forget, their memories can be confirmed rather easily by having the infant encounter the same situation again. In their day-to-day lives, the associations that infants form are often confirmed. Parents repeatedly drive cars, take their infants to the supermarket, vacuum the house, read books, feed, diaper, and play with the baby. In short, they perform tasks over and over again, helping infants reactivate memories of those scenes and confirm associations between actions and consequences.

## Manipulating memories

Finally, we need to consider more complex cognitive problems. How and when do infants learn to put pieces of information together to solve problems? After watching his children use a stick to obtain an object that was out of reach, Piaget suggested that such behavior did not appear until the last stage of the sensory motor period. This simple experiment has since assumed broad significance. Not only does it indicate tool use (Parker & Gibson, 1977), it suggests that the organism can transform an image. What then are the mental abilities that are needed to use a tool, such as a stick, to solve a problem? To solve these kinds of problems, infants must imagine the stick going to the object and helping pull the object closer (Bates, Carlson-Luden, & Bretherton, 1980). This kind of imagery obviously requires that the child hold an object in memory. It also requires that infants be able to manipulate the image of the stick so that they can imagine the problem being solved. Normally, such images and the child's manipulation of them occur inside the child's head. All we can see are the behaviors that result. On occasion, however, Piaget saw his children externalize these images and manipulate them to solve a problem. In this look at the workings of a child's mind, Piaget is playing with Lucienne who is 16 months old. Piaget hides a familiar watch inside an empty match box.

> I put the chain back into the box and reduce the opening to 3 millimeters. Lucienne is not aware of the functioning of the opening and closing of the match box and has not seen me prepare the experiment. She only possesses two preceding schemes: turning the box over in order to empty it of its contents, and sliding her fingers into the slit to make the chain come out. It is of course this last procedure that she tries first: she puts her finger inside and gropes to reach the chain, but fails completely. A pause follows during which Lucienne manifests a very curious reaction.
>
> She looks at the slit with great attention; then several times in succession, she opens and shuts her mouth, at first slightly, then wider and wider!
>
> (Then) Lucienne unhesitatingly puts her finger in the slit, and instead of trying as before to reach the chain, she pulls so as to enlarge the opening. She succeeds and grasps the chain. (Piaget, 1952, p. 337–338)

In this case, Lucienne practiced the image present in her mind—making the slit larger—by opening and closing her mouth. Lucienne demonstrates the thought processes needed to convert static images of objects into images that can be altered to solve problems. As noted earlier, this ability to represent and manipulate images transforms the child's cognitive processes from an action based organization to a symbolic one.

**Continuity and discontinuity in development**

We can see from this sojourn through infant visual perception, memory, imitation, and forgetting, that Piaget's influence permeates the research on cognitive development in infancy. Being guided by Piaget does not mean that researchers have been confined by his views. When observations seem to veer from Piaget's proposals, researchers have examined those deviations carefully. The notion of stages is an example of a theoretical issue that has occasioned considerable debate.

Piaget delineates stages to highlight the new skill that is being acquired, even though it is understood that the stages are the result of a continuous process of change. This view, that development is characterized by distinctly different stages, has not been particularly popular with American psychologists. Nevertheless, studies of infant cognition repeatedly find many of the same milestones that Piaget saw in infancy (Wachs & Hubert, 1981; McCall, Eichorn, & Hogarty, 1977; Kagan, 1979; White & Watts, 1973).

There is widespread recognition that infants in the first month or so have limited cognitive skills (McCall et al., 1977; Sameroff & Cavanaugh, 1979). The change from these reflexive behaviors to the more controlled and purposive behaviors of the two- to seven-month-old seem to be well established.

The majority of researchers have also described a major change in the infant's cognitive skills that occurs around eight months of age (Kagan, 1979; McCall et al., 1977; Starkey, 1981; White & Watts, 1973). This change is best described as the onset of symbolic functioning. The infant is no longer confined to understanding the environment in terms of actions. The ability to remember, visualize, and search opens the door to a new and more powerful way of understanding the world.

At 18 months, there is another milestone—the development of language (Kagan, 1981; McCall, Eichorn, & Hogarty, 1977; Uzguiris, 1976). Perhaps this cognitive advance has received so much attention because it is easier to study what children say than what children think. Whatever the reason, the onset of language completes the transition from action to thought.

It is a tribute to Piaget's genius that many of the milestones he outlined have been duplicated in studies that use very different methods. Two generations of psychologists have painstakingly built on Piaget's description. We now have a clearer picture of how vision, memory, imitation, and the object concept develop. The increased understanding makes emphasizing one particular event or stage much less important.

## THE ROLE OF EARLY EXPERIENCE

There is a certain satisfaction in being able to trace the infant's cognitive development from the reflexes of the newborn to the problem solving skills of the two-year-old. Although our understanding is far from complete, we can determine whether infants have coordinated schemes for exploring the world, if they have an object concept, and whether they have progressed to the levels of reconstructive memory, deferred imitation, and problem solving skills. Describing events is only the first step in the scientific enterprise. Psychologists would like to know if an infant's cognitive skills relate to later behavior and development. Attempts to answer this question have taken many forms. Psychologists have asked whether an infant's progress can be accelerated. If one aspect of development is accelerated, does that mean the next milestone of development will be accomplished earlier? Researchers have also asked whether there is any relationship between an infant's cognitive development and later intellectual development. The remainder of this chapter will consider the role of early experience in the larger context of the child's subsequent development.

First let us examine whether a particular aspect of an infant's cognitive development can be accelerated by providing appropriate experience or practice. In the 1960s, Burton White argued that infancy was a critical period for the development of intelligence. He also argued that we could learn to structure the experiences of infancy to assure optimal development (White, 1971). To prove his point, White and his colleagues went into an institution for infants and designed environments that they thought would enhance the child's cognitive development.

One of their first experiments was based on Piaget's observation that three-month-old infants who are trying to coordinate their eyes, hands, and mouths spend a lot of time examining their hands. These infants watch their hands rotate and seem spellbound when both hands meet in front of their face. White decided that if he could make infants' hands more obvious, they would notice

**Figure 6—13**                    **The effect of early experience**

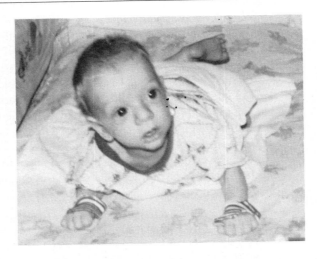

This infant's red and white striped mitts make his hands easier to see. Hence, he coordinates his eyes and hands earlier than infants who are not wearing bright mittens.

them sooner. Then the whole scenario of sensory motor development might be accelerated. He devised red and white striped golf gloves for infants that he called "find-me-mitts" (see Figure 6–13). With these gloves on, infants began to watch their hands early in the second month. The infants without the mittens did not find their hands until the third month (White, 1971).

The mittens were a small modification of the environment designed especially to help infants find their hands and begin to examine them. White did not stop with small modifications of the environment. He wanted to enrich every aspect of the environment so the infant would receive stimulation of all the senses. To this end, he changed the white hospital sheets for multicolored print sheets. He added colorful crib bumpers covered with cartoon characters. White instructed the nurses to give the infants in the enriched group extra handling each day. He also had the nurses change the infants' positions so they could follow the activities in the ward. Finally, he added a special mobile that featured highly contrasting colors, several toys, and a mirror (see Figure 6–14). By the time the infants in this environment were 3½ months old, they spent much more time attending to visual presentations than other infants. They also coordinated the schemes of looking, grasping, and sucking much earlier than the infants in the orphanage who did not have these experiences. This massive enrichment accelerated some aspects of development by as much as 1½ months in infants who were only 4 months old. There was, however, a price to pay for this acceleration. For a month after the mobile was added to their environment, infants in the enrichment group cried much more than infants in the control group. White reasoned that a gradual increase in stimu-

**Figure 6—14**  **Enriching an infant's environment**

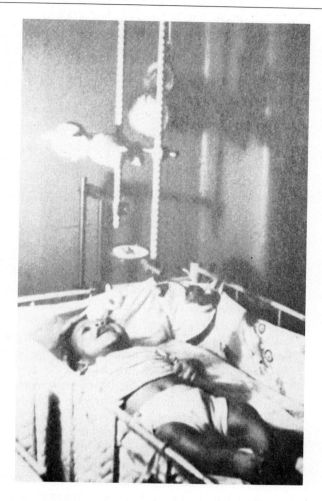

Infants in an institution were provided with this mobile when they were 36 days old. They learned to coordinate their eyes and hands a month earlier than infants who did not have a mobile. The visual enrichment provided by the mobile also helped these infants develop a long attention span.

Source: Reprinted by permission from White, Burton L., & Held, R. J. (1966). Plasticity of sensorimotor development in the human infant. In J. F. Rosenblith, & W. Allismith (Eds.), *The causes of behavior*, II (pp. 60–70). Copyright 1966 by Allyn & Bacon, Inc., Boston.

lation might accomplish the same acceleration of cognitive skills without the emotional upset. In his next experiment, he replaced the mobile with two pacifiers that were mounted on the crib. After the infants were accustomed to this change, he substituted the mobile. The infants were not as upset by this gradual change in stimulation, and they achieved flexible coordination of their eyes, hands, and mouth before they were three months old (White, 1971).

There are several lessons that can be drawn from White's experiments. First, he has demonstrated that experiences will accelerate the acquisition of specific sensory motor skills. Second, he has shown that infants can be overstimulated. Finally, he has documented the importance of a match between the infant's skills and the environment. The need for this kind of match reflects Piaget's view that development proceeds gradually through the processes of assimilation and accommodation. Stimulation that is geared to the needs of the child achieves the same acceleration as massive stimulation, and it is accomplished without the emotional side effects.

Although White's experiments are a compelling demonstration of acceleration during infancy, they are not the final word. His infants were in an institution and despite the good intentions of the staff, they received much less stimulation than infants raised at home. White comments that the large, complex mobile might not have been too much stimulation for home-reared infants who have a wealth of visual experience during the first month of life. Perhaps, then, the acceleration achieved by White would not appear in a group of infants that were raised at home.

A second question left unanswered by White's experiments concerns the long-term effects of experience. White's studies tell us that acceleration of specific skills was achieved, but we do not know whether the short-term changes he established were translated into changes a year or several years later. To answer these questions, we need to examine the effects of extra stimulation on infants who are being raised at home, and we need to follow a group of infants who have received extra stimulation for a long period.

Simoneau and Decarie investigated the first issue—whether stimulation would accelerate the development of home reared infants. They were guided by Piaget's observation that coordination of the looking, grasping, and sucking schemes is necessary for the development of an object concept (Whiteley, 1981). They reasoned that if infants achieved eye-hand-mouth coordination early, this coordination might help them explore objects and, hence, hasten the development of the object concept.

To test these notions, Simoneau and Decarie (1979) gave three-month-old infants a test of object constancy. Then one group received training designed to coordinate looking and grasping. Infants were guided through sequences where they looked first at an object; then the experimenter helped them reach for it and bring it to their mouths. After a month of this training, these infants understood objects better than infants who did not have the training. These intervention studies demonstrate that an infant's rate of development can be accelerated by providing specific experiences. The question of whether or not these experiences have a lasting effect is much more complex.

One way to determine long-term effects is to provide particular experiences to a sample of infants and then follow these infants for several years. The most famous follow-up of infant experiences was conducted by Harold Skeels in an Iowa orphanage in the 1930s. Because the orphanage was crowded, 13 of a group of 25 infants were moved from the orphanage to a home for the mentally retarded. The 13 children were judged to be mentally retarded. Their average score on an intelligence test was 64.3, well below the standard of 100 that is considered normal. The 12 children who stayed at the orphanage had an average intelligence rating of 86.7. The children taken to the home for the mentally retarded were received warmly by the older residents. The infants were played with, loved, and stimulated by the adult women. Most of the children were "adopted" by one of the adults, and the other women served as adoring aunts. After 18 months of this stimulation, the children's intelligence scores had jumped to 92.8. Over the same period, the infants who stayed at the orphanage had lost considerable ground. Their average intelligence score was now 60.5. The near normal performance of the children at the institution for the mentally retarded made them easy to place in adoptive homes, and 11 of these children were adopted. These 11 children maintained an IQ in the normal range (101.4).

A follow-up of all 25 children as adults (aged 25 to 35) indicated that the 11 children who were adopted maintained their normal status. They were all self-supporting. Half had graduated from high school, and five had attended college. As a group, they did not differ from the rest of the U.S. population according to educational or occupational criteria. Their 28 children were of average intelligence (IQ = 104) and were progressing normally in school (Skeels, 1966).

The group that remained at the orphanage did not fare as well. One died as an adolescent, and four remained wards of the state. As adults, only half had completed third grade and only one had any education beyond eighth grade. Only one of these adults could be described as occupationally successful. The rest, if employed at all, held part-time jobs or jobs at their institutions (Skeels, 1966).

Most psychologists cite this study as evidence of the positive effect of stimulating environments. Other explanations are possible (Longstreth, 1982). The children were very young when initially tested, and infant assessments of intelligence are not good predictors of later intelligence. Furthermore, the group that remained in the orphanage were children who could not be placed. This suggests that they had some obvious deficit. Their decline over the years should be expected. Despite these reservations about the Skeels experiment, other researchers have found similar gains by children who were adopted before the age of two (Clarke & Clarke, 1976; Dennis, 1973).

Naturally occurring experiments like these prompted psychologists to design programs to enhance the development of infants who might otherwise arrive at kindergarten ill-prepared to learn. The impact of these programs has been followed closely.

In Florida, a program initiated by Ira Gordon sent paraprofessionals from the local community into homes to show mothers how to play stimulating games with their children. The weekly home visits began at three months of age and continued for one, two, or three years. Gordon found that if the infants were in the program for two years, they learned easily in kindergarten.

He notes that not only did the infants benefit, but their mothers developed more sophisticated attitudes about child rearing. They were more aware of their child's development, had appropriate ways to praise and punish their child, were concerned about language development, and made an effort to provide stimulating experiences for their child (Gordon, 1975).

While Gordon's infant program focused on teaching the parents, a project in North Carolina focused on teaching infants. Infants, put in day care before they were three months old, maintained normal intellectual growth through three years of age. The control children began to decline after the first year. Hence, by two years of age, the children in the experimental group had a significant intellectual advantage over the control children (Ramey & Haskins, 1981).

The effectiveness of infant intervention programs continues to be debated. The fact that infants are involved mediates against random assignment of children to intervention programs. Therefore, control groups are often composed of infants who differ in systematic ways from the infants in the intervention group. When statistical analyses are reported, about half of the programs appear to have an impact. When more clinical conclusions are drawn, almost all of the programs appear to be effective (Simeonsson, Cooper, & Scheiner, 1982).

There are many political, economic, and ethical questions about programs for infants. To some extent, they are based on an *innoculation* theory of child development (Zigler, 1975). This is the notion that providing specific experiences at an early age will innoculate children against poverty, school failure, and unstimulating environments. Such a view is not realistic. Many psychologists have demonstrated that when the intervention stops, intellectual growth begins to decline. To really be effective, the stimulating environment has to continue, as it does when children are adopted.

Conducting infant stimulation programs has made it clear that being a parent requires skill, devotion, and time. Most mothers provide their infants with all three. Having these skills provided by someone else is a very expensive proposition. Hence, before such programs are instituted on a larger scale, politicians want to see long-term results that document their effectiveness.

There are also many ethical questions that have to be decided before infant stimulation programs will be common. Some psychologists feel it is unethical to maintain control groups since infants in such groups would clearly profit from the stimulation. If control groups are not maintained, it is difficult to make a convincing case for the effects of the programs. Other ethical questions cloud the picture further. Is it appropriate to take over the parenting of infants? One can argue that it is justifiable ethically and economically because it would only last for one generation. The children in these programs will then be integrated into the culture, just as the children in the Skeels study were. As adults, they will be able to provide appropriate parenting for their children. This "pro" argument also suggests that the financial burden, while heavy initially, will be returned to society in years to come because the children who have benefited will be productive members of society.

The other side of this argument emphasizes the importance of the mother-infant bond and objects to the notion that part of the mother's role would be usurped by a day-care program. The importance of the family unit must be maintained, according to this view, and any invasion of the family prerogative by the state is unwarranted. Instead, these researchers feel that breaking the intergenerational poverty cycle should begin with programs designed to help parents help their children. They also counter the "pro" arguments by noting that we have no convincing evidence that an infant stimulation program will remove all of the vestiges of being raised in poverty.

These issues, presented here in their most extreme form, quickly move beyond the scientific information that is available. We have seen that early experiences can affect cognitive development, that stimulating environments can influence intellectual development several years hence, and that some of the effects of early deprivation can be reversed if the environment is improved. But translating these results into a meaningful social policy is not easy.

### SUMMARY

The chapter began by recognizing those psychologists who have ventured into the difficult area of infant research. They have devised a host of ingenious methods that allow us to delve into the workings of the infant's mind. Moving beyond observations, they have found ways to directly assess the infant's growing cognitive skills. Recording heart rates, sucking responses, and the electrical activity of the brain have given us new insights into the infant's cognitive growth.

To chart the course of cognitive development in infancy, the newborn's beginning skills were cataloged. Infants are born with many functional ways of understanding their environment. Vision, grasping, hearing, sucking, smelling, tasting, and touching are all present. These initial skills are the foundation for the cognitive changes described by Jean Piaget during the sensory motor period. During the first month of life, these beginning patterns of behavior are practiced until they are flexible ways of exploring the environment. As infants gradually gain control over each of these skills, they are able to integrate two or more simple behaviors. The isolated behaviors of the newborn give way to complex action patterns, or schemes, that infants use to understand their environment. One of the major milestones of the sensory motor period—the object concept—evolves from the actions of infants. The object concept is important because it signals the beginning of the child's ability to represent the environment, and it paves the way for the gradual ascendance of thought. At the end of the sensory motor period, children can encounter an obstacle or a barrier and imagine a way to overcome it. They can imitate actions they witnessed days earlier. They can solve problems and use tools. The thoughts that were initially derived from actions have begun to dominate the child's behavior.

Piaget's description of cognitive changes during infancy prodded psychologists to look more closely at the first two years of a child's life. Since Piaget first published his classic books on infant development, there have literally been thousands of studies examining infants' cognitive skills. As a result, we now have detailed information concerning what an infant prefers to examine, when visual abstractions are formed, how long an infant remembers, when an infant can recreate an experience, and when imitation and problem solving begin.

Any review of the sensory motor period typically generates new appreciation for human infants. From birth they are searching, attentive, and persistent in their attempts to understand their world. In two years of actively interacting with the environment, they make dramatic advances in perceiving, knowing, remembering, and thinking. Even these advances are only part of the story. Infants make similar, impressive strides in social development. The cognitive skills that worked so well in understanding objects take on an added dimension when they are applied to people. In the next chapter, we will finish the chronicle of infant development by tracing the social development of the infant.

# CHAPTER 7

# Social development in infancy

Although the physical and mental development of the child are important, the most critical aspect of the infant's environment is the people who care for the child. Human infants cannot obtain food for themselves, they cannot walk or crawl to safety, they cannot express or satisfy their needs in any direct way. For all of these basics of survival, newborns depend on other people.

In terms of the survival of the species, this total dependency could be very dangerous. Suppose parents decided not to care for their infants. In many other species, the parents take no interest in their offspring. These animals typically produce a huge number of eggs. By chance, some of them hatch and survive to reproduce. Oysters exemplify this strategy. They produce 500 million eggs a year, but provide no parental care. A similar strategy would never work for humans. Producing hundreds of offspring and hoping that a few survive would exhaust both the mother and the resources of the environment. A different strategy had to evolve to insure the survival of our species (Figure 7–1).

Having parents who take care of the young was an obvious solution to the problem. Providing such care has become a major factor in the survival of the great apes—humans, gorillas, orangutans, chimpanzees, and gibbons (Johanson & Edey, 1980). Human adults produce few infants, and should these infants not survive, the species would soon be in danger of extinction. Hence, parental care and social systems that insure the health of the young are critical to the survival of our species. In this chapter, the social systems that surround the infant will be explored.

The attachment that develops between the primary caretaker and the child is one of the first examples of a social tie that helps insure an infant's survival. Although the primary caretaker does not have to be the mother, it usually is. For convenience and to avoid the dispassionate label of primary caretaker, this tie will be referred to as the mother-infant attachment. While the attachment between mother and infant may be the most important one, the father-infant relationship has been receiving increasing attention. Psychologists are beginning to realize that the father makes his own unique contribution to the infant's social development. It is also important to trace the emergence of the child's social skills. As with cognition, infants are not passive. They can maintain, enhance, or reduce their mother's or father's attention by their behavior. In this context, individual differences between infants will be explored. Whether

**Figure 7—1**             **Caring for the young**

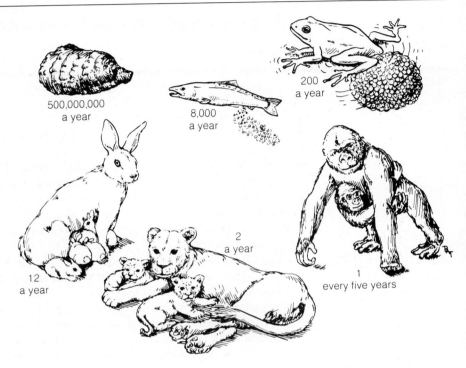

500,000,000
a year

8,000
a year

200
a year

12
a year

2
a year

1
every five years

Reproductive strategies in animals vary enormously. The oyster relies on maximum egg production and provides no parental care. In the great apes, nearly all of the emphasis is on parental care and the birthrate is reduced to a minimum.

Source: Johanson, D. C., & Edey, M. (1981). *Lucy* (pp. 322, 323). New York: Simon & Schuster.

a child is seen as difficult or easy, whether the child cries a great deal or very little, whether the child sleeps 8 hours or 12 hours may facilitate or hinder the parent's feelings of attachment. Finally, we will consider what happens to children when some families fail to care for them adequately. Abuse, neglect, and abandonment indicate that the systems that normally insure the infant's health and well-being have failed.

## THE DEVELOPMENT OF ATTACHMENT

Attachment is a general term describing the affectionate ties that develop between parents and their offspring, especially between the mother and child. Attachment, as it is used in the field of developmental psychology, refers to an enduring affectionate tie that one person forms to another specific person (Ainsworth, 1973). Developing an attachment is an ongoing process. It is most noticeable during the first year of life because the infant's attachment changes so obviously during this period.

Attachment differs from the bonding that was described in Chapter 4. Bonding is a rapid process that takes place during the period surrounding birth. Bonding describes the parents' feelings for the newborn. The bonding that takes place at birth is a one-way street, from parent to child. It fosters the parents' emotional commitment to a specific newborn. The baby is only required to be present, although it certainly helps to have a responsive and alert baby. Bonding is most aptly described as one aspect of the ongoing attachment process.

## Imprinting

For many years, it was assumed that attachments between parents and children were the end result of learning. This view was initially challenged by the work of two ethologists, Konrad Lorenz and Eckard Hess. As ethologists, they studied the natural history of a behavior. They gathered information on when specific behaviors were displayed, how these behaviors changed during the life cycle, and how the environment affected these behaviors. They suggested that each species has built-in patterns of behavior that insure survival and keep the mother and infant together. In birds, *imprinting* is one of the built-in behaviors that ties the newborn to its mother.

Konrad Lorenz began his imprinting studies when he was five years old. As many youngsters might, he badgered his parents for a pet duck. Despite his father's gloomy predictions concerning the fate of the duck, Lorenz's wish was granted (Hess, 1973). The duck became very attached to Lorenz and would follow him everywhere. Although Lorenz did not realize it at the time, these are the signs of imprinting.

In subsequent years, Lorenz and Hess devoted many hours to observing imprinting in a variety of birds. They wanted to know what caused newly hatched goslings to follow their mothers. By accident, they discovered that there is nothing particularly impressive about the mother. Goslings will follow the first object they see move. In the natural habitat, this would almost always be the mother goose. In the laboratory, it could be a model of a goose, a football, or even Lorenz himself. Imprinting is common among birds. It takes place during a relatively short period early in life (the first 21 hours in the case of a goose) and has several long-term consequences. If birds are imprinted on humans, they will act permanently tame around humans, a desirable consequence for scientists working with birds. A less desirable consequence is that the birds will not be interested in mating with birds (see Figure 7–2).

Hess and Lorenz studied imprinting in many species of birds. In the process, they gave the methods of ethological analysis a new scientific respectability and demonstrated the value of in-depth studies of species-specific behavior.

## Attachments in primates

Despite the impact that Lorenz and Hess had on the study of behavior, there was still the feeling that imprinting was only important in a few species of birds. Newborn humans are very different organisms. The leap from imprinting in geese to attachment in humans might not have been made without the addi-

**Figure 7—2**     **Imprinting**

*International Crane Foundation*

This whooping crane was imprinted on humans. As a result, a human has to perform a mating dance to encourage her to lay an egg.

tional information provided by Harry Harlow and his colleagues at the University of Wisconsin.

Harlow's primary scientific interest was studying how learning occurred. Harlow used monkeys as subjects because they were more tractable than children. One disadvantage of working with monkeys is that monkeys are very susceptible to many diseases, and an outbreak of disease could easily destroy an entire group of laboratory monkeys. Hence, when a serious disease threatened his laboratory monkeys, he isolated the infant monkeys. They grew up germ free, but the isolation they experienced dramatically altered their social development. Instead of being curious and playful, the isolated monkeys were fearful and withdrawn. Harlow was intrigued by the changes he saw and designed an important series of experiments to examine the role that the mother played in the social development of monkeys (Harlow, 1958).

**Figure 7—3**　　　　　**Contact comfort**

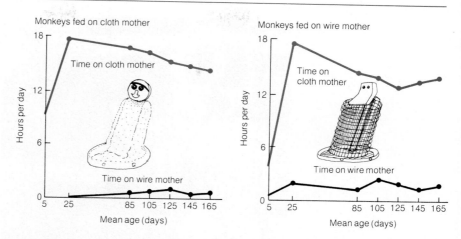

Monkeys fed by the wire mother spent little time with her. They preferred the cloth mother and spent between 13 and 17 hours a day enjoying the "contact comfort" she provided.

Source: Harlow, H. F., & Zimmerman, R. R. (1959). Affectional responses in the infant monkey. *Science, 130,* 421–432.

The prevailing scientific position was that infants became attached to their mothers because their mothers provided them with food. In a disarmingly simple experiment, Harlow provided two surrogate mothers for each monkey, one that provided food and one that did not. The mother that provided food was constructed of wire. The other mother was covered with soft terry cloth. To everyone's surprise, the infant spent many hours clinging to the terry cloth mother and made only quick trips to the wire mother to nurse. Food was not the source of the infant's attachment; something as intangible as comfort was (see Figure 7–3).

Harlow probed the nature of the infant's attachment to these surrogate mothers by putting mechanical spiders and windup bears in the infants' cages (Harlow & Zimmerman, 1959). Confronted with these frightening "monsters," the infants dashed to their soft mothers and grasped the terry cloth tightly. Infants with wire mothers had no such haven, and they threw themselves on the floor, hid their heads, and rocked back and forth.

The infant's attachment to these terry cloth mothers was evidenced in other ways. When the terry cloth mother was present, the infant would venture away from her to explore a toy in the cage. If something startled these monkeys, they could dash to their mother again, summon their courage as they clung to her, and then venture off again. Within minutes, an infant monkey could be transformed from a frightened, quaking recluse to a bold adventurer. The terry cloth mother supplied the courage by providing comfort (see Figure 7–4).

**Figure 7—4**     **The importance of attachment**

*University of Wisconsin Primate Laboratory*

Attachment figures provide a base for exploration and the courage to explore. This monkey is emboldened by his contact with the mother and will soon be able to explore the object that initially frightened him.

Harlow's monkeys demonstrated that even an inanimate terry cloth mother is a powerful force in the infant's development. The mother provides a source of comfort, a haven in the event of stress, and a base from which to explore. The unyielding wire mother offered none of these. Harlow's studies and conclusions drew attention to the crucial role that appropriate mothering plays in a monkey's development. The stage was set for similar investigations with humans.

## HUMAN ATTACHMENTS

John Bowlby, a British psychoanalyst, became interested in the attachment between mother and infant when he was investigating the development of children living in orphanages. Building on the work of the ethologists and the work with primates, he reasoned that the newborn of every species has particular behaviors or signals that they use to attract the attention of their mothers and keep their mothers nearby (Bowlby, 1969, 1973, 1980). Any behavior that initiates, maintains, or elicits proximity to the mother is identified as an attachment behavior. As a group, these behaviors form the *Attachment Behavioral System*. According to Bowlby, the Attachment Behavioral System is specifically designed to protect the infant from harm. Through this system, human infants (*a*) develop obvious preferences for specific people, (*b*) express these preferences clearly once object permanence is achieved, (*c*) object angrily and cry if separation occurs, and (*d*) seek comfort from this person if the environment seems threatening (Main, 1981).

## The infant's signals

Newborn humans are not able to function independently. They are able to function in concert with someone else—usually the mother. In fact, the infant has a remarkable repertoire of skills that can be used to influence the caretaker. Bolby suggested that human infants signal their parents by crying, smiling, sucking, and clinging.

**Crying.** An infant's cry is an especially strong signal that tends to bring the mother into contact with her infant. Mothers become concerned when they hear infants cry as evidenced by changes in the mother's heart rate (Donovan, Leavitt, & Balling, 1978). Throughout the first year, mothers respond to this signal by picking up their children.

The communication provided by a crying infant is more differentiated than you might expect. Mothers believe they can tell from an infant's cry whether their child is hungry, angry, hurt, tired, or bored. "Oh, she's really mad about something" or "Time to eat" are standard responses to infants' cries. Sceptics argue that the cries are the same, but the mother interprets a whole series of events before labeling the cry. For example, when the child first wakes up, the mother knows that hunger is the most likely possibility. If her son has just been fed, then boredom or gas become possibilities. Wasz-Hoechert, Lind, Vuorenoski, Partanen, and Valanne (1968) were the first to prove that attentive mothers could understand the language of crying. They recorded the first cry the child gave at delivery, the cry when the baby was pinched or pricked, and the cry of a child who had not been fed for four hours. Then they asked adults to pick out the birth cry, the pain cry, and the hunger cry. The different types of cries were identified with great accuracy especially by mothers, midwives, and children's nurses. The differences between the cries are also obvious when tracings of different cries are examined. Two cries of a four- and five-day-old infant are presented in Figure 7–5. The darker tracing indicates a louder cry. The first cry is more rhythmical as indicated by the clear pattern. The second cry is angry and uncontrolled as indicated by the fuzzy, indistinct pattern.

Once psychologists agreed that infants had several different cries, they began to look closely at crying. The cries of premature infants differed from the cries of full-term infants. Children with Down's syndrome had a different pattern to

**Figure 7—5**    **Spectrogram of an infant's cries**

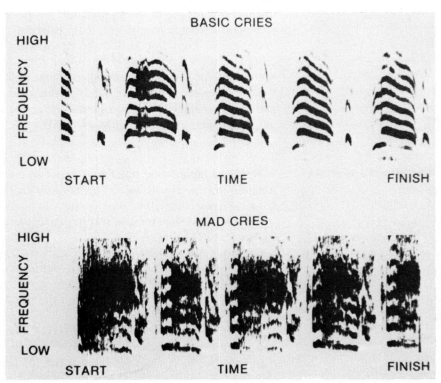

*Courtesy Dr. Peter H. Wolff*

Two spectrograms of a baby crying for about five seconds. The top picture represents a sequence of four repeated cries by a four-day-old baby boy. The bottom picture shows a sequence of five angry cries by a four-day-old baby girl. The fuzziness in the picture of the mad cries represents the hissing sounds caused by the excess air which the angry baby is forcing through her vocal chords. The differences between two infants' cries can be seen and can probably be heard by adults who spend a lot of time with infants.

their cries (Dunn, 1977). Now psychologists suspect that neurological abnormalities may be detectable by looking at a visual tracing of an infant's cry.

On a day-to-day basis, the cries of normal infants begin differently, but if the crying continues, it falls into a basic, rhythmic cry. Peter Wolff (1969) suggests that parents recognize this basic pattern and interpret it as meaning "everything is normal." When a cry veers from the basic pattern, they begin to search for a cause. The cry is a very basic way that the child signals the parents; and what it lacks in subtlety, it makes up for in urgency. Most parents quickly recognize the specific cry of their infant (Wiesenfeld, Malatesta, & DeLoach, 1981) and find it very difficult to ignore this signal (Zeskind, 1980).

**Smiling.**    Smiling is another signal that keeps the mother responding to the infant. Since social smiling is not stable until the second month of life, the infant has to rely on reflexive crying to maintain proximity earlier. During the second month, the infant begins to smile broadly at the mother, to indicate excitement by bicycling movements of the arms and legs, and to coo and vocalize (Emde, 1980). Parents usually find this combination irresistible and spend hours talking to and playing with their infant. The cycle of loving interaction, with the mother and infant responding to each other, strengthens the mother's feelings for her infant and maintains her caring, protective attitude. Mothers spontaneously comment on their infant's awakening sociability saying, "she's so much fun now, she smiles and laughs and gets really excited when we play." From Bowlby's point of view, mothers are responding to a new set of signals from the child.

**Clinging, crawling, and walking.** Few parents can resist the outstretched hands of their five-month-old infant. Reaching and clinging extend the child's attachment behaviors and also presage the more active role that the infant is beginning to take in maintaining proximity. When babies begin to crawl and walk, they are no longer limited to signaling the mother. Now they can maintain proximity by their own actions.

This brief and incomplete list of attachment behaviors indicates how infants first signal the mother and later maintain proximity by their own actions. It fails to describe the complex and reciprocal interaction that the mother and infant develop during the first year. To understand these subtle interchanges that are the basis of the Attachment Behavioral System, we must investigate the mother's response to the infant and the changes in the nature of the infant's attachment.

**The infant's changing attachment**

The feeling or bond that the mother develops at birth is toward a specific infant. This bond helps insure that the mother recognizes her particular infant and develops a commitment to the child. The attachment behaviors that the newborn displays are not nearly so specific. The crying of the newborn is not even directed toward people. It is the infant's reflexive way of expressing hunger, pain, discomfort, or boredom. Even the beguiling smile of the six-week-old infant is not directed specifically at the mother. Any adult that engages the baby in play will see the same beaming face and bicycling legs. The attachment behaviors that are directed specifically at the mother do not begin to appear until approximately six months of age (Emde, 1980).

In evolutionary terms, it would probably make more sense for human infants to become attached to their mothers the first day. But the infant's cognitive skills are not sophisticated enough to recognize a particular person. Furthermore, the infant's senses are not coordinated enough to understand that the person singing, diapering, and nursing are all one individual. An attachment to a specific person must await the attainment of these sensory motor milestones. Once infants recognize their mother in a variety of poses and situations and once their senses are integrated, they are cognitively equipped to form an enduring attachment (Kagan, 1979).

**Attachment**

*Sue Markson*

The infant reaching is one of several attachment behaviors designed to keep the infant close to the mother. John Bowlby suggests that these proximity seeking behaviors help protect the infant and insure its survival.

The attachment of the infant to one person is followed by a series of changes in the infant's reaction to other adults. At four months, infants gurgle and smile at a strange grandmotherly woman who peers into their crib. At 10 months, the approach of this stranger may frighten infants and cause them to cling to their mothers.

Once a firm attachment to a specific adult has been established, infants begin to show their distress when this adult leaves. Notice that this attachment behavior also has cognitive undertones. Crying when the mother leaves and searching for the mother indicate that infants can remember the absent person. In Piaget's terms, the infants have learned that objects (and people) are permanent.

The infant's contribution to the Attachment Behavioral System seems limited at birth. As infants master cognitive skills, their attachment behaviors are directed toward a specific person. By the time infants are mobile, they have some ability to remember, can manipulate images, and have usually developed an enduring emotional tie to a specific person. Developing this tie depends as much on the mother's responses as it does on the infant's changes. Let us switch the focus of the discussion to consider the mother's role in the Attachment Behavioral System.

**The mother's response to her infant**

The mother's attachment to the infant begins before birth and is influenced by several personal variables. The mother's self-esteem, the quality of care she received as a child, and whether her baby was planned can all affect her relationship with her infant. As discussed in Chapter 4, the events surrounding birth typically cement the bond that the mother has for her infant and commit her to caring for this specific child. The quality of this bond probably serves as the foundation for the nurturing and caring that continues through the first year.

The mother's role in the Attachment Behavioral System begins by meeting the child's needs. Mary Ainsworth, who has done more than any other researcher to test Bowlby's theory in a systematic way, first demonstrated the importance of the mother's response to the child's signals. She and Silvia Bell found that mothers who responded promptly and consistently to their infant's cries were rewarded later. By one year of age, these infants cried less than those whose mothers did not respond promptly (Bell & Ainsworth, 1972). Their study, and several cross-cultural investigations of mothers who carry their infants constantly, scotched the folk view that you spoil a baby by picking it up. On the contrary, infants who were cuddled early in life were content with less physical contact at one year of age. But infants who were left to cry during the first months of life continued their excessive crying at one year.

Bell and Ainsworth's results also gave credence to Bowlby's view that crying is a species-specific signal designed to keep the mother close. Babies seldom started crying while their mothers were attending to them. Crying typically occurred when the mother was working some distance from her infant. The crying alerted the mother, and she responded to her infant's signal by establishing contact. Bell and Ainsworth noted that the mothers in their study usually did not feel the diaper to see if it was wet or go get a bottle. They picked up the baby and began soothing and rocking. When these techniques are used, most infants stop crying very quickly (Byrne & Horowitz, 1981). This cycle of behavior—including the infant's signal, the mother's prompt response, and the ending of the signal—support Bowlby's view that crying is one of several attachment behaviors designed to keep the mother close. Interestingly, if the mothers responded promptly, the infants stopped crying promptly. Bell and Ainsworth suggest that infants learn that their cries will be answered and their needs will be met. Hence, once they are picked up, they stop crying.

Meeting the infant's needs in a prompt and solicitous way is part of a cycle called the Attachment Behavioral System. The cycle can begin with the baby's cries signaling the mother. When the mother responds to the infant, the aversive crying stops. The mother feels she is effective and proceeds with meeting the infant's needs. The caretaking that takes place forms a backdrop for the special interaction that characterizes mothers with their infants. These "waltzes" or "dances" are 10- to 20-minute periods of intense social play that typically accompany changing a diaper or nursing a child (Stern, 1974; Condon & Sander, 1974). After the baby is full, warm, and dry, mothers often begin a playful interaction. Opening with a drawn out "Hiiiii, baaby," they play patty-cake or tickling games. They sing songs, pull the baby to standing positions, bounce the laughing baby gently on their knee, or show them a favorite toy. All the while, the mothers use exaggerated facial expressions and speech. Mothers continue this interaction as long as their infants smile and respond. But if the infant looks away or begins to cry, the mother immediately decreases the level of stimulation (Stern, 1977).

These intense play sessions are thought to heighten the attachment between mother and infant. The mother and infant both learn to "read" the other's signals. In addition, infants have a chance to become familiar with their mother's face, and they learn to associate their mother with these playful interludes. The cycle that started with the infant's signal often concludes with a playful interaction that enhances the Attachment Behavioral System. This brief description does not do justice to the complexity and richness of the Attachment Behavioral System. It does outline some of the steps that we have been able to examine (see Figure 7–6). The system can begin with a smile from the infant or it can begin with the mother nursing or the father tickling the child. Similarly, the interaction can end when the child becomes tired and cranky or when the father's or mother's attention is needed elsewhere.

**The father's attachment**

The cycle of interaction that has been described is not limited to the mother. Any adult can respond to the child's signals. Fathers who diaper and dress the child are just as capable of extending the caretaking into play as the mother. Caretaking is an easy way to begin playing with the child, but it is not the only one. A smile from the infant can signal the father that the child is ready for roughhousing. This rough-and-tumble play enhances the father's attachment in the same way that patty-cake enhanced the mother's attachment. Because the infant's signals are not directed initially at any particular person, fathers, grandmothers, babysitters, and siblings can become familiar faces and partners in playful interactions during the first months (Yogman, Dixon, Tronick, Als, & Brazelton, 1979). By 8 to 12 months, infants will often be attached to these people as well as to their mothers. Psychologists were initially surprised that infants could be attached to several adults during the first year. So much emphasis had been put on the mother-infant relationship that other relationships had seldom been studied. The Glasgow study was the first to point out that as many as 70 percent of the infants became very attached to their playful fathers during the first year (Schaffer & Emerson, 1964). Infants who were initially attached only to their mothers extended this attachment rapidly to grandparents, siblings, and especially to fathers. Schaffer and Emerson also demonstrated that being attached to more than one person did not weaken that

**Figure 7—6**     **The Attachment Behavioral System**

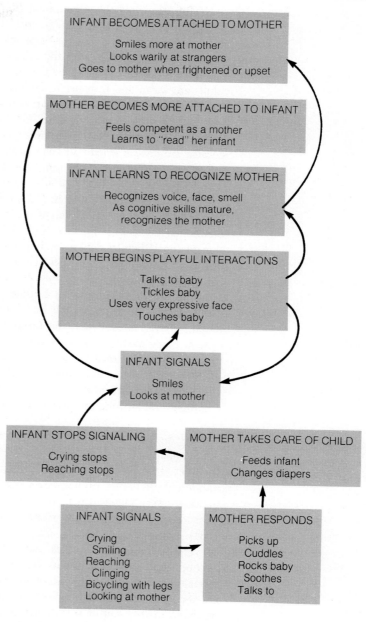

INFANT BECOMES ATTACHED TO MOTHER

Smiles more at mother
Looks warily at strangers
Goes to mother when frightened or upset

MOTHER BECOMES MORE ATTACHED TO INFANT

Feels competent as a mother
Learns to "read" her infant

INFANT LEARNS TO RECOGNIZE MOTHER

Recognizes voice, face, smell
As cognitive skills mature,
recognizes the mother

MOTHER BEGINS PLAYFUL INTERACTIONS

Talks to baby
Tickles baby
Uses very expressive face
Touches baby

INFANT SIGNALS

Smiles
Looks at mother

INFANT STOPS SIGNALING

Crying stops
Reaching stops

MOTHER TAKES CARE OF CHILD

Feeds infant
Changes diapers

INFANT SIGNALS

Crying
Smiling
Reaching
Clinging
Bicycling with legs
Looking at mother

MOTHER RESPONDS

Picks up
Cuddles
Rocks baby
Soothes
Talks to

The Attachment Behavioral System encompasses all of the behaviors the infant uses to keep the mother close. During the early days, crying is the most effective behavior. Later, the infant is able to keep the mother close by smiling, reaching, clinging, looking, and bicycling with the legs. Once infants can walk or crawl, they can play a more active role in staying near the mother. The infant's Attachment Behavioral System meshes with maternal behaviors to promote attachment.

attachment bond in any way. In fact, the infant with an intense attachment to one person was likely to be attached to other adults as well.

Having examined the Attachment Behavioral System, it is easy to see how infants can form multiple attachments. The number of people infants are attached to depends on how many people meet the child's needs in a warm, responsive way and play with the infant. If only the mother takes the time to play with the infant, she will be the focus of the infant's attachment. If several adults are warm and responsive, infants may be attached to all of them. Nevertheless, being attached to several adults does not mean that the attachments take exactly the same form. After the Glasgow study, psychologists began to examine the infant's attachment to the father as well as the mother. In the last decade, we have learned that each parent makes a unique contribution to the infant's social development. Let us look at the father's specific contribution (Lamb, 1982d).

For years, the father's attachment to the infant was minimized. Freud and Bowlby stressed the importance of the mother-infant relationship and scarcely mentioned the father. Furthermore, the animal studies reinforced the exclusion of the father by demonstrating that maternal behavior was mediated by hormones (Rosenblatt & Siegel, 1975). Because it is difficult to identify the fathers in most primates, scientific interest in the father was minimal. Several events in the 1970s caused this attitude to change.

The same animal researchers that documented the role of hormones in maternal behavior proved that the hormonal influence is short-lived. A second system, based on the mother's recognition of the infant and the mother's bond to the infant, takes over as the hormonal system wanes. Fathers can participate in this second system as readily as mothers. As described in Chapter 4, fathers who are present during the delivery of their baby or who are actively involved with their child during the first days of life develop a bond similar to the mother's.

Other animal studies indicated that there is more plasticity in the father-infant attachment system than there is in the mother-infant attachment system. In other words, a father can be very involved with his infant or he can be indifferent. Whether or not he is involved depends on three factors. First, males are very involved with their offspring in species where the mother and father form a monogamous relationship for long periods (Parke & Suomi, 1981). Some primate fathers, like the marmosets and the gibbons, participate actively in the care of infants and seem very attached to particular infants. Second, males can only be involved if the female allows them to be. Rhesus monkeys in the wild usually deny the fathers access to infants. These mothers are very protective of their infants and allow few intrusions from males in the troop. In nuclear families of rhesus monkeys that were established at the University of Wisconsin, the females allowed the fathers more contact with the infants. As a result, the adult males were very involved with the infants (Suomi, 1977). Third, even though the rhesus monkey fathers could be described as attached to the infants, their attachment did not mimic the mother's. Mothers could be seen holding the infants, nursing them, and retrieving the infants when they strayed. Fathers, on the other hand, never nursed, seldom retrieved, and did not spend time holding their infants. Instead, they protected, groomed, and roughhoused with their infants. Hence, if we are going to look at father involvement, we need to examine behaviors other than the cuddling that is so characteristic of the mother.

These animal studies tell us that hormones are not as salient for long-term attachments as we previously thought. Furthermore, the father's responsiveness to the infant can be molded by the environment, and the attachment is likely to be built on rough-and-tumble play and protection rather than caretaking.

Recent evidence suggests that these same characteristics apply to humans (Pedersen, 1980). Human fathers can take care of their infants if they are needed. Mothers who have had a Caesarean birth and need time to recuperate, typically turn over the care of the newborn to the father (Parke, 1981). In this situation, most fathers perform the caretaking skillfully. Husbands and wives in today's society often prefer to share the child care. In homes where both the mother and father work, fathers typically participate actively in caring for the children (Hoffman, 1977).

**Fathers prefer play**

*Jean-Claud Lejeune: Stock, Boston*

Fathers prefer to play with their children in a rough-and-tumble fashion. This form of interaction is as likely to result in secure attachments as the mother's more gentle talking and caressing.

We also see that the father-infant relationship usually compliments the mother-infant relationship (Parke & Suomi, 1981). Fathers take special delight in being the child's playmate (Kotelchuck, 1976; Parke, 1981). Mothers talk to their infants; fathers touch them. Mothers play patty-cake; fathers throw them into the air (Power & Parke, 1981). These different styles of interaction are seen in the first days of life, and they continue to characterize parental involvement throughout the toddler and preschool periods (Lamb, 1981; Clarke-Stewart, 1978). Furthermore, these styles of interacting do not change when the roles of the mother and father change. Even when fathers are the primary caretakers, their interaction with the child is infused with playful asides (Lamb, Frodi, Hwang, Frodi, & Steinberg, 1982). The different styles that mothers and fathers adopt when playing with their children shape the parent-child relationship. Both the caretaking style of the mother and the playful style of the father produce strong infant attachments.

## PATTERNS OF ATTACHMENT

The path that infants and their fathers and mothers take in the process of becoming attached is sometimes not as straight or as ideal as the path that has been described. Instead, there are several patterns of attachment, ranging from the securely attached child who is trusting and curious, to the anxious infant who is not comforted by the mother's presence. Because the attachment process is one of the first social achievements of the infant, it is important to examine these different outcomes. Before a discussion of these patterns will be meaningful, we must digress for a moment to describe how the infant's attachment is measured.

**The Ainsworth strange situation**

Attachment behaviors are most obvious when the mother leaves the infant or when she is reunited with the infant after a brief separation. Hence, Ainsworth and Wittig (1969) devised a set of carefully regimented episodes called the *strange situation* that involve the mother leaving and returning (see Figure 7–7). In the strange situation, the infant and the mother begin by playing in a comfortable room filled with toys. Then a stranger enters the room. After talking with the mother, the stranger approaches the baby. At this point, the mother leaves the room quietly, leaving the infant and the stranger together. Approximately three minutes later, the mother returns, the stranger leaves, and the baby's attention is redirected to the roomful of toys. As soon as the baby is engaged with the toys, the mother leaves again, this time announcing her departure by saying bye-bye. The baby is alone for three minutes before the same stranger enters. In the final episode, the mother returns and greets the baby (Ainsworth, Blehar, Waters, & Wall, 1978).

Observers watch the baby's reaction in each situation. They note how distressed the infant is when the mother leaves, how effective the mother is at soothing the infant after her return, how the infant reacts to the stranger, and

**Figure 7—7**  **Ainsworth's strange situation**

| Number of episode | Persons present | Duration | Brief description of action |
|---|---|---|---|
| 1 | Mother, baby, & observer | 30 seconds | Observer introduces mother and baby to experimental room, then leaves. |
| 2 | Mother & baby | 3 minutes | Mother is nonparticipant while baby explores; if necessary, play is stimulated after 2 minutes. |
| 3 | Stranger, mother, & baby | 3 minutes | Stranger enters. First minute: Stranger silent. Second minute: Stranger converses with mother. Third minute: Stranger approaches baby. After 3 minutes, mother leaves unobtrusively. |
| 4 | Stranger & baby | 3 minutes or less* | First separation episode. Stranger's behavior is geared to that of baby. |
| 5 | Mother & baby | 3 minutes or more† | First reunion episode. Mother greets and/or comforts baby, then tries to settle the baby again in play. Mother then leaves, saying "bye-bye." |
| 6 | Baby alone | 3 minutes or less | Second separation episode. |
| 7 | Stranger & baby | 3 minutes or less | Continuation of second separation. Stranger enters and gears her behavior to that of baby. |
| 8 | Mother & baby | 3 minutes | Second reunion episode. Mother enters, greets baby, then picks baby up. Meanwhile stranger leaves unobtrusively. |

Summary of procedures in the strange situation.

*Episode is curtailed if the baby is unduly distressed.
†Episode is prolonged if more time is required for the baby to become reinvolved in play.

Source: Ainsworth, M. D. S., Blehar, M. C., Waters, E., & Wall, S. (1978). *Patterns of attachment* (p. 37). Hillsdale, NJ: Lawrence Erlbaum.

whether the infant is able to explore and play during the different episodes. Ainsworth and her colleagues have now watched hundreds of infants in the strange situation and they report that most of the infants fall into one of three patterns of attachment—secure, anxious, or ambivalent infants (Ainsworth et al., 1978).

**Secure infants**

The majority of infants (between 50 and 65 percent) could be called securely attached. Infants in this group have developed very positive relationships with their mothers during their first year. The infants seem competent and self-assured while they explore the toys in the room. When the mother leaves, the infants are distressed but the mother's return is joyous. Secure infants cling to their mother on her return and nestle close to her, initially refusing to be put down. The secure infant is comforted quickly by the mother's embrace and appears happy by the end of the session.

When these infants are observed at home, their security and confidence are even more obvious. They are so sure that their mothers are accessible and will respond promptly that they seldom cry when their mothers go to another room in the house. At home, these mothers are warm and responsive and initiate many playful interactions with their children. The mothers lavish physical contact on their infants and provide reassurance and comfort when it is needed. As a result, by the end of the first year, these infants seldom cry (Main, 1981).

**Anxious/avoidant infants**

Babies who avoid their mothers in the strange situation bear little resemblance to the infants just described. During the reunion episodes, these infants ignore their mothers. When they are picked up, they wiggle and squirm. They are often very friendly to the stranger, and this friendliness contrasts sharply with their avoidance of their mother. Throughout the strange situation, they seem captivated by the toys. Unlike the secure infants, they are not distressed when the mother leaves and do not seem afraid or angry.

Observations of these infants in their homes suggests that the mother's behavior has blocked the path to a secure attachment. The mothers are often angry and irritated by their babies. Instead of providing tenderness, warmth, and sensitivity, these mothers are rejecting and rigid. Unfortunately, this pattern of attachment characterizes between 20 and 30 percent of the infants who have been observed (Main, 1981).

**Ambivalent infants**

A few infants (less than 10 percent) seem ambivalent in the strange situation. They certainly are not as secure as the first group. They seem to seek contact with their mothers, yet when it is offered, these babies resist it. Furthermore, they do not seem to derive much comfort from the contact their mothers provide. Despite the fact that the mother's presence is not very comforting, these infants are very distressed when their mothers leave the room. Often, they are distressed even before she leaves, seemingly because of the stranger's presence.

At home, the mothers of these infants are much less responsive to the infant's crying, smiling, and signaling than mothers whose infants are securely attached. These mothers are not rejecting or rigid, and they seem to enjoy hugging their infants. What these mothers seem to lack is a sense of timing. They do not seem to be able to read the baby's signals clearly. Hence, they try to cuddle the infant when the infant wants to play, and they offer a toy when the infant needs a hug.

**Other factors in attachment**

By observing infants at home during the first year and then putting mothers and infants through the strange situation, Ainsworth proved that the mother's acceptance, sensitivity, promptness, and responsiveness during the first year were related to the strength of the infant's attachment. Ainsworth's view meshed nicely with Bowlby's notion that the infant's signals begin a series of interactions between mother and infant that ultimately promote a secure attachment. Although Ainsworth's results were consistent with Bowlby's theorizing, there could be other explanations. Both the ineffective interaction during the first year and the lack of attachment in the strange situation might be due to something else—such as a separation at birth or prematurity.

Before the mother-infant relationship could be convincingly cited as the root of attachment, some of these other factors had to be ruled out. A factor that seemed like a prime candidate to explain both the mother-infant interaction and the attachment was whether the mother and infant were separated at birth. Such a separation interrupts the bonding process and might also interfere with the attachment process. Two studies have shown, however, that separations between the mother and infant at birth do not play a role in the infant's attachment one year later (Hock, Coady, & Cordero, 1973; Rode, Chang, Fisch, & Sroufe, 1981). Although attachment may initially build on the bond developed at birth, the period surrounding birth is not a good indicator of whether an infant will be securely attached one year later (Lamb, 1982c). Mothers and infants who were separated at birth were able to overcome this separation, and by one year to 18 months, their attachment patterns were normal.

Other variables such as social class, the number of siblings in the family, and the sex of the infant were likewise of little importance in whether an infant was securely attached or anxiously attached one year later (Main & Weston, 1981; Rode, Chang, Fisch, & Sroufe, 1981). The evidence clearly points to the conclusion that attachment at one year is determined by the nature of the mother-infant interaction during that year.

Remember, though, that infants are not passive recipients of their mother's care. The infant helps determine how well the mother can carry out her responsibilities. Low birth-weight infants, for example, may cry more, need to be fed more, and hence tax the mother's skills (Ainsworth et al., 1978). Similarly, infants who have medical problems as newborns may make the mother's job more difficult (Waters, Vaughn, & Egeland, 1980). These infants often cry for extended periods of time and are slow to smile when the mother begins her playful interactions. When observed in the strange situation at one year, these toddlers are often classified as ambivalent. As Ainsworth notes, the mother seems loving, but her timing is off. Perhaps the mother's timing is off because it is so difficult to coordinate her behavior with the infant's erratic behavior. These studies just remind us that mother-infant interaction is always a two-way street with both participants responsible for and contributing to the attachment that results.

**Multiple attachments**     Over a third of the infants studied by Ainsworth were not securely attached to their mother at one year of age. Many of these infants were, however, attached to their fathers. Despite the fact that the father is more at home rough-

## HOW BLINDNESS AFFECTS THE INFANT'S SIGNALS

Because of their handicap, blind children are not able to provide one of the standard attachment signals—eye contact. In this moving passage, Selma Fraiberg, who has worked with blind infants and their parents for 20 years, describes how this affects the adult-infant interaction.

I began the developmental study of blind infants 12 years ago. I gradually became aware of many differences in my behavior toward blind infants when I watched myself with sighted infants. Many of these feelings are still with me, and catch me by surprise. Yet, I think I am reasonably without prejudice toward the blind and, as far as I can judge, my feelings have not been an impediment in my work.

The first self-discoveries came to me in New Orleans when David Freedman and I began our study of a five-month-old blind baby, Toni. We had been visiting Toni for six months when we were asked by a social agency to evaluate another blind baby, Lennie, then nine months old. We arranged for a home visit.

Somebody had made a mistake. Lennie was not blind. We found a neglected baby lying in a filthy crib. If we exerted ourselves in testing, we elicited brief regard of our faces and tracking. It was the absence of sustained fixation that had led someone to believe that Lennie was blind when he was three months of age. Since that time he had been reared as a blind child and as the unwanted 14th child in an impoverished family.

After concluding our testing and a long discussion with the mother, I began to write up notes for a social agency referral. As I put the observations in sequence, I made notations on the conditions that elicited visual regard. I was describing Lennie's responses to my voice when something struck me as strange. It was my monolog. But I always talk to babies I told myself. No. I don't always talk to babies. I don't talk to Toni in the same way.

I searched my memory. It was true. I did very little talking when I was with Toni. This troubled me. Toni was a responsive and endearing child. Lennie depressed me. I enjoyed holding Toni. I had to overcome some feelings of revulsion when I held Lennie. But I talked to Lennie. What was the reward? When I searched my memory again, I came up with two pictures. When I talked to Lennie long enough, I elicited brief moments of visual fixation of my face and a meeting of eyes. When I sustained his fixation long enough, I elicited a ghost of a smile.

Later, I could make use of this self-observation when I was with Toni. I talked to her more frequently, but always I had the sense of something missing, something that should be coming back to me from Toni. There was of course no fixation of my face. And something else was missing. Although Toni smiled frequently in response to her mother's voice, she rarely smiled to our voices as observers. Later, in the course of years, I was to learn much more about the stimuli that evoke smiling in the blind infant. The voice, even the voice of the mother, does not automatically evoke smiling in blind infants. I missed that in Toni. I still miss it in blind infants, and my team members share this feeling with me. What we miss in the blind baby, apart from the eyes that do not see, is the vocabulary of signs and signals that provides the most elementary and vital sense of discourse long before words have meaning.

Fraiberg, S. (1974). Blind infants and their mothers: An examination of the sign system. In M. Lewis & L. A. Rosenblum (Eds.) *The effect of the infant on its caregiver.* New York: John Wiley & Sons.

housing, when the infant's attachment needs are heightened by the strange situation, infants seek out their fathers and cling to them just as they do with their mothers. Notice, however, that the infant's attachment to the father develops independently of the attachment to the mother (Lamb, 1982d). Infants can be securely attached to both parents, one parent, or neither parent (Lamb, 1978). It is often the case that infants who are not securely attached to their mothers are securely attached to their fathers (Grossmann & Grossmann, 1981). Although children who are securely attached to both parents exhibit the most confidence in social situations, the infant's social development seems to proceed normally as long as infants are attached to at least one parent (Main & Weston, 1981).

## THE IMPORTANCE OF ATTACHMENT

As children approach their first birthdays, the majority of infants have established a harmonious relationship with their parents, characterized by sensitivity and trust. These securely attached infants derive comfort and pleasure from their interaction with their parents. Other infants are very anxious around their parents and do not seem comforted by contact with either their mother or father. A third group seems ambivalent. These last two groups are often lumped together in a second category loosely labeled anxious or insecure. The child's attachment status at a year is of more than passing interest. The patterns of attachment established during the first year influence a variety of cognitive and social achievements in later years.

**Social skills**

Securely attached infants are unusually confident and happy in a variety of social settings, and this advantage lasts well beyond infancy. Pastor (1981) describes securely attached two-year-olds as sociable, friendly, and cooperative. When playing with others, these children actively initiate social contact.

The advantage of being securely attached persists through preschool. At the University of California at Berkeley, Wanda Bronson observed securely and anxiously attached infants 3½ years after they had been observed in the strange situation. Infants who had been securely attached to their mothers were sought by other children as playmates, were sympathetic when their friends were distressed, and were regarded as leaders (Bronson, 1981).

Securely attached children are also more cooperative when asked to do something. If, for example, a mother asks a child to "stop banging the broom," the child could obey and begin sweeping, the child could continue banging in the same manner, or the child could bang the broom harder, swinging it wildly back and forth. If children are insecure, they are more likely to actively disobey (Londerville & Main, 1981) and bang the broom harder. Securely attached children are more likely to cooperate, not only with the mother, but with other women as well.

It is easy to see how the infant's social skills can benefit from a sensitive, caring relationship with the parents. Bowlby would predict that the advantages of a secure attachment would extend beyond the social realm. What advantage, if any, does the child gain in the areas of personality or cognitive development?

**Personality variables**

Toddlers need to establish their autonomy. From 18 to 30 months, they should explore and investigate their world. To do this, they need to leave their parents for short periods of time. Alison Clarke-Stewart has shown that toddlers can leave their mothers and explore independently if they were securely attached as infants. These children are confident about their relationship to their mothers and need less physical contact (Clarke-Stewart & Hevey, 1981). In

Clarke-Stewart's view, these children are well on their way to becoming autonomous, independent, and competent.

In contrast, the anxious infant has trouble leaving the mother to explore. Anxious infants sought physical contact just as often at 30 months as they did at 18 months. These infants cannot leave their mothers and hence seem more dependent, somewhat immature, and less autonomous (Clarke-Stewart & Hevey, 1981). The security that an infant feels in the first year can still be seen in personality factors three to five years later. Kindergarten students, who had been securely attached as infants, adapted readily to changes in their schools and were able to cope with frustrating tasks and difficult problems better than children who were not securely attached as infants (Gove, Arend, & Sroufe, 1979).

Infants who were securely attached are self-directed and curious as toddlers and preschoolers. The more anxious infants do not explore as much and seem less curious. These infants cannot tolerate the short separations from their mothers. The words curious and self-directed suggest that the effects of attachment spill over into the cognitive sphere.

**Cognitive skills**

The independent exploration that characterizes securely attached infants facilitates cognitive progress in several areas. As two year-olds, these children delight in exploring and using tools (Matas, Arend, & Sroufe, 1978). Objects and the details of objects fascinate them. They laugh and smile when they discover new characteristics of toys (Main, 1981). When they encounter an environmental obstacle, they are enthusiastic, persistent, and effective in solving the problem (Sroufe, 1979). Their exploration also contributes to well developed spatial skills (Hazen & Durret, 1982).

Language development is another area where securely attached infants have an advantage. Presumably, the positive interaction that was established between the infant and the mother sets the stage for the acquisition of language. Mothers who were sensitive and warm during the first year are likely to display similar qualities when speaking to and listening to their toddlers' initial attempts at speech (Londerville & Main, 1981). These children learn to mimic their mothers readily and soon develop an extensive vocabulary. It is not surprising that their language development progresses very rapidly (Connell, as cited in Ainsworth et al., 1978).

The child's positive attitude toward the environment might be expected to affect scores on intelligence tests. Being securely attached, however, is not particularly advantageous when it comes to broad assessments of infant intelligence or assessments of attention span or symbolic play (Main, 1981).

In summary, being attached to an adult during the first year continues to influence development well after the first year. There is growing evidence that the infant's attachment is important not only to social relationships but to personality variables and selected cognitive skills. Over time and across situations, the quality of the attachment relationship continues to influence later behavior in predictable ways (Pastor, 1981).

This quick review of the importance of attachment might create the impression that the strange situation is a crystal ball that will tell us what will befall the child for years to come. But there is no mystery involved. A secure attachment indicates a caring, trusting relationship which, in all likelihood, will continue into the toddler and preschool years. The continuing relationship contributes to all the social, personal, and cognitive tasks the child encounters. Likewise, an insecure attachment at one year heralds more years of difficult communication that are likely to hinder the child in various social, personal, and cognitive tasks. The strange situation is one indicator of the mother-infant interaction just as blood pressure is one indicator of a person's health. It does not mean that the mother-infant relationship is impervious to change. Although mother-infant attachments are very stable in middle-class families (Waters, 1978), they tend not to be as stable in disadvantaged families (Thompson, Lamb, & Estes, 1982). Furthermore, changes in the family environment may alter the mother-infant relationship. The mother returning to work or a shift in the caretaking arrangements is often accompanied by a change in the mother-infant relationship. The attachment between the mother and infant may have to be renegotiated at these points (Thompson, Lamb, & Estes, 1982).

If the mother-infant attachment is open to change, then it is appropriate to ask if it can be strengthened. If the attachment can be improved, will that tip the balance toward a more favorable direction on later social, personal, and cognitive tasks? These questions are being actively investigated. The preliminary results indicate that we can provide guidance that will enhance the infant's attachment (Egeland & Sroufe, 1981). Whether this will be accompanied by long-term benefits is still not known.

### SEPARATION

Establishing a secure attachment to at least one parent is the major social task of the first year. Infants who have accomplished this have an advantage in several areas of personal, social, and cognitive development. There are some awkward corollaries to secure attachments. When a stranger is present, toddlers may cling to their mothers, hide behind her skirt, or cry. This phenomenon, known as *stranger anxiety*, begins soon after children demonstrate a preference for the mother and reaches a peak between 18 and 30 months. With the mother there to provide comfort and protection, children will soon venture forward to investigate the intruder or will ignore the stranger while they go about their play. If the mother leaves or the stranger approaches, the toddler's anxiety will set off attachment alarms, crying, or both.

A second corollary of a secure attachment is *separation anxiety*. On occasion, toddlers who are attached to their responsive, accepting mothers experi-

## CASE HISTORY OF A SEPARATION

John Bowlby has described the feelings of abandonment that toddlers feel when the mother leaves. In the following case, Jane was prepared for the separation, she was familiar with the substitute caretakers, and her father came to visit daily. Still, the separation takes a toll.

Jane, aged 17 months when she came into care, was the youngest of the four children James and Joyce Robertson fostered whilst their mothers were having a new baby. She was a lively, attractive child who had been cared for by her young mother with devotion and imagination. Both parents expected high standards of obedience and Jane already understood many of their prohibitions.

Familiarizing Jane with the foster-family was extended over several weeks and proved more difficult than it was with the two older children in the study. By the time Jane came into care, however, she was fairly well at ease in her new surroundings, and, when the moment came, was willing to accept full mothering from the substitute at hand.

For the first three days Jane was gay and lively. Both the gaiety and the intense smiling she directed at her foster-parents seemed, however, rather artificial and intended to elicit answering smiles; and when she stopped smiling her face became tense and blank.

The impression gained by the Robertsons that these smiles were artificial and intended to placate was amply confirmed later by Jane's mother. After seeing the film record of these early days she commented, "Jane smiles a lot like that after I've been angry with her and she's trying to placate me."

By the fourth day Jane's mood had changed. No longer gay, she was often restless and cross, and was prone to cry irritably. She tended also to suck her thumb and wanted to be nursed. The impression she gave the foster-parents was of a child "under stress and . . . at times bewildered."

It happened that the foster-parents lived in the same block as Jane's parents so that when Jane was playing in the communal garden, which the families shared (with others), she was no distance from the gate to her parents' garden. For the first four days she seemed not to notice the gate. On the fifth, however, she went to it, tried to open it and failed. Looking over the wall into the empty garden, she shook her head, ran back to the communal garden and then seemed uncertain which way to go. The following day she tried the gate again and this time it opened. Running down the path she tried next to open the door to her parent's apartment. Unsuccessful, she returned, shut the garden gate carefully and then spent some minutes peering at the empty house. On returning to her foster-mother's home that day she resisted entering and for the first time since leaving her mother uttered the word "mama."

On each of the 10 days Jane was away, her father visited for an hour. At first she played happily with him and cried when he left. Towards the end of her stay, however, she seemed pointedly to ignore him whilst he was there, but as soon as he made to leave she clung to him and cried.

When mother arrived to take her home Jane recognized her immediately. At first a little uncertain and shy, she was soon smiling in a sweet, perhaps placatory, way. The game of putting pennies into a purse that she had been playing with her foster-mother she switched quietly to her mother, who was thereafter expected by Jane to take over all her care.

For a time after Jane returned home relations between her and her parents were strained. Sometimes she conformed to their wishes, at others she did the opposite. Their attempts to correct her by smacks led to outbursts of crying of a strength not seen before.

By the end of her 10 days in care Jane had seemed to be firmly attached to her foster-mother and reluctant to give her up. For that reason the foster-mother visited the home several times during the early weeks. At first she was warmly welcomed by Jane, but as Jane's renewed relationship to her mother became more secure the visits created conflict and Jane seemed hardly to know towards which of them to go.

ence a sudden separation. Hospitalizations, vacations, business trips, divorce, and death are just a few of the situations that could involve lengthy separations. Almost every toddler experiences shorter separations—during weekends or while the mother works. It is not surprising that some of these separations disrupt a child's attachment. John Bowlby observed the behavior of toddlers (between 12 months and three years) during long separations and found that these children experienced three different sets of feelings as their attachment turned into detachment (Bowlby, 1973).

**Active protest**

During the first day or two of a separation, children protest wildly—crying, screaming, shaking their beds, and actively searching for their missing parents. If their mother reappears during this period, she is greeted enthusiastically and the child's protest stops.

**Despair**

The active protesting is gradually replaced by mourning, withdrawal, and a general sense of hopelessness. Children who are separated from their parents for longer than a week are no longer crying and protesting. They are passive, quiet, apathetic, withdrawn, and utterly miserable. The toddler's longing for the mother is not, however, devoid of emotion. Often it is accompanied by anger and hostility. Children in residential nurseries express this anger by being sullen and hostile toward those who try to care for them. Anger is even obvious when the mother returns. Rather than rushing to their mothers, these toddlers often respond by crying or walking away. They seem to ignore or even actively reject their mother's fervent hugs and kisses. According to Bowlby, the child's response is a mixture of anger and ambivalence. Fortunately, the toddler's feelings are only temporary. A little patience and reassurance by the mother typically reestablishes the secure relationship that existed prior to the separation.

**Detachment**

If a separation continues for several months, most children begin to forget their mother and start to build new relationships. Unfortunately, the relationships that they now form may bear the scars of their broken attachment to their mother. New relationships may be tentative and superficial and not serve the same purpose that the trusting-caring attachment of the first year did. If the mother returns before the detachment has progressed too far, she may be able to gradually reestablish the relationship. If the child is completely detached, her efforts may not be successful (Bowlby, 1980).

**Preventing detachment**

Bowlby's views on separation were gleaned from his observations of toddlers who found themselves abruptly placed in unfamiliar environments with unfamiliar adults—often for as long as a week or two. This situation is much more extreme than most of the separations toddlers experience. Still, the thought that a separation might disrupt the parent-child relationship has caused parents to cancel vacations, delay surgery, and feel guilty about leaving the child, even for short periods.

**The Linus phenomenon**

© 1956 United Features Syndicate, Inc.

The Linus phenomenon refers to the child's attachment to inanimate objects. Blankets can take on all of the characteristics of an attachment figure for a short period of time. Linus's famous blanket can destroy enemies as well as provide comfort and security.

The feelings of abandonment that children experience during a separation can be reduced in several ways. Other familiar, caring adults can take care of the child. If the infant is attached to both parents and the mother has to leave the child for a few days, the father's presence will keep the child from becoming overly distraught. Grandparents and babysitters who have already established trusting relationships with the child can see the child through separations with a minimum of disturbance (Bowlby, 1973).

Leaving children in a familiar environment with their favorite toys and blankets also helps. Charles Schulz, the creator of "Peanuts", always portrays Linus with a blanket. In fact, Linus cannot venture into the world without his blanket. It offers comfort while instilling trust and confidence. If deprived of his blanket, Linus is reduced to staring vacantly into space or screaming. The Linus phenomenon is common in toddlers because, for a short period of time, blankets can serve many of the same purposes as attachment figures (Passman & Weisurg, 1975). Similarly, stuffed animals and dolls can offer solace during brief separations, providing the toddler is attached to them.

The separation between parents and child rarely has to be complete. Phone calls from the parents and pictures of the parents assure the child that the mother will return (Passman & Longeway, 1982). Adhering to the mother's routines, especially at bedtime, seems to minimize the loss that children feel. These preventive measures can delay the despair seen in children plunked into residential nurseries (Bowlby, 1973).

Bowlby's picture of the distressed toddler in a strange environment surrounded by strange adults has prompted pediatricians to reevaluate hospitalizations for toddlers. If there is a choice, procedures are handled on an outpatient basis or hospitalizations are delayed until the child can understand that the separation is necessary and temporary. When the situation demands that the toddler be hospitalized, visiting hours are unlimited and the mother can often stay at the hospital with her child. Even if the mother cannot stay with her child, a separation of a week or less while the child is hospitalized has no long-term effects on the child's social development (Rutter, 1979). Children do become extremely distressed, however, if they have recurrent problems that require several hospital stays or if they have to stay in the hospital for long periods of time.

Psychologists and parents have also become sensitized to the toddler's feelings of grief and abandonment during and after a separation. If parents understand the reasons for their child's anger and hostility and if they know that some of these feelings are common, they can deal with their child lovingly. With Bowlby's description in hand, psychologists can advise parents on situations that provoke separation anxiety and make recommendations that will forestall the deterioration of attachment.

## FAMILY CONFIGURATIONS AND ATTACHMENT

When the extended family was common, there were usually several adults—grandparents, aunts, uncles, and grown cousins—in addition to the mother and father, who could become attachment figures. These adults were present, and if they took an interest in the child, an attachment blossomed. Hence, there were several adults who might care for the child and substitute for the mother if it became necessary. Incidentally, this is still the dominant family configuration in many cultures.

In westernized countries, the extended family has gradually been replaced by the nuclear family. In the nuclear family there are only two adults, the mother and the father, who are deeply involved with the child. Good neighbors and babysitters might serve as an extended network; but the parents perform most of the caretaking, and the mother is typically the primary caretaker.

The 1980 census indicates that the nuclear family configuration is not as pervasive as it was during the 1960s and 1970s. Twenty percent of the children in the United States spend part of their lives in a single parent family (Lamb, 1982a). When single parents remarry, and they typically do within three years, the children become part of a stepfamily or blended family. Today, one in every five children is a member of a blended family (Einstein, 1982). Single parent families and stepfamilies mean that at least one of the natural parents is absent. Working mothers become absent parents during the hours they are employed. All of these changes in the configuration of the family raise questions concerning the infant's development. Do infants form secure attachments in these varying settings?

**Working mothers**

Twenty years ago, the topic of working mothers would never have appeared in a chapter on infancy, simply because mothers of infants rarely worked. Today, it is very common (Hoffman, 1980). Some of these women are professionals who launch careers in their early 20s and marry a colleague along the way (Wilkie, 1981). In their middle 20s they decide to have a child. They are committed to both their family and their career and try to balance the demands of each.

Divorced women are also common among the ranks of working mothers.

Often these mothers have to work. Their job as a parent is made doubly difficult as they try to hold down a job and serve as the primary source of the child's love and security.

As we have seen, the development of a secure attachment depends on a close mother-infant relationship. Are working mothers able to promote this kind of relationship with their infants? To answer this question, we can look briefly at historical accounts of mothers' roles, cross-cultural evidence, and empirical studies.

Before formulas were widely available, wet nurses were sometimes necessary for mothers who were unable to nurse their children. The wet nurse took over one of the most important and intimate motherly functions soon after birth. Still, she did not preclude the development of an attachment between the mother and child. Nannies were, and still are, a colorful mother substitute in England. To many children, the nanny is a combination caretaker, storyteller, tutor, and disciplinarian. Children often spend much more time with their nannies than with their mothers, but they still develop strong attachments to their mothers (Gathorne-Hardy, 1972).

When other cultures are examined, it becomes clear that most mothers do not devote all of their time to caring for their infant (Minturn & Lambert, 1964). In South America, Mixtecan mothers have sole responsibility for their infants for about six weeks, and they retain primary responsibility for four to five months. After this time, they often leave the child with friends, relatives, or older siblings while they work. In the Orient, Okinawan mothers believe that infants are godlike, and that the infant's every whim should be indulged. Hence, they rush to the aid of a crying newborn. The mother's indulgence is short-lived, however, and care of the infant is soon shared with a grandmother or another nursing mother. Similar stories can be told of families in villages in India and Africa. For a short period of time—six weeks to six months—the mothers assume primary responsibility for their children. After this, they do not relinquish responsibility, but they do have substantial help from other female relatives, older siblings, and occasionally fathers. In all of these cases, the infant develops a strong attachment to the mother.

These historical and cross-cultural accounts indicate that children can develop secure attachments even though they are mothered by several people. Well controlled experiments have reached similar conclusions. Schaffer and Emerson (1964) provided the first clear evidence that the important factors in attachment were how responsive and sensitive the mothers were, not how many hours a day they spent with their infants. In fact, the relative unimportance of the amount of time spent was highlighted by the fact that many of the infants had formed a strong attachment to the father who spent most of his daytime hours working. When they were home, however, these fathers played a key role in feeding, diapering, and playing with the infant. This interaction provided the base for a close father-infant relationship. If fathers can work and still become attachment figures, then so can mothers. Unlike the situation with fathers, when mothers work, day care becomes an issue.

**Day care**

Apprehension surrounds infant day care in the United States. Yet, quality day care for infants has been common in other countries for many years, and the dire forecasts concerning the development of these infants have not occurred. In the United States, day-care centers have been gradually throwing off this shadow as investigations show that infants can thrive in day-care settings (Kagan, Kearsley, & Zelazo, 1978).

One example comes from a university operated day-care center at Harvard University. Infants became part of a day-care program when they were between three and five months of age. From that point, they attended the center approximately seven hours a day, five days a week until they were 2½ years old. Despite the long hours away from their mothers, 90 percent of them went to their mothers and not their caretakers when they were put into Ainsworth's strange situation (Kagan, Kearsley, & Zelazo, 1978). Jerome Kagan, the director of the study, points out that the home environment and the mother continue to exert a powerful influence over the child even though the mother works full time.

Arlene Ragozin of Harvard also investigated the attachments of children who were cared for in a day-care center. Rather than using the strange situation, Ragozin observed mothers and infants in their homes. Like Kagan, she finds that day care is compatible with normal patterns of attachment (Ragozin, 1980).

A blanket endorsement of day-care for infants is, however, premature (Smith, 1981). Day care programs associated with universities are usually meticulously designed to meet the needs of infants. Other programs might not be as successful (Belsky, Steinberg, & Walker, 1982). Furthermore, many mothers who cannot afford to have their infants in a day-care center arrange infant care at the homes of women in their community. These more casual arrangements may not foster secure attachments (Vaughn, Gove, & Egeland, 1980). Unfortunately, single parents, who are financially stressed and have the greatest need for stable, responsive child care, are often the least able to find or afford such care (Vaughn et al., 1980).

This brief look at variations in mothering provides convincing evidence that infants can form secure attachments even if they are cared for by several people. Whether a mother works is not as important as whether she is responsive to her infant when she is home and whether she has a stable, loving mother substitute caring for her infant (Anderson, 1980). Being cared for by the mother, father, and a baby-sitter who are all loving, responsive, and concerned is a far cry from the unresponsive care that used to be the norm in institutional settings. Any child-care arrangement that involves frequent changes in the person caring for the child is not likely to foster a secure attachment. Having revolving caretakers means that infants are forming anxious attachments (Vaughn et al., 1980) or that attachment bonds are being continually formed and broken. Neither situation instills much trust in adults. If working mothers can find a responsive adult who will be a stable figure in the infant's life, secure attachments will follow.

**Stepparents and
single parents**

The children in single parent families and stepfamilies have to learn to accept separations. If they are toddlers when their parents separate, they are very likely to protest, then mourn their lost parent. Whether they become detached depends on the course of the relationship. It is possible for the absent parent to maintain a close relationship, but there are many circumstances working against it (Hetherington, Cox, & Cox, 1982). The responsibility for maintaining a secure attachment shifts to the remaining parent, typically the mother. Given the child's outbursts of anger and hostility and the mother's own emotional turmoil, maintaining a close mother-infant relationship is a continuing struggle (Hetherington, Cox, & Cox, 1982). When interviewed, children of divorce and children in blended families often recall their feelings of loss, fear, and insecurity (Einstein, 1982; Wallerstein & Kelly, 1980). Although these feelings attenuate over time, many stepchildren feel that their insecure feelings remain close to the surface (Einstein, 1982).

There is no standard family configuration in today's society. Stepfamilies, single parent families, families where mothers work full time, nuclear families, and extended families exist side by side. The variation in families does not preclude the development of secure attachments. Infants can and do develop secure attachments in all of these settings. There is little doubt, however, that secure attachments are achieved more easily in some family configurations than others. The children most likely to experience difficulty seem to be children in single parent homes (Lamb & Bronson, 1980; Lamb, 1982a). Whether this is due to the time pressure that single parents face, the financial difficulties that affect most single parent families, or to the unstable day care arrangements that these children often experience is not known (Vaughn et al., 1980). Although a single secure attachment seems to be sufficient for normal social development, having secure attachments to both parents confers some social advantages (Main & Weston, 1981). Obviously, infants are more likely to develop two secure attachments in families that include both parents.

## CHILD ABUSE AND ATTACHMENT

Ainsworth and Bowlby both suggest that the attachment between the mother and infant mirrors the nature of their interaction. If this is true, then abuse and neglect during infancy should have dramatic and consistent consequences for attachment. We know that toddlers who experience abuse relate to adults in atypical ways (George & Main, 1979). In a day-care setting, they are aggressive and harass the supervising adults both physically and verbally. Their relationships with peers are also unusually aggressive. Abused toddlers avoid adults. When they do approach an adult, they come from the side or backstep toward the adult (George & Main, 1979). These unusual social behaviors are probably derived from the punitive relationship that exists between parents and toddlers.

Psychologists, pediatricians, and social workers have all contributed to our understanding of abuse through retrospective studies of abusive families. In a *retrospective study*, a particular sample, such as abused children, is identified. Then researchers look for common denominators in the family's history. Are all of the mothers from a particular socioeconomic class? Is lack of education a common factor? Do the mothers share some common event, like a separation from the child at birth? Such studies are very helpful in isolating important factors. The story of DES unfolded through a retrospective study. A physician carefully studied the history of the patients and found a common factor—all of the girls' mothers had taken DES during pregnancy. Evidence obtained from retrospective studies has to be verified by other studies.

*Prospective studies* have several advantages over retrospective studies because they start with a large sample of subjects and follow the subjects forward. Hence, researchers do not know at the beginning of the study which children are abused. Therefore, they are less apt to bias the information they gather on the home or the mother-infant interaction. Also, in prospective studies the investigators actually observe the mother and infant interact. Abusive mothers are very apt to distort information about how they interact with their infants. Hence, relying on the mother's account is not very satisfactory. In a prospective study, researchers follow the family and observe the mother-infant interaction from early in life. If some of the parents in the sample begin to abuse their infants, the researchers will know exactly what kind of mother-infant relationship existed prior to the abuse. In sum, prospective studies can pinpoint the relationship between abuse and the social skills of the child at a later time.

Byron Egeland and Alan Sroufe are conducting such a prospective study of attachment. They began their study with 267 pregnant women from lower socioeconomic backgrounds. The investigators expected that some of the infants born to these mothers would be abused and neglected during the first 18 months. When the infants were 3, 6, 9, and 12 months old, the investigators visited the mother's home. They noted evidence of violence, poor physical care, and unsanitary conditions. They also looked for evidence that the infant was being neglected. Extreme neglect was indicated if the infant had untreated wounds, if there was no place for the infant to sleep, if hazards were common in the home, if the mother never bothered to change diapers or clothing, and if the mother left the infant without arranging for substitute care (Egeland & Sroufe, 1981).

By 12 months of age, four of the infants had been physically abused, 3 had been neglected and abused, and 24 infants had been severely neglected. These 31 infants formed a subsample of infants receiving inadequate care. Egeland and Sroufe then observed these children in the strange situation and compared them to a subsample of infants who were receiving excellent care from their mothers. The differences at 12 months are astounding (see Figure 7–8). Seventy-five percent of the infants receiving excellent care were securely attached. Only 38 percent of the infants receiving inadequate care were securely attached. A quarter of the infants receiving inadequate care were anxiously attached. These results are consistent with the view that mothers who reject and abuse their infants foster an anxiously attached child.

A surprising number of children in the inadequate care group had developed ambivalent attachments to their mothers after the first year. Although mothers of children in the ambivalent group did not reject their infants outright, their lives might be described as chaotic. Some of the mothers in this group were using drugs, some were emotionally distraught, and others were just with-

**Figure 7—8**     **Attachments of abused children**

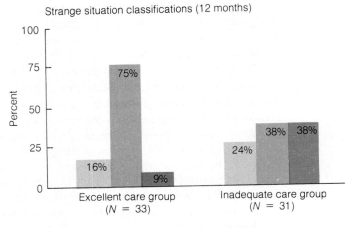

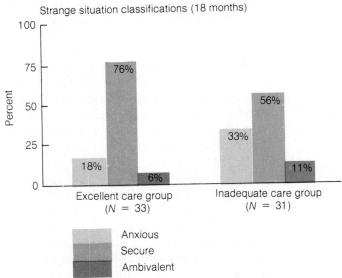

Percentage of infants in each care group who are securely attached, anxiously attached, or ambivalent at 12 and 18 months.

Source: Egeland, B. A., & Sroufe, A. L. (1981). Attachment and early maltreatment. *Child Development, 52*, 44–52.

drawn. Whatever the reason, their infants received inconsistent care through-out the first year. As a result, these toddlers were ambivalent toward their mothers when observed in the strange situation.

At 18 months of age, Egeland and Sroufe evaluated the attachment between these mothers and infants a second time. The infants receiving excellent care remained securely attached. The attachment pattern had changed in over half the infants receiving inadequate care. All but one of the children in the am-bivalent group had made up their minds. They were now either secure or anxious in their attachment. Five children became more secure during the six-month interval. The authors offer some tentative explanations for these infants' newfound security. First, by the time their toddlers were 18 months old, the mothers' lives were more stable and they seemed more content. Second, grandmothers and other family members had come to the aid of some of these floundering mothers. Providing support for the mother and helping the mother achieve some stability might be two interventions that would help ambivalent infants become more securely attached.

All in all, the results of this continuing prospective study indicate that in-fants of abusive, neglectful, rejecting, and inconsistent mothers have some difficulty becoming securely attached. The positive note is that if the family's circumstances improve, the infant can still forge a secure attachment (Egeland & Sroufe, 1981).

If abuse and neglect are the infant's lot rather than care and commitment, the social milestones of infancy are likely to be affected. The effects of contin-uing abuse inhibit the mother-infant interaction, and social patterns of behav-ior, like attachment, that would normally develop, are nipped in the bud.

## TEMPERAMENT

During the first year, the parent-infant relationship serves as the foundation for the development of social skills. If the parents are caring, responsive, and sensitive to the infant's needs, the parent-infant relationship has a good start. What about the infant? Infants come into the world with a set of behaviors that actively influence the mother-infant interaction. Furthermore, this behavioral repertoire differs enormously from one infant to another. The course of an infant's development is managed by the parents, but it is also influenced by the child's temperamental characteristics.

During the 1950s, individual differences between infants were largely ig-nored by researchers, and all of the infant's behaviors were attributed to the mother. If an infant cried excessively, the mother was not successfully under-standing the child's signals. If the infant did not sleep through the night, then the mother was somehow encouraging wakefulness. Alexander Thomas and Stella Chess of New York University took exception to this attitude. As with innumerable other parents, they were impressed by the striking differences in their own children's behavior, even in the first month of life. Their profes-sional observations further convinced them that the individuality they saw was not due to the parents. So began a 25-year crusade to demonstrate that the temperamental characteristics of each infant guide development.

To find evidence for their position, Thomas and Chess began a series of longitudinal studies in which they studied infants from two to three months of age to young adulthood (Thomas, Chess, Birch, Hertzig, & Korn, 1963; Thomas & Chess, 1977; Thomas & Chess, 1980; Thomas & Chess, 1984). During the early phases of their research, they identified nine different categories that could be used to describe an infant's temperament (see Figure 7–9). Then these temperamental variables were reevaluated as the children went through infancy, toddlerhood, preschool, elementary school, and adolescence. Thomas and Chess interviewed parents, talked with teachers, and saw

**Figure 7–9**          **Temperamental characteristics**

1. *Activity Level:* the motor component present in a given child's functioning and diurnal proportion of active and inactive periods. Protocol data on motility during bathing, eating, playing, dressing, and handling, as well as information concerning the sleep–wake cycle, reaching, crawling, and walking, are used in scoring this category.
2. *Rhythmicity (regularity):* the predictability and/or unpredictability in time of any function. It can be analyzed in relation to the sleep–wake cycle, hunger, feeding pattern, and elimination schedule.
3. *Approach or Withdrawal:* the nature of the initial response to a new stimulus, be it a new food, new toy, or new person. Approach responses are positive, whether displayed by mood expression (smiling, verbalizations, etc.) or motor activity (swallowing a new food, reaching for a new toy, active play, etc.). Withdrawal reactions are negative, whether displayed by mood expression (crying, fussing, grimacing, verbalization, etc.) or motor activity (moving away, spitting out new food, pushing away new toy, etc.).
4. *Adaptability:* response to new or altered situations. One is not concerned with the nature of the initial responses, but with the ease with which they are modified in desired directions.
5. *Threshold of Responsiveness:* the intensity of stimulation that is necessary to evoke a discernible response, irrespective of the specific form that the response may take or the sensory modality affected. The behaviors utilized are those concerning reactions to sensory stimuli, environmental objects, and social contacts.
6. *Intensity of Reaction:* the energy level of response irrespective of its quality or direction.
7. *Quality of Mood:* the amount of pleasant, joyful, and friendly behavior as contrasted with unpleasant, crying, and unfriendly behavior.
8. *Distractibility:* the effectiveness of extraneous environmental stimuli in interfering with or in altering the direction of the ongoing behavior.
9. *Attention Span and Persistence:* two categories that are related. Attention span concerns the length of time a particular activity is pursued by the child. Persistence refers to the continuation of an activity in the face of obstacles to the maintenance of the activity direction.

Enduring temperamental characteristics.

Source: Thomas, A., & Chess, S. (1981). The role of temperament in the contributions of individuals to their development. In R. M. Lerner & N. A. Busch-Rossnagel (Eds.), *Individuals as producers of their development* p. 236. New York: Academic Press.

the children on a regular basis. Their goal was to trace the effect, if any, that temperamental qualities in infancy had on psychological development. The result is an unparalleled series of studies describing temperament during the first 20 years of life.

## Temperamental characteristics of infants

Imagine the difficulty associated with identifying temperamental variables in infants. Most of the adjectives we use to describe an adult's temperament—such as aggressive or hostile—are difficult to apply to infants. Thomas and Chess's first achievement was to describe nine temperamental characteristics that could be used to accurately characterize an infant.

The first category considers how active a child is. Some infants are awake 9 hours a day, others 16 hours. Both infants can be healthy and normal, yet their sleeping times differ by seven hours.

Thomas and Chess also found that some infants fall naturally into a regular schedule, while others are seldom predictable. This characteristic could influence the mother-infant interaction. The mother can be prepared for the regular child who eats every four hours. It is hard to plan when your infant could be awake and hungry in the next two hours, or three hours, or four hours.

Infants also differ in how well they adapt to their environment and how they approach new experiences. Some infants love their first baths, wolf down their first solid food, and are not disturbed by long trips. They approach new experiences readily, and changes in the environment do not seem to upset them. At the other end of the continuum are infants who scream through their first bath, spit out their first solid food, and seem upset for two days after a trip.

Two other factors that distinguish between infants are the level of stimulation that provokes crying and the intensity of the cries. A doorbell is enough to jolt one infant into alertness. Another infant will sleep right through a siren. When some infants are hungry they cry vociferously. Others let you know that they are hungry, but their cries do not convey the same sense of urgency.

Mood is another temperamental characteristic that differentiates infants. We have all seen infants who are basically placid and happy. We have all heard about infants who are less content. Even psychologists were amazed when they recorded the actual number of minutes that 10 infants spent crying during a day. One infant cried for only seven minutes; another cried for more than an hour (Rebelsky & Black, 1972). Finally, Thomas and Chess pointed out that infants differ in how easily they are distracted and the length of their attention span.

## Patterns of temperament

These nine temperamental variables did not occur randomly in the infants Thomas and Chess studied. Several temperamental variables clustered together forming constellations of temperament. Three such temperamental styles have been studied extensively—the Easy Child, the Difficult Child, and the Slow-To-Warm-Up Child.

**The Easy Child.**  Easy infants adopt a regular schedule early in life. They enjoy the new experiences common during the first year of life. When the environment dictates a change, they adapt quickly and their general mood is positive. When these infants are upset, the intensity of their reaction is mild or moderate. Approximately 40 percent of the children studied by Thomas and Chess could be characterized as Easy Children.

**The Difficult Child.**  The difficult infant does not seem to have a schedule. Mothers can only predict that the Difficult Child will be unpredictable. When new experiences are offered, the Difficult Child withdraws. Adapting to any change in the environment is a laborious process. These infants cry a great deal and are intensely aroused by slight changes in their environments. Only about 10 percent of the infants in Thomas and Chess's study were rated difficult.

**The Slow-To-Warm-Up Child.**  A third constellation, the Slow-To-Warm-Up Child, was also identified. Like the Difficult Child, this infant withdraws when new situations are encountered and is slow to adapt. However, unlike the Difficult Child, the withdrawal reaction is mild. In addition, the Slow-To-Warm-Up Child is less likely to be negative and irregular. Approximately 15 percent of the children fit this pattern.

Only 65 percent of the children fit neatly into one of these categories. Even within these three categories, children vary widely in how much they manifest a particular trait. Remember, also, that all three temperamental styles are considered normal. Thomas and Chess were the first to try to educate parents to the wide range of behavioral styles that normal children can display.

**Stability of temperament**

Thomas and Chess succeeded in isolating temperamental variables in infants. The next step was to look at the stability of these temperamental characteristics over time. If an infant displays all of the characteristics of a Difficult Child for six months but then is transformed into an Easy Child, the value of the temperamental categories is limited. If, however, children show these characteristics consistently over several years and in many situations, then they might be used to predict behavior.

Of the nine temperamental variables charted by Thomas and Chess, the five used to predict the Easy and Difficult Child seem to be the most stable (Persson-Blennow & McNeil, 1982; Thomas, Chess, & Korn, 1982). The child's activity level, regularity, adaptability, mood, and intensity of response are all moderately stable from 6 to 12 months (Martin & Wachs, 1981). Ratings that are made when the children were two, three, four, and five years old also indicate that some of the temperamental variables are stable over longer periods of time (Thomas & Chess, 1977; Thomas, Chess, & Korn, 1982; Carey & McDevitt, 1978). Between five and seven years of age, as children make the transition to school the question of stability becomes more complex. Some children are remarkably consistent in their temperamental characteristics from infancy to elementary school. Other children show less consistency (Thomas & Chess, 1981).

One of the reasons for the lack of consistency may be that our measures of temperamental variables are not very sophisticated (Rutter, 1982). Is adaptability expressed the same way in infants, preschoolers, and schoolchildren? Are parents aware of how adaptable their child is at school? Because of problems like these when parents are interviewed or fill out questionnaires, psychologists have looked for other ways to assess temperament. Direct observations might yield more satisfactory ratings of temperament, but these take long periods of time, especially if one is to sample several situations in which temperamental characteristics would be obvious.

Because temperamental variables during infancy are not always predictive of temperamental characteristics years later, a few psychologists have been tempted to dismiss the impact of temperamental variables altogether (Bates, 1980). Remember, however, that there are few indicators during the first few months of life that permit consistent predictions. As we have seen, both prematurity and complications at birth are mitigated by a favorable environment. Development is an ongoing process, and parents, infants, and the environment all make a substantial contribution. Furthermore, the infant's contribution can be altered by the parents' responsiveness or by the impact of the environment. Thomas and Chess (1980) have used the concept *goodness of fit* to convey the way that the child's temperamental characteristics mesh with the parents' propensities and the environment.

## Goodness of fit

At any age, if the demands from the parents and the environment fit with the child's capabilities, then psychological development proceeds in a healthy direction. There is a good fit between the child and the environment. If, however, the parents or environment demand behavior that the infant is temperamentally unable to provide, then unfavorable psychological functioning will occur—a poor fit exists. Intuitively it seems that the Easy Child should find a good fit. Likewise, the Difficult Child should encounter dissonant demands from parents or the environment. This is not always the case (Thomas & Chess, 1981).

Some parents are able to respond constructively to the Difficult Child's pattern of behavior. One parent took pride in his young son's lusty cries. Despite the intensity of the crying, a good fit existed between the parent's expectations and the child's temperament.

The Difficult Child may frustrate a parent at one point and delight a parent at another. One girl in the Thomas and Chess study embodied all of the dubious qualities of the Difficult Child. Her parents were highly critical of her behavior. Her father interpreted her inability to adapt as stubbornness and punished the girl severely. This poor fit soon led to a neurotic behavior disorder. The girl would explode in anger. Her peer relationships deteriorated, and she was repeatedly reprimanded for pulling the hair of her classmates. For years, the child's temperament and the demands of her parents did not mesh. At 10 years of age, the girl began to display a real talent for music and drama. This brought approval and respect from parents, teachers, and classmates. Her intense negative reactions and her inability to adapt were now accepted as part of her artistic temperament. She began to get along better with her parents, and within a few years, she was symptom free. The poor fit of her early years was replaced by a good fit between the girl's temperament and the demands of her parents (Thomas & Chess, 1977).

Even if the parents are tolerant of the child's temperament, the environment may contain obstacles to a good fit. This was illustrated in a sample of Puerto Rican children who lived in small apartments in New York City. There were

---

## CASE HISTORY OF A DIFFICULT CHILD

Carl requested a discussion after his first term in college because of feelings of depression and inability to cope with the academic and social situation at college. He had made virtually no friends and found studying difficult.

The longitudinal data showed that in earlier life Carl had been one of our most extreme Difficult Child temperamental types, with intense, negative reactions to new situations and slow adaptability only after many exposures. This was true whether it was the first bath or first solid foods in infancy, the beginning of nursery school and elementary school, first birthday parties or the first shopping trip. Each experience evoked stormy responses, with loud crying and struggling to get away. However, his parents learned to anticipate Carl's reactions, knew that if they were patient, presented only one or a few new situations at a time and gave him the opportunity for repeated exposure, Carl would finally adapt positively. Furthermore, once he adapted, his intensity of response gave him a zestful enthusiastic involvement, just as it gave his initial negative reactions a loud and stormy character.

In his later childhood and high school years Carl met very few radically new situations. He lived in the same community and went through the neighborhood school with the same schoolmates and friends. Academic progression was gradual and new subjects were not introduced abruptly. He had sufficient time to adapt to new demands, and generally became enthusiastically involved with a number of activities. As a result,

he developed an appropriate positive and self-confident self-image. He played the piano and spoke with animated zest of his pleasure in this activity. He was asked in the interview, "Do you remember what happened when you first started piano lessons?" He thought for a moment and a startled expression came over his face. He described how he had asked his mother if he could take lessons, and she said yes—but she insisted on one condition, that he stick to the lessons for six months, no matter how he felt, and then, if he wanted, he could give them up. He agreed, started and began by "hating it." But he stuck to the bargain and six months later his mother asked if he wanted to quit. His answer was, "Are you crazy? I love it!"

When Carl went off to college, however, he was suddenly confronted with a whole series of new situations—strange surroundings, an entirely new peer group, new types of faculty approaches, school schedules and a complex relationship with a girl student. Again, his temperamental responses of withdrawal and intense negative reactions were expressed. Other possible reasons for his difficulties were explored—dependency needs for his parents, sexual conflict, anxiety over academic demands, peer competition—but no evidence of any of these was elicited.

Only the one discussion was necessary with Carl, and consisted primarily in clarifying for him his temperamental pattern and the techniques he could use for adaptation.

---

Thomas, A., & Chess, S. (1977). *Temperament and development* p. 165–167. New York: Bruner/Mazel.

no playgrounds in their neighborhood, and the streets were too dangerous for playing. The children with high activity levels had no place to let off steam, and the restrictions on their physical activity soon caused a great deal of stress. Over half of these children were labeled hyperactive before they were nine. Only one of the middle-class children, who lived in larger houses and had ample play areas, was referred to the clinic for hyperactivity (Thomas, Chess, Sillen, & Mendez, 1974).

It is important to note that a poor fit can occur with Easy Children. Unreasonable demands from perfectionistic parents often cause problems even when the child is adaptable, predictable, easygoing, approaches new experiences readily, and has a moderate activity level. In other cases, parents may be unhappy with their Easy Child because they consider the child a pushover. Easy Children do not demand the same attention as Difficult Children, and their positive traits may actually deny them needed attention (Thomas & Chess, 1981). For the most part, however, a good fit is obtained with an Easy Child. Difficult Children and children who are Slow-To-Warm-Up need to be in environments that are flexible and responsive if they are to find a good fit.

## The importance of temperament

Temperamental characteristics do not irrevocably determine the course of development. Rather, they are one set of factors that guide the development of the individual. These characteristics provide a background of consistency, but they can be muted or exaggerated by the way they mesh with parents, environments, schools, and teachers. Given these qualifications, it is still important to recognize the role that temperament plays in psychological development. Difficult Children have often posed problems for unsuspecting parents. In Thomas and Chess's study, only 10 percent of the children were difficult. Yet, they made up almost a third of the behavioral problems that were identified in later years (Rutter, Korn, & Birch, 1964).

When the characteristics of the Difficult Child are combined with either physical or cognitive handicaps, the child is even more likely to develop behavioral problems. If a retarded child exhibits all of the characteristics of the Difficult Child, the probability of a behavior disorder is 100 percent. If a retarded child has only two of the characteristics, the probability of a behavioral disorder declines to 40 percent (Thomas & Chess, 1981). The presence of the temperamental characteristics of the Difficult Child adds another vulnerability and significantly increases the incidence of behavioral disturbance (Rutter, 1982).

In normal children, characteristics of the Difficult Child also predict problems in the future. Nursery school teachers were asked to rate the temperaments of some of the children Thomas and Chess were studying. If children were in the highest 25 percent for negative mood or mood intensity, they were likely to be a behavioral problem. All of the children rated in the top 10 in negative mood and intensity developed behavioral problems (Thomas & Chess, 1981).

Difficult Children present the most striking relationship between temperament and adjustment. Their irregularity, withdrawal, and inability to adapt combine with their frequent negative moods and their intense responses to make day-to-day living an endurance contest. Difficult infants cry at a higher frequency than easy infants (Boukydis & Burgess, 1982). They also sleep about 9½ hours compared to almost 12 for the easy infants (Weissbluth, 1981). Some researchers suggest that the difficult temperament is a sign of neurological immaturity (Field, 1982). The Easy Child seems to be more organized at one month of age than the difficult infant (Martin & Wachs, 1981). Despite these constitutional variables, Difficult Children who are lucky enough to have a supportive environment typically negotiate the milestones of infancy and childhood easily.

In conclusion, the child's temperamental characteristics guide the course of development. During the first three years, the child's temperament is an important ingredient in the interaction patterns that parents and children develop. As such, it is fair to conclude that temperament influences the course of both normal and deviant psychological development. But the role of temperament at any age can never be considered in isolation. Easy Children can be born into families that cherish their child's sunny disposition or into environments where they are ignored because they are not demanding. Similarly, Difficult Children may find devoted parents who pave the way for their child and greet outbursts with patience and tolerance, or they may be born into unyielding environments that demand regularity and adaptability.

**Temperament and social development in infancy**

Since Thomas and Chess isolated temperamental characteristics of infants and documented their role in psychological development, other investigators have become interested in the way temperament affects the infant's social relationships. It is easy to see how the infant's temperamental characteristics could influence the mother-infant interaction. If an infant is smiling rather than crying, the mother can be playful and relaxed. If the infant is calm and regular, the mother is less likely to be exhausted. If the infant has mild reactions, the mother's soothing efforts are likely to be successful. All of these variables can influence how responsive, sensitive, and committed the mother can be. They should also influence the patterns of attachment that develop.

Susan Crockenberg at the University of California at Davis has tried to establish the relationships between temperament, mother-infant interaction, and attachment. She studied infants and their mothers for one year, seeing them shortly after birth, at three months, and at one year. Crockenberg's goal was to find out whether the newborn's temperament influenced the mother-infant interaction, and whether this could, in turn, be seen in the patterns of attachment that developed. Not surprisingly, 40 percent of the irritable newborns were anxiously attached a year later. Only 16 percent of the calmer infants were anxiously attached.

When Crockenberg related this to the mother-infant interaction, she found that whether or not the mother had some help or emotional support was important. If the mothers of irritable infants had little support, they were likely to be less sensitive to their infants. At one year, this lack of sensitivity was expressed in an anxious attachment. If a father or a grandmother helped, or even if a sympathetic pediatrician listened, these mothers could be sensitive and responsive to their infants. At one year, their irritable infants were securely attached (Crockenberg, 1980). The effect of temperament became obvious when Crockenberg applied the same test to the calmer infants. These infants developed secure attachments despite the social milieu. Even if their mothers were unresponsive, these easygoing infants cried little and were quickly calmed. Both Crockenberg and Michael Rutter (1978) suggest that Easy Children are not as bothered by unresponsive environments, and that they can endure more discord without showing any ill effects.

As expected, no simple relationship exists between temperament and attachment. One can predict that a Difficult Child is more likely to try the mother's patience than an Easy Child. Furthermore, if the mother has no support, the interaction between her and the child can quickly become strained. The quality of the interaction is then reflected in the child's attachment at one year.

Difficult Children continue to exert important influences on their environment during the toddler stage. The mothers of difficult toddlers can quickly become embroiled in intense conflict. In one observational study, the investigators kept track of the conflicts that developed routinely between toddlers and their mothers. During the course of several hours, they noticed that two-year-olds infringed on some household rule or threatened to do some mild damage every five minutes (Lee, 1981). The mothers typically tried to control the child. With Easy Children, this control took a mild form, and the incidents were quickly forgotten. This very common interaction pattern takes an insidious turn with a Difficult Child. Difficult children approach trouble more often. Their mothers respond, and knowing the mischief their toddlers can create, they usually warn the child repeatedly or physically restrain the child. Difficult toddlers react to their mother's interference in a characteristically intense way. They ignore her warnings, talk back, or immediately return to the scene of the crime. This pattern of conflict, frustration, and exasperation is much more noticeable at two years of age than it was at six months or one year. Difficult Children can make the terrible twos live up to their name (Lee, 1981).

Temperamental characteristics have the potential to alter the child's social relationships. If the mother is discouraged by the difficult infant's activity, irregularity, and intense reactions, the relationship can be negative. Remember, though, that 60 percent of the irritable infants developed secure attachments. This is a tribute to their mothers' patience and responsiveness and perhaps to the support the mothers received from husbands and grandparents. As difficult infants become toddlers, their temperamental characteristics again strain the fabric of the mother-infant relationship. Thomas and Chess argue that temperamental characteristics which fit poorly with the demands and expectations of the parents are a major source of behavioral disorders during childhood.

## SUMMARY

Social development during infancy is a cooperative venture. The principal actors are the primary caretaker (typically the mother) and the infant. The mother's role requires her to be sensitive to the child's needs and to respond to them. The caretaking that she provides sets the stage for other playful interactions. The infant initially signals the mother by crying. In a few weeks, smiling, cooing, looking, and bicycling with the legs can also be used to alert the mother. The infant, alert and happy after being fed and changed, can respond to the mother's playful activities.

Both the mother and infant benefit from these playful interchanges. The mother's attachment is enhanced by the child's attentive cooing and smiling. Also, the mother learns how to read her child by seeing what causes laughter and what causes the child to look away. The infant learns to recognize the mother, and over a period of months this recognition turns into attachment.

The reciprocal interaction between mothers and their infants has been labeled the Attachment Behavioral System. In Bowlby's view, this system of signals and responses has developed over the ages to protect children and insure their survival. In the latter half of the first year, infants begin to develop a specific, enduring attachment to their mothers. The quality of this attachment depends on the harmony that exists between mother and child and can be assessed in Ainsworth's strange situation. Securely attached infants have mothers who have been sensitive, responsive, and committed during the first year. Children whose mothers have been rejecting are more likely to be anxiously attached. A few children seem to be ambivalent in their attachments.

The attachment pattern that children show in the strange situation is important because it is related to later performance on a variety of social and personal measures. If cognitive skills depend on the mother-infant relationship, then the attachment pattern is likely to influence these skills as well.

The attachment pattern indicates the harmony that exists between mother and child. Disruptions to the mother-infant relationship, such as the mother returning to work or a long absence, can affect the child's attachment. During and after such disruptions, the relationship between mother and child has to be renegotiated. A secure relationship can usually be reestablished if the mother demonstrates the same sensitivity and caring that made her an attachment figure initially.

The father's role in the infant's social development was ignored for years. Investigations in the last 10 years have demonstrated that the father makes a unique contribution to the infant's social skills. Fathers are perfectly capable of providing the necessary caretaking, but they prefer to play with their infants. Their particular specialty is rough-and-tumble play. The roughhousing that characterizes the father-infant relationship is just as likely to lead to a strong attachment as the gentler talking and tickling that the mother engages in. Investigations have also demonstrated that infants can be attached to several people. In fact, the child who is attached to both parents handles the social tasks of preschool with ease.

Since attachment is such a critical aspect of social development during infancy, psychologists have examined environments that foster secure attachments and environments that are associated with anxious attachments. Not surprisingly, infants who have been abused or neglected are very often anxiously attached to their mothers. Children in single-parent families and children who have unstable caretaking arrangements may also have trouble developing secure attachments. The knowledge that we have about the attachment process may soon allow us to intervene to strengthen attachments or to help mothers who are not establishing a harmonious pattern of interaction.

Infants are not passive partners in the mother-infant interaction. Their contribution to the mother-infant relationship and to other social interactions is mediated by individual differences in temperament. Alexander Thomas and Stella Chess have devoted much of their professional careers to describing these temperamental characteristics and tracing their influence on later development. Their descriptions of the Easy Child, the Slow-To-Warm-Up Child, and the Difficult Child highlight the wide range of normal temperaments that infants evidence. By describing how these temperamental characteristics mesh with the demands of the environment, Thomas and Chess have affirmed the fact that social interaction, even with infants, is a two-way street.

# PART 3

The mind's eye

**Communication in other species**

Vervet monkeys
Dolphins and whales
Language in the great apes
Limitations of signing in the great apes

**Language areas in the brain**

**Language acquisition in humans**

Phonology—understanding the sounds of language
Pragmatics—understanding the use of language
Semantics—unraveling the meaning of language
Syntax—decoding the order of words

**How does the child master language?**

Biological factors
Imitation
Conceptual progress

**The language environment**

Motherese
The effect of motherese on language development
A responsive environment
Individual differences in language acquisition
Bilingual environments

**Summary**

# CHAPTER 8

# The ability to communicate

Communication has long been regarded as the hallmark of the human species and is popularly thought of as one of the complex skills that differentiates us from all other species. Perhaps we are the only species to communicate using words. However, bees, ants, birds, primates, dolphins, and whales also communicate. In fact, all animals that live in social groups use communication to maintain their social structure and to insure the survival of the species. This communication often includes gestures, postures, territorial markings, alarms, and mating rituals.

Although we are primarily interested in human language, looking first at communication in other species can be instructive. It is unlikely that language sprang up *de novo* in humans. It is more likely that it represents a continuing adaptation of skills that are evident in some form in other species. Looking at how other animals communicate may help us understand how and why language developed in humans.

The speech of humans is more flexible than the limited communication of animals. Our greatly increased capacity to communicate depends, in part, on the organization of our brains to interpret and produce language. Hence, this chapter includes a discussion of the language centers of the brain.

Language acquisition in humans proceeds systematically. During the years from one to five, children learn most of the complexities of their native language without any specific tutoring. Thanks to two decades of work by psycholinguists, we can chart, with some precision, the steps children take in acquiring language. But psychologists have very different answers to the question, how do children learn language?

One group suggests that children learn language because their brains are wired to learn language. In its strongest form, this view argues that the environment has only a token effect on language acquisition.

The effect of the environment is not so easily dismissed. It is certainly the major force in determining which language a child speaks. If you are born in an English-speaking country and your parents speak English, you will learn to speak English. The environment can have dramatic effects on language. Deaf children grow up in a linguistically impoverished environment which affects their cognitive skills as well as the way they communicate. Other less dramatic aspects of the environment may also influence the child's language. How the mother speaks to the child, whether or not the parents read to the child, whether the child is born first or later, and whether the home is bilingual are all environmental variables that bias language acquisition.

When discussing language, one can hardly avoid discussing thought. Is language just a superficial layer of words that reflects our underlying concepts and thoughts? Does language prime the development of thoughts? Because language and thought are intertwined, answers to these questions are difficult. But increasingly, psycholinguists have been trying to examine the relationship between language and thought.

## COMMUNICATION IN OTHER SPECIES

For decades, it has been obvious that animals communicate. The mode of communication can be a rigid system of signals and an equally inflexible system of responses such as those that characterize the mating rituals of many species. Animals can also communicate through a dominance hierarchy or by establishing a particular territory. These methods of communication lack the subtlety and flexibility of human communication. Are there other animals that vocalize and gesture as a way of communicating with their peers?

**Vervet monkeys**

Vervet monkeys, which live in Africa (see Figure 8–1), give very specific alarm calls for different predators. When a snake is spotted, adult vervets give a particular alarm call. The alarm communicates the specific nature of the danger, including whether or not the snake is poisonous (Ristau & Robbins, 1982). The other vervets immediately stand on their tiptoes and step gingerly through the bushes. The effect is as clear as if a human yelled, "Snake!" to other humans. The vervets use a different call to indicate that an eagle is nearby. When this call is given, the animals look at the sky and run into dense bush. A third alarm warns the monkeys of the approach of a leopard and sends the monkeys scampering up trees. Each call communicates a different type of danger, and each call is followed by behaviors that will minimize the danger to the individual animals (Seyfarth, Cheney, & Marler, 1980).

This is not the entire story of communication among vervets. The young vervets have to learn when to give the appropriate alarm. Although adult vervets seldom give false alarms, infants have been known to give the eagle alarm when pigeons approach or leaves fall. As infants learn that pigeons and falling leaves pose no danger, they limit their alarm calls to the more dangerous eagle. Most adult vervets carry their categorization a step further. They reserve their eagle alarm for the martial eagle.

**Dolphins and whales**

Dolphins and whales are also able to communicate vocally. They produce both tones and clicks when in their natural settings. At the very least, these sounds communicate distress. Jacques Cousteau reported that a young sperm

**Figure 8—1**     **Vervet monkeys communicating**

*Wrangham: Anthro-Photo*

When a snake is spotted, adult vervets give a particular alarm call. The other vervets stand on their tiptoes and step gingerly through the bushes.

whale became entangled in the propeller of his research ship, *Calypso*. Within minutes, the calf's distress signals had attracted 27 female sperm whales (Bonner, 1980).

Bottle-nosed dolphins are well known for the remarkable performances they give at amusement parks and water shows around the country. In one of these exhibitions, the trainer asks if there are any people celebrating birthdays in the audience. When the inevitable hands go up, the dolphins respond by saying, "Happy Birthday." Later, a seemingly stubborn dolphin repeatedly refuses to do the next trick. When asked by the trainer what he wants, the dolphin replies in understandable tones, "More fish" (Prescott, 1981). Although these are impressive tricks, they do not qualify as language (Herman, 1980). The dolphins have simply been trained to mimic a few human sounds. They have no particular intent to communicate, and they have no understanding of what they are saying.

Dolphins, however, do vocalize, using clicks and at least 30 different whistles (Dreher, 1966). When these whistles were taped and played back to a pool of dolphins, it was clear that they were meaningful. One of these whistles caused the dolphins to "talk" back. Another led to sexual arousal. When certain whistles were played, dolphins became subdued, or searched the pool, or thrashed excitedly in the pool. Dreher argues that the information content of the whistles constitutes a kind of dolphin alphabet. More conservative scientists suggest that these whistles are closer to a human frown, sigh, or giggle (Linehan, 1979).

The communication systems that have been described have an important purpose in the social structure of vervets, dolphins, and whales. It is impossible to read accounts of vervets and dolphins communicating without being impressed by the conceptual development that seemingly accompanies these communications. Yet these systems lack the complexity, flexibility, subtlety, and nuance of human language.

## Language in the great apes

For decades, psychologists have wondered if animals could master the complexity and nuance of our language. In the 1940s, Keith and Cathy Hayes raised a chimp, named Viki, in their home and attempted to teach her language. Although Viki learned to understand many of the verbal commands and responded to many words that the Hayes used, she only learned to produce three recognizable words in six years (Hayes, 1951). In a similar experiment, an orangutan learned to speak four words in approximately 12 months (Laidler, 1980). Although the investigators who worked with these apes are unanimous in their opinions that their students showed great conceptual awareness, the attempts to teach them to vocalize met with limited success.

To Beatrice and Allen Gardner, the conclusion that chimps could not learn language seemed premature. They argued that the vocalization experiments were destined to fail because chimps and orangutans have none of the vocal apparatus necessary for articulate speech. But chimps do use gestures in their natural habitats (van Lawick-Goodall, 1973). The Gardners reasoned that teaching a chimp sign language might be much more successful. Therefore, in the late 1960s, the Gardners began to teach American sign language (Ameslan) to Washoe, a one-year-old female chimpanzee.

When Washoe was an infant, she lived in a trailer in the Gardner's backyard. In these settings, she was surrounded by caretakers who signed to her continually. Their objective was to put Washoe in a linguistically stimulating environment similar to a child's language environment. Washoe responded by learning over 130 signs and by combining these signs to indicate her wants and needs (see Figure 8–2).

Since Washoe's success, a whole troop of chimps, two gorillas, and an orangutan have been taught American sign language (Ristau & Robbins,

**Figure 8—2**                                   **Signing in the great apes**

| Relation | Koko | Washoe* | Deaf children† |
|---|---|---|---|
| Nomination | That cat; that bird. | That food; that drink. | |
| Recurrence | More cereal; more pour. | More fruit; more go. | Cookies more; please more. |
| Nonexistence | Me can't. | Me can't. | Good finished. |
| Affected person, state | Sorry me; me good. | Washoe sorry. | (Me) angry; want open. |
| Attributive | Hot potato; red berry. | Drink red; comb black. | That pink; red shoes. |
| Genitive | Koko purse; hat mine. | Baby mine; you hat. | Barry train. |
| Locative | Go bed; you out. | Go flower; look out. | Daddy work; (me) go home. |
| Dative | Give me drink. | Give me flower. | Give me orange. |
| Agent-action | You eat; me listen. | You drink; Roger tickle. | Me eat; man work. |
| Action-object | Open bottle; catch me. | Tickle Washoe; open blanket. | Eat cracker; grab boy. |
| Agent-object | Alligator me (chase). | | Daddy shoe (take off). |

Two-word sentences signed by Washoe, Koko, and a deaf child.
*Examples drawn from Gardner and Gardner (1971, 1973).
†Examples drawn from Klima and Bellugi (1972) and Schlesinger and Meadow (1971).

Source: Patterson, F. (1978). The gestures of a gorilla: Language acquisition in another pongid. *Brain and Language*, 5, p. 90.

1982). These apes have shown humor, deception, pathos, anger, and conceptual skill in their communications with humans. Koko, the gorilla, asked for a drink by signing "thirsty drink mouth." When the trainer brought some juice, Koko was asked where she wanted it. Koko laughingly signed "nose," then "eye," then "ear." Finally, the joke over, Koko signed "drink" and opened her mouth (Patterson & Linden, 1981). Using language to joke implies an openness and flexibility in the communication system.

Another index of flexibility in the use of language is the invention of new words. Human children who are learning language often delight their parents by creating new words. The chimps and Koko created words that described the world from their vantage point. Moja, a chimp, dubbed Alka-Seltzer the "listen drink" (Gardner & Gardner, 1979). Lucy, another chimp, called a radish a "cry hurt food" (Fouts, 1974). Once learned, a sign could be used to describe a broad range of objects. After learning a sign for a drinking straw, Koko used it to describe several long, thin objects—cigarettes, a pen, and a car radio antenna (Patterson & Linden, 1981). Similar generalizations are common when human children acquire language (Clark, 1973; Bowerman, 1978a). The word moon, for example, was used by one child to refer to the moon, a cake, round marks on windows, postmarks, and the letter "O."

The apes in the sign language projects learned more than the names of objects. At times, the chimps and Koko have used their language skills to insult their peers, to deceive their trainers, and to express their feelings. The expression of feelings is illustrated by Koko's graphic description that she was "red rotten mad" (Patterson & Linden, 1981).

Perhaps the most compelling example of the value of the gestural language to the chimps is the fact that there are many reported instances of chimps signing to each other (Fouts & Budd, 1979; Gardner & Gardner, 1980). Critics argue that these instances are rare. Fouts retorts that expecting two chimps to sign to each other all of the time is the equivalent of teaching two college students a few words of Japanese and then expecting them to speak only in Japanese. The natural communication system of the chimps is usually more efficient. Furthermore, there are so few signing chimps that the question of chimp-to-chimp communication has not had a chance to be answered. Currently, Roger Fouts has Washoe, her adopted infant, and several other signing chimps at a compound at the University of Washington in Seattle. In this setting, the chimps often sign to each other and they have taught Washoe's infant several signs (Fouts, 1982). Penny Patterson is also gathering information on gorilla-to-gorilla signing. She has extended her project to include a male gorilla, Mike. Should Mike and Koko mate, their infant would be the first to have two signing parents.

**Signing between two great apes**

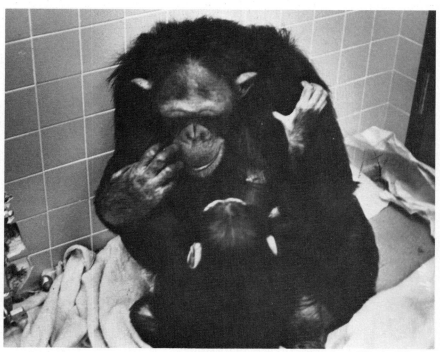

*Friends of Washoe*

Chimps have used sign language to communicate with each other.

Source: Fouts R. S., & Budd, R. L. (1979). Artificial and human language acquisition in the chimpanzee. In D. A. Hamburg & E. R. McCown (Eds.), *The Great Apes* (p. 390). Menlo Park, CA: Benjamin/Cummings Publishing.

**Limitations of signing in the great apes**

The linguistic accomplishments of the chimps and Koko were initially received with skepticism, then hailed as evidence that language was not the exclusive domain of humans. As more research has been completed, psychologists have recognized that the sign language of chimps and gorillas has certain limitations (Terrace, Petitto, Sanders, & Bever, 1979; Ristau & Robbins, 1982). First, only a small number of signs are used for most of the communications. Second, to date all of the apes seem to master a set vocabulary. Their language skills stop improving (Terrace, 1981). Of course, this may be a limitation of their conceptual system, not of the language they have learned. It may also be due to the teaching methods used in the various projects. A third limitation that linguists are especially concerned about is the limited *syntax* (word order) that chimps use. When human infants put their first two words together, they usually adhere to a specific word order. The chimps and Koko have been less constrained by such rules. This prompts critics to conclude that chimps and gorillas do not use syntax. Investigators working with the chimps point out that word order is not as important in sign language as it is in spoken language. Further, they argue that the chimps have their own signing dialect. Roger Fouts admits that he signs "with a heavy chimp accent" (Fouts, 1982).

On the basis of his work with a chimp named Nim, Herbert Terrace points out that the language chimps use is often an imitation of a sentence just signed to them. Further, he notes that the long sentences signed by chimps are often redundant. "Give orange me give eat orange me eat orange give me eat orange give me you" is a 16-word sentence produced by Nim (Terrace, 1979). But the information conveyed is no more complex than that contained in a three-word sentence. Terrace (1981) is quick to remind us that when the length of a child's sentences increases, so does the complexity.

The most severe criticism is that these apes have no understanding of the signs they use (Savage-Rumbaugh, Rumbaugh, & Boysen, 1980). What seems to be conversation is really an elaborate system of imitation and a long game in which the apes simply perform the same signs as in the past. These authors want proof that the chimps understand the meaning of "drink" when they sign it. In response, the psychologists working with Koko and the chimps point out that unique combinations of signs, like "water bird" to describe a swan and "cry hurt food", would never have been created if the apes did not understand what they were signing. Nor would the chimps sign to each other or sign when they are alone if the signs were not meaningful.

Although the language skills of apes are limited, the use of a gestural language has greatly increased the ability of Koko and the chimps to communicate with humans. In the process these apes have displayed some unexpected conceptual skills (Wood, Moriary, Gardner, & Gardner, 1980). Also, the signs that Koko and the chimps have mastered and put together do resemble, in some respects, the early language of children (Ristau & Robbins, 1982). The similarity to some aspects of children's thought and language suggests that communication has a lengthy evolutionary past, and that communication skills may be supported by biological structures in the brain.

## SIGNING WITH AUTISTIC AND RETARDED CHILDREN

Teaching sign language to chimps and gorillas has been so successful that it was only natural to ask if sign language might increase the communication skills of children who are retarded or autistic.

Autistic children are often identified by their language disturbances. Some have no recognizable speech or are limited to a few standard vocalizations. Other autistic children repeat whole phrases that they have heard, a symptom called echolalia. Just establishing communication with these children is difficult.

Prior to the use of sign language, language training programs often involved thousands of trials to establish a few sounds like "ba" or "ka." Even with this kind of arduous training, autistic children seldom used speech spontaneously or learned to use rules that would let them expand their speech beyond the specific phrases they were taught.

Over 100 autistic children have now been exposed to sign language and their ability to communicate has improved immeasurably (Bonvillian, Nelson, & Rhyne, 1981). The early learning of signs may be slow. But once the child learns that objects and actions have manual labels, learning progresses rapidly. Although some children only mastered a few signs, several learned over 350 signs. Forty percent of the children used the signs they learned spontaneously, and many of the children produced complex signed sentences. Happily, the new communications skills these children learned were not limited to the training situation; they were used with other adults and in other environments (Bonvillian et al., 1981).

Why do signs work when speech fails? With both autistic and retarded children, the use of sign language bypasses the disturbed speech system. This detour may enable the child to use areas of the brain that are not damaged. Teachers report that it is easier to teach signs than sounds. You can mold the child's fingers and guide the hands through the appropriate movements. Many signs resemble the object they represent. This concreteness makes the signs easy for retarded or autistic children to learn and remember.

Sign language has some disadvantages as an alternative to speech. Parents are reluctant to learn sign language. They cling to the hope that their child will learn to speak. The years they spend hoping could be years filled with communication via signs. Unfortunately, these years spent hoping might also mean that the child will not learn to sign as quickly (Bonvillian, Nelson, & Rhyne, 1981).

Perhaps signing offers some uncharted advantages. Learning to communicate with signs may facilitate other symbolic skills. Phillip Brody, a teacher in Los Angeles, has been experimenting with sign language as a means of teaching reading to trainable mentally retarded children. The students in his class have IQs between 25 and 50. Children at this level have enormous difficulty learning to read when standard teaching methods are used. Progress is slow, and learning to recognize one or two words a month normally requires hours of one-to-one coaching. Phil's students were typical. Before coming to his class, not one of them could read, and few could recognize even a single letter of the alphabet. Now several students know thousands of words.

Brody began teaching sign language to the students just to alleviate communication problems. When he saw how quickly they learned signs for objects, he decided to try teaching the signs for letters. The same children who had not been able to learn the alphabet using verbal techniques now succeeded using signs. The next step was words, and to Brody's surprise, the children began to read (Elias, 1981).

The optimism generated by the initial success with sign language needs to be followed by careful research. Research is needed to examine the effectiveness of sign language with a variety of populations and under differing circumstances. Researchers might also investigate other symbolic skills that might be facilitated by signing.

## LANGUAGE AREAS IN THE BRAIN

Early in the 19th century, it was widely believed that the two halves of the brain were identical. As the century progressed, several physicians challenged this view and paved the way for the identification of language areas in the brain. The first, a country doctor named Marc Dax, studied patients who had suffered strokes (a disruption of blood flow to the brain). During a stroke, the brain is deprived of oxygen and some brain cells may be destroyed. Dr. Dax reported that all 40 of his patients who had lost their speech after a stroke had damage to the left side of their brain. The patients who had stroke damage to the right hemisphere of the brain did not lose the ability to speak. Dax concluded that the two halves of the brain have different functions and that speech is controlled by the left half of the brain. These first homey observations were soon replicated and served as the impetus for a scientifically based understanding of the language areas of the brain (Springer & Deutsch, 1981).

In most individuals, the left hemisphere of the brain is specifically organized to acquire language. If you are right-handed, the chances are 95 out of 100 that the areas that control speech are located in the left hemisphere of your brain. Even if you are left-handed, your speech centers will still be located in the left hemisphere 70 percent of the time (Rasmussen & Milner, 1977).

These speech-control centers have two main functions: to interpret language and to produce language. The first speech center to be pinpointed was called Broca's area in honor of Paul Broca, a French surgeon. Broca was responsible for identifying the precise region of the left hemisphere that caused labored and hesitant speech when it was damaged (see Figure 8–3). A patient with the speech disorder called Broca's *aphasia* might describe an upcoming dental appointment in the following way. "Monday . . . Dad and Dick . . . Wednesday, nine o'clock . . . 10 o'clock . . . doctors . . . and . . . teeth" (Geschwind, 1979, p. 186). The same kinds of errors are evident in the patient's writings. But most patients with Broca's aphasia can sing fluently—probably because the retention of melodies is in the undamaged right hemisphere.

Broca's work was primarily concerned with patients who had trouble producing speech. Once Broca showed that a specific area of the brain was involved in speech, other neurologists began to examine related deficits. Karl Wernicke, a German neurologist, noted that stroke victims could sometimes speak fluently, but their words lacked meaning. Autopsies on Wernicke's patients indicated damage to a different area of the left hemisphere, now known as Wernicke's area (see Figure 8–3).

Stroke patients who suffer damage to Wernicke's area show no hesitancies in speech, but their words do not convey meaning. A patient with Wernicke's aphasia described a picture of two boys stealing cookies behind a woman's back as, "Mother is away here working her work to get her better, but when she's looking the two boys looking in the other part. She's working another time" (Geschwind, 1979, p. 168).

Both Broca and Wernicke identified regions of the brain that were important

**Figure 8—3**　　　　　　　　　　**Language areas in the brain**

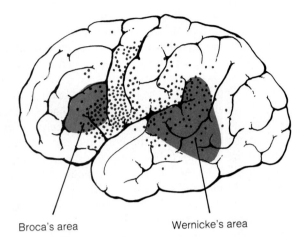

Broca's area　　　　　　　Wernicke's area

Wernicke's area helps the individual interpret the meaning of words. Broca's area is involved in putting words together to form sentences. The two areas are connected by a series of fibers. The cortex surrounding these areas is critical for language acquisition.

Source: Geschwind, N. (1979). Specializations of the human brain. *Scientific American, 241,* p. 186.

to speech. Damage in Broca's area disrupts the production of speech, while lesions in Wernicke's area interfere with the patient's ability to interpret events. Broca's and Wernicke's discoveries were major milestones in understanding the brain's role in language. Another milestone occurred when Wilder Penfield, a Montreal neurosurgeon, discovered that direct electrical stimulation of the tissue around Broca's and Wernicke's areas caused patients to stop talking, to stutter, or to forget the names of words. Using this technique, Penfield was able to map the areas in a particular brain that were involved in language and speech (see Figure 8–4).

Penfield's technique is a blessing to patients who must undergo brain surgery, because surgeons can avoid any areas that might disrupt speech. The mapping technique also provided more complete information about the connections between the speech centers of the brain. We now know that, in most adults, the speech centers of the brain are located in the left hemisphere and that no similar speech centers exist in the right hemisphere. Further, we know that these two main speech areas are directly connected by a bundle of nerve fibers and that all speech-related areas can be electrically mapped if the need arises (Penfield & Roberts, 1959).

When we pair this anatomical information with the person's behavior, we can begin to form a model of language and speech. The meaning or concept that a person wants to convey in conversation probably arises in Wernicke's area. The idea is then transferred to Broca's area where it is fashioned into a coherent sentence. The sentence is then spoken by the muscles of the mouth,

**Figure 8—4**                    **Mapping language in the brain**

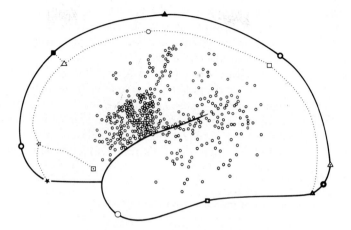

Wilder Penfield discovered that stimulating points along the surface of the cortex with a small electrical current interrupted speech. Using this technique, neurosurgeons have been able to map the language areas of an individual's brain.

Source: Springer, S. P., & Deutsch, G. (1981). *Left brain, right brain* (p. 195). San Francisco: W. H. Freeman.

lips, tongue, and larynx (Geschwind, 1979). This built-in organization of the brain coordinates the language the child hears and interprets the events the child experiences. All of these factors are necessary for language acquisition.

## LANGUAGE ACQUISITION IN HUMANS

In the 1930s, when child development was a fledgling field of inquiry, the study of language consisted largely of counting the number of words that children of different ages knew. As Piaget's work became available, the field changed. Developmental psychologists were intrigued by the stages of infant development that Piaget had outlined. They began to examine the stages children pass through as they acquire language.

One group, led by Roger Brown at Harvard University, taped the speech of three children who were just beginning to use language. These children were code named Adam, Eve, and Sarah (Brown, 1973). Over a period of four years, Brown and his students listened to phrases such as "eat sweater" and "byebye dirty" in an effort to understand the steps in language acquisition. Since these early years, psycholinguists have recorded the early words and phrases of children in dozens of languages. After listening collectively to thousands of hours of children's speech, psychologists have agreed that acquiring a language demands, at the very least, that the child master the sounds, the form, the meaning, and the order of words in that language.

**Phonology—
understanding the
sounds of language**

Children usually utter their first words around their first birthday. This event, recorded faithfully in baby books by proud parents, marks the end of the prelinguistic stage of language acquisition just as it marks the beginning of language. During the prelinguistic period, children learn the textural features of their language, how to take turns in a conversation, and what speech sounds are used in their language.

Sensitivities to sound are part of the newborn's built-in equipment. As we have noted in earlier chapters, low frequency sounds tend to soothe, while high frequency sounds alert the infant. Speech sounds are especially interesting to the newborn and produce a wave of electrical activity in the left hemisphere of the brain (Molfese, 1977). In addition to being sensitive to human speech in general, infants can discriminate very small differences in sounds, like the

**Mothers transmitting the language**

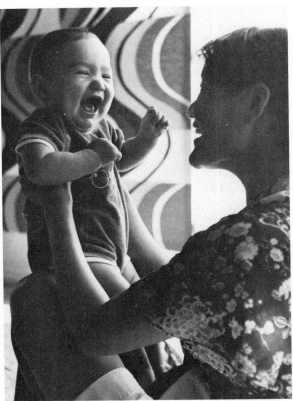

*Emilio A. Mercado: Jeroboam*

Mothers exaggerate their facial expressions and their tones when speaking to infants. Such exaggeration helps infants begin to understand the feelings and tones that accompany speech.

distinction between "P" and "B." Even though infants can hear these differences, they still have to learn that these differences are important in their language. This takes considerable exposure to the language.

To illustrate this point, the deVilliers named two dolls Bok and Pok. Then they asked children to, "Put the hat on Bok" or, "Give Pok a ride in the wagon." Children under 18 months had a great deal of difficulty performing the task. If the dolls were named Bok and Zav the children had no trouble. The deVilliers' experiment demonstrates that even though our brains can detect small differences in speech sounds soon after birth, this sensitivity must be meshed with an understanding of language before children can interpret the differences between sounds (deVilliers & deVilliers, 1982).

Humans produce a wide variety of sounds. During the first months of life, all children can produce the guttural sounds of German, the rolled "r's" of Spanish, and the click sounds common to some African languages. But producing sounds and speaking a particular language are two very different accomplishments. Cooing and babbling begin in the first three or four months of life. Many a father has rejoiced to hear his five-month-old produce the sound "dada." But this sound is not meaningfully associated with daddy and will not be for several more months. In the meantime, infants may crawl around the house uttering an endless string of "da's" to every object that is encountered. Gradually, this babbling begins to sound more like speech. Pauses and stops punctuate the babbling, and the infant's voice rises and falls as if an exciting story is being told. Of course, the content is still gibberish.

When the first recognizable words do appear, they are likely to be repeated consonant vowel combinations like "dada," "baba," "papa," "mama," and "wawa." It is no accident that in most languages, the childish versions of the words mother and father are repeated consonant-vowel sounds.

Because producing sounds is difficult, a child's early speech tends to simplify the pronunciation of words. "Doggie" becomes "goggie," "spoon" is shortened to "poon," and "guck" describes both a truck and a duck (deVilliers & deVilliers, 1979). For four to five years, children work on closing the gap between their pronunciation and the adult pronunciation of the same word. Even school-aged children will still trip over words with several syllables and call their favorite food, "fsighetti."

Although the brain is tuned to speech from the first weeks of life, interpreting sounds and producing them in the right combinations requires many months of concentrated practice. In linguistic terms, infants must master *phonology*—the sound system of language—before they can use the language fluently.

## Pragmatics— understanding the use of language

Patricia Greenfield, a psycholinguist at UCLA, was amazed at how readily her daughter could communicate using only single words. The child conveyed meaning by combining her single words with actions, objects, gestures, and intonation. Intrigued, Greenfield undertook a study of how two children used *pragmatic* aspects of communication to heighten the effectiveness of their single-word sentences (Greenfield & Smith, 1976).

Infants learn about some of the pragmatic aspects of language long before they speak. They learn how language is used, how a conversation flows, and what rules are necessary to keep conversations going. In other words, they learn the form of communication.

The social interaction between the mother and the child provides infants with a great deal of information about the pragmatics of language. The universal game of peek-a-boo is a perfect nonlinguistic training ground for learning to switch roles. Infants also learn how to gain and hold their mother's attention by maintaining eye contact and smiling (Brown, 1980). In face-to-face play, during feedings, and during diaper changes, the mother stimulates her child to respond (Stern, 1981). The conversation that results is initially very one-sided because the mother has to play both roles.

Oh, you are a funny little one, aren't you, hmm?
Aren't you a funny little one?
Yes. (Snow, 1977, p. 4)

Gradually the conversation becomes less lopsided and the mother's questions are answered by coos, gestures, and finally words (Kaye & Charney, 1980).

Prelinguistic children often use gestures to demonstrate that they understand some of the pragmatics of communication (Wolf & Gardner, 1981). Janeen, a 13-month-old, stands on her tiptoes and points to a favorite ball that has been put on the fireplace mantle. Toddlers often point to objects they want and steer their mother's attention in the direction they are pointing. They can also be very inventive about communicating their wants and needs. Amber, an 11-month-old, handed her mother a windup bear, then took her mother's hand and put it on the windup key. All the while she looked pleadingly into her mother's eyes. It is common for toddlers to grab their mother's hand and drag them into the nursery to retrieve some precious toy that is out of reach. Once toddlers have an object, they might hand it to you or hide it from you. Larry, at 12 months, did not want his mother to take his blanket. He held it tightly to his body and turned his back on his mother.

Children can get the attention of another person, make requests, and show possession by using gestures. Even when children begin to talk, they augment their limited vocabulary with gestures that add more meaning.

Learning the pragmatics of language continues well beyond the prelinguistic stage of language acquisition (Flavell, Speer, Green, & August, 1981). Children and adolescents learn about the form of conversations when they learn not to interrupt. Speakers signal their intentions to end their talk with a phrase like "in conclusion." During a conversation, speakers often check to see if the listener is following by asking a question. As listeners, we acknowledge that we have heard what has been said by nodding our heads. We register amazement, disgust, and excitement appropriately, and we check to make sure we have understood what the speaker intends. By considering the context and the inton-

**Gestures**

Gestures add meaning to the early speech of children. Even though the child can only speak in single-word sentences, adults usually understand what the child is communicating because of the context, the use of gestures, and the child's intonation.

ation accompanying a remark, we know whether the speaker is being funny, sarcastic, or serious (Ackerman, 1982; Garvey, 1977). All of these skills allow us to initiate conversations, to keep them flowing smoothly, and to end them. In short, we have a working command of the pragmatics used in language.

**Semantics— unraveling the meaning of language**

In addition to understanding phonology and pragmatics, the toddler has to learn what words mean. The turning point in Helen Keller's struggle to acquire language came when she realized that the finger spelling games she played with her teacher could be used to convey meaning. In a dramatic scene by a water pump, Helen suddenly realized that her teacher was spelling the word for water. In that moment, the world of language opened to Helen because she finally understood the link between symbols and objects.

What was a milestone for Helen Keller is readily accomplished in the day-to-day activities of the infant. As infants develop cognitively, they realize that objects have an independent existence. Once they have mastered object permanence (see Chapter 6), attaching a symbol to objects seems to come naturally. By 18 months, toddlers often badger their parents endlessly with the question, "Whasis?" They want to know what label goes with each object.

Attaching a label to an object is only the beginning of understanding and conveying meaning. Most objects have several labels. Each label conveys a different meaning. The label "Bowzer" tells you about one specific dog. "Irish setter" conveys a different set of information. "Dog" and "mammal" are even more general categories. Each label can be appropriately attached to a dog. How does a child learn these different symbols and when to use each one?

Children first learn proper nouns—like "Gramma" and the names of siblings and pets (Bowerman, 1978a). These labels are the easiest to master because there is one label for each person. But deciphering the meaning of most words is more complex. When one word like "dog" includes Saint Bernards, cocker spaniels, and Chihuahuas, the toddler must become a miniature sleuth to figure out what "dog" means. Does dog refer to big animals, barking animals, furry animals, four-legged animals, or is a dog some combination of these characteristics? We cannot question children directly about how they decide what dog means because their language is so limited. Instead, we must study how they use the word. We then learn that children often *overgeneralize* or *overextend* words.

Overextension refers to the child's use of one word to refer to many similar objects. The word "vov-vov" was first used by one toddler to refer to a dog. Later, it was generalized to kittens, hens, all of the animals at a zoo, and a picture of pigs dancing (Moskowitz, 1978). Within a few months of learning the word, it had come to denote many animals. In the next few months, the use of "vov-vov" was gradually restricted, until finally, it was used only for dogs.

This process of labeling an object, overextending that label to other similar objects, and then gradually restricting the use of that label is common during language acquisition. Psycholinguists have examined this process closely hoping to find clues about how children extract meaning from words. Three possible explanations have been offered—feature analysis, designing a prototype, and intentionally overextending.

**Feature analysis.** Both Eve Clark (1977) and Katherine Nelson (1979) have argued that the child extracts a single feature, or sometimes a set of features, that seems to characterize the object. Children trying to decide what dog means might attend to some salient perceptual characteristic like the dog's size or the fact that dogs have four legs. Alternatively, the child might focus on how an object is used. For example, a ball is something that can be thrown, and it rolls and bounces. Once an important feature has been established, other similar objects will be given the same label. Children add additional features or qualifications to their concepts as needed. In the case of dog, they might add "furry" and "barks." Once these new features are added, chickens will no longer be called dogs because they do not bark, and pigs will be eliminated because they do not have any fur. As the process of feature analysis continues, the child's understanding of the word dog becomes more accurate.

*Feature analysis* seems like a long and difficult process for a toddler to go through (Greenberg & Kuczaj, 1982). One seldom sees a child conducting elaborate or time-consuming comparisons when they shout "goggie" at a horse.

**Prototypes.** Because deciding that a dog is furry involves abstract processing, psycholinguists have looked for simpler explanations for overextensions. Instead of analyzing features, children form an image or *prototype* of what a model dog might be (Greenberg & Kuczaj, 1982). Then when they encounter anything remotely similar, they label it goggie.

This view of how children acquire meaning has recently received a lot of attention (Kuczaj, 1982). If children maintain an image or prototype, they do not have to isolate abstract features like "round" and then compare two objects to see if they are round. It is reasonable, given the image children have of the moon, that they might see a postmark, flash to their image of the moon, and label the postmark "moon."

**Intentionality.** The two preceding views suggest that children's linguistic understanding undergoes continual revision until something akin to the adult meaning is reached. Some psycholinguists argue that perhaps the child's concepts do not undergo much change. What changes is the sophistication of the language that children use to describe objects. Werner Leopold's daughter Hildegard used "wau-wau" (her version of dog) to designate a pair of slippers that had a puppy's face on them. She knew the word shoe. Why didn't she call her slipper shoe instead of "wau-wau"? Perhaps she was pointing out that here indeed was a puppy on the tip of her slippers (Leopold, 1939).

It is possible that some of the overextensions children use are caused by a limited vocabulary. Suppose a child has restricted the word dog to four-legged, furry, medium-sized, living objects that bark. Then the child encounters a cow. The child might very well call the cow goggie because it is the word that best fits the concept. In this case, the meaning derived for the word dog is accurate, but a limited vocabulary prevents the child from correctly labeling this new animal (Greenberg & Kuczaj, 1982).

As is often the case in psychology, there is probably some truth in all three explanations of how the child decides the meaning of words (Boswell & Green, 1982). Children may initially form prototypes of words. They may also attach meaning to one or two features of a word and then extend that meaning. On other occasions, they may mislabel because their vocabulary is limited or because they intend to note a particular similarity. In all of these explanations, overextensions of labels are seen as a clue to the child's thought processes (see Figure 8–5). Psycholinguists do not agree on exactly what children are thinking when they overextend. But they do agree that this process is important and that answers to some of the puzzles of language acquisition can probably be found in overextensions.

Two-year-olds overextend words frequently. Preschoolers make mistakes by abstracting meanings from words that have somewhat similar meanings. Melissa Bowerman (1978b) points to the semantic adjustments that preschoolers make in verb use. As early as two years of age, the children she studied had used the verbs "make" and "put" correctly. Then as three- to five-year olds, they began to confuse them. "You put a place for Eva" and, "I make some butter my sandwich." Bowerman argues that the child's confusion comes from the belated recognition that "put" and "make" share some aspects of meaning.

**Figure 8—5**  **Overextensions in early speech**

| Child's lexical item | First referents | Other referents in order of occurrence | General area of semantic extension |
|---|---|---|---|
| Moo | Moon | Cake<br>Round marks on windows<br>Writing on windows and in books<br>Round shapes in books<br>Tooling on leather book covers<br>Round postmarks<br>Letter "O" | Shape |
| Bow-wow | Dog | Fur piece with glass eyes<br>Father's cufflinks<br>Pearl buttons on dress<br>Bath thermometer | Shape |
| Kotibaiz | Bars of cot | Large toy abacus<br>Toast rack with parallel bars<br>Picture of building with columns | Shape |
| Bébé | Reflection of child (self) in mirror | Photograph of self<br>All photographs<br>All pictures<br>All books with pictures<br>All books | Shape |
| Vov-Vov | Dog | Kittens<br>Hens<br>All animals at a zoo<br>Picture of pigs dancing | Shape |
| Ass | Goat with rough hide on wheels | Things that move: animals, sister, wagon . . .<br>All things with a rough surface | Movement<br><br>Texture |
| Tu-tu | Train | Engine<br>Moving train<br>Journey | Movement |
| Fly | Fly | Specks of dirt<br>Dust<br>All small insects<br>Child's own toes<br>Crumbs of bread<br>A toad | Size |
| Quack | Duck on water | All birds and insects<br>All coins (after seeing an eagle on the face of a coin) | Size |

**Figure 8–5 *Concluded***

| Child's lexical item | First referents | Other referents in order of occurrence | General area of semantic extension |
|---|---|---|---|
| Ko-ko | Cockerel's crowing | Tunes played on a violin<br>Tunes played on a piano<br>Tunes played on an accordion<br>Tunes played on a phonograph<br>All music<br>Merry-go-round | Sound |
| Dany | Sound of a bell | Clock<br>Telephone<br>Doorbells | Sound |

Children often identify horses and cows as "doggie." They have overextended their label for dogs to animals that are somewhat similar. In time, the meaning of the word is narrowed to the adult meaning.

From the Acquisition of Language by B. A. Moskowitz. Copyright © 1978 by *Scientific American,* Inc. 

The confusion, rather than indicating a backward step in language acquisition, indicates that the child is beginning to integrate the meaning of verbs.

For many years, the study of semantics took a back seat in language acquisition. However, psycholinguists studying the child's language soon realized that one-word sentences and even gestures convey meaning. They were forced to acknowledge that not all meaning comes from word order, but that the child is conveying meaning long before two words are put together (Bruner, 1975). Now semantics is recognized as a critical aspect of language acquisition.

## Syntax—decoding the order of words

Linguists have attached great importance to *syntax*—the way words are combined. The order of the words tells us what the speaker intends. "The ball hit Mommy" and, "Mommy hit the ball" convey two entirely different meanings. Learning language involves more than learning the names of objects. It involves more than stringing words together. "The accident the truck smashed in car a red" is a string of words. But these words defy interpretation because they do not conform to syntactical rules. Syntax dictates how we combine words and allows us to express relationships between words.

Linguists have always been fascinated with the internal structure of adult language. However, the rules children use to form sentences are very different. Furthermore, children's rules change as their language skills become more sophisticated. Let us follow the child's progress from the first words to the mastery of past tenses, plurals, and questions. Along the way, we will see why children produce such unique statements as "Everyone knows those are feets!" "My teacher holded the baby rabbits," and "Why garage door?"

**Holophrases—one-word sentences.** By 18 months, most children have a limited vocabulary and use one-word sentences called *holophrases*. "Gone," "Mommy," "Cookie," and "There" are all examples of one-word sentences produced by Allison Bloom (Bloom, 1973). They are interesting because children do not choose words like "a" or "the," even though these are the most frequently used words in the English language. Instead, children choose words that will convey meaning. Usually these words are nouns, although words like "There," "Up," and "More" are also prominent (Bloom & Lahey, 1978).

The first holophrases consist of a word that is spoken in isolation. Even these single words can convey meaning. "Up" shouted gleefully while a child is teetering on daddy's shoulders certainly conveys a different meaning than the pleading "Up" spoken by a child who is standing on the ground with outstretched arms. The child's intonation and the context usually allow us to interpret these one-word sentences accurately.

These early, isolated words are soon replaced by words that are chained together. At 21 months, Allison engaged in the following dialogue with her mother after her mother suggested that Allison take off her coat (Bloom, 1973, p. 51):

| Mother's speech | Allison's speech |
|---|---|
|  | Up. Up (points to her neck). |
| What? | Neck. Up. |
| Neck? What do you want? What? | Neck. |
| What's on your neck? | Zip. Zip. Up. |

Although each of Allison's words constitutes a single-word sentence, by using different words successively she manages to convey her meaning. Allison wanted her mother to zip up her coat and seemed to have this thought clearly represented in her mind from the beginning of the conversation (Bloom, 1973, p. 51). Because Allison's speech was limited to single-word sentences, she had a difficult time communicating with her mother.

**Duos—two-word sentences.** Holophrases are soon replaced by combinations of words. The first words a child strings together are often unexpected and certainly ungrammatical from an adult's point of view. We seldom see two-word sentences like, "A hat" or, "The book." The combinations that children produce are often composed of two nouns: "Baby basket", or "Mommy bathroom." What are children trying to convey?

To answer this question, Roger Brown (1973) laboriously cataloged all of the two-word sentences of Adam, Eve, and Sarah, as well as several children who spoke Swedish, Spanish, Finnish, and Samoan. When he completed his catalog and put similar sentences together, he discovered a startling consistency.

Almost all of the children's sentences fit into nine different kinds of statements (see Figure 8–6). In their two-word sentences, children talked about what they were doing, what they wanted others to do, and what was happening around them. They did not talk about the future or the past; nor did they construct hypothetical situations. Their early speech gave voice to relationships that they had discovered during the sensory motor period and that had been laboriously organized during the first 18 to 24 months of life.

Children's first, crude sentences are about the people, actions, and objects they have been exploring. Notice that in the duos children construct, there are no plurals, the verbs are not conjugated, and these omissions often make the sentence difficult to interpret. It helps if the context is included. Then we know that "eat table" does not refer to a dog gnawing on the table leg, but to the fact that another child is eating at the table. Similarly, "fly roof" could mean the child intends to fly, that there is a fly on the roof, that the roof is flying or, and this was the context for the remark, that a bird flew from the birdfeeder

**Figure 8–6**     **The words of babes**

| | |
|---|---|
| Agent action | Car go. |
| | Mommy fix. |
| | Daddy read. |
| Action object | Hit ball. |
| | Read book. |
| | Eat raisin. |
| Agent and object | Mommy pumpkin. |
| | Eve lunch. |
| | Mommy sock. |
| Agent location | Fly roof. |
| | Sit chair. |
| | Eat table. |
| Entity and location | Mommy outside. |
| | Lady home. |
| | Car garage. |
| Possessor and possession | Daddy chair. |
| | My teddy. |
| | Mommy nose. |
| Nomination | That teddy. |
| | That hat. |
| Nonexistence | All gone dirty. |
| | Dog away. |
| | No hat. |
| Recurrence | More milk. |
| | More noise. |

Almost all of the sentences that toddlers produce can be placed in one of the nine categories listed above. This is true regardless of the language the child learns. These universal sentences suggest that children's early words express concepts that have been acquired during the sensory motor period of development.

to the roof. Parents, interpreting their child's early language, have the benefit of knowing what aspects of the situation prompted the child's remark. Hence, the child's ungrammatical utterances are responded to appropriately. Frequently, the parents cannot interpret their child's two-word utterances. These communication failures push children to extend their language and convey their meaning more precisely.

**Three words and beyond.** As the child's sentences become longer, the relationships that are expressed become more complex. The child now says "I walking" or "I walked" instead of "I walk." What used to be "Adam ball," and as such, could be interpreted as "Adam wants the ball," "Adam has the ball," or "That is Adam's ball" is turned into a more precise statement, "Adam's ball." As children venture beyond the two-word stage, they learn how to indicate the possessive, how to distinguish between the present and the past, when to use "a," "an," and "the," and to use prepositions like "on" and "in." As Roger Brown (1973) examined the linguistic progress of Adam, Eve, and Sarah, he made two observations. He noticed that the three children deciphered these grammatical complexities at decidedly different rates. Eve had mastered all of these rules by the time she was 27 months old. Adam did not use them fluently until he was four years old. But, in spite of their speed at acquiring these rules, all three children learned them in precisely the same order. When the deVilliers verified these conclusions in a larger study (de-Villiers & deVilliers, 1973), psycholinguists became convinced that learning the rules of English proceeds in a systematic, thoughtful manner. What seems to happen is that children listen to the language that surrounds them, then filter it through their own concepts before constructing their sentences. By listening, children learn that their parents' language follows certain rules. From two to five years of age, the child struggles to untangle these rules.

**Negatives.** Learning to construct a negative sentence follows a series of steps. Toddlers, who do not know how to express a negative, often shake their heads "No" (Pea, 1980). By 18 months, a head shake can be punctuated by a defiant "No!" In the next step, the toddler puts "No" with another word and produces combinations like "No doggie" and "No wet." The negative usually precedes the other word. When three-word combinations are formed, "No" is likely to be outside of a normal two-word combination, as in "No doggie bite." In the next step, the child realizes that adults put the negative in the middle. Trying this, the child says, "Doggie no bite." A final modification is to change the form of the negative to doesn't. The end product, "The doggie doesn't bite," is a perfectly acceptable adult version of a negative sentence. Once mastered, the child's understanding of negatives is applied to all negatives. The child can now use "can't," "won't," and "don't" appropriately in an endless array of sentences.

**Plurals.** The rule for forming plurals is also acquired in a series of steps. In English, however, the rule for forming plurals has many exceptions. Once children have adopted a rule, they may not know the exceptions. For example, Kai had often played a game with his mother that involved naming the parts of the body. During this game, he had consistently used the word feet. As a four-year-old, he knew plurals were formed by adding an "s." Hence, when his cousin said "Look at my foots," Kai was amused. He looked at his mother and said, "Did you hear that? David said 'foots.' Everyone knows they are 'feets'."

Kai's use of plurals demonstrates another common progression in language acquisition. A child will often use a correct construction for months, then replace it with an incorrect one, before gradually returning to the correct form (Slobin, 1971). Initially, the correct constructions that children use are imitations. As children learn a rule, they use it, sometimes overextending it. This still signals progress because now they are not just imitating; they are applying the rule that says add an "s" to form a plural.

Once children learn a rule, they are not very responsive to corrections. Jean Berko Gleason reports the following attempt of a mother to influence her child's speech.

**Child:** "My teacher holded the baby rabbits and we patted them."
**Mother:** "Did you say your teacher held the baby rabbits?"
**Child:** "Yes."
**Mother:** "What did you say she did?"
**Child:** "She holded the baby rabbits and we patted them."
**Mother:** "Did you say she held them tightly?"
**Child:** "No, she holded them loosely." (Gleason, 1967)

In a similar study, one mother repeated the correct form eight times with little impact on her son's speech (Moskowitz, 1978).

**Questions.** As with forming a negative sentence, asking a question requires numerous rule changes. In the child's first attempts, such as "Where we can go?" or "Why garage door?" the child merely adds a Wh-word to the normal word order. In English, to ask questions correctly the verb comes before the subject as in "Where is your house?" On occasion, children are so confused about the position of the verb that they will include it twice. "I don't know where is the woods is?" (Hakuta, 1975). Once children understand how to form the question, you would think they could ask about anything. But Bloom, Merkin, and Wooten (1982) note that questions that begin with "what," "where," and "who" are the easiest for children to ask. Learning to ask "how," "why," and "when" are more difficult.

Tag questions literally take years to master (Dennis, Sugar, & Whitaker, 1982). A tag question is a sentence that is turned into a question by adding a "tag" on the end. "John will be home late, won't he?" and "I made a mistake, didn't I?" both illustrate tag questions. The use of tags differs markedly from culture to culture. In French, a single tag, *n'est-ce pas*, serves as an all-purpose version of "isn't that right?" In English, each tag is different and changes depending on the subject and verb of the sentence. To trace children's understanding of tag questions, Roger Brown and Camille Hanlon (1970) enlisted the aid of puppets. One puppet would say, "John will be late." A friendly alligator puppet would then add, "John will be late, won't he?" After several such demonstrations, a child is asked to be the alligator. Most children eagerly accept, and in the process of playing the alligator, they display their developing understanding of tag questions. Because tag questions are so complex, they offer a good illustration of the process that children go through to decipher the rules of speech and the correct syntax (Dennis, Sugar, & Whitaker, 1982).

The acquisition of language seems to be a tedious proposition. At the minimum, the child has to learn phonology, pragmatics, semantics, and syntax. It is important to remember that children do not divide language this way. They are intent on learning to communicate, not mastering phonology or semantics. Roger Brown (1980) notes that despite our good intentions and the fact that we have made unquestionable strides in understanding a child's speech, we may have conceived of the whole psycholinguistic learning process much too simply and mechanically. The art of conversing is more than the sum of these skills. Tracing the child's language progress from immature to mature forms does not tell us why the child changes rules. Nor does it tell us about the effects of different environments. Considering these issues adds another layer of complexity and additional dimensions to the study of language.

**Language Acquisition**

"Well, Billy uses badder English than me."

Children follow a series of rather precise steps in acquiring adult grammar.
Source: Keane, B. (1982, July 8). The family circus.

## HOW DOES THE CHILD MASTER LANGUAGE?

The steps a child goes through in acquiring language as well as the different systems of knowledge the child must understand have already been described. We have, however, sidestepped a critical question—namely, how does the child accomplish these feats? One of the reasons for approaching this question cautiously is that it requires speculation about what children are thinking. Such excursions inside the child's mind are fraught with controversy. Psycholinguists can agree that children use plurals before they understand possessives. We have only to look at continuous records of children's speech to obtain detailed information on that question. To decide how the child learns language we have to be part scientist, part theoretician, and part soothsayer. With this caution in mind, let us turn to explanations of how the child acquires language.

**Biological factors**

Noam Chomsky (1975) believes that children learn grammar because of certain genetically determined predispositions. In support of this view, he presents five main arguments. First, humans are the only species that use language. Second, the brain is specifically designed to support language. Third, language has a biological base. Fourth, language acquisition proceeds in a similar way in children all over the world. Finally, learning language is far too complex to be accomplished by a child unless it is built in. There is some evidence for each of these statements.

From our earlier discussion, we know that a number of species communicate vocally, including dolphins, whales, birds, monkeys, and the great apes. The communication systems that these animals use lack the flexibility of human language, but they contain some of the same elements. When a gestural language has been used, chimps, gorillas, and orangutans have been able to communicate. Still, when we look at the overall linguistic capabilities of other species, it seems fair to conclude that human language retains many unique features.

Most psychologists agree that the human brain is specifically designed to process language. The two areas of the brain discussed earlier seem unique to humans. The more debated issue is whether these areas of the brain warrant the claim that language development is genetically determined. Many other skills, like vision and hearing, are supported by particular areas of the brain; but visual and auditory experiences still play a part in the adult's ability to see and hear.

The existence of a sensitive period for language acquisition is a third argument used to buttress the view that language is biologically based (Lenneberg, 1967). Drawing from clinical cases and neurological evidence, Lenneberg concludes that being exposed to language prior to puberty is essential to fluent speech. He points out that adults learning to speak a second language will always retain an accent. Children, however, can learn a second language free of any accent. Surgical evidence also supports the notion of a sensitive period.

Surgery that would disrupt language in an adult has a transient effect on young children. A child under five who has the entire left half of the brain removed will have few linguistic deficiencies. An adult who must have similar surgery is likely to have long-lasting and severe language impairments (Krashen, 1975). Genie, the isolate described in Chapter 5, had almost no exposure to language until she was 13 years old. The language she was able to learn at that point deviated in significant ways from normal speech. These studies support the concept of a *sensitive period* for language acquisition. But the position that language acquisition is limited to a more absolute *critical period* has not been supported (Snow & Hoefnagle-Hohle, 1978).

If language acquisition progresses similarly despite the fact that children are learning very different languages and despite the influence of the environment, then scientists can point to *language universals* as proof that language is built into the child. As mentioned previously, children from all parts of the globe construct their initial sentences to describe agents, actions, and objects in their environment. Hence, this might be considered a universal in language acquisition. Once children begin producing possessives, plurals, etc., they do so in accordance with the language they are learning. This means that specific universals are difficult to find. More general strategies, however, such as attending to the ends of words, might be universal.

At times, the complexity of language is bewildering. Hence, it is not surprising that some linguists believe that the brain is predisposed to untangle this complexity. In its most naive form, however, this argument amounts to throwing up your hands and saying, "There is no way to explain how children acquire language; therefore, it has to be biological." Chomsky phrases the argument in less absolute terms. Because learning language is so complex, there may be an "underlying biological matrix that provides a framework" for the growth of language (Chomsky, 1978, p. 200). If this is the case, then psycholinguists need to be able to identify the specific skills that form the matrix.

An analogy from the visual system will help illustrate the kinds of skills that might be needed for deciphering language. In reviewing infants' visual skills, we noted that the infant's eyes were attracted to edges and sharp contrasts. An infant's language areas could be predisposed to notice the order of words or the endings of words. Slobin (1973) suggests that the brain is primed to use specific strategies to decode speech. Specifying what these strategies are is very different from throwing up one's hands at the complexity of language.

To summarize, biological factors form a base for the acquisition of language. Further, some specific skills that help the child understand language are built into the system. We know that an infant can distinguish sounds that are nearly identical. Other more complex strategies might also be built into the system. Such strategies would have to be very general, otherwise human language would be no more flexible than the Vervet's communication system. Biological factors can help us understand how a child learns language. Acknowledging the role of biology, however, does not preclude other explanations of how language is learned.

## Imitation

Imitation is often included among explanations of how children learn language. Imitation is obviously a factor because children learn to speak their parents' language. But if you consider the early language that children produce, it is unlike adult language. Parents do not model "Bye-bye dirty," or "Eat table" for their toddlers. For this reason, psycholinguists are ambivalent about the role of imitation. What is important, in their view, is that children must be exposed to the structure of the language they are learning. Having an adult produce well-formed sentences seems to prime the child to model a shortened version of the sentence.

**Model:** "It goes in a big box."
**Eve:** "Big box."
**Model:** "I will not do that again."
**Eve:** "Do again." (Brown, 1973, p. 76)

In these examples, Eve is not mindlessly imitating the model. The sentences that are produced are evidence of active processing. The child extracts information that she can reproduce and that fit with her current understanding of language. Bloom, Hood, and Lightbown (1974) report that children seem to imitate words and structures that they are just beginning to learn. Children who are actively trying to express possession might imitate a possessive in their mother's speech. Three months later if you looked at the same children, they would no longer be imitating possessives. Now they would be imitating more complex structures.

Children differ markedly in their propensity to imitate. When Lois Bloom and her colleagues observed the speech development of four children from different families, they found that two of the children were frequent imitators, while the other two rarely imitated. Since all four were learning language satisfactorily, one has to conclude that imitation is just one of several possible strategies that children can use to decipher the structure of language.

The imitation studies that have been mentioned are all longitudinal studies. Such studies are expensive and time consuming. To shorten the process somewhat, researchers have tried to elicit imitation by playing Simple Simon. In the following exercise, 32-month old Peter is instructed to imitate exactly what Simple Simon says.

| **Simple Simon Says** | **Peter** |
|---|---|
| 1. This is a big balloon. | This a big balloon. |
| 2. This is broken. | What's broken? |
| 3. This is broken. | That's broken. |
| 4. I'm trying to get this cow in here. | Cow in here. |
| 5. I'm gonna get the cow to drink some milk. | Get the cow to drink milk. |
| 6. You made him stand up over there. | Stand up there. (Bloom & Lahey, 1978, p. 250) |

Peter's attempts to reproduce Simon's exact words are not very successful. If we were using these sentences to assess Peter's language skills, we would conclude that Peter needed to work on several grammatical structures. We would be very surprised to learn that Peter had actually produced all of these sentences the preceding day! Why did he fail the imitation task? What was different? Slobin and Welsh (1973) explain that on the previous day Peter had intended to convey meanings in a specific context. His active involvement in the situation made it easier for him to generate complex sentences. Simply asking the child to imitate reduces his active involvement and hence does not elicit his best effort.

From the studies reported here, we can conclude that imitation is a strategy that some children use to help them understand the structure of language. By itself, however, it cannot account for how the child produces language. The imitation studies are unanimous in concluding that much more is happening when a child imitates than a mindless reproduction of speech.

**Conceptual progress**

Both of the preceding explanations allude to conceptual skills that help the child understand language. The biological explanation cites conceptual strategies that guide the child. Even the imitation explanation takes the view that the child's imitations are thoughtful, active reproductions, rather than passive mimicry. Given the importance of the child's thought processes in these explanations, it is not surprising that many psycholinguists regard thought as the key to the acquisition of language.

According to Piaget (1962), language builds on the sensory motor skills described in Chapter 6. Once infants understand objects and can form images of those objects, they learn the names of objects. As infants explore their environment, they see relationships between people, objects, and actions. When they combine words to form their first sentences, it is these relationships that they describe (Brown, 1973).

If thought is the key to language, then the primary function of language is to allow the child to express thoughts that would otherwise exist silently. It follows, too, that more complex thoughts would give rise to more complex language. Dan Slobin (1966) gives the example of children acquiring the ability to talk about the hypothetical. In Russian, the actual construction of hypothetical statements is easy, but even though the language requirements are minimal, children do not use the hypothetical until very late in development. The reason, Slobin suggests, is that thinking about what does not exist requires very sophisticated thought processes. As children acquire the cognitive skill to think about hypothetical events, they will also acquire the language forms to talk about it. Slobin (1978) calls this the waiting-room metaphor. Linguistic skills remain in a waiting room until children's thought processes mature. Once children can think about the past or the hypothetical, they must decipher the language used to express their thoughts. Only then can the thought be verbalized (see Figure 8–7).

**Figure 8–7**  **Language and thought**

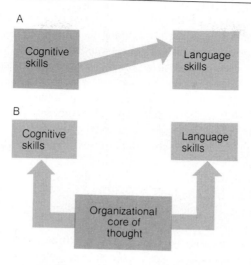

The waiting-room metaphor is illustrated in diagram A. In this view, language skills must wait until the child develops cognitive skills. Only then can words be learned to express the concept. An alternative view suggests that both cognitive and language skills depend on a symbolic core (diagram B). If this is the case, language skills and cognitive skills should develop along separate lines. But since they both depend on the child's organization of the world, they should follow correlated patterns.

To test the hypothesis that thought precedes language, investigators have charted children's sensory motor development, while faithfully recording their language. In general, these studies find that children acquire an object concept before they produce their first words, and that one-word sentences require the sophisticated skills of the final stage of sensory motor development (Bloom, Lifter, & Broughton, 1981). More complex language skills also seem to be linked to conceptual development (Cromer, 1981). When children say "Mommy nose" as they point to their mother's face, it is clear that they understand the possessive. Nevertheless, the possessive form does not appear in their language for several months. Presumably, it takes that long for the child to map the correct language onto the thought.

This view of how language is learned solves many of the problems that we have raised about language. Acknowledging that language builds on the infant's understanding of the world provides a bridge between prelinguistic thought processes and language. All of the pragmatic skills that infants learn during the prelinguistic period can now be used to serve language (Bruner, 1975). Recognizing the link between thought and language makes it clear that language does not just suddenly spring forth at one year of age. It also offers an attractive alternative to Chomsky's view that the acquisition of syntax must be genetic.

Although conceiving language as developing from thought solves several problems, it raises others. In some children, language does not seem to depend as heavily on thought (Cromer, 1981). For instance, David Ingram (1981) studied a little girl who produced two-word sentences before she reached the highest stage of sensory motor development. Her language development did not depend upon mature conceptual development. As exceptions to the waiting room theory have been reported, psycholinguists have looked at other possible relationships between language and thought. Perhaps thought does not precede language; perhaps the two advance in a parallel fashion and become intertwined during the preschool years (Vygotsky, 1962). Perhaps language development influences thought as well as the reverse (Bloom, 1981). Figure 8–7 diagrams these different relationships. The first diagram of the waiting-room metaphor shows the one-way street going from thought to language. The second depicts an inner core of symbolic awareness that fosters both thought and language. Because both thought and language depend on this inner core, they will both advance at a similar rate. But each will have its own pattern of growth.

In this section, we have examined three answers to the question, "How do children learn language?" One answer points to the importance of biological predispositions. Another suggests that imitation is a critical factor. A third places the responsibility on the child's conceptual development. Each answer accounts for some of the evidence we have concerning language acquisition. Language areas do exist in the brain. Children do imitate. All three of these answers acknowledge the importance of thought. Trying to pick one of these explanations over the others is a little like trying to decide whether an elephant is best described by referring to the trunk, the ears, or the gargantuan legs. To use one of these descriptions and exclude the others would mean the description of the elephant would be incomplete. Until we have a more cohesive view of how children acquire language, we will have to be content with describing the elements we think are important. In all likelihood, biology, imitation, and conceptual skills are all necessary for a complete description of language acquisition.

## THE LANGUAGE ENVIRONMENT

In the 1950s, many psychologists believed that language was shaped solely by the mother or primary caretaker. When the child's random babbling began to sound like "Mama," the mother showed her pleasure by reinforcing the child with hugs, kisses, and attention. As a result, the child kept repeating "Mama." Sounds were shaped into words, and words were shaped into sentences by the reinforcing mother. The end product, many years later, was adult speech (Bijou & Baer, 1965). This behavioristic view clashed openly with Chomsky's notion that the environment played a minimal role in shaping language. He believed that the child was born to speak and that the mother's speech simply triggered the learning of the parent language (Chomsky, 1978).

Neither of these positions, especially in an extreme form, can withstand much scrutiny. If mothers shape the child's speech gradually by reinforcing the child, why does the child replace a correct plural like "feet" with the incorrect plural "feets" (Slobin, 1971)? The genetic view does not fare much better. If any adult speaker can trigger the child's innate skills, then television should do the job. Such an environment, however, does not trigger language (Hoff-Ginsburg & Shatz, 1982). Infants born to deaf parents can often hear, but they need to interact with an adult. Despite liberal use of the TV as a model, these children initially learn to sign.

These two explanations take diametrically opposed positions on the importance of the environment. The truth is that the child's environment figures heavily in language acquisition. But it is not the simple role outlined by the early behaviorists, nor is it a trigger as Chomsky might argue. It is a complex combination of parents stimulating the child, modeling speech, and being aware of the child's language skills. In this section, we will describe the ways language environments enhance or inhibit language development. We will examine the impact that parents have on the child's language, the effect of stimulating or impoverished environments, and the course of language acquisition in individual children. The discussion will also refocus our attention on the fact that language is basically a social phenomenon (Bates, Bretherton, Beeghly-Smith, & McNew, 1982).

## Motherese

Both fathers and mothers change their speech patterns when they talk with small children (Kavanaugh & Jirkovsky, 1982). These adaptations are often labeled *motherese* to indicate that the way parents talk to their toddlers is so different that it almost qualifies as another language. The language parents use is specifically designed to acquaint the child with the sounds, use, meaning, and order of the language.

**Phonology.** When parents play with their infant, their speech is exaggerated. They speak to their child in a high-pitched voice that ranges from secretive whispers such as, "I'm going to get you," to high frequency, excited squeals such as, "Oh, you're so silly." The "Big Bad Wolf" is drawn out into a menacing growl, and "Little Red Riding Hood" is delivered in a high register singsong. Parents speak slowly and distinctly, placing greater stress on important words. All of these modifications are designed to attract the child's attention and to provide an intelligible model of the sounds the child must master (Chapman, 1981).

**Pragmatics.** Parents adopt a conversational model long before their children can converse. When a father asks his three-month-old a question, he pauses expectantly, then answers the question himself. Hence, even during the prelinguistic period, infants learn to take turns and to read the gestures, intonations, and facial expressions of their fathers. Infants learn that they can initiate and terminate an interaction. By the time children are able to produce two-word sentences, they are well aware of the obligations one has in a conversation. They also know that to communicate, you must get the attention of another person and then convey your message. Since children are not very good at continuing conversations, parents usually assume this role (Chapman, 1981).

**Semantics.** To learn language, the model of language must be tied to the child's activities. If the child is playing with a clown and the caretaker repeats "clown" several times, the child is likely to associate the word clown with the object. When children are just beginning to talk, parents use a lot of one-word sentences (Chapman, 1981). Even when their sentences are longer than one word, such as "That's a book," the first two words will be spoken quickly. "Book," however, will be louder, will be stressed, and will be drawn out. It will probably be repeated in the next breath. The child will have no doubt that the word book is applicable to that object. One of the child's most difficult tasks in language acquisition is dividing the flow of language into separate words. Initially, the stream of language may sound like a run-on sentence: "Howareyouthismorning?" Segmenting language into words is much easier if parents use one-word sentences or stress the critical word (Shatz, 1982).

When children begin to speak, parents' sentences change. Now they emphasize the same semantic relationships that Roger Brown found in Adam, Eve, and Sarah's early speech. The parents' sentences are suddenly filled with agents, actions, and objects. Parents interacting with their children talk about: objects disappearing— "The doggie's gone"; events reoccurring— "More applesauce?"; and people possessing—"That's Mommy's purse" (Snow, 1977). By talking about the child's world, parents help the child label the ongoing activities.

Language games are another parental strategy that help the child understand the meaning of words. These games are always played in the same way. Hence, once children understand the structure of the game, they can play, even if they have a very limited vocabulary (Snow, Dubber, & deBlauw, 1982). As an example, Ninio and Bruner analyzed one of these structured language games—reading a picture book. The children in their study ranged from eight-month-old infants who had no speech to 18-month-old toddlers who were just beginning to talk. Ninio and Bruner found that in the reading situation, parents limited their statements to about four kinds of sentences. They would say "Look," then ask a question that began with "What." At the end of the interaction, they would label objects and then give the child feedback. Here is an example:

**Mother:** Look!
[Child: touches picture.]
**Mother:** What are those?
[Child: vocalizes and smiles.]
**Mother:** Yes, they are rabbits.
[Child: vocalizes, smiles, and looks at mother.]
**Mother:** [Laughs] Yes, rabbit. (Ninio & Bruner, 1978, p. 6)

As the children in this study became older, their part in the game changed from touching the picture to producing recognizable labels. But the structure of the game remained the same. When the children progressed to the point of naming the rabbits, the parents almost always reinforced the child by laughing, saying yes, or repeating the name. Ninio and Bruner regard this sequence as one of many structured games that parents use to introduce children to the meanings of words.

**Syntax.** The syntax that parents use with toddlers is simple and repetitive. Let us listen in on a conversation where "motherese" is being spoken. In this case, a father is speaking to his 20-month-old daughter.

Get the shoe.
Yes, get the shoe.
Go get the shoe.
Let's put Debbie's shoe on.
Is this Debbie's shoe?
Yes, this is Debbie's shoe?
Point to the shoe.
Where is Debbie's shoe?
Is your shoe on your foot?

This one-way conversation illustrates the syntactic conventions of motherese. Notice how repetitive the father's speech is. The child hears "shoe" nine times. Most of the time the word "shoe" is the last word in the sentence. This makes it easier for the child to distinguish shoe from the other words in the sentence. While hearing the word, the shoe is present and is being put on her foot. The sentences that the father uses are very short. As the child begins to produce two-word sentences, parents adjust their language. They begin to expand these simple combinations. The child's rather uncomplicated "Daddy car" is expanded into the more meaningful, "Yes, daddy's washing the car."

Parents seem to have an intuitive grasp of their child's language skills. With each step the child makes, the parents' language becomes slightly more complex. During the period from 12 months to 4 years, children's sentences expand from one word to five or six words. As the child progresses, parents lengthen their sentences so that they stay two to three words longer than the sentences the child produces (Chapman, 1981).

Parents also modify the complexity of their sentences. Although parents use questions when speaking to prelinguistic children, they avoid the more complex forms. Only after children demonstrate that they understand cause and effect do parents begin to ask the child "Why" (Hood & Bloom, 1979).

Although motherese is directed toward helping the child through the maze of language, parents seldom correct the grammatical mistakes their young children make (Brown, 1973). The ungrammatical, "Why the dog won't eat," is answered, "I don't think she feels good." If the mother noticed the aberrant form of the question, she ignored it. Parents do correct children who mislabel a picture. When Sarah said, "There's the animal farmhouse," her mother responded, "No, that's a lighthouse." Parents correct their children when the statement is not factually correct, but they turn a deaf ear to most of the ungrammatical constructions their children produce (Brown & Hanlon, 1970).

Motherese is an index of the parents' sensitivity to the language their child understands and uses. It is also an index of how responsive the parents are. Motherese provides the child with a well-formed, easy-to-understand, and intelligible model of language. Perhaps the most amazing part of motherese is that no one instructs parents in how to speak it. Parents make these speech modifications quickly and seemingly without thinking. Snow (1972) listened to mothers addressing their two-year-old and 10-year-old children. Mothers used simple constructions with the two-year-olds, but switched to much more elaborate ones with the 10-year-olds. When asked, the mothers said they were not aware that they altered their speech and that they were not consciously providing different models of language for the children.

**The effect of motherese on language development**

The preceding account of parents' speech modification is interesting. However, an important question is what effect these modifications have on language acquisition. If parents do not shorten their sentences, modify their intonation, ask endless questions, and expand sentences, does the child's language acquisition suffer? Or, stated positively, does motherese facilitate the acquisition of language?

This seems like an easy question to answer, but it is not. We have listed a dozen ways that parents alter their speech when talking to children. It may be that all of these are necessary to introduce language to a child. It may be that just a few modifications are necessary to spur the child's understanding and use of language. Some modifications may be reflected in more advanced speech the next day. Other modifications may not have an impact for six months (Horowitz & Sullivan, 1981).

At least two of the modifications of motherese give clear evidence of facilitating language. If the parents ask questions and if the parents expand their child's early sentences, the child is likely to make rapid linguistic progress (Hoff-Ginsberg, 1982). Questioning children seems to focus their attention on the subject. The fact that a question demands a response keeps the child involved. Using questions, then, is primarily an attention-getting device. Expanding sentences assists language more directly. When parents expand a child's sentence, they show the child how the sentence could be said with all the flourishes of adult syntax (Hoff-Ginsberg & Shatz, 1982). They also provide a model of language that is slightly more complex than the child's. This slight discrepancy between the adult's speech and the child's speech facilitates the child's mastery of language. Children seem to learn rapidly when information is presented at a level that is slightly above their own.

**A responsive environment**

Modifying the intonation and simplifying sentences seems to come very naturally to most parents. What seems to vary enormously is when and how often parents provide this language model for their children.

Some parents are constantly talking with their children. While children are being diapered and dressed, parents carry on a conversation about the clothes, naming each article several times. During the bath, parents again use simple, short sentences to talk about parts of the body, water, and the toys that are floating around the tub. At lunch and storytime, the infant's environment is again described in detail, using simple, repetitious sentences.

In other homes, this monologue is missing. Parents dressing their child rely more on commands, urging the child to "hold still" and limiting the conversation to instructions like "turn around." During lunch, the child is warned "don't spill" and is urged to "drink your milk." The description of the environment is missing entirely, and the mother is not attentive to the child's activities. It is not surprising that children in these homes learn language more slowly than children who are treated to a running monologue that links language with the child's activities (Hoff-Ginsburg & Shatz, 1982).

Perhaps a more compelling demonstration of the importance of the mother's responsiveness is provided by two case histories collected by Evelyn Thoman (1981) as part of the Connecticut Longitudinal Study. Thoman began observing children the day after birth and followed the children intensively for five weeks, spending entire days at their homes. When the children had their first and third birthdays, they were visited again.

After examining over one million pieces of information, Thoman concludes that the mother-child interaction during the first five weeks after birth forms a pattern that will ultimately influence language, emotional, and cognitive development. She describes two mothers, who are anonymously labeled Alpha and Beta. These two mothers represent the extremes of mother-infant interaction. Although they did not differ in the amount of time they devoted to taking care of their infants, Alpha played, stimulated, and looked at her child twice as much as Beta.

When Thoman evaluated these infants at one year of age, Beta's infant cried for 51 minutes during the six hours of observation. Alpha's baby cried for six minutes. On an intelligence test, Alpha's child had an IQ of 112. Beta's infant had an IQ of 74. The assessment of language indicated that the lack of interaction had seriously affected the language skills of Beta's child. Thoman's point is that patterns established in mother-infant relationships during the early weeks of life were good predictors of the child's emotional, intellectual, and linguistic sophistication at one year of age. Of course, the pattern that is established also depends on the infant. An unresponsive infant could certainly alter the level of the mother's play.

Thoman's position is echoed by other investigators interested in language. They find, not surprisingly, that children who learn language rapidly have attentive, responsive mothers (Farran, 1982). Responsive mothers attend to the child's gestures, repeat the child's immature sentences, and encourage exploration. In the process, they link their speech to the child's activities (Schachter, 1979).

If an unresponsive mother can affect her child's language, then we need to ask why some mothers are not responsive. Catherine Snow suggests that social class is a factor. She presents a convincing picture of the woman living in poverty, who does not have the time or the mental or physical resources to be responsive to her child (Snow, Dubber, & Blauw, 1982). Parents from the lower socioeconomic classes use simple speech patterns and short sentences. This is called a *restricted language code*. The language environment they provide their children is more likely to focus on concrete occurrences and describe ongoing events. In contrast, middle-class parents use an *elaborated language code*. Their sentences are longer, more complex, and are more likely to deal with abstractions (Bernstein, 1966).

If the restricted code of lower-class parents is transmitted to children, their language skills may gradually fall behind. Some evidence for this position comes from the Abecedarian project in North Carolina. The lower-class mothers in this study used many commands when speaking to their children and adopted an authoritarian style of child rearing. Infants of some of these mothers were placed in an environment especially designed to foster language skills. By 3½ years of age, these children had well developed language skills and could use language to play, to explore, and to communicate. Children who had not had the advantage of the elaborated language environment had fallen far behind (Ramey, MacPhee, & Yeates, 1982).

Another variable that is often discussed in connection with language delays is parental education. Schachter (1979) examined the mother-infant interaction patterns in a group of well-educated black mothers, a group of well-educated white mothers, and a group of poorly educated black mothers. The two well-educated groups were responsive to their infants. The poorly educated mothers were not. Rather than repeating or expanding their child's language, these poorly educated mothers repeated the same commands to the child, getting louder each time. They ignored the child's activities and language. The differences in Schachter's three groups were all related to education. No differences existed between the two racial groups. Educated mothers of both races asked more questions, described current events more often, spent more time reading to their children, and issued fewer commands.

Family instability can also affect language. Family instability can mean having several adult caretakers; it can mean that siblings assume a large share of the responsibility for the child; and it can mean that few routines are followed in the home (Farran, 1982). These changes might well dilute the language environment surrounding the child and reduce the responsiveness of the environment.

Motherese involves specific modifications of speech that help the child learn language. In an earlier section, these modifications were presented dispassionately. Evelyn Thoman (1981) points out that we do not really capture the mother-infant interaction if we leave out the affective side of their communication or if we ignore the other features of the environment. The parents' social class, their education, and the family's stability are all part of the larger environment, and all of these variables can affect the opportunities for interaction as well as the mother's motivation to play with her child.

## Individual differences in language acquisition

The discussion so far gives the impression that all children follow exactly the same steps as they learn language. Overall this is true. Children first use one-word sentences, then two-word sentences that describe their world. Furthermore, they acquire more complex constructions in the same order. But within these steps, children do differ. Katherine Nelson (1973, 1981) was the first to notice the different learning styles children use. Some children emphasize nouns in their early speech. As many as 35 to 40 of their first 50 words will be nouns. Dianne Horgan (1980) refers to these children as "noun lovers." Noun lovers are especially common among the first children of middle-class parents. The parents delight in labeling every object in the environment. These children seem to absorb language with ease and are often regarded as precocious.

Their counterparts, those children who are not as enthusiastic about nouns, are called "noun leavers." They are usually from lower socioeconomic backgrounds. They are not as likely to be first-born children. They are often left-handed. When they learn to talk, their language focuses on relationships. They are likely to use a lot of stock phrases like, "Have a good day," "See you later," and "How about."

Dianne Horgan's daughter, Kelly, is a left-handed noun leaver. Only 17 of her first 50 words were nouns. She was slower to develop language than most of the children in the literature. But her language was wonderfully expressive, and she often invented her own labels for objects. Her first questions did not begin with "What" or "Where." She asked, "How about daddy go get a hamburger?" and, "How about what you want to eat?" Kelly used a lot of expressions in her speech. "How about" was one that she adapted for asking questions. Kelly did eventually go through a phase of noun learning. But even when she used nouns more, her speech still differed from the speech of noun lovers (Horgan, 1980). It is interesting that all of the left-handed children that Horgan tested were like Kelly. Perhaps these children were processing language in a different manner, at least initially.

The search for different learning styles among children soon turned into a search for different styles among mothers. Keith Nelson (1980) points out that some mothers hog the floor, and the children have little chance to speak. This style may affect how children behave in conversations even though it does not affect their understanding of the language. The tendency of some mothers to expand their child's sentences has already been mentioned. While some mothers expanded more than half of the child's statements, other mothers rarely expanded a sentence. Because the toddler's conversational skills are limited, it is usually the mother who determines the length of a conversation. It can be just one turn for the mother and one for the child. Or, it can be 8 or 10 turns. At four years of age, children who have engaged in longer conversations have superior communication skills (Nelson, 1980).

Individual differences are a factor in learning language. These differences remained in the background while the general process of language acquisition was explored. Now that we understand the broad outlines of language, investigators are devoting more attention to the different styles that children use to acquire language and the different ways parents convey information about language.

**Bilingual environments**

Whenever environmental effects are discussed, a question is raised about bilingual children. Does a bilingual environment enhance or inhibit language acquisition? Does the sensitive period for language acquisition affect the individual's ability to learn a second language? These questions have never been more important. The linguistic isolation that characterized the United States for so many years is over. The need for everyone to be able to speak a second language becomes more obvious every day. Hence, we need to explore the acquisition of a second language with as much ingenuity as we have devoted to studying the first language.

Specific areas of the brain facilitate the acquisition of the first language. What happens to these areas when two or more languages are learned? The answer seems to depend on when the second language is learned. If both languages are learned in infancy, they are likely to be coded in the left hemisphere just as a single language. If, however, a second language is learned after infancy, the right hemisphere becomes more involved (Lambert, 1981).

The *language mapping* technique developed by Penfield is one way to examine whether two languages are processed differently in the brain. To date, two bilingual and four trilingual subjects have participated in cortical mapping studies prior to neurosurgery (Whitaker, Bub, & Leventer, 1981). During this procedure, the subjects were asked to name objects while electrical stimulation was applied to the surface of the brain. When brain tissue around the language areas was stimulated, it became clear that the languages the subjects spoke were processed in somewhat different areas of the brain (see Figure 8–8).

Learning two languages during the first years of life has some advantages. If both languages are learned simultaneously during infancy, they will be well integrated. A second language learned later is likely to remain more compartmentalized. Proof comes from an association experiment conducted in Canada. The bilingual subjects were asked to think of one word that could be used to relate *chaise* (chair), "food," "desk," *bois* (wood), and *manger* (to eat). The subjects who had learned French and English as infants were more likely to think of the correct answer "table" than subjects who had learned the languages sequentially (Lambert, 1981).

The literature on bilingual children has often hinted that the younger you are when you learn a second language, the easier it is to learn (Lenneberg, 1967). Learning a language after puberty is not only supposed to be slower, it is supposed to be less successful than normal first language learning (Krashen, 1975). Actually, adults can make very rapid progress when they must learn a second language. Catherine Snow and her Dutch colleague, Marian Hoefnagel-Hohle (1978), studied 51 English-speaking children and adults who went to Holland for a year. They were tested three times during their first year as

**Figure 8–8**  **Bilingual brains**

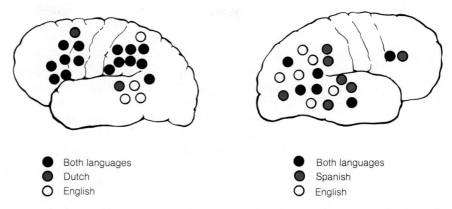

● Both languages
◐ Dutch
○ English

● Both languages
◐ Spanish
○ English

Individuals who speak two languages may have additional areas of the brain devoted to language. In the bilingual individuals pictured, some areas of the brain coded both languages, some coded only one language. The dark circles indicate areas in which both languages were coded. The other circles indicate areas in which only one language was coded.

Source: Whitaker, H. A., Bub, D. & Leventer, S. (1981). Neurolinguistic aspects of language acquisition and bilingualism. *Annals of the New York Academy of Sciences, 379*, p. 72.

they tried to pick up the language at school or work. The 12- to 15-year-olds learned the language most rapidly. At the end of a year, they had almost achieved native fluency. The adults learned the language quickly at the beginning of the year, but their improvement slowed after the first three months. For the 6- to 10-year-olds, the reverse was true. Although these children started slowly, by the end of the year, they had almost mastered the language. The slowest learning occurred in the youngest subjects (three to five years). This study has made psycholinguists question the younger-is-better notion. A more appropriate conclusion seems to be that children and adults use somewhat different processes to learn a second language (McLaughlin, 1981).

Discussions of bilingual children inevitably spark a debate about whether their cognitive development is affected. One side argues that bilingual children will encounter problems in abstract thinking and problem solving if they have not fully developed cognitively in at least one language before they learn a second (Cummins, 1980). Early studies that compared the cognitive skills of bilingual and monolingual children reported a host of deficits in the children who spoke two languages (Lambert, 1981). But when the studies were examined closely, it became obvious that many of the bilingual children were from the lower social classes. The children who spoke only one language were middle- and upper-class children. The differences in cognitive skills could well have been due to the difference in social class.

When monolingual and bilingual children have been matched on age, sex, and social class, as in several Canadian studies, the bilingual children have consistently achieved higher scores on a variety of cognitive assessments. Bilingual youngsters in Montreal were more intelligent, achieved higher grade levels on achievement tests, and did better in French (the language used in the schools). Peal and Lambert (1962) add that the bilingual children had "developed a more diversified structure of intelligence and more flexibility of thought."

The Canadian studies have since been replicated in Singapore, Switzerland, South Africa, Israel, and New York. These studies paint a picture of benefits, not deficits, accruing to bilingual children. Children who can speak two languages have a cognitive and linguistic flexibility that surfaces in tests of creativity, divergent thinking, and problem solving. Lambert (1981) concludes that bilingualism enhances the flexibility of a host of cognitive processes.

Lambert is quick to point out that in all of these studies, the second language conferred additional status and was never intended to replace the first. If minority children find that learning English means giving up their culture or attaching less importance to it, they are likely to be ambivalent. In addition, if they are not fluent in the second language but are urged to give up the first, their cognitive and academic proficiency may be affected (Cummins, 1980). The advantages of bilingualism are most likely to occur when children are encouraged to be proud of their native language and culture while they learn a new language.

Snow's study of children learning Dutch did indicate that occasionally the new language caused some interference with the old language. This was most common during the preschool years. The confusion preschoolers experience results from having to untangle two languages simultaneously. Because they have to sort out the sounds, words, order, and rules for two languages, children raised in bilingual homes often experience short delays in language development. Normally, the different vocabularies and grammatical rules are straightened out by the time the child begins school.

## SUMMARY

Communication is critical to the survival of many animals. Even a brief look at communication skills in the animal kingdom reveals a surprising array of behaviors, gestures, sounds, and alarms that convey information. Despite the variety of these communications, no other species has developed as flexible or open a communication system as humans. The very uniqueness of our language makes it a challenge to explore.

Children seem to acquire language in a twinkling. They learn so readily and with so little overt tutoring that it is tempting to conclude that languages are easy to learn. They are not. The mastery of the sounds, meaning, form, and order of human language is a tremendously complex process. Because languages are so complex and because children learn them so readily, many psycholinguists are persuaded that some facility for language is built into the brain. The language areas of the brain and the universal steps that children follow in the early stages of language acquisition support this view.

Recognizing the importance of these areas of the brain does not preclude a major role for the environment. The short, simple, repetitious sentences that parents use when speaking to a toddler provide the keys to adult syntax. In addition, parents weave language around the child's actions, helping link objects and words.

Children's thoughts form part of the foundation for language. The fact that children talk about agents, actions, and objects in their early sentences is taken as evidence that they are mapping language onto events that they understand cognitively. Hence, to study language, psycholinguists have taken a longer look at the concepts the child acquires before language is used. Specifically, children must understand the permanence of objects before they can attach a word to them.

The fact that some children love nouns and some children leave them has awakened researchers to the individual styles that characterize a child's early language. These styles appear to have biological as well as environmental underpinnings.

Learning a second language poses an intriguing puzzle to psycholinguists, partly because how you learn the language seems to depend on when you learn it. Two languages learned in infancy are interwoven, but languages learned after five or six seem to be kept somewhat separate. Despite some thoughts to the contrary, adults are certainly able to acquire a second language readily. It may be that they use a different process to learn the language, but they can still learn efficiently.

The study of language is inextricably tied to the study of thought. Psychologists separate them when possible, trying to understand the factors that drive each skill. But our ultimate objective is to understand the development of all of the child's cognitive skills—language, thought, images, and memories. In the next chapter, the discussion of cognitive development will extend to the child's thought processes.

**Structuralism**

    Jean Piaget
    Assumptions and major concepts
    The functioning of the child

**Stages of development**

    Sensory motor development
    Preoperational thought
    Concrete operations
    Formal operations

**The keys to cognitive progress**

    The development of the central nervous system
    Disequilibration
    Experience
    Social transmission
    Other factors influencing cognitive development
    Evaluation of the structuralist theory

**Summary**

# CHAPTER 9

# Cognitive development

Mature thought is boundless, flexible, and diverse. Adults can hypothesize about the future. They can relive the past. They can imagine events that have never occurred. They can solve problems systematically and logically. They can isolate information from past experiences and apply that information to current tasks. In short, their cognitive skills are highly developed. In contrast, infants lack all of these skills. Instead they have a repertoire of reflexes and their brains are organized to help them obtain information about the environment; but their cognitive powers are limited to processing the sights, sounds, and tastes of their immediate environment. During the years from infancy to adulthood, the immature sensations of the infant are gradually replaced by the adult's multifaceted thinking skills. This chapter describes the steps infants take as they move from sensations and reflexes toward the flexible thought of adults.

Cognitive development is a complex subject because the gap between the reflexes of infants and the cognitive skills of adults is so large. But there is a further complication. Psychologists do not agree on the course of cognitive development. Two major schools of thought exist, and each describes a different path to adult thinking skills.

The first school, described in this chapter, reflects the pervasive influence of Jean Piaget and is known as the structuralist position. The second school, presented in Chapter 10, is properly labeled as an information processing position and emanates from experimental psychology and studies of adult thought. Although the two positions share some common ground, they diverge at many points. As the two positions are presented and evaluated, the reader will get a firsthand view of the importance of theory in child development. Hence, these chapters are not only about cognitive development, they are about the way psychologists approach this topic.

This chapter begins by introducing Jean Piaget. The initial focus on one man is useful because he is the one most directly responsible for translating the philosophical tenets of structuralism into a description of cognitive development. A knowledge of Piaget's background helps the reader understand the mixture of biology and philosophy that influences his views. But the structuralist view is not limited to Piaget. In Geneva, he surrounded himself with many capable scientists, and it is really more accurate to speak of the Genevan position when presenting research from Piaget's laboratory.

Although Piaget is known most widely as a stage theorist, his position incorporates much more than separate stages of development. Hence, a section on the assumptions of structuralism is included to provide a framework for the consideration of stages. The discussion then moves to a detailed description of the thought processes used by infants, preschoolers, school-age children, and adolescents. The structures that define each age group are outlined and current experiments that extend, refine, or refute Piaget's ideas are considered. In a final section, the factors that encourage cognitive progress are considered and the structuralist position is evaluated.

## STRUCTURALISM

Structuralism owes such a debt to Piaget that the discussion must begin with his formulations concerning cognitive development. To really grasp Piaget's theory, we need to understand the forces that shaped his thoughts. A brief biographical sketch will introduce the man and his ideas.

**Jean Piaget**

Piaget began his scientific career at the tender age of 10 when he published his observations of an albino sparrow in a professional journal. His biological bent during these early years was strong, and he actively pursued zoology and the study of shellfish. His contribution to the field was regarded so highly that he was offered a position as the director of a museum before he completed high school. Despite this early recognition, Piaget's godfather was chagrined that young Jean's education was so narrowly confined to the sciences. He introduced Piaget to philosophy and to the debates about the nature of man that had aroused Descartes and Rousseau. Piaget, an apt pupil, soon became interested in the study of knowledge, formally known as epistemology. By the time he entered college, Piaget was well acquainted with two views of the world— the sciences, where facts are king, and philosophy, where ideas reign supreme. To Piaget, both approaches were incomplete. From his vantage point, the ideas of the philosophers were never formally tested. Their acceptance or rejection seemed to depend solely on the quality of the author's arguments. On the other hand, facts in the sciences often remained isolated. As a result, they lacked the power of more integrated theories. Piaget concluded that to really understand a phenomenon, one had to gather facts into cohesive ideas and subject those ideas to empirical tests. Throughout his life, he was impatient with *empiricists* who collected isolated facts and never attempted to mold them into a coherent view of a phenomenon. But he was equally impatient with philosophical arguments that eschewed the objectivity of data (Bringuier, 1980).

After completing his undergraduate degree and his doctorate in biology, Piaget turned to the fledgling field of psychology. He was exposed to the ideas of Freud and studied clinical psychology at the Sorbonne in Paris. While in Paris, he was hired to help with the tedious process of standardizing an intel-

**Jean Piaget**

*Courtesy World Health Organization*
Jean Piaget's contributions to developmental psychology changed the face of the field.

ligence test that was being developed in Alfred Binet's laboratory. While asking hundreds of children the same questions, Piaget discovered that children who did not know the correct answers often gave similar wrong answers. These answers reflected their way of reasoning about the question and made perfect sense from their point of view. As Piaget thought about the reasons for the wrong answers, he decided that the younger children approached the questions differently than the older children who gave the correct answer. This insight became a major tenet in his theory of cognitive development. The thought processes used at different ages are not just more sophisticated—they are qualitatively different (Ginsburg & Opper, 1979).

This quick sketch identifies three sets of experiences that helped frame Piaget's views of cognitive development. The first was his introduction to science and the study of biology. His view of cognitive development begins by acknowledging that we are biological organisms subject to the same biological forces as other animals (Piaget, 1971). The second was his fondness for philosophy. One of Piaget's major goals was to understand how children acquire knowledge. He even called himself a genetic epistemologist, a title that underscored his interest in both biology and knowledge. A final thread that was woven into this theory came from Binet's laboratory. Here he gained insight into children's thought processes and began to formulate practical notions about how to investigate the evolution of knowledge.

The rest of Piaget's long career was devoted to studying the structure of thought and examining the evolution of knowledge from infancy to adulthood. In 1921, he accepted a post as Director of Research at the Rousseau Institute in Geneva. At the institute, he conducted and directed research that lead to more than 40 books and hundreds of articles covering almost every aspect of a child's thought processes. Piaget interviewed children about the movements of the sun and moon. He asked them about the passage of time. He invented stories about disobedient children to see how his young subjects perceived right and wrong. His interest in how the child perceived the world led him to investigate the child's understanding of physical causality and the properties of objects. His research included his famous studies of his own children during infancy and extended to an investigation of adolescent logic that has become a classic in developmental psychology.

Over the years Piaget devised an interview technique called the *clinical method*. Unlike standardized interviews in which all children are presented with the same list of questions, the clinical method allows the answers of the child to guide the investigator's questioning. Piaget also realized early in his career that asking children questions was not nearly as informative as watching them manipulate common objects and describe their conclusions. So he devised problems that required children to demonstrate their thinking skills. Many of these problems have become standards in the field of developmental psychology precisely because they let us watch the child's thought processes in action.

Piaget's life was disciplined and constructed around his research and writing. He seldom took vacations, unless they were working ones. His only respites from work were his long bike rides on Saturday and reading an occasional novel. Even on Sundays, he worked in his study, producing four or five pages of text (Bringuier, 1980). His consuming passion was understanding the acquisition of knowledge.

**Assumptions and major concepts**

**The child as an active organism.**   At the heart of the structuralist theory is the assumption that children are active organisms capable of directing their own activities and extracting information from the environment. Infants build their understanding of the world from their actions (Piaget, 1954). Similarly, adolescents need to play with a puzzle if they are to solve it. Active involvement with a problem does not, however, always require physical manipulation of objects. Mental manipulation or thinking about a problem is a form of active involvement used by older children and adults (Piaget, 1970; Kuhn, 1981).

The emphasis Piaget places on the active child has sometimes been construed to mean that children cannot be taught. Readers of Rousseau will recognize Piaget as a kindred spirit, for both men endorse unfettered exploration and believe that children should be encouraged to draw their own conclusions

(Piaget, 1964). However, to interpret these beliefs as an indictment of all teaching is to oversimplify Piaget's theory and to miss his point. Piaget and other structuralists would recommend providing an environment for children that is appropriate for their level of thought. In such an environment, children would be encouraged to explore. The conclusions they drew from their exploration would become an integral part of their thought structure—not a feeble copy of someone else's. Throughout the school years, then, teaching should mean providing an environment for exploring math, language, science, and history, and encouraging children to investigate, draw conclusions, revise, and generalize from their experience. To facilitate thought, teachers could question a child's reasoning, offer other points of view, and challenge conclusions, rather than merely providing the right answer. In short, Piaget feels that teachers should serve as guides to the knowledge of the world, but acquiring that knowledge is really the child's province (Piaget, 1970).

**Constructivism.** Piaget insists that children are actively exploring, processing, and evaluating their environments, even when they are sitting quietly. As a by-product of their exploration, children constantly augment their conceptions of the world. New conceptions form the base for further exploring, and the cycle of constructionism begins again. As the cycle is repeated and extended, children's thoughts begin to approximate adults' thoughts. In a constructivistic view, then, each new understanding builds on the child's old understanding, but carries the thinking a step further (Furth, 1969). A parallel exists in language acquisition. As described in the previous chapter, children first put the negative word at the beginning of a sentence, then in the middle of the sentence, and finally they use the adult form of the negative. Children's thought follows a similar progression beginning with a global, unintegrated conception of objects or causal relationships, and proceeding gradually to more mature concepts.

Constructivism also assumes that current concepts determine how you react to new events or information. If you understand adding and subtracting, you can use these operations as a basis for understanding multiplication. But you would have a great deal of difficulty understanding how to solve quadratic equations. In Piaget's view, the knowledge or the structure of numbers that allows addition can be extended to understand simple multiplication. This structure or organization is not sufficiently complex to extend quickly to quadratic equations.

Constructivism implies a direction to development (see Figure 9–1). Each new understanding of the world becomes more similar to mature thought. The notion that there is a specific direction to development also suggests that there are logical truths for the child to discover. Gravity is an example. On our planet, objects that are released fall to the ground. Within a few months, infants learn to look down for objects that have been released. A child reared on a space shuttle might develop a different conception because objects do not fall in a weightless environment. Because all children experience the effects of

**Figure 9–1**                **Constructivism**

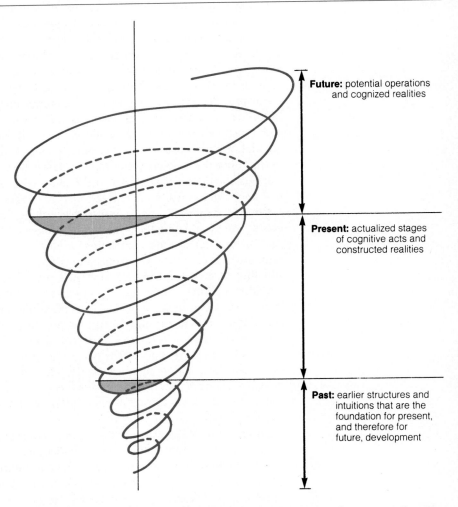

Future: potential operations and cognized realities

Present: actualized stages of cognitive acts and constructed realities

Past: earlier structures and intuitions that are the foundation for present, and therefore for future, development

The structuralists assume that knowledge is constructed from earlier, more rudimentary understandings.

Source: Langer, J. (1969). *Theories of Development (p. 96).* New York: Holt, Rinehart & Winston.

gravity, the permanence of objects, and the flow of liquids, the concepts that they construct are similar.

The view that children construct their own reality follows from the basic assumption that children are active organisms. But this global concept does not tell us how children accomplish this task. To understand how this occurs, we need to look at exactly what happens when children explore their environments.

**The functioning of the child**

An infant, a kindergarten child, a high school senior, and an adult all construct their knowledge in a similar way—they *adapt* to their environment and *organize* the information they encounter in the environment. It is important to emphasize that the processes of learning are the same throughout the life span because Piaget is often portrayed as a stage theorist and the constant processes that shape cognitive development are ignored.

**Adaptation.** The child has two ways of adapting to the environment. The first is *assimilation* and refers to the fact that children's structures determine how they understand an object. To illustrate the process of assimilation, let us consider infants who have learned to grasp objects. They assimilate objects to this grasping behavior. They grasp things that are not normally grasped, like noses and hair, thereby forcing objects to fit with what they already know (Langer, 1969). This distortion of reality through assimilation is also found in adolescents and adults. To assimilate information, children do not have to adapt their structures. The new information and events are forced to fit the existing concepts.

The other half of the child's ability to adapt to the environment is *accommodation*. When children accommodate, they modify their existing structure. Infants who previously grasped hair and noses now modify that grasp. They accommodate their grasping structure to take into consideration the different aspects of a person's hair and nose. Children cannot learn their ABCs one day and read the next. Each new change has to be integrated into the existing structure.

Accommodation and assimilation are complimentary processes that occur simultaneously. Using these two processes, children can adapt readily to their environment, assimilating new information to their current structures, and modifying their old structures to incorporate new information (see Figure 9–2).

**Organization.** Adaptations do not insure cognitive advances. Children must organize the information that results from their exploration and remember it; otherwise they will have to continually relearn the same information. In Piaget's view, the child's activity and construction result in an organized body of information called a *structure* (Furth, 1969). Structures describe the child's whole approach to the environment. Bruner captures the wholism and integration that characterize structures when he comments, "The position of a piece on a chessboard, the function of a word in a sentence, a particular facial expression, the color or placement of a (traffic) light cannot be interpreted without reference to the person's internalized rules of chess or language, the conventions he holds concerning human interaction, the traffic rules in force in his mind" (Bruner, 1976, p. 4). In other words, children and adults maintain an internalized *organization* of various aspects of the world.

Structures also include ways to transform information. If you know that all dogs are mammals and that "Dustmop" is a dog, then you can transform those two statements to gain a new bit of information—"Dustmop" is a mammal. The ability to transform information adds a new dimension to thought. Our

**Figure 9—2**                              **Adaptation**

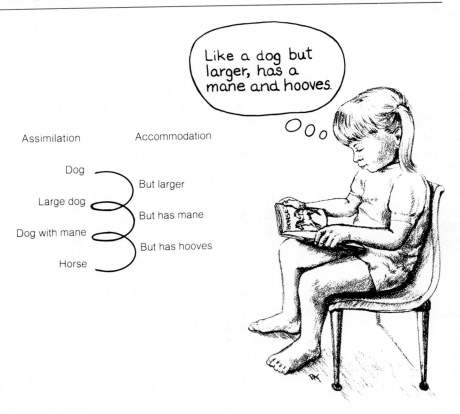

Adaptation involves the complimentary processes of assimilation and accommodation. These two processes allow the child to understand new objects and events in the environment.

Source: Flavell, J. (1977). *Cognitive Development,* Englewood Cliffs, NJ: Prentice-Hall.

knowledge is no longer limited to actual experiences. We can consider events that have not been explored.

The principle of inertia is a good example of how transformations can extend our thought. Simply stated, the principle of inertia asserts that if nothing obstructs the movement of an object, say a car, the car will keep going forever. Because friction and air resistance are always present, we will never observe a car rolling merrily along with an empty fuel tank. But we can transform our information about friction and air resistance and imagine what would happen if they did not exist. In the process, we would rediscover the principle of inertia (Inhelder & Piaget, 1958).

Structures are dynamic and change as new information is gleaned from the environment (Inhelder & Piaget, 1979). New structures are constantly being created from old ones. Each new structure is more stable because it encompasses more information about the world. As new, more complete structures are formed, they subsume the earlier structures. If, as an adult, you were confronted with an object that you could not identify, you could revert to the action modes of the sensory motor stage. For example, college students, when asked to experiment with four colorless liquids, often begin by smelling them. As an adult, you have all of the transformations of an adult available to you, yet you can also use the actions of a child.

Although a person's structures are constantly being revised, we can describe the child's structures at a single point in time. Think of cognitive development as a 16 millimeter film with each frame representing the child's evolving cognitive structures. If we stop the film on all five-year-old children and examine just that frame, we are likely to see that they think about the world in similar ways. The stages that Piaget and his colleagues described are best understood as such individual frames of an ongoing film (Inhelder, 1962).

Understanding structures is sometimes difficult because a structure is an abstraction from the data that then becomes important in its own right (Tomlinson-Keasey, 1982). Such abstractions are very common in science. The equator is not a painted line encircling the globe, but it does exist as the dividing line between the northern and southern hemispheres (Feldman & Toulmin, 1975). Structures are similar. You cannot see them just as you cannot see the equator, but they describe the thoughts of the child and the transformations that the child is capable of executing (Inhelder & Piaget, 1979). While weighing your own reaction to the notion of structures, keep in mind the essentials from Piaget's point of view. Structures result from exploration, they represent the child's integration of knowledge, they include ways to transform that knowledge, and they are dynamic, not static.

**Equilibration.** Many of the concepts that are important to Piaget's theory reflect his early biological training. This is especially true of *equilibration*. Equilibration refers to the coordination between the child's exploration and the structures that result from that exploration. The two are complimentary. At any particular moment, children may encounter a new event or new information or even think about familiar information in a new way. This may disrupt the child's structures and cause a state of disequilibrium. But children have the means to restore equilibrium. They can accommodate their current structures to the new information, or they can distort the new information to fit an already existing structure. As children progress from infancy to adulthood, they achieve broader and more integrated structures. These reflect successively higher levels of equilibrium (see Figure 9–1).

To summarize, children are active organisms who explore their environment and use that exploration as a basis for constructing concepts. They gather the sum of their knowledge into a coherent totality—a structure of thought—that includes concepts as well as ways to transform information. The two aspects of this process, the exploration and the structure that results, proceed in tandem through the process of equilibration.

This completes a short list of the concepts that Piaget uses to explain how children acquire knowledge and advance cognitively. These same processes are used throughout the life span. But Piaget does more than give us this general set of processes. Remember that he was intrigued with the wrong answers that children gave on IQ tests. After outlining the processes a child uses to acquire knowledge, he stops the film of cognitive development and examines the different structures used by infants, preschoolers, school-age children, and adolescents.

## STAGES OF DEVELOPMENT

Piaget described four major stages of development. The stages actually denote four qualitatively different thought structures. During the sensory motor period (birth to 2 years), actions are the primary mode of interaction with the environment. During the preoperational period (2 to 6 years), the child begins to use symbols. Only during the last two stages, concrete operational thought (7 to 11 years) and formal operational thought (12 to 16 years), do children become skilled at transforming information. As the stages are described in more detail, remember that the ages given are approximate. To Piaget, the structure defines the stage, not the child's age.

**Sensory motor development**

The first stage, sensory motor development, occupies approximately the first two years of a child's life. As described in Chapter 6, infants gradually modify their reflexes and begin to systematically explore their environments. Action is the dominant mode of interacting with the environment during the sensory motor period. Infants have to throw, grasp, bang, and suck on objects to understand them. These actions are the precursors of thought.

Toward the end of the sensory motor period, the child begins to use symbols. Piaget first noticed these symbols while watching his children search for objects that had disappeared. At 19 months, Jacqueline faced three different screens spread on the floor. Piaget showed her a toy bear, then hid it in his hand and moved his hand slowly under the first screen, the second screen, and under the third screen. Jacqueline searched immediately under the third screen. Her reaction suggests that she formed a mental image of the toy bear and followed it under all of the screens. If she did not find the toy bear on the first try, she extended her search, reversing the order that her father followed while hiding the toy bear. Jacqueline's search pattern demonstrates that she can remember the sequence of her father's actions. More importantly, she can reverse that image when conducting her search (Piaget, 1954). Here, then, is one of the first indications that an infant can form a symbol, remember it, and transform it (see Figure 9–3). Such symbols usher in the stage of preoperational development.

**Figure 9—3**          **Mentally reversing an action**

*Sue Markson*

A complex game of hide-and-seek suggests that even infants can mentally reverse the actions they have seen. This child follows the toy under one of the three screens. His perseverance in looking for the toy indicates that he can form a symbol, remember it, and transform it.

**Preoperational thought**

The use of mental symbols is the single most important feature of the preoperational period. The development of this skill is traced in Figure 9–4. In Phase 1, which occurs during the sensory motor period, children explore objects, registering how the object looks, feels, smells, tastes, and sounds. This exploration fosters the formation of an object concept. The next step toward

**Figure 9—4**          **Development of symbols**

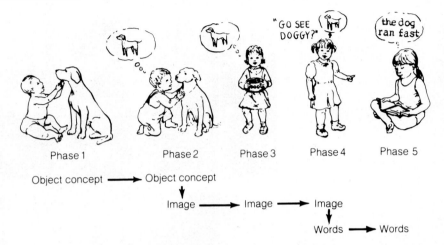

Phase 1          Phase 2          Phase 3          Phase 4          Phase 5

Object concept ⟶ Object concept
                        ↓
                      Image ⟶ Image ⟶ Image
                                            ↓
                                          Words ⟶ Words

Phase 1. Children explore objects and register how they feel, look, taste, touch, and sound. This exploration leads to an object concept at about eight or nine months of age.

Phase 2. Once children understand the characteristics of an object, they can form images of those objects.

Phase 3. Children can recall an image without the object being present. This is the first symbol and is the basis for all symbol use.

Phase 4. Words are attached to the image. Now children can talk about objects and events that have already occurred or will occur in the future.

Phase 5. As children move through preoperational thought and into concrete and formal operations, words become useful symbols that are no longer tied to images.

thought (Phase 2) occurs when children have such a comprehensive understanding of the object that they are able to form an image of it. On occasion, the process of forming an image is very overt. Toddlers can imitate an airplane by extending their arms and running around the house. This action mimics some of the characteristics of a plane and helps cement the child's image (Piaget, 1962). In Phase 3, images exist even though the object is not present. Children can recall situations and events from the past. They do not need an object to trigger their image. At this point, the image is separated from the immediate situation, and symbols, as opposed to actions, begin to assume much more importance in the child's life (Piaget, 1962). As parents supply the names for objects, children attach labels to the images they have formed (Phase 4). In later years, the image will no longer be necessary. Adolescents and adults can represent abstract events using words, mathematical notation, or formulas.

The use of symbols is most obvious in the child's acquisition of language. Words, attached to images, allow children to express their thoughts, experiences, and needs. The acquisition of language, from ages two to seven, coincides with the preoperational stage of thought. But the use of symbols is not restricted to language. Whenever children substitute one object for another, they create a symbol. A three-year-old playing house designates her friend as the Daddy, reserves the role of Mommy for herself, and recruits three stuffed animals as children. The friend, the child, and the stuffed animals are all symbols. A child pushing a flat block methodically across the floor and accompanying it with a syncopated "choo choo choo choo" is using the block to symbolize a train. Even a preschooler's drawing that looks like random brush strokes might be a symbol for the Empire State Building with King Kong on top (Gardner & Winner, 1982).

Until recently, psychologists have concentrated on language and have not systematically investigated other symbol systems. Howard Gardner and his colleagues are beginning to rectify this oversight. The longitudinal study that they are conducting as part of Project Zero follows the emergence of symbols in music, art, and play (Wolf & Gardner, 1981).

Because the ability to represent and create symbols is critical to cognitive development, any theory that proposes a sequence for the emergence of symbols is sure to capture the interest of researchers. Piaget suggested that images mediate between actions and symbols, that symbols begin to direct the child's actions, and that the use of symbols does not automatically confer sophisticated thinking skills. Each of these ideas has been explored in the decades since Piaget's first writings.

**Imagery, imitation, and action.** Piaget's view of the emergence of symbols emphasizes the role of imagery, imitation, and action. An image is the earliest symbol available to a child. Words come later and are attached to these early images. In some respects, the formation of images via imitation is the most important aspect of the emergence of symbols because images form the foundation for other symbols (Sinclair, 1975). Despite the importance that Piaget accorded to imagery, it has provoked the least research of all of his ideas.

Imagery, as an experimental topic, was ignored for years because it was so difficult to verify experimentally. Asking people about their images reminded psychologists of introspectionism, a topic that fell into disfavor early in the century. Allan Paivio (1971) was among the first to apply rigorous experimental techniques to the study of imagery in adults. His research established imagery as a useful vehicle for processing information and demonstrated that using both words and images to process information was superior to relying solely on words.

Investigating imagery in young children is a challenge to psychologists because the language skills of young children are so limited. Toddlers may have images even though they cannot tell us about them. Marian Perlmutter (1980) found a three-year-old who reacted to a bottle of honey by saying that she liked the chocolate stuff her mother used to give her, but not the yellow stuff. The mother confirmed that she used to put chocolate syrup or honey in the child's bottle, but added that the child had given up her bottle when she was 14 months old.

Because language skills are so variable in toddlers and preschoolers, psychologists have tried to study the child's images by looking at imitation and action. These processes are more visible than imagery, and theoretically, they are the precursors of images.

Peter Wolff and Joel Levin (1972) devised a memory task that incorporated action. Two toys were presented to preschoolers, and the children were instructed to remember the toys as a pair. One group of children was allowed to play with the toys; another group simply studied them. Actually playing with the toys helped the children remember which toys were paired. Presumably, the action component led to an image of the toys together. These results and the results of several follow-ups (Wolff, Levin, & Longobardi, 1974; Saltz & Dixon, 1982) provide support for Piaget's emphasis on actions forming images. "Until approximately the age of five, the generation of a percept or a dynamic image depends on concomitant motor output" (Wolff & Levin, 1972, p. 546).

For imitation to enhance the use of symbols, it must be deferred. Piaget explains this as the ability of the child to recreate the image at a later time and under different circumstances. Piaget's observations of his own children include several records of how children recreated an event to enhance their understanding. In one instance, the feet of a toy clown were caught in the top of Jacqueline's dress. She struggled to remove the doll's feet. As soon as she succeeded, she tried to reenact the scene. When she failed with the clown, she substituted her fingers and mimicked the scene. Piaget (1962) argues that Jacqueline recreated the events to help her represent what had happened.

When young infants imitate, they often try to reproduce an exact copy of the original, including irrelevant actions and gestures. Kenneth Kaye (1982) observed this in six-month-old infants. Mothers were told to show their infants how to obtain a toy by reaching around a Plexiglas barrier. As the mothers demonstrated, they often waved their hands to attract the infant's attention. Within a short time, the infants began to reach around the Plexiglas. As they did, many of the infants waved their hands (Kaye, 1982).

Imitation in older infants, toddlers, and preschoolers is typically much less exact. Actions that simply resemble a model are often used to represent what happened. Piaget, playing with 11-month-old Jacqueline, struck the notes of a xylophone with a little hammer. Jacqueline, having no hammer, drummed on the table (Piaget, 1962). Toddlers and preschoolers sometimes select a single feature of the model to help them represent the action. A train's whistle, an airplane's wings, or a doctor's stethoscope can recreate a complete image of a train, an airplane, or a doctor.

Summarizing the evidence on imagery, imitation, and action during the preoperational period is difficult. Imagery has only been recognized as a useful mode of processing information in the last decade, and the information that is available on toddlers' use of imagery is primarily anecdotal. Despite the lack of information about imagery, psychologists have had some success investigating imitation in toddlers and the effectiveness of action in toddlers. Incorporating either of these into memory experiments seems to help toddlers remember. The act of remembering an event and recreating it either through imitation or ac-

**Imagery, imitation, and action**

*Sue Markson*

Imitating an object helps the child form a mental image of that object. Such imitation is very common during the preoperational period.

tion is proof that the toddler is representing information symbolically. Hence, despite the fact that we cannot see the child's imagery at work, many psychologists accept its existence from the imitation and actions of the child.

**The power of symbols.** According to Piaget, the emergence of symbols and the gradual ascendance of thought over action are the hallmarks of the preoperational period. These advances make it possible for children to plan and regulate their own behavior. This directive function of thought can be seen in the way preschoolers use language. Over 50 years ago, Piaget (1926) noticed that at school much of the speech of six- and seven-year-olds was not specifically intended to communicate. Instead, language was used to announce what was happening at the moment and to direct action. Witness the following monologue by Lev.

> Lev sits down at his table alone: "I want to do that drawing, there . . . I want to draw something, I do. I shall need a big piece of paper to do that."
> Lev knocks over a game: "There! Everything's fallen down."
> Lev has just finished his drawing: "Now I want to do something else."
> (Piaget, 1926, p. 37)

The monologues observed by Piaget are intriguing and support his description of symbols accompanying and then directing action. Other psychologists, however, have offered a different interpretation of these same monologues.

Lev Vygotsky, a Russian psychologist, agreed with Piaget that preoperational children regulate their behavior by talking aloud. But in Vygotsky's view, these solitary monologues have a different origin and serve a different purpose. Initially, the speech of adults controls children's behavior. For example, a father might shout "Stop!" at a 10-month-old approaching an electrical outlet. The father's tone inhibits the child's behavior even though the words are not understood. Over time, the directives of adults begin to convey specific meanings, as when children are told to drink their milk. By three years of age, children begin to direct themselves. At first, these directives take the form of monologues similar to Lev's. But these monologues are quickly internalized and become *inner speech* or verbal thought (Vygotsky, 1962). Language now comes in two guises: internal language that is intended solely for the child and directs behavior as thought; and external language that is intended to communicate with others (Flavell, 1977).

The main difference between Piaget's and Vygotsky's theories is the origin of the language that directs action (Zivin, 1979). Vygotsky believes that this directive behavior has a social base and is transmitted via language. Through language, children emulate and internalize their parents' directives. Kaye (1982) characterizes this position as an "outside-in" view. In other words, the language originates outside the child and is internalized.

In contrast, Piaget presents an "inside-out" view. He feels that the important developments occur within the child. The child's actions lead to symbols. Once symbols in the form of images are present, thought can begin to direct action. If Piaget is right, any symbols, images, or words should have the power to regulate behavior. If Vygotsky is right, language should be the only regulating mechanism (Bronckart & Ventouras-Spycher, 1979).

Walter Mischel and his colleagues have investigated children's ability to regulate their own behavior. Four-year-olds were promised a pretzel if they could wait for an unspecified period. If they found that they could not wait, they were to ring a bell and they would receive a marshmallow. As the children waited, they displayed a range of self-regulatory behavior.

> When the distress of waiting seemed to become especially acute, children tended to reach for the termination signal, but in many cases seemed to stop themselves from signaling by abruptly creating external and internal distractions for themselves. They made up quiet songs ("Oh this is your land in Redwood City"), hid their heads in their arms, pounded the floor with their feet, fiddled playfully and teasingly with the signal bell, verbalized the contingency . . . prayed to the ceiling, and so on. In one dramatically effective self-distraction technique, after obviously experiencing much agitation, a little girl rested her head, sat limply, relaxed herself, and proceeded to fall sound asleep (Mischel, Ebbesen, & Zeiss, 1972, p. 215).

Mischel conducted another study that relied exclusively on imagery. Children were asked to imagine the marshmallows that were rewards had been transformed into clouds. This nonverbal technique was also successful in regulating behavior (Mischel & Baker, 1975).

In a more practical study of the use of images, Pamela Cole and Nora Newcombe (1983) told children working on a task to imagine that they shut a door between themselves and a noisy distraction. Shutting the door in their imagination made the room quiet again and removed the distraction. With this technique, children were able to continue concentrating on the task. The children reported no difficulty in using images and even elaborated on the images.

These three studies demonstrate that self-control is not derived exclusively from verbal techniques (Flavell, 1977). Language is useful in regulating behavior (Meichenbaum, 1977), but other symbols can also be used effectively. Piaget was correct in assuming that a variety of symbols could direct behavior. Vygotsky was wrong in one sense, but his experiments called attention to the social aspects of symbols, an aspect that Piaget's theory neglected.

Vygotsky's concern with social roles can be seen in the work of several contemporary psychologists. Howard Gardner agrees with Piaget about the contribution of actions and knowledge to the emergence of symbols. But Gardner also sees the value of Vygotsky's emphasis on social knowledge. The following vignette illustrates the toddler's early grasp of social roles.

> J, at 14 months, sees his father shake a dust mop out of the window. Later that same day, J finds a broom in the closet and drags it out. He pulls it to the window where his father had shaken out the mop and tries to push it up. When he has no luck, he goes off in search of his father, who hangs onto him, as J tries shaking the broom out the window. (Wolf & Gardner, 1981, p. 305–306)

Being able to imitate complex sequences is a clear sign that children distinguish between agents, actions, and objects. As described in the chapter on communication, such discriminations are obvious in the early phases of language acquisition.

Gardner's view represents a compromise between Piaget's position that symbols emerge from the child and Vygotsky's position that symbols are a product of the social setting. Both the child's action and the social setting are now seen as elements that contribute to the emergence of symbols and the regulation of behavior.

**Egocentrism.** The use of symbols represents a major cognitive advance over the actions common during the sensory motor stage. Still, the thoughts of preoperational children are very limited. In discussing these limitations, Piaget suggested that during the preoperational stage of development, thought is *egocentric*. In other words, events are understood only from the child's perspective. This is not to say that children purposefully ignore the perspectives of others; they simply are not aware that their experiences and the experiences of others differ (Piaget, 1926). Thought, play, and language are seemingly bound by this egocentricity.

To demonstrate what he meant by egocentrism, Piaget built a landscape of three mountains from *papier-mâché*. The mountains had different heights. One mountain had a red cross on it, a second was snow capped, and the third had a small house (Piaget & Inhelder, 1956). Piaget asked children to sit on one side of the mountains and, from that vantage point, to indicate what a doll sitting across the table would see. Preoperational children had trouble seeing the mountains from the doll's perspective. When asked what the doll saw, these children usually answered that the doll's view was the same as their own. These results prompted Piaget to conclude that the egocentric child "appears to be rooted to his own viewpoint in the narrowest and most restricted fashion, so that he cannot image any perspective but his own" (Piaget & Inhelder, 1956, p. 242).

The three mountains task requires the coordination and transformation of several bits of information (Cox, 1980). Children have to imagine what the doll is seeing and select that particular view from several photographs. In addition, they must ignore the view they see. When Piaget concluded that children are egocentric, did he mean that they did not know that the doll saw a different view, did he mean that children could not decide what the different view was, or did he mean that they were transfixed by their view and failed to consider others?

In the last decade, psychologists have tried to tease apart some of these factors. Eleanor Leung and Harriet Rheingold (1981) found that 12-month-old toddlers pointed at objects they wanted their mothers to look at. Toddlers who point are seemingly aware that their mother's view may be different from their own. Another simple but dramatic experiment reinforced this conclusion. Jacques Lempers at the University of Minnesota asked toddlers to show their mothers a photograph glued to the inside of a cube. The two-year-olds immediately turned the photo toward their mothers. The 18-month-olds also turned the photo towards their mothers, but they tried to adjust either their position or the cube so that they could still see the photograph. As early as 18 months, then, children know that other people see a different view of the world (Lempers, Flavell, & Flavell, 1977).

The photo task poses few problems for children because it is much simpler than the mountain task, the child controls what everyone sees, and no complex transformations of thought are required. Perhaps removing the complex transformations from the mountain task would make it easier. Helene Borke (1975) tried this. She had a muppet from *Sesame Street* point out how a scene looked from several vantage points. She also let children take an active part in the task. After this practice, the children found the mountain task much easier.

A fair conclusion seems to be that when the mountain task is simplified or when children are given strategies that help them coordinate all of the necessary information, they are able to visualize the perspective of another (Gelman, 1979). Before concluding, however, that preoperational children are not egocentric, let us look at another situation.

When using language, preoperational children sometimes have trouble seeing a different perspective. Krauss and Glucksberg (1977) asked children and adults to describe the objects pictured in Figure 9–5. Their descriptions had to be specific enough to allow another person to identify the object. Suppose you were listening to the labels created by these nursery school children. Could you pick out the "Strip-stripe," the "Eagle," or the "Wire"? All of these labels were given to the third object. Adults' descriptions were much more specific. They described the third object as "A zigzag with lines going in all different directions." It is important to note that the younger children were not generating words at random. The boy who created "Strip-stripe" could find that object if the experimenter asked. He knew what a "Strip-stripe" looked like even if no one else did. Results like these support the view that young children are not

**Figure 9–5**    **Egocentric speech**

| FORM | CHILD'S INITIAL DESCRIPTION | | | | | ADULT'S INITIAL DESCRIPTION |
|---|---|---|---|---|---|---|
| | 1 | 2 | 3 | 4 | 5 | |
| 1 | Man's legs | Airplane | Drapeholder | Zebra | Flying saucer | Looks like a motor from a motorboat. It has a thing hanging down with two teeth. |
| 2 | Mother's hat | Ring | Keyhole | Lion | Snake | It looks like two worms or snakes looking at each other. The bottom part looks like the rocker from a rocking chair. |
| 3 | Somebody running | Eagle | Throwing sticks | Strip-stripe | Wire | It's a zigzag with lines going in all different directions. |
| 4 | Daddy's shirt | Milk jug | Shoe hold | Coffeepot | Dog | It's like a spaceman's helmet; it's got two things going up the sides. |
| 5 | Another Daddy's shirt | Bird | Dress hold | Dress | Knife | This one looks something like a horse's head. |
| 6 | Mother's dress | Ideal | Digger hold | Caterpillar | Ghost | It's an upside-down cup. It's got two triangles, one on top of the other. |

When asked to describe objects so that another child can identify them, preschoolers give very egocentric responses. Adults, on the other hand, give longer, more complete descriptions.

very good at considering the needs of their listeners. But the story does not end here.

The task devised by Krauss and Glucksberg required the coordination of several bits of information. Not only did the children have to label a novel picture, they had to consider the listener's vocabulary and experience if they were to communicate effectively. The fact that preoperational children were not successful in this task does not necessarily mean that they never modify their speech for their listener.

Marilyn Shatz and Rochel Gelman (1973) demonstrated that four-year-olds can adjust their speech for their listeners. Four-year-olds were asked to tell an adult about a toy, and then tell a two-year-old about that same toy. When talking with two-year-olds, these preoperational children used short, simple sentences and tried to direct the toddler's attention to the toy. With adults, the four-year-olds used longer sentences, asked questions, voiced their own thoughts, and qualified the information. In short, they modified their language to fit the skills of their listener (Gelman, 1979).

Here again, we see that the difficulty of the task affects egocentrism. When children have to coordinate several pieces of information, they are likely to seem egocentric. John Flavell and his colleagues have tried to look systematically at the skills children must possess to perform these different tasks. The simplest Level 1 tasks, like showing pictures to an adult, only require children to identify what another person sees. Coordinating perspectives is not required in these tasks. Level 2 tasks require more complex assessments. Children must understand that people seeing an object from several perspectives see it somewhat differently. A picture of a turtle placed on top of a table can be right side up to the child and upside down to the experimenter. Coordinating these two perspectives is difficult for three-year-olds. Furthermore, brief explanations and demonstrations do not seem to make it any easier (Flavell, Everett, Croft, & Flavell, 1981).

Piaget argued that egocentrism pervaded the preoperational child's thought, language, and play. Recent research in this area suggests, however, that egocentrism is not responsible for the child's immature thought. Preoperational children can take the perspective of another person. They understand that an adult can be looking at a different scene. They can and do alter their speech depending on the person listening. What Piaget called egocentrism seems to be more accurately described as an inability to coordinate perspectives, not an inability to understand that people have different perspectives. The coordination of perspectives, and for that matter the coordination of several bits of information, requires the more flexible thought structures of concrete operations.

To summarize, preoperational thought focuses on symbols, how they emerge, how they transcend actions, and their limitations. Piaget recognized that the use of symbols is a monumental step in cognitive development. Once symbols are acquired, the child can represent objects that are no longer present. Freeing the child's thought processes from the immediate situation permits the child to transcend the constraints of time and space and opens the door for operational thought (Ginsburg & Opper, 1979).

**Concrete operations**     The preoperational child's limited ability to transform information is rectified with the advent of *concrete operations*. Children previously unable to approach problems systematically now demonstrate the ability to organize information logically. They begin to classify and order their environments (Inhelder & Piaget, 1964) and to coordinate information from several spheres. These logical skills are a major advance over the unorganized symbols of the preoperational period.

To describe concrete operations, it is useful to first look at some of the specific knowledge that children acquire. After seeing what concrete operational children know and how they differ from preoperational children, we will assess the logical strategies that must accompany this knowledge. Piaget examined the child's abilities in a host of areas. Our discussion will be limited to the child's ability to classify, order, and conserve.

**Classification.**   Being able to classify events and objects into larger categories brings order to the world. For adults, days are grouped into weeks, months, and years. The knowledge that it is Monday provides adults with a great deal of information. We know that it is the beginning of the workweek, that the next day is Tuesday, and that there are five days until the weekend. This single bit of information allows us to draw many other conclusions because Monday is part of a larger organization of knowledge.

Preoperational children lack this kind of organization. When asked to name the days of the week, a five-year-old girl might respond, "Sunday, Monday, Yesterday, Wednesday, and (after a long pause) November." To a preoperational child, this is perfectly logical since yesterday has the word day in it and she celebrates her birthday in November. The classification system that preoperational children use for days of the week is not the same as adults use. It is a gangly, undisciplined grab bag that contains a lot of miscellaneous information about days.

Inhelder and Piaget have traced the development of classification skills from the loose collections of preschoolers to the disciplined categories of adults. They presented children with a group of geometric shapes (see Figure 9–6A) and asked them to "put together those that are alike." Some of the youngest children selected a few of the shapes and put them together to form a complex object like a "house" or a "bridge" (see Figure 9–6B). Another strategy preschoolers used was to put several objects in a line. The boy that constructed the line in Figure 9–6C began with triangles, but was not able to follow through with that category. After two triangles, he started selecting squares. Neither his line (Figure 9–6C) nor the complex objects (Figure 9–6B) are actually a class because the objects included do not share a defining property (Inhelder & Piaget, 1964).

Between five and seven years of age, children begin to sort objects into real

**Figure 9—6**　　　　　　　　**Classification**

A. Objects to sort

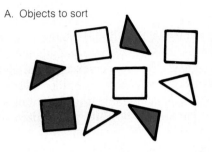

B. Preoperational arrangement

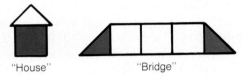

C. Preoperational arrangement

D. Hierarchical classification

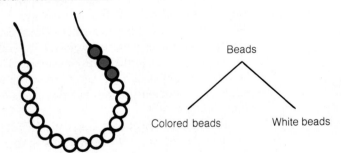

Classification skills are assessed by asking children to sort a collection of objects like those in (A). The collections in (B) and (C) illustrate two ways that preoperational children sort objects. They really don't use a defining characteristic to form a class. Hierarchical classification is illustrated in (D). To answer correctly, children have to group both colors of beads into the higher order category beads.

classes. All of the squares are put in one pile, and all of the triangles in another. This is certainly a step forward from building bridges. But the child's thought processes still lack the flexibility of adult thought (Ginsburg & Opper, 1979). Once the objects have been sorted by shape, these children have trouble resorting them by color. Considering two dimensions at the same time also poses problems. To demonstrate this, Ellin Kofsky (1966) showed preoperational children an arrangement of objects like the ones in Figure 9–6A and asked whether there were more blue objects or more squares. This is a more difficult question than it might seem because children have to sort the objects by color first, resort by shape, and compare the totals. The answers the children gave indicated that many of them were unable to understand that the objects could belong to several categories.

Mental transformations are also required when children are presented with the objects in Figure 9–6D and asked, "Are there more colored beads or more beads?" Preoperational children are overwhelmed by the abundance of colored beads and have difficulty forming the superordinate class beads. Hence, they answer that there are more colored beads. To Piaget, this proves that the children cannot think about the larger class and its subdivision simultaneously. They focus or center on one subclass, ignoring the whole (Ginsburg & Opper, 1979). Once children can transform information, the logical aspects of the classification task begin to override the perceptual cues. Children learn to *decenter* and consider both the subdivisions and the entire collection. As a result, children can count the colored objects and the square objects separately. Furthermore, they know that the class, beads, contains both color beads.

Complete classification systems often include several hierarchical steps. A good example, studied by most college students, is the biological classification system of phyla that includes organisms ranging from bacteria to mammals. Adults can move up and down such a classification system with ease. They know that all birds are animals, but that all animals are not mammals. They are able to compare abstract criteria and include parts of several classes in higher order classes.

The game "20 questions" has been used as an indicator of a child's ability to use information from different classes (Siegler, 1977). To play, a category is defined, like letters, numbers, or animals. Participants are allowed to ask yes or no questions until they think they know what the moderator has selected. Six-year-olds playing this game are often unable to use the information they have obtained. One little girl was trying to identify a number between 1 and 100. She used her first question to ask if the number was over 50. When told that it was, she asked if the number was 27. Obviously, this child does not understand the class of numbers between 50 and 100 and could not relate 27 to that class (Ronning, 1977).

Being able to move up and down a complex, hierarchically arranged classification system takes years of experience with the objects being classified. In many cases, abstract operations are required. These are the province of the last stage of cognitive development—formal operations.

The ability to classify begins in infancy and proceeds through a series of steps before reaching the plateau of adult functioning. In infancy, similarities are noted. Infants demonstrate by their actions that they see similarities between objects. Jonas Langer (1980) describes a one-year-old girl who began a play session by dropping all of the square blocks. Midway through the session, she switched her attention to circular rings and began dropping them. She was able to differentiate between the two kinds of blocks and separated them in her dropping game. As a three-year-old, she will begin calling one set squares and the other circles. When preoperational children add these symbols to their repertoire, they are able to communicate about their loose classification systems. The concrete operational child organizes objects in meaningful ways according to a single defining property and is able to form hierarchical classes. Formal operational children advance further when they understand abstract and complex classification systems that contain multiple hierarchies.

**Seriation.** Being able to order objects is another logical skill used daily by

**Figure 9—7**            **Seriation**

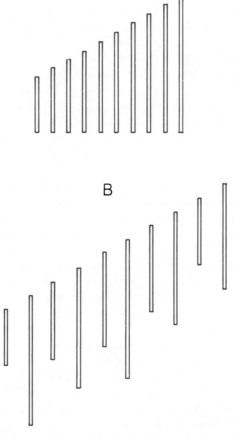

Seriation refers to the order of objects. When preoperational children are asked to put 10 sticks (A) in order from the smallest to the tallest, they sometimes focus on just one end of the stick. Their arrangement looks like (B) with only the tops of the sticks in line.

adults. People are either tall, of medium height, or short. Air temperatures range from over 100 degrees Fahrenheit to below freezing. Students' examinations are assigned grades ranging from A to F. Even members of the opposite sex are ordered from 1 to 10 on some abstract scale of attractiveness. Establishing an order to information and assigning numbers to that order is another way of organizing the world.

The ordering system that preoperational children use is as elementary as their classification system. They understand the extremes of an order—tall and short, hot and cold—but arranging the world in fine degrees is very difficult. Inhelder and Piaget (1964) discovered these difficulties by asking preoperational children to arrange a group of sticks from the tallest to the shortest (see Figure 9–7). A common strategy among the three-year-olds was to arrange one end of the sticks appropriately and ignore the other end (see Figure 9–7B). This is a familiar error among preoperational children; they are unable to decenter their attention and hence cannot organize the tall and short sticks in one arrangement (Voyat, 1982).

If the children could arrange the sticks from tallest to shortest without error, Piaget gave them a second set of sticks and asked them to integrate these new sticks into the first set. Being able to order both sets of sticks demonstrates that children are able to coordinate information from several sources—a hallmark of concrete operational thought.

Attaching numbers to an arrangement of objects increases the complexity of a task. Because of "Sesame Street" and nursery schools, most three-year-olds are able to count to 20. Their counting, however, is not meaningfully related to objects, and they do not necessarily use one number to correspond to one object. In Piaget's terms, they lack one-to-one correspondence. Hence, three-year-olds can count the objects in Figure 9–8A and have 10 the first time and 12 the next. Furthermore, the two different totals are not inconsistent to them! To explain this lapse, Piaget began to study conservation.

**Conservation.** It is a major discovery to children that the number of items in a display does not change when the arrangement changes. Whether 10 pebbles are arranged in a straight line, a circle, or a star, the number of elements remains the same; in other words, they are conserved. The ability to conserve means that the child is able to discern the unchanging elements in a situation. Piaget followed the child's growing understanding of conservation by presenting tasks in which number, mass, weight, and volume remained the same.

One of the standard Piagetian tasks for assessing the child's understanding of number is to present two rows containing the same number of objects, but arranged so that one row is longer than the other (see Figure 9–8A). When asked if one row has more objects, preoperational children are likely to decide that the longer display has more objects (Voyat, 1982). Of course, this is incorrect, but it reflects the child's current understanding. Preoperational children have spent some years learning that longer displays typically contain more objects (Flavell, 1977). The logical error is that they cannot coordinate this intuitive understanding of length with the more precise information they obtain by counting. The problem, as in the classification tasks and some of the perspective taking tasks discussed earlier, lies in children's inability to coordinate all of their information.

Gelman (1972) describes the preoperational child's difficulty. She points out that giving the correct answer to this task requires much more than an understanding of numbers. It is true that children have to know how to count. But they also have to attend to the different rows and coordinate the length of the displays with their counting. Finally, they have to map language onto the logic they are using so that they can explain what they are thinking to the experimenter. Gelman concludes that logic is only one of the skills necessary to respond to conservation tasks. This explains why children can conserve number when they are four or five, but cannot conserve mass until they are seven or eight.

Conservation of mass is probably the best known of all the tasks devised by Piaget. Children are shown two identical clay balls (see Figure 9–9). Once they agree that the balls are equivalent, the experimenter transforms one into the shape of a hotdog or a pancake and asks the child if the two shapes are still equivalent. Then they are asked whether the two objects contain the same amount of clay. Their responses are a good indicator of their thinking.

David, aged seven, responds, "Since you rolled it out, it is fatter."

**Figure 9–8**  **Conservation of number**

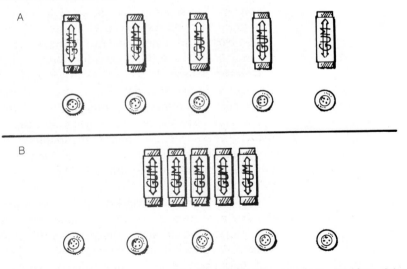

Two rows containing the same number of objects are presented in (A). One of the rows is then lengthened as in (B). Children are asked if one row has more, the same, or less than the other. Preoperational children usually decide that the longer array has more objects.

**Figure 9—9**     **Conservation of quantity**

In conservation problems, children are presented with clay balls, glasses of liquids, and containers of marbles that are initially equal. Then one of the containers is transformed. Preoperational children are persuaded by the perceptual changes that the quantity has changed. Concrete operational children remember that they were equal and that nothing has been added or subtracted; hence they know that the quantities are still equal. They use logic to answer the question and ignore the distracting perceptual cues.

> Gail, aged eight, answers, "I can imagine in my eyes if I rolled it back it would be the same."
> Lisa, aged eight notes, "It is just shaped into something different; all of the clay's still there."
> Julie, aged seven, notes, "It's smaller there, but bigger there." (Tomlinson-Keasey, Eisert, Kahle, Hardy-Brown, & Keasey, 1979)

David's answer indicates that he is confused by the perceptual cues. He centers on one aspect of the transformed ball and decides that the ball has grown. Gail, who has attained the stage of concrete operations, indicates that she can reverse the effects of the transformation. This mental operation called *reversibility* adds flexibility to thought that the preoperational child does not have. Lisa's logical answer notes that the initial equivalence has not been changed. Julie's response indicates that she can decenter. Unlike David, she no longer focuses on a single cue to answer the question.

The classification, seriation, and conservation problems that Piaget posed illustrate the logical advances that characterize concrete operational thought. The word operations is important because children in this stage operate on symbols. They examine particular dimensions of objects and organize that information into classes and subclasses. They coordinate several different items of information and order objects. Finally, they mentally reverse physical transformations and decenter.

When Piaget first described the skills of preoperational and concrete operational children, psychologists thought that children made a massive conceptual leap that enabled them to use mental transformations. Years of research have shown that the leap is actually a gradual accrual of information, logic, and language about specific problems. There is no magic moment when a child suddenly becomes concrete operational. Whether or not the child can coordinate the information requirements of any specific task depends on how difficult the task is, how compelling the perceptual cues are, how much experience the child has had, how the questions are phrased, and so on (Gelman, 1982; Brainerd, 1978).

---

### HUMOR

The development of concrete operational thought leads to a definite change in such logical skills as conservation, seriation, and classification. But the same thought processes have other effects, outside the logical domain. The operations of reversibility and the ability to think about relationships seem to be central to the appreciation of humor based on double meanings. Jokes, riddles, and puns require children to shift from the obvious meaning of some key word and consider one or more additional meanings (McGhee, 1979). When children can understand that words can be used in several contexts, they can appreciate the jokes listed below.

Order! Order in the court!
Ham and cheese on rye, please, Your Honor.
Waiter, what's this fly doing in my soup?
It looks like the breast stroke, sir.
I saw a man eating shark in the aquarium.
That's nothing. I saw a man eating herring in the restaurant.
Call me a cab.
You're a cab.

Prior to the period of concrete operations, children often do not understand why these jokes are funny (Shultz & Horibe, 1974).

---

**Formal operations**

According to Piaget's theory, the stage of *formal operations* is the culmination of cognitive growth. Between the ages of 11 and 16, mental operations are completely integrated and thought attains a flexibility unrealized at the earlier stages. Students are no longer limited to mental transformations of concrete objects. They can abstract from the reality of a problem and consider alternatives or alterations in the problem. In formal thought, ideas begin to dominate concrete experimentation, and students' thinking processes are designed to find answers to questions.

To assess formal operations, Piaget devised 15 tasks that require systematic experimentation and integration of information. The chemicals task depicted in Figure 9–10 explores a student's ability to generate combinations and to test hypotheses. Students are presented with four odorless, colorless liquids, and the experimenter demonstrates that adding a fifth agent, labeled *g*, to a flask results in a yellowish color. The student's task is to duplicate that color. Inhelder and Piaget (1958) recorded the approaches used by children 5 to 12 years of age as they worked on this problem.

Preoperational children were not systematic in their approach to the problem. Their thinking was intuitive and magical. They suggested that the color comes from the water if you shake the container, or that the color flies away to another beaker or becomes invisible (Inhelder & Piaget, 1958).

Concrete operational children approached the problem a bit more systematically, and began to explore one or two possibilities.

**Figure 9–10**                    **Formal operations**

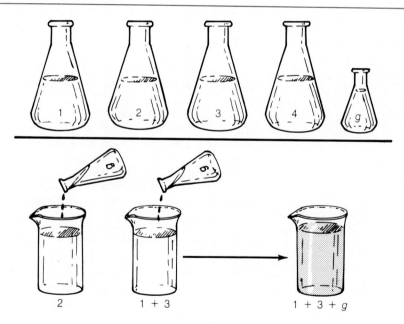

The chemicals task was devised by Inhelder and Piaget to assess formal thought. Four similar flasks contain colorless liquids: (1) diluted sulphuric acid; (2) water; (3) oxygenated water; (4) thiosulphate. The smaller flask, labeled *g*, contains potassium iodide. Two glasses are presented to the subject; one contains liquids 1 + 3, the other contains liquid 2. While the subject watches, the experimenter adds several drops of liquid *g* to each of these glasses. The liquid in the glass containing liquids 1 + 3 turns yellow. The subject is then asked to reproduce the color, using all or any of the liquids in the five flasks.

Source: Inhelder, B., & Piaget, J. (1958). *The growth of logical thinking from childhood to adolescence.* New York: Basic Books.

REN (age seven) tries $4 \times g$, then $2 \times g$, $1 \times g$, and $3 \times g$: "I think I did everything . . . I tried them all."

"What else could you have done?"

"I don't know."

We give him the glasses again: he repeats $1 \times g$.

"You took each bottle separately. What else could you have done?"

"Take two bottles at the same time." He tries $1 \times 4 \times g$. then $2 \times 3 \times g$. . . .

When we suggest that he add others, he puts $1 \times g$ in the glass already containing $2 \times 3$ which results in the appearance of the color: "Try to make the color again."

"Do I put in two or three?" . . . No, I don't remember any more, etc. (Inhelder & Piaget, 1958, p. 111)

Ren has to be prodded to combine more than one substance. When he does add more substances, he does not keep track of his efforts. Hypotheses and ideas are not yet guiding his behavior. Contrast his performance with ENG's.

ENG (age 14) begins with $2 \times g$, $1 \times g$, $3 \times g$, and $4 \times g$: "No, it doesn't turn yellow. So you have to mix them." He goes on to the six two-by-two combinations and at last hits $1 \times 3 \times g$. "This time I think it works."

"Why?"

"It's $1 \times 3$ and some water."

"You think it's water?"

"Yes, no difference in odor. I think that it's water."

"Can you show me?"

He replaces $g$ with some water: $1 \times 3 \times$ water. "No, it's not water. It's a chemical product: it combines with 1 and 3 and then it turns into a yellow liquid." (He goes on to three-by-three combinations . . . .) "No, (2 and 4) aren't the same as the drops: they can't produce color with 1 and 3." (Then he tries $1 \times 3 \times g \times 2$). It stays the same with 2. I can try right away with 4 ($1 \times 3 \times g \times 4$.) It turns white again: 4 is the opposite of $g$ because 4 makes the color go away while $g$ makes it appear." (Inhelder & Piaget, 1958, pp. 120–121)

The chemicals task requires students to combine elements in a systematic way. Although not as systematic as college students, ENG sees the need to record his trials and to experiment with all of the chemicals. Once all of the combinations have been explored, students must evaluate the data, isolate the importance of each chemical, and mentally organize the results.

The chemicals task is just one of several problems devised to highlight the differences between concrete operational thought and formal operational thought. Other more familiar problems involve if . . .then statements.

If this is Los Angeles, then the freeways are jammed.

1. This is Los Angeles. What can you say about the freeways?
2. This is San Francisco. What can you say about the freeways?

3.  The freeways are jammed. What can you say about the city?
4.  The freeways are empty. What can you say about the city?

Students are given the first if . . . then statement as a postulate and asked to logically derive information from that statement so that they can answer the four other questions. At the stage of formal thought, students can make the abstract transformations needed to deduce that if the freeways are empty, this cannot be Los Angeles (Kuhn, 1977; Moshman, 1979).

These problems illustrate the major differences between concrete operational thought and formal operational thought. Students who think formally are able to shift from focusing on a single aspect of the situation to a consideration of all the possibilities. They can take the results of concrete operational experimentation, restate them in propositional form, and further operate on them. This gives the student greater flexibility of thought. As is obvious from the if . . . then example, formal operational students frequently move beyond the actual information given. As a result, they can speculate about worlds that do not exist, they can evaluate political systems they have not experienced, or they can predict technological advances that will not materialize for years. The thought processes foreshadowed by the elementary transformations of the concrete operational child come to fruition in the balanced, flexible, cohesive thought of adults.

Like so many of Piaget's formulations, formal thought has generated widespread interest (Neimark, 1975). Psychologists, educators, mathematicians, chemists, and physicists have studied formal operations to gain insight into abstract thought processes. They began their studies by asking if everyone reached the stage of formal thought (Neimark, 1981).

When assessments of formal thought were conducted outside Switzerland, investigators were shocked to discover that many college students did not investigate all of the possibilities or systematically check the hypotheses they formed (Johnson-Laird & Wason, 1977). Indeed, many college professors argued that the skills characteristic of formal thinkers were not apparent in their students. Psychologists wondered, laughingly, if Piaget was the only person ever to achieve formal operational thought. It is true that many college students do not respond to all of their professor's questions logically. Often students are grappling with a new field, trying to learn the new vocabulary, the classification system, and the orderings that characterize that field. Until this more concrete information is understood, students will have trouble forming hypotheses about the subject area and investigating them systematically.

The recognition that students need to have some background in a subject area before they are able to think formally has occasionally been misinterpreted to suggest that formal thought requires high levels of education. A few investigators have also suggested that formal thought is restricted to highly industrialized societies (see Modgil & Modgil, 1976). Both of these views ignore the fact that formal operations evolve from the classifications and orderings of concrete operations. For example, the Kalahari Bushmen have a limited formal education and a minimal understanding of industrialized societies. Yet, they apply formal operational skills to hunting. The process of tracking an animal involves inferences and hypothesis testing that are clearly formal operational.

> Determining, from tracks, the movements of animals, their timing, whether they are wounded and if so how, and predicting how far they will go and in which direction and how fast, all involve repeated activation of hypotheses, trying them out against new data, integrating them with previously known facts about animal movements, rejecting the ones that do not stand up, and finally getting a reasonable fit, which adds up to meat in the pot. (Tulkin & Konner, 1973, p. 36)

The formal thought of the Kalahari Bushmen begins with concrete knowledge about the animals' tracks, how they move, and what happens when they are wounded. This information is woven together by the abstract thought processes of formal operations.

We can conclude from this brief review that adolescents acquire formal operations sometime between 11 and 16 years of age. The beginning ability to make multiple transformations first appears during this age span, but applying formal operations to all fields seems to be a lifelong endeavor. Education does not guarantee the deductive power of formal thought, nor does the lack of a formal education exclude formal thinking. These studies provide an awareness that formal operational thought depends on concrete understandings. In addition, the familiarity of the task, the student's background in the area, some biological considerations, and even the student's personality will influence whether children can use inference and logic to solve a particular problem (Pascual-Leone & de Ribaupierre, 1979).

Knowing that adolescents do not approach all areas logically has led researchers to ask whether students can be taught to think formally. Students can be taught the correct answers to the chemicals task, but that does not mean they will be able to use formal thought in other problems. Similarly, if formal operations tasks are simplified, children as young as six can solve them (Ennis, 1978). But it is doubtful that these children have been transformed into formal operational thinkers (Kuhn, 1977; Moshman, 1979). Perhaps a better way to approach this question is to look at how students acquire formal operations.

Deanna Kuhn and her students and colleagues have tried to understand how formal thought is acquired. In one study, Kuhn and John Angelev (1976) found that merely exposing ten-year-olds to a problem-rich environment over a 15-week period enhanced their thinking skills. Over a four-month period, this exposure was as effective as having an adult demonstrate the solutions to problems. Kuhn's data emphasize the student's active role in constructing formal operational solutions to problems. Such an approach fits with Piaget's stance and explains why individuals in less industrialized societies reason so formally while hunting, but might think airplanes are magic birds.

# THE KEYS TO COGNITIVE PROGRESS

The corpus of Piaget's work has proved invaluable as a description of cognitive development. The actions of infants are superseded by the symbols of the toddler. The mental operations that emanate from symbols are initially restricted to simple transformations. With experience, these operations expand to include the hypothetical events and logical inferences that denote formal operations. While most psychologists agree that children's thinking progresses according to these steps, they do not agree on finer points of the theory or what causes the child to move from one stage of thought to the next.

The structuralists stress equilibration, the child's own activities, and biological factors, but also include social, physical, and cultural experiences. Many other psychologists feel that Piaget underestimates the importance of social and cultural factors and overestimates the importance of internal factors. Let us look at the issues in this debate.

**The development of the central nervous system**

In 1958 Inhelder and Piaget suggested that formal thought reflected, in part, the development of the nervous system. In the intervening 25 years, we have accumulated much more information about the development of the brain. We know that the process of surrounding nerves with fatty tissue, called *myelination*, continues into adulthood in some areas of the brain (Wiggins, 1982). Further, the frontal lobes which are associated with high level reasoning skills are among the last areas to myelinate (Yakovlev & LeCours, 1967). We also know that the electrical signals from the brain go through a period of intense maturation at puberty (Eeg, 1980). Even head circumference, which is an index of brain development, undergoes a growth spurt during puberty (Eichorn & Bayley, 1962). Whether or not these changes in the nervous system prime formal thought is not known. The leap from biology to behavior is so large that most researchers are content to point to the changes in the brain as interesting events that might be important to formal thought.

Herman Epstein (1978) has carried the comparison of brain development and cognitive development a step further than most researchers. He notes that head circumference goes through three growth spurts—the first between birth and 2 years, the second around 7 years, and the third around 12 years (see Figure 9–11).

The alignment between these periods of brain growth and Piaget's stages of cognitive development seems to be more than fortuitous according to Epstein. In his view, growth spurts in the brain mark the formation of new cerebral connections. To support this, he cites the fact that cell division ceases before age two. The brain, however, continues to become heavier into adolescence. The additional weight comes from more extensive networks of axons and dendrites, myelination, and the growth of the cells in the brain. When head circumference increases dramatically, the brain is changing dramatically, and behavioral changes might be expected to follow (Epstein, 1979).

**Figure 9—11**          **Periods of rapid brain growth**

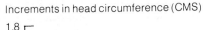

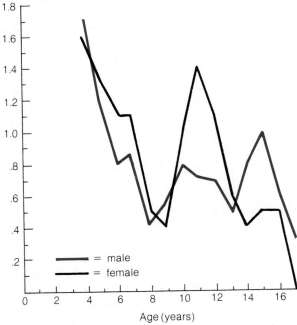

Age (years)

Head circumference, which is a reliable indicator of brain growth, shows growth spurts during infancy, at about seven years, and again at puberty (Eichorn & Bayley, 1962). Epstein believes that these changes could be a factor in the development of higher level thinking skills.

Source: Epstein, H. T. Correlated brain and intelligence development in humans. (1979). In M. E. Hahn, C. Jensen, & B. C. Dedek (Eds.), *Development and evolution of brain size (p. 116)*. New York: Academic Press.

Epstein draws his conclusions from correlational data. These data only tell us that two events are related, not that one event causes the other. Conclusions about whether growth spurts in the brain cause cognitive progress must be regarded as speculation until we find noninvasive methods that are highly sensitive to internal changes in the brain. Computerized (CAT) scans are beginning to be used to assess brain development in premature infants (Murakami, Nakamura, Mizojiri, Aida, & Matsuo, 1981). The procedure, however, is not routine and does not provide a detailed analysis of brain development.

Although we have not been able to establish whether specific changes in the brain affect cognitive development, we do know that normal cognitive development is dependent on an intact brain (Mehler, 1982). Furthermore, we know that the normal development of the brain depends on transactions with the environment (see Chapter 5). Hence, acknowledging the importance of the brain to cognitive development does not preclude the environment.

**Disequilibration**

According to Piaget, the contradictions that become apparent as children tackle logical problems cause them to ask more questions and to seek more information until they begin to doubt their first solution. Their doubts indicate a certain *disequilibrium* that forces them to rethink their answers to problems like conservation and classification. As they reconsider the problem, they often revise their earlier views. Piaget (1977) regards this process, which depends on the creation of disequilibrium, as the central mechanism in cognitive change. Like brain development, disequilibrium is essentially an internal variable. It is a state that occurs when all of the information does not fit the child's structures.

In the 1970s, investigators tried to capitalize on this internal force by presenting children with experiences that would create cognitive conflict. Deanna Kuhn reasoned that if children saw another person classify objects using a more advanced strategy, they might experience disequilibrium. Hence, Kuhn designed her experiment so that an adult would model a different classification strategy. She began by asking children, aged three to eight years, to sort objects of varying shapes and colors. She then had the adult model perform the task while the child watched. The model purposely sorted the blocks using a strategy slightly more advanced than the child's strategy (+1), a strategy less advanced than the child's (−1), the same strategy (0), or a strategy considerably more advanced than the child's (+2). Kuhn reasoned that the +1 model would create the most disequilibrium in the child and that if disequilibrium forces children to rethink their strategies, these children should advance more. Models at the child's own stage or at the stage below the child's should not induce any disequilibrium because the child already understood these strategies (Kuhn, 1972).

This experiment was designed to test Piaget's notions about disequilibrium, but it also tested the influence of a model. If children just blindly imitate a model, they should copy the model's strategy regardless of that strategy's level.

The results of this experiment supported the position that a moderate discrepancy (+1) between the model's and the child's strategy promoted the most cognitive progress. Children who watched the +1 model showed sustained change in their classification skills. Children who watched a model at their own level or a lower level seldom changed the way they approached the problem. The children who watched the model at a considerably higher level (+2) did not imitate the model's advanced classification skills (+2); instead, these children moved up one level in their classification skills. Kuhn takes this change—to a level that was never modeled for the child—as an indication that there is a step-by-step progression for classification skills.

Kuhn's experiment was an earnest attempt to examine the effect of disequilibration on cognitive change. Since then, many of her conclusions have been reinforced by other investigations (see Beilin, 1980; & Pinard, 1981). Training young children in the use of concrete operations is most successful when these children are on the verge of concrete operational thought (Beilin, 1978). At this stage, the contradictions are apparent to the child and seem to set the wheels of change in motion.

**Experience**

The experiences of children can propel them to higher levels of thought. Piaget discussed the effects of experiences with objects at great length, noting that experiences are particularly important during infancy. Experiences that require thinking are also useful if the child is to advance readily to concrete operational thought or formal operational thought. When Piaget discusses experience, he seldom mentions whether the environment is stimulating or whether children have been taught to add and subtract. He prefers to look at experience as the product of the child's self-directed activity. In his view, such activity enhances the disequilibrium the child perceives, thereby promoting cognitive progress.

To examine the effects of self-directed activity, Deanna Kuhn and Victoria Ho (1980) compared children who directed the investigation of problems with children who watched as the problems were explored and solved. After 11 weeks of dealing with formal operational problems, the directors were thinking at a higher level than the children who watched. Both of the groups did learn something about isolating variables and investigating hypotheses. However, observation was not as useful as directing the experiment.

**Social transmission**

The culture has an impact on cognitive development. Few of us could equal the Kalahari Bushmen's tracking expertise, despite our skills in formal thinking. Such information is not an active part of our culture. The knowledge of our culture is transmitted through social agents—parents, teachers, and peers—to each new generation. Thanks to these agents, children do not have to constantly reinvent the wheel, the computer, or the space shuttle. But the role that Piaget allots to social agents is a limited one, because children's ability to understand is limited. We cannot teach an infant algebra or a preschooler calculus. Social transmission of knowledge must mesh with the child's level of thought.

**Other factors influencing cognitive development**

The child's activities, the disequilibrium that accompanies the child's actions, and the development of the central nervous system are all internal variables that have been related to cognitive progress. While recognizing that such internal variables are important, we need to mention several qualifications. First, all of these variables, despite the fact that they are characterized as internal, require environmental input. Kuhn's conclusions often mention the child's internal processes; yet her experiments provide proof that children advance in environments that promote thinking. Thus, the need for continuing stimulation from the environment is obvious, even from a structuralist view. To sort through hypotheses and reorganize concepts into higher order systems, the environment must be stimulating enough to engage the child.

Another reason to qualify the role of internal variables is that they do not explain why some children make progress, while others do not. In experiments that document the importance of self-directed activity or disequilibrium, not all of the children that begin at the same level advance (Inhelder, Sinclair, & Bovet, 1974), nor is their progress always sustained (Brainerd, 1978).

A third qualification is that young children have been trained to give concrete operational answers using a variety of methods that do not emphasize the internal activity of the child (Beilin, 1980; Brainerd, 1978). Teaching preoperational children to use verbal rules to solve the conservation problem has been very successful. The experimenter explains the rule that "nothing was added or taken away so the number remains the same" (Beilin, 1980). Providing verbal feedback, tutoring, demonstrating the reversibility of concrete transformations, and contradicting the child have all prompted concrete operational responses from children who were initially preoperational. Of course, these methods focus on what is happening in the environment and ignore what is happening in the child. Many of these techniques could also produce disequilibrium in the child and foster a reorganization of the child's thinking.

Part of the problem in isolating the factors that promote cognitive development comes from the tasks themselves. As we have seen, even a simple task like number conservation confounds the child's knowledge of number, knowledge of language, memory, experience, and logical skills (Brainerd, 1977; Siegel & Hodkin, 1982). When a child does not respond logically to these problems, it could be due to the immature logic being used, but it could also be a function of any of the other variables (Keating, 1979).

Tom Trabasso and his colleagues have shown that many of the tasks used to assess cognitive development are influenced by memory (Austin, Ruble, & Trabasso, 1977; Bryant & Trabasso, 1971). When the language required in a task is similarly minimized, young children give logical answers to concrete operational tasks (Siegel & Hodkin, 1982). Even changing a single word in a sentence could lead to a different answer. Children shown a picture of four boys and two girls were told; "Here are kindergarten children. These are the boys and these are the girls and these are the children. Who would have a bigger birthday party, someone who invited the boys or someone who invited the children?" When many of the children answered incorrectly, Markman changed the question to, "Who would have a bigger birthday party, someone who invited the boys or someone who invited the class?" Now children compared the groups accurately (Markman, 1981, p. 205).

Because the tasks used to assess cognitive development are so sensitive to language and memory, critics have concluded that they are useless as indicators of cognitive progress. These critics have substituted tasks that separate the effects of memory, logic, or language. But simplifying logical problems in an effort to isolate important variables has a built-in danger. The essence of concrete operational thought is the coordination of information, and simplifying the tasks to reduce the memory skills or the language skills may alter the cognitive requirements of the task so much that you are no longer measuring what you initially intended (Larsen, 1977). Despite this warning, psychologists have learned a great deal from trying to separate the influences of memory, language, and logic (Siegler, 1978). We will direct our attention to these studies in the next chapter.

**Evaluation of the structuralist theory**

Any evaluation of Piaget's 60 years of work in cognitive development and the thousands of investigations that have built on his observations is likely to oversimplify the issues. It is important to keep in mind that the goal of most experiments emanating from the structuralist position is to understand the growth of knowledge. Hence, the focus is on the action of the sensory motor period, the symbols of the preoperational period, the transformations of concrete operations, or the abstractions of formal operations and on how the child moves from one form of thought to another. Piaget was not really concerned with whether the process of logical development can be hastened or whether some children progress more rapidly than others. He was intent on charting the course of cognitive development. In this he has largely succeeded (Beilin, 1980). His description of the changes in the logical skills of children and adolescents is unparalleled in developmental psychology. Few other theorists have even tried to describe the whole process of logical development from birth to adulthood.

Another index of a theory's value is its impact on the field. Piaget's theory has generated research, sparked controversies, and added new ways of thinking about a phenomenon. By these measures, Piaget's theory is a resounding success. Piaget's description of cognitive development has altered the course of developmental psychology and influenced researchers in such diverse specialties as infant memory, language development, imagery, conditional reasoning, and moral judgments. In addition, Piaget's influence has spilled over into half a dozen other disciplines including education, anthropology, philosophy, and sociology.

Despite the elegance and general serviceability of Piaget's structuralist perspective, it does not provide a complete picture of cognitive development. Structuralists, in their desire to outline normative growth, have paid little attention to individual differences in cognitive development. Nor have they looked at patterns of cognition. Despite their adherence to an interaction model, their experiments have focused on the child's struggle to understand the world. In the process, the importance of external variables has often been minimized. Finally, the focus on structures often leads to experiments in which several cognitive skills are confounded. These skills could easily be investigated separately. Cognitive development certainly includes the development of perception, imagery, memory, and language. In the next chapter, these separate aspects of cognitive development will be considered.

## SUMMARY

The structuralist approach has a long philosophical history that Piaget adapted to the study of cognitive development. He combined structuralism, his biological background, and his penchant for interviewing children about their thoughts. The result is a complex and all-encompassing description of how the child's thought patterns change from infancy to adulthood.

To understand the structuralist approach, it is necessary to deal with the assumptions and major tenets that guide the approach. The first principle is that children are actively involved and direct their interactions with the environment. Most of the other tenets of Piaget's theory are derived from this single assumption. Because children are the primary mediators of their cognitive progress, they interpret the events of the environment, decide what actions to take, and reorganize their thought processes when necessary. They accomplish this by adapting to the environment and organizing the information that they glean from the environment.

After Piaget described the general process of cognitive development, he studied the different ways children organize their world. The sensory motor period, the preoperational period, the concrete operational period, and the formal operational period each have a central focus that describes the child's approach to the environment. The actions of the sensory motor period yield to the symbols of the preoperational period. As the child sorts and organizes the world, the language and symbols mastered during the preoperational period begin to be transformed in simple ways. These elementary transformations are the essence of concrete operational thought.

Perhaps the transition from preoperational skills to concrete operational thoughts is the most impressive change in cognitive skills. Certainly, it is the most researched. Once children are able to switch perspectives and transform information, their approach to the world is altered. The transformations that are endemic to concrete operational thought are seen in the jokes and puns that captivate children in the primary grades. The child's social skills suddenly evidence a maturity that was lacking during the preschool years. Academic abilities blossom as the classifications and conservations of arithmetic and reading become clear.

The simple transformations of the concrete period are woven into the systematic thought of formal operations. At this level, thinking skills become more flexible and complex. Adolescents can escape the reality that has bound much of the younger child's thinking. They can consider and explore all of the possibilities, including possibilities that have never existed. Formal thought is the capstone of Piaget's theory, and systematic approaches to problems dominate thought throughout the adult years.

While Piaget's general description of cognitive development has been widely accepted, the reasons for the child's development have not. Structuralists focus on internal variables, like disequilibrium, self-directed activity, and the development of the nervous system. Other psychologists feel that these variables do not give sufficient credit to the environmental variables that modify the way a child approaches a problem. Literally hundreds of experiments have been conducted to examine the factors that enhance cognitive development. Most psychologists now agree that children can be guided to the logic of concrete operations.

The structuralism of Piaget and his colleagues provided a new approach to cognitive development and has spurred investigations in virtually every area of developmental psychology. The result has been an explosion of information about all aspects of children's thinking. It does not diminish Piaget's contribution to point out that detailed investigations of Piaget's ideas have uncovered flaws, gaps, and contradictions and have prompted alternative views of cognitive development. Chapter 10 will introduce these alternatives.

# C H A P T E R   1 0
## Cognitive skill

Humans display a complex repertoire of cognitive skills. To learn, we have to smell, taste, see, hear, or feel the events in the environment. Once we feel the dew on the grass, see the letters on the page, or hear the ambulance's siren, the information is carried from the sense organs to the brain. In the brain, the information is stored so that the next time we encounter dew, letters, or sirens, we recognize them. In humans, cognitive skills even extend to retrieving these memories at will. This chain of events, known as information processing, occurs so effortlessly that we seldom take the time to analyze the component processes. But each step in this chain involves complex interactions between the environment and the brain. In this chapter, we will analyze the separate processes in the chain and look at how they develop.

The perceptual processes of seeing, hearing, and touching are honed early in life and represent the initial phase of information processing (Lawrence, Kee, & Hellige, 1980). As adults, we often take these senses for granted. In deaf children, however, information is not carried to the brain via the ears. Similarly, blind children do not get any visual input. These sensory impairments disrupt the normal chain of information processing. Looking at how these disruptions affect cognitive skills tells us something about the importance of this first sensory level of information processing.

The attentional processes that guide what we see, hear, and touch are another cognitive skill. Being able to attend means that children can focus on a particular task. Hyperactive children and children with minimal brain damage often have attentional deficits. These children are recognized early as having learning problems. Their attention deficits typically mean that these children will have difficulty solving more complex cognitive problems (Amado & Lustman, 1982).

Strategies for storing information vary depending on the age of children and their particular skills. Strategies for remembering become progressively more complex and organized as children mature. We can remember a person's name by constructing an image, by repeating the name silently, or by weaving the name into a known organization. Upon meeting Mrs. Surfass for the first time, we can transpose her into an image of a surfer, or we can concentrate on her face and rehearse her name several times, or we can code her as Fred's accountant. All of these strategies are likely to help us remember her.

The final stage of cognitive processing is retrieving stored information. What would life be like without the ability to retrieve information? A famous neurological patient, N. A. could tell you. N. A. suffered an injury to his brain in a fencing accident. Although he recovered and appeared to be normal, his memory was obviously impaired. When introduced to a psychologist named Wickelgren, N. A. asked,

> "Wickelgren, that's a German name, isn't it?"
> The doctor said no, it wasn't.
> "Irish?"
> "No."
> "Scandinavian?"
> "Yes, it's Scandinavian."
> After talking with N. A. for about five minutes, Dr. Wickelgren went into his office for another minute. When he returned, he was again introduced to N. A. who asked,
> "Wickelgren, that's a German name, isn't it?"
> The doctor said no, it wasn't.
> "Irish?"
> "No."
> "Scandinavian?"
> "Yes, it's Scandinavian." (Lindsay & Norman, 1977, pp. 434–435)

In N. A., one of the links in the chain of information processing is broken so that even a simple introduction cannot be retrieved. In other respects, N. A.'s cognitive skills appeared to be normal.

After considering the chain of cognitive skills that is invoked for even simple learning and recognition, we will consider more complex cognitive tasks. Memory is a good example of a complex cognitive skill that begins as a perceptual process and requires individuals to organize, store, and retrieve information. Solving logical problems or thinking about multifaceted issues also requires the child or adult to organize and reorganize stored information. On a moment's notice, we can use our stored information about college professors and courses to help a friend decide what courses to take. We can also use our stored information about mathematics to solve an algebraic equation. In these and other problem solving situations, we convert old information into a form that can be used to answer some new question.

Perceiving, attending, coding, storing, and retrieving allow us to think deductively and solve problems. Let's look at the development of these skills in children.

## PERCEPTUAL SKILLS

Perceptual skills become organized early in life. The newborn has some initial ability to receive information through all of the senses. During the first year, this initial equipment becomes more organized and each of the senses becomes integrated with the others (see Chapter 6). Once all of the senses are working together and can share the information that is received, the child is able to extract information about the environment very efficiently (Collins & Hagen, 1979). Although each of the senses has some unique aspects, in general, the perceptual systems function in similar ways. At the simplest level, the senses respond to isolated features of the environment. As the child develops and the brain becomes more organized, perceptual systems process larger and more organized units of information.

**Feature detection**

*Feature detectors* are the first level of perceptual experience (Haith, 1980). The visual and auditory centers of our brains initially respond to elementary features of the environment. Straight lines, angles, high notes, and differences in tone are some of the simple features that the brain detects early in infancy. Although feature detectors are part of the perceptual system throughout life, they yield to other more complex perceptions in the first few months of life. In essence, these simple, isolated features of the environment begin to be analyzed and organized (Shepard, 1982; Neisser, 1976; Posner, Pea, & Volpe, 1982).

Feature detection by itself will not explain perception; it is really just the beginning of perception. The brain extracts the information from dozens of features and organizes it. Here is an example from the visual system.

**Organization**

In English-speaking countries, the separate features of vertical, horizontal, diagonal, or curved lines are organized during the preschool years into the letters A through Z. In Japan, these same features are organized into あ and ん. Perceiving letters is an organization that is added to the initial detection of features. Perceiving words requires still another level of organization. This development, from isolated features to organized patterns, illustrates the ongoing interplay between the environment and the brain. After some experience and practice with culturally important visual stimuli, the brain recognizes and responds to them very efficiently (see Figure 10–1).

A similar process occurs when sounds are heard. Newborns recognize the differences between sounds (see Chapter 8), but the stream of language does not have any meaning. Within a year, toddlers are able to understand some of the directives and sentences they hear. The language now has an additional level of organization, and children are able to isolate words from the stream of language. As with letters, the organization into words varies depending on the culture. Few of us could separate the Japanese greeting *konnichiwa* into its word segments. Even understanding words is not enough. Whether we interpret the sounds *ai-s-k-r-ee-m* as "ice cream" or "I scream" depends on the sentence. This represents a higher level of organization.

A newborn responds primarily to isolated features in the environment. Within a few months, the brain and the child's experiences begin to impose organization on the environment. Consider the photograph in Figure 10–2. At

## Figure 10—1      Alphabets from different cultures

cat — English

Japanese

Arabic

KOT — Russian

The word cat takes many forms in alphabets from around the world. Yet by school age, the brain recognizes and responds very efficiently to these culturally determined ways of expressing cat.

first this appears to be an abstract photograph. Your visual system is certainly detecting all the isolated features in the photograph, but you do not see anything in particular. If, however, you are told that this is a photograph of a dalmatian walking along a path and sniffing, your brain begins to impose a different organization on the photograph. The dalmatian, facing the left, soon begins to pop out of the photograph whenever you look at it. The organization of this perception is directed by your brain (Lindsay & Norman, 1977).

The processes of seeing and hearing that initially seem to be simple and straightforward are very complex. Reading the sentence, "Something wicked this way comes" requires students to perceive, analyze, and organize the printed message. Lindsay and Norman (1977) depict these cortical processes as a group of demons recording information in a central place, say a chalkboard (see Figure 10–3). On this chalkboard, all the feature detectors (depicted as "D" demons) have isolated the features on the right-hand side of the board. Simultaneously, specialist demons ("S") are trying to organize the featural information so they can decipher the next word in the sentence. Meanwhile, if the supervisor is a Ray Bradbury fan or has read *MacBeth*, the analysis will be cut short because the sentence is familiar. The chalkboard analogy highlights the flurry of cortical activity involved in perceiving information in the environ-

**Figure 10—2**        **Perception and the brain**

When you first glanced at this photograph, you probably did not see the dalmatian that is facing to the left and sniffing along the path. Once you locate the dog, in about the center of the photograph, it is hard to look at the photograph without seeing the dog. Your brain often guides the way perceptions are organized.

Source: Lindsay, P. H., & Norman, D. A. (1977). *Human Information Processing (p. 12)*. New York: Academic Press.

ment. The feature detectors and organizers are busily doing their job. All the while, the person's background, attention, and individual skills are operating to form, evaluate, discard, and reform hypotheses about what exists in the environment.

**Disruptions in perception**

Perceiving events in the environment is the first step in the chain of information processing. Blind and deaf children are unable to perceive some of the events in their environments because of an impairment in the sensory system. What happens to the later phases of information processing when one of the perceptual systems is disrupted?

Children who are congenitally deaf provide a partial answer. Because deaf children perceive no sounds in the environment, they have no speech models to imitate and no stream of language to segment. Under these conditions,

**Figure 10–3**        **Pattern recognition**

Analyzing a sentence is a complex process. The brain's feature detectors, here indicated by "D" demons, have listed the features that are appropriate on the right side of the chalkboard. Another crew of demons wear an "S" to indicate that they perform some special task. Some of the specialists try to organize the features and decide what word is being used. Other specialists decide whether the word is a noun, a verb, or some other part of speech. All of the specialists work together with the supervisor and the feature detectors to figure out the sentence.

Source: Lindsay, P. H., & Norman, D. A. (1977). *Human Information Processing (p. 282)*. New York: Academic Press.

learning to talk becomes an almost impossible task (Liben, 1978). Deaf individuals typically substitute a signed language for spoken language (see Figure 10–4). Sign language is a fully expressive and autonomous language (Schlesinger & Namir, 1978). Since it does not exercise the language areas of the brain, the deaf child's brain becomes organized in a somewhat different fashion than the hearing child's brain (Liberman, 1982).

The consequences of early childhood deafness extend far beyond the sensory realm and the inability to speak. Reading and writing pose monumental problems (Brooks, 1978). Deaf children are taught to read by matching a ball or a picture of a ball with the letters b-a-l-l. This intensive training works well for isolated words, but it does not help the child understand the rules of grammar. As a result, sentence analysis and comprehension suffer (Quinn, 1981). In a national survey of deaf individuals, the 19-year-olds scored at the fourth-grade level when they were asked to determine what a written paragraph meant.

Constructing sentences is also a problem. Deaf children have great difficulty with the structure of sentences and grammar. Kathryn Meadow cites some examples of sentences written by deaf high school students applying for admission to Gallaudet College.

> I began to love it as to be my favorite sport now.
> She told him that there was a fitted place to put.
> To his disappointed, his wife disgusted of what he made.
> The doctor believes that a sickness woman would live within three or four weeks.
> This room was small and many furniture lay crowdly. (Meadow, 1975, p. 460)

Deficits in speech, reading, and writing are perhaps not surprising since they all rely on a language system the deaf child cannot experience. But this may not be the end of the cognitive problems for the deaf child. Hearing language could prime the brain to deal, not just with the stream of language, but with all sequential information (Liberman, 1974). Consider the following problem; "John is taller than David, but shorter than Mike. Who is taller, David or Mike?" Answering this question is very difficult for deaf students (Furth & Youniss, 1971). Some of the difficulty comes from not being able to understand the question, rather than an inability to think (Furth, 1971). Deaf children have no trouble remembering a sequence of lights. They do, however, have problems if the sequential task requires a knowledge of words (Tomlinson-Keasey & Smith-Winberry, 1983).

Like a stone thrown into a pond, the consequences of deafness ripple outward, marring a host of secondary processes including language acquisition, reading, and writing. Even distantly related processes, like memory and problem solving, may be impaired if the material the child is asked to remember or think about is linguistically organized. A flaw in the perception of sound, then, disrupts the whole chain of information processing.

**Figure 10—4**     **Sign language**

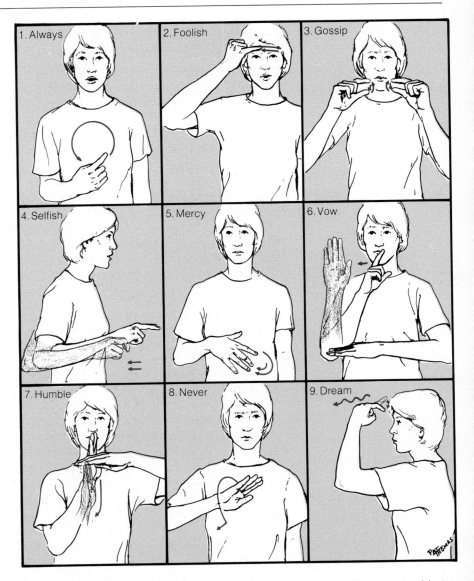

American sign language is a fully expressive language. Signs exist for concrete objects as well as abstract ideas. The signs are put together in an orderly way to express thoughts. Signed poetry exists, and even rhythmical "songs" can be signed.

Source: Riekehof, L. (1963). *Talk to the deaf*. Springfield, MO.: Gospel Publishing House.

## ATTENTION

At a crowded and noisy restaurant, we have no trouble blocking out the conversations of others and attending to what our friends are saying. If we become bored with the conversation and our eye is caught by the distraught woman at the next table, we can easily switch our attention to the argument she and her escort are having. This ability to attend selectively is very important to survival. We can select a particular aspect of the environment and concentrate on it. In the meantime, we monitor the rest of the environment with less intense interest.

The phenomenon of selective attention was initially studied by Broadbent (1958, 1977). It was obvious, he argued, that people did not attend to all of the stimuli in the environment. To do so would overwhelm the perceptual equipment and create chaos for the organism. If, as you are reading this book, you are registering the furniture you are sitting in, the sensations from your feet, the conversation from across the hall, and the music from the radio, you are probably not getting much from your reading. There is a limit to the attention that can be deployed (Lindsay & Norman, 1977). You can demonstrate this yourself. While you are hurrying to class with a friend, ask her to multiply 15 times 37. Chances are she will slow the pace or stop while she solves the problem. The attention needed to concentrate on the arithmetic task interferes with the performance of the other task—walking. In the laboratory, the interference that occurs when we ask students to perform two tasks simultaneously indicates how much attention each task takes (Posner & Boies, 1971). Selective attention and allocation of attention to particular tasks are important information processing skills.

In children, these skills begin to develop as early as three or four years of age (Miller & Zalenski, 1982). Preschoolers understand that noise is distracting if they are trying to concentrate on a task. They also acknowledge that interest in a subject is an important factor in determining their attention span. By 12 years of age, children's attention can be directed in a flexible way and they can decide to attend to particular parts of the environment (Zelniker & Jeffrey, 1979). At this point, they no longer focus on the most prominent aspect of their environment. Instead, they pick out the information that is most useful (Hale, 1979).

**Individual differences in attention**

Attention, like perception, influences processes that occur later in the chain of cognitive skills. In fact, attention in infants is regarded as one of the earliest indicators of later cognitive functioning (Lewis & Brooks-Gunn, 1981). Michael Lewis tested infants who were three months old on a task requiring visual attention. Twenty months later, he gave these same children IQ tests. The infants who had been most successful at the attention task had the highest IQs. Intuitively, it makes sense that attention is one of the vanguards of information processing. Infants who are able to concentrate and deploy their attention should acquire a better understanding of their environment than infants who have trouble focusing their attention.

Individual differences in attention during the early months are probably related to the functioning of the central nervous system. Arthur Jensen (1981) suggests that such small differences in the functioning of the central nervous system have a cumulative effect. Over a period of dozens of years, these differences might mean that a person acquires substantially more information and organizes that information into more sophisticated and flexible conceptual systems.

**Attentional disorders**

Another way of isolating the importance of attending is to look at older children who have trouble attending. Such deficits are prominent in hyperactive, learning disabled, and impulsive children. The most recent psychiatric handbook of mental disorders (DSM III) lists *attentional deficits* as a distinct syndrome (American Psychiatric Association, 1980). Children in this category are typically inattentive and impulsive. By the time they are 10 they have usually been referred to a mental health professional. Teachers complain that these children do not finish what they start, do not seem to listen, are easily distracted, and have difficulty concentrating. Of course, the reason they are referred to mental health professionals is because they are not performing well in school. Psychologists evaluating these children have noted that their attentional difficulties follow a pattern. These children have no trouble directing their attention to a task initially. The problems arise if they must maintain their attentive state over a long period of time (Pihl & Niaura, 1982).

Children with attention problems are victims of a vicious cycle of superficial information processing. They do not look and listen carefully or reflect on their experiences in a thoughtful manner. As a result, the conclusions and deductions they draw about their environments are based on fleeting perceptual cues. Relying on such fleeting impressions means that the child does not form subtle or complex concepts. The impoverished concepts hinder the next set of transactions with the environment and the cycle continues (Douglas & Peters, 1979).

The cycle just described examines behavior. Hebb (1976) tried to link this behavioral cycle to the functioning of the brain. Normally as the brain becomes organized, cell assemblies are formed. These cell assemblies work together to recognize complex and familiar stimuli. But higher order cell assemblies are not the final step. If children can direct their attention to the events in the environment, they can actually recruit additional neurons to help them perform the task at hand, whether it be recognizing faces, solving problems in logic, or reading words. As Hebb puts it, higher order cell assemblies become "enriched with associative connections interwoven like a tapestry" with the ongoing mental activity. By using both cell assemblies and associative connections, the mental activity "co-opts and imposes its own order widely throughout the brain" (Hebb, 1976, p. 313). Of course, the lack of these associative connections means that children are not as immersed in the activity.

Children with attentional problems have often been labeled as *hyperactive*. Actually, the high activity level is not as serious or as long lasting as the attentional problems. Studies that follow hyperactive children into adolescence find that while their activity level has decreased, they continue to have serious problems attending and concentrating (Amado & Lustman, 1982). As a result, these adolescents do not perform well in school, despite average or above average intelligence.

Summarizing what we know about attentional factors in children is a little dangerous since there is so much to learn. Nevertheless, we do know that attentional factors appear early in development (Anthony & Graham, 1983) and are related to the child's ability to perform cognitive skills in later years. Attentional deficits have been linked with problems in the central nervous system, but the exact nature of the organic deficit is not clear (Rutter, 1981). Follow-ups of children with attention problems suggest that these problems continue into adolescence and adulthood. As one of the early factors in the chain of information processing, attentional deficits influence higher order cognitive processing. Attention is not a single step in the chain of information processing, but a repeating part of a continuing cycle. As such, many theorists suggest that attention is one of several executive or control processes that determine how different individuals perform cognitive tasks (Kagan, Klein, Finley & Rogoff, 1977).

## MEMORY

Our lives are enriched by memories. If prompted, we can all relive a terrifying experience, a momentous occasion, a humiliating event, or a wondrous moment. The process of retrieving experiences from the past—remembering—is one of the most complex information processing skills. As an introduction to this skill, let us look at a man with an extraordinary memory.

Arturo Toscanini achieved international reknown as a conductor. His flawless memory for music has become part of the legend surrounding the man. One widely reported anecdote begins with the second bassoonist coming to Toscanini just before a concert. The bassoonist was very upset as he had just discovered that the key for the lowest note on his instrument was broken. He asked Toscanini what was to be done. Toscanini shaded his eyes, thought for a moment, and then said, "It is all right—that note does not occur in tonight's concert" (Marek, 1982, p. 414).

Another story reports that Toscanini wanted to perform Joachim Raff's Quartet No. 5. He and his assistants diligently searched in the libraries and music stores for the score. When their search failed to turn up a copy, Toscanini, "who had probably not seen the music for decades, wrote the entire movement down, with all the dynamic marks." When a collector found a copy and checked it against Toscanini's version, he only found one error (Marek, 1982, p. 415).

Toscanini's memory for music was strengthened by his ability to hear a composition while reading it. He had only to glance at a page, and he heard the music in his imagination (Marek, 1982).

Other cases of flawless memories exist in the psychological literature (Neisser, 1982), and several will be presented in this chapter. They are interesting because they provoke the same questions that memory researchers are trying to answer. Is the ability to remember the same mechanism in everyone? If so, how is the basic skill of memory elaborated? Is it elaborated in differing directions? Does one kind of memory precede another during development? Perhaps the best way to begin answering these questions is to look at the earliest memories of children.

**Earliest memories**

I remember a bright, shiny pair of black shoes. I was skipping and watching these shoes. I know now that I was going to a birthday party and that these were new black patent shoes with a strap across them, but my memory is really just a picture of those shoes on my feet skipping. (Estimated age, three)

I remember bright lights coming at me very fast and being very afraid and running. My parents have told me that I was almost run over, but I don't remember most of what they tell me. I only remember that it was dark except for these headlights and I was trying to reach the curb. (Age as confirmed by parents, three)

I remember a yellow cloth. That's all I remember, but it is very clear in my mind. It's really like a bright yellow square. I asked my mother if she knew why I should remember such a crazy thing and at first she didn't know. Then she remembered that the nurse in my doctor's office used to lay babies on this bright yellow square to give them shots. (No estimation of age)

I was standing on the floor of a room looking up at a stairway. I can still see the planks on the stairs. I have this vivid image of the stairs and my father standing at the top of the stairs. I don't know why this sticks in my mind. (Estimated age, three)

These are the earliest memories of four college students. Students were asked to "remember an event from early in your life. It doesn't have to be a complete memory, but think of the earliest fragment of memory or experience that you can. Once you have this memory firmly in mind, try to estimate how old you were at the time." These memories are interesting, but asking students to do this has several drawbacks. First, asking for memories may uncover the person's earliest memories, but such queries may also uncover stories that parents have retold (Piaget, 1962), images that have come from photographs, or vivid images of events that never really occurred (Brown & Kulick, 1982). Asking people to estimate their age at the time of their memory introduces another source of error. Most early memories are somewhat fragmented, and estimates of how old the person was at the time could err by as much as a year or two. Finally, even if these memories are firmly etched in people's minds, we often have trouble verifying the reported events.

In the examples, the students have tried to isolate their memories and to report them just as they exist without any embellishments. The yellow square and the staircase are not embedded in any larger context in the students' memories. If we could revisit the scene, it might become clear why these particular fragments are etched so clearly in memory.

Despite the anecdotal and somewhat subjective nature of these attempts to look at early memories, we can draw some conclusions from these studies. Early memories are usually images. There are virtually no extended conversations associated with early memories. These images can be auditory or even olfactory as well as visual. Many people remember the smell of a grandmother's house or a particular basement. Early memories often involve some motor activity on the part of the child—like skipping or running. Also, an emotional component is common in early memories. About 50 percent of these memories are about joyful, exciting experiences. Another 30 percent are fearful experiences or unpleasant memories (Waldvogel, 1948).

It is interesting that early memories are reported consistently at about the same age. Although there are scattered reports of memories in the first two years, most adults begin to report an occasional event from around the time of their third birthday (Waldvogel, 1948). After that, memories become more common, more elaborated, and more complete.

**Memories of two- and three-year-olds**

These early memories were all reports by adults who had scanned the recesses of their minds for memories from 15 to 20 years earlier. We certainly cannot conclude from this that children have no memories until they are three. A three-year-old can remember many events from the past (Perlmutter, 1980). In the chapters on infancy, we noted that recognition of the mother's voice and smell occurred during the first few weeks of life. At approximately eight months, infants form an object concept. Once past that milestone, infants often search for objects and people they cannot see (Braine & Eder, 1983). Toddlers seem to learn the locations of many objects. Their agitation when the cookie jar is opened, their repeated crawling toward garbage cans and other areas that are off limits indicate that they readily remember locations (Ashmead & Perlmutter, 1980).

Psychologists agree that infants can recognize familiar people and events. Such recognition memories are reactivated on a continuing basis because mothers reappear, diapers are changed in the same place, baths reoccur, and food appears at the same table or highchair. How long would infants remember a particular person if that person was not present to reactivate that recognition?

In laboratory studies, toddlers demonstrate rather short memories (Perlmutter, 1980). But in recent more naturalistic studies, toddlers have remembered events from many months in the past.

Judy DeLoache (1980) is one of the investigators who decided to look at children's memories in more natural settings. She went to children's homes with a "Big Bird" toy. She hid the toy while the children, aged 18 to 24 months, watched. After three to five minutes of waiting, these children walked immediately to the hiding place. When the wait was extended to 30 minutes, 60 minutes, or even overnight, 80 percent of the children still remembered where "Big Bird" had been hidden. When the task was made more complex, by hiding three toys in different locations, the children were able to retrieve the specific toy that was requested. The toddlers were not just remembering a place; they had coded a specific toy in a specific place.

Two-year-olds even develop simple strategies to help them remember. They do not group similar objects, they do not repeat "Big Bird is hidden in the oven," and they do not build an elaborate structure to help them remember. Such strategies require more verbal skill and logical sophistication than toddlers have. Instead, two-year-olds try to stay near the hiding place or keep looking at the hiding place. They also try to remember by doing something that will make the hiding place distinctive, like putting their hand on the box that is hiding the toy (Wellman, Ritter, & Flavell, 1975).

Two- and three-year-olds can report what happened at Christmas, what animals they have seen at the zoo, and what happened on an airplane flight. Although most of the episodes have occurred recently, some two-year-olds have reported events that took place when they were only 14 or 15 months old. In several cases, the parents were able to confirm the accuracy of the child's memory and the details that the child reported. These memories are particularly impressive because the events occurred and were put into long-term memory before the child could talk (Nelson & Ross, 1980; Todd & Perlmutter, 1980).

The fact that children remember events before they acquire linguistic skills means that their memories are not stored in a linguistic form. How, then, are they stored? Nelson and Ross (1980) comment that spatial locations figure prominently in the youngest children's memories. Children remember the location of objects readily, and they have people and events placed in spatial configurations. The spatial character of toddlers' memories supports the view that early memories are stored as images. After children develop language, they can use their new linguistic skill to access the image and describe it.

This view of toddlers' memories ascribes much more skill to toddlers than earlier views. What has changed? Spatial memories are obvious when studies are done in the child's home instead of the laboratory setting. The toddler has no spatial organization of unfamiliar environments like laboratories. Studies conducted in the home also allow us to see how the environment cues memories. Nelson and Ross (1980) point out that toddlers are not very skilled at retrieving their own memories. They have to be cued by the environment.

### Spatial memories

*J. R. Holland: Stock, Boston*

Toddlers' memories seem to be spatially organized. We see evidence of their memories when they search for a favorite toy in a familiar place.

Once these early memories are cued, children produce accurate and detailed representations of those events. Kenny, a toddler, illustrates this cuing procedure.

Kenny was 20 months old when he first visited his great grandmother's house. While waiting for dinner, Kenny's dad devised a new game that kept the boy outside and preserved his grandmother's knickknacks. The game called "Toss-the-stuffed-monkey-into-the-air," was a huge success. A year later, Kenny made a second trip to his great grandmother's house. The moment he stepped out of the car, he rushed to the spot of the game and began throwing his monkey into the air. His parents reported that the game had not been played in the intervening months. Kenny's memory was cued by the scene of the previous fun, even though it occurred many months earlier. Katherine Nelson states categorically that all memories of very young children are cued by some aspect of the environment.

Children's earliest memories are unique in several ways. They are spatially organized. They are coded as images. They must be cued by the environment.

They do not require language. The adult's memory system is much more complex. How does this early memory·skill evolve into the multifaceted adult system? To answer this question, we must first look at the development of imagery and then the development of memory.

## THE DEVELOPMENT OF IMAGERY

Shereshevskii, otherwise known as S, has achieved an unsought notoriety in cognitive psychology because of his unique visual memory. His story begins when he angered his newspaper editor as a cub reporter. The editor began each day by detailing lengthy assignments. He included specific details and particular instructions for the reporters. S never took any notes, but when asked, he could repeat the assignments verbatim. The editor was amazed and sent S to a prominent Russian neuropsychologist, A. R. Luria. Luria maintained his friendship with S for over 30 years and published a small volume detailing S's incredible memory.

When Luria tried to probe the limits of S's memory, he found none. S could easily reproduce 70 words or numbers in a series. Furthermore, he could reverse the order of the series. He only needed a three- or four-second pause between each number in the series and he could reproduce whatever he heard.

Luria also discovered that S could reproduce these words or numbers months or years later with no loss in accuracy. Some of the recall sessions occurred, without warning, 15 or 16 years after the original session. "S would sit with his eyes closed, pause, then comment: 'Yes, yes. . . . This was a series you gave me once when we were in your apartment. . . . You were sitting at the table and I in the rocking chair. . . . You were wearing a gray suit and looked at me like this. . . . Now, then, I can see you saying . . .,' and with that he would reel off the series precisely as I had given it to him" (Luria, 1968, p. 12). Because S's images were so durable, he retained images of events that occurred early in his infancy. He reports several images from before he was one year old.

When S did make an error in recall, it was usually an error of perception, not of memory. For example, he was asked to remember a series of words that included the word "egg." In his mind, he put the egg against a white wall and when he was recalling the words, the egg blended with the background and he did not see it.

After finding that S's memory had no limits and seemed to be infinitely durable, Luria concentrated on studying the process S used to remember. The most notable characteristic was the visual impressions that S formed. When he heard or read a word, it was immediately converted into a visual image. Even numbers had a visual counterpart; 6 was a man with a swollen foot, while 87 was a fat woman and a man twirling his mustache.

S's images were especially vivid, probably because they incorporated both visual and auditory characteristics. He described one person as having a "crumbly, yellow voice" and thought a 2,000 CPS tone sounded like pinkish, red fireworks. When he heard or read words, he saw vivid, colorful images. S also relied on associations. After many years as a mnemonist, he was able to generate abstract images quickly. For America, he formed a picture of Uncle Sam; for Bismarck, he evoked an image of a statue of Bismarck. Once the image was in his mind, he had no trouble remembering it.

The case history of S provides a vivid illustration of the power of imagery in memory. Although S's imagery was unique because it was so powerful, imagery is used commonly to remember information. Answer this question in your mind. Where is the salt kept in your home? When most students answer, they report that they can see their particular salt shaker in the kitchen cupboard or on the table. This is a visual image, and it is this representational skill that we are trying to examine as a component of information processing. We are interested in how imagery helps us process information. We are interested in how the ability to use imagery changes during development, and we are interested in how imagery interacts with other representational skills to help us remember.

## Imagery and information processing

Let us begin with the first question. What role does imagery play in information processing? Some psychologists believe that imagery functions like perception. Ronald Finke (1980) reminds us that perception involves responses at all levels of the visual system (see Figure 10–3). Images could also activate information processing mechanisms at many levels. To these psychologists, then, imagery can have many different and interesting behavioral effects.

Ernest Hilgard (1981) presents some fascinating support for the position that an image may have an effect similar to perceiving an object. The image Hilgard introduces is actually a hypnotic hallucination. To produce this hallucination, Hilgard asks a subject, let us call him Bob, to sit in the middle of three chairs and to converse with another person, Jim. After Bob has studied Jim's appearance in some detail, Bob closes his eyes. The experimenter invites Jim to move to the chair on the other side of Bob. The experimenter does this in a voice that Bob is sure to hear. At the same time, the experimenter signals Jim not to move. To make the hallucination convincing, Hilgard adjusts the empty chair and thanks Jim for moving. When Bob opens his eyes and looks at the empty chair, he reports that he sees Jim. They even converse a bit with Bob hallucinating both Jim's appearance and his remarks. When Bob is asked to look at the chair that Jim is actually sitting in, he is surprised and may look back and forth. Finally he announces that it looks like Jim is seated in this chair, too. Now the most surprising part of the experiment unfolds. Bob is told that one of these figures is a *hallucination* and is asked to decide which one is real. Bob may ask both Jims if they are real. Typically, he reports that both claim to be real. He also reports that they both seem solid and warm (Hilgard, 1981).

The hallucination produced by the hypnotized students has perceptual effects similar to those of the actual person. Bob seems to be able to touch, feel, see, and hear the hallucination he has created. In fact, his perceptions are so convincing that he cannot rely on them to signify which of the Jims is a figment of his imagination.

Another demonstration of the power of imagery comes from the relatively new field of sports psychology. Swimmers trained to generate vivid mental images of themselves swimming have been able to improve their athletic performance (White, Ashton, & Lewis, 1979). The conclusion is that practice using mental imagery has some of the same behavioral benefits as physical practice. Whether or not such training is effective seems to be influenced by the person's ability to generate vivid imagery (Ryan & Simons, 1982). S's images as a child were so vivid that sometimes he would be laying in bed thinking about going to school and forget to go. He actually thought he was already on his way to school.

These studies suggest that mental imagery is a functional skill in the chain of information processing and that, like perception, it influences processes that occur later in the chain (Block, 1981). A second conclusion is that producing an image is really a constructive process, like producing perceptions. If this is the case, then images are subject to the same organization and analysis that characterize perception.

**Figure 10—5**        **Eidetic imagery**

**Imagery in children**

The images of children may not be like adult images. *Eidetic imagery*, for example, is much more common in children than in adults. An eidetic image is an unusually vivid image that is a faithful representation of the environment. People with eidetic imagery can look at a page and later visualize that page so vividly and accurately that they can read it. Although these reports have filtered down through psychological history, adults who can demonstrate this skill are rare (Stromeyer, 1982). But roughly five percent of the children between 6 and 12 can "see" an image after a picture they have been shown has been removed (Haber, 1979). The 10-year-old boy in Figure 10–5 is one of over 50 children that Haber found who could demonstrate eidetic imagery.

---

**Figure 10–5 *Concluded***

---

A few children have the capacity to see, in their mind's eye, pictures that are no longer present. After a picture is removed from an easel, they report that they still see an image, they use the present tense in describing the image, and they can scan the image just as they would if it were still present. A 10-year-old boy describes the Indian and Animals picture after it is removed:

**Experimenter:** Can you see it?

**Subject:** Yes, I can see the white and blue sky and the ground has two different shades of green in it with some blue on it . . . and I can see two different squirrels, one is gray, and the Indian's holding him in his hand and he's eating a nut. The one on the ground—he's red with a white stripe on him. There are three birds in the air—they're green, orange—they've got some red on them.

**E:** Can you see the birds' mouths?

**S:** No, I can see the deer and the cloth on the Indian's belt, it has many colors on it, yellow is the biggest color—and I can see his bow he's holding, it's got zigzag red on it.

**E:** Anything else—any other animals?

**S:** There's three rabbits—two of them are brown and one of them is white—the one brown and white one are next to each other and there's a brown one in the right-hand corner.

**E:** What are they doing?

**S:** The one over in the right-hand corner is jumping and the other two are just standing around.

**E:** Tell me more about the Indian.

**S:** Well—

**E:** Start at the top and move down.

**S:** Well, he's got a headband on—he doesn't have a shirt on; he's got a belt on with a cloth hanging out which is red, yellow. He's got Indian moccasins on—I think they're brown.

**E:** Has he got anything else on?

**S:** No.

**E:** Anything else you can tell me—and tell me if any of the parts go away.

**S:** The rabbits and birds are going away (pause) and the sky (pause) that's it—it's all gone. (Haber, 1979, pp. 585–586)

Source: Haber, R. N. (1979). Twenty years of haunting eidetic imagery: Where's the ghost? *The behavioral and brain sciences, 2,* 583–629.

The actual skill of eidetic imagery, however, is different from the folklore that surrounds it. The images these children form do not last long. They will begin to fade in two to five minutes. Even while children can see the image, they do not see a complete representation. Their image has the same kinds of gaps and elaborations that we find in any other kinds of memory (Haber, 1980). Haber suggests that this image is directly tied to the visual channel. If children blink their eyes repeatedly, the image disappears. If children want to prevent images from forming, they simply have to name each of the items in the picture and no visual image develops. To account for this, Haber suggests that "eidetic children have two modes of processing visual stimuli: a visual mode, which leads to a visual image, and a verbal rehearsal mode, which blocks the image" (1979, p. 590).

Haber and others have tested adults, looking for the same skill that children display. But in adults the incidence of eidetic imagery drops to almost zero. This difference is curious and invites speculation. One explanation simply states that children lose their imagery much as they lose their baby teeth. But this hypothesis is not supported by data. In the only longitudinal study on record, children remained eidetic for five years (Leask, Haber, & Haber, 1969). Furthermore, young children are not better at eidetic imagery than older children.

Another explanation centers on the more primitive and concrete aspects of imagery and suggests that as more advanced cognitive processes develop, imagery disappears. The fact that children with eidetic imagery have a range of IQs, a range of reading skills, and a range of abstract thinking skills argues against this hypothesis. But the fact that primitive peoples rely more heavily on imagery suggests that this hypothesis has some merit.

A final explanation has been dubbed the neurological hypothesis. According to this view, eidetic imagery occurs because of neural immaturity. To test this, experimenters have examined children with neurological deficits and older subjects (70 to 90 years old), expecting to find a greater proportion of eidetic imagery. The results from these studies have been inconsistent. Some have found a high percentage of eidetic imagers, while others have not (Haber, 1980).

Ralph Haber argues that true eidetic imagery is so rare and startling that it does not fit into any developmental picture. Gummerman and Gray (1971) believe, however, that eidetic imagery represents the extreme of an ability that is present in all of us to some degree. Their position is supported by a recent study in which children and adults were shown simple and complex pictures (Pezdek & Chen, 1982). Pictures of a clown or a street scene (see Figure 10–6) were presented to fourth graders and college students. The extra detail in the complex pictures was not essential to the theme of the picture, but if you did not attend to the details, you might not recall whether you had seen the picture. The adults found complex pictures more difficult to recognize than simple pictures. Perhaps adults just code the main theme of the picture and ignore the details. The children did equally well recognizing the simple and complex

**Figure 10—6**                    **Remembering pictures**

SIMPLE            COMPLEX

*Courtesy Thomas O. Nelson*

The complex pictures used in this experiment add details to the main theme of the simple picture. However, if you do not encode the details, you might not recognize the picture.

pictures. Perhaps this skill is a less sophisticated version of the imagery reported by Haber.

**Imagery as an aid to memory**

Eidetic imagery is interesting as a phenomenon, but it does not seem to account for how children usually remember information. In fact, children with eidetic imagery occasionally report that it interferes with other cognitive processes. S, whose imagery was especially vivid, read very slowly because the images he formed tumbled into each other. It is not surprising, then, that some psychologists have argued that imagery is superfluous as a memory aid (Pylyshyn, 1973). Imagery, however, was also a central part of S's memory skill, and earliest memories are typically images. Perhaps, then, imagery can help children remember.

After a provocative article by Richard Anderson (1975) describing the *key-word* technique, many researchers began to look at how elementary school children use imagery (Pressley, Levin, & Delaney, 1982). We now know that creating an image around a keyword can improve memory in both experimental and educational settings. An example comes from a study in which eighth graders were asked to remember 12 fictitious people and their accomplishments (Shriberg, Levin, McCormick, & Pressley, 1982). These 12 people were introduced using short paragraphs:

> Animal owners all over the world are impressed that Charlene McKune has taught her pet cat how to count. The cat can count to 20 without making any mistakes. Moreover, the remarkable cat can do some simple addition. It took many months of patient training to teach the cat these skills, and Ms. McKune rewarded him with a large bowl of spaghetti after every successful session. Finally, last week, the local university presented the cat with an honorary diploma. (p. 242)

To use the keyword method, students selected one word that helped them remember the person's name. In the case of Charlene McKune, raccoon was selected as a keyword because it rhymed with McKune. The next step was to build an image around the keyword (see Figure 10–7).

Groups of children who were given keywords and pictures that summarized the information in the paragraph were able to remember the "famous" people, their accomplishments, and the incidental details much better than students who only studied the paragraph. A third group was given the keyword and told to create their own image. These students also remembered more than the

**Figure 10–7**     **Imagery as a mnemonic device**

The keyword method relies on imagery to help the child remember. Children develop images that include all the details of the story they are trying to remember.

Source: Shriberg, L. K., Levin, J. R., McCormick, C. B., & Pressley, M. (1982). Learning about "famous" people via the keyword method. *Journal of Educational Psychology, 74*, 238–247.

control group. As a result of these experiments, imagery is being recognized as a potent tool for remembering, and school-age children are being taught how to use imagery (Pressley, 1982).

Preschoolers and toddlers are not very good at using imagery to help them remember (Cramer, 1981). Perhaps, though, the problem is the difficulty of the tasks, not the inability to use imagery. Typically, in these experiments, children are given two nouns (bee and ring) and asked to remember them as a pair (Kee, Bell, & Davis, 1981). In order to remember them, children have to construct a link between the words, remember the words, and remember the link. These kinds of mental transformations are difficult for preoperational children. The fact that they have trouble generating these links is really not a good indicator of whether they use imagery.

Michael Pressley and his colleagues believe that imagery is an effective tool for remembering even in preschoolers. But to see this facilitative effect, the experimenter has to provide the links between the nouns. When both the key-word and an illustration are presented to help the child link the image with the word, children as young as three are able to learn Spanish vocabulary words easily. If they have to create their own image, they did not learn any better than children in a control group (Pressley, Levin, & Delaney, 1982).

Not all researchers are as enthusiastic about the keyword method. Some regard it as a sideshow trick, arguing that the new memories are not organized or integrated with other knowledge the child has learned. To answer these critics, psychologists need to demonstrate that elaboration strategies help children retain information over a long period of time and that such a strategy, once it is taught, will be transferred to a variety of memory tasks (Rohwer, 1980).

Despite these objections, research on imagery has increased our understanding of information processing. We know that preverbal memories are predominantly spatially organized images. We also understand that these images are not easily retrieved by the toddler. The images have to be cued by the immediate environment. As preschoolers become more verbal, these early images are linked with language and can be retrieved more easily.

During elementary school, children learn more complex cognitive strategies—forming associations, rehearsing, and elaborating the information. When imagery is wedded to these strategies, it is an effective aid to recall (Wooldridge, Nall, Hughes, Rauch, Stewart, & Richman, 1982). Imagery, then, seems to be an initial way of processing the environment that gradually becomes integrated with language based strategies and conceptual strategies (Herman, Roth Miranda, & Getz, 1982).

## THE DEVELOPMENT OF MEMORY

Adults have better memories than children. Psychologists want to know why and they want to know how adults' memories differ from children's. At least four factors have been examined to account for the superior memories of adults. The first is the development of more efficient strategies for remembering. Preschoolers lack the skill to help themselves remember (Fabricus & Wellman, 1983). College students rehearse, organize, and sometimes outline material they need to remember. A second difference between children and adults is the amount of knowledge these two groups have at their disposal. An adult's information about the world provides a rich context for building associations and remembering. This contextual base is just being formed in children. A third, more controversial difference is the capacity of children's and adults' memories. Finally, a person's awareness about the process of remembering changes. This awareness, called *metamemory*, allows adults to evaluate memory strategies and choose effective ones for each task.

To trace the development of memory, we will follow the changes in children's strategies, knowledge, memory capacity, and metamemory. Before we do this, we need to further dissect the process of memory. In an information processing model, memory is a combination of several distinct processes (see Figure 10–8). To remember something, we need to encode the information. After information is encoded, we need to store it in memory. Finally, we need to develop strategies that will enable us to retrieve that information. These three processes seldom occur in isolation, but separating them conceptually helps psychologists devise experiments that will emphasize the retrieval process or the encoding process (Bjorklund & Hock, 1982).

Experimenters also distinguish between short-term and long-term memories. Information that needs attention immediately is stored in short-term memory. The different processes discussed in this chapter are carried out on information stored in short-term memory. For this reason, short-term memory is also known as working memory. But short-term memory is limited. Only a few storage and processing activities can be carried out at a given time (Dempster, 1981). Long-term memory or permanent memory is not limited to current activities; it contains the sum of the individual's experiences. Furthermore, the capacity of long-term memory is unlimited (Farah & Kosslyn, 1982). Long-term memories can be retrieved weeks, months, or decades after the event has occurred. Many of us remember a telephone number long enough to dial it, but the next day cannot retrieve it. The number was only in short-term memory. The distinctions between encoding, storing, and retrieving and between short-term and long-term memory will become clearer as we discuss strategies, knowledge, memory capacity, and metamemory in children and adults.

**Strategies to enhance memory**

A *mnemonic strategy* is an action or plan undertaken to assist memory. Preschool children often fail to produce such strategies and are unaware of their usefulness. So they are not very good at producing them (Flavell & Wellman, 1977). School age children do see a need to do something to help them remember. They begin to generate simple strategies like repeating words or instructions that they must remember. The strategies that junior high school children use range from simple rehearsal to building complex organizations

**Figure 10—8**          **Short-term memory**

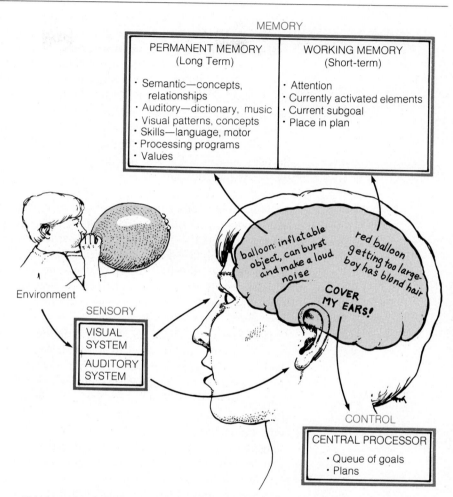

This illustration is a working model of the human information processing system. The environment is coded through the sensory system and passed to the memory system. Here it is compared with information we carry in long-term memory. The appropriate long-term memories are activated and become working memory. The working memory, also known as short-term memory, is a work space for ongoing cognitive activity. Working memory, in concert with the central processor, decides on a course of action and carries it out. The action could be responding or storing information in long-term memory or merely deciding that no response is necessary.

Source: Dodd, D. H., & White, R. M., Jr. (1980). *Cognition: Mental structures and processes.* Boston: Allyn & Bacon.

that will cue recall. As these memory strategies are discussed, notice that complex strategies, if they are used at all, are not discovered until about age 12 (Neimark, 1976). Perhaps this is because the more sophisticated strategies require the child to combine several kinds of mental processes.

**Using language to cue memories.**   Initially, toddlers rely on a spatial representation of their environment. Between 2 and 2½ they begin to respond to language to cue their memories. Catherine Sophian (1982) demonstrated this by having children under 2 and children who were 2½ search for a hidden toy. In an observational condition, the children saw the experimenter hide the objects. In a verbal condition, the children were told where the object would be hidden. In the verbal condition, toddlers had difficulty using the verbal cue to help them find the toy, but finding the toy was easy if they were given the observational cue. The older children were more adept with the verbal cues, even though they were only six months older.

This study is probably not surprising to mothers who have asked their toddlers about a circus they attended earlier in the week. Initially, such a question evokes blank stares. If the mother can retrieve a program or a book about the circus, the child's memories come pouring out. The program cues the child's visual memory directly. The verbal cues are less successful at this young age. Verbal cues become more important in retrieving memories as development proceeds. For the majority of adults, verbal cues have become the dominant way of retrieving information.

**Rehearsal.**   Rehearsing, or repeating the information to be remembered, is another mnemonic strategy used early in life. If children are asked to remember the word *bear*, they will probably mouth "bear." Even before children begin repeating the actual words, they can visually rehearse the location of an object. One three-year-old trying to remember in which of two cups a bear was hidden, looked at the correct cup and nodded "yes," then looked at the other cup and vigorously nodded "no" (Wellman, Ritter, & Flavell, 1975). By kindergarten age, many children rehearse spontaneously. At this age, children can be readily taught to rehearse a list of words they want to remember (Asarnow & Meichenbaum, 1979).

More complex rehearsal strategies evolve during the school years. Suppose the children are asked to remember 16 items with 1 item presented every five seconds. After the word *plum* is presented, first or second grade children chant "plum, plum, plum" until the next word is presented. By eighth grade, children use the five seconds to rehearse the whole list instead of just the most recent word (Pressley, Heisel, McCormick, & Nakamura, 1982). Their rehearsing sounds like this—"plum, bear, dog, plum, bear, dog." Children who use this strategy, instead of the simpler one, remember more of the 16 words. High school students continue to refine the art of rehearsal. They organize the list and plan how they will put the list into memory as well as how they will retrieve it during the test (Brown, Bransford, Ferrara, & Campione, 1983).

**Organized recall.**   Suppose a list is composed of words from different categories—food, animals, and articles of clothing. Third graders hearing this list might use the only strategy they know—rehearsal—to help them remember. Even when they are asked to group the words, they form random groups of words that are not meaningfully related (Corsale & Ornstein, 1980). Junior high school children decide spontaneously that if they group the words in a meaningful way, they will remember more of them (Bjorklund & Hock, 1982). A look at their recall indicates that they remember "ice," "pitcher," and "spoon" together. This strategy is called *category clustering* (Corsale & Ornstein, 1980). Organizing material into meaningful categories is a familiar strategy to college students who are studying for exams (Moely, 1977).

*Chunking* is a similar mechanism. If asked to remember six numbers, it helps to chunk them into two groups of three. Instead of remembering 4 6 2 3 0 9, adolescents remember four hundred and sixty-two and three hundred and nine. Adolescents have no trouble recoding isolated numbers into chunks, but children between 5 and 12 show little spontaneous chunking (Lange, 1978).

**Verbal elaboration.** Instead of giving children lists of words to remember, psychologists often investigate memory by asking children to remember paired items (cat and apple, turkey and rock, good evening and *buenos noches*). In these experiments, children are asked to remember the pairs together so that when "cat" is presented later, the child can respond "apple." One strategy for remembering the pairs is called *elaboration* and involves generating an image or sentence in which the two words are related. Visual elaboration as described involves creating images in the keyword technique. In verbal elaboration, the child creates a sentence linking the two words. Because bizarre sentences are more effective mnemonic aids, a student might generate, "The turkey hatched the rock" or, "The turkey pushed the rock off the cliff." Using such elaborations, children in nursery school can remember paired items (Pressley, 1982).

Adolescents elaborate material without prompting (Rohwer, 1980). Younger children rarely generate this strategy on their own. Furthermore, even if younger children are taught to elaborate, they have difficulty combining all of the mental processes needed to use the strategy successfully. They have to be prompted to remember the sentence they created. Adolescents immediately try to remember the link they created between the two words (Rohwer, 1980). These results are important because they illustrate the problem young children have in putting all of the elements of memory together. They can successfully elaborate, encode, and store the information, but without special help, they have problems retrieving it.

Elaboration takes more time than rehearsing or responding to a cue. The words have to be elaborated before they can be stored. They are then encoded. Because this process requires organization early in the memory process, few people practice the strategy. If, however, people practice this or similar strategies that involve associations, they can rival the performance of S in remembering lists of words or numbers. At Carnegie Mellon University, an undergraduate student was trained to elaborate digits and to generate meaningful associations for them. Over an 18-month period, he practiced remembering digits for one hour a day. At the end of his training, the number of digits he could remember had skyrocketed from 4 to 79. This phenomenal improvement was due to complex elaborations of three or four digits. The subject was an avid runner and had stored in memory a variety of times for races varying in length from a half-mile to a marathon. He used these times to elaborate strings of three or four digits. For example, he coded the string 3492 as 3 minutes 49.2 seconds—close to the world record for the mile. His ability to remember a long series of numbers attests to the power of elaboration (Ericsson, Chase, & Faloon, 1980).

Strategies for learning vary depending on the task and the age of the learner. The two-year-old who keeps his eye and his hand on the cup hiding the M&Ms is using a strategy. Strategies used by school-age children are more sophisticated, but are still likely to be patchy and fragile (Brown, Bransford, Ferrara, & Campione, 1983). Even among college students, it is seldom the case that we see an immediate application of the most systematic and logical strategies.

Even this truncated look at strategies demonstrates that strategies for remembering information are more varied, more efficient, and more sophisticated in adults than in children. Changes in strategies, however, do not entirely explain the development of memory. We can teach children the strategies that adults use, but children will still not remember as well as adults. Similarly, if we prevent adults from using particular strategies, they still remember more facts than children (Chi, 1978). To understand the development of memory, we must look beyond strategies.

## The development of knowledge

The second advantage that adults have over children is that adults have years of knowledge and experience tucked into long-term memory. The sum of this knowledge is often called a person's *semantic memory*. It includes factual information, like when the first humans landed on the moon, relational information, like how a tree and a saw are related; and procedural information, like how to add three and four. VP, another extraordinary mnemonist, demonstrates the utility of semantic memory (Hunt & Love, 1982).

VP was born in Latvia in 1934 and moved repeatedly during the Second World War. His wandering exposed him to many languages, and he learned to speak German, Latvian, Russian, Estonian, Spanish, French, Latin, and English. This base of languages helped VP develop associations for information that he wanted to remember.

As a child, VP attended schools that stressed rote learning. He credits some of his memory skill to this early training and to the fact that the schools were more authoritarian than today's schools. VP's IQ was 136. Not surprisingly, his performance on the IQ tests was strongest on those subtests that required memory. He also achieved unusually high scores on tests that required perceptual speed. He noticed the tiniest details of presentations and could code them very rapidly.

**Figure 10—9**          **War of the ghosts**

One night two young men from Egulac went down to the river to hunt seals, and while they were there it became foggy and calm. Then they heard war-cries, and they thought: "Maybe this is a war-party." They escaped to the shore, and hid behind a log. Now canoes came up, and they heard the noise of paddles, and saw one canoe coming up to them. There were five men in the canoe and they said:

"What do you think? We wish to take you along. We are going up the river to make war on the people."

One of the young men said: "I have no arrows."

"Arrows are in the canoe," they said.

"I will not go along. I might be killed. My relatives do not know where I have gone. But you," he said, turning to the other, "may go with them."

So one of the young men went, but the other returned home.

And the warriors went on up the river to a town on the other side of Kalama. The people came down to the water, and they began to fight, and many were killed. But presently the young man heard one of the warriors say: "Quick, let us go home; that Indian has been hit." Now he thought: "Oh, they are ghosts." He did not feel sick, but they said he had been shot.

So the canoes went back to Egulac, and the young man went ashore to his house, and made a fire. And he told everybody and said: "Behold I accompanied the ghosts, and we went to fight. Many of our fellows were killed, and many of those who attacked us were killed. They said I was hit, and I did not feel sick."

He told it all, and then he became quiet. When the sun rose he fell down. Something black came out of his mouth. His face became contorted. The people jumped up and cried.

He was dead.

A year after reading this story, VP was able to reproduce whole sections of it exactly as it was told. In all, he retained 70 percent of the nouns and verbs used in the original story.

Source: Hunt, E. and Love, T. (1982). The second mnemonist. In V. Neisser (Ed.) *Memory observed.* San Francisco: W. H. Freeman.

VP's memory was tested using several standard procedures. In one, he read a short story called "War of the Ghosts" (see Figure 10–9) and was asked to recall the story one hour later. A year after the original reading, he was called in unexpectedly and asked to repeat the story. At that time, VP recalled not only the plot, but actually used 70 percent of the nouns and verbs used in the original story.

VP relied on associations to remember information. In one experiment, he was presented with nonsense syllables like XIB and asked to generate associations for that syllable. Most students do this by interchanging or dropping letters, or by remembering a word that is acoustically similar, like FIB. VP, however, developed semantic associations. In response to XIB, he associated X with the signature of an illiterate. IB reminded him of Women's Lib. Thus, "illiterate woman" could be used to retrieve the syllable XIB (Hunt & Love, 1982). When asked to explain how he remembered other nonsense syllables, VP explained that one syllable was similar to a Latin proverb, another was similar to an American political scientist, a third resembled the Latin word for swan, and a fourth reminded him of the Hebrew word for gentile.

From this brief sketch, we can see that part of VP's skill was a function of languages he knew. These provided a very rich store of information to build associations. A second part of his skill came from his ability to construct associations quickly. Moments after a nonsense syllable was presented, VP had formed an association. Finally, his whole educational experience was focused on acquiring and retrieving information (Hunt & Love, 1982).

Ulric Neisser (1982) suggests that VP's skills are a superior form of the semantic memory skills we all use. An example of how semantic memory functions in a typical population of college students is described in a classic experiment by Benton Underwood (1982). Students were shown dozens of words like "table" or "fork" at a rapid rate. Then they were shown another set and asked to identify those they had seen earlier. The mistakes the students made were as instructive as the correct responses. Students often thought that "chair" and "knife" had been included in the first set of pictures. These students' mistakes demonstrate the relationships that exist in our minds. Information that we perceive does not just register in our brains in an isolated way. Seeing a picture of a table or a fork activates a whole network of associations (Anderson, 1981). The objects involved may be quite different, like a table and a chair, but they share this regular relationship that makes them part of the network (Rohwer, 1980). As a result, they can be tapped by a single association.

Some information processing theorists believe that the increase in semantic memory is the catalyst for increased memory as we get older. Chechile and Richman (1982) present the position succinctly: The basic memory system is functioning at age five in the same way that it functions in adulthood. Retention increases with age because of the richer semantic memories one accumulates. A test for this hypothesis would be to find a subject in which children have more expertise than adults. If knowledge, or semantic memory, is critical to memory, these children should outperform adults.

Michelene Chi (1978) designed such a test. The children she examined were, on the average, 10 years old and had participated in a local chess tournament. The adults were graduate students who knew how to play chess. Both groups were asked to remember a particular arrangement (see Figure 10–10). Despite the fact that adults could bring all of their sophisticated memory strategies to bear on this task, the children were much better at remembering the chessboard. The children's greater knowledge of chess helped them organize the pieces and remember the relationships more efficiently. When Chi presented these same children and adults with another memory task—repeating digits— the adults remembered many more than the children. Chi argues that the reason these children excelled in the chess tasks was because of their greater knowledge and organization of the game. In short, they had richer semantic memories than the adults.

Since Chi's article appeared, other psychologists have touted the importance of the child's semantic memory (see Siegler, 1983). Limited knowledge constrains a person's approach to a subject, be it chess, algebra, or geography. A larger knowledge base means that finer discriminations and relationships will be understood quickly (Chi & Koeske, 1983). College students at Yale Univer-

**Figure 10-10**          **Knowledge in memory**

*Joel Gordon*

Some children acquire a great deal of knowledge about the game of chess. When these children are compared to adults who are not as knowledgeable about chess, the children remember chessboards better.

sity learned new information about Ted Kennedy in moments, but new information about unknown people was quickly forgotten (Anderson, 1981). Prior knowledge about a person creates a network that allows individuals to integrate new information easily.

**Memory capacity**

Psychologists have always assumed that adults have more memory capacity than children. This conclusion was based on scores of studies in which children could not remember as many words, as many letters, or as many numbers as adults. The underlying metaphor was that the mind was a container: little people have little containers and bigger people have bigger ones (Brown & DeLoache, 1978). Recently, however, this notion has come under attack. Frank Dempster's exhaustive review of the literature (1981) on memory span led him to conclude that school-age children and adults have the same memory capacity. If this is the case, then improvements in memory occur because of changes in strategies, knowledge, and metamemory, not basic capacity.

Still, this position is not endorsed by all information processing theorists.

Juan Pascual-Leone (1980) and Robbie Case (1978) argue the reverse—that memory span or M space increases with age. Pascual-Leone has even specified the rate of increase and has tried to tie this increase to changes in brain physiology. As we have seen, young children seldom generate memory strategies. Pascual Leone and his colleagues believe that the use of strategies is directly linked to the growth of working memory. To prove this, Pascual-Leone taught children of the same age but with different memory capacities an elaboration strategy. The children with larger memory capacities learned more efficiently.

Robbie Case's position is a bit different. He believes that the total processing space of both children and adults is limited. He states that as children become more efficient at remembering, they require less of this limited space. The net effect is that more space seems to be available (Case, Kurland, & Goldberg, 1982). To demonstrate this, Case had adults and children count. The adults had to count in an artificial language. Because remembering this language took so much of their memory space, the adults could only remember as many numbers as six-year-olds. The results from experiments like this have convinced Case (1980) that psychologists and educators need to be aware of the limits of memory capacity. When the load on working memory is decreased, children can often solve problems that otherwise would befuddle them.

**Metamemory**

The interest in metamemory, or what children understand about remembering, was sparked by John Flavell (Flavell, 1971, 1981; Flavell & Wellman, 1977). Prior to his work, psychologists had been content to document the continuing improvement in the ability to encode and retrieve information. Flavell pointed out that these skills were accompanied by a heightened awareness of memory processes. Flavell's initial work pointed to the development of metamemory between the ages of 4 and 12 (Flavell & Wellman, 1977; Kreutzer, Leonard, & Flavell, 1975). More recent investigations have extended the improvement in metamemory into adolescence (Pressley, Heisel, McCormick, & Nakamura, 1982; Waters, 1982).

To date, metamemory research has shown that children have to develop an appreciation for the difficulty of memory tasks (Lawson, 1980). They need to realize that they will have more difficulty remembering 10 words than 3 words, and that they will have to do something to devise a strategy to remember 10 words. As we have seen, preschoolers do not realize that it takes special effort to remember information (Corsale & Ornstein, 1981). By third grade, children have quite an array of strategies to help them remember. When asked how she would remember to bring her skates to school the next day, a third grader detailed a long list of strategies.

> I could put them in my book bag, or set them on the table. Or I could always write myself a note, and put it up on my bulletin board. Or I could tell my mom to remind me. Or I could take them to school the day before and just leave them there.

> A kindergarten boy responded to the same question with a candid, "I would forget." (Kreutzer, Leonard, & Flavell, 1975, p. 151).

Determining whether a child understands the process of metamemory is useful, but it is only the first part of the problem (Brown, 1978). We must then ask whether understanding the memory process enhances memory skills (Cavanaugh & Perlmutter, 1982). In other words, does children's knowledge about memory influence their behavior?

The connection is not as direct as developmental psychologists might like to think. Elementary school children, who understand the usefulness of categorizing words, do not necessarily use this strategy when they are asked to remember a list of words (Salatas & Flavell, 1976; Cavanaugh & Borkowski, 1980). Perhaps these children were too young to apply their knowledge about remembering to actual tasks (Waters, 1982). Studies using older children have had more success in showing that metamemory is a factor in remembering information (Schneider, 1982)

Improved awareness of memory may not affect isolated tasks. Being aware, however, could determine how widely children apply a strategy that they have learned (Kurtz, Reid, Borkowski, & Cavanaugh, 1982). Retarded children profit immediately from being taught a memory strategy (Brown & Palincsar, 1982), but they have no idea when to apply the strategy or how to adapt it to a slightly different task (Campione & Brown, 1978). They seem to lack the understanding that this new strategy can be put to use on a variety of tasks (Kendall, Borkowski, & Cavanaugh, 1980). In essence, these children lack metamemory.

Given these results, psychologists have concluded that applying memory strategies to a variety of tasks requires metamemory (Borkowski, in press). From a practical standpoint, this means that educators must not only teach children how to use a strategy like elaboration, they must instruct students when the strategy is most valuable, how it augments other strategies, and what can be expected if you use it (Pressley, Heisel, McCormick, & Nakamura, 1982).

The development of memory is not a single process that follows an obvious path. Children begin by remembering spatial locations, and their memories are cued by environmental contexts. Gradually, they learn to use language to cue their spatial memories and they learn to integrate language with images. During the elementary school years, children begin to generate strategies to help them remember and they become aware of the skills that are needed to remember. Both strategies and metamemory continue to develop into adolescence and young adulthood. Of course, each day children learn more about their world. This increase in knowledge plays a major role in the child's ability to encode, store, and retrieve information in everyday situations.

## HIGHER ORDER COGNITIVE PROCESSES

In addition to the basic processes that have already been discussed, information processing theorists have investigated a variety of other, more complex skills, such as cognitive mapping, problem solving, and scientific reasoning (Morrison & Manis, 1982; Pick & Rieser, 1982; Sternberg, Guyote, & Turner, 1980; Siegler, 1978, 1983). To understand how psychologists approach these more complex cognitive skills, we will examine some studies involving problem solving and scientific reasoning.

Robert Siegler began his assessment of scientific reasoning with a close examination of tasks that Inhelder and Piaget used in their research on formal operational thought. He modified one of these tasks—the balance beam—and began a detailed study of how children reason about scientific issues. The task itself is deceptively simple. A balance beam (see Figure 10–11) that has four equally spaced pegs on each side of a fulcrum is presented. The child is asked to place metal weights on each side of the balance and then to predict whether the balance will remain level or tip to one side.

After years of studying problems like this, Siegler (1983) concludes that to understand scientific reasoning, we need to understand what rules the child devises to solve problems. In the balance task for example, young children initially attend only to the weight that is put on the balance. Their rule might be: "If the number of weights is the same on each side, the balance will remain level; otherwise it will tip." Several years later, the child's rule still includes weight, but now the child considers the distance of that weight from the fulcrum.

**Figure 10–11**                    **Scientific reasoning**

Balance scale apparatus

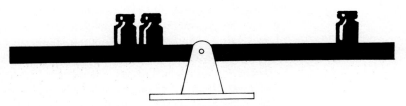

Rule I. If there are the same number of weights on both sides, the balance will be level. If the number of weights is uneven, the side with the most will go down.

Rule II. Both weight and distance from the fulcrum are important, but weight is the determining variable.

Rule III. Both weight and distance are important factors. If they are equal, the balance will be level. If only one of those factors is the same, the other will determine the outcome. But if both factors are different (i.e., different weights on different pegs), one can't tell what will happen.

Rule IV. The force from the fulcrum is equal to the distance multiplied by the weight. The side with the greater force will go down.

Siegler believes that scientific reasoning is based on rules. Young children form rules that account for some of the facts. When children discover that their initial rules are incomplete, they modify them to encompass more of the facts. Over a period of years, their rules begin to take the same form as adult rules. On the balance problem, five-year-olds use Rule I. Seventeen-year-olds use Rule III but can learn rule IV easily.

Source: Siegler, R. S. (1978). The origins of scientific reasoning. In R. S. Siegler (Ed.), *Children's thinking: What develops?* Hillsdale, NJ: Lawrence Erlbaum.

Once psychologists have identified which rule a child is using, they can predict whether or not a child will answer correctly and what kinds of errors the child will make. Understanding what rule the child is using also means that we can direct the child to more comprehensive rules. If we know that the child only attends to the weight on the balance beam, we could devise a situation where the weight is uneven but the balance still remains level. Demonstrating that weight is not the only factor might prod the child to consider other factors. Siegler concludes that a child's scientific reasoning is based on rules.

Forming rules seems like a reasonable way for children to organize the information they have garnered from the environment. But the process is not a smooth one. Deanna Kuhn suggests that forming these rules is a complex, circuitous process. In her experiment, children came into the laboratory for several experimental sessions in which they were asked to solve problems. From one experimental session to another, the children would change their strategies and forget what they had already discovered about a problem. Achieving a stable and comprehensive solution to a particular problem required several sessions in which detours and regressions of thought were common. Students were reluctant to give up rules they had formed earlier. Their inability to discard old rules and formulate new ones was a major obstacle to learning (Kuhn & Phelps, 1984).

Children may formulate rules to help them organize information from their environments. This is not, however, the only way to organize information. Rules may work well for older children trying to solve problems. But, as mentioned in Chapter 8, rules require too much analysis to be a common mode of information processing in young children (Farah & Kosslyn, 1982).

If children do not form rules, how do they organize the information they encounter? A second suggestion is that children store every example of a concept like "dog" in memory. This strategy is called the *exemplar* model. Notice that it does not require any analysis of the dog. Every time children encounter a dog, they will remember that dog. If this is the case, then how do all of these isolated representations get organized into a category called dog?

A third explanation is that children develop a *prototype* of a dog based on their experience and then fit new examples of dogs to that prototype. As a child's information about dogs becomes more extensive, the prototype is modified. Trying to document the existence of prototypes in a child's mind poses a challenge for psychologists. In one attempt, children and adults were asked whether a particular bird fit the prototype they had formed. The question, "Is a robin a bird?" received an immediate yes. The question, "Is a penguin a bird" required more time. Presumably both the children and the adults had to compare the penguin to their prototype of a bird before they could answer (Farah & Kosslyn, 1982).

Perhaps all three of these strategies are used at different times during development. Kossan (1981) found that seven-year-olds preferred a nonanalytic exemplar approach when they were asked to remember imaginary animals. The 10-year-olds in her study were more likely to analyze the characteristics of the animals and form rules. Rules offer an efficient way to handle information. They are used by older children and adults and are especially valuable for cognitive tasks that require problem solving. Exemplars allow children to form concepts without engaging in lengthy analysis. Perhaps this is the mode of concept formation used by younger children. The prototype explanation allows children to make comparisons even if the object is not familiar. When children were shown a wombat, they decided rather quickly that it was an animal. When asked whether an ant was an animal, they took a much longer time to answer. The point is that familiarity with an object does not guarantee we will immediately be able to categorize it. Ants are familiar, but they are not similar to a prototype that children have formed for "animal." A wombat, despite its unfamiliarity, fits neatly into this prototype (Anglin, 1977).

The question, "How do children organize information?" has several answers. A tenable hypothesis is that exemplars are used until children acquire a certain amount of experience with a category, such as birds. Once the child knows a few birds, a prototype of a bird can be formed. This is finally translated into a set of rules about what constitutes a bird.

Another suggestion is that strategies to organize information may vary depending on the task. Problem solving and scientific reasoning seem to require children to experiment and form rules. Organizing information about animals and birds may be better served by using exemplars and prototypes.

## EVALUATING THE INFORMATION PROCESSING APPROACH

The information processing model begins by drawing a parallel between children's mental processes and computer operations. Using this analogy, information processing theorists try to examine the cognitive processes that occur between environmental events and the child's response to those events. This allegiance to a computer model is not followed strictly by all information processing theorists. In actual practice, information processing covers a number of theories and research paradigms. The computer model serves more as a framework for diverse approaches than an agreed upon model. No doubt, the reader noticed that as the actual studies in perception, attention, memory, imagery, and problem solving were reviewed, the computer analogy drifted to the background.

Information processing theorists specify the precise nature of the processes that characterize cognition. If the process to be studied is memory, then this process is divided into its component parts and each segment is tested. Specific memory strategies are evaluated. The importance of knowledge as a factor in memory is assessed. Even the developmental course of the memory is measured and quantified.

Thanks to this demand for precision, psychologists understand much more about the variety of processes that children use to understand their environment. We know how children use imagery, how they deploy their attention, how they think about the process of memory, and how they approach complex problems.

In terms of empirical strategies, this advantage can turn into a handicap from a theoretical perspective. Because information processing theorists are working on so many processes from so many vantage points, the field sometimes seems fragmented, and researchers are accused of focusing on narrow domains of behavior (Kail & Bisanz, 1982). The breadth of processes under study is impressive, but this breadth tends to preclude any overriding integrative theory. Despite these difficulties, a few investigators have recently tried to draw some of the findings together (Anderson, 1982; Case, 1980, 1981; Pascual-Leone, 1980; Siegler, 1983). In the next few years, we will undoubtedly see more attempts to weave the findings into a coherent theoretical form.

A major concern of developmental psychologists is describing and understanding the cognitive changes that occur from infancy to adulthood. Information processing theorists have been accused of minimizing these changes. Robert Kail and Jeffrey Bisanz (1982) point out, however, that developmental changes are described for each process. The changes that occur in imagery are specified. The increasing complexity and organization of memory is described. Strategies used by two-year-olds and college students are compared. Nevertheless, this approach is very different from the whole child approach of the structuralists.

A final disadvantage of the information processing approach is that efforts to understand the reasons for change are just beginning (Brown, Bransford, Ferrara, & Campione, 1983). The descriptions of how a four-year-old and a 10-year-old remember are very valuable, but these descriptions seldom include information about how the four-year-old's memory is transformed into the 10-year old's version. When such interpretations have been offered (Case, 1981; Siegler, 1983), they have borrowed heavily from Piaget's approach to change.

Information processing theorists have been at the forefront of research on individual differences in cognitive development. Their investigations have revitalized a field that was mired in controversy. Such research is valuable because it describes the whole spectrum of skills like imagery, memory, or problem solving. In this chapter, we have focused on some of the separate skills that are used to process information. In the next chapter, the last in the section on cognitive development, we will look at individual differences in cognition.

## SUMMARY

The information processing approach to cognitive development grew out of the experimental tradition of the behaviorists. But behaviorism ignored the mental operations that occurred between environmental events and responses to those events. The information processing theorists realized that perception, attention, memory, imagery, and various problem solving skills determined the child's response. They wanted to investigate these operations, but they wanted to do so in a precise, scientific way. Adopting the computer model allowed them to define separate processes for acquiring information.

The computer model was also used to organize this chapter. We began with the processes that are most directly related to the external environment—the perceptual processes. The next skills we considered—attention and imagery—are less dependent on the external environment. Finally, memory and problem solving were discussed. These processes sometimes occur with little reference to the external environment. This organization portrays information processing as a chain of events and conveys the impression that information processing occurs in a strict sequence. This is not an accurate reflection of how information processing occurs. Of course, children have to analyze the stimulation in the environment. When they do, perception and attention are primary skills that the child uses. The child's information and knowledge also influence the analysis. In fact, all of the processes that have been discussed can be used whenever the child begins to interact with the environment. The child can attend to something, begin to process it, find a contradiction, go back to the environment, and then immediately integrate the information into long-term memory. No set sequence of information processing is followed religiously. Instead, different processes are tapped at different times to help children understand their environments.

The development of imagery was traced from the toddler's earliest spatial memories to the visual imagery of S. Thanks to the information processing theorists, imagery is recognized as a vital skill that everyone applies during the early years of information processing. Furthermore, we are recognizing that imagery, once integrated with language skills, can be a valuable aid to memory. The literature hints that imagery can be developed far beyond our current understanding and may have uses in school, sports, and psychotherapy. It is obvious from this sketch of imagery that individuals differ in their ability to use visual imagery. Children with eidetic imagery and adults like S have skills that most of us lack. Nevertheless, the suggestion from information processing is that we all have some skill with images, but we lack information about how to use that ability effectively.

The development of memory begins soon after birth with the recognition of familiar sights, sounds, and tastes. By one year of age, the child demonstrates that some information is stored in a spatial memory. Although two-year-olds obviously store information, retrieving those memories is difficult. Cues from the environment are necessary. As language is learned, the earliest spatial memories become integrated with language. The child's increasing skill with language helps organize concepts and memories. During the elementary school years, several changes occur that influence memory. First, the child's store of knowledge increases. Second, the child begins to use strategies to aid memory. Third, the child develops an awareness of memory, called metamemory. Finally, the child's memory capacity may change. By adolescence, memory is aided by the use of a wide variety of strategies and a substantial body of accumulated knowledge.

When children are asked to think, they must organize the perceptions, memories, and images they have gathered from the environment. To answer a question about birds, children may rely on exemplars. To decide whether a wombat is an animal, they may refer to their prototype of an animal. To decide how weight and distance interact on a balance, they may abstract rules. All three of these processes help children organize information from the environment.

Trying to understand the child's mind is a formidable, but fascinating task. It is little wonder that many developmental psychologists devote their careers to studying some aspect of cognitive development. Their efforts are yielding insights that ultimately will help us develop everyone's cognitive potential.

# C H A P T E R   1 1

# Individual differences in cognition

Measuring individual differences holds an honored place in the field of psychology and traces its beginnings to an English biologist, Francis Galton (Anastasi, 1958). Both Galton and Charles Darwin were grandsons of a noted physician, Erasmus Darwin. Perhaps this illustrious heritage sparked Galton's interest in heredity; perhaps it was his keen interest in the theory proposed by Charles Darwin. Whatever the reason, he began to collect information on whole families to demonstrate the inheritance of specific talents. He soon realized that a large number of people would have to be objectively measured before the degree of family resemblance could be specified. Galton, undaunted by the difficulty of the task, set up a psychometric laboratory at the International Health Exhibition. For three or four pence, interested individuals could come into his laboratory and be measured for weight, sitting and standing height, arm span, breathing capacity, strength of pull and squeeze, force of blow, reaction time, keenness of sight and hearing, color discrimination, and judgments of length (Forrest, 1974).

As in modern psychology laboratories, the instruments occasionally malfunctioned. Galton complained that some of the customers punched the pad used for recording the force of a blow so hard that they broke the equipment. When he strengthened the equipment, some customers sprained their wrists. What better testament to individual differences! Despite these problems and occasions when "rough persons entered the laboratory who were apparently not altogether sober," Galton was pleased with his laboratory (Galton, 1885). He collected information on over 10,000 people including such celebrities as the prime minister, William Gladstone. When the exhibition closed, Galton moved his laboratory to a permanent location.

Galton believed that a person's intellectual level was based on information acquired through the senses. He reasoned that the most intelligent people acquired their superior knowledge through finely discriminating sensory processes (Galton, 1883). Hence, he felt that measurements of mental capacity should focus on assessments of sensory discrimination and motor coordination. He developed the Galton whistle to assess hearing and the Galton bar for visual estimations of length. He even included reaction time as a useful measure of coordination. A hundred years after Galton's studies, reaction time returned to the forefront of differential psychology.

## Galton's anthropometric laboratory

# ANTHROPOMETRIC
# LABORATORY

### For the measurement in various ways of Human Form and Faculty.

*Entered from the Science Collection of the S. Kensington Museum.*

This laboratory is established by Mr. Francis Galton for the following purposes:—

1. For the use of those who desire to be accurately measured in many ways, either to obtain timely warning of remediable faults in development, or to learn their powers.

2. For keeping a methodical register of the principal measurements of each person, of which he may at any future time obtain a copy under reasonable restrictions. His initials and date of birth will be entered in the register, but not his name. The names are indexed in a separate book.

3. For supplying information on the methods, practice, and uses of human measurement.

4. For anthropometric experiment and research, and for obtaining data for statistical discussion.

Charges for making the principal measurements: THREEPENCE each, to those who are already on the Register. FOURPENCE each, to those who are not:— one page of the Register will thenceforward be assigned to them, and a few extra measurements will be made, chiefly for future identification.

The Superintendent is charged with the control of the laboratory and with determining in each case, which, if any, of the extra measurements may be made, and under what conditions.

H. & W. Brown, Printers, 20 Fulham Road, S.W.

*Historical Pictures Service, Chicago*

An announcement for the laboratory that Francis Galton set up in England in 1884. Over a period of years, Galton measured over 10,000 individuals on a variety of sensory and cognitive skills.

Galton's *anthropometric* laboratory pioneered the idea of measuring individual differences using purely objective assessments. Galton's contribution to the field of differential psychology did not end there. He devised basic statistical methods to help him cope with the avalanche of measurements from his laboratory. Finally, he was the first to hypothesize the existence of a general mental ability (Jensen, 1980).

Galton's work intrigued generations of students including his countryman, Charles Spearman, who formulated the two-factor theory of mental organization (Spearman, 1927). Following Galton's lead, he felt that intellectual activities evolved from a general ability. Pursuing this notion, he found that all measures of complex mental performances are positively intercorrelated. In other words, peope who are good at seeing what is missing in a picture are also good at sentence-completion tasks, abstract reasoning, analogies, and problem solving (Herrnstein, 1982). All of these tests, then, measure some common factor. Spearman labeled this general factor g. In addition to g, each intellectual activity requires specific information or an s factor (see Figure 11–1). Spearman argued that assessments of intelligence should concentrate on measuring the general or g factor that all intellectual skills share. It would be futile to measure specific factors since they are limited to particular activities.

The interest in individual differences that blossomed in England at the turn of the century was also evident in other countries. In France, Alfred Binet wrote that intelligence "consists of two principal things: perceiving the external world and then taking up these perceptions again in the memorial state, handling them, and meditating on them" (Binet, 1890, p. 582). Binet and his colleagues had given the measurement of intelligence a great deal of thought even before the Minister of Public Instruction asked them to devise a method

**Figure 11–1**    **Spearman's two-factor theory**

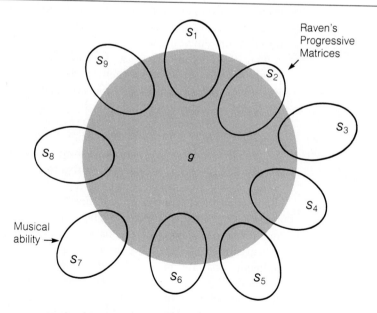

An illustration of Spearman's two-factor theory of abilities. All tests measure a general factor g that is common to mental tests as well as a specific factor s that is unique to each test. Some tests, such as those that assess musical ability, have a great deal of specific variance. Others, like the Raven's Progressive Matrices, are primarily g.

Source: Jensen, A. R. (1980). *Bias in Mental Testing (p. 214)*. New York: Free Press.

for identifying mentally retarded children. The scale Binet developed, unlike Galton's anthropometric measures, sought to measure a wide variety of complex mental processes. His scales were an immediate success because they were simple, included exact directions, contained brief but varied tasks, and provided age standards. They were adapted for use in many countries.

In 1916, Lewis Terman published an adaptation of Binet's scale in the United States called the Stanford-Binet. From this time, testing the differences between individuals has flourished in the United States. Tests became an integral part of the evaluation of soldiers during World War I. Assessments of personality began to appear, and these were soon followed by tests of attitudes and interests (Anastasi, 1958). The growing use of such measures meant that entrance to college, exemption from the draft, and scholarships were determined by how well individuals performed on tests. As test scores began to play a major role in people's lives, they became the focus of anxiety, public scrutiny, and controversy (Cronbach, 1975).

No one denied that differences in ability existed. The arguments centered, instead, on the reason for these differences. A few psychologists argued that the differences were innate; but many more believed that experiences, or the lack of experiences, determined a child's ability. Otto Klineberg represented the view of the 1950s when he wrote, "The teacher has the right to assume that under similar conditions both the range of capacities and the average capacity of various groups will almost certainly be the same" (Klineberg, 1952, p. 953). The assumption was that any differences in cognitive skills could be traced to the environment.

The 1960s began with researchers summarizing the evidence that experience played a substantial role in intellectual development (Hunt, 1961). The political and social climate of the 1960s brought social reforms, a distrust of IQ tests, and an optimism about our ability to alter intelligence. The role of heredity was not denied, but the emphasis was on the child's experiences (Cronbach, 1975).

The glow of idealism soon faded from this staunch environmental position. The hastily established, large-scale programs of the 1960s did not produce the miracles that optomistic psychologists had promised (Cronbach, 1975). Psychologists realized that there were limits to the changes that could be expected regardless of the environment. The rethinking of positions that occurred did not cause a replaying of the nature-nurture controversy. In the intervening years, researchers asked and answered questions about the predictability of intelligence tests and the stability of intelligence. They asked questions about the importance of environmental variables, including play, nutrition, stimulation, the behavior of parents, the impact of schools, and even the impact of stressful events. Responding to the criticism that IQ tests were culturally biased, researchers experimented with ways of removing cultural variables from the intelligence equation. They tried assessments that relied on mazes or repeating patterns. They tried assessments that were based on biological variables such as evoked potentials. They tried physiological indices like reaction times.

All of these investigations opened new areas of differential psychology. This chapter will examine these branches of the field of individual differences.

Before proceeding, however, it is appropriate to confront the emotionally charged atmosphere that is part of the treatment of individual differences. Scientific controversy is often productive. It moves the field forward by highlighting flaws in experiments and directing attention to any unwarranted assumptions that investigators have made (see Jensen, 1980, 1982 for examples). But when scientific controversies erupt into the public forum, the time-consuming and meticulous methods of science are often pushed to the background, and popular views may tend to override data-based arguments. The popular press is not bound to present both sides of an issue, and the limited space in popular magazines promotes presentations of complex issues that are often disturbingly superficial (Herrnstein, 1982).

Controversy about the use and abuse of mental tests has often been aired on the public stage and fueled by the media. Too often, these criticisms are not tied to empirical studies, or they are lopsided presentations of the issue. In looking at the information on individual differences in cognition, we have to adopt a dispassionate stance and try to evaluate the information that is presented. This is not easy because the issues are complex, and fair conclusions often rest on the appropriateness of complicated statistical procedures. Nevertheless, we need to try to sort through the research in a rational way. It is only by getting an accurate picture of factors that affect individual differences in intelligence that we can realistically help all children achieve their potential.

## MEASUREMENT ISSUES

To measure a complex trait or behavior, it has to be defined. How we define "intelligent" or "well-adjusted" plays a central role in its measurement. For example, if we define intelligence as having knowledge about the culture, then we might ask people how far it is from New York to Los Angeles or what is the height of an average American man. If, however, we define intelligence as the ability to adapt, we might ask children to tell us what they would do if they saw thick smoke coming from the window of a neighbor's house. Intelligence is often defined as the ability to use logic. Questions that reflect this definition take the following form: "A mother sent her boy to the river to bring back exactly 3 pints of water. She gave him a 7-pint can and a 4-pint can. Show me how the boy can measure out exactly 3 pints of water using nothing but these two cans and not guessing at the amount" (Terman & Merrill, 1972). If all of these questions seem to measure plausible aspects of intelligence, you might design a test that includes a variety of different kinds of questions. In fact, the examples above are taken from two widely used intelligence tests—the Stanford-Binet and the revised version of the Wechsler Intelligence Scale for Children (WISC-R).

Solving the definitional problem is just the first task that psychologists must confront to construct a test. Psychologists also have to worry about the reliability and the validity of a test, and they have to be sure that their test is properly standardized. Each of these three issues needs to be understood before we turn our attention to individual differences in cognition.

**Reliability**

The *reliability* of a test is its consistency. If you measure a friend's height on one day and she is 5'2", you accept that measurement. Another measurement the next day should yield the same result. If the second measurement shows her to be 5'8" or 6'2", the measuring instrument is not reliable. Similarly, intelligence tests have to yield consistent scores to be useful. An easy synonym for reliability is repeatability because repeated testings over a short time period should duplicate the first score.

**Validity**

A second fundamental question to be asked about any test is how *valid* it is. In other words, does it measure what it purports to measure? How would you decide whether a test is really a measure of intelligence? You might ask teachers to rank order their students according to intelligence. Then you could compare your test results to the teacher's ranking. You might compare your test scores with other assessments of intelligence. In essence, the scores you obtain from your test must be compared to some other independent assessment of intelligence. Rank in class, teacher's ratings, job success, and SAT scores are some of the outside measures that have been used to check the validity of intelligence tests.

If you compare IQ tests with other assessments of intelligence and your test puts people in the same position as the second assessment, you should be able to conclude that your test is valid. Unfortunately, with measures of intelligence, the conclusions are not that simple. Suppose we want to validate the IQ test we have constructed by comparing it to rank in a high school class. Who is to say that rank in high school is not biased in the same way as the test? If this is the case, then you have two biased instruments yielding the same result rather than one assessment validating the scores of the other (Kempthorne & Wolins, 1982). Of course, it is conceivable that this criticism could never be answered. No matter what measure is suggested, critics can always claim that it is a biased measure.

**The standardization sample**

Francis Galton gathered measurements on over 10,000 English subjects. By determining the average height or reaction time of those 10,000 people, Galton obtained a norm for his sample. Any individual could be compared to this norm and be told, "You are shorter than 90 percent of the subjects I have tested" or "Your reaction time is faster than 83 percent of the subjects I have tested." The norms for a test are the baseline of comparison. Hence, it is important that the norms reflect the larger population accurately. Currently, test producers go to great lengths to insure that the *standardization sample* for

# IQ TESTS ON TRIAL
## Larry P. et al. v. Wilson Riles

In 1971 the parents of seven black children filed a suit against Wilson Riles, the Superintendent of California Schools. Each of the children had received an IQ score below 75 on an individually administered IQ test. Based on this test, the children had been placed in special education classes. The thrust of the lawsuit was that the intelligence tests used to place children in these classes were discriminatory.

The basic issue in the case was the overrepresentation of minority students in special education classes. The prosecution argued that intelligence tests lead to black children being unfairly labeled as "retarded." Furthermore, the effects of the hour-long test continued to limit the children's educational and occupational opportunities years after the test was administered.

The court ruled in favor of the children and placed a moratorium on all IQ testing of black children. Some of the court's reasoning is given in the following excerpt of the decision:

They (the plaintiffs) claim that they are not mentally retarded and that they have been placed in EMR classes on the basis of tests which are biased against the culture and experience of black children as a class, in violation of their fourteenth amendment right. In fact, plaintiffs have presented evidence, in the form of affidavits from certain black psychologists, that when they were given the same IQ tests but with special attempts by the psychologists to establish rapport with the test-takers, to overcome plaintiffs' defeatism and easy distraction, to reword items in terms more consistent with plaintiffs' cultural background, and to give credit for nonstandard answers which nevertheless showed an intelligent approach to problems in the context of that background, plaintiffs scored significantly above the cutting-off point of 75. (Larry P. v. Wilson Riles, 1972)

Since this landmark case, the arguments for both the prosecution and the defense have been published widely. The prosecution and defense based their cases on the following issues.

### Prosecution's arguments

1. The items from IQ tests are drawn from the white middle-class culture. As such they cannot measure the intelligence of black children.

2. Whites have more opportunities when they are young and this gives them an advantage over blacks on the test.

3. The language of black children may differ substantially from the language used in the test. Here again, white children have an advantage.

4. Motivational factors during the administration of the test may be affected by the race of the examiner and may contribute to the fact that black children often perform poorly.

5. The tests are standardized on a white sample, with only a token or representative number of blacks in the standardization sample. This means that the tests should not be used with black children.

6. IQ tests are an easy way for schools to avoid their responsibility to educate both black and white children. (Lambert, 1981)

### Defense's arguments

1. The IQ tests are not the reason for the overrepresentation of minority children in special education classes. Males are also overrepresented in these classes and no one argues that IQ tests discriminate against males.

2. Special education classes do not stigmatize children for life. Studies have shown that children who attend these classes have higher incomes and more stable marriages than children who are not labeled "retarded."

3. IQ tests are an objective measure of skills. Without IQ tests, recommendations for special classes would be left to teachers' judgments which are not as accurate or as unbiased as IQ tests.

4. IQ tests predict scholastic achievement for minority children as well as they do for other children.

5. Having an examiner from a different racial group makes little difference in the performance of children on standardized IQ tests.

6. When the items of the IQ tests are actually analyzed, those that are portrayed as biased are often shown to be fair to all groups.

a test is an accurate reflection of the entire population. The sample includes rural and urban dwellers, individuals from different geographic regions, upper and lower income families, and of course, males and females.

It is interesting that until the 1970s, few of the intelligence tests included a representative sample of minority groups. This was one of the salient factors in banning IQ tests in New York, Chicago, Los Angeles, and Houston. Critics argued that since minorities were not included in the standardization sample, the scores of minorities could not be compared to the norms (Lambert, 1981). As a result, test producers have become far more conscientious about including a representative sample of minority children in the standardization sample. Currently, all of the widely used tests include minorities in the standardization sample. However, the norms are still overwhelmingly based on a single group. The inclusion of small numbers of children from minority groups satisfies the statistical requirements, but it still means that the norms by which minorities are judged are determined largely by scores received by the majority. Critics of IQ tests argue that this comparison is not fair (Mercer, 1977) and have proposed some measures that consider the culture of the child. Before we can understand these criticisms, we need to examine two of the most popular intelligence tests and two of the tests that have been suggested to reduce the impact of the culture.

**The Stanford-Binet**

The Stanford-Binet includes items for each of 20 age groups beginning at two years and continuing through a category called Superior Adult III. Children begin the test at an age level where they can pass all of the items. They continue answering items until they reach an age level where they fail all of the items. A 4½ year-old, for example, might pass all of the items at that level, four of the items designed for five- and six-year-olds, and none of the items for the seven-year-olds. This child's total score is then compared to age-mates' scores and is translated into an IQ of 115.

The Stanford-Binet meets high standards of reliability and validity (see Figure 11–2). It includes nonwhites in the standardization sample of 2,100. Critics of this test argue that it places too high an emphasis on verbal skills and memory items, and that the single IQ score it yields does not accurately represent the pattern of strengths and weaknesses that characterize most children.

**The Wechsler IQ tests**

David Wechsler had a different approach to the measurement of intelligence. He concentrated on a few abilities that were considered important to intelligence and constructed 12 subtests that measured these skills. Six of the subtests focus on verbal skills, asking children to define *diamond* or to explain how a cat and a mouse are alike. Six other subtests examine performance skills. As part of these tests, children are asked to tell what item is missing in a picture or to arrange pictures so that they tell a story (see Figure 11–3).

These 12 subtests (only 10 are usually administered) yield a verbal IQ, a

**Figure 11—2**          **Stanford-Binet intelligence test**

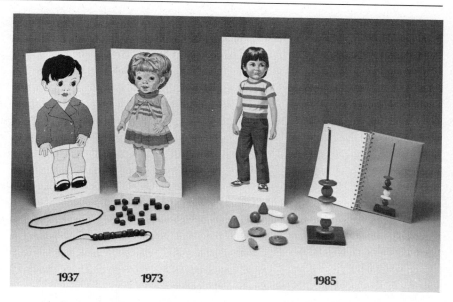

1937          1973                              1985

The Stanford-Binet was one of the first IQ tests used in this country and has remained a favorite for testing younger subjects. Through the years, the test has been revised. When children are asked to identify parts of the body in 1985, they are shown a picture that can be viewed as either a boy or girl. The matching beads task has also been changed so that the child who has trouble putting beads on the string is not penalized.

Source: These Stanford-Binet materials will be included in the fourth edition, Copyright 1985 by the Riverside Publishing Company. Reproduced by permission of the publisher.

performance IQ, and a full-scale IQ. In addition, the test yields a profile of a child's abilities on the various subtests. Based on this profile, psychologists can sometimes tell whether a child has concentration problems or was particularly anxious while taking the test.

The three Wechsler tests are the Wechsler Preschool and Primary Scale of Intelligence (WPPSI), the Weschler Intelligence Scale for Children-Revised (WISC-R), and the Wechsler Adult Intelligence Scale-Revised (WAIS-R). The WPPSI is used for children between 4 and 6½ years of age. The WISC-R covers the years between 6 and 16, and the WAIS-R is designed for individuals between 16 and 74 years of age.

The Wechsler tests meet stringent psychometric standards for reliability and are widely recognized as valid indicators of intelligence (Sattler, 1982). All three of these tests include a representative sample of minorities in the standardization population. The major criticism leveled at the test itself is that there is some latitude in how an examiner scores the items. Critics argue that these subjective judgments can become a source of bias.

**Figure 11–3**            **The Wechsler Intelligence Scale for Children—Revised (WISC-R)**

*Information* (30 questions)

How many legs do you have?
What must you do to make water freeze?
Who discovered the North Pole?
What is the capital of France?

*Similarities* (17 questions)

In what way are pencil and crayon alike?
In what way are tea and coffee alike?
In what way are inch and mile alike?
In what way are binoculars and microscope
  alike?

*Arithmetic* (18 questions)

If I have one piece of candy and get another one,
  how many pieces will I have?
At 12 cents each, how much will 4 bars of soap
  cost?
If a suit sells for half of the ticket price, what is the
  cost of a $120 suit?

*Vocabulary* (32 words)

ball              poem
summer       obstreperous

*Comprehension* (17 questions)

Why do we wear shoes?
What is the thing to do if you see someone drop-
  ping their packages?
In what two ways is a lamp better than a candle?
Why are we tried by a jury of our peers?

*Digit Span*

Digits Forward contains seven series of digits, 3 to
9 digits in length (Example: 1-8-9).
Digits Backward contains seven series of digits, 2
to 8 digits in length (Example: 5-8-1-9).

*Block Design* (11 items)

The task is to reproduce stimulus designs using
four or nine blocks. An example of a Block Design item is shown below.

*Picture Completion* (26 items)

The task is to identify the essential missing part of
the picture.

*Object Assembly* (4 items)

The task is to arrange pieces into a meaningful
object. An example of an Object Assembly item
is shown above in column 2.

*Coding*

The task is to copy symbols from a key. An example of the Coding task is shown below.

| 1 | 2 | 3 | 4 | 5 | 6 |
|---|---|---|---|---|---|
| √ | ⌐ | ‖ | ө | ⁄ | ◊ |

| SAMPLE | | | | | | | | | | | | | | |
|---|---|---|---|---|---|---|---|---|---|---|---|---|---|---|
| 2 | 1 | 4 | 6 | 3 | 5 | 2 | 1 | 3 | 4 | 2 | 1 | 3 | 1 | 2 | 3 |

The WISC-R includes 10 subtests that measure different aspects of intelligence. The
questions above illustrate the kind of questions that are asked. These are not actual questions from the test.

Source: Sattler, J. M. (1982). *Assessment of Children's intelligence and special abilities* (pp. 143–144).
(2d ed.). New York: Allyn & Bacon.

**The SOMPA**

When the WISC-R is administered to minority children, many of them
receive low scores and are subsequently recommended for special education
classes. Jane Mercer believes that many of these placements are in error and
that the IQ scores minority children receive are a reflection of their very different cultural experiences. To compensate for these differences, she has proposed an alternative assessment—the System of Multicultural Pluralistic Assessment (SOMPA).

As part of this assessment, a child's IQ on the WISC-R is translated into an
Estimated Learning Potential. Children with very different cultural backgrounds would be considered to have normal learning potential if their IQs fell
between 73 and 95 (Mercer, 1977). Mercer argues that because they have
normal learning potential, placing them in special education classes is inap-

propriate and will limit their educational opportunity unnecessarily (Mercer, 1979).

As with any new testing procedure, the value of the SOMPA must be determined through research. Initial studies have indicated that using the SOMPA sharply reduces the number of children from all ethnic groups who are recommended for special education classes (Reschly, 1981). If special education classes are harmful to students, this is a blessing. But special education classes do not necessarily reduce students' chances for achievement or impede their development (Lambert, 1981). The SOMPA has also been criticized because it dilutes our ability to predict a student's achievement (Yonge, 1982). As Fred Brown (1979) points out, giving weekend duffers a handicap can make their net golf scores resemble the professionals' scores. But what do these transformed scores tell about the golfing skills of players in each group? The critics of SOMPA are really asking whether SOMPA scores are stable and if they will predict achievement as well as IQ tests.

**Raven's Progressive Matrices**

The best known and most widely used test designed to reduce cultural factors is the Raven's Progressive Matrices. This test has been used in over 1,000 studies and has been given in countries all over the globe. The sample items shown in Figure 11–4 illustrate how the test requires people "to form comparisons, reason by analogy, and develop a logical method of thinking, regardless of previously acquired information" (Raven, 1938, p. 12).

Three different versions of the test are available. One is for children, one for preteens and adults, and a third for individuals who are very intelligent. Because the test requires no verbal skills, it has been successfully used with deaf individuals and in testing students who are not fluent in the language of the examiner. Despite these important advantages, the Raven's Progressive Matrices has two major drawbacks. The first is that it is not well standardized. The second is that it is such a pure measure of general intelligence that it is not as good at predicting scholastic and vocational achievement as IQ tests that have a larger verbal component. Apparently some assessment of verbal skills is necessary to predict success accurately. Even though the Raven's Progressive Matrices is a *culture-free* test, these drawbacks limit the test's usefulness.

The attempts to develop culture-reduced tests or culture-free tests have to be called disappointing. When the cultural factors are eliminated, tests lose some of their ability to predict performance in school or success on the job. Perhaps all this says is that academic and vocational success require some understanding of the culture and some ability to function within its boundaries.

## THE STABILITY OF INTELLIGENCE MEASURES

The *stability* of a trait refers to the consistency of a person's score over time. This is a different issue than the reliability of a test. We can measure height reliably but we do not expect a child's height to be stable. Many IQ and achievement tests are highly reliable, but that does not mean that these scores

**Figure 11—4**            **Raven's Progressive Matrices**

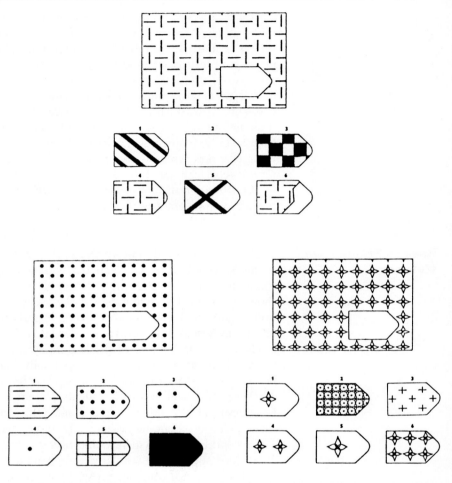

Raven's Progressive Matrices require no verbal knowledge or information about a culture. For each matrix, students must select the one alternative that would most logically fill the blank space.

will remain stable. Bloom (1964), for example, indicated that children acquired about half of their mature intelligence by age four. Piaget and his colleagues point to several changes in how children think. If IQ tests tap these newly learned skills, then children will undoubtedly answer more of the test questions correctly. But remember that an individual's performance is compared to the average performance of that age group. A change in IQ means that the child's position relative to the rest of his or her peers has changed.

**Infant IQ tests**

Intelligence tests for infants are extremely difficult to construct. The primary problem is that infants have few behaviors that we can identify as being direct precursors of later intellectual skills. Motor skills can be reliably assessed but are not particularly good predictors of later mental skills.

In an attempt to circumvent this problem, Nancy Bayley (1969) designed both a mental scale (Mental Developmental Index) and motor scale (Psychomotor Development Index). The mental scale consists of 163 items that assess an infant's perception, attention, memory, and ability to imitate and solve problems. Beginning at two months, infants receive credit if they recognize their mothers. At 6 months, infants are expected to look for a fallen spoon, and at 12 months they should be able to turn the pages of a book. The motor scale includes 81 items that cover the major milestones such as grasping, sitting, standing, and walking.

The Bayley tests are the most reliable and the most valid assessments of infants that are available. They are not, however, dependable predictors of an individual's later intellectual skills (Bayley, 1970; McCall, 1981). Scores obtained prior to the age of six months are likely to be negatively correlated with intelligence test scores at age four. Even IQ scores obtained when children are 21 months old have little or no relationship to adult intelligence (Honzik, MacFarlane, & Allen, 1948). Further, infant IQ tests cannot be used to identify which children at ages four or seven will be labeled gifted (Willerman & Fiedler, 1977). Test scores obtained before four years are reliable and stable over short periods of time, but they have little long-term predictive value for a specific child (Jensen, 1980).

Infant IQs are not predictive for several reasons. First, infants grow and change rapidly. Second, the skills they can perform are only distantly related to adult intelligence. Third, it is difficult to get an accurate index of infants' abilities because they may be tired, hungry, afraid of strangers, or uninterested in the tasks. In fact, below five years of age, "one can better predict what a child's IQ will be at age 15 from a knowledge of the average IQ of the parents than from any test score obtained on the child" (Jensen, 1980, p. 281). If infant IQ tests are such poor predictors, why do such tests even exist? The reason is that they are quite accurate in identifying developmentally disabled children. Infants who score in the mentally retarded ranges during their first year and a half are likely to obtain low IQs later in development, and many of them will be functioning in the mentally retarded range during the school years.

The largest study to document this relationship is the Collaborative Perinatal Project (Broman, Nichols, & Kennedy, 1975). In this project, the Bayley Mental Scale was administered at eight months, the Stanford-Binet at four years, and the Wechsler Intelligence Scale for Children (WISC) at seven years. Over 30,000 children from every part of the country, including 16,293 black children, were tested. The infant IQ test (Bayley Mental Scale) that was administered at eight months was a good predictor of severe mental retardation at seven years of age.

**Stability of IQs during the school years**

By five or six years of age, IQs are much more stable. The critical variable at this age is how long an interval elapses between tests. If the interval is only a few months, the two test scores will be very similar. If five or more years elapse, the correlations will be lower (Jensen, 1980). Several longitudinal studies have reaffirmed this conclusion. Marjorie Honzik and her colleagues studied 150 infants from 21 months to 18 years of age. They obtained a measure of mental performance almost every year during those 16 years. They found that test scores from successive years were quite stable. However, test scores given every three years showed more variation. Figure 11–5 indicates that the scores were still stable over a three-year period if the children were older. The correlation between tests given at 2 and 5 years (.32) is not much better than chance, but the scores obtained at 9 and 12 or 13 are very similar.

What happens if the interval between tests is 12 years? Honzik and her co-workers indicate that during this interval almost 10 percent of the children show IQ increases or decreases on the order of 30 points. Nevertheless, most children do not demonstrate dramatic changes in IQ after age six. A recent study reports that the correlation between the WPPSI given at age 5½ and the WISC-R given at 16½ was .86 (Yule, Gold, & Busch, 1982). This is almost as high as test-retest reliability coefficients, yet the two tests were given 11 years apart. Despite this impressive group correlation, predicting any individual's IQ from a test given at age six is risky. One boy's IQ changed by 50 points over an interval of 12 years. It is interesting that this massive change did not occur overnight, but took place slowly over a period of years (see Figure 11–6). A particular child being evaluated may be one of the few who will show steady declines or increases in IQ. For these reasons, psychologists continually caution against using IQ tests for long-range predictions concerning individual children. Assessments of a child's IQ must be kept up-to-date to be accurate.

**Figure 11–5**

**How stable are IQ scores?**

| Age | Correlation |
|---|---|
| 2 × 5 years | r = .32 |
| 3 × 6 | .57 |
| 4 × 7 | .59 |
| 5 × 8 | .70 |
| 7 × 10 | .78 |
| 9 × 12 | .85 |
| 15 × 16 | .70 |

How stable are IQ scores over a three-year period? The older the child, the more stable the scores. When two-year-olds are tested and then retested as five-year-olds, the correlation is not much better than chance. The predictability from 9 to 12 years is, however, very high.

Source: Honzik, M. P., MacFarlan, J.W., & Allen, L. (1948). The stability of mental test performance between two and eighteen years. *Journal of Experimental Education, 17,* 309–323.

**Figure 11—6**     **Case studies of children with changing IQ scores**

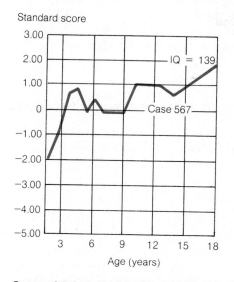

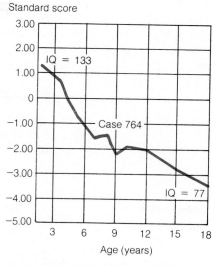

## Case with increasing mental test scores

*Case 567.* The early preschool history of this girl (the period of her lowest test scores) was characterized by the critical illnesses of her mother and brother and the emotional and financial strain that these entailed. Further, the girl had very poor muscle tonus, fatigue posture, and was very shy and reserved. At 6½ years she had pneumonia. From 10 on, while still reserved, she had many supports in her life—music, athletic success, summer camps, the honor roll at school. Eighteen years marks her first year in college and away from home and her first really completely satisfying social life, which resulted in great expansiveness. Both parents are college graduates who did advanced work in their fields.

## Steadily decreasing mental test scores

*Case 764* is an example of a gradual lowering of IQ from 133 to 77, and sigma scores from +1 to −3. She is an only child, born when the mother was 44, the father 37. The estimated IQ of the mother is 65 to 70. The father is a skilled mechanic. The parents went to school until age 14.

Obesity began in late preschool years and increased steadily until medical advice was finally followed at age 14 (height 5′2″, weight 160 lbs. at 13). Weight was normal at 17. There were, however, no IQ variations in relation to these physical changes. She was always overindulged by the mother, who lived to feed her and keep her young, and who was always complaining that her daughter never gave her enough affection.

A few individuals show continuing changes in IQ over the years. These changes occur gradually over several years and underscore the importance of having up-to-date IQ scores on individuals if a decision is being made about their progress.

Source: Honzik, M. P., MacFarlane, J. W., & Allen, L. (1948). The stability of mental test performance between two and eighteen years. *Journal of Experimental Education, 17,* 309–323. A publication of the Helen Dwight Reid Educational Foundation.

In sum, the stability of IQs depends on two factors—how old the child is at the initial testing and the length of the interval between tests. Older children who are retested at short intervals have stable IQs. Younger children retested after many years are not likely to demonstrate the same consistency. The two case histories in Figure 11–6 suggest some of the reasons for a lack of consistency.

## PREDICTING BEHAVIOR FROM INTELLIGENCE

Intelligence tests and, more generally, tests that measure $g$ are good predictors of how people will function in a variety of settings. Scholastic success, occupational success, and even adjustment are related to intelligence.

**Scholastic achievement**

Children with high IQs learn more quickly, get higher grades, and achieve higher educational levels than children with low IQs. Intelligence tests in the elementary grades even predict achievement in cognitive or scholastic skills that the child has not encountered. The Wechsler Preschool and Primary Scale of Intelligence (WPPSI) does not require reading or spelling and is usually administered to preschoolers. Yet IQ scores obtained with this test predict how well children will read after one year of instruction (Krebs, 1969) and how well they will read, spell, and perform arithmetic operations after they have completed 11 years of school (Yule, Gold, & Busch, 1982). These results are an impressive testament to the ability of IQ tests to predict later scholastic achievement.

Intelligence predicts achievement in some areas better than others. Performance in academic subjects like English, math, and science is related to IQ more than performance in music, art, and typing. Presumably, this is because academic subjects require more $g$, while others require more $s$.

The fact that a child's IQ predicts achievement does not mean that intelligence and achievement are perfectly correlated. In elementary school, the correlation is between .60 and .70; by college it has decreased to .40 and .50; and it goes even lower in graduate school (Jensen, 1980). Intelligence becomes less important in graduate school because everyone is extremely bright. Hence, the differences that we see hinge on aspects other than intelligence. During the elementary years, IQ accounts for about half of the variation in achievement. The other half is accounted for by motivational factors, attitudinal factors, and family factors (Walden & Ramey, 1983).

The relationship between IQ and achievement implies that there is a relationship between intelligence and learning. Intelligence is important to learning, especially when the material the child must learn is complex or hierarchical or when it requires insight or reason. It is interesting that IQ differences are most important in the early phases of learning a task (Jensen, 1980).

It should be obvious that intelligence is related to educational achievement.

Does intelligence in childhood predict adult educational achievement? In a longitudinal study that followed children from the preschool years into adulthood, Robert McCall (1977) noted that as early as seven years of age, the child's IQ was significantly correlated with adult educational status. The correlation, however, is not high enough to make accurate predictions about a particular individual. Factors other than IQ also influence educational attainment. Bright but disadvantaged children, for example, may lack the resources to attend college.

**Occupational achievement**

The relationship between occupational level and IQ is more of a *threshold phenomenon* than a straight correlation. A threshold phenomenon means that you need a certain level of intelligence to function in a field, but after that level is achieved, other variables determine how successful you will be. People at all levels of intelligence can be successful at jobs that require little training and involve minimal responsibility. But as you progress up the occupational ladder to jobs with the highest status ratings—scientist, lawyer, physician, engineer—the minimal intelligence level that is necessary increases. Eighty students who were accepted into medical school at the University of Oregon demonstrate how high this threshold can be. Their IQ scores ranged from 111 to 149 with a median of 125. The lowest IQ in the class, 111, is higher than the IQs of 77 percent of the population (Matarazzo, 1972). Another example from a less scientific field illustrates the same principle. The IQs of police officers and fire fighters range from 96 to 130 with a median of 113. Highly intelligent people can be found among the ranks of unskilled laborers and Nobel Laureats, but few professional, technical, or highly skilled jobs employ many people with IQs below 100.

Because a low IQ limits the fields one can enter, it would seem that low IQs would be more predictive of occupation level than high IQs, but high IQs are also correlated with occupational status. Lewis Terman studied 1,500 geniuses (IQs above 140) for 60 years. These highly intelligent children achieved a much higher occupational level than would normally be expected. Over 85 percent of the men in his study were lawyers, engineers, college professors, major business managers, financial executives, scientists, physicians, educational administrators, top business executives, and accountants. The gifted women in Terman's study did not achieve the same occupational levels. It is worth noting, though, that Terman's study began in 1921 when the children were about 11. His subjects reached adulthood in the era of the 1930s when professional women were somewhat rare. The women in his study were highly active in volunteer organizations, but only a few had careers (Terman & Oden, 1959).

A more recent study indicates that perhaps intelligence in women is becoming more predictive of occupational level. McCall's group of females entered the labor force in the 1970s, and the IQs they attained at age seven were a good predictor of their adult occupational levels.

**Intelligence and adjustment**

Intelligence tests seem to measure ability, and it is not surprising that this general ability level would have an impact on scholastic and occupational achievement. It is less obvious how *g* would influence personal variables such as whether a person is well adjusted or maladjusted. Nevertheless, studies of gifted individuals from junior high age to senior citizens indicate that highly intelligent individuals are also well adjusted (Hogan & Weiss, 1976; Stanley, 1979; Oden, 1968). As adults, the gifted children studied by Melita Oden were better adjusted than the normal population. They lived longer, had fewer illnesses, were less likely to abuse alcohol, and were seldom arrested. As a group, they report a satisfaction with their lives that is not paralleled in the normal population (Terman & Oden, 1959).

What about the lower end of the IQ scale? Is there a disproportionate amount of maladjustment in people at this level? There certainly is a disproportionate amount of crime (Heilbrun, 1982). Delinquents predominantly come from the lower half of the IQ distribution. This is true regardless of racial ties or social class (Hirschi & Hindelang, 1977; Jensen, 1980). In other words, whether the delinquents were black, Oriental, or white, or whether they were from a higher or lower class family was not as important as whether their IQ was between 70 and 90. It goes without saying that the majority of teenagers with IQs in this range are not involved in delinquent or criminal activities, and it is also obvious that many intellectually able young people do become involved in criminal activities. Nevertheless, the probability of a police record is greater among individuals with IQs between 70 and 90.

It is wise to remember that all we are sure about is the relationship between IQ and adjustment. The cause of the relationship is not clear. One suggestion is that the low IQ means that these individuals are not very clever and are caught breaking the law. If this is the case, then the correlation is spurious. Other investigators suggest that the low IQ is accompanied by frustration that often leads to criminal behavior (Jensen, 1980). A suggestion that has received recent empirical support is that individuals with low IQs are not very good at controlling their impulses. This leads them to violent confrontations and crimes more often than individuals with better impulse control (Heilbrun, 1982).

To summarize, measures of intelligence are highly correlated with a variety of other complex behaviors including school achievement, occupational level, and adjustment. It is not stretching the truth to say that standard intelligence tests predict personally and socially significant behavior better than any other psychological construct. Given these correlates of intelligence, it is understandable that psychologists have devoted considerable energy to programs that might increase IQ. As Jensen (1981) points out, an individual increase of five IQ points is almost meaningless, but this relatively small increase could be very significant for the entire culture. An increase of five points in the population's IQ would double the percentage of people who scored over 130 and halve the percentage of people who scored below 70. The educational, social, and economic consequences of even this small change would be tremendous. With this in mind, let us turn to a discussion of differences in intellectual abilities.

## PATTERNS OF COGNITIVE SKILLS

**Sex differences in intelligence**

Arguing that women are smarter than men or vice versa is guaranteed to irritate about half of the population. For this reason, many of the psychologists who construct IQ tests have taken special care to minimize any differences between the sexes on their tests. Both the Stanford-Binet and the Wechsler scales have been designed to minimize sex differences. In some cases, items that showed large sex differences were simply discarded. More often, some items that favor each sex are included. This guarantees that, overall, the differences in IQ between sexes will be minimal (Jensen, 1980). Other tests, like the Raven's Progressive Matrices, were constructed without reference to sex differences. If sex differences in intelligence were important, they should be evident on these tests. The Raven's Progressive Matrices, as well as other tests that measure general intelligence, yield similar scores for males and females (Jensen, 1980).

The one interesting sex difference that occurs in large-scale studies of general intelligence is that more males than females are found at both extremes of the IQ continuum (Hendrickson, 1982). Males are more likely than females to have IQs below 70 and to be placed in special education classes (Lehrke, 1978). There are also more males than females at the upper end of the IQ scale (Terman, 1925; Benbow & Stanley, 1980; Hendrickson, 1982). Psychologists have sometimes disputed this result saying that surveys of extremely bright children have just failed to identify all of the girls. This seems unlikely because teachers recommend more girls than boys for gifted programs. A more likely explanation is that boys' IQs are more variable than girls' (Jensen, 1980). This explanation is compatible with the fact that both males and females have an average IQ of 100. Despite this difference in variability, then, psychologists of both sexes happily conclude that sex differences in general intelligence *g* do not exist. The differences that do crop up are actually differences in specific abilities *s*.

As these sex and racial differences are discussed, it is important to remember that the differences reported are mean differences. They do not describe an individual's level of functioning. Despite the fact that women, in general, are more verbal, many men are highly skilled verbally. The largest difference we will consider is the male superiority in spatial skills. Yet over one-quarter of the females tested still exceed the performance of the average male.

**Verbal skills.** From age 10 or 11 through adulthood, girls surpass boys on a wide variety of tests that assess verbal skills. This includes standard verbal tasks like spelling and punctuation and extends to higher level skills such as the comprehension of written text and complex logical relationships (Maccoby & Jacklin, 1974). The differences between the two sexes, however, are quite small in absolute terms.

**Quantitative skills.** Until puberty, males and females receive equivalent scores on math tests. After puberty, males routinely score higher. The differences are not large, but they are consistent. Males, for example, account for 56 percent of the children with exceptional math talent, while females account

**Figure 11—7**          **Spatial skills**

*Spatial visualization.* The subject is asked to visualize the three-dimensional object that will result from folding a two-dimensional pattern. In the item shown here, the subject is to determine which of the five boxes at the right can be made from the pattern shown at the left.

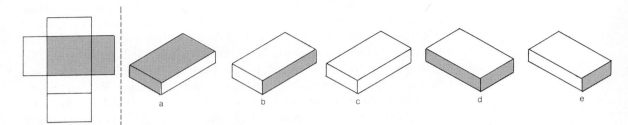

a          b          c          d          e

*Imbedded figures.* In these items, also called Gottschaldt figures after the German psychologist who invented them, the subject must be able to analyze complex figures into their simpler components to find which of the several figures in the bottom row contains the figural component in the top row.

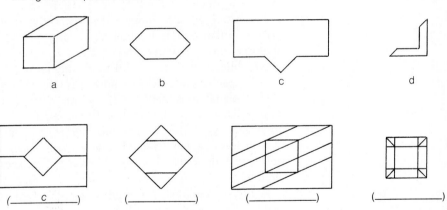

a          b          c          d

(___c___)     (_____)     (_____)     (_____)

Spatial skills are one of the few areas in which large sex differences exist. The items above assess spatial skills.

Free Press, a Division of Macmillan, Inc. from *Bias in mental testing* by Arthur R. Jensen. © 1980 by Arthur R. Jensen.

for 44 percent (Benbow & Stanley, 1980). These differences remain even when girls have been as interested in math and taken as many math courses as boys. One explanation that is often given for this sex difference is the clear-cut male superiority in spatial skills.

**Spatial ability.**     Males are significantly better than females at tests that require spatial skills. Males can find a target figure in a complex pattern and rotate geometric figures to find a match more readily than females (see Figure 11–7). Male superiority on spatial tasks is so pervasive that everyone agrees it exists. Like verbal and quantitative differences, sex differences in spatial skills become clearest after puberty.

**Memory.** The patterns of cognitive functioning reported so far have focused on differences in intellectual skills after puberty. Several analyses of the WISC-R reveal a sex difference in younger subjects in memory skills. Females score better than males on items that require certain types of memory (Jensen & Reynolds, 1983).

To summarize, neither males nor females routinely outperform the other on tests of general intelligence. When an occasional study finds differences in overall intelligence, the size of the difference is trivial. Sex differences in specific cognitive skills are more common. These differences are typically small, but they are found consistently among adolescents. The only large sex difference is found in spatial ability.

## Racial differences in intelligence

The topic of racial differences is at least as explosive as sexual differences. When given a standard IQ test like the Wechsler, Orientals are given a 6- to 11-point edge over whites (Lynn, 1982), and whites are given a 15-point edge over blacks (Jensen, 1980). These differences have been found repeatedly in studies that span several decades. Few psychologists take issue with the fact that groups of individuals from different racial backgrounds receive different scores on IQ tests. The fireworks really center on two other issues. The first is whether the differences that are reported actually represent differing levels of skills or whether they are an artifact of the testing procedures. The second question, that follows if the differences are not due to testing procedures, is what causes the differences.

**Test Bias.** The fact that racial groups differ in the scores they receive on IQ tests does not automatically mean that the tests are biased. Tests are designed to highlight differences between individuals. The question is whether or not the differences that appear actually reflect differences in ability. Bias can creep into the testing process from many different directions. Perhaps the process of deciding who will be tested is biased. Perhaps there is some aspect of the actual administration of the test that discriminates against one racial group or benefits another. Perhaps the items in the test systematically discriminate against one group. Or perhaps the tests predict well for one group and not as well for others. These are just a few of the many possible sources of bias. Let us examine the research that assesses how these variables affect IQ scores.

IQ tests are often thought to underestimate the abilities of black children. If this is true, the tests should not predict achievement among black children accurately. Most large-scale studies like the prestigious Coleman report on the Equality of Educational Opportunity indicate that standardized tests accurately predict achievement for minority children (Coleman, Hobson, McPartland, Mood, Weinfeld, & York 1966). Despite such results, when IQ tests came under fire in the 1970s, the American Psychological Association commissioned a panel of experts to investigate the charges of test bias. They, too, concluded that IQ tests predict success as accurately for black students as they do for other students (Cleary, Humphreys, Kendrick, & Wesman, 1975). More recent studies have only reinforced this conclusion (Reschly & Sabers, 1979; Eckland, 1980; Blau, 1981). Predictions of success are, however, far from perfect for any racial group, and the errors associated with making individual predictions have already been mentioned. Still, these errors do not occur significantly more often among one of the racial groups.

To keep the controversy in perspective, we also need to ask what alternatives are available if we discard tests. The alternatives of teachers' recommendations and supervisors' judgments are far less objective than a test. Tests have identified many children from the lower socioeconomic classes who have superior abilities. These children might well have been overlooked if less objective measures were used.

Other critics of IQ tests have suggested that the test items are biased, the testing procedures are biased, and even that the process by which children are chosen to be tested is biased. All of these contentions have been dispelled by recent research. The process used to recommend children for testing has not been found to be discriminatory (Mercer, 1977). Particular items that have been the subject of attacks are actually answered correctly by as many minority children as white children (see Figure 11–8). The comment that white examiners frighten black children and inhibit their performance has not received support. White examiners are just as likely to get an accurate assessment of a child's intelligence as black examiners (Lambert, 1981; Sattler & Gwynne, 1982).

A consideration of this research has lead many psychologists to conclude that IQ tests are not biased (Clarke, 1980). One expert comments "that the tests . . . are not holding back black children. But something is" (Economos, 1980). If we accept the judgment that the tests are not as flawed as many psychologists, lay people, and judges have previously believed, we are left with explaining the differences between races.

Richard Lynn, in a provocative article in the journal *Nature*, confronts the task of explaining the IQ differences between whites and Orientals. He points out that during the past 20 years, Japanese children have shown an increase of seven IQ points, making Japanese children the smartest in the world. An astonishing 10 percent of the children in Japan have IQs over 130 compared to 2 percent of the children in the United States and western Europe.

Some researchers attribute this dramatic increase in the intelligence of Japanese children to improved health and nutrition. Others cite the emphasis on preschool experiences, family and social pressure to excel, and the rigorous preparation for exams. Harold Stevenson finds no mystery in the difference between the IQ scores of Japanese and American children. In the first grade, Japanese children spend 25 percent of their day studying math. Their American counterparts spend 14 percent (Mohs, 1982). Japanese children also attend school for seven hours a day, six days a week, and have only a short vacation in the summer. This intense educational program and the social discipline

**Figure 11—8**          **Bias in test items**

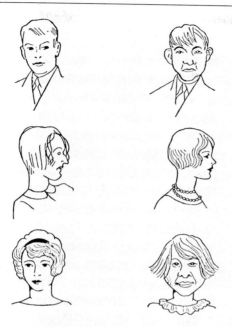

The "aesthetic comparison" test of the Stanford-Binet scale (1937 and 1960) at Year IV-6. Of each pair of faces, the examiner asks "Which one is prettier?" A passing score is three out of three correct.

This item was criticized because in all cases the "correct" picture had Anglo-Saxon features. But when black and white children were given this item, it was the easiest of the seven items for the black children. For the white children, it ranked third.

This item required children to identify the missing part. It was criticized as unfair to black children because combs with widely spaced teeth are common in the black culture. The research indicates that this item was easier for black children than white children.

Critics of IQ tests often decide that a particular item is biased just by looking at the item. To determine if an item is biased, research must be done. In the above two cases, studies indicated that the items were not biased.

Free Press, a Division of Macmillan, Inc. from *Bias in Mental Testing* by Arthur R. Jensen. © 1980 by Arthur R. Jensen.

from the culture provide a combination guaranteed to maximize the child's potential.

The same variables apply to the differences between blacks and whites in the United States. When social class is controlled, the IQ spread between black and white children is reduced to 12 points. In most studies, social class is determined by a single variable like parents' education or occupation. When a more complex set of socialization factors—the mother's educational level, her

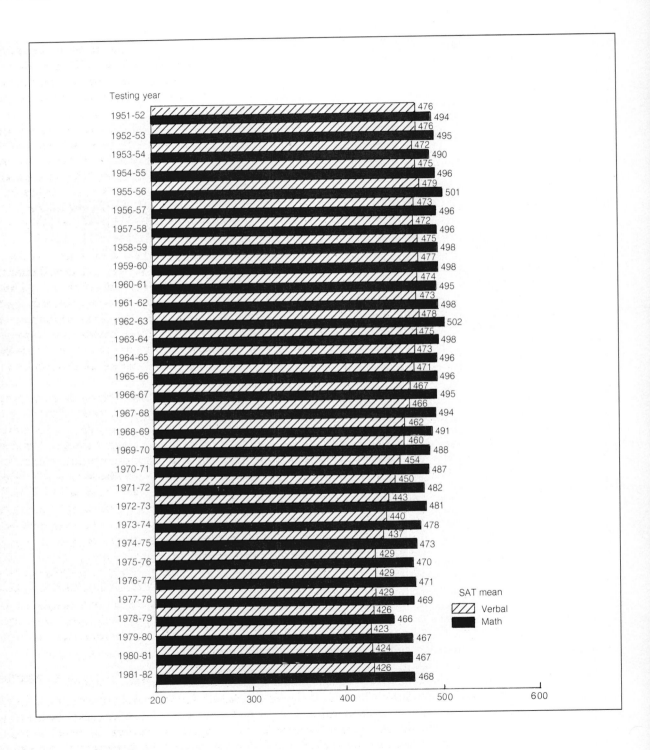

Testing year

| | |
|---|---|
| 1951-52 | 476 / 494 |
| 1952-53 | 476 / 495 |
| 1953-54 | 472 / 490 |
| 1954-55 | 475 / 496 |
| 1955-56 | 479 / 501 |
| 1956-57 | 473 / 496 |
| 1957-58 | 472 / 496 |
| 1958-59 | 475 / 498 |
| 1959-60 | 477 / 498 |
| 1960-61 | 474 / 495 |
| 1961-62 | 473 / 498 |
| 1962-63 | 478 / 502 |
| 1963-64 | 475 / 498 |
| 1964-65 | 473 / 496 |
| 1965-66 | 471 / 496 |
| 1966-67 | 467 / 495 |
| 1967-68 | 466 / 494 |
| 1968-69 | 462 / 491 |
| 1969-70 | 460 / 488 |
| 1970-71 | 454 / 487 |
| 1971-72 | 450 / 482 |
| 1972-73 | 443 / 481 |
| 1973-74 | 440 / 478 |
| 1974-75 | 437 / 473 |
| 1975-76 | 429 / 470 |
| 1976-77 | 429 / 471 |
| 1977-78 | 429 / 469 |
| 1978-79 | 426 / 466 |
| 1979-80 | 423 / 467 |
| 1980-81 | 424 / 467 |
| 1981-82 | 426 / 468 |

SAT mean

Verbal
Math

200    300    400    500    600

# THE RISE AND FALL OF NATIONAL TEST SCORES

High school seniors heading for college are well acquainted with the Scholastic Aptitude Test (SAT). It is the most widely administered achievement test in the United States. Each year, well over a million students spend three hours agonizing over the answers to English analogies and mathematics equations. It comes closer than any other test to assessing the academic preparation of high school seniors. Unfortunately, from 1963 to 1980, the average scores on the SAT dropped precipitously. In 1976, the College Entrance Examination Board, worried about the potential pool of scholars available to society, appointed a panel whose mission was to discover the reasons for the decline in test scores.

The first place the panel looked was the test itself. Was the test more difficult? Students who took both the 1963 version and the 1973 version provided the answer. Not only was the 1973 test not harder, it was easier.

The next place to look was at the sample of students who took the test each year. If more women, or more minorities, or more students from the lower quartiles of the class were taking the test, the mean scores could be affected. In the 1960s, many more students embarked on a college career, and the panel found that this different mix of students did account for between two thirds and three fourths of the decline in those years. However, after 1972, the composition of the students taking the test has not changed, but the scores have continued to decline.

The panel then decided to see if all of the students taking the test were receiving lower scores. They found that the decline in scores was not limited to low-ability students. The declines occurred among all types of students—black, white, male, female—from all types of backgrounds, and from both private and public schools. These initial analyses confirmed a real decline in the basic skills of all high school students.

Teachers have argued for years that the curriculum in high school has lost its academic focus.

The panel confirmed this, pointing to courses like Executive English and Children's Theatre that had replaced traditional English. As a group, they felt that "less thoughtful and critical reading is now being demanded and done, and that careful writing has apparently gone out of style" (CEEB, 1977, p. 27). The panel commented that mathematics preparation had not been diluted in the same way as English preparation and that the decline in math scores was less noticeable than the decline in English.

The panel considered several other factors associated with the high school, such as grade inflation, absenteeism, the level of difficulty of textbooks, and reduced homework. In all of these areas, the high school of the 1970s had laxer standards than the high school of the 1950s and early 60s. A final factor in the high school curriculum that was mentioned by the panel was the decreased competence of teachers in contemporary high schools.

The family did not escape the panel's scrutiny, but the relationships between family factors and test scores were harder to document with firm data. The family certainly underwent significant changes, and the panel felt that these could have a bearing on SAT scores, but positive conclusions were elusive. Watching television was shown by several studies to be negatively related to achievement. The panel concluded that television detracts from homework, competes with school, and has contributed to the decline in SAT scores.

The panel did not stop with trying to explain the declining scores. They made a series of recommendations designed to explore the SAT decline further and to remedy it. Since the panel's report, more attention has been focused on public education in the United States. The harbinger of change seems to be in the air. A return to academic requirements, more required courses, and higher standards in teacher selection seem to be on the horizon.

Source: Eckland, B. K. (1982). College entrance examination trends. In Austin, G. R., & Garber, H. *The Rise and Fall of National Test Scores* (p. 13). New York: Academic Press.

expectations, and the way she disciplines her children—are controlled, the IQ disparity between blacks and whites decreases even more (Blau, 1981). Looking at these results, psychologists are prompted to argue that the differences in IQ scores are primarily due to environmental variables. To buttress their case, they point to adoption studies and intervention programs. These studies often find that differing circumstances can alter the child's IQ by 6 to 16 points.

When sex differences were discussed, the cognitive strengths and weaknesses of males and females were discussed. The same approach has been used with racial differences. Cecil Reynolds and Arthur Jensen (1983) selected black and white children who had the same IQ scores and examined their performance on different aspects of the IQ test. Black children scored better than whites on tasks that required children to remember a string of numbers, to do mental arithmetic, and to code information. White children had an advantage when they were asked to assemble pieces of a puzzle, to arrange pictures to tell a story, and to demonstrate their comprehension of a situation. Surprisingly, there were no differences in the subtests that assessed information and vocabulary. This is surprising because critics of IQ tests typically argue that blacks have a distinct disadvantage in these two areas. This profile approach suggests that black children do especially well on tasks that require sustained attention while white children are better at spatial tasks.

Explaining racial differences in IQ scores is a delicate task. Those who would argue that the differences result from environmental variables can point to cultural discrepancies, educational experiences, and parental expectations that influence Orientals, whites, and blacks differently. Those who would argue that biological variables account for the difference try to equate for these differential environments and expectations. In the next section, we will consider the impact of both biological and environmental variables on intelligence.

## BIOLOGICAL FACTORS IN INTELLIGENCE

**Genetic factors in intelligence**

The evidence for a genetic component in intelligence is overwhelming and is accepted by most thoughtful psychologists (Albee, 1982). The size of the genetic component is more often a source of contention. As described in Chapter 2, behavioral geneticists and experts in statistics agree that genetic factors account for 50 to 80 percent of a person's IQ score (Bouchard & McGue, 1981; Herrnstein, 1982; Baker, Defries, & Fulker, 1983).

Even if the heritability index is as high as .80, the IQ of two children with the same genes may differ by as much as 25 IQ points if one is reared in a stimulating environment and the other in an unstimulating one (Cronbach, 1975). The environment, then, can be the difference between a borderline IQ of 75 and a normal IQ of 100. It can be the difference between an average IQ of 105 and a gifted score of 130. These differences are certainly large enough to warrant continued attention to a host of environmental factors that enhance or reduce IQ. As pointed out in the preceding section, even an increase of five points across a large segment of the population would benefit society enormously. Acknowledging the role of heredity in the IQ equation does not mean that environmental factors have no effect nor is it a reason to despair about the role of intervention programs. It does mean that we should examine all influences if we are to help children achieve their potential.

**Chronometric
analyses**

The two intelligence tests we have examined, as well as many other mental assessments, ask questions about the culture or ask children to remember information they have learned in school. Critics of intelligence tests continue to argue that such questions are biased (Dorfman, 1980) or are a function of the child's experiences (Dirks, 1982). To answer these critics, researchers have tried to find assessments of intelligence that are free of any cultural or intellectual content. Reaction time and other *chronometric analyses* fit the bill.

**Reaction time.** As early as 1868, a Dutch physiologist, F. C. Donders, wrote that it should be possible to determine "the time required for shaping a concept or expressing one's will" (Donders, 1969). He and Galton assumed that mental processes took a quantity of time and that this time factor could be measured. But their early attempts to measure these processes were not very successful, and Binet's approach to measuring intelligence was. Interest in mental chronometry lapsed for over half a century, then reemerged when intelligence tests came under fire. Currently, researchers from several areas of psychology are interested in the time it takes to perform mental processes. Today mental chronometry refers to "the study of the time course of information processing in the human nervous system" (Posner, 1978, p. 7). Reaction time is one of the most prominent measures being investigated.

Galton, you remember, thought reaction time might be a measure of general intellectual ability. But he measured only simple reaction time—how long after hearing a sound could a person press a button. He must have been disappointed when his assessments of reaction time showed no relationship to intellectual functioning. Choice reaction time, however, is a different story. In a choice reaction time setting, the child must respond to one of several possible choices. The console shown in Figure 11–9 illustrates a choice reaction time situation. Children begin with their index finger on the home button. When any one of the eight bulbs on the console lights, the child turns it off by pressing the button directly under that light. That is all there is to the task. There are no questions on New York or Greece, no arithmetic problems to solve, and no memory tasks. Removing one's finger as quickly as possible is all that is required. The only variation in the task is the number of lights involved. Covers can be attached to the console so that only one light or as many as eight lights are showing. When there are more lights visible, it takes the individual longer to respond.

The task is so simple that even preschool children understand the task and perform it easily. This one task, then, can be used with people from 3 to 93 years of age, and the scores that are obtained can be compared directly.

**Figure 11–9**    **Measuring choice reaction time**

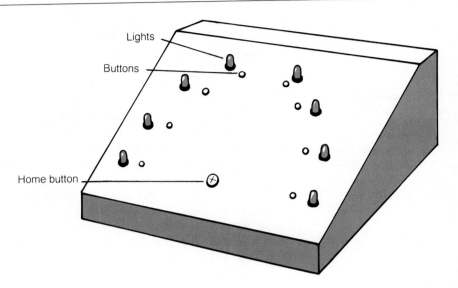

Lights

Buttons

Home button

In a test of choice reaction time, students start by placing their finger on the home button. When one of the lights on the console comes on, the student responds by pressing the button under the light. A timer measures how long it takes for the students to remove their finger from the home button and how long it takes to turn off the light. Several studies have indicated that there is a relationship between performance on this task and intelligence.

Source: Free Press, a Division of Macmillan, Inc. From *Bias in Mental Testing* by Arthur R. Jensen. © 1980 by Arthur R. Jensen.

The correlations between choice reaction time and intelligence are in the range of $-.40$ to $-.60$ (Carlson & Jensen, 1982). Shorter reaction times are related to higher IQs (see Figure 11–10). This relationship holds with college students (Jensen & Munroe, 1979), ninth graders (Carlson & Jensen, 1982), mildly mentally retarded adults (Vernon, 1981), and severely retarded children (Jensen, Schafer, & Crinella, 1981).

This surprisingly high correlation between a measure as uncomplicated as choice reaction time and a trait as complicated as intelligence prompts the question, what is being measured? Jensen speculates that choice reaction time measures the conduction efficiency of the nervous system. Jerry Carlson believes that the level of arousal and attention may also play a role in the reaction time test (Carlson, Jensen, & Widaman, 1983). The relationship between choice reaction time and intelligence provides compelling evidence that differences in mental skills are not simply a reflection of home environments or the learning that has taken place at school. Some much more fundamental process is involved.

In Jensen's experiments, no information about the culture is required. The

**Figure 11–10**  **Is choice reaction time related to intelligence?**

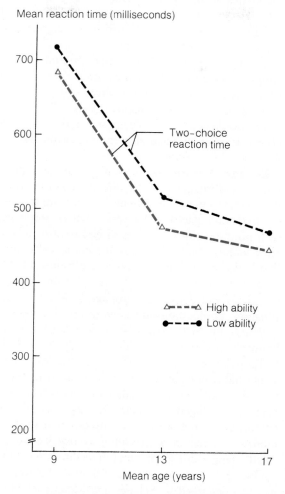

Mean reaction time (milliseconds)

△—△ High ability
●—● Low ability

Two-choice
reaction time

Mean age (years)

Nine-year-olds who scored in the top 5 percent on the Raven's Progressive Matrices required less than 700 milliseconds to respond in a choice reaction time situation. Their peers, from the 40–45th percentile of the Raven's Progressive Matrices, took well over 700 milliseconds to respond. Thirteen-year-olds had a distinct advantage over their peers with less ability. The same relationship occurred when 17-year-olds were tested.

Source: Keating, D. P., & Bobbitt, B. (1978). Individual and developmental differences in cognitive processing components of mental ability. *Child Development, 49,* 155–169.

same basic experiment, however, can be used to assess learned information. Saul Sternberg (1966) substituted letters of the alphabet for the lights on the console. After seeing an array of one to seven letters, for example a, s, c, and b, the letter z is presented. The person has to decide whether the letter was present in the earlier array. Notice that in this experiment, the person has to review information that has just been stored in short-term memory. Sternberg found that scanning short-term memory takes longer if seven letters are presented than if two letters are presented. The results from both Jensen's and Sternberg's reaction time experiments suggest that reaction time is actually measuring a central mental process.

The rebirth of interest in mental chronometry is a recent phenomenon. Attempts to measure mental processing time are expanding beyond the simple situations described above into areas that require searching long-term memory and solving complex problems (Davies, Sperber, & McCauley, 1981; Simpson & Lorsbach, 1983). We are still at the beginning stages of sorting out what choice reaction times and performance on tests like the Scholastic Aptitude Test have in common.

**Evoked Potentials.** Another way of reducing cultural influences on measures of intelligence is to directly measure how the brain responds to events that occur in the environment. To measure the electrical activity of the brain, electrodes are placed on the scalp. The person is seated in a quiet environment with no distractions. A series of flashes of light or clicks is presented. When a click sounds, the brain responds automatically, producing an electrical pattern that looks like a flutter of waves (see Figure 11–11). Over a number of trials, a computer sorts the normal activity of the brain from the brain's response to the clicks and derives the *average evoked potential.* As in the reaction time situation, no questions are asked or puzzles posed.

When this method was being developed, researchers found that individual brains differed in reaction time. As early as 1965, these differences were related to IQ (Chalke & Ertl, 1965). Since this early finding, the results have been somewhat confusing. Whether the brain is responding to clicks or lights seems to make a difference. Whether the individuals being measured are below average in intelligence or above average also changes the results. Perhaps the confusion stems from the slightly different methods that are used. The technology involved in determining averaged evoked potentials is complex, and small changes in experimental procedures may cloud the results.

One of the most recent innovations in the averaged evoked potential research was first described by Schafer and Marcus (1973). They designed two settings in which averaged evoked potentials were measured. The first setting was the same as described above. The person simply sat in a chair and waited for the clicks to be presented by the experimenter. In the second situation, the subjects actually initiated the clicking sounds by pressing a button. Because they were in control, they knew exactly when each click would be heard, and their brains responded very quickly. The difference in the brain's response time when the experimenter controlled the clicks and the brain's response time in the two settings is an index of *neural adaptability.* Large differences in the two situations mean that subjects respond very quickly when they know what is coming. Small differences mean that it does not matter if the person knows the click is coming. This measure of neural adaptability is strikingly related to intelligence (Schafer, 1979). Hospital technicians and people with a doctoral

**Figure 11—11**　　　　　　　**Averaged evoked potentials and intelligence**

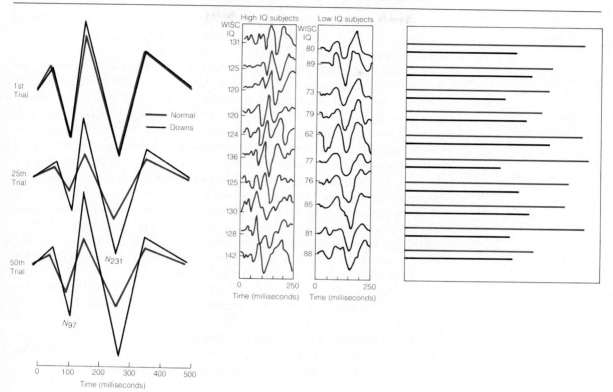

When normal adults and Down's syndrome adults first hear an auditory click, their brains respond similarly. By the 25th click, the normal adults are able to predict the sound and their brains respond differently. At the 50th trial, the Down's syndrome adults have exactly the same curve as they did on the first trial, but the normal adults have adapted.

Individuals with high IQs have more complicated evoked potentials as indicated by the number of squiggles in the tracing. If you think of each tracing as a piece of string that can be stretched, the high IQ subjects will have longer "string measures."

Sources: Schafer, E. W. P., & Peeke, H. V. S. (1982). Down syndrome individuals fail to habituate to cortical evoked potentials. *American Journal of Mental Deficiency, 87,* 332–337.

Hendrickson, A. E. (1982). The biological basis of intelligence Part I: Theory. In H. J. Eysenck (Ed.), *A model for intelligence.* New York: Springer-Verlag.

degree show very different levels of neural adaptability. Severely retarded residents of a state hospital also show differences in neural adaptability that correlate with measured intelligence (Jensen, Schafer, & Crinella, 1981).

Another example of differences in neural adaptability is taken from a comparison of Down's syndrome adults and normal adults. These two groups listened to a series of clicks presented every two seconds over a loudspeaker. The regularity of the stimulation meant that the individual could anticipate when the click would sound. As the clicks were repeated, the response pattern of normal adults changed (see Figure 11–11). In essence, their brains adjusted to the sounds. The Down's syndrome adults, however, have the same pattern of response to the 25th click and the 50th click as they do to the first click (Schafer & Peeke, 1982). This evidence strengthens the argument that differences in neural adaptability are related to intelligence.

Averaged evoked potentials may also measure the complex functioning of the central nervous system (Blinkhorn & Hendrickson, 1982). According to this view, intelligent individuals will have complex evoked potential patterns. How is such complexity measured? You begin by assuming that the evoked potential tracing reflects the complexity of the message that has been transmitted through the brain. Because each little squiggle is important, psychologists began sticking pins into the tracing and then threading a piece of string through the pins. The statistic of interest was the straightened length of the string. The computer has now eliminated the need for string, but the measure is still called the *string measure* (Eysenck, 1983). The correlation between the string measure of central nervous system functioning and intelligence as measured by a culture-fair intelligence test is on the order of .7 (Blinkhorn & Hendrickson, 1982; Hendrickson, 1982). In other words, the string measure accounted for half of the individual's performance on the IQ test.

The relationship between averaged evoked potentials and intelligence is intriguing. Years of research are still needed to streamline the technique and isolate the factors that are involved. Researchers are attracted to the method because measuring electrical potentials removes any vestige of culture or experience. Ultimately, this method may help determine if a factor like the efficiency of neural transmission is important to intelligence (Schafer, 1979).

## ENVIRONMENTAL FACTORS IN INTELLIGENCE

Prenatal circumstances and birth factors are environmental influences that can either enhance or inhibit the development of the brain. These factors are most critical during the periods of rapid brain growth that occur prenatally and during early infancy (see Chapter 5).

**The impact of nutrition on behavior**

**Malnutrition.**  The importance of adequate nutrition during the period of rapid brain growth was discussed in Chapter 5. Children need enough nutrients to fuel cell division during the prenatal and early postnatal months. Does nutrition make a difference after that point? This question is difficult to answer experimentally because of the ethics involved in supplementing some children's diets while other children do not receive supplements. Answering this question also requires longitudinal studies of children's diets and assessments of their intelligence. Even if we are able to establish a relationship between diet and intelligence, we have to eliminate other variables that might explain the relationship. Despite these difficulties, the effects of diet on intelligence are considered so important that various national and international agencies have tried to collect information on the effects of proper nutrition.

The country of Columbia, South America, was the site for one long-term study concerned with the effect of nutrition on intelligence. This project focused on three-year-olds who had suffered severe malnutrition and included an educational component, nutritional supplements, and information on health and hygiene. Children who stayed in the program for several years were taller, heavier, and had higher scores on cognitive assessments (McKay, 1978). But it is certainly possible that the educational program, not the nutritional supplement, was responsible for the cognitive changes (Bejar, 1981).

A second study done in Guatemala confined its intervention to nutritional supplements (Barrett, Radke-Yarrow, & Klein, 1982). One hundred and thirty-eight chronically malnourished children were studied from birth to school age. The children came from several villages outside of Guatemala City, where 80 to 85 percent of the children were undernourished. Some of these villages received additional protein and calorie supplements from the Institute of Nutrition of Central America and Panama. Other villages were not as fortunate.

To assess the impact of the additional nutrients, psychologists tested six- to eight-year-old children who fell into three distinct nutritional groups. The first group received nutritional supplements from birth to four years of age. Their mothers had also received extra protein and calorie supplements while they were pregnant. Overall, their nutritional history was good. A second group received some supplements during infancy, prompting the conclusion that these children had an adequate diet. The children in the third group did not receive nutritional supplements on a regular basis. These children were described as undernourished.

Supplementing the mother's diet during pregnancy and improving the child's diet during the first years of life had unexpected effects on the behavior of the children when they reached school age. The children with healthy diets were outgoing and social, had moderate activity levels, and were interested in their environments. Furthermore, they expressed their feelings, showing both anger and joy more often than the other children. These differences were primarily social. Modifying the children's diets also altered their performance on some cognitive tasks. Children who received good supplementation were able to persist on a task and follow directions better than their peers. The dietary supplementation seemed to help them focus their attention. In the villages with the poorest nutrition, the children who received extra calories were more successful on the block design subtest and had higher scores on a battery of cognitive tests. In this study, providing supplemental nutrients had long-term effects on both socioemotional behavior and cognitive skills (Barrett, Radke-Yarrow, & Klein, 1982).

The children who had inadequate diets provided a sharp contrast. They had problems maintaining their attention and appeared apathetic. In addition to their general lack of expressiveness, they seemed unable to organize their behavior (Barrett, Radke-Yarrow, & Klein, 1982).

Specific deficiencies in a child's diet or the ingestion of toxic substances can also affect a child's intellectual functioning. Iron deficiency is associated with attentional problems and memory deficits (Pollitt & Leibel, 1976). Some of these deficiencies can be remedied by adding iron to the diet of anemic children (Walter, Kovalskys, & Stekel, 1983). Anemic children in India who were given extra iron in their diet jumped 17 points on the performance section of the WISC. Similar children who did not receive the supplements gained six points (Seshadri, Hirode, Naik, & Malhotra, 1982). The authors argue that visual-motor coordination is improved by the iron supplements, perhaps because the functioning of the brain is more efficient.

Lead is one of the most extreme examples of a substance that alters the functioning of the brain. If large amounts of lead are ingested, then a severe inflammation of the brain occurs causing mental retardation and, in the most severe cases, death (Lowenstein, 1982). Lead poisoning, usually caused by children eating lead-based paint, was quite common a few decades ago. Today lead-based paints are no longer used. Currently, health officials are concerned about the more subtle effects of the small quantities of lead in the air. Small amounts of lead in the bloodstream pose a hazard to the normal mental development of children (David, Grad, McGann, & Koltun, 1982). Not all children are affected by these small concentrations of lead. For those who are, however, the damage to the brain is irreversible. Long ago, allergists suggested that particular foods might also affect the functioning of the brain in susceptible individuals. Unpredictable behavor, tantrums, bedwetting, and seizures are just a few behaviors that can be triggered by offending foods (Crook, 1980; David, Grad, McGann, & Koltun, 1982). The most controversial extension of this view is that particular foods cause hyperactivity.

**Nutrition and hyperactivity.** Hyperactive children have attentional problems and usually do not perform well in school. The search for solutions to these children's learning problems has run the gamut of treatments from medication to diet to behavioral modification. Investigators trying to understand the attention problems of these children have recently decided to study neurotransmitters in the brain. Different foods do affect the concentration of neurotransmitters in the brain (Cottet-Emard, Peyrin, & Bonnod, 1980). This could mean that hyperactive children have more trouble metabolizing neurotransmitters than other children (Shekim, Davis, Bylund, Brunngraber, Fikes, & Lanham, 1982). If this is the case, then hyperactive children could accumulate some substance in their brain that makes them overactive and decreases their attention span.

Benjamin Feingold, a physician, suggests that as many as 50 percent of hyperactive children can be helped by a diet free of food additives and dyes (Feingold, 1975). Feingold's diet has been greeted with great enthusiasm by desperate parents. Parents' groups around the country extol the virtues of the diet and decry the use of medication to control hyperactivity. Controlled experiments, however, have not been as enthusiastic. Some children are helped by the diet, but many are not (Stare, Whelan, & Sheridan, 1980). After several careful studies, the Nutrition Foundation (1980) reported that the diet poses no risks for children. On the positive side, they also noted that a family that adheres to the diet undergoes changes, as a family, that are frequently beneficial to the hyperactive child.

In specific instances, the Feingold diet has had a marked effect on behavior. One 3½-year-old boy who had daily seizures alternated between the Feingold diet and a regular diet. The number of seizures per day increased three to four times when the child returned to the regular diet (see Figure 11–12). After a year of strict adherence to the diet, the child's seizures stopped and his medication had been substantially reduced (Haavik, Altman, & Woelk, 1979). The authors note that although the diet had a clear effect on the seizures, it did not affect the boy's hyperactivity.

The medical community and the public have become more concerned about possible effects of particular foods and food additives on hyperactive children. In the United States, approximately 5,000 different additives are generally recognized as safe (Traxel, 1982). Some people are sensitive to these additives (Crook, 1980). Recent experiments, therefore, have focused on individual sensitivities to isolated additives. James Swanson and Marcel Kinsbourne (1980), for example, gave hyperactive children a large dose of nine food dyes and compared their learning skills to a group of children given a placebo. The food dye capsules impaired the hyperactive children's ability to remember an animal that had been paired with a number. The same capsule of food dyes had no effect on children who were not hyperactive.

**Figure 11–12**  **How diet affects behavior**

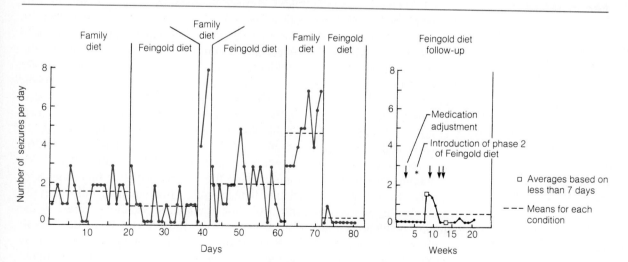

A three-year-old boy who had daily seizures when fed a normal diet had fewer seizures when he followed a strict diet that eliminated foods containing preservatives and additives (the Feingold Diet). By maintaining the diet, he was able to reduce his medication and remain seizure free.

Source: Haavik, S., Altman, K. & Woelk, C. (1979). Effects of the Feingold diet on seizures and hyperactivity: A single-subject analysis. *Journal of Behavioral Medicine, 2,* 365–374.

Although the controversy about whether an altered diet can affect learning is far from being settled (Forbes, 1982), we are beginning to understand the effects of nutrition on the brain. Everyone agrees that adequate nutrition is most important during the period of rapid brain growth. When the brain is no longer growing rapidly, nutrients are the fuel for the brain's functioning. The nutrients we eat on a day-to-day basis alter the functioning of the brain in subtle ways. These subtle changes are extremely difficult to document, in part because the blood-brain barrier (see Chapter 5) insulates the brain from the rapid fluctuation of nutrients in the blood-stream. Despite this barrier, the brain ultimately derives its nutrients from the blood supply, and toxic substances like lead cross the barrier and damage the brain. The absence of an essential mineral such as iron can also affect the functioning of the brain. A small segment of the population is probably sensitive to food additives such as dyes and preservatives, just as a small segment is sensitive to wheat, milk, and corn (O'Banion, Armstrong, Cummings, & Stange, 1978). It is certainly possible for these dyes and additives to affect the central nervous system. Nevertheless, supposing that all hyperactive children will be helped by a diet like Feingold's is like trying to fit all children with the same size shoe. Research has to deal with individual reactions to specific chemicals before we will understand the relationship between the foods we eat and the functioning of the central nervous system.

**Family influences**

Children grow up in families and spend the majority of their childhood years interacting with the individuals in these small social systems. It follows that the search for environmental factors that affect the child's intelligence should focus on the family. Maternal intelligence and educational level, whether or not the family is intact, the number of siblings, and social class are all family variables that relate to intelligence. These factors are not, however, independent (Willerman, 1979). Intelligent women are likely to stay in school, marry a successful man, and limit the size of their families. The intelligent behavior of their children is a product of the entire system, not any single variable. Hence, we need to look at the separate family factors related to intelligence and then try to understand how the entire system functions to produce an intelligent child.

Family background is implicated in the intellectual accomplishments of adults. But many of the variables that look like environmental influences are confounded with genetic influences. For example, an extensive library in the home might be counted as an environmental variable, yet its existence typically reflects the parents' intellectual interests. To untangle the effects these factors have on intelligence, psychologists have turned to adoption studies (Horn, Loehlin, & Willerman, 1979).

Sandra Scarr and Richard Weinberg (1976) have tested both black and white children who were adopted by middle-class families. After several years in their adoptive homes, the black children had IQs above the national average of 100. They were also doing well in school. Their IQ scores and educational attainments were much higher than would be expected given the occupations and educational achievements of their biological parents.

A French study confirmed these effects. Working-class women with at least two children put one of the children up for adoption. The children were adopted by upper-middle-class families. Several years later, the children in the higher socioeconomic environment had an average IQ of 110. Their siblings, who had remained with the mother, had an IQ of 94. The two groups of children also differed in school achievement. Eighty-seven percent of the adopted children were doing well in school, but 55 percent of the children who stayed with their biological mothers had failing grades (Schiff, Duyme, Dumaret, Stewart, Tomkiewicz, & Feingold, 1978). The improved family environment provided by the adoptive families increased IQ and promoted skills, values, and attitudes that fostered success in school (Scarr, 1981).

These studies verify the impact of the environment on both intelligence and school achievement, but they are not very helpful in delineating the specific characteristics of the environment that enhance intellectual development. The potentially important factors are many. First and foremost is the mother.

**Mother-child interaction.** Mothers set the intellectual tone in the home. They determine the level of stimulation that will surround the child, they model the language the child will acquire, they establish the types of control that will be used, and they suggest values and attitudes that the child will learn.

Language provides a good example of the pervasive influence of the mother on the infant, toddler, and child. Middle-class mothers respond to their infants and preschooler's speech with extended sentences designed to inform. These mothers ask questions, repeat their child's sentences, and expand the two-word utterances that are the child's first sentences. While they are providing this language model, they are attending to and responding to the child's efforts to construct sentences (Hoff-Ginsburg & Shatz, 1982). Lower-class mothers rely more on commands and instructions. When their child does not respond, they are likely to repeat the same command (Schacter, 1979). These differences in transmitting the language may seem small, but they can affect the child's language, social skills, problem solving strategies, and coping style (Ramey, MacPhee, & Yeates, 1982).

The mother's importance to the developing child has been given a preeminent role in the research of Burton White (1978). He began his 10-year research project by trying to identify the characteristics of a competent six-year-old. Early in his project, he discovered that he did not need to wait until the children were six; he could identify the competent children by the time they were three. He reasoned that because the mother is the primary caretaker prior to age three, she must be the primary force behind the child's competence. He began observing mothers interacting with their toddlers and found that mothers of competent children were particularly effective in three areas. First, they designed safe, accessible, and interesting environments for their toddlers. They allowed the child to explore and to feel the satisfaction of functioning

**Does the mother's behavior affect intelligence?**

Mothers who allow their child to explore but who remain attentive to possible danger have children who are confident and competent when they attend school.

autonomously. Second, the mother was an accessible and interesting consultant who provided help, comfort, and companionship on request. Third, the mother disciplined the child in a firm and consistent fashion. Despite this firmness, the interaction between the mother and her child was characterized by warmth and affection.

Burton White's study was designed to describe environments that produced competent children. He reasoned that once we knew which variables were important, we could teach parents to provide that type of environment, or design programs that would provide that environment. If we know that reading to children helps them read when they attend school, or that asking preschoolers questions helps them develop fluid language, we can help parents be more effective (Henderson, 1981). This does not mean that all parents have to imitate middle-class mothers. It does mean that within every culture, parents can expose their children to a wide range of interesting and stimulating activities (Henderson, 1981).

**Father-child interaction.** For years, the role of fathers was ignored in the psychological studies of child development. When fathers were studied, it was the effect of their absence, rather than their presence, that was investigated. Early studies agreed that father absence was related to poor achievement in school (Deutsch, 1960) and to reduced IQ scores, especially in boys

(Deutsch & Brown, 1964). The suggestion was also made that a father who was absent during the early years of life was more devastating scholastically than father absence that occurred later (Santrock, 1972).

As with many of the correlations that have been reported in this chapter, this correlation has been questioned. Critics have suggested that the correlation between father absence and poor scholastic achievement was really the result of a constellation of family factors that were altered when the father left or died (Herzog & Sudia, 1973). Most prominent among these factors was the reduced income in the families now headed by mothers. After Herzog's criticism, two large-scale studies looked at families in which the fathers were absent (Broman, Nichols, & Kennedy, 1975; Svanum, Bringle, & McLaughlin, 1982). Both of these studies found that the boys in these families had lower IQs and lower school achievement. These differences, however, disappeared when the socio-economic class of the families was taken into consideration.

More recent studies have moved away from the father-absent, father-present dichotomy and have asked, instead, whether fathers who spend time with their sons enhance the child's cognitive development. In these studies, all of the fathers are present, but some are more available to their children. Having the fathers present minimizes the financial and emotional upheavals that confounded the studies on absent fathers. With these variables controlled, the impact of the father on cognitive development is still evident. Fathers who interact with their infants have boys who score higher on infant IQ tests (Pedersen, Rubenstein, & Yarrow, 1979). If fathers are available to their school-aged sons, the boys solve problems readily (Reis & Gold, 1977), are rated as brighter by their teachers (Ziegler, 1979), and receive higher grades (Blanchard & Biller, 1971).

Assessing the amount of time that the father is available is one way to measure the father's impact on the child's cognitive development. Measuring the quality of the interaction between father and son is an additional refinement. Warm, supportive fathers are likely to have sons with high IQs (Radin, 1981). Authoritarian, hostile fathers seem to inhibit their son's cognitive growth, perhaps by making the boys anxious in learning settings (Harrington, Block, & Block, 1978). Fathers who interfere or take over also have a negative effect on their sons' cognitive skills (Radin, 1981). The exact reason for this effect is not clear. When the father takes over, it could be that the son's sense of autonomy is threatened. Perhaps the child just retreats from the task and does not exercise his problem solving skill. In any case, it is safe to conclude that fathers who are present, involved, and supportive have a positive effect on their son's IQ. This effect does not seem to be a function of social class, race, or income, but emanates from the actual interaction between father and son.

Fathers do not influence their daughters' cognitive development as directly. Despite this general conclusion, girls seem to benefit intellectually if they are given autonomy and if the father is supportive, but not interfering (Radin, 1981; Levy-Shiff, 1982). In attempting to explain this difference between boys and girls, psychologists have offered two suggestions. The first is that girls are

**Fathers also make a difference**

*Michael Hayman: Stock, Boston*

Warm, supportive fathers are likely to have sons with high IQs. Fathers seem to have less impact on their daughter's IQs.

better able to cope with the vagaries of the environment and are not as susceptible as boys to a variety of stresses including absent or uncaring fathers (Lehrke, 1978). The second suggestion is that girls are simply influenced more by their mothers than their fathers (Bayley & Schaefer, 1964).

Norma Radin offers this succinct summary of a father's role in cognitive development. "A father influences his children's mental development through many and diverse channels: through his genetic background, through his manifest behavior with his offspring, through the attitudes he holds about himself and his children, through the behavior he models, through his position in the family system, through the material resources he is able to supply for his children, through the influence he exerts on his wife's behavior, through his ethnic heritage, and through the vision he holds for his children" (1981, p. 419).

**Family structure.** Family size, the spacing of siblings, and the birth order of a particular child all relate to intelligence (Henderson, 1981). In general, children from large families will receive lower scores on IQ tests than children from small families. Recognize, though, that the number of children in the family is related to socioeconomic status.

The first child in a family has an advantage when it comes to achievement. He or she is more likely to go to college and graduate school than children born later. Studying the list of National Merit Scholars in any particular year will show that firstborn children are more prevalent than children born later. In fact, in most indices of occupational and intellectual distinction, firstborns appear more often than expected. The explanation for this success given most often is that parents had the time and were motivated to stimulate their first-born child.

Robert Zajonc has formulated a theory, called the confluence model, based on similar reasoning. He argues that the greater the intelligence of the family as a unit, the greater the opportunity for intellectual development. Adults are more stimulating than children, and older siblings contribute more to an intellectual atmosphere than younger children. Having a sibling who is very close to your age is, according to the theory, detrimental to intellectual development because it dilutes the intellectual environment. The same is true of large families. The intellectual environment is much more limited than in small families (Zajonc & Markus, 1976). Despite the appeal of this theory, attempts to verify it have not been impressive (Henderson, 1981). Socioeconomic status is consistently more important in IQ determinations than family size, birth order, or spacing of siblings.

**Socioeconomic status.** Socioeconomic status is one of the best predictors of intelligence and academic achievement (Henderson, 1981). What are the causes of the association between social class and intelligence? It seems unlikely that the amount of money a family earns or the father's job is critical to a child's intelligence. More plausible is the notion that intelligent individuals obtain a good education, become successful, and earn enough money to move into the middle or upper classes. They also have intelligent children, but that is not directly linked to their socioeconomic status.

**Stress.** Stress is a powerful factor in adult behavior, illness, and coping (Selye, 1979). For some reason, stress has not been as widely studied in children. Recently, however, Bernard Brown and Lilian Rosenbaum concluded that stress can affect the growth of intelligence. They based their findings on several thousand seven-year-olds who reported their problems. Some children had no problems, while others reported more than 15. The problems included physical ailments, domestic problems, divorce, and the death of a friend or relative. Intelligence scores on the WISC declined from 105 in the sample of children who had no problems to 91 in the sample that had more than 15 problems (Brown & Rosenbaum, 1983). This survey approach masks many other issues that may affect the child's functioning, but it indicates that children are not immune to the problems that surround them.

Divorces and family disruptions are a common source of stress. As many as half of the children born in the 1970s will spend some time living with only one parent (Hetherington, 1981). No one is certain whether the dissolution of the family affects intelligence, but divorces are followed by a spiral of events that could affect intellectual functioning. Divorces often mean that children have minimal access to their fathers. When parents separate, the financial resources of the family are divided. Income for the woman and her children drops as much as 30 percent (Hoffman, 1977). The financial problems of the family are compounded by the fact that many divorced women have limited job skills. Even if the mother can find a full-time job, the children are often left in temporary and erratic child-care settings. The whole household is disorganized and the nurturing, structured environment advocated by psychologists dissolves into a conflict-ridden power struggle (Hetherington, Cox, & Cox, 1978).

As we have seen, when fathers are present, when socioeconomic status is high, and when devoted caretakers are available, children are most likely to achieve. Divorces may alter that achievement by changing the child's circumstances. Divorced mothers are not as successful in providing stimulating home environments as married women (MacKinnon, Brody, & Stoneman, 1982). The optimistic note in the divorce literature is that the chaos and disruption are usually temporary. The effect on the child's achievement may also be temporary.

**The systems approach—the Abecedarian project**

Family and societal variables that influence intelligence do not act in isolation. Each one becomes part of the whole pool of influences that, over the years, contributes to or detracts from intellectual development. This rippling effect of isolated variables is underscored in the Abecedarian project conducted in North Carolina. The typical child in this project came from a family headed by the mother. The mothers had few resources, their IQs were in the low 80s, their incomes were below $1,500 a year, and they had a 10th-grade education. The mother's lack of resources meant that the children in her family had a high probability of failing in school and being diagnosed as cases of *psychosocial retardation*.

Infants from these high-risk families were enrolled in the Abecedarian day-care program as early as six weeks of age and continued to attend the day-care center until they were ready for public school. The day-care experience they received was especially designed to foster language development and to produce appropriate and adaptive social behavior (Ramey, MacPhee, & Yeates, 1982). A control group of infants from the same population were not enrolled in the day-care program but were provided with social services, medical services, and nutritional supplements. The two groups have been compared on a variety of indices for five years. The results show how the mother, child, and social system influence each other.

**Effects on the child.** Social and cognitive changes in the children were apparent by two years of age (Ramey & Haskins, 1981). The children in the project were more attentive, more adaptive, and more cooperative than the control children. Their language skills at 3½ were similarly superior. This constellation of language and social skills provided these high-risk children with better ways of coping with the world. In addition, the day-care children enjoyed a consistent advantage in IQ scores. Although the two groups had identical scores at 12 months, by 24 months the experimental group had a decided advantage that has been maintained through five years of age (see Figure 11–13). At five years of age, only 11 percent of the day-care children had IQ scores below 85, compared to 39 percent of the control children (Ramey, MacPhee, & Yeates, 1982).

The project has also made a difference in how the children approached life. The children from the day-care project came to believe that they controlled their success (Walden & Ramey, 1983). In their minds, effort and hard work were the keys to academic achievement. This determination was evident in the

**Figure 11–13**         **Intellectual effects of the Abecedarian project**

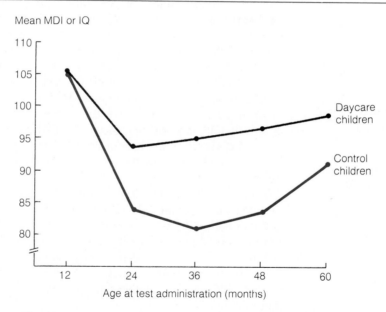

The Abecedarian project provided day care for infants who were "at risk" for school failure. Day care began during the first months of life and continued until the child began attending public school. At two years of age, the day-care children received much higher IQ scores on the Bayley Scales of Infant Development. During the next three years, both groups were given the Stanford-Binet. The day-care children maintained a significant advantage over the control children during these years. At five years of age, the children were given the Wechsler Preschool and Primary Scale of Intelligence. The day-care children still had a six-point advantage.

Source: Ramey, C. T., MacPhee, D., & Yeates, K. O. (1982). Preventing developmental retardation: A general systems model. In D. K. Detterman & R. J. Sternberg (Eds.), *How and how much can intelligence be increased.* Norwood, NJ: Ablex.

classroom where the children paid close attention and were not easily distracted. The efforts of the day-care children were translated into higher levels of academic achievement in public school. The authors conclude that the day-care intervention weakened the relationship between IQ and academic achievement and strengthened the relationship between motivational factors and achievement. Clearly, the project had a major impact on the academic level of the child (Ramey, MacPhee, & Yeates, 1982).

**Effects on the mother.**  The mothers in this project were from very low income families; they were typically black and young. Their interactions with their children were characterized by an authoritarian attitude, but they were not hostile or rejecting. These mothers used a large number of commands when they spoke to their children. An interesting change in the mother-child interaction occurred as a result of the language and social skills the children acquired in day care. By 36 months, the children in day care were communicating easily with their mothers. They asked their mother to watch their activities or join them in a tea party. These language and coping skills promoted play activities that were enjoyable for both the mother and child. At the same time, the shared play helped blunt the authoritarian style of the mother.

**Effects on the family.**  When the children in the Abecedarian Project were 4½ years old, an interview with the mothers was conducted. To the surprise of the interviewers, the experimental mothers now had more education than the control mothers and were employed in jobs that required higher levels of skill. At the beginning of the study, the groups had similar educational and occupational backgrounds. Having the child in a full-time, high-quality day-care program relieved the mother of the burdens of child care and allowed her to improve her occupational skills or continue her education. These changes are important in assessing the total project because they are permanent and help draw these high-risk families closer to the mainstream of society.

If only changes in intelligence are considered, the 6.96 point spread that separated the experimental and control children at five years may not seem very impressive. But if you consider how many of these children have moved into the normal range of the IQ scale and away from the range associated with special class placements, delinquency, and lack of occupational skills, the differences become more impressive. Furthermore, if we add the other effects on the child and the mother-child interaction, the project certainly merits close attention.

Perhaps over many years the Abecedarian project would not induce higher IQ scores but will be felt in other ways. This was the case when Head Start children were evaluated years after their preschool experience (Collins, 1983). When observed between 3 and 15 years later, the Head Start children were not distinguished from their peers by markedly different IQs. But they had not been placed in special education classes as often as their peers, nor had they been asked to repeat grades as often. As a group, they were less likely to drop out of high school, they had better attitudes toward school, and their achievement scores were higher than similar children who had not graduated from a Head Start program (Lazar & Darlington, 1982). These two projects illustrate the long-term ripple effects that are now recognized as an outcome of large-scale intervention programs. IQ tests tell us nothing about personal and social development, about changes in the family situation, or about attitudes and motivational variables. To evaluate the benefits as well as the drawbacks of social programs, psychologists must examine the whole constellation of variables that affect achievement (Brown & Campione, 1982).

In the final analysis, the point of intervention programs is to alter the pattern of achievement, not the IQ. It is clear that interventions such as Head Start and the Abecedarian project do not raise the child's IQ dramatically. The interventions, however, are important in terms of maximizing the child's potential and increasing the child's ability to function in the mainstream of society. In the final analysis, such functional changes overshadow the importance of IQ.

## SUMMARY

Measuring intelligence has been an integral part of psychology since Galton's first tentative attempts to measure individual differences at a world's fair. The issues involved in measuring such a complex trait are themselves complicated. The first set of issues is whether the tests measure the trait accurately. The tests that are currently used must meet accepted standards of reliability and validity. They must also be standardized using an appropriate population. The most widely accepted tests of intelligence, the Stanford-Binet and the three Wechsler scales, satisfy these requirements. Furthermore, they have demonstrated their usefulness repeatedly by predicting scholastic achievement and occupational success among diverse groups of people.

Despite their ability to predict behavior, or maybe because of it, the tests have come under increasing fire from several segments of the population. In the last decade, the issue of whether the tests are fair has been taken to the courts. As a result, many of the criticisms have been carefully investigated. More often than not, detailed studies have shown that the test scores are not as biased as many people believe. Despite this support for IQ tests, the search for tests that do not require any knowledge of a specific culture holds many attractions. Tests like the Raven's Progressive Matrices that require minimal language skills have been devised and used successfully. Tests like the SOMPA, that try to take the child's cultural background into account, have also been proposed.

A new tack in the assessment of intelligence has emerged in the last few years. Psychologists are again contemplating physiological measures as an index of intelligence. Both reaction time and averaged evoked potentials have been proposed as reasonable ways to assess the biological basis of intelligence. The fledgling state of research in these areas simply means that we must be hesitant about drawing firm conclusions.

A summary of the environmental factors that affect intelligence should emphasize three points. First, a large number of environmental factors that are correlated with intellectual development have been identified. Many of these, like maternal education and IQ, are intertwined and cannot be separated from biological factors. A second point, highlighted in the Abecedarian project, is that these environmental factors are embedded in a network or system of variables whose effects radiate beyond the mother or her child. Finally, the mere number of variables that seem to be implicated in intellectual development means that it is simplistic to think of intelligence as the product of single, isolated factors.

The studies reported in this chapter demonstrate that the environment can influence intelligence at the cellular level, the physiological level, or the social level. At the cellular level, genetic status, nutritional factors, and insults to the organism, like anoxia or lead poisoning, can affect intelligence. At the physiological level, reaction time, evoked potentials, and neural adaptability are related to intelligence. At the social level, the family system, the community, the school, the relationship between parent and child, and the child's ability to cope with society are important. At every level, intellectual functioning can be enhanced or disrupted. Models of intelligence must admit all of these factors, from cellular to social, and they must acknowledge that these factors interact with each other.

# PART 4

## Widening social and personal horizons

**Theories about the family's influence**

Freud's theory of the mother-child relationship
Erickson's psychosocial stages

**The changing role of the family during development**

Families during infancy
Families of toddlers
Families with preschoolers
Families of school-age children
Families with adolescents
The family's response to males and females
Early families and late families

**Alternative family patterns**

Families with two working parents
Divorce and its consequences

**Child abuse and neglect**

What constitutes child abuse?
Patterns of abuse at different ages
The abused child
The abusive parent
Preventing child abuse

**Summary**

# CHAPTER 12
## The family's influence

The helplessness of the newborn and the long period of dependency that is characteristic of humans mean that infants must be fed, sheltered, and protected. For most mammals, the mother takes the responsibility for sheltering her young and protecting them from harm. As we move up the evolutionary ladder to primates, the responsibility for the young is more widely shared. For example, in chimpanzee groups and gorilla groups, both the males and females protect infants. Dianne Fossey's sensitive account of gorillas (1983) shows that males not only protect, they provide nurturance and emotional support when the mother has been killed or has left the group (see Figure 12–1). Among humans, the functions of the mother and the father in the social unit called the family are much more complex. Families certainly provide shelter, protection, and nurturance, but they also affect the child's cognitive skills, self-esteem, attitudes, and motivation. In this chapter, we will discuss the importance of the human family and describe how it affects children from infancy to adolescence.

Families are undergoing rapid changes. The skyrocketing divorce rate means that single parent families and stepfamilies are as common now as they were rare a generation ago. The increasing number of women working outside the home has also altered family patterns. As women have been given more equality in their career options, many have chosen to have their families later in life and to limit the size of their families. With both parents working, fathers have been participating more in the routines of child care. Even with the father's help, mothers have had to make a variety of arrangments for their children while they work. These fundamental changes in the family and the society mean that children's lives are altered in complex ways.

As a first step in understanding how contemporary family patterns shape the child, we need to look at traditional families and outline those family patterns that help a child thrive. Once these patterns are presented, deviations will be considered. Teenage parents, single parents, and stepparents offer the child a somewhat different socializing force. The impact of these slightly different patterns can be positive as well as negative. As we consider these patterns, we will discuss the importance of the father, the ways that maternal employment affects the family, and the effects of a divorce on the lives of children.

After considering a variety of family styles, we will look specifically at envi-

**Figure 12–1**                    **The role of fathers**

Male baboons, chimpanzees, and gorillas protect infants and offer them security.

ronments that are detrimental to the healthy development of the child. Abusive parents provide an extreme example of an unsupportive environment. When a child is physically, emotionally, or sexually abused, it signals a breakdown in the family unit. For the safety of the child, it is important to be able to identify the troubled family. If efforts to predict and prevent abuse fail, we must try to mend the family unit that is torn by violence.

## THEORIES ABOUT THE FAMILY'S INFLUENCE

**Freud's theory of the mother-child relationship.**

Freud was one of the first theorists to draw attention to the importance of the family unit. His theory, however, focused on the mother-child relationship. The mother was, in his view, "unique, without parallel, established unalterably for a whole lifetime as the first and strongest love-object and as the prototype of all later love-relations" (Freud, 1964, p. 188). Freud believed that the mother's behavior determined how well adjusted her children were and what personality traits they exhibited. Infants were seen as passive and dependent. If they were not cared for properly, they would remain passive throughout their lives, always searching for a mother to care for them. If mothers did not allow their infants enough pleasure in sucking, as adults they would always seek the oral pleasure they missed as an infant (Baldwin, 1981). Infants whose needs were met in a reasonable way would not fixate on oral pleasures. They would progress to the next stage. Of course, they might retain some vestiges of the pleasure derived from the oral stage such as smoking a pipe or kissing.

After the passive pleasures of the oral stage, the child moved to the anal stage. During this period, the mother's influence was equally critical. Freud felt that mothers who began toilet training too early or were too harsh in their punishments caused children to be obsessed with cleanliness, to be defiant, or to feel timid because they were ashamed (Miller, 1983). Mothers must allow their two- and three-year-olds some gratification of impulses; but they must also encourge self-control (Miller, 1983).

Assuming the mother and child negotiated these first two stages successfully, they would next embark on the phallic stage. By age four, in Freud's scheme, the source of pleasure had moved to the genital area. Children express this new interest by asking questions about sex differences and babies. Once a boy discovers the difference between the sexes, he supposedly desires his mother. But his feelings are rebuffed and his repressed desires serve to shape masculine interests and values. For girls, the development of feminine characteristics is very different. Upon discovering that she has no penis, the girl supposedly feels inferior and develops the passive nature that Freud believed was characteristic of women (Crain, 1980).

Many of these tenets of Freudian theory have been challenged and carry little weight in current developmental theories of personality. They do underline, however, the critical role that Freud attributed to the family. Children could be timid, obsessive, defiant, or passive depending on how their mothers treated them during the early years.

## Erikson's psychosocial stages

Although Erikson was a psychoanalyst and actually studied with Anna Freud, he moved away from the sexual stages postulated by Freud and offered instead a series of psychosocial conflicts that the child must negotiate. Like Freud, he placed enormous importance on the family and believed that family interaction patterns shaped the child's personality (see Figure 12–2).

According to Erikson (1963), a healthy adjustment means that the child resolves several basic conflicts in a positive way. The first conflict centers around the development of trust. Infants thrive when their caretakers are predictable and reliable. Before they are a year old, these infants realize that their needs will be met. Infants whose needs are not met, whose parents are inconsistent and neglectful, can fail to develop this basic trust.

The second conflict the child faces is between autonomy and shame. Erikson talks about toilet training, but for Erikson, this training is just one of several areas in which the child has to learn to control impulses. While parents tolerate a certain amount of messiness when infants eat, the throwing of food

**Figure 12–2**    **Erikson's psychosocial stages**

| Psychosocial conflict | Significant people | Favorable resolution | Unfavorable resolution |
|---|---|---|---|
| First year:<br>Trust versus Mistrust | Mother | Child begins to trust adults | Suspicion |
| Second year:<br>Autonomy versus Shame | Parents | Self-control; self-esteem | Doubts about abilities; self-conscious |
| Three to five years:<br>Initiative versus Guilt | Family | Ability to direct and initiate activities | Fear of punishment; denial |
| Six years to adolescence:<br>Industry versus inferiority | School | Performs tasks competently | Feels inadequate or inferior |
| Adolescence:<br>Identity versus Role Diffusion | Peers; models | Confidence in self; forms coherent identity | Diffused sense of identity |
| Young adulthood:<br>Intimacy versus Isolation | Friends; spouse | Forms intimate relationships with friends of both sexes | Self-absorption; isolation |
| Middle age:<br>Generativity versus stagnation | Becomes a mentor | Establishing and guiding the next generation | Repulsion; individual interpersonally adrift |
| Retirement years:<br>Ego-Integrity versus Despair | Humans | Acceptance of life cycle | Fear of death |

Erik Erikson outlined eight psychosocial conflicts that had to be resolved during development. In each case, successful resolution of the conflict primed the child or adult to tackle the next stage. An unsuccessful resolution of the conflict made it difficult to resolve the next conflict in a positive way.

Source: Erikson, E. H. (1963). *Childhood and Society*. New York: W. W. Norton.

or the intentional spilling of milk is likely to be met with a stern rebuke. Two-year-olds who love to say no are allowed some autonomy, but they also have to compromise. Socialization during this period means achieving a balance between the child's impulses and the parents' expectations. The healthy resolution of this conflict yields a child who is autonomous, confident, and independent. If parents behave autocratically and ridicule a child, the child fails to develop a sense of autonomy. The result is a toddler with lasting feelings of dependency and shame.

From three to six, the child makes plans and sets goals. William Crain (1980) reports that in a single day his five-year-old son embarked on several personal projects. He used blocks to build a tall tower. He used the bed for a jumping contest. Finally, he initiated a family outing to an adventure movie. With a sense of trust and some feelings about their own autonomy, children delight in initiating projects and carrying them through. If parents intrude excessively into these projects or outline every step of a child's day, this initiative is squelched. Parents who let the child initiate activities and offer the child a chance to succeed, allow for the fullest development of healthy personality characteristics.

Major changes in the child's development occur between the ages of 6 and 11. If development is proceeding positively, children become industrious and competent. In earlier eras, children accompanied their parents as they hunted, farmed, cooked, or sewed. They learned the rudiments of the skills they needed to survive. In contemporary society, children undertake culturally meaningful tasks at school. They learn to read. They study math. They relive the culture's history. The danger in this stage is the feeling some children develop that they are inadequate or inferior. The negative feelings at this stage can be a result of peers who tease a child, teachers who are constantly pointing out inadequacies, or societies that discriminate against particular groups. The parents are still important, but other social agents begin to influence their child's development.

Erikson outlines four more stages (see Figure 12–2). Each one involves a social conflict that can be resolved positively or negatively. Parents seem to be central to the positive resolution of the first three stages and to play lesser roles in later stages.

Erikson's model provided developmental psychologists with much food for thought. The view of the family guiding the child through the early phases of growth and development is powerful. Few psychologists disagree that the well-adjusted adult is one who negotiates the various crises and phases of childhood successfully. But developmental psychologists today take issue with several of Erikson's proposals. The effect of even the most negative events during child-hood can be alleviated or exaggerated depending on whether or not the environment is supportive. Psychologists today also quarrel with the view that the mother is the main socializing agent. Fathers have been recognized as important partners in child rearing. They make a distinct and important contribution to the development of their children (Bell, Johnson, McGillicuddy-Delisi, & Sigel, 1981). Furthermore, Erikson ignored the effect that the child has on the family. Research in the last decade has made it clear that the child makes a unique contribution (Bell & Harper, 1977).

Psychologists today are likely to look at the family as a system. Each member of the family influences that system. Although the psychological impact of each member is important, the family configuration is also affected by financial, social, and biological stress (Sameroff & Seifer, 1983). Competent adults, then, reflect the totality of an everchanging set of forces (Block, 1982).

## THE CHANGING ROLE OF THE FAMILY DURING DEVELOPMENT

Erikson pointed out that the family is not a static unit. It constantly changes, responding to the needs of the child and the changes in society. It would be inappropriate for a family to treat two daughters—one an adolescent, the other an infant—the same way (Zeigler, 1983). Yet adjusting to the individual needs of the child may be difficult for parents. A father who feels uncomfortable with his newborn son is not excluded from the child's affections forever. This same father and son may establish a close relationship once the boy is old enough to communicate. Likewise, a mother who loved the cuddly, dependent stage of infancy may become exasperated when her adolescent questions the rules.

Charting the ideal family for each period of development is a little brazen given the current state of psychological information. Nevertheless, we know something about what families need to provide if their infants, toddlers, pre-schoolers, school-age children, and adolescents are to become competent adults.

## Families during infancy

Infants are helpless and depend on their caretakers for nurturance and suste-nance. Although Freud exalted the mother and her ability to undertake this role, we know that the first loving relationship can be provided by any adult who is committed to the child. Adoptive parents, grandparents, and unrelated adults can replace the biological mother. The requirements are one or two adults who are sensitive to the child's needs, who respond to these needs in a caring way, and who encourage the emotional attachment that presages healthy development (Stern, 1977).

Mary Main (1981) studied a group of infants who were followed during their first year of life. At one year of age, some of the children were angry, they recoiled from contact with their mothers, and they were not securely attached. Looking at these children as newborns, she found that they were cuddly and loving. Furthermore, they cried about the same amount as another group of infants who were securely attached, loving, and curious one year later (Main, 1981). Main could see no differences in the infants who became angry one-year-olds and those who became loving one-year-olds. The most obvious dif-ferences were not in the infants, but in the mothers. The mothers of the angry one- year-olds seemed reluctant to touch their children when they were infants. Many times these mothers provided adequate care, but they did it in a wooden way.

This study provides a particularly graphic example of the role that the family plays during the first year of life. Love is transmitted through touching, peek-a-boo games, tickling sessions, and a general responsiveness and sensitivity to the infant's needs. If the mother cannot provide this environment, other adults can. Mary Main (1981) even suggests that day-care centers staffed by loving, responsive, and dependable adults may compensate for unhealthy relationships at home.

## Families of toddlers

The toddler requires a different set of responses from the family. At this age, children need to be confident that the caretaker—father, mother, babysitter, or teacher—is available, but they also need to begin to explore the world. Many investigators studying toddlers have reported on the child's first tentative journeys away from the mother (Matas, Arend & Sroufe, 1978). First children make certain of the mother's position and her attention, then they move cautiously away, checking back two or three times to make sure that their mother is still watching (Sorce & Emde, 1981). These checks allow the infant to make contact and obtain "emotional refueling" (Mahler, Pine, & Bergman, 1975). As the children gain confidence, they check back less frequently. In the familiarity of their own home, toddlers may be comfortable as long as they can hear their mother in another room. In an outdoor setting, children set their own boundaries for exploration. One-year-olds seldom venture further than 25 feet (seven meters) from their mothers, but three-year-olds are secure playing much further away (Rheingold & Eckerman, 1971). Of course, if a stranger appears or children become frustrated or stressed, they will seek the security that their mother provides.

Families of toddlers need to encourage the child's beginning flirtations with independence. This is accomplished by being available and allowing the child some freedom. Burton White (1978) stresses the transition that parents must make from the infancy to the toddler stage. Parents should allow their toddlers to investigate the house. Creating a space that the child can explore is one way for parents to maintain a supervisory, assisting role rather than a restricting, confining one.

Separations from the parent pose difficulties for toddlers. The easiest way to help these children tolerate the separations that are necessary for work, vacations, or even shopping trips is to acquaint the child with the new setting and the adult who will be in charge. Once the new adult is seen as a substitute parent and the new environment becomes familiar, most children are quite happy to be in a different environment for some part of the day.

## Families with preschoolers

Compared to toddlers, preschoolers are very worldly. They can march into nursery schools without a tear, respond to simple requests, and indicate their knowledge of the world by counting to 10 or singing the ABCs. During this period, the family needs to continue its support, but the unquestioned indulgence accorded infants is no longer appropriate.

Diana Baumrind (1967) has delineated the characteristics of families that produce active, outgoing preschoolers. She began by watching 110 three- and four-year-olds while they played at nursery school. Over a period of three to five months, observers noted whether or not the child was mature, self-reliant, cooperative, friendly, easygoing, domineering, purposeful, independent, and achievement oriented. Based on these ratings, Baumrind divided the children into three groups. Pattern I children were the most mature and were characterized as competent, independent, self-reliant, curious, assertive, and self-controlled. Pattern II children were more discontent, insecure, and apprehensive. They sometimes appeared withdrawn and distrustful. Pattern III children were very immature. As a group, they retreated from novel or stressful experiences and were very dependent. They lacked the self-reliance and self-control of the other two groups of children.

After assessing the children, the next steps were to observe the parents playing with their children and to interview the parents. She made appointments with each family and observed them through dinner and bedtime preparations. This time of day is particularly rich in family interaction because the whole family is present and are concentrating on several tasks—preparing dinner, cleaning up, and getting the children ready for bed. The home observations helped Baumrind decide how much control the parents exercised, what kinds of demands they made of their preschoolers, how well they communicated with their children, and how loving they were.

It came as no surprise that parents who were loving and communicated well with their children had competent, secure children. More surprising was the fact that the parents of these self-reliant children expected mature behavior. Furthermore, the parents maintained control over the child, determining and enforcing bedtimes, table manners, and household rules. The following sequence illustrates one of hundreds of interactions recorded by Baumrind's research team.

[Family is at the dinner table. Boy gets up.]
**Father:** "Hey, sit down!" [Yells, but good naturedly.]
[Boy sits and finishes milk. Boy gets up.]
**Father:** "What do you say, Todd?"
**Boy:** "Excuse me please."
**Father:** "What?"
**Boy:** "Excuse me please."
**Father:** "OK"
**Boy:** [on way out] "Tomorrow I'm not going to say it because I said it two times." (Baumrind, 1967, pp. 65–66)

The father in this interaction maintains control and has specific expectations about his son's behavior at the dinner table. In contrast, the immature children in Pattern III lived in families that were somewhat disorganized. The parents spent little time training the child to be independent and did not communicate which behaviors were appropriate and which were not. As a group, though, these parents were quite nurturant (see Figure 12–3).

Seeing the relationship between the mature behavior of preschoolers and the family environment prompted Baumrind to delineate three child-rearing strategies. She saw some parents as *authoritarian*, some as *authoritative*, and some as *permissive* (Baumrind, 1971).

Authoritarian parents dominate the home and maintain rigid control over every aspect of the child's behavior. These parents do not encourage a verbal give-and-take with their child, insisting instead on their views. The occasionally harsh demands of the parents exist in an atmosphere that is not particularly nurturing.

Authoritative parents direct their child's activities, but they listen and consider the specific feelings and suggestions of the child. They also explain why a specific decision has been made. Finally, the direction they provide is carried out in an atmosphere of acceptance and warmth. Such parents let a child

**Figure 12–3**　　　　　　　　　　**Families with preschoolers**

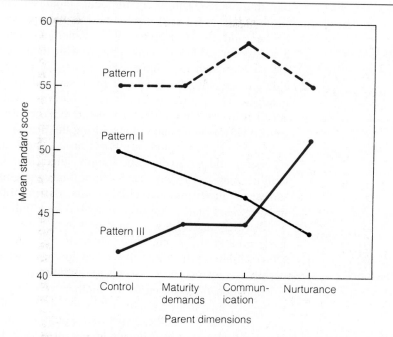

Parents who maintain control, demand mature behavior, communicate with their children, and lavish love on their children have competent, responsible preschoolers (Pattern I). Parents who are less loving and communicate poorly have preschoolers who are less competent.

Source: Baumrind, D. (1967) Child care practices anteceding three patterns of preschool behavior. *Genetic Psychology Monographs, 75, 73.*

explore all the aspects of interpersonal growth. These children come to understand that in some situations their desires are likely to be met; in others, they are not. Both sets of experiences seem to be part of building a mature understanding of the world.

Permissive parents set no standards for the child's behavior. They accept the child in an almost unquestioning fashion. They make few demands and allow the child to determine the activities for the day. These parents are available as resources, but they exercise little control and do not communicate with the child. When these children begin nursery school, they are oblivious to realistic bounds or controls. They appear irresponsible, immature, and dependent.

It should be emphasized that all of these families provided some nurturance and control, and all of them made some demands on their children and communicated with them. The parents' placement in the authoritative, authoritarian, or permissive group indicates their relative use of these child-rearing techniques. About one quarter of the parents did not fit neatly into any of these categories (Baumrind, 1971).

Baumrind's study reports a set of relationships. It is tempting to conclude that the different family environments produced the behavior patterns of the children. We must remember, however, that parents are responding to a particular child (Bell & Harper, 1977). Pattern I children may be so mature that it is easy for parents to communicate with them. Given the child's maturity, the parents' high expectations are also likely to be met. Perhaps Pattern III children are not ready to listen or to respond to their parents' demands for maturity. The permissive family resembles the ideal family during infancy. It is certainly possible that their immature child continues to provoke the indulgence that was more appropriate during the first year of life.

Baumrind's conclusions are based on a sample of white families who were successful and well educated. Family interaction in lower-class or minority families may not follow exactly these same patterns. To assess a lower-class sample, Walter Emmerich (1977) contacted almost 600 families who had children in Head Start programs. He looked for children who completed activities without help and who were engrossed in activities rather than wandering aimlessly around the room. Such children received high scores for autonomy. Other children who constantly asked for help, wanted attention, and lacked persistence were given low scores for autonomy.

Emmerich then turned to the mothers. He interviewed them and watched while they taught their children how to sort a set of blocks. During the interview, he asked the mothers what they would tell their children on the first day of school. Answers like "Don't holler" and "Mind the teacher" were called *imperative communications*. Answers that explained why one should mind the teacher and told the child what to expect were called *instructive communications*.

To examine mother-child interaction, Emmerich asked mothers to teach their children how to sort eight blocks that were different sizes, colors, and shapes. Some mothers took over the task and did it for their children. Other mothers explained the task and acted as an assistant rather than the director.

The boys in Emmerich's study were affected most by their mother's behavior. Mothers who discussed the first day of school with their sons and provided encouragement, guidance, and support during the sorting task were more likely to have autonomous sons. High levels of maternal control provoked rebellion or dependency. Girls were affected less by their mother's efforts at control, but they responded very positively to their mother's warmth. Boys seemed to be suspicious if their mothers suddenly expressed a warm and caring attitude, especially if their mothers had been cold and indifferent.

In both Baumrind's and Emmerich's studies, the parents' ability to communicate and their expectations are associated with maturity and autonomy. It is interesting that the authoritarian behaviors of some of the Head Start mothers interfered with the boys' bids for autonomy, but did not seem to affect the girls.

## Families of school-age children

The school-age child provides a different challenge for parents. The child is away from home for long periods, the peer group has emerged, and the school is making demands on the child. How does the family change to cope with these new factors? For one thing, parents relax more. School-age children are not as demanding as preschoolers, yet they are not as worrisome as adolescents (Strommen, McKinney, & Fitzgerald, 1983). Another change is in the relative power of the family members. Parents are no longer the masters. Because they no longer have to direct mundane activities like dressing the child and tying shoes, parents and children can enjoy more equal status.

One of the biggest changes from preschool is the child's rapidly expanding competence. The parents' major task is to promote this competence and then bestow the independence that should accompany competent behavior. One of the dangers of this period is that the parents' response to a situation will not reflect an up-to-date assessment of the child's competence. The family must remain flexible about their children and be willing to acknowledge, accept, and encourage change. Competent children are likely to be granted more independence. Some families can send an eight-year-old on a short flight to relatives with little worry. Others are aghast at the idea and are convinced that their child could never handle such a trip.

How do parents promote the competent, independent behavior of their school-age children? Again, one of the clearest answers comes from Diana Baumrind's laboratory (1977). She reevaluated her preschool subjects when they were eight and nine years old. She sought the children who took initiative, assumed control, and tackled their problems head-on. When she found children like this, she looked at her ratings of their parents taken five years earlier. These children were likely to come from homes with authoritative parents. Baumrind also found children who were passive, seemingly helpless, and very dependent. Her records indicated that these children had been raised in permissive homes. If the parents had been described as authoritarian in the previous study, the children were neither initiators nor passive. But if parents were still using an authoritarian strategy with their school-age child, their sons were likely to express little initiative and have no interest in school. Baumrind's study is especially valuable because it is one of the few in which parental strategies were actually observed and related to the child's behavior five years later. Other investigators who have relied on interviews have come to similar conclusions.

Stanley Coopersmith (1967) studied families with school-age children. He began by assessing a group of 10- to 12-year-old boys on self-esteem. Many of the boys were pleased with their lives and their accomplishments. They approached the world with a confident air, took challenges in stride, and expected that they would succeed. Unfortunately, other boys in the sample had less favorable views of themselves. They were anxious, depressed, and did not express much emotion.

After identifying the children who had either high, medium, or low self-esteem, Coopersmith visited the families of these boys and interviewed the mothers about their child-rearing practices. The results are presented in a book that is now a classic in developmental psychology—*The Antecedents of Self-esteem*.

Coopersmith found that preadolescent boys with high self-esteem received nearly total acceptance from their parents. The atmosphere in the family was nurturing and democratic. Less expected was the fact that these families had clearly defined rules that they enforced. The limits and rules that the families adopted were reasonable, and more important, they were appropriate to the age of the child. The rules were not enforced in an arbitrary or inflexible fashion, but they were enforced. Coopersmith concludes that definite and enforced limits are associated with high, rather than low, self-esteem. Although his study was done with preadolescent boys, it was later extended to females. Essentially the same family patterns were found to be associated with high self-esteem in girls (Sears, 1970).

Coopersmith's conclusions about the antecedents of self-esteem sound strikingly like Baumrind's conclusions about the antecedents of competent preschool children. The parents Coopersmith describes are certainly nurturing, they exercise control in a rational way, their demands consider the age of the child, and they communicate with their children. Coopersmith goes a step futher and attempts to explain why the parents' rules enhance the child's self-esteem. When clear rules exist, children can decide for themselves whether they are reaching the standard expected of them. Therefore, children who live with rules and limits have a definite advantage because they know when they have performed well and can derive personal satisfaction from their performance.

In contrast, the home that provides few standards for behavior leaves the child adrift. Children in such families do not know what is expected, and even the limited expectations may change on a daily basis. Hence, they are dependent on the evaluation of others. The formation of self-esteem is hindered because children must rely on their parents to tell them whether or not their behavior is acceptable.

Coopersmith's study is not without flaws. Like Baumrind's, it was limited to middle-class white families. Furthermore, the parents simply recalled how they treated their children. No independent verification or observation took place. Despite these reservations, Coopersmith's study replicates many of the features that Baumrind found in families of younger children. When two studies using very different measures obtain results that are so similar, both studies assume more importance.

Families of school-age children maintain many of the strategies that worked well with preschoolers. But several new facets of family interaction become important. The members of the families are on a more equal footing. Parents relinquish some of the omnipotence they had when their children were younger. Now parents can enjoy the child's burgeoning competence. Each new area of competence signals another step toward independence, and parents must remain flexible enough to allow the child to grow. Flexibility, however, does not mean permissiveness. Parents who maintain control and establish reasonable limits help their children understand what is expected and provide a boost in self-esteem.

## Families with adolescents

Adolescents are often portrayed as posing especially difficult problems for families. The basis of the problems, and they have often been exaggerated (Grinder, 1978), is the adolescent's need to establish his or her own identity. Adolescents move away from their families in the sense that they no longer adopt all of their parents' values and opinions. They question, modify, and reshape their family's beliefs in the process of formulating their own values. During this process, adolescent boys are likely to initiate conflict with their mothers. If the boy is not yet physically mature, mothers react to their son's hostility by becoming more rigid. During this period, family conflict increases. As the boy changes physically, mothers begin to defer to their son's wishes and family relations become more harmonious (Steinberg, 1981).

Parents need to be supportive and offer perspective to adolescents struggling with their identity (Seltzer, 1982). The active phase of parenting, which required constant nurturance, close direction, and supervision, gives way to a more subtle relationship. Caretaking functions are minimal. Instead, cognitive expressions of affection such as "I'm really proud of you" augment physical expressions of affection. In fact, the whole family's interaction, although grounded in emotional ties, takes on more cognitive overtones. Now parents are valued for their information on subjects as diverse as careers, cars, mortgages, and marriage (Seltzer, 1982). The supportive home also serves as a haven for the adolescent. Parents offer support and encouragement and provide a refuge when the turmoil of adolescence is greatest.

In families with adolescents, nurturing and communicating are still important, even if their form changes. Control also remains an important factor for the development of self-esteem in daughters (Leahy, 1981), but control combined with punitive discipline has a negative effect on sons.

The successful family, whether its charges are infants or adolescents, is a safe harbor, a place where developing children and adolescents are guaranteed acceptance, where their conquests and disappointments will be listened to with a supportive ear, and where their ventures will be encouraged and monitored.

## The family's response to males and females

Boys and girls provoke different responses from parents. Fathers, especially, are likely to behave differently when they are playing with their sons than when they are playing with their daughters (Parke, 1981). This differential treatment begins in infancy, with the father lifting and tossing his newborn son and cuddling his newborn daughter (Lytton, 1980). As the children grow, fathers concentrate on encouraging the physical and intellectual development of their sons, but are more concerned that their daughters are feminine (Parke, 1981).

Mothers offset this somewhat by providing extra cognitive stimulation for their daughters.

Fathers tend to enforce sex-role standards in both boys and girls. Even in play situations, they are apt to discourage boys who pretend to be nurses and encourage them if they want to play cowboys and Indians. Generally, fathers are more likely to accept their daughter's desires to play with toys that are labeled masculine and are less likely to interfere if girls adopt a masculine role (Langlois & Downs, 1980).

Even the teaching of preschoolers is approached differently depending on whether the child is a boy or girl. With boys, parents focus on the task at hand and maintain control of the interaction. With girls, such control is not necessary and mothers and fathers adopt a more relaxed, cooperative teaching style (Frankel & Rollins, 1983).

During the school years, parents supervise girls more, give them more household chores, restrict their activities, and are more likely to insist on knowing where their daughters are (Block, 1983). Boys are given somewhat more freedom to explore and have fewer controls and restrictions. These treatments can have "cumulative, powerful, and general effects" on the child's ability to adapt (Block, 1982, p. 293). Boys, who are exploring with minimal supervision, are more likely to encounter new and unpredicted situations. Thus, they are forced to improvise and devise a strategy to handle the situation. Girls, operating under their parents' watchful eyes, become more adept at developing and maintaining relationships (Block, 1983).

The family atmosphere sets the tone for the sex-typing that becomes most salient during adolescence. A boy's sex-role identity takes a direct cue from the father. If the father dominates the home, making all of the decisions and functioning as resident disciplinarian, boys are very apt to fit the "macho" stereotype. If the father and mother share the decision making and the family atmosphere is warm and supportive, the boys are likely to have a more moderate masculine orientation. If the father is passive and lets the mother run the family, boys are less likely to use their fathers as role models (Parke, 1981).

In all of the studies reviewed, warmth has been deemed a desirable parental trait. Nothing has altered this view with regard to boys. Available and nurturant fathers promote competence, personal adjustment, and success in males from preschool age to adulthood. In recent years, investigators have questioned the effect that complete acceptance and nurturance have on females. The new research suggests that an atmosphere that is unquestioningly nurturant promotes passivity in girls. Baumrind (1977) broaches this view by noting that biology and society conspire to create passivity in women. To counter this, parents need to provoke their daughters and challenge them to achieve. Fathers who are demanding, challenging, and somewhat abrasive appear to raise the most competent and independent daughters (Baumrind, 1978). Exposure to vigorous, thought-provoking interaction, coupled with praise for independence and achievement, may save girls from the "compassion trap" which lures them toward conformity and lack of self-determination (Radin & Russell, 1983).

Why do males thrive when their parents are unconditionally nurturant? The answer, according to Baumrind, is that for men biology and society conspire to create independent adults. Hence, they do not need the extra push that women need. This view is a departure from standard child-rearing advice, yet more and more studies are suggesting that parental strategies have a different effect on males and females (Leahy, 1981).

## Early families and late families

We have discussed the role of the family through the changing ages of the child. The parents' ages may also be a factor. Teenage pregnancies continue to increase, as do pregnancies to women who are over 35. Each of these groups brings a different set of life experiences to the family.

Teenage families have been characterized as unrealistic about mothering and unresponsive to their infants (Epstein, 1980). In many cases, their unresponsiveness has turned into abuse (Egeland & Brunnquell, 1979). The teenage mother's plight is often aggravated by financial and social difficulties that result directly from her early, and many times unwanted, pregnancy (Phipps-Yonas, 1980). The teenager's immaturity and her frustration at her plight do not foster an attitude of unqualified acceptance toward the infant.

On the other end of the age range is the career woman, who decides that the biological clock is running out, and it is now or never. These women are typically well-educated, financially secure, and mature. They have stable relationships with their husbands, and they have made a deliberate decision to have a child. These mothers are devoted to their infants and will go to great lengths to fulfill the child's needs.

In these brief descriptions, "early" families seem to offer infants few advantages and "late" families seem to offer many advantages. This conclusion confounds the age of the mother with educational and financial factors. Perhaps "early" mothers would be just as effective as late mothers if they had similar social advantages. Psychologists from the University of Washington were able to study a sample of women who varied in age but were similar on other variables (Ragozin, Basham, Crnic, Greenberg, & Robinson, 1982). Most of the women in their sample were married, had completed high school, and were primarily homemakers. They varied in age from 16 to 38. The older mothers in this sample reported greater satisfaction with their role as a parent than the younger mothers. They were also willing to commit more time to their new infant. Furthermore, their behavior with their infants demonstrated their sensitivity, responsiveness, and love. These conclusions, however, were only typical of the older woman with her first child. Adding another baby to an already existing family held less appeal for the older woman. The authors conclude that a measure of maturity helps women make the necessary commitment to an infant. Young mothers, even many in their early 20s, did not find being a parent particularly rewarding (see Figure 12–4).

This section began by promising to outline family strategies that enhanced a child's development. Despite the gaps in our information and the tentative

**Figure 12—4**    **Maternal age and caretaking skills**

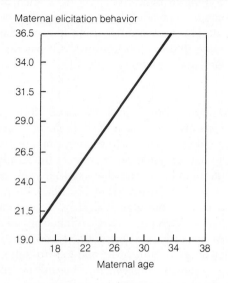
Maternal elicitation behavior

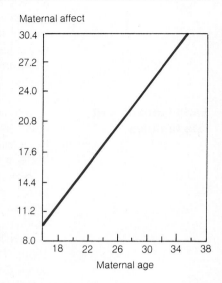
Maternal affect

Teenage mothers are less interested than older mothers in playing with their infants. Young mothers also display less affection than older mothers when they interact with their children.

Source: Ragozin, A. S., Basham, R. B., Crnic, K. A., Greenberg, M. T., & Robinson, N. M. (1982). Effects of maternal age on parenting role. *Developmental Psychology, 18,* 631.

conclusions, a reasonably detailed picture of families that produce competent, well-adjusted children has been painted. This portrait of the family is, however, only one of many family arrangements that exist in today's society. We need to turn our attention to variations of the family and examine their effect on the child's development.

## ALTERNATIVE FAMILY PATTERNS

The traditional family consists of a father who works, a mother whose responsibilities are confined to the home, and two or more children. This traditional picture is actually very recent (Lamb, 1982a). Women have always assumed the primary responsibility for children, but when humans were hunters and gatherers, the women were the gatherers. In societies where this still exists, infants accompany their mothers to the fields and older children are left with siblings or cousins. Furthermore, in these cultures men are not exempt from child-rearing responsibilities; they have to teach the boys the skills they need to survive.

The industrial revolution has been blamed for assorted societal woes and some of the changes in the family can be traced to that period. The husbands left the fields and began working in the factories. Even then, wives typically worked alongside their husbands. Michael Lamb suggests that women stopped working only when the husband's wages could support the family comfortably—less than one century ago. Even when mothers began to stay home, the normal family was a group that included the parents, children, grandparents, aunts, and uncles. As families became more mobile, the extended family was replaced by the nuclear family. Hence, the nuclear two-parent family that we define as traditional actually has a very short history (Lamb, 1982a).

This glimpse of families in the past gives us more perspective on what is and is not traditional. Certainly, it should make us question the extreme stance that all deviations from the traditional pattern are bound to destroy the fabric of society. Some changes have negative consequences, others have little effect, and some may have positive consequences. As we examine how alternative family patterns affect children, we need to be alert to all of these possibilities.

## Families with two working parents

Having a mother who works outside the home seems like a minor deviation from the traditional family pattern, but it changes the family system in major ways. Before we consider these effects, it is appropriate to note that working mothers who are employed are not all career oriented, nor are they all supplementing their husbands' income. Many women must take jobs in order to feed their families. If we are to assess the effect of the working mother on children, we must consider how mothers feel about their jobs. If they would rather not be working, the effect on their families will be different than if they have made a deliberate decision to pursue a career. It is also possible that for some women, not working could have adverse effects on the family. If the mother feels dissatisfied at home and her self-esteem suffers, the family can be unfavorably affected (Lamb, 1982b). The mother's ability to juggle satisfactorily the dual demands of a career and a family also hinge on support from the father. If he is threatened by the wife's career, she is less likely to receive encouragement and help from him. The point to remember is that "the mother works" is only one fact that describes a family. It operates in concert with many other facts that must be considered if one is to describe how the family functions.

**Working mothers with infants and toddlers.** In the United States, over 40 percent of mothers return to work before that child is one year old (Cordes, 1983). This represents a striking increase from 20 years ago when few mothers with infants worked outside the home (Hoffman, 1980). This change in society has raised the question, "Can women with children this young meet the dual responsibilities of a career and an infant?"

One way to answer this question is to look at the critical tasks of infancy and see how infants fare when their mothers are employed. The first year is critical for forming an emotional attachment (see Chapter 7). Such an attachment depends on sensitive and responsive caretaking. In the 1950s, experts cautioned that maternal employment was synonomous with child neglect, and the World Health Organization condemned day care arguing that it produced "permanent damage to the emotional health of a future generation" (World Health Organization, 1951). In the 30 years since then, we have learned that the actual consequences of maternal employment are tame when compared to these predictions.

Infants and toddlers often appear angry or withdrawn when their mothers first return to work. But this is a temporary response. The child's long-term adjustment seems to depend on the quality of the substitute care. When women are successful in finding a substitute mother, the child's attachments to both the mother and the substitute caretaker are strong (Kagan, Kearsley, & Zelazo, 1978; Hock, 1980). When the child's care is haphazard or the caretaker changes frequently, attachments are more likely to be insecure (Lamb, 1982b; Schwartz, 1983). Even insecure attachments are not an indictment of the working mother. Michael Lamb suggests that the child's insecurity reflects the mother's lack of commitment to parenthood and could have been present even if she were unemployed (Lamb, 1982b). Working mothers who value their role as a parent are able to forge a secure attachment with their children, regardless of the number of hours they work. When they come home in the early evening, they play with their infants, talk with them, and touch them. To the researchers watching, it seemed that the mothers were using the time to reestablish their relationship with their infants (Pedersen, Cain, Zaslow, & Anderson, 1982).

Cognitive skills are difficult to assess during the first year, and to date, few investigators have studied infants whose mothers returned to work shortly after the child was born. In the two available studies, the children of employed mothers have been better adjusted than children whose mothers did not work. However, the boys of the mothers who worked had somewhat lower IQs (Gold & Andres, 1978c; Gold, Andres, & Glorieux, 1979). In her summary of these studies, Hoffman (1980) concludes that continuous full-time mothering during the preschool years is associated with adolescent boys being more intellectually able, but also more conforming, fearful, and inhibited.

Many women with infants want or need to work. They also want to devote adequate time and attention to their infants. One way that these seemingly conflicting goals can be met is through an infant-leave policy. Many industries and institutions currently have maternity leaves, but these only last a few weeks and are designed to help the mother recover from the pregnancy. Infant leave, in contrast, would recognize parenting as a legitimate reason for taking leave from the job and would be available to both fathers and mothers. The length of the leave would be at least 6 months, although most psychologists would prefer it to be 12 months long.

In 1974, Sweden incorporated an infant-leave policy that allowed either parent up to seven months leave after the birth of a child. The leave policy has allowed mothers time to develop a relationship with their infants. Unfortunately, few fathers have taken advantage of the policy. In the first year, only 2 percent of the fathers asked for even a day of leave. To increase participation in the program, the Swedish government began a nationwide advertising campaign showing wrestlers, soccer players, and other masculine heroes holding their infants, feeding them, and taking them for a stroll (see Figure 12–5).

**Figure 12—5**    Increasing paternal participation in infant care

*Courtesy Försäkringskasseförbundet, Stockholm*

This poster was part of a national campaign in Sweden to encourage fathers to take advantage of the infant-leave policy available to parents. Famous sports figures are shown taking an interest in infant care.

Despite this campaign, less than 10 percent of the fathers avail themselves of the infant leave policy (Lamb & Levine, 1983).

Mothers who have infants and choose to work have their hands full. The task of maintaining a job and being a responsive mother requires energy and commitment. Mothers who have supportive and helpful husbands and stable, loving child-care arrangements are able to provide an environment in which the child thrives. Mothers who do not give their infants adequate attention and whose child-care arrangements are haphazard can expect more negative outcomes.

**Working mothers and school-age children.** Maternal employment has several positive effects on the school-age child. The children benefit by being in a family that has increased income and more status (Moen, 1982). The children also have role models of women who are successful outside the home and of men who help around the house. For girls, this is translated into career aspirations (Hoffman, 1980). For sons, it fosters a more complex view of the women's role in society and a willingness to share the household chores. When mothers work, they model the message that effort and hard work pay. This message can influence the child's willingness to work in school (Piotrkowski & Katz, 1982). Working mothers usually have organized homes and expect their children to contribute to the household chores. We have already seen that such organization is related to high self-esteem. The final advantage is that children are encouraged to be independent—a benefit for both sexes, but an especially important one for females (Hoffman, 1977).

On the negative side, boys of mothers who work sometimes do poorly in school (Gold & Andres, 1978b). The mother working may also strain the father-son relationship in lower-class families. Michael Lamb suggests that these strains occur because the culture interprets a working mother as an indication that the father has failed.

**Working mothers and adolescents.** The positive aspects of a mother working outweigh the negative aspects when the children in the family are adolescents. The benefits described for school-age children become even more salient during adolescence (Gold & Andres, 1978a). At least part of the reason for the positive effect on adolescents is that mothers who work grant their sons and daughters independence less grudgingly.

Of course, single mothers who work are less likely to reap the benefits listed here and may have to cope with difficult financial circumstances, time pressures, and their own futures. These additional stresses are a good reason to consider single parent families separately.

**Divorce and its consequences**

The dissolution of the family is one of the most serious and, simultaneously, one of the most common problems that children in contemporary society face. A divorce leaves its mark on both parents and children. Families adjust to minor disruptions like moving to a different house or the arrival of a new baby, but the disbanding of the family opens deep emotional wounds that

### School-age children

Joel Gordon

Frank Siteman: Stock, Boston

Household chores provide children with an opportunity to demonstrate their competence.

require years to heal. The emotional impact of a divorce is enough to jar most well-adjusted individuals. The financial problems and legal entanglements that accompany many divorces compound the emotional turmoil. Furthermore, the divorce is never the end of the stress. Divorces are typically followed by a period in which the family is a single parent household. The single parent household evolves, in time, into a stepfamily. Each of these additional changes requires new adjustments on the part of the children.

**The divorcing family.** Psychologists who have studied divorce agree that there are no victimless divorces. Divorce is an emotionally wrenching process for adults as well as children. Fathers, normally a bastion of strength, report severe emotional distress during the period following the separation from their wives. Isolated from their family in a temporary, and often unsatisfactory living arrangement, they find that they cannot cook, their clothes get dirty, and they do not know how to function in a supermarket (Hetherington, Cox, & Cox, 1978). In addition to these practical difficulties, they acknowledge that their emotional state makes it difficult to sleep or concentrate on their jobs (Jacobs, 1982).

The personal crisis that accompanies divorce temporarily alters the mother's view of the world and her personal style (Doherty, 1983). Mothers report feeling lost in the homes they have shared with their husbands. Every knick knack is a harsh reminder that they have failed as wives. The financial uncertainty of their future makes them question their ability to raise their children alone. Coping with their own anger and depression saps their ability to deal with their children's emotional distress.

Children show their emotional distress in varied ways. Preschoolers may begin wetting the bed or stuttering. School-age children may be afraid to spend the night at a friend's house. Adolescents may withdraw into a shell or become engrossed with their friends, their school, or their work. The children's anger, depression, and feeling of abandonment is compounded by the disorganization that seems to descend on the home.

The atmosphere of crisis subsides over the ensuing weeks and months, but the emotional difficulties continue. Mavis Hetherington and her colleagues at the University of Virginia were the first to chart the aftermath of divorce (Hetherington, Cox, & Cox, 1978). They studied 24 preschoolers whose parents had just separated and 24 preschoolers who came from intact homes. During the two-year period following the separation, the investigators interviewed the mothers, made visits to the home, observed the children in nursery school, and administered a variety of tests to the mothers and their children.

The results of this study showed that the emotional distress that accompanies divorce is still evident in all family members one year after the divorce. After two years, the healing process is well underway. The family has reorganized and is likely to be functioning satisfactorily, even if it is not functioning as smoothly as an intact family.

Hetherington and her colleagues found that divorce disrupts all of the relationships in the family. The most extreme changes were seen in the relationship between fathers and their children. Immediately following the divorce, most fathers saw their children frequently. Two years later, the majority of the fathers saw their children less than once a week. Most of the fathers felt that they had lost their children. Eight fathers who had been very committed to their children could not endure the pain of being weekend fathers and purposely reduced their visits. A few of the fathers thought that their relationship with their children had improved, primarily because they could interact with their children in an atmosphere that was not clouded by conflict.

The mothers also experienced upheavals in their relationships with their children. Their sons, formerly loving and compliant, became defiant and hostile. Mothers described their continuing battle with their sons as a "struggle for survival" and "declared war." One year after the divorce, the boys were aggressive, demanding, and would not listen to reason. The girls, on the other hand, were compliant, whiny, and dependent. The mothers seemed unable to cope with the situation. Unlike the mothers in intact families, recently divorced mothers did not communicate well, were less affectionate, were inconsistent, and had minimal control over their children. Fortunately, during the following year, the mothers regained control, imposed some organization on the home, and improved their communication. After two years, the divorced families looked more like the intact families.

Hetherington concludes that divorcing families are in crisis, and that the repercussions for the family reach a peak approximately one year after the divorce. During the second year, the family begins to recover and reorganize. The process proceeds more quickly with girls than boys. Two years after the divorce, the stress in mother-son relationships was still obvious. Despite the turmoil caused by the divorce, many of the parents felt that their relationships with their children were better than they had been during the tense period preceeding the divorce. This prompts Hetherington (1981) to conclude that a stable, divorced family is better for children than a family in constant conflict.

Hetherington's experiment, like many ground-breaking studies, raises as many questions as it answers. All the families in her study were headed by mothers. Would families headed by fathers have the same difficulties? Might the fathers experience more difficulty with their daughters? Hetherington's study was confined to middle-class families in comfortable circumstances. Would the results from families in less favorable circumstances be the same? What about older children? Would they have as much trouble adjusting to the divorce?

Answers to some of these questions came from a longitudinal study conducted by Judith Wallerstein and Joan Kelly (1980). They studied almost 100 children for 10 years after their parents divorced. Included in their sample were children from 2 to 18 years of age. Their surprising finding was that the emotional trauma of the divorce lingered for one third of the children. Even after five years, these children and adolescents were depressed, lonely, felt unloved, and expressed disappointment with their relationships with their parents. Of course, this means that two thirds of the children were functioning adequately or had survived the breakup without major effects. Wallerstein and Kelly also note that the divorce did not have a precipitous effect on school grades. Most of the children maintained grades that were similar to those they received before the divorce. Despite these positive notes, the majority of children wished that their parents would reconcile and felt that the predivorce family was preferable to their current situation.

Ten years later, children of divorce still see themselves as vulnerable and deprived. They are eager for monogamous, lasting marriages. This goal seems to elude many women. A significant number seem "to be drifting from job to job and from man to man" (Wallerstein, 1983). College students, whose parents had divorced 10 years earlier, report that their relationships with their parents were more distant and less affectionate than students from intact families (Fine, Moreland, & Schwebel, 1983).

Given the long-term consequences of divorce, researchers have turned their attention to the different circumstances that might ease the child's adjustment to the divorce. Parents who continued their conflict and bitterness hindered the child's adjustment (Emery, 1982). No matter what the age or sex of the child, adjusting to the divorce was easier if the children could maintain an intimate relationship with both parents (Hess & Camara, 1979). If the custodial parent took over the reins and got the family functioning again, the children adjusted faster. Those children who adjusted well were intelligent and socially mature prior to the divorce (Kurdek, Blisk, & Siesky, 1981). These personal characteristics helped them negotiate the crisis (see Figure 12–6).

As more couples face divorce, the alternatives for handling the divorce have increased. Settlements that award the parents joint custody of the children are much more common and are mandated by law in some states. Friendly divorces in which the former couple maintain contact and seem generally caring and respectful are also being reported more often (Ahrons, 1981). These changes in the way society responds to divorce are bound to influence the children.

Joint custody is often seen as a partial answer to the deleterious effects of divorce (Clingempeel & Repucci, 1982). Proponents point out that both parents remain involved with the child, thereby reducing the child's feeling of abandonment. However, critics argue that having two parents involved in decisions increases the conflict. More psychologists are looking at continuing parental conflict as one of the major sources of the child's problems (Emery, 1982). Psychologists advocate clear structure and some serenity after the divorce, not more conflict. Critics also feel that having children alternate between their mother's and father's homes confuses the child (Steinman, 1981). For several years, these arguments about child custody raged without the benefit of any empirical research. We are now beginning to see studies that examine the child's adjustment when both parents are awarded custody.

Joint custody has two pragmatic advantages. First, there are fewer custody cases that return to court (Ilfeld, Ilfeld, & Alexander, 1982). Presumably, this means that at least the parents are satisfied with the arrangement. Second,

**Figure 12—6**     **Children's adjustment to their parents' divorce**

### Earl—A child who coped successfully

Earl, age 11, a handsome boy in jeans and well-worn tennis shoes, talked about his plans for the future. His main interest currently was sports, but he had reluctantly concluded that this was not a good career choice and that he would become an architect, like his father, "Because it's more worth my time and it's easier to get a job." He confirmed that he liked school because "I like to learn and I like physical ed."

About the divorce, Earl offered, "A long time ago it was really bad, but it's better now. I see my dad every weekend, as much as I used to before the divorce." But, if he had a problem he went to his mother. "It's easier to talk to her because I know her longer."

Earl's teacher described him as a gifted student. She added that he was especially sensitive to other children's feelings. Sometimes he would say to his teacher, "Have you noticed that Susie is sad today?" The teacher had been impressed with his tactful leadership and his perceptive remarks. When he suggested an idea to a group, he would say, characteristically, "Why don't we try it this way?" Earl had close friends and was popular with his classmates. His teacher said, "He seems aware of both adult and peer levels and can relate accordingly."

When we met Earl shortly after his parents separated, he was profoundly hurt and frightened. He refused for several years to accept the divorce as final despite his father's almost immediate remarriage. By the time of the second follow-up, Earl had recovered his very good developmental pace. His sensitivity to other people may well have been enhanced by his own successful mastery of the family travail.

### Barbara—An unhappy child

Barbara, age 11, looked pretty, but still painfully thin, almost emaciated. Throughout the session, her neediness was striking, as it had been on the earlier occasions that we had talked. And as we parted, she kissed me, clung to me tightly, and asked me to return to see her, begging to know exactly when I would do so.

As Barbara entered the playroom, she busied herself with a dollhouse and began to construct a fantasy story which could have been a childish rendition of *Waiting for Godot*. She arranged the family dolls around the dinner table, which was set with careful attention to detail. The dolls in all their finery sat quietly awaiting the imminent arrival of the daddy doll who never appeared. It soon became clear that "waiting for daddy" was a central fantasy which was repeated endlessly as if frozen in time.

Barbara moved rapidly after this from game to game. Her attention span was short and her restlessness approached hyperactivity. Once she asked for a piece of clay to take home with her and she smelled it repeatedly. She spoke openly and sadly of her loneliness and her great yearning for her father. She dictated a note to him which she asked me to deliver, which read, "Dear Daddy—I love you. Please, please come to see me." Barbara described her relationship with her mother as improved. She explained that her mother's anger had diminished and that she was no longer as frightened, "She doesn't throw things anymore." Barbara said that she was against divorce because, "It is bad. I will never, never, never divorce."

Barbara was poorly parented in the postdivorce period by a father who visited capriciously and made dazzling promises he failed to keep, and by a mother who was herself slowly recovering from an agitated depression precipitated by the father's infidelity and his remarriage to a much younger woman. Barbara seemed unable to integrate the divorce and the separation from the father, or to find sufficient nurturance in her relationship with her depressed mother, whose life was additionally burdened by economic problems, her lack of economic skills, and her ambition to make her way as a creative writer. We considered the child very troubled, in urgent need of psychological intervention, supportive parenting, and a stable life arrangement.

Five years after their parents' divorce, a third of the children are still dissatisfied with their lives. Barbara is one example. Another third, like Earl, have adjusted and are content.

From *Surviving the Breakup* by Judith S. Wallerstein and Joan Berlin Kelly. © 1980 by Judith S. Wallerstein and Joan Berlin Kelly. Reprinted by permission of Basic Books, Inc., Publishers.

fathers who share their child's lives through a joint custody arrangement are
less likely to default on child support (Luepnitz, 1982). This translates into
more financial security for the child. Other possible advantages of joint custody
were outlined by Deborah Luepnitz based on her interviews of 50 parents,
some of whom were awarded joint custody. She found that in all of the joint
custody arrangements, both parents were highly involved with the children. In
several exclusive custody families, the other parent no longer maintained any
contact with the children. As we have seen, losing contact with a parent is
particularly devastating to a child. Luepnitz (1982) also points out that joint
custody parents have a periodic respite from the responsibilities of parenting.
They are less likely than single parents to report feeling "burned out."

Joint custody is a very recent legal alternative that may help children maintain contact with both parents. It certainly is not a complete answer. The adults
have to get along well enough to share decisions and communicate about the
children's needs. Joint custody also means that each of the adults is tied to
their ex-spouse. The person's opportunities to move out of the state, sever the
ties with the past, and start fresh may be limited by the custody arrangement.

**Single parent families.** Living in a single parent home represents another alternative to the traditional family. Over one third of all marriages now
being formed will end in divorce (see Figure 12–7). This means that close to
50 percent of the children of the 1990s will live in a single parent family
sometime during their childhood (Camara, Baker, & Dayton, 1980). Currently, more than 11 million children live with only one of their parents (Lowenstein & Koopman, 1978). Just as a nuclear family has advantages and dis-

**Figure 12–7**                                        **Families from 1960–1990**

**Living arrangements of children under 18 years old, United States, 1960–1990**

| Living arrangement | 1960 | 1970 | 1978 | 1990 |
|---|---|---|---|---|
| Total number (thousands) | 64,310 | 69,523 | 63,206 | 64,776 |
| Percent | 100.0% | 100.0% | 100.0% | 100.0% |
| Living with two parents | 87.5 | 83.1 | 77.7 | 71 |
| With two natural parents | | | | |
| Both married once | 73.3 | 68.7 | 63.1 | 56 |
| One or both remarried | 5.7 | 5.0 | 4.4 | 4 |
| With one natural parent | | | | |
| and one stepparent | 8.6 | 9.4 | 10.2 | 11 |
| Living with one parent | 9.1 | 13.4 | 18.6 | 25 |
| With mother only | 7.9 | 11.5 | 17.0 | 23 |
| With father only | 1.1 | 1.9 | 1.6 | 2 |
| Living with neither parent | 3.4 | 3.5 | 4.0 | 5 |

Paul Glick predicts that the number of children living with their natural parents will decrease to 56 percent by 1990 while children living with only one parent will increase to 25
percent. Another 11 percent will be living in stepfamilies.

Source: Glick, P. C. (1979). Children of divorced parents in demographic perspective. *Journal of Social
Issues, 35,* 170–182.

## THE LEGAL SIDE OF CHILD CUSTODY

When parents seeking a divorce cannot agree on the custody of the children, the courts are often asked to make the decision. The way courts handle this difficult decision has changed dramatically through the ages. Prior to 1900, fathers were routinely awarded custody. Mothers, being unemployed and the property of men, had few rights.

From 1920 to 1960, judges argued that it was in the best interest of the child to stay with the mother. The notion that children needed their mothers during the "tender years" came to mean that all children, not just infants, would be better off with their mothers.

In the 1960s, men began to demand that they be considered in custody decisions. Men charged that they were being discriminated against and that they had equal rights as parents. By 1980, 15 states had passed laws stating that women and men are to be judged equally as potential custodians.

In 1980, California went a step further by passing a bill which states that joint custody will prevail "unless it can be proved by a parent that sole custody is in the best interests of the child" (Foster & Freed, 1980, p. 25). The statute goes on to say that if the court feels that joint custody is not appropriate, it must consider "which parent is more likely to allow the child . . . frequent and continuing contact with both parents . . ." (Foster & Freed, 1980, p. 26). Now several states have similar joint custody statutes. The new laws mean that judges have several options in awarding custody.

*Sole custody* gives one parent the physical custody of the child. The parent with custody makes most of the decisions regarding the child's life. The parent without custody is awarded visitation rights according to a particular schedule.

Despite the changes in the laws, this is still the most common type of custody decision, and in 9 cases out of 10, sole custody is awarded to the mother.

*Split custody* divides the children between the two parents. Some of the children live permanently with the mother and some live permanently with the father. Judges often award boys to the father and girls to the mother when this type of decision is made.

*Joint custody* means that both parents are involved in making decisions about the child's life. It does not necessarily mean that the children spend half of the time with each parent. The important feature is that both parents share the responsibilities and rights of child rearing.

*Joint physical custody* is a variation of joint custody. Children spend half of their time with each parent. Such an arrangement is most convenient when both parents live in the same school district. Nevertheless, there are cases in the literature in which children spent one year with their father on the East Coast and the next year with their mother on the West Coast. The psychiatrist in this case notes that "not surprisingly, all three of the children suffered from an assortment of psychiatric problems" (Gardner, 1982, p. 233).

One of the most novel twists on joint custody has the parents move in and out of the family house while the children stay in the same neighborhood, retain their friends, and attend their local school. This is not usually a satisfactory long-term solution because parents can seldom readjust their household every three or six months.

Judges commonly report that custody decisions are the most difficult decisions they must make. The new options available do not necessarily make the decisions any easier.

advantages when compared to an extended family, so a single parent family has advantages and disadvantages when compared to a nuclear family.

All investigators agree that single parents are shouldering a heavy burden. Whether male or female, single parents report being overwhelmed by the demands on their time. Job-related activities and child-care responsibilities often conflict, and even if a parent can deal with these major tasks, more routine responsibilities like household maintenance, financial planning, and social obligations suffer. The limited energy and resources of the single parent mean that the child's environment is likely to be less stimulating than the environment provided by two parents (MacKinnon, Brody, & Stoneman, 1982).

Children in a single parent family are given considerable responsibility and have a status that is more equal to the adult's (Weiss, 1979). Children must help maintain the functioning of the household. A man with three daughters, aged four to nine, described the family during the breakfast rush.

> It is a matter of survival. Each of the kids has a chore. Patsy makes her bed in the morning when she gets up. That is one less job I have to do. Shirley gets the cereal down if we are having cereal. Lenore clears the table and puts the dishes in the dishwasher. While one is in the bathroom, the other has something to do. By the time we leave the house in the morning, the beds are made, the table is cleared, and the dishes are put away in the dishwasher. (Weiss, 1979, p. 100)

In addition to helping with day-to-day activities, children in a single parent family are often given responsibilities that would normally be performed by a spouse. Sons fix the plumbing, daughters serve as hostesses, and older children care for younger ones. Single parents also find themselves consulting their children on long-term decisions that affect the family. Preteen children and teenagers are involved in discussions about whether a child needs braces, the kind of insurance the family needs, and budgeting the family income. These additional responsibilities are a mixed blessing. Teenagers seem especially able to rise to the occasion and demonstrate competence, maturity, and independence.

Younger children, thrust into positions of responsibility, may be forced to grow up too fast. Playing with friends, going to school, and doing homework may be ignored so that the child can help the parent cope. In some homes, the parent's job means that no one is available to provide the emotional support and structure that foster development. Ten-year-olds who have no supervision for several hours a day can begin to feel insecure and alone (Rickard, Forehand, Atkeson, & Lopes, 1982). The effect of living in a single parent home, then, varies depending on the age of the child. It could also vary according to the child's individual strengths and the parent's skill at juggling responsibilities.

Children in single parent families often receive lower scores on IQ tests than their peers in two parent homes (Hetherington, Camara, & Featherman, 1983). The differences, however, are small (three to four points), and they often disappear when socioeconomic status is considered. Clearer differences exist in the area of school achievement. The demands of the single parent home often prevent high levels of achievement in school. In fact, males from single parent families complete fewer years of school than males with two parents (Hetherington, Camara, & Featherman, 1983).

Most of the studies of single parents have been conducted on families headed by the mother. It is certainly possible that homes headed by fathers offer a different list of advantages and disadvantages.

**Families headed by fathers.** Contemporary fathers are devoting more time to their children and are deriving greater satisfaction from their role as a parent (Hoffman, 1983). When these men divorce, they are likely to maintain more involvement with their children, either through a joint-custody arrangement or by being the exclusive parent (Thompson, 1983). It becomes important to ask, then, how children fare with their fathers. The answer seems to be that single parent fathers are as able as single parent mothers (Berry, 1981). This conclusion is, however, based on a select group of fathers who have exclusive custody. Less than 10 percent of the single parent families in the United States are headed by fathers (Hetherington, 1981). In general, these fathers are well-educated, financially secure, and in professional positions. A more random sample of fathers might not be as successful (Katz, 1979).

Single parent homes headed by fathers are not without problems. Just as the mothers felt they were at war with their sons, fathers who are the heads of families have more trouble with their daughters (Warshak & Santrock, 1983). Girls living solely with their fathers were demanding, dependent, and immature when compared with girls who lived with both parents. John Santrock points out, though, that the effectiveness of the parent was more important than whether the father or mother headed the household. Children in authoritative homes were competent and independent. Children in permissive or authoritarian homes were sometimes angry, dependent, and withdrawn (Santrock & Warshak, 1979). A similar result was reported by Joyce Lowenstein and Elizabeth Koopman (1978). They found that which parent headed the family made no difference in the boys' self-esteem. The more critical factor was the boys' relationship with the noncustodial parent. The boys with the most frequent contacts maintained the highest levels of self-esteem.

When totaling the advantages and disadvantages of a child living with only one parent, it is important to remember that single parent homes usually result from divorces. It may be the divorce and the conflict surrounding the separation that disrupt children, not the single parent home. The death of a parent, for example, does not cause the same long-term behavior problems as a divorce (Emery, 1982). Having two parents who live in harmony would certainly be preferred to having only one parent, but having two parents is not an advantage if they are in constant conflict. The single parent home, despite its drawbacks, offers advantages over a home filled with tension and hostility (Hetherington, 1981).

Although our information on single parent homes is limited, one fact is clear. Most single parent families are temporary. Five years after a divorce or a death, the majority of the parents have remarried (Hetherington, Camara, & Featherman, 1983). This sets the stage for a new family relationship—the stepfamily.

**The stepfamily.** Children have a fresh set of problems when either parent decides to remarry. The first obstacle is the child's resentment of the new mother or father. After some years in a single parent household, children may not welcome an intrusion into the relationships that they have carefully carved with each parent. Clinical case histories show that some children intentionally sabotage their parents' new relationships. A remarriage signals the end of the child's fantasy that their biological parents will reconcile (Visher & Visher, 1979). Children also suspect that they will lose contact with the noncustodial parent if he or she remarries. The evidence to date suggests that this fear is realistic. Before either parent remarries, 67 percent of the noncustodial parents (usually the father) maintain contact with their children. Once the father remarries, only 40 percent maintain contact with their children. If both parents remarry, the percentage of fathers who maintain contact drops to 34 percent (Furstenberg, 1981).

The addition of a stepparent to the single parent family can often help the children (Santrock, Warshak, Lindbergh, & Meadows, 1982). Another adult provides emotional support and raises the level of cognitive stimulation in the home. The presence of a stepfather in the family tends to minimize the cognitive deficits that boys without a father normally show (Chapman, 1977). The stepparent also contributes in less direct ways. With another adult to help, the biological parent can spend more time with the children and provide more nurturing. The positive effect that the stepparent has can also be seen in cognitive development. When children from stepfamilies, nuclear families, and single parent families are compared, the children from single parent families usually fare the worst (Clingempeel & Reppucci, 1982).

Despite these possible advantages, the obstacles to a harmonious stepfamily are formidable. Remarriages are more likely to end in divorce than first marriages. Further, the presence of children from a previous marriage increases the probability that the second try will fail (Clingempeel & Reppucci, 1982).

The alternative family patterns considered in this chapter include working mothers, divorcing families, single parent families, and stepfamilies. Many other possibilities exist. Grandparents are seeking and being awarded custody. Gay couples are adopting children. Children are being raised in communes or foster homes. Each of these alternatives influences the development of the child, and despite the obvious disadvantages of many of these alternatives, they can be effective for some children. The variety of family patterns that can be successful suggests that psychologists should identify characteristics of a healthy family. Once these characteristics are identified, parents can try to make sure they are available to the child regardless of who heads the family.

## CHILD ABUSE AND NEGLECT

The first responsibility of parents is to protect and nurture their children. In abusive families, this fundamental responsibility is ignored, causing dire consequences for the child. Child abuse was not viewed as a social problem in the 18th and 19th centuries, not because it did not occur, but because physical abuse of children was accepted and even encouraged. Harsh discipline was seen as a necessary part of raising a child. Religious leaders condoned physical abuse to strengthen the child's moral values and break children of their evil impulses (Williams, 1980b). The entire society approved of beating children, and child-rearing advice sometimes recommended ice water baths to subdue infants and switches for beatings (DeMause, 1980). No legal protection for children was available because children were regarded as their parents' property. The case of Mary Ellen Wilson, which was brought to court in 1874, marked a turning point in society's attitude. Mary Ellen had been cruelly beaten and neglected by her family, but concerned friends and neighbors could find no way to protect her. Finally, community leaders appealed to Henry Bergh, who was the president of the Society for the Prevention of Cruelty to Animals. He was able to bring the child to the attention of the court. Mary Ellen was granted protection, and her guardians were sent to prison (Williams, 1980b). The irony that animals enjoyed more protection than children was not lost. By the turn of the century, 161 communities in the United States had established social agencies to protect children. These social agencies rescued children who lived in abusive circumstances and offered legal advice and services. To really protect children, however, these agencies needed more power.

In the 1960s, pediatricians and radiologists began to dramatize the injuries and fatalities inflicted on children by their parents. The *Battered Child Syndrome*, a name coined in 1962 by Henry Kempe, signaled the beginning of a nationwide effort to understand and curtail child abuse. These efforts have led to intensive studies of troubled families and have at least outlined the dimensions of the problem. The problem is severe. Murder has become one of the top five causes of death in children under 14 (UPI, 1982), and over 1 million children a year are abused in some fashion (Kaplan & Pelcovitz, 1982).

**What constitutes child abuse?**

Initially, professionals limited their attention to cases where the child suffered severe physical abuse. This definition excluded children who desperately needed to be protected from sexual abuse, emotional abuse, or neglect. Current definitions include all of the above categories, and some agencies include children who have been diagnosed as *failure to thrive* (see Figure 12–8). These differing definitions of child abuse have made it difficult to estimate the number of children affected. The annual figure of 1 million underestimates the total number of children who suffer indignities at their parents' hands. Emotional abuse is rarely reported and difficult to prove. Sexual abuse makes children feel ashamed and confused. Often these children do not even tell their parents. As we will see, most physical abuse is not so severe that it leads to hospitalization. Therefore, much of this abuse escapes detection. If estimates of abuse included these undetected and unreported cases, the number of children abused would be substantially higher (Williams, 1980a).

**Patterns of abuse at different ages**

Stories of infants who were scorched in scalding bath water, thrown across the room, or smothered under pillows appear frequently in the media. These stories leave the impression that the most common victims of child abuse are infants and toddlers. Actually, children under two account for less than 20

**Figure 12—8**          **Failure to thrive**

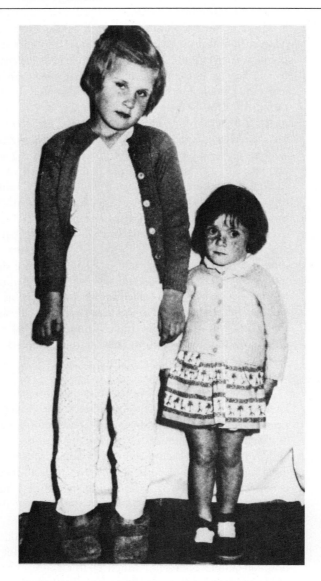

The taller child in this picture, who is of average height for her age, is five years, one month old. The other child is only nine months younger. This child's short stature was caused by neglect. The lack of a nurturing environment can slow a child's growth. When these children are hospitalized and removed from their rejecting parents, they gain weight rapidly and begin to catch up with their peers.

Source: From Franklin, A. W. (1977). *The Challenge of child abuse.* New York: Academic Press. Frontispiece.

percent of abused children (American Humane Association, 1979). Their injuries are so severe that they require medical treatment. Hence, the child is brought to the attention of professionals. Despite treatment, an estimated 10,000 children die each year as a result of abuse and neglect (Kadushin & Martin, 1981). Abuse of school-age children is more common than abuse of infants and toddlers. But school-age children are less likely to have injuries that require medical treatment. As a result, the abuse is seldom reported to authorities.

Sexual abuse has often been ignored in discussions of abuse and neglect. Much less information is available about sexual abuse, primarily because it is the most underreported form of abuse (Kempe, 1978). Sexual abuse accounts for approximately 10 percent of all abuse, and the victims are typically girls under 12 (Kaplan & Pelcovitz, 1982). In the majority of cases, a parent or guardian is the abuser (Rimsza & Niggemann, 1982). Although most parents warn their children about strangers, they forget to mention that children need to be leery of friends and relatives, too. The clinical literature is full of case histories of women who, as young girls, were approached by their grandfathers with the following line: "Good girls do this for Grandpa and *never* tell their mothers." In one such case, sexual abuse began at age 5 and continued until the girl was 13 (Lewin, 1981).

Father-daughter incest is the most common form of sexual abuse and is usually nonviolent. Sexual abuse is also more common in stepfamilies. The female children in these families are not biologically related to the males. Sexual behavior boundaries are not as clear in these families, and cases of stepfather-stepdaughter incest are becoming increasingly common (Perlmutter, Engel, & Sager, 1982).

Child rape or more violent sexual exploitation is likely to come to the attention of authorities. Regardless of whether or not the sexual abuse is violent, children and adolescents who timidly tell a neighbor, a grandparent, a teacher, or a school nurse about sexual abuse should not be discounted. In many cases, the children have been warned not to tell anyone and are very frightened. Adults must remember that children do not ordinarily fabricate stories of detailed sexual activities (Adams-Tucker, 1982).

**The abused child**

Initially, studies of child abuse focused on the parents. Researchers wanted to know what characterized abusive parents and what triggered outbursts of temper that ended in assaults on the child. As data were collected, it became clear that the children who were abused were alike on several dimensions. As reported in Chapter 4, infants with low birth weights and premature infants are more likely to be abused than normal weight infants (Lynch & Roberts, 1982). Children who are premature or below normal weight account for between 20 to 30 percent of abused children, but only 2 to 8 percent of the population (Lynch & Roberts, 1982).

Once investigators were alerted to the fact that particular children provoked

## DIAGNOSING AN ABUSED CHILD

In order to prevent child abuse and neglect, professionals need to be able to identify children who are abused or neglected. Although a medical examination may suggest abuse, the parents are likely to explain that the child was hurt in an accident. In such cases, psychologists are often asked to evaluate the probability of abuse. Psychologists are usually not able to say, absolutely, that the child has been abused or neglected, but they can identify characteristics of the child that are similar to those of abused and neglected children.

Medical symptoms may include physical scars or marks. Abused children may also be very small for their age. However, many abused children do not bear any obvious physical marks or medical symptoms. In such cases, abuse is identified by psychological symptoms and behaviors.

Withdrawal is a common symptom among abused children. Often the child is socially isolated and appears severely depressed.

Catatonia is another characteristic of abused children. To test for this, psychologists have the child stand in a particular spot. Then the child's arm is positioned so that it is raised and extended. An abused child will hold this pose for several minutes while the psychologist ignores the child and talks to the parents (MacCarthy, 1977).

Abused children are very aware of their environments. When they enter a new situation with a strange adult, they are "hypervigilant." By being very alert and watching the adult's every move, the child may be trying to avoid situations that have led to punishment in the past. When being interviewed by a psychologist, these children appear very tense. They become distracted and anxious at the slightest noise.

The abused child has been severely punished for failing. Hence, these children are likely to avoid new situations in which they might fail. When asked questions that they cannot answer, the abused child is likely to become very restless, change answers, or refuse to answer (Rodeheffer & Martin, 1976).

Martin and Beezley (1976b) offer the following summary of the characteristics that are prevalent in abused children:

| Characteristics | Percentage of children displaying trait |
|---|---|
| 1. Impaired capacity to enjoy life. | 66% |
| 2. Psychiatric symptoms—enuresis, tantrums, hyperactivity. | 62 |
| 3. Low self-esteem. | 52 |
| 4. School learning problems. | 38 |
| 5. Withdrawal. | 24 |
| 6. Opposition. | 24 |
| 7. Hypervigilance. | 22 |
| 8. Compulsivity. | 22 |
| 9. Overly mature behavior. | 20 |

Few abused children will display all of these characteristics, but a child who displays several of these symptoms could well be a victim of child abuse or neglect.

abuse, they found many special characteristics of abused children. Stepchildren, mentally retarded children, children with congenital defects and physical handicaps, and children with chronic illnesses are more likely to be abused than normal children (Lightcap, Kurland, & Burgess, 1982; Parke & Lewis, 1981). Abused children may also have difficult temperaments. When a child's temperament leads to a lack of responsiveness or creates other frustrations for the parent, physical abuse becomes more likely. Chronic crying and irritability, two of the hallmarks of difficult children, are often cited by parents as the precipitating factor in an abusive episode (Kaplan & Pelcovitz, 1982). Children who are normal, healthy, and responsive do not always escape abuse, but children who are premature, have constitutional defects, or an erratic temperament are more probable targets.

Infants, of course, have no control over their arrival, their appearance, or the other characteristics that engender their parents' violence. Older children do. The abused child sometimes seems to invite attacks by purposefully antagonizing parents. Carol George and Mary Main (1979) compared abused children in child-protection centers with another sample of children from families under stress. All of the children were between one and three years of age. The abused children assaulted their peers and harassed their caretakers more than the stressed children. It is impossible to determine from this experiment whether the child's aversive behavior or the parents' abuse came first. Perhaps it is enough to know that the parent-child interaction has disintegrated into a cycle characterized by hostile children and abusive parents.

With school-age children, disrespectful remarks are as likely to provoke abuse as unacceptable behavior. A detailed report on child abuse in the state of Wisconsin includes the parents' account of what triggered abusive incidents. As many as 60 percent of the incidents involved the child talking back, sassing, cussing, or being verbally aggressive. In each case, the interaction between parent and child was tense but under control until the child became verbally abusive.

> Rosemarie, 13, was taping a song that was on the radio and told her mother to be quiet. When she wasn't, Rosemarie swore at her, which made Mrs. B. angry. She threw her tea at Rosemarie, pushed her to the floor, kicked her in the back and hit her with a belt.

> Mrs. F had left home for approximately two months prior to the incident. Her five-year-old son Larry resented her return home because of his feeling of being previously rejected. Larry kept calling his mother a "bitch." Mother whipped him with a belt, causing welts.

> Ruth, 16, had been pouting because mother would not let her go ice skating. She became angry and refused to complete a craft project promised for school. Mother ordered her to do it. Ruth sassed her mother, who then grabbed her, shook her and slapped her, bruising her cheek near her eye. (Kadushin & Martin, 1981, p. 118–119)

Infants, toddlers, school-age children, and adolescents who are abused are not necessarily passive or random targets for adult violence. Some aspect of their behavior, whether intended or not, primes the parent's loss of control. Looking at the victims as contributing to their own abuse may seem callous and misdirected, but defining the child's contribution is necessary if we are to understand what happens in families that resort to abuse. Only then can we prevent the abuse and protect the child. The fact that children trigger their parents' rage does not absolve the parents from the final responsibility for the violence.

**The abusive parent**

Protecting one's own child would seem to be one of the strongest human drives. Something fundamental must go awry for parents to attack and, in many cases, kill their own offspring. Some psychologists view attacks as isolated incidents provoked by a particular catalyst such as the father's drinking or the child's disrespectful remarks. To others, the violence is the culmination of an unhappy childhood filled with unmet needs. Sociological factors are prominent in explanations of child abuse because abuse occurs most frequently against a background of poverty and isolation. An ecological approach meshes the psychological history and social circumstances of the parents with the child's particular characteristics and an environmental trigger. To evaluate these different explanations, we need to consider them in more detail.

**Psychological model.** When abusive parents are interviewed about their own childhood, they frequently tell a story of parental loss, rejection, and abuse. According to the psychological model, this disturbed relationship leaves them emotionally crippled. As adults, they still have unmet needs for love and support that they transfer to their children. Their fantasy is that their new baby will finally provide the loving relationship they have craved. The parents' expectations are so high that few infants can meet them. When the child does not respond immediately to the parent's attention, or if the child's demands seem insatiable, the parent interprets this as rejection, and the stage is set for abuse.

Researchers trying to document the validity of this scenario have focused on three issues. First, were abusive parents abused as children? Second, do abusive parents have unrealistic expectations that they impose on their children? Third, do these parents have personality defects that promote violence? Let us examine these questions in turn.

Abusive parents have more troubled childhoods than other parents (Friedrich & Wheeler, 1982). However, parents who do not abuse their children sometimes tell similar stories of childhoods marred by rejection and abuse. Yet, as adults they do not abuse their children. Why do some parents translate their unmet needs into abuse while others with similar histories transcend their experience and become adequate, supportive parents? The answer must lie outside the childhood experiences of the parents.

The second question concerns the unrealistic expectations that abusive parents hold (Twentyman & Plotkin, 1982). One mother thought that her six-month-old baby was willfully having a bowel movement at an inconvenient time. Furthermore, she extended her interpretation of her son's behavior and decided that the boy was stubborn and would grow up to be delinquent unless she taught him a lesson (Kempe & Kempe, 1978). Such unrealistic expectations are only part of the problem. Abusive mothers adopt a very negative style when they interact with their children (Egeland & Brunnquell, 1979). They are more likely to use physical punishment for common misbehaviors and are less likely to reason with the child (Friedrich & Wheeler, 1982). Both the unrealistic expectations and the inappropriate discipline point to gaps in the parents' knowledge about children.

The third question concerns personality traits that differentiate abusive parents. Abusive parents are less able to empathize with their children, are more hostile, and are more impulsive than groups of parents who do not abuse their children (Friedrich & Wheeler, 1982). Mothers who abuse their children are frequently immature and depressed (Lynch & Roberts, 1982). On personality inventories, abusive mothers appear anxious and lack confidence (Hyman, 1981). They are also more likely to be subtly hostile and rejecting (Main, 1981). But 90 percent of the parents who abuse their children show no evidence of severe pathology (Kempe & Kempe, 1978). Questionnaires are no better at predicting abuse. These instruments will identify potential abusers, but they will also erroneously identify 100 parents who will not abuse their children for every five correct identifications (Starr, 1979).

The psychological model receives scattered support from a variety of studies, yet the basic flaw remains. For each of the variables that predict abuse, we can find many exceptions. Other factors that promote or discourage abuse must be operating.

**The sociological perspective.** Overcrowding, poverty, unemployment, and isolation are some of the social factors that appear frequently in abusive families. Abusive parents are found at all levels of society, but parents from lower socioeconomic settings are more likely to abuse their children. Fathers who abuse their children often come from the ranks of the unemployed and unskilled. Single parents who have little relief from their child-care duties occasionally become exasperated and resort to abuse. In one study, 60 percent of the abusive mothers were the sole parent. Of the fathers who abused their children, 25 percent were managing their families on their own (Kadushin & Martin, 1981).

Isolation is another common characteristic of abusive families (Salinger, Kaplan, & Artemyeff, 1983). The adults in these families often have no personal friends, relatives, or co-workers that they regard as confidants (Parke & Lewis, 1981). In fact, as shown in Figure 12–9, they actively avoid social entanglements (Garbarino & Stocking, 1980). It is interesting that the length of time a family has lived at a particular location is a factor in child abuse. Moving not only increases short-term stress, but it pulls the network of friends and relatives out from under the parents. These social networks—whether in an Amish community, an urban ghetto, or a suburban neighborhood—tend to control parents' behavior toward their children (Warren, 1981).

Despite the fact that social variables are related to child abuse, the same objection that was lodged against the psychological explanation can be lodged against the sociological explanation. The majority of families that live in stressful circumstances do not abuse their children. Both the psychological and so-

**Figure 12—9**                    **Social networks of abusive parents**

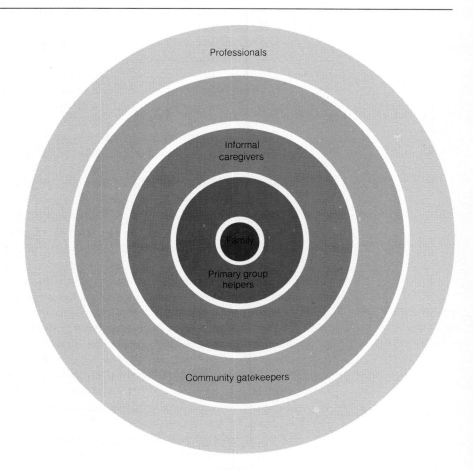

A family's social network can be diagrammed as a bull's-eye with the family at the center. Most families have a primary group of helpers that might include their extended family and godparents. These adults are close to the family and maintain an intimate relationship with the family. One circle removed from the family are informal caregivers, like aunts, friends, and neighbors. Community resources, like the church, are more removed from the family. Professionals such as doctors, psychologists, and social workers are even more remote. Child abuse occurs frequently in families encapsulated in a thick ring of privacy. These parents are isolated from their primary group and their extended family. Intervention programs that try to penetrate this isolation may help protect the children in the family.

Source: Gottlieb, B. H. (1981). The role of individual and social support in preventing child maltreatment. In J. Garbarino & S. H. Stocking (Eds.), *Protecting children from abuse and neglect.* (p. 49). San Francisco: Jossey-Bass.

ciological explanations isolate important pieces of the abuse puzzle, but these explanations need to be woven together with the child's contribution and considered in the context of the community and society.

**The ecological approach.** The ecological model considers the child, the psychological makeup of the parents, and the social stresses of the family (Garbarino, 1982). By considering all of these factors, the model moves away from blaming the abuse on an aberrant child, a sick parent, or a violent society. Instead, it considers the whole process of family functions within the society. Ross Parke and Nancy Lewis (1981) present such an ecological model. They comment on the mismatch between the level of stress that abusive parents experience and the resources and skills that these families have available to solve their problems. As a family's level of stress increases, the need for support and coping skills increases. If supportive adults or additional coping strategies are available, the tension may subside. Unfortunately, abusive parents are often isolated, the support systems they can invoke are minimal, and their financial, intellectual, and emotional resources are limited. As a result, a premature infant, an active child, or a teenager who is involved with drugs may heighten the level of stress to the point where parents begin to lose control.

**Preventing child abuse**

The initial reaction to some of the tortures inflicted on children was to remove the child from the family. In some cases, this certainly is the best strategy (de Castro, Rolfe, & Hippe, 1978). But removing hundreds of thousands of children every year would strain child protective services to the breaking point, would interfere with the basic unit of society, and would constitute an invasion of the family's privacy. Besides, foster care is not always an attractive alternative. Children who are adopted or fostered are not exempt from abuse (Korbin, 1981). Restructuring the family so that it is a reasonable and safe environment is preferable, if it can be accomplished (see Figure 12–10). To this end, intervention programs have tried to extend the parents' repertoire of disciplinary techniques, to reduce the child's deviant behavior, and to direct the resources of the community to help the troubled family. Let us look at the success of these various intervention strategies.

The first strategy involves reducing the stress on the parents, especially during periods of crisis. In essence, this strategy acknowledges that raising children is sometimes frustrating, that some children may be particularly difficult, and that the parents need some help and support in dealing with the child. Parents Anonymous and community "hot" lines are quick ways for parents to find a supportive, empathetic adult.

Other informal and formal support systems can help the family. The church, the neighborhood, and relatives that live nearby are obvious examples of informal sources of support. As we have seen, abused families are often isolated, so they may need more formal support systems. Many prevention programs have devised ways to give the parents some time off, especially when

**Figure 12–10**                    **Preventing child abuse**

The T. family became involved with our treatment program when Jack T. sought help in controlling his impulses to hit Jacky, his 10-month-old son. Mr. T., a 40 year-old, intermittently employed housepainter, was referred to us by his counselor at an alcoholism treatment center. He could not tolerate Jacky's crying, which he felt was designed to manipulate him. His request for help was perceived with a sense of urgency, since he had previously abused two young daughters. Both of these children sustained multiple fractures and were subsequently placed in foster homes and eventually adopted. The T.'s first child died as a result of crib death, but may have also been abused. Jacky was apparently conceived to relieve the T.s' emptiness and depression caused by the loss of the three older children. This represented their final attempt to succeed as parents.

It soon became clear to us that Jack's impulses to hit his son were experienced mainly when he returned home for dinner, hungry and tired. At this time, he became enraged if Jacky was not quietly sleeping.

If Jacky was being fed by Mrs. T. or if he was crying and fussing, Jack experienced mounting resentment. After a short period in individual psychotherapy, Jack recognized that he felt neglected and jealous of his son when the latter was being cared for by Mrs. T. Jack recalled painful memories about his early childhood as a foundling and a foster child. He remembered being hungry and lonely. He was always the last to be fed, as the natural children of the foster parents came first. Jack could also identify with Jacky's cries of hunger, since he had suffered from malnutrition in one of his foster homes. He realized how these experiences left him ill-prepared to function as a devoted parent.

The therapist helped Jack deal with his vocational problems. As Jack was able to get more painting jobs, his self-esteem rose and he became less "rivalrous" with his infant son. Jack was also encouraged to continue to control his drinking through participation in Alcoholics Anonymous.

The T. family was followed for four years during which Mr. T. never hit his son.

In some cases, the abusive parent makes significant progress through individual psychotherapy. In this case, both the father's unemployed status and his experience as a child were contributing to his abusive behavior. Insight gained during therapy helped the father control his behavior and his environment.

Source: Green, A. H. (1980). *Child Maltreatment.* New York: Jason Aronson.

the family is in a crisis. Free babysitting services, 24-hour drop-off centers, day-care centers, and mothers' helpers are some of the formal programs that give the parents a chance to marshall their resources. The availability of these resources does seem to reduce child abuse (Garbarino & Crouter, 1978). Remember, though, that parents who use these services are typically those who recognize a potentially dangerous situation and are therefore motivated to defuse the situation.

A second strategy is parent education. Although it is impossible to predict who will abuse their child, we can identify families at risk and offer them information about parenting. This kind of program can reduce the unrealistic expectations that isolated parents harbor. It can also increase the father's participation in the child-care routines (Parke, Hymel, Power, & Tinsley, 1980).

An involved father relieves the mother's stress and strengthens the bond between father and child. Parents seem most eager to attend classes about child care during the periods prior to and after birth. Parents of older children will often attend classes designed to help the family through a crisis.

As with the use of community resources, attending classes is strictly voluntary. Neither supportive agencies nor educational approaches touch parents who believe that their frequent and severe beatings are justified. One parent in the Wisconsin study exemplified these feelings when he said, "Not only would I have done it again, I would have done it sooner" (Kadushin & Martin, 1981, p. 217).

A third strategy involves shoring up the bond between parent and child early in life. This can be done by noting the parents' reactions and comments during the prenatal period and also during labor and delivery. Parents identified as high-risk can then be offered a variety of support systems. In one program of this kind, the pediatrician took a personal and long-term interest in the family, calling the parents and offering support every week or so (Kempe & Kempe, 1978). A control group of high-risk parents received no additional support. During the first 17 months, five children from the control group were hospitalized for abuse or neglect. The group that had received additional professional support had several cases of neglect, and many of the families had abnormal patterns of parenting—but none of the children were hospitalized for physical abuse (Kempe & Kempe, 1978).

A fourth strategy focuses on the child. The goal in these projects is to reduce the child's crying, whining, teasing, yelling, and aggression (Issacs, 1982). Parents are taught how to talk with their children, when and how to praise their children, and how to make reasonable bargains. Watching the families interact after the training indicates that the mothers and the children have benefited from the program. The child's aversive behaviors have been cut in half (Reid, Taplin, & Lorber, 1981; Wolfe & Sandler, 1981). Of course, the hope is that the child's new demeanor will help parents maintain control. But this has not been demonstrated. Nor do we know whether the changes will last. In one of the few studies that followed families for one year after the treatment, the investigators found that the mothers and children gradually returned to their old habits (Wahler, 1980).

Are any of these strategies successful? It is surprising that we have very few answers to this question. Some programs indicate that the majority of families have been helped (Isaacs, 1982). This conclusion, however, is not based on a decreased incidence of abuse. It is based on the fact that families have learned how to interact in more positive ways. Very few studies have followed abusive parents for any length of time. In those that have, the conclusions are more guarded (Sudia, 1981).

Clara Johnson (1977) recorded all of the families offered protective services in Nashville, Tennessee and Savannah, Georgia over a three-year period. She found that approximately 60 percent of the reported children had been abused again during that interval. More ominous is the fact that the repeated incidents were likely to involve more serious injury. She concluded that the services offered by the protective agencies were not altering the abusive interaction patterns of the families.

Even when an intervention program is successful in reducing the physical abuse, a disheartening number of parents (68 percent) continue to reject their children or react to them in a hostile way (Martin & Beezley, 1976a). In one oft-cited case, professionals worked with 23 abusive families for almost two years. At the end of the treatment, the majority of mothers still did not accept their battered children (Baher, 1976).

Large-scale studies reinforce the conclusion that altering parent-child relationships is not easy. The Berkeley Planning Associates covered 1,724 parents that were treated in 11 different projects. They found that 30 percent of the parents continued to abuse the child while they were being treated. Overall, though, these children fared better than those whose parents received no formal treatment (Cohn & Collignon, 1979).

Health professionals continue to struggle with the issue of child abuse. Although some of the precursors to abuse have been identified, we cannot accurately differentiate parents who will lose control and injure their child from those who neglect their child or from those who maintain a normal relationship with their child. Once abuse has occurred, protective agencies have offered a variety of services, including professional and community support, therapy, information on child rearing, and child-management classes. These programs have certainly saved many children from injury and have undoubtedly saved some lives. But just as frequently, they fail to protect the child from further abuse (Sudia, 1981). Transforming families that are abusive and negative into ones that are loving and supportive will require more than cursory efforts. Even intensive intervention strategies may do no more than provide a neutral or indifferent environment for the child.

## SUMMARY

The family is vital to the child's physical, emotional, and cognitive development. The importance of the mother was recognized by theorists beginning with Freud. Now the entire family unit is seen as contributing to the child's development. The child can flourish or flounder depending on the environment provided by the primary caretaker and the supporting members of the family.

In this chapter, we have traced the family's impact on children as they move from infancy through adolescence. At each period of development, the family has to adjust its responses to the differing needs of the child. Infants need to be provided with total protection and responsive, consistent, loving care. Toddlers need to be encouraged to explore the world under the watchful eye of an adult. Preschoolers need to move outside the family, but they still look to the family for care, support, and direction. School-age children need to have rules and limits set by their parents. When parents have high expectations for their children and combine these expectations with nurturance and understanding, their children are likely to be competent, independent, and secure. Adolescents require a somewhat different approach. The emotional ties of earlier years are present even if they are not as overt, but the close direction of earlier years gives way to a constant interchange about activities. The home still provides essential support and encouragement to the child.

Individual differences between children, even children in the same family, often require parents to modify their behavior. Boys demand more freedom than girls, yet they want to know that their parents are supportive. Girls need to be challenged and occasionally provoked into taking the initiative. These individual differences mean that a description of the ideal family must always be open to modification.

The families typically described in studies of child rearing are two-parent families in which the father works and the mother's responsibilities are centered around the home and family. Other family patterns abound, and these are likely to pose some problems for the child and also offer certain advantages. Evaluating the effects that working mothers, single parent families, stepfamilies, and divorce have on children is not straightforward. Each family environment, regardless of how it is organized, must be considered as a working unit and evaluated in terms of how well it functions. Even single parents, who are beset by dozens of demands, have been able to minimize the negative impact of a divorce by establishing an authoritative atmosphere in the home and helping the children maintain a relationship with the other parent.

Abusive parents provide an extreme example of a poorly functioning family unit. As society has become more sensitive to child abuse, it has recognized that physical abuse is only one form of mistreatment. Emotional abuse, sexual abuse, and neglect are seldom reported to authorities, yet are obstacles to healthy development. The parents' history, the social circumstances of the family, and even the children themselves can contribute to an explosive situation. Prevention programs have tried to educate parents about child development, establish or reestablish strong bonds between the parents and child, alter the child's behavior, and defuse any crisis that arises.

Promoting the optimal development of children must be a primary goal of any society. To accomplish this, we must look first to the family. This basic unit of society maintains the primary responsibility for children, and despite the changes in the form of the family, it is likely to retain that responsibility. One of the easiest and most effective ways to influence children is to promote family environments that will meet the child's needs.

# CHAPTER 13

# Friendships and social development

Aristotle said, "No one would choose a friendless existence on condition of having all the other good things in the world." Aristotle's view voices the essential role of friends in the development of children. Should anyone doubt this role, they have only to read the poignant story published by Anna Freud and Sophia Dann (1951) about six small children brought to England from a concentration camp after World War II. These three-year-old German-Jewish children had been separated from their mothers since before they were one year old and had developed an intense attachment to each other. When separated, they constantly asked to return to the group. When a child was absent, the remaining five immediately wanted to know when that child would return. While they were tender, loving, and concerned about their peers, they were suspicious or indifferent toward adults. If the adults interfered with their group, the children became actively hostile.

In this situation, the peers actually provided the kind of relationship normally provided by the family. Furthermore, these children were effective in their efforts as substitute parents. A follow-up of these children 35 years later indicated that they were leading productive lives (Hartup, 1983). In the case of these six children, the peer group assumed the role of the parent. Normally the peer group has different roles, namely, fostering a sense of belonging, facilitating social comparison, and enhancing social skills.

Being able to establish and maintain friendships is a unique skill that children learn from peers. Children need to know how to join group activities, how to be a member of a group, how to manage conflicts that develop between group members, and how to be sensitive to everyone's needs. Many of these skills are subtle, and there is little direct instruction in "How to be a friend." As early as nursery school, however, there are many subtle exchanges that teach a child these skills.

[David and Tony are sitting together at the drawing table]

**David:** Do you like my drawing?
**Tony:** No.
**David:** You have to like it.
**Tony:** I don't have to like it if I don't want to.
**David:** Why?
**Tony:** I don't like it, that's why. (Rubin, 1980, p. 8)

In this scene, David is being taught the difficult lesson that peers, unlike parents, do not marvel at everything the child produces. This is only one of the lessons playmates teach.

Children relate to each other early in life, and as children develop, peers provide a variety of experiences. Still, peers are not important in the lives of newborn infants. Parents provide for infants, assuming responsibility for their physical well-being, providing love, and introducing the child to the world. As infants become toddlers, preschoolers, and then skip off to school, the social circle surrounding them gradually expands to include siblings and playmates. Whereas two-year-olds spend only 10 percent of their time playing with other children, preadolescents and adolescents spend 50 percent of their time with peers (Hartup, 1983). By adolescence, the peer group has taken its place alongside the family as a major socializing agent.

We can see the changing importance of peers in a child's development by looking at the responses different aged children make to the question, "What is a friend?" Tony, age three, responds, "We are friends because we know each other's names." Julie, an eight-year-old, says, "Friends don't snatch or act snobby, and they don't argue or disagree. If you're nice to them, they'll be nice to you." A 13-year-old acknowledges a different role for a friend when she says, "A friend is someone that you can share secrets with at three in the morning with Clearasil on your face." In adulthood, friends allow the free expression of emotion, the sharing of privacy, and the discussion of personally crucial themes. Friends also provide support and remain committed to a person despite interpersonal conflict (Rubin, 1980). For a toddler, a friend is a playmate, and little else is expected. But as the child becomes an adult, a friend begins to signal a long-term caring relationship that is predicated on intimacy, trust, and loyalty (Berndt, 1981). The development of friendships and intimate relationships is of lifelong importance; hence, the skills that spell success or failure in interpersonal relationships deserve to be described in some detail.

What do peers offer another child? In some areas of development, the peer group complements the parents' efforts in the home. For example, parents are often the first source of social values, but in time peer groups will modify those values. In such areas as clothing, the peer group offers the child an entirely different perspective than parents. The peer group also provides an arena for social experiences that parents cannot provide. In the family, parents are the authorities. Among peers, the person in charge must be determined. Children and adolescents struggle through a process of competition, cooperation, and aggression to determine who will fill various social roles.

Peers present a second socializing force for the child. By looking at children with their peers, we can watch the processes of moral development, trace prosocial behaviors such as sharing and helping, and examine the beginnings of aggression.

# THE INCREASING IMPORTANCE OF FRIENDS

**Infants and friends**

For many infants, their first playmate is an older sibling. Infants without siblings, however, often play with other infants. Zick Rubin describes his son's first play group, formed at the tender age of eight months.

> Four infants—three of them still crawlers, one beginning to walk—were placed in a living room and instructed by their mothers to get to know each other. That is, after all, what a play group is for. Unconcerned about these parental designs, the babies ignored one another . . . .
>
> Even at the earliest sessions, however, there were isolated instances in which one baby approached and made physical contact with another. For example, "Vanessa takes Elihu by surprise by crawling to him, screaming, and pulling his hair. Elihu looks bewildered. Then he starts to cry and crawls to his mother to be comforted." Such episodes of hair pulling, poking, and pawing when the babies were eight and nine months old did not appear to involve hostile intent. Instead, they seemed to reflect the babies' interest in exploring one another as physical objects. When Elihu crawled over to another baby's stroller and started to bend the passenger's nose, his actions and manner were indistinguishable from the way in which he handled toy animals, bath toys, and other objects that interested him. (Rubin, 1980, p. 15–16)

From this amusing scene, we can see that infants are interested in other children, but they lack the understanding that another child can initiate activities as well as respond to the child's curious poking (Hay, Nash, & Pederson,

### Social interaction between infants

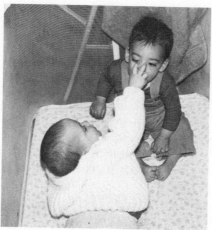

*Bill Aron: Jeroboam*

Infants notice each other and are curious about each other, but they are not able to sustain social interaction.

1983). Infant play lacks the social give-and-take of adult interaction. When one infant makes an overture to another, it is as likely to be ignored as it is to evoke a response (Vandell, Wilson, & Buchanan, 1980). Clearly, infants at this age find other children interesting, but they are not skilled at sustaining a social interaction. Friendships and peer relations exist only in the loosest sense (Hartup, 1983).

**Toddlers and friends**

Near their first birthday, the infants' awareness changes. Now a child will offer a playmate a toy—smiling, vocalizing, and looking at the child. When the second child responds by taking the toy, there is a chain of socially directed behaviors, with some apparent connection between them. This reciprocal awareness marks the beginning of social interaction, and even in toddlers, these short social encounters take many forms.

Cooperation begins a few months past a child's first birthday. Two toddlers, who could not walk without assistance, managed to get around together by holding on to opposite sides of a toy cart. When one of them took a step, the other was forced to take a corresponding step to stay upright (Rubin, 1980). Investigators have also reported seeing altruistic behavior in children this young. A 14-month-old child hearing an infant cry, clumsily offered a pacifier and tried to stroke the child's head. Of course, the interaction may have a less positive flavor, as when a 15-month-old grabs a teddy bear from the arms of another toddler and vanishes around the corner. Aggressive interactions like these occur during this age period, but they are not as common as positive interactions (Rubenstein & Howes, 1976).

Peer exchanges among toddlers illustrate the beginnings of cooperation, aggression, and empathy (Howes, 1983). If toddlers know each other, they are likely to spend more than half of their time in activities that include the other child. Their social exchanges may involve a long sequence of mutual interaction (Rubenstein & Howes, 1976). Toddlers who do not know each other and are thrust together in a playroom are not nearly as socially oriented (Mueller & Brenner, 1977).

Even at two years of age, the peer group offers some unique opportunities for the child. Few parents can maintain a high interest level in jumping off a step 20 times. Toddlers, however, delight in such repetition. In fact, two-year-olds have already learned that if they want to talk or be reassured they should find an adult, but if they want to run, jump, and play, peers are more willing partners. This leads Judith Rubenstein and Carollee Howes (1976) to suggest that peers provide a context in which toddlers can practice specific skills and extend their understanding of the environment.

The social encounters of toddlers are more advanced than the curious exploring of the first year. First, the two children alternate behavior; there is a give-and-take to the interaction. Second, each toddler contributes to the interaction. Remember that during infancy, the mother often played both her own part and the baby's part in social exchanges. When playing with peers, toddlers share the responsibility for their interaction. Despite the increasing complexity and the obvious enjoyment that toddlers derive from social encounters, they still form a minor part of the child's life.

**The preschool years**

Preschoolers are more social than toddlers. In early descriptions of play behavior, toddlers were observed as engaging in solitary play while preschoolers interacted with other children and cooperated in play groups (Parten, 1932). It appeared from these observations that the solitary play of toddlers gradually gave way to increasing social involvement and cooperative play. Closer examination, however, has shown that such discrete characterizations are misleading (Hartup, 1983). Preschoolers have not given up solitary play, but their solitary play is more sophisticated and complex than the solitary play of toddlers. Toddlers are not confined to solitary play. They often engage in social interactions, but their interactions are immature. By preschool, some of these immature social interactions, like tantrums, are replaced by cooperation. In short, preschoolers engage in the full spectrum of social interaction—cooperation, competition, aggression, affiliation, and altruism. Compared to toddlers, the social behavior of preschoolers is extended and multifaceted (Furman & Bierman, 1983). Many social skills valued in our society emerge during this age period.

**Figure 13–1**   **Solitary play and cooperative play**

Peter Menzel: Stock, Boston         Elizabeth Crews: Stock, Boston

Cooperative play and isolated play are both common among nursery school children. Some children enjoy solving problems by themselves and undertaking projects that only one person can work on. Other children enjoy playing together.

Preschoolers have also become much better communicators. They are effective in getting the attention of another child. They can listen attentively, ask questions if they need more information, and look at the speaker. Furthermore, these children have learned to change their speech to fit the needs of the situation or their listener. Developing these basic communication skills allows preschoolers to carry on extended social interactions. In a continuing Star Wars saga, for example, preschoolers can assume the roles of the central characters, confront and demolish the enemy, and celebrate their victory. Much of this extended interaction depends on newly acquired language and communication skills.

Dominance hierarchies are another social innovation during the preschool years. These hierarchies were initially explored using the same methods that comparative psychologists used in studying dominance in chimpanzees, gorillas, and rhesus monkeys. Observers would code the aggressive encounters between two children and identify which child dominated and which child submitted. On the basis of many such encounters, the observers outlined a

**Figure 13–2**            **Dominance hierarchies**

*Charles Gatewood*

As early as nursery school, children form a dominance hierarchy. Unlike monkeys, however, the dominance hierarchy among children changes as they pursue different goals. Children sitting on the bench during baseball season may star in the school play or win the spelling bee.

hierarchy—ranking each child from the most dominant to the least dominant (Savin-Williams, 1979). Among nursery school children, the number of aggressive encounters over a six-week period is limited. Many children had no aggressive interactions during the observations. This left the resulting dominance hierarchy with many gaps. The observers also noted that dominance in one setting (playing on swings) does not guarantee dominance in another setting (see Figure 13–2). It became clear that a different measure, not necessarily tied to aggression, was needed to define the social status of the children.

Another way of establishing a child's social status is through the attention a child receives (Chance & Jolly, 1970). Children who are the objects of peer attention are likely to be popular, talkative, and sociable. They are also able to deal with aggressive children effectively (Vaughn & Waters, 1981). A child's rank order, in terms of attention received, is likely to be established early in the school year and remain stable. The highly ranked children are watched and imitated because of their social skills. The lower ranked children are probably watching to learn how to handle a variety of social exchanges. A child's rank in the attention hierarchy is also a powerful reflection of the social organization in the nursery school.

In nursery school, friendship networks or affiliative structures usually consist of pairs of children with several other children on the outskirts of the play group. Preschoolers form these networks daily during play periods. Being included or excluded from these friendship networks are recurring themes among the nursery school set. Making friends is no easy task. Preschoolers have to learn the subtle social skills that facilitate entrance into a network because any pair of children may protect their play by denying other children access to their group. The following interchange took place while David, Josh, and Jonah were in the sandbox:

**David** [to Josh]: Will you help me make some soup?
**Josh:** Yeah—and Jonah can't play, right? (Rubin, 1980, p. 49)

Refusing the third child admission to the group seems to solidify the social bond between David and Josh.

It is important to note that exclusion or inclusion is not based solely on long-term friendships. In nursery school, the most frequent reason for excluding a child is that the intruding child is the wrong sex.

[Jake and Danny are on the big swing together]
**Laura** [running up, excited]: Can I get on?
**Jake** [emphatically]: No!
**Danny** [even more emphatically]: No!
**Jake:** We don't want you on here. We only want boys on here.
[After Laura leaves, I ask Jake why he said that]
**Jake:** Because we like boys—we like to have boys. If Laura gets on here, I'll put fire in her eye. (Rubin, 1980, p. 102)

Why preschoolers exclude the other sex is an interesting question. Lisa Serbin argues that sex segregation is instilled by the culture, and if the culture would respond differently, such segregation would disappear. To test her notions, she asked two nursery school teachers to promote cross-sex play. When a boy and girl played cooperatively, the teachers voiced their approval by saying to the class, "I like the tower John and Kathy are building with the blocks." Similar comments made frequently over a two-week period had a clear effect on cross-sex play. Before the teachers expressed approval of cross-sex play, only 5 to 6 percent of the play groups involved children from both sexes. At the end of the trial, cross-sex play had increased by 20 percent. However, when the teachers stopped making positive comments, the children returned to their earlier patterns (Serbin, Tonick, & Sternglonz, 1977). The immediate return to old patterns suggests that the change wrought by the teachers was artificial and that other forces act to keep play groups segregated.

Zick Rubin (1980) has suggested that one of the forces that affects play is the particular behavioral style of children. Boys gravitate toward rough-and-tumble play and prefer outdoor activities (DiPietro, 1980). Girls enjoy dramatic play and table activities (Sprafkin, Serbin, & Elman, 1982). The behavioral styles of the two sexes may be so different that children feel more comfortable with their own sex and hence develop more social bonds within their same sex.

Same-sex play groups are often encouraged by the culture (Hartup, 1983). Parents, teachers, and social institutions unwittingly keep the sexes in separate play groups. A junior high school teacher defended separate teams this way; "Some of the boys are pretty strong and can hit that ball pretty hard. So it might be a good idea to have a girls' softball team and a boys' softball team. We really don't want anyone to get hurt" (Schofield, 1981, p. 65). Regardless of the reason for children playing with members of their own sex, the pattern of children's preferences for play partners is clear in nursery school, becomes stronger through the grade-school years, and persists into early adolescence (Schofield, 1981). Many of society's values and stereotypes are transmitted to the child through these boy and girl groups that begin during the preschool years.

**School-age children**    School-age children make major strides in the cognitive arena. These intellectual awakenings have an immediate and direct effect on social skills. Children can now transmit complex information clearly and supply additional information if their listener needs it. Communication skills like these are necessary if children are to cooperate on a task. Altruism also depends on cognitive skills. Before children can be concerned about others, they must be able to take the perspective of another person. In fact, being able to see the world through another's eyes is a major cognitive advance that guides a host of social skills (Selman, 1981).

The more sophisticated cognitive skills of the school-age child translate into long-term, stable friendships. Friendship groups often last through the school year, and many children maintain their friendships over several years. This

**Figure 13–3**        **Sociogram**

Number of students = 21
Boys                = 13
Girls               =  8

Sociograms are used to examine the interpersonal relationships of groups. By doing a sociogram on a class of elementary students, psychologists and teachers can locate isolated children and take steps to bring them into the group. In this class, Anne and Don are extremely popular. Each was named by five classmates as a person, "I particularly like." Edgar and Betty were not selected by any of their classmates and seem to be isolated from the class.

Source: Northway, M. L., & Weld, L. (1957). *Sociometric testing*. Toronto: University of Toronto Press.

stability means that friendship groups may be identified and studied. *Socio-grams* are the most popular way to study such groups.

The sociogram in Figure 13–3 indicates that three of the children from this classroom are very popular; they were listed as "children I especially like" by five other children in the class. In sociometric terms, these children might be called *stars* (Gottman, 1977). The class also has two *isolates*—children not named as a friend by anyone. After using a sociogram to identify isolates, teachers can begin activities that will bring these children into the group. They can also enlist the aid of a star to bring out a child who is more isolated.

What determines whether children are isolates or stars? A host of personal characteristics have been named—physical attractiveness, athletic skill, intel-lectual ability, and friendliness. Children with intellectual skill or athletic skill are admired by others and sought as friends. Attractive children are perceived as friendly and not aggressive (Langlois & Stephan, 1977). For this reason, they seem more approachable, and it is easier to converse with them. Friendly and sociable children have no trouble initiating conversations with peers, and they maintain their popularity by including other children in their play. They seem secure and able to approach anyone. But the characteristics that predict popularity in young children do not guarantee popularity in adolescence. The social skills required of older children are both more elaborate and more subtle than the concrete helping, cooperating, and sharing that we see in preschool-ers (Dweck, 1981).

One of the most surprising characteristics of popular children is that they tend to be the second or third child in a family. Their position in the family may force these children to develop tolerance, to learn how to negotiate, and to accommodate to the family (Miller & Maruyama, 1976). These survival skills give them an edge in relating to peers.

Between 5 and 10 percent of elementary school children are isolates. These children seem to antagonize their classmates or to have personally unattractive characteristics. Being fat, a trouble maker, or hyperactive are all likely to di-minish the popularity of a child. Still, the majority of the isolated children do not fall into these categories. Their problem seems to be caused by a lack of fundamental social skills.

Steven Asher and his co-workers have conducted extensive interviews with children who are isolates. Typically, these researchers pose a hypothetical sit-uation for the child: "How can you play with two boys who are playing a board game?" Although these children often give reasonable responses like "ask if I can play," they are much more likely to suggest aggressive strategies such as "take the game" or "punch them" (Asher & Renshaw, 1981). When asked how they would initiate a social interaction, isolated children cannot form a strategy. Their lack of social sophistication has prompted efforts to teach these children how to be more sociable.

A film depicting preschoolers interacting with other children was used to teach isolates social skills. For several weeks after the film, the children who saw the film were more successful in their interactions with other children

(Asher & Renshaw, 1981). Aggressive behavior in preschoolers has also been modified by simple verbal instruction from the teacher to the child (Zahavi & Asher, 1978). These studies have established that certain social skills can be taught and that a child's aggressive social behavior can be modified. However, they do not tell us whether these modifications make the child more popular.

Sherri Oden and Steven Asher (1977) addressed this issue by coaching third and fourth graders in how to be friends. They taught the children how to participate, cooperate, communicate, and how to be supportive. The children in the coaching condition began to be accepted by their peers, and one year later they were still gaining in peer acceptance (see Figure 13–4). Children who received no coaching were still perceived as isolates.

Isolates who lack social skills can be taught some of these skills (Ladd, 1981). In coaching sessions, children are taught to monitor their social behavior. Many isolates are not aware of the impression they create. This is illustrated by one girl's surprised statement during a coaching session, "You mean what I do affects whether kids like me or not?" (Asher & Renshaw, 1981, p. 289). Once this cognitive awareness is established, children can successfully monitor their own social behavior.

Not all of the attempts to help isolates have been successful. John Gottman (1983) argues that we don't know enough about how children make friends to intervene appropriately. We do know that how children make friends depends

**Figure 13—4**          **Changing friendship groups**

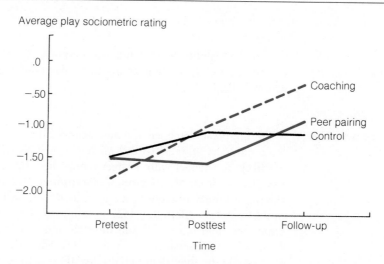

Children who were initially identified as isolated were coached on how to be friends. They made steady progress in social skills over the course of a year. Repeated socio-grams show that these children gradually became more accepted by their peers.

Source: Oden, S., & Asher, S. R. (1977). Coaching children in social skills for friendship making. *Child Development, 48,* 495–506.

## MAINSTREAMING

One of the principal arguments advanced for mainstreaming is that both retarded children and nonretarded children can benefit from social contact with each other. The contact hypothesis argues that mainstreaming retarded children into regular classrooms will increase understanding and acceptance of these children by their peers.

This hypothesis has not received much support. Normal children have not been very accepting of retarded children who are placed in their classrooms. If given a choice, they always select other normal children as partners. Perhaps this is not too surprising because normal children will have more in common with other normal children. Another result suggests that mainstreaming does not enhance the social acceptance of the mentally retarded child. The normal boys actually rejected the retarded children who were mainstreamed more often than retarded children who were segregated in their own classes.

In subsequent studies, these results have been repeated. Retarded children who are main-

streamed are given lower social status ratings than retarded children who were segregated in their own classrooms. It seems that greater contact between retarded and normal children does not increase the social acceptance of the retarded child. Actually, the reverse has been true.

In attempting to explain these results, Jay Gottlieb has suggested that retarded children misbehave in the classroom and are rejected because of their conduct. When retarded children were perceived as competent and did not disrupt the classroom, they were more likely to be accepted. He concludes that contact between normal and retarded children will not, by itself, produce attitude changes. If the normal children are going to accept the retarded children, the retarded children must behave appropriately. Hence, he suggests that mainstreaming of any child be delayed until any unusual behaviors have been changed into more acceptable behaviors.

Adapted from Gottlieb, J., & Leyser, Y. (1981). Friendship between mentally retarded and nonretarded children. In S. R. Asher & J. M. Gottman (Eds.), *The development of children's friendships*. New York: Cambridge University Press.

on (*a*) their ability to exchange information, (*b*) their skill in establishing a common ground, (*c*) their ability to resolve conflicts, and (*d*) their communication skills.

**Adolescents and their peers**

During preadolescence and adolescence, the peer group expands to include large numbers of peers. Although boys and girls still have a best friend, they are likely to interact with a larger group, like the cross-country runners, or to have friends from several groups—the runners, the drama club, and the band. Friendship lines in adolescence become drawn on the basis of similarities and mutual interests (Berndt, 1982). Friends are the same age, the same sex, the same race, and have common interests and activities. Having a friend means more to an adolescent than having a playmate means to a preschooler. Friends are confidants; they demand loyalty; they require support during periods of personal difficulty. Such interpersonal commitment is not part of toddlers' or preschoolers' friendships.

It is hard to know whether two people become friends because they have similar interests or whether they are neighbors or classmates and consequently become more similar over time. Unfortunately, few longitudinal studies have examined this question. In one study, Denise Kandel (1978) tested children in the fall and spring of the school year. She was interested in three groups— friendships that were maintained throughout the school year, friendships that had been severed, and new friendships that were formed during the school year.

When friendships did not last, Kandel found that the two students did not share the same educational goals or aspirations at the beginning of the year. Students who became friends during the year shared similar goals, interests, and even political orientations. Friends that remained close all year were even more similar in their attitudes at the end of the year than they were at the beginning of the year (Kandel, 1978).

This brief description of the changing nature of peer interaction provides a foundation for the study of several areas of social development, including interpersonal skills, moral development, and prosocial behavior. In these areas, the social influence of peers meshes with the child's cognitive skills and life experiences to fuel development.

## INTERPERSONAL DEVELOPMENT

Robert Selman (1981) began his research on interpersonal development by noting the changes in the way children perceive friends. Since then, he has woven the various phases of friendship or interpersonal interaction into a model of social-cognitive development. His model links the different ways children view friends with changes in the child's cognitive processes. In Selman's view, the cognitive skill needed for interpersonal development is the ability to understand the other person's perspective. As this skill develops, so does the child's concept of friendship.

We have discussed the fact that infants consider other children as objects. Although toddlers and preschoolers recognize that other children are not objects, their ideas of friendship are rooted in convenience. For toddlers and preschoolers, a person is a friend because they live near you, or they have nice toys to play with, or they play with you. At this age, awareness of the other child's thoughts and feelings is not part of the friendship. Robert Selman calls this Level 0. At this level, children really do not select friends, and they have only rudimentary understandings of another person's thoughts and feelings.

At Level 1, children approximately four to nine years old see friendships as one-way streets. Children understand that other children have different opinions, but their own desires and views dominate their behavior. For these children, a friend is a person who does what you want; the friend's feelings are not very important. Friendships are formed and ended quickly and easily because friendships are not perceived as long-term associations. Matthew, age five, exemplifies this level when he answers that Larry is his best friend, "Cause he plays with me a lot" (Damon, 1977, p. 154).

Level 2 occurs between the ages of 6 and 12. At this level, reciprocity between friends becomes important. Friendship is now subjective, and playing with a person does not automatically establish a friendship. Friends demonstrate that they are trustworthy through specific acts of kindness. When Betty, a 10-year-old, was asked why she liked Karen, she replied, "Because she's nice, she gives me jewelry and candy, and I give her things too" (Damon, 1977, p. 158). At Level 2, children are able to evaluate their own feelings and those of their friend. As a result, school-age children often compare, cooperate, and compromise to maintain their friendships.

Mutual concern is evident in friendships at Level 3 (about 9 to 15 years of age). Friendships are now bonds built over time, and friends become psychological comrades as well as playmates. A friend is someone who can be counted on to help when one feels sad, lonely, or anxious. Jack, age 13, describes this new component of friendship when he says, "You need someone you can tell anything to, all kinds of things that you don't want spread around" (Damon, 1977, p. 163). To Selman, this new level of awareness is made possible by the child's ability to think about relationships with other children.

The relationships of older adolescents and adults, Level 4, demand a more sophisticated view of interpersonal relationships. At this level, people are less

**Figure 13–5**                    **Social development in an abused child**

When first admitted to the school at age 14, Tommy, who had a history of severe social deprivation and abuse, frequently hid under his desk out of fear of teachers and peers. Gradually, however, he began to form a close tie to his teacher; this tie was based, however, almost entirely on a one-sided "you-give-I-take" interaction, characteristic of Level-1 understanding of the nature of friendships. By the end of his second year, Tommy formed his first real peer relationship.

Rather than being based on what is usually the source of an adolescent friendship—sharing feelings and establishing a common bond of trust (Level 3)—Tommy's relationship was based on playing and sharing toy trucks with a younger child in his class. This relationship also exemplified a Level-1 notion of friendship. In his occasional attempts to make new friends, Tommy would approach the target child with a toy to share or would go up to other children and try arbitrarily to join in their play. If the other did not respond in kind, Tommy would become upset and leave, not

realizing the effect of his own inadequate social strategies. The occasional child who attempted to form and maintain a friendship with Tommy in a more age-appropriate way—by more mutual sharing of ideas, feelings, or activities, for example—was not responded to, was rebuffed, and would give up the effort.

Tommy's behavior illustrates the one-way level-1 notions of friendship. When children who demonstrated a higher-level understanding of making friends approached him, Tommy was not able to respond in kind, and his low-level social approaches were rejected by same-age peers. Hence no relationships were formed.

Our description of interpersonal development helps us place Tommy's behavior along a developmental continuum. It leads us to look at Tommy's social interaction strategies and to see him not simply as overly angry, hostile, or unfriendly, but as a child whose way of making friends is developmentally lagging behind that of his peers.

Adapted from Selman, R. L. (1981). The child as a friendship philosopher. In S. R. Asher & J. M. Gottman (Eds.), *The development of children's friendships*. New York: Cambridge University Press.

likely to maintain exclusive relationships. They recognize that relationships have a variety of forms including acquaintances, colleagues, social friends, and intimate friends.

Selman's model is a description that links the cognitive realm and the social realm, and it is a description that can be used to follow a child's social development (Gurucharri & Selman, 1982). The case of Tommy (see Figure 13–5) suggests how this model might be used to understand interpersonal growth.

To Selman, the different phases of friendships are coordinated with the child's ability to understand and relate to different points of view. As children move from preschool to adolescence they first acknowledge, then consider, then evaluate other people's perspectives.

Interpersonal development does not depend on cognitive development or social experiences, but the interdependence of these two variables. Once psychologists recognized the interdependence of social experiences and cognitive skills, they asked if these same variables were linked in other areas of development. Psychologists found that children often conceptualize and reconceptualize their experiences in the social world. This realization gave rise to the area of inquiry called social cognition (Shantz, 1983). Interpersonal development is one area where social cognition is important; moral development is another.

## MORALITY

As children develop an awareness of their friends' thoughts and feelings, they begin to see conflicts. Childhood conflicts arise from the different desires of two friends. Adult conflicts take more varied forms. These conflicts set the stage for moral development.

The moral dilemma Sir Thomas More faced is often cited as an example of a man's personal views conflicting with society's. As King Henry VIII's Lord Chancellor, Thomas More held the highest judicial office in England and was highly regarded as a statesman and scholar. When the king wanted to divorce his first wife to marry Anne Boleyn, Thomas More objected. In the ensuing quarrel, More resigned from his post. The king proceeded to replace the Roman Catholic Church with the Church of England and named himself as head of the new church. Thomas More refused to swear allegiance to the new church or to the king as its leader. He was tried for treason and beheaded (Scarisbrick, 1970).

Moral decisions like Thomas More's consist of four components: (*a*) interpreting the situation, (*b*) comparing opposing views of the situation, (*c*) making a decision about a course of action, and (*d*) carrying out that action (Rest, 1983). Initially, More had to consider the meaning of King Henry's actions and the consequences. As part of the second component, More had to evaluate the views of the Pope, the king, and the queen. More arrived at his decision to defy the Crown after he considered his family, his country, and the personal danger involved. Carrying out his decision and enduring the infamous Tower of London required inner strength as well as certainty about his course of action. The question for psychologists, then, is how does this morality develop?

**The development of
morality**

An adult's moral beliefs are the result of cognitive development and years of experience with peers. The cognitive aspect of morality is clear from the earliest years. Just interpreting the flow of events in the world requires considerable cognitive sophistication. When six-year-olds are asked to describe what happened during a short film, they describe the movements of the characters and report the events they observed. They seldom make inferences about the character's feelings or intentions (Shantz, 1983). In one instance, a six-year-old used great detail to describe a fence that appeared in the film and to tell who climbed it. His recall was accurate, but the fence was not relevant to the central theme of the film (Flapan, 1968). The boy had not acquired the cognitive skills to abstract the main points of the film.

Andrew Collins and his colleagues report similar results when children watch television programs. Seven-year-olds often misunderstand the motives of characters and miss relevant cues. They also have trouble integrating information from various parts of the show (Collins, Wellman, Keniston, & Westby, 1978). It is safe to conclude from these studies that young children miss some of the complexity of most moral dilemmas and ignore the less direct ramifications. A second conclusion is that mature moral decisions depend on a certain level of cognitive development. Until children can interpret the events surrounding a conflict, their reasoning about the conflict is likely to remain superficial. Young children have to learn to interpret, code, and process events before they can evaluate them.

The cognitive foundation of moral judgment is obvious from these examples. We need to examine the role of peers, too. For this, we turn to Piaget. Prior to Piaget, psychologists believed that values and a sense of justice were passed directly from the parents to the child. Piaget introduced a different perspective. He suggested that peers, not parents, were the important agents in transmitting the norms of society. Piaget believed that adults were usually so overbearing about moral teachings that they lost their effectiveness with children. In a group of peers, children have to cooperate in order to continue playing. This cooperation provides a foundation for moral reasoning.

Some of Piaget's views developed as he watched children in Geneva playing marbles. The rules of the game—the shape of the ring, how many marbles were initially put in the ring, who took the first turn—were initially regarded as "sacred and untouchable, emanating from adults and lasting forever" (Piaget, 1948, p. 18). As children played more often, they realized they could alter the rules and put 15 marbles in the ring instead of 5. The only condition was that everyone had to agree to the rules before the game began (see Figure 13–6).

Rules, then, evolve from peer interaction. By 10 or 12 years of age, children are no longer constrained by their parents' rules for play. Because no authority exists, the children learn to negotiate and coordinate plans, to settle disagreements, and to make and enforce rules and promises. These experiences teach children that social rules can be used to coordinate social activities. By cooperating, children learn that they can attain goals that would otherwise be unattainable. They also learn to consider the perspective of others (Rest, 1983).

**Figure 13—6**          **The rules of the game**

*Bruce Kliewe: Jeroboam*

Children initially think the game of marbles has an absolute set of rules. After playing for a while, they understand that they can modify the rules. From such games, children learn that rules evolve from peer interaction.

Although Piaget believed that peers were the critical social agents for the development of moral judgments, he gave equal importance to reasoning. In his classic volume *The Moral Judgment of the Child,* he focused attention on the cognitive processes that must accompany moral development. Young children conform to social norms determined by their parents. Right and wrong are only understood in terms of the parents' definitions. Further, parents are the ultimate source of justice. Piaget calls this the *morality of constraint* because morality is imposed by some external agent. As children's understanding of the social world changes, so does their understanding of morality. Junior high students consider the justice of a decision and its fairness to all individuals. Piaget calls this the *morality of cooperation.*

As always, Piaget provides interviews with children to support his views. Before the interview begins, the children might listen to the following story:

> There was a little boy called Julian. His father had gone out and Julian thought it would be fun to play with his father's ink pot. First he played with the pen, and then he made a little blot on the table cloth.
>
> A little boy who was called Augustus once noticed that his father's ink pot was empty. One day that his father was away he thought of filling the ink pot so as to help his father, and so that he should find it full when he came home. But while he was opening the ink bottle, he made a big blot on the table cloth. (Piaget, 1948, p. 118)

When the interview begins Const, who is seven, repeats both stories correctly. When asked which boy is naughtier Const replies, the one who made the big blot. When asked why, he answers, "Because it was big."

Nuss, a 10-year-old, sees the issue differently. The naughtiest is "the one who made the little stain, because the other one wanted to help" (Piaget, 1948, p. 126).

Answers like Const's that focus on the amount of ink spilled are, in Piaget's view, indicative of the morality of constraint. Const knows that spilling the ink is wrong, and his cognitive skills make no allowances for extenuating circumstances. Nuss's view considers what is just. According to Nuss, it is not fair to punish a child who is trying to be helpful and cooperative. Nuss's views reflect the morality of cooperation.

Piaget's interviews with children added force to his suggestion that morality is rooted in a child's understanding of the social world. But his interviews with children were not acceptable as scientific data (Rest, 1983). An alternate scheme was proposed by Lawrence Kohlberg.

Lawrence Kohlberg (1958) pursued the notion that children's reasoning about moral dilemmas changed during development. In his dissertation, Kohlberg presented short stories to boys who were 10 to 16 years of age. In each story, the main character faced a moral conflict (see Figure 13–7). Students listened to these stories and were asked questions about the dilemma. In the Heinz dilemma, they are asked about stealing an expensive drug to save a life. The boys' responses to this question fell into three categories or levels—*preconventional reasoning, conventional reasoning, and postconventional reasoning.* In the first level, children decide whether or not stealing is right based on authority figures and the possibility of punishment. A 10-year-old's answer in the following interview is typical of this level.

**Interviewer:** Why shouldn't you steal from a store?

**Subject:** It's not good to steal from the store. It's against the law. Someone could see you and call the police. (Kohlberg, 1976, p. 36)

The reasoning used by this student is preconventional. It revolves around the child's own interests or those of other isolated individuals. The needs of society are not considered. The same subject, seven years later, has an entirely different response to the question. In his new answer, society's needs have become the most important aspect of his reasoning.

**Interviewer:** Why shouldn't you steal from a store?

**Subject:** It's a matter of law. It is one of our rules that we are trying to help protect everyone, protect property, not just to protect a store. It's something that's needed in our society. If we didn't have these laws, people would steal, they wouldn't have to work for a living, and our whole society would get out of kilter. (Kohlberg, 1976, p. 36)

This reasoning is typical of the conventional stage. The subject is concerned about the good of society as a whole. He is no longer an isolated individual trying to avoid trouble, but a member of a larger group—society.

**Figure 13–7**                    **Heinz' moral dilemma**

In Europe, a woman was near death from a special kind of cancer. There was one drug that the doctors thought might save her. It was a form of radium that a druggist in the same town had recently discovered. The drug was expensive to make, but the druggist was charging 10 times what the drug cost him to make. He paid $200 for the radium and charged $2,000 for a small dose of the drug. The sick woman's husband, Heinz, went to everyone he knew to borrow the money, but he could only get together about $1,000, which is half of what it cost. He told the druggist that his wife was dying and asked him to sell it cheaper or let him pay later. But the druggist said, "No, I discovered the drug and I'm going to make money from it." So Heinz gets desperate and considers breaking into the man's store to steal the drug for his wife.

1.   Should Heinz steal the drug?
1a.  Why or why not?
2.   If Heinz doesn't love his wife, should he steal the drug for her?
2a.  Why or why not?
3.   Suppose the person dying is not his wife but a stranger. Should Heinz steal the drug for the stranger?
3a.  Why or why not?
4.   (If you favor stealing the drug for a stranger.) Suppose it's a pet animal he loves. Should Heinz steal to save the pet animal?
4a.  Why or why not?
5.   Is it important for people to do everything they can to save another's life?
5a.  Why or why not?
6.   It is against the law for Heinz to steal. Does that make it morally wrong?
6a.  Why or why not?
7.   Should people try to do everything they can to obey the law?
7a.  Why or why not?
7b.  How does this apply to what Heinz should do?

The Heinz story is used to probe a person's thoughts about a moral conflict.

Source: Colby, A., Kohlberg, L., Gibbs, J., & Lieberman, M. (1983). A longitudinal study of moral judgment. *Monographs of the Society for Research in Child Development, 48,* No. 200, p. 77.

At 24 years of age, the same subject has yet another approach to the question about stealing.

**Interviewer:** Why shouldn't someone steal from a store?

**Subject:** It's violating another person's rights, in this case to property.

**Interviewer:** Does the law enter in?

**Subject:** Well, the law in most cases is based on what is morally right so it's not a separate subject, it's a consideration.

**Interviewer:** What does "morality" or "morally right" mean to you?

**Subject:** Recognizing the right of other individuals, first to life and then to do as he pleases as long as it doesn't interfere with somebody else's rights. (Kohlberg, 1976, pp. 36–37)

This response reflects postconventional moral reasoning. Now the person's commitment to society is based on the moral issues involved, and laws are simply society's attempt to institutionalize this morality. Stealing is wrong because it violates the rights of individuals, which are more important than laws and society.

Kohlberg and his colleagues have argued that the developmental sequence from preconventional to conventional to postconventional reasoning is invariant. In other words, one stage of moral reasoning must precede the next. Also, the earlier stages of moral reasoning are essential to the acquisition of the most advanced stages. A number of longitudinal studies have been conducted to test this stage model of moral reasoning. The most impressive is a 20-year longitudinal study of the boys originally interviewed by Kohlberg for his dissertation (Colby, Kohlberg, Gibbs, & Lieberman, 1983). These men, who have been interviewed repeatedly over 20 years, seldom deviated from the sequence of stages that Kohlberg proposed. At age 10, about 80 percent of the subjects used preconventional reasoning. By age 16, 80 percent had switched to conventional reasoning. Postconventional reasoning did not appear until 24 years of age (Colby et al., 1983). In the 20-year follow-up, not one of the men reached a new stage in the sequence without going through each preceding stage (Colby, et al., 1983). Their findings provide strong support for the stage model. They also demonstrate that changes in moral reasoning occur slowly (Nisan & Kohlberg, 1982). Many of the men participating in Kohlberg's study showed no changes between testing sessions that were four years apart. In fact, adults who were not attending college remained at the same stage regardless of the interval between tests (Rest, 1983).

Kohlberg's and Piaget's views of moral reasoning are similar in several ways. Both described changes in the child's moral reasoning. Both believed that cognitive skills mediated the development of moral reasoning. Both attributed some of the change in moral reasoning to peer interaction. Interacting with peers fosters a willingness to cooperate, and cooperation is basic to all social systems. Peer interaction also builds feelings of equality and reinforces the view that everyone is entitled to a common set of legitimate rights. Finally, the give-and-take among peers forces young people to take the role of the other.

The power of role taking has been shown in several studies which have brought peers together to discuss controversial topics. In weekly sessions, students discussed a topic chosen from the newspaper, such as abortion or capital punishment. The discussions were heated and brought out many perspectives. After a series of these discussions, the participants reasoned at a higher level when confronted with moral dilemmas (Blatt & Kohlberg, 1975). Students who have leadership positions in clubs are also required to deal with many points of view. It is not surprising that these students also use higher levels of moral reasoning (Keasey, 1971). Both of these studies suggest that opportunities to interact with peers and see several points of view will ultimately alter a person's approach to moral dilemmas.

There are other factors that influence moral development in children. Parents are heavily invested in transmitting values about the culture. Formal schooling is also correlated with moral reasoning. Actually, education is the best predictor of an individual's level of moral reasoning and is a better predictor than age (Colby et al., 1983). This was demonstrated by Rest (1979a) who compared medical students with practicing physicians, college students with adults having a college education, and high school students with adults having only a high school education. In spite of the large age differences within each group, groups with comparable educations gave similar reasons for their moral judgments.

## Evaluation of Kohlberg's theory

Kohlberg's view of moral development has spawned hundreds of studies on morality. From this point of view, his theory is one of the most successful in developmental psychology. However, his views have also encountered serious criticism.

The interview which is the heart of Kohlberg's theory provides a wealth of information. However, it is not standardized—not everyone is asked the same questions—and the scoring is not entirely objective. Although many psychologists defend the interview as necessary to probe an individual's reasoning (Damon, 1977), others have argued that the procedure is unscientific and subjective (Brainerd, 1978). In response to these objections, psychologists have tried to standardize the assessments and the scoring of morality (Colby et al., 1983; Gibbs, Widaman, & Colby, 1982). James Rest (1979b) has devised a standardized procedure—*the Defining Issues Test*—to measure moral judgment. The Defining Issues Test asks students to consider many of the same moral dilemmas as Kohlberg's test, but it has a multiple choice format for answers. The administration of the test is entirely standardized as is the scoring. While this procedure also has drawbacks, using both the Defining Issues Test and the Moral Judgment Interview provides two valuable and overlapping perspectives about the development of moral reasoning.

Both ways of assessing moral development find systematic changes with age. Students taking the Defining Issues Test are likely to achieve somewhat higher moral judgment scores than students responding to a Kohlberg interview. The multiple choice format may allow them to recognize an explanation that they would not be able to produce in an interview.

A final criticism of the moral judgment literature is that it deters us from the real question, which is how to facilitate the development of moral behavior. The reasoning used during moral interviews may not be related to a person's actual behavior in a conflict. This criticism raises another question—What is the relationship between moral reasoning and moral behavior?

## The relationship between moral reasoning and moral behavior

Kohlberg's theory of moral development concentrates on the change in moral reasoning from childhood to adulthood, but it ignores the person's behavior. To see if moral reasoning predicts a person's behavior in an actual moral dilemma, psychologists must evaluate people who have taken a stand on a moral issue (Blasi, 1980). To this end, Peace Corps volunteers, civil rights protesters, delinquents, students who cheat, and Good Samaritans have been given the Defining Issues Test or a Moral Judgment Interview. Typically, the adult's ability to reason about a situation is related to moral behavior (Blasi, 1980). The relationship is not always strong, and other factors are important (Emler, Renwick, & Malone, 1983). Nevertheless, Peace Corps volunteers and Good Samaritans are likely to use postconventional reasoning. Delinquents and students who cheat are likely to use preconventional reasoning.

If moral reasoning and moral behavior are not perfectly correlated, we must ask what factors determine whether people will act according to their convictions. At least three factors have been suggested. First, adults must be convinced of the righteousness of a position. Perry London (1970) and his colleagues interviewed 27 Christians who made a decision to help persecuted Jews in Nazi Germany. Although many of these rescuers fell into their roles by chance, they persevered in their mission once they became involved. One rescuer initially agreed to help his secretary, whose husband was Jewish. This rescuer's compassion for one man turned into a four-year crusade during which 200 Jews were saved. This particular man continued his efforts despite great personal expense and considerable danger.

Second, London detected an adventurous spirit among the rescuers. The most blatant example was a civilian who rescued a Polish underground leader from jail. The rescuer walked into the jail and told the jailers he had secret verbal orders to take the man. The orders were too secret to be written and from too high a source to be questioned, implying that the orders came from Hitler. The jailer released the prisoner (London, 1970, p. 246). London suggests that this adventurous nature helped rescuers overcome the fear that might normally dissuade people from acting on their convictions.

Finally, the rescuers shared a strong identification with at least one of their parents. One man described his mother and her humanitarian values in detail; another pointed to his father's lifelong commitment to ending prejudice. This characteristic is consistent with psychological findings that nurturing adults who modeled concern for others had a decided effect on a child's altruism.

The morality of individuals in contemporary society is constantly questioned. In this section, we have reviewed the factors that contribute to morality. Moral judgments depend on a certain level of cognitive development, but high levels of cognitive development do not guarantee high levels of moral reasoning. The individual's social experiences and education are also part of the complex, but even these factors do not predict who will actually take a moral stance. Making the commitment to follow one's convictions seems to depend on chance encounters, the personality of the individual, and the person's models of moral behavior.

The literature on moral development and the moral dilemmas we have considered have been concerned primarily with rules, laws, authorities, and obligations. Nancy Eisenberg-Berg (1979) argues that these moral dilemmas are directed toward constraining negative behaviors—stealing, lying, and breaking laws. She feels that psychologists should be equally concerned with positive behaviors such as sharing, cooperation, altruism, and helping. Her views are shared by many contemporary developmental psychologists who are examining the acquisition of *prosocial* behaviors.

## PROSOCIAL BEHAVIOR

Do humans have a basic nature—one that is inherently good or evil? Writers like William Golding have portrayed positive social actions—sympathy, generosity, cooperation, and helpfulness—as a thin veneer, held tenuously in place by social norms. In his classic, *Lord of the Flies*, he describes the crumbling of prosocial behaviors when English schoolboys are stripped of this veneer. Anthropological observers have sometimes echoed this opinion. They point to the Ik, a mountain tribe in Uganda, as an actual example of Golding's scenario. When this tribe of hunters was driven from their hunting grounds, their society disintegrated into small ruthless bands concerned only with survival. Aggression, deceit, lying, stealing, and murder became the norm (Turnbull, 1972). To some, the Ik offered proof of the inherent evil of humans.

An account of the social interaction among members of the Hopi Indians provides a more positive assessment of the nature of humans. Cooperation is the mainstay of the tribe, and having a "Hopi good heart" means trusting and respecting others, being concerned for the whole group, and finding inner peace (Dennis, 1965).

When psychologists entered this argument, they pointed out that neither of these tribes could be used as examples of the basic nature of the human race. Instead, they argued that prosocial behavior, like most behavior, results from biological, psychological, economic, and historic events (Mussen & Eisenberg-Berg, 1977).

**The development of prosocial behavior**

Prosocial behavior is defined as positive action directed toward another person without any expectation of reward or reinforcement (Mussen & Eisenberg-Berg, 1977). Children as young as 14 months soothing a crying infant, preschoolers sharing their last piece of bubble gum with a friend, and adolescents taking time to tutor a classmate are examples of prosocial behavior.

To study prosocial behavior, psychologists headed initially to the laboratory where they devised a series of ingenious experiments to assess generosity, cooperation, and helping. In a typical experiment, children played a game, solved a puzzle, or performed a task for which they received a prize. The prizes were candy, money, or toys. After the game phase of the experiment, children were given the chance to donate some of their winnings to a less successful child or an orphan. The amount they donated was an index of their altruism.

Researchers then altered this basic design so that children observed an adult who generously donated their prizes or an adult who refused to donate. This variation assesses the importance of a role model for instilling prosocial behav-

**Prosocial behavior**

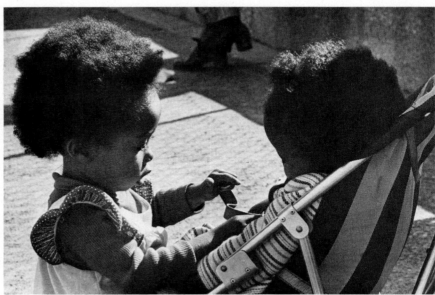

Brent Jones: Click/Chicago

If we observe toddlers carefully, we will see them caring for others, sharing with others, and trying to help.

iors. It is not surprising that observing models who generously donate their winnings increases a child's immediate donations. What is surprising is that watching a generous model still has an effect on altruism months after the experiment (Grusec, Kuczynski, Rushton, & Simutis, 1978).

Another variation of the basic prosocial experiment incorporates an adult who is warm and nurturing (Yarrow, Scott, & Waxler, 1973). The attempt in these experiments is to recreate in the laboratory the situation that exists in the home. In one of the most extensive experiments of this kind, an adult spent about five hours over a two-week period establishing herself as supportive and caring. With a second group of children she was not nurturant; she remained aloof, ignoring the children's requests and being distant and unhelpful.

After the pattern of interaction was established, some of the children saw the model actually help another woman who had banged her head. This additional condition created four groups of children. The first group had a nurturing model who helped others. The second group also had a nurturing model, but the children never saw her help anyone. The third and fourth groups had models who were distant and aloof. However, the third group saw their model help someone while the fourth group did not.

About two weeks after the first phase of this experiment, the children were individually taken to another home where they visited a mother and her baby.

Almost all of the children in the first group spontaneously offered to help the mother pick up spilled buttons or retrieve toys the baby had dropped. Children from the other three groups were less likely to help (Yarrow, et al., 1973). From studies like this, psychologists have concluded that in order to instill prosocial behaviors, parents have to be warm and caring, but they also have to live by the principles that they are teaching.

Other approaches to the study of prosocial behavior include asking children to respond to hypothetical stories or observing their behavior in natural settings. In one of the few longitudinal studies of toddlers' prosocial behaviors, mothers were trained to observe their own infants. The mothers provided detailed and objective accounts of how their children reacted to the distress of others and how those reactions changed over a nine-month period. Children who were not a year old watched curiously or responded with a frown when someone else was upset. On occasion, they burst out crying. By a year and a half, the child's agitation had subsided when someone else was distressed. Now the children tried to comfort the person by patting them or touching them. By two years of age, the children had developed a wide repertoire of behaviors that they used to comfort another person. They gave toys to a child who was suffering, made suggestions about how to help, offered sympathy, brought others to help, and in their own way, tried to make the person feel better (Radke-Yarrow, Zahn-Waxler, & Chapman, 1983).

These naturalistic studies provide convincing evidence that children exhibit prosocial behaviors long before they are three. The fact that they can respond compassionately does not necessarily mean that they will always respond compassionately. At this age, children are just as capable of ignoring or even taunting someone in distress. The important point is that the capacity for prosocial behavior is present in toddlers.

Among preschoolers, prosocial behaviors are even more common. During 100 days of observation, Lois Murphy (1937) observed preschoolers help teachers, help other children in distress, warn children of danger, protect and defend other children, and ask adults to assist a peer. Some of the children Murphy observed were never helpful, but she saw many instances of giving and caring.

Observational studies provide information about the frequency of prosocial behavior. However, they do not tell us what children are thinking when they assist other children. Nancy Eisenberg-Berg decided to ask. She and Cynthia Neal (1979) waited until a child shared a toy with a peer or comforted a child in distress. Then they asked, "Why did you do that?" The children never mentioned pressure from teachers or fear of punishment as a reason. Their answers were couched in prosocial terms: "I wanted to"; "He's my friend"; "She was hungry." As we will see in the section on aggression, preschoolers are not candidates for sainthood. Nevertheless, they are capable of cooperative, helpful, sensitive, and generous behavior in a variety of interpersonal situations.

Among school-age children, we might expect to see prosocial behavior become more differentiated and more complex. This expectation is not necessarily supported by the available research. Several investigators who have compared grade school and preschool children have found that the younger children were more cooperative and more generous (Radke-Yarrow et al., 1983). Older children, however, detect subtle cues that indicate another person's distress. They are also able to make deductions about what has happened and to abstract from that situation. But it is not clear that they help the child any more frequently than younger children.

Factors other than age determine whether or not a child will cooperate with peers, share with friends, or help others. In the past decade, psychologists have investigated personal, biological, familial, and cultural variables in an attempt to uncover the secrets of prosocial behavior.

## Factors that influence prosocial behavior

**Biological variables.** Sociobiologists have recently tried to revise the gloomy picture of human nature painted by early philosophers. These researchers point to a kind of altruism that occurs in many species. Birds and monkeys warn their neighbors of impending danger. The termite as well as the chimpanzee engage in cooperative behavior that benefits the species. Sociobiologists argue that among mammals, maternal behaviors, many of which are genetically controlled, provide examples of altruistic behavior because the mother puts the infant's welfare and safety first.

An extreme case of altruism occurs when one member of a species sacrifices its life for the others. For example, the honeybee often forfeits its life so that the queen bee and the hive will survive. Higher up the biological scale, we see mothers, fathers, aunts, and uncles who risk their lives to defend their young. Dian Fossey describes what happens to a troop of gorillas every time poachers capture a baby gorilla. Observing a captured infant, Fossey notes that it "had come from a group of about eight animals and . . . all the family members had died trying to defend the youngster" (Fossey, 1983, p. 112).

Sociobiologists emphasize the genetic factors that influence prosocial behavior. They point out that cooperation between members of a species increases survival. Hence, the genes of altruistic animals are passed to the offspring. Despite the evolutionary sense of this position, it is currently impossible to separate genetic factors from familial and cultural influences that affect humans. As critics of the sociobiological stance point out, human behavior is more complex than the behavior of honeybees and incorporates more environmental determinants, such as family factors, cultural influences, and personal variables.

**Family factors.** As we have already seen, warm, nurturing parents who model cooperation and generosity have been found to have children who are helpful, generous, and cooperative. It is tempting to conclude that nurturing parents automatically instill prosocial behaviors in their children. Such a conclusion is an oversimplification. Parental nurturance, by itself, does not always predict prosocial behavior. Loving parents who seldom discipline their children, or do not communicate well, or do not model prosocial behavior may find that their children lack prosocial skills. A more accurate conclusion is that nurturance is one of the child-rearing techniques related to prosocial behavior (Radke-Yarrow et al., 1983). These techniques include the parents' disciplinary methods and their expectations.

Parents use a host of techniques to discipline their children. Some parents assert their power through physical punishments, withholding privileges, or threatening the child. Other parents withdraw their love and ignore their children. Still another technique involves reasoning with the child. Parents using this method explain to their children how their actions affect others.

Of these three techniques, reasoning with the child is thought to elicit the most prosocial behavior. According to Martin Hoffman (1970), parents who reason with a child bring out the child's empathetic feelings, while parents who assert their power are likely to arouse fear and anger. When power-assertion techniques are used, control and responsibility remain with the parent. The child does not internalize any altruistic attitudes.

Hoffman's views have generally been supported. From preschool through grade school, boys and girls are likely to share more, be more generous, and come to other children's aid if the reasons for such behavior have been explained (Mussen & Eisenberg-Berg, 1977). In contrast, parents who assert their power are likely to heighten a child's hostility and decrease prosocial behavior (Dlugokinski & Firestone, 1974).

These disciplinary techniques are only one part of a larger picture. There are parents who assert their power about some issues, but do it within a broader atmosphere of love and respect for the child (Henry, 1980). Zahn-Waxler and her associates give the example of the mother who reprimands her child by saying, "Don't you see you hurt Amy—don't ever pull hair!" Such harsh messages also include an explanation. This combination of techniques is likely to foster prosocial behavior (Zahn-Waxler, Radke-Yarrow, & King, 1979). The authoritative parents described by Diana Baumrind are a good example of parents who control their children and assert their power on occasion, but communicate the reasons for their decisions and surround the child with love.

The parents' expectations also impart important lessons about cooperation and generosity. As children mature, they are often asked to assume some responsibilities within the family. Simple tasks like emptying the garbage, feeding pets, and setting the table give the young child a sense of the cooperation that is necessary in a home. Children who assume these responsibilities are likely to share with others and be cooperative (Staub & Jancaterino, 1975). This finding is reinforced by studies showing that children reared in extended families and rural environments are altruistic. In both of these situations, everyone has responsibilities from an early age.

The atmosphere provided by parents is a critical factor in the development of prosocial behavior in children. But describing that atmosphere scientifically has proved difficult. Nurturance and reasoning are two important ingredients, but these mingle with techniques for control and the parents' ability to communicate. Loving parents who live by the golden rule are imitated by their children. If parents combine their nurturance with explanations that reinforce prosocial behavior, the children are likely to be generous, supportive, and caring. Forced obedience is less likely to encourage prosocial behavior. Less extreme control techniques like expecting mature behavior and assigning responsibility are likely to stimulate the child to behave in a caring way.

**Cultural influences.**   The influence of culture on prosocial behavior must not be overlooked. Evidence from the Ik and the Hopi show that cultural influences can interact with family patterns and override family interactions. Cooperation is a hallmark of some cultures, and this belief is passed to the children. Other cultures emphasize the competitive nature of life and pass along the subtle message that children should look out for themselves.

At UCLA, Millard Madsen has devised an experimental procedure to assess the cooperative spirit of children. In a board game played by four children, any child can prevent another from winning. But if the children cooperate, they can all win. Children reared in rural environments are usually eager to cooperate, saying, "You go first, then I'll go, then he'll go," and so on. Children reared in urban environments are more suspicious of the other children and often refuse to cooperate. The differences between rural and urban children are evident in all of the cultures tested (Madsen & Shapira, 1977).

The differences between cultures are equally interesting (see Figure 13–8). Mexican and Israeli children are more likely to cooperate than American children, prompting researchers to suggest that the Mexican and Israeli cultures strongly value a cooperative attitude. This is certainly true in the Israeli Kibbutz. Children are initiated into communal living early in life, and cooperation is a central tenet of the culture (Spiro, 1963).

The cultural push for cooperation is not always as obvious as it is in Israel. In Mexico, subtle cultural values encourage altruism. The female role is highly regarded, and women make major contributions to the economy. Extended families that place a priority on cooperation are also common. Finally, children growing up in these cultures are expected to take responsibility for tasks that have an economic impact on the family (Whiting & Whiting, 1975).

**Personal variables.**   Any discussion of prosocial behavior must include a description of individual variables. Sex and intelligence may affect whether individual children will share, cooperate, or help. It was a surprise when investigators reported few sex differences in cooperation, offering comfort, sharing, and helping behaviors (Radke-Yarrow et al., 1983). Girls do tend to be more empathetic than boys and often express more sympathy when someone is distressed. However, when actually confronted with a crying infant, boys as well as girls express concern and try to help (Zahn-Waxler, Friedman, & Cummings, 1983).

We might suspect that children with a high level of intelligence would also exhibit high levels of prosocial behavior. This is not the case. High levels of intelligence help children think about a variety of ways to cooperate or help. However, children with an average level of intelligence are just as eager and

**Figure 13—8**      **Cultural differences in prosocial behavior**

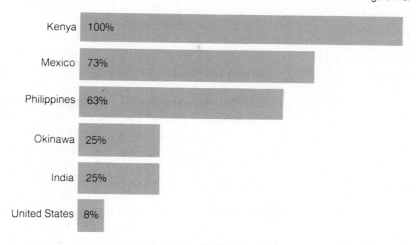

Percent of children from six cultures who were more altruistic than the average child.

When compared with children from five other cultures, children from the United States are not very altruistic. Fewer than 10 percent were more altruistic than the average. In Kenya, all of the children were more altruistic than the average child.

Source: Radke-Yarrow, M., Zahn-Waxler, C., & Chapman, M. (1983). Children's prosocial dispositions and behavior. In E. M. Hetherington (Ed.), *Handbook of Child Psychology* (Vol. 4). New York: John Wiley & Sons.

willing to help. Hence, intelligence is not considered a very important factor in prosocial behavior (Radke-Yarrow et al., 1983).

The answer to the question, "What factors influence prosocial behavior?" is in some ways a surprise. Many of the standard personal variables like age, sex, and intelligence do not have a marked effect on the child's prosocial behavior. The family environment and the cultural setting appear to be more important determinants of whether a child expresses concern for others.

## AGGRESSION

Aggressive behavior is the antithesis of prosocial behavior. Aggressive children, rather than contributing to the family or the school or sharing and cooperating with their peers, are a disruptive, negative force. Aggressive, violent adults tear at the very fabric of a democratic society. In the nuclear age, aggressive cultures have the means to annihilate life. Understanding the development of aggression is, therefore, a continuing concern of social scientists.

Several decades of research have shown that aggression is a complex behavior, and its biological roots can be altered, channeled, or encouraged by the family and the culture. Even defining aggression is not a simple task. A business executive who works with a single-mindedness and resolve is often labeled aggressive. A mother defending her young against predators is described as aggressive. A mass murderer is also labeled aggressive. In order to focus the discussion, psychologists usually limit their definition of aggression to behaviors aimed at harming another (Parke & Slaby, 1983).

**Biological bases of aggression**

Although the biological causes of aggression were ignored for many years, researchers now recognize that genetic, hormonal, and biochemical factors play a role in aggressive behavior (Simmel, Hahn, & Walters, 1983). Konrad Lorenz, a nobel prize-winning ethologist, was among the first to draw attention to biological factors in aggressive behavior (Lorenz, 1966). Lorenz showed that aggression helped species adapt and survive. For example, fighting for a territory preserves limited food supplies and spreads animals over a large area. Fighting for a mate assures that the strongest animals reproduce. Finally, fighting to protect the young insures the continuation of a species. As an ethologist, Lorenz focused on lower animals, and his book is sprinkled with anecdotes about aggressive behaviors in fish, geese, dogs, zebras, and baboons. Critics have argued that the same principles do not apply to humans. Lorenz admits that experience and learning play a much larger role in humans than in other animals. His primary point is that "aggression, far from being a diabolical, destructive principle . . . is really an essential part of the life-preserving organization of instincts" (Lorenz, 1966, p. 48).

**Genetic factors in aggression.**   By interbreeding strains of mice, we can produce aggressive mice (Hewitt & Broadhurst, 1983). But these mice only show aggressive behavior when other environmental and biochemical cues are present (Lagerspetz & Lagerspetz, 1983). These studies substantiate Lorenz's view that the genetic potential for aggression is part of our biological makeup. They also demonstrate that this potential is not automatically transformed into actual instances of aggression. Hormonal fluctuations, biochemical changes in the brain, family factors, and cultural demands all determine whether the potential for aggressive behavior is expressed.

**Hormonal influences on aggression.**   Psychologists have amassed convincing evidence that hormones organize and energize aggression (Tieger, 1980). In animals whose hormone levels can be manipulated, young females who are exposed to male hormones exhibit more masculine behavior and more aggression throughout their lives (Svare, 1983). Likewise, males who do not receive the standard dose of androgens engage in less fighting behavior as adults. Their central nervous system is less sensitive to situations that stimulate their male peers to aggression.

In humans, we must depend on accidents of nature to decide if male hormones organize the brain differently. June Reinisch (1981) located a group of males and females whose mothers took male hormones during the first trimester of pregnancy. It is during this period that the male hormones organize the human brain. If these brief exposures to male hormones altered the organization of the brain, it should be apparent as the children develop.

Reinisch was able to assess the potential for aggression in 17 females and 8 males who had been exposed to hormones prenatally. She asked these children to react to six situations involving conflict. In one situation the children were told: "You're walking down the street. Some kid is mad at you and comes up and hits you. What do you do?" The children could respond by saying they would hit the other child, call the other child stupid, leave the scene, or tell an adult. Reinisch then gave the same test to their brothers and sisters. The children who were exposed to the male hormone were more likely than their siblings to think of physical aggression as a way of solving a conflict (see Figure 13–9). Their brief exposure to male hormones was more important than age or birth order in determining whether they gave aggressive responses to these questions.

In addition to organizing the brain, hormones can activate behavior. A sudden dose of *testosterone* stimulates aggressive behavior in animals. Levels of testosterone in the bloodstream are related to fighting behavior in male rats and rhesus monkeys. Even female primates become more aggressive if they receive injections of testosterone (Joslyn, 1973).

In humans, psychologists examined the activating role of high levels of hormones by studying prisoners with a history of violent crime. As often as not,

**Figure 13–9**                 **Hormonal effects on aggression**

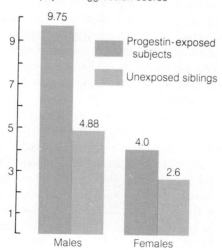

Mean physical aggression scores

Two groups of children were asked what they would do if confronted with several situations. The children who had been exposed to hormones *in utero* were more likely to suggest that physical aggression was an appropriate solution to the problem.

Source: Reinisch, J. M. (1981). Prenatal exposure to synthetic progestins increases potential for aggression in humans. *Science, 211,* 1171–1173.

though, these prisoners had no unusual hormonal profiles (Scott, 1983). What became apparent, however, was that the surge of hormones during adolescence may be related to some types of aggression. Sixteen-year-old boys with high levels of testosterone were more impatient and irritable than boys with lower levels (Olweus, Mattson, Schalling, & Low, 1980). These boys also relied more on physical and verbal aggression when they were threatened or provoked by other boys (Mattsson, Schalling, Olweus, Low, & Svensson, 1980).

It might be tempting to conclude that testosterone controls whether a male will attack when provoked. Observations of a troop of rhesus monkeys make it clear that such simple, one-way relationships between hormones and aggression are unlikely. Male rhesus monkeys are not very tolerant of strange males. When strange animals are introduced to the troop, the resident males are likely to band togther to challenge and attack the newcomer. Rather than fighting back, the attacked males become submissive. In the process, their level of circulating testosterone drops as much as 80 percent (Rose, Gordon, & Bernstein, 1972). When these monkeys were attacked, their hormonal levels decreased. These unexpected results suggest that the relationship between aggression and hormones is often indirect and not well understood.

Sex differences in aggression are thought to stem from the organizing and activating functions of hormones. Such differences appear early in life (Maccoby & Jacklin, 1980), continue through childhood, adolescence, and adulthood (Cairns, 1979), and exist in every culture that has been studied (Whiting & Whiting, 1975). On most indices, boys are more aggressive and are likely to retaliate aggressively (Whiting & Edwards, 1973). When two children are playing and one is a boy, the likelihood of an aggressive incident occurring is high. Two girls seldom erupt into aggressive squabbles (McGrew, 1972). Girls do express aggression, and some investigators report that girls are more verbally aggressive than boys (Feshbach, 1970). Overall, the expression of aggression in girls tends to be less frequent, more subtle, and more indirect than in boys (Brodzinsky, Messer, & Tew, 1979).

**Environmental factors that influence aggression**

Early studies of aggression in children were usually conducted in laboratories. In an oft-repeated experiment, children came to the laboratory and watched an adult or another child punch an inflated plastic doll. This "Bobo" doll would bounce back up each time it was knocked down. After watching others punch the Bobo doll, the children were taken to a playroom. Once in the playroom, these children engaged in more aggressive play than children who had not watched the Bobo doll being punched. The researchers concluded that children imitate aggressive behavior. Critics of these studies argued that children might not imitate aggression if they were studied in a more natural setting.

To answer these criticisms, Eron and his colleagues began a 20-year study of aggression under more natural conditions. Initially, they assessed aggression in 875 third-grade children. They also interviewed the parents to determine what kind of punishment was used in the home, how close the family was, and how the parents dealt with their child's aggression. They also coded the television programs the child liked. Ten years later, when the children were 19, the investigators conducted another set of interviews with 50 percent of the original subjects. In 1981 when the adults were 30 years old, they were interviewed a third time. Here are some of their intriguing findings.

First, they found that parental use of physical punishment was an important factor in aggression. Children who were rejected and punished harshly dealt with others the same way (Eron, 1982).

Second, they found that children, especially boys, who were aggressive at 9 years of age were still aggressive at 19. They were three times as likely to be arrested as their nonaggressive peers (Eron, Walder, Huesmann, & Lefkowitz, 1978). As a group, the aggressive boys reported that statements such as, "I feel like picking a fight or arguing with people" described them. Finally, they admitted to "ripping people off."

Third, these investigators found that viewing violent television in the third grade predicted aggression 10 and 20 years later. The effect of television on these boys was so pronounced that the authors concluded "a preference for watching violent television in the third-grade time period is a cause of aggressive habits later in life" (Eron et al., 1978, p. 233).

In their discussion of these results, Eron and others argue that the most important predictors of aggression are sociocultural events and the child's identification with the parents. Because aggression was so stable, the authors imply that aggressive behavior is not easily altered. These statements have been actively pursued by other psychologists.

**The stability of aggressive behavior.** The fact that aggressive males maintain their aggressive stance has now been documented in a host of long-term studies (Olweus, 1979). Boys rated as highly aggressive are likely to remain in that category. Unaggressive boys seldom become extremely aggressive. The strength of this relationship is demonstrated by the correlation between measures of aggression given at two different times. The correlations, ranging from .65 to 1.00 over a one-year interval, are almost as high as correlations between intelligence tests (Olweus, 1979). This pattern held whether aggression was determined by teachers' ratings or observational data.

Aggressiveness is also stable over longer time periods and does not disappear after adolescence. Dan Olweus (1982) suggests that aggression becomes part of a general antisocial behavior pattern as males reach adulthood. Adolescents who exhibited a variety of antisocial behaviors such as fighting, theft, alcohol abuse, and truancy continued to have serious antisocial tendencies throughout adulthood (Robins, 1978). Boys who were rebellious and hostile in junior high maintained that attitude as adults (Block, 1971). These longitudinal studies suggest that aggressive, antisocial behavior is a continuing component of some men's personality (Olweus, 1982).

Concluding that aggression is a somewhat stable trait does not mean that we can predict criminal violence or recidivism among violent prisoners. Children who are aggressive in school seldom become violent delinquents (Farrington, 1982). Factors other than a tendency toward aggressiveness are part of the profile of violent criminals.

Nor does the conclusion that aggression is a stable trait give special weight to biological factors. Aggressive individuals tend to select activities that allow them to express their aggressiveness (Kung Fu instead of cultivating a garden). Once boys have selected a Kung Fu class, they are likely to share experiences and become friends with a particular set of peers who maintain an interest in aggressive activities (Bullock & Merrill, 1980). Patterns of family interaction can also sustain aggression. These patterns begin very early in life.

**The family.** Aggression begins at home. Between 84 and 97 percent of all parents use physical punishment (Parke & Slaby, 1983). Even when parents do not believe in spankings, most children can watch their siblings or their parents fight (Straus, Gelles, & Steinmetz, 1980). As children develop, they observe and model the aggressive tactics that their siblings and parents use to solve problems.

Family interaction patterns may be a factor in long-term aggressive behavior (McCord, 1979). Joan McCord identified three facets of the family that predicted criminal behavior 30 years later: (1) When they were children, the criminals had not had much parental supervision; (2) the parents were in constant conflict; (3) the mother was not affectionate. Dan Olweus also found that aggressive boys had mothers who rejected them or were indifferent. This cool relationship was obvious during the first four or five years of life and was especially likely to foment aggressiveness in "hot-headed" boys (Olweus, 1980).

It is easy to say that both the child and the family contribute to aggressive behavior, but how, exactly, is such aggression maintained? Gerald Patterson (1982) and his colleagues at the Social Learning Center in Oregon have tried to determine what happens in families of aggressive children. In their studies, psychologists visit the home and observe the family. All members of the family must be present and must be in one of two rooms designated by the observers. During the observation period, the family cannot make phone calls, cannot watch television, and can have no guests. Under these circumstances, the members of the family are forced to talk with each other, and the interaction can be revealing.

Patterson believes that aggressive behavior in the child is fostered by ineffective parenting skills. The parents cannot discipline the child. Part of their ineffectiveness is due to the child's temperament. Aggressive children respond to punishment by becoming even more aggressive. The parents then vacillate in their punishment or give in to the child. On different occasions, the parents try disapproval, nagging, and scolding. None of these techniques work. As the vicious cycle continues, the parents begin to ignore positive behaviors and focus on the fights the child starts (Patterson, 1982). In an effort to establish their authority and to gain control over the explosive outbursts of the child, the parents become very punitive or stop trying to control the child (see Figure 13–10).

**Figure 13—10**                    **The aggressive child and the family**

Observation of an interaction between the mother and her aggressive child

| Time frame 1 | Time frame 2 | Time frame 3 |
|---|---|---|
| Behavior: Mother ("clean your room") | Child (begins whining) | Mother stops asking |

|  | *Short-term effects* | *Long-term effects* |
|---|---|---|
| Mother | Child stops whining | Mother will be more likely to give in when the child whines |
| Child | Mother's nagging stops | Child is more likely to whine when next asked to clean room |

An example of family interaction going awry. The mother cannot tolerate the whining and hence quits asking her child to clean the room. The short-term effect is positive because the whining stops. But the long-term effect is negative. When she next tells her child to clean the room, the child is very likely to begin whining again. To avoid the whining, the mother may eventually stop asking the child to do any chores.

Source: Patterson, G. R. (1980). Mothers: The unacknowledged victims. *Monographs of the Society for Research in Child Development, 45,* No. 186.

Patterson's view that the aggressive child is part of an ineffective family system is reinforced by several studies of delinquents. Parents of delinquent teenagers are not effective as managers (Loeber, Weissman, & Reid, 1983). They supervise the child's activities less, they know less about the child's whereabouts, and they have less control over their children's friends (Wilson, 1980). Teenagers who are not monitored by their parents are more likely to be antisocial, to break rules, and to be reported to the court.

Aggressive children bring a constellation of traits into any setting that affects how they are treated. Aggressive children are usually very active, may have academic problems, and behave inappropriately around peers. As a result, they are rejected by their peers and are regarded suspiciously by teachers (Milich, Landau, Kilby, & Whitten, 1982). Within a family, one aggressive child may cause the entire family to move in a negative direction. Patterson notes that in such families, interaction between family members is avoided because it is so destructive.

Parents, however, can modify the child's aggression by controlling the home environment. They can monitor their own behavior and model nonaggressive solutions to problems. They can limit access to aggressive toys, limit exposure to violent television programs, maintain some control over the selection of peers, and keep abreast of their child's activities. They can reward children for cooperation and other prosocial behaviors. They can explain the harmful effects of aggression. Even nursery school children learned alternate ways of solving problems when the teacher explained that fighting was not acceptable (Zahavi & Asher, 1978). Parents and teachers can help older children explore a variety of techniques as substitutes for fighting (Feshbach & Feshbach, 1982).

Children who are labeled aggressive early in life will have continuing confrontations with their parents, their peers, their teachers, and perhaps law enforcement officials (Patterson, 1982). Programs that help parents and children alter or manage this aggression could benefit everyone.

**Peers.** After the family, a child's peers are the most important socializing agents. Peer groups both inhibit and encourage aggression. The formation of dominance hierarchies among children and adolescents is one way to regulate peer interaction and avoid continuing aggressive interchanges (Parke & Slaby, 1983). The dominance hierarchy determines the boss. As long as that particular hierarchy is maintained, aggression within the group is limited. Among nursery school children, dominance is determined by toughness and physical prowess. As adolescence approaches, a boy's athletic skill and sexual maturity determine his place in the dominance hierarchy. By high school, a child's intelligence, creativity, and skill in nonphysical activities begin to determine who is dominant (Savin-Williams, 1980).

Peers also maintain a subtle set of standards about acceptable behavior. Children who deviate from this standard with aggressive behavior are likely to be isolated from the group (Dodge, 1982). The effect of this isolation varies. Some youngsters modify their behavior and reenter the group. In this case, the peer group is an effective socializer. Other children, relegated to the status of outsiders, may never learn more appropriate ways to resolve conflicts. They remain outsiders.

**Negative influence of peers**

*George W. Gardner*

Teenage gangs, especially in urban areas, tend to encourage aggression and violence among their members.

Peer groups can also promote aggression. In many cities, adolescent gangs encourage high levels of aggression. Members who break the law, are aggressive toward others, and confront the police, are awarded high status by their peers.

**What elicits aggression?**   As we have seen in the preceeding sections, the answer to this question is more complex than psychologists originally thought. Frustration at almost any age—from infancy through adulthood—can provoke aggression. In fact, the relationship between frustration and aggression was so obvious that psychologists of an earlier era believed frustration and aggression were always linked (Dollard, Dobb, Miller, Mowrer, & Sears, 1939). Frustration, however, does not always lead to aggression, nor is it the only situation that provokes aggression. Contemporary views of aggression recognize that in humans, as in animals, the built-in, "fight-or-flight" mechanism is a whole system of reactions triggered by stressful events in the environment (Berkowitz, 1983). Events that produce pain or distress are likely to provoke aggression in humans.

The child's cognitive skills also mediate aggressive responses (Dodge, 1982). After being struck by a classmate on the playground, a girl has to decide why the other child hit her. Was the classmate kidding, is she a good friend, was it an accident, or was it malicious? The child's decision about her classmate's intentions influences the way she responds. If she decides the other child was malicious, she must then decide what action to take. If the classmate is quite a bit bigger, she might decide to call a teacher. If the classmate is smaller, she might ignore the incident. Cognitive processing influences the child's interpretation of events and what action she will take.

If cognitive skills are important modifiers of aggression, perhaps aggressive children do not think about their reactions. This is, in fact, the case. Aggressive children are often impulsive and unable to delay gratification (Patterson, 1982). Another cognitive error made by aggressive boys is that they automatically view their peers as hostile (Dodge & Frame, 1982).

As part of their cognitive processing, children review the ways that they might respond to an attack by another. It is at this point that cultural norms play a role. If the culture supports and encourages physical violence, the child is more likely to start a fight. Television is an important part of our culture, and as we see in the next section, it tends to support and encourage aggressive behavior.

**Television and aggression**

Television is one of the most pervasive influences in American life. Children in the United States spend more time watching television than they spend in school or communicating with their parents (Singer, 1983). Since children spend so much time watching television, it is naive to think that it has no impact on them. The more realistic question is what kind of impact does television have?

In a 1982 report, the surgeon general stated that television is an important influence in the lives of children. In the next chapter, we will discuss how television affects cognitive development, social stereotypes, school achievement, family relationships, prosocial behavior, and consumer practices. In this section, we will limit the discussion to the effect that television has on aggression.

The daily television shows that children watch depict life punctuated by violence. Does this violence influence the child's aggressive behavior? Eli Rubenstein (1983) points out that there are only three possible answers to this question: (1) Television has no significant relationship to aggressive behavior; (2) television reduces aggressive behavior; (3) television increases aggressive behavior. Almost all of the studies conducted during the last decade support the third conclusion. No studies of any consequence support the second conclusion. Occasionally, however, a study, such as one conducted by a television network, concludes that television violence has no significant long-term effects on aggression (Milavsky, Kessler, Stipp, & Rubens, 1982). Nevertheless, the bulk of the evidence points overwhelmingly to the conclusion that televised violence is connected to later aggressive behavior (Pearl, Bouthilet, & Lazar, 1982).

The world of dramatic television presents an unrealistic view of life (Gerbner & Gross, 1980). Men outnumber women four to one. These men are centrally concerned with maintaining power. Violence is the key to power. Hence, 80 percent of all prime time and weekend programs contain violence. Between four and eight violent episodes occur during every hour of prime-time television. When weekend programming is included, physical aggression occurs between 10 and 20 times per hour (see Figure 13–11). By the time the average child graduates from high school, he or she will have witnessed 13,000 violent deaths on television.

The impact of this violence is most obvious in children who watch television the most. These children are more likely to fight with their parents, to become delinquents, and to become involved in fights than children whose television viewing is limited (McCarthy, Langner, Gersten, Eisenberg, & Orzeck, 1975). Although these studies, some of which were longitudinal, are compelling, they have a major drawback. They rely on correlational data. The television industry points out that scientists cannot infer that television causes aggression from correlational data. The television industry suggests that these children may be bored and unhappy. That is why they watch so much television and also why they are so aggressive. The implication is that the children would be aggressive whether or not they watched television.

To counter this argument, two researchers introduced television to a remote northern Canadian community. They assessed aggressive attitudes before and after television was introduced. Children who watched long hours of television showed an increase in aggressive attitudes, while those who seldom watched television showed a decrease in aggression (Granzberg & Steinbring, 1980).

Another way to prove that watching violence on television increases aggression is to conduct laboratory experiments during which some children are ex-

**Figure 13-11**    **Violence on television**

Violent acts per hour
(prime time and weekend)

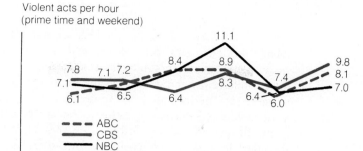

11.1
8.4    8.9
7.8    7.1    7.2
7.1                8.3
6.1    6.5    6.4        7.4    9.8
6.4    6.0        8.1
7.0

- - - ABC
——— CBS
——— NBC

1973-74    1974-75    1975-76        1977-78    1978-79

Violent acts per hour
(prime time)

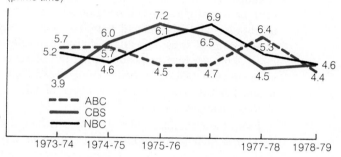

7.2    6.9
5.7    6.0    6.1
5.2        5.7        6.5    6.4
4.6    4.5    4.7    5.3    4.6
3.9            4.5    4.4

- - - ABC
——— CBS
——— NBC

1973-74    1974-75    1975-76        1977-78    1978-79

Antisocial acts per hour
(prime time and Saturday morning)

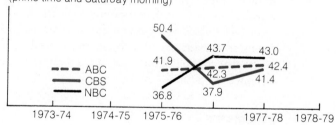

50.4
43.7    43.0
41.9            42.4
42.3    41.4
- - - ABC
——— CBS    36.8    37.9
——— NBC

1973-74    1974-75    1975-76        1977-78    1978-79

Acts of Physical Aggression
(prime time and Saturday morning)

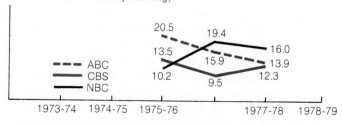

20.5
19.4
13.5        16.0
15.9    13.9
- - - ABC    10.2        12.3
——— CBS        9.5
——— NBC

1973-74    1974-75    1975-76        1977-78    1978-79

The number of violent incidents during prime-time television ranges from 4 to over 7 per hour. When weekend programming is included, the number of violent incidents ranges from 6 to 10 per hour. Children watching television both evenings and weekends see about 50 antisocial acts every hour.

Source: Adapted from Comstock, G. (1982). Violence in television content: An overview. In E. Pearl, L. Bouthilet, & J. Lazar (Eds.), *Television and Behavior: Ten years of scientific progress and implications for the eighties* (p. 116). Washington, DC: U.S. Government Printing Office.

574

posed to televised violence and others are not. After the experimental treatment, the children's behavior is recorded for a period of time. Such experiments have been conducted since the 1960s and have shown that children, adolescents, and adults become more aggressive after viewing portrayals of violence. The increase in aggression is not limited to certain forms of televised violence. Violence in cartoons, fantasy programs, and in realistic programs all increase the aggressiveness of viewers (Parke & Slaby, 1983). Nor is the effect limited to children in the United States. Similar results have been reported in Australia, Finland, Poland, Canada, and Great Britain.

Perhaps the most compelling data in support of the proposition that violence on television increases aggressive behavior come from compilations of the hundreds of studies of television and aggression. In one compilation, 76 percent of the studies found a significant relationship between television and aggression, while 19 percent found no relationship (Andison, 1977). Another compilation of over 200 studies found that televised violence had its biggest effects on aggressive behavior during the preschool years. After these impressionable years, television had a reduced effect on aggression until the children reached adolescence. Then the effect of television on aggression increased sharply for males (Hearold, 1979).

From these findings, psychologists conclude that watching violent television programs increases aggressiveness. Although any single study may contain flaws, the evidence from so many different researchers all over the world is difficult to refute. Over the last 20 years, the effects of television have been studied in the field, in the laboratory, with people of all ages, and with people who live in vastly different cultures. In the main, the same conclusion is repeated—televised violence increases aggressive behavior. In most researchers' minds, the existence of a long-term as well as a short-term relationship between the viewing of violence and a viewer's subsequent level of aggression is no longer in doubt.

## SUMMARY

During infancy, other children provoke curiosity, but very little interaction actually takes place. Toddlers do play with other children, but their social skills are not very complex or sophisticated. During preschool, the social interactions of children blossom. Cooperation, competition, aggression, affiliation, and altruism all become an obvious part of the child's life. Social skills are honed and practiced throughout the grade school years leading to a more mature understanding of friendship. Reciprocity between friends becomes important, and children consider their friends' feelings as well as their own. During adolescence, friendship becomes a mutually binding pact. Friends recognize both the rights and the responsibilities that are part of that friendship.

Learning to play with peers and forming friendships are significant aspects of a child's development. However, the influence of peers extends to other social arenas. Indices of moral development, prosocial behavior, and aggression tell us how children relate to peers and how they cope with the expectations of society.

Moral dilemmas arise when children's desires conflict with the desires of others or with the rules of society. School children initially respond to a moral dilemma in terms of their own interests. This preconventional reasoning is replaced by conventional reasoning as young adults realize that society cannot function without rules to guide people's behavior. A small number of individuals move one step further—to postconventional reasoning. They realize that moral issues really precede laws. Making mature moral judgments is only one step on the path to moral behavior. A devotion to the cause, a sense of adventure, and a family that has modeled high standards of moral behavior increase the likelihood that moral judgments will be converted to moral behavior.

Morality is typically associated with what people should not do. Equally important is understanding how children develop notions about what they should do. Cooperating, sharing, and helping are examples of prosocial behaviors that psychologists would like to encourage in everyone. In one sense, this is not hard—even toddlers have been observed sharing their toys or responding in a caring way to the distress of another person. Parents can encourage prosocial behavior by providing a loving environment and simultaneously modeling prosocial behavior. In addition, parents need to explain their own actions to their children and expect mature behavior from the child. Forcing obedience is less likely to enhance the child's spontaneous prosocial behavior.

Aggressive behavior is often perceived as the opposite of prosocial behavior. This is certainly an oversimplification. Aggression that defends the family or the territory insures the survival of the species. Aggressive behavior is most likely to present a continuing problem when the child's behavior is supported and encouraged by the family and the culture. The family often encourages aggression by modeling such behavior. The child imitates the aggression and learns to rely on aggression to solve problems. An aggressive child can eventually disrupt the entire family. The parents, unable to discipline the child effectively, become overly punitive or relinquish control altogether. The culture can also encourage or inhibit aggressive behavior. Watching television, a daily activity in Western cultures, contributes to aggressive behavior, especially in children who watch violent programs for hours on end.

**The effects of school**

> The school's effect on cognition
> Nonacademic effects of schooling

**The structure of the school**

> The traditional and open classroom
> Cooperative and competitive learning
> Competition

**Teachers**

**Student diversity**

> Gifted children
> Academically handicapped students
> Differences in conceptual style
> Differences between the sexes

**Television as an adjunct to the school**

> Television and cognitive functioning
> Television and prosocial behavior
> Attitudes and values learned from television
> Providing information

**Summary**

# CHAPTER 14
# Schools

Schools are responsible for educating our children, bringing stability to the culture, and instilling cultural values. But cultures differ in the values they choose. The following letter, written by the Indians of the Five Nations, illustrates the different goals of education. The letter was a response to officials at William and Mary College who had invited the Indians to send their young braves to school.

> You who are wise must know, that different nations have different conceptions of things; and you will therefore not take it amiss, if our ideas of this kind of education happen not to be the same with yours. We have had some experience of it: several of our young people were formerly brought up at the colleges of the northern provinces; they were instructed in all your sciences; but when they came back to us . . . (they were) ignorant of every means of living in the woods . . . neither fit for hunters, warriors, or counsellors, they were totally good for nothing. We are, however, not the less obliged by your kind offer. . . and to show our grateful sense of it, if the gentlemen of Virginia will send us a dozen of their sons, we will take great care of their education, instruct them in all we know, and make men of them. (Drake, 1834, p. 27)

Schools must prepare young people to function in the culture. In the 1700s, this meant that Indians taught their braves to hunt, to wage war, and to help others. In the 1980s, schools try to develop the potential of all children, regardless of race or sex. In terms of literacy, this means not simply being able to sign one's name or being able to read and write, but being able to function in the contemporary social setting (Resnick & Resnick, 1977). Typically, this means obtaining at least a 12th-grade education. Having the entire population of a country complete 12 years of school would be an unprecedented achievement. The United States is still far short of that goal. Nevertheless, there have been tremendous strides in reaching that goal. In 1870, only 2 percent of the 17-year-olds in this country graduated from high school (see Figure 14–1). In the 1980s, more than 75 percent of our young people will finish high school (Copperman, 1978).

Although the school's first mission is to develop academic skills, that mission flows into other areas. Schools have become concerned with the child's development in nonacademic areas. Teachers encourage social behavior, try to en-

**Figure 14—1**

**Education in the United States**

| | Percentage of 17-year olds graduating from high school | Percentage of 18—21 age group enrolled in higher education | Percentage of age group 25 and older who completed four years of college |
|---|---|---|---|
| 1870 | 2% | | |
| 1890 | 4 | 3% | |
| 1900 | 6 | 4 | |
| 1910 | 9 | 5 | 3% |
| 1920 | 17 | 8 | 3 |
| 1930 | 29 | 12 | 4 |
| 1940 | 51 | 15 | 5 |
| 1950 | 59 | 27 | 6 |
| 1960 | 65 | 37 | 7 |
| 1970 | 76 | 46 | 11 |
| 1975 | 75 | 45 | 13 |
| 1981 | 75 | 60 | 30 |

In the United States, three quarters of our young people graduate from high school and over half receive some form of higher education.

Sources: Cooperman, P. (1978). *The Literary Hoax.* New York: William Morrow; Coleman, W. T., & Selby, C. C. (1983). *Educating Americans for the 21st Century.* Washington, DC: National Science Foundation.

hance self-esteem, and even oversee the child's sexual education. Even beyond these responsibilities, the school undertakes specific training to meet society's needs. This often means socializing children from other countries, offering job training, and training specialists to carry the nation forward in technical areas.

In this chapter, we will examine the school's progress, successes, and failures in achieving these very high goals. We will look at the structure of the schools, the importance of teachers, the variety of students, and how other institutions affect the child's learning. As we describe the impact that school has on developing children, it will become clear that the culture can work against or mesh with the intentions of the educational system.

## THE EFFECTS OF SCHOOL

Does attending school affect intelligence? The answer seems obvious. Where else would one learn about hieroglyphics, the Pythagorean theorem, or the 103d element? However, a more critical question is whether formal schooling enhances children's thinking skills and their ability to solve problems. The research behind this question tells an interesting story.

**The school's effect on cognition**

Harold Stevenson and his colleagues traveled to jungle villages in Peru and compared the children living there with children from Detroit, Michigan, and Lima, Peru. The children in the jungle villages had little experience with books, radios, and other technology. The children in Lima and Detroit grew up surrounded by technology. In both the jungle villages and the city, some of the children attended school while others did not. The research team was interested in how the groups that attended school would differ from those who did not. When they compared six-year-olds who attended school with six-year-olds who did not, they found that attending school had a decided impact on cognitive processes (Stevenson, Parker, Wilkinson, Bonnevaus, & Gonzalez, 1978).

The children who did not attend school continued to live in unchanging and relatively unstimulating environments. They did not learn to code information in systematic ways, to categorize it, or to remember it effectively. The three groups of children who did attend school, whether they lived in the city of Lima, a jungle village in Peru, or the barrios of Detroit, showed comparable improvements in cognitive skills. This does not mean that all of the children profited equally from the school experience or that schools equalized the initial differences between the groups. It means that attending school had an impact on all three groups of children.

Within each environment, individual differences between students were great. Some children from the most impoverished village environments thrived in school and performed well on every assessment. Some from the most affluent urban environments seemed to make little progress in cognitive development.

The three environments were chosen because each was expected to yield a different picture of child development before the age of five. But the effects of the environments were not as substantial as expected. Children from the villages lived without telephones, newspapers, or mail service. No roads existed, and access to the villages, even by foot, was sometimes limited. One local radio station provided news from the rest of the world. Life in these villages was not conducive to the development of verbal skills. However, these children often achieved remarkable scores on tests of visual discrimination and seriation. Different environments produce a pattern of cognitive strengths and weaknesses that corresponds to the child's experiences. It is misleading to categorize environments as culturally enriched or impoverished, because even the villages provided some enriching experiences.

If we accept the fact that formal education produces a different pattern of cognitive strengths and weaknesses, the next goal is to describe that pattern. Barbara Rogoff has spent years trying to understand how formal education affects basic cognitive skills such as perception, organizing memory, and problem solving (Rogoff, 1981).

Children who attend school learn to interpret perceptual cues in a systematic and analytical way. As a result, they can analyze a perceptual presentation (see Figure 14–2). Children who attend school also show improved memory performance, especially when the memory task requires them to organize information. This is an interesting distinction and one that goes back thousands of years to the earliest Chinese educational system (Knight, 1940). When someone teaches students how to organize information for efficient memory, they

**Figure 14–2**                               **Embedded figures**

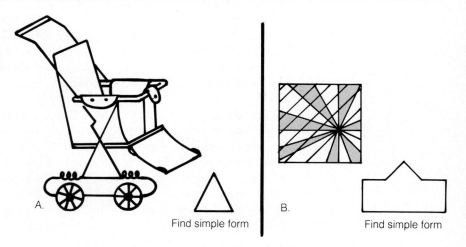

Finding shapes that are embedded in figures is easier for children who have attended school. It is also an area in which students exhibit large individual differences. The first figure (A) is part of a test for preschoolers. The second figure (B) is designed for school-age children.

Sources: Coates, S. W. (1972). *Preschool Embedded Figures Test.* Palo Alto, CA: Consulting Psychologists Press; Oltman, P. K., Raskin, E., & Witkin, H. A. (1971). *Group Embedded Figures Test.* Palo Alto, CA: Consulting Psychologists Press.

use these strategies very effectively. Yet children who have not learned these strategies have difficulty discovering them independently.

Schooling helps children organize information. They begin to use categories such as food, toys, and animals to think about their environment. Unschooled children are more likely to form categories that are functional, such as "A stove is for cooking." The use of functional categories may persist in adults. An unschooled peasant was given the following items—hammer, saw, log, hatchet—and asked which three were similar. "They all fit here! The saw has to saw the log, the hammer has to hammer it, and the hatchet has to chop it. And if you want to chop the log up really good you need the hammer. You can't take any of these things away, there isn't any you don't need!" (Luria, 1976, p. 58). Even though three of the objects were tools, the peasants' category included the log because it was used with the tools.

Transforming abstract information is another skill that children learn in school. Most junior high children would have no trouble with the following syllogism: In the Far North, where there is snow, all bears are white. Novaya Zemlya is in the Far North, and there is always snow there. What color are the bears there? (Luria, 1976). Children who have not attended school are likely to regard this as a ridiculous proposition. Because they have trouble accepting the first fact, they cannot transform the information to answer the question.

# HOPE STIRS IN THE GHETTO

Of all the problems that beset the nation's educational system, one of the most intractable has been the plight of the inner-city high school. Crippled by crime, underfunding, and racial strife, the schools have been unable to motivate students who play hooky and mark time. Academic performance has been abysmal. But now there are signs that some ghetto high schools, despite their appalling problems, are making substantial progress.

▶Morris High, the South Bronx, New York. When Frances Vazquez, 35, became the principal of Morris in 1979, the school was racked by violence. Located in one of the most depressed neighborhoods in the nation, Morris had an enrollment of 1,700 pupils that was 35 percent black and 65 percent Hispanic, many of them recent immigrants from the Caribbean and Latin America. "When I first arrived, I would not have used the staircase," recalls Vazquez. "Groups of kids were hanging around the halls and simply not attending classes."

Vazquez is in her office by 6:15 AM to run a program that now balances hard work and discipline with understanding and support. Students and their parents must sign contracts with the teacher to certify that they understand course requirements. Half an hour's homework is demanded in every subject every night.

The results are impressive by any standard. Last year the number of suspensions was down to 32, from 200 in 1978. Reading and achievement scores have risen, and there is a new sense of optimism and confidence in the halls. Of this year's 300-plus seniors, 85 percent will go on to attend college (acceptance letters are plastered on one wall).

▶Albert Sidney Johnston High, Austin. Three years ago, the school had a largely vocational curriculum with a student body almost entirely composed of minority students. It lagged behind all other Austin schools academically. Recalls Principal Adan Salgado: "We were the doormat of the district."

Then Johnston had to deal with a new problem that turned out to be its inspiration: a 1980 court-ordered desegregation plan resulted in busing half of its students from white sections of town. When white parents began protesting against the new plan, Johnston's faculty became determined to improve the school. Led by Salgado, who can call most of his 1,700 students by their first names, the administration began beefing up the academic program, installing the school system's first computer center and adding advanced courses in French, Latin, math, biology, and chemistry. White enrollment has grown from 44 percent during the first year of busing to 50 percent this year. A total of 29 white students have left private schools to ride a bus 45 minutes each morning to Johnston. In 1980, 90 percent of the students were below grade level in math; by 1982, the figure had improved to 54 percent.

▶George Washington Preparatory High, Los Angeles. Only four years ago, Washington High would have matched most people's Hollywood image of the blackboard jungle. "Morale here was terrible," recalls Margaret Wright, a leader of the parents' group. "The rooms were dirty, and 90 percent of the teachers were rotten."

Then, in 1979, George McKenna, a tough-minded former civil rights activist, became principal at the age of 37, which made him the youngest administrator ever appointed to the office in a Los Angeles high school. He moved quickly to upgrade expectations; he added the word preparatory to the school's name, underlining its new, no-nonsense commitment to high academic standards. He also replaced 85 percent of the teachers, banned radios and Walkmans, and imposed a dress code.

McKenna's hard-line approach to learning is paying off. Violence and absenteeism have dropped dramatically, and seniors' test scores for basic skills, while still below the city level, increased by an average of four points this year in every subject.

**Child in school**

*Owen Franken: Stock, Boston*

Attending school helps develop specific perceptual and thinking skills.

From these differences in cognitive skill, Rogoff (1981) concludes that schools enhance children's ability to search for general and abstract rules. In addition, children are able to put specific instances into larger, more inclusive categories. What happens in school that makes children adopt a more general mode of thought? Barbara Rogoff (1981) suggests that instruction in the verbal mode encourages thinking. The language that is used is removed from everyday context and helps children consider events in the abstract. Writing, too, requires analysis of material and helps students abstract from common occurrences. Children also receive specific instruction in how to define, organize, and classify material. This instruction seems to have a significant impact on children who have attended school.

Despite this evidence, several national commissions in tne United States have argued that the best predictor of a child's success in school is the home environment. The "school's output depends largely on a single input, namely the characteristics of the entering children. Everything else—the school budget, its policies, the characteristics of the teachers—is either secondary or completely irrelevant" (Jencks et al., 1972, p. 256). A decade later, we can begin to see the flaws in this conclusion (White, 1982). Schooling will not erase individual differences in ability. These will occur regardless of class size, teacher characteristics, or curriculum. But that does not mean that schools have no impact on students. The more critical question is do schools actualize the potential of all students?

Michael Rutter and his associates have tried to answer this critical question. They visited 12 secondary schools serving lower and lower-middle socioeconomic youths in London. They discovered that the schools did make a difference in actualizing the child's potential (Rutter, Maughan, Mortimore, & Ouston, 1979).

Rutter began by testing all of the students. Rather than giving them intelligence tests, he measured whether they were learning what the school was teaching. He also looked at truancy, delinquency, behavior in school, attendance, and employment. He reasoned that instead of counting the number of students in the classroom or looking at the age of the building, he should look at the emphasis placed on learning. Accordingly, when he evaluated schools, he looked at homework assignments, whether the homework was checked, and whether the teachers planned their courses. Another area of interest was discipline: how the teacher handled behavior problems, how much time teachers spent with the students, how they rewarded students, and how much time they actually spent teaching. He also investigated how the school treated students. He assessed the freedom given to students, the responsibilities they were given in the school environment, and how much they participated in the activities offered by the school.

When all of these ratings were completed, Rutter compiled a profile of the most successful schools, the moderately successful schools, and the least successful schools. The successful schools emphasized academics, had a clear system of rewards and punishments, and encouraged independence in students. These schools had a supportive administration that set the tone for both teachers and students. Such schools had a startling impact on students (see Figure 14–3). Children attending these schools performed well even if they did not have superior ability. In the least successful schools, students floundered academically. The homework assignments were sporadic, and classes lacked a clear organization. Student morale and interest were low. Students who attended these schools did poorly on exams that measured achievement.

Rutter's study is just one of several recent studies demonstrating that schools do make a difference. The school's academic policies, the teachers, and their emphasis on academics have a major impact on the student's performance (Rutter, 1983). The factors that have the least impact are physical factors such as school enrollment, the age of the building, and the physical appearance of the school. Even though schools do not erase individual differences in ability, they "can foster good behavior and attainments, and even in a disadvantaged area, schools can be a force for the good" (Rutter et al., 1979, p. 205).

Schools everywhere have begun to reorganize so that they reflect the new understanding of the school's impact (see box). School administrators are increasing their emphasis on academics, promoting pride in their campuses, expecting higher quality work, and requiring homework. Principals realize that they must enlist parents as partners in the educational enterprise and establish an atmosphere that facilitates learning. Part of this atmosphere includes high academic expectations and active teaching. (Brookover, Beady, Flood, Schweitzer, & Wisenbaker, 1979).

**Nonacademic effects of schooling**

Schooling was initially designed to teach academic skills. Attending school also affects attitudes, self-esteem, and understanding of the culture. Several social experiments such as Head Start and Follow Through have achieved no-

**Figure 14–3**          **The effects of schools**

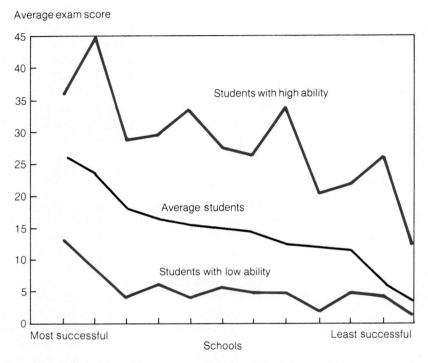

Average exam score

Students with high ability

Average students

Students with low ability

Most successful

Schools

Least successful

Students attending the most successful schools do well regardless of their entering skills. In the least successful schools, even the best students perform poorly.

Source: Rutter, M., Maughan, B., Mortimore, P., & Ouston, J. (1979). *Fifteen thousand hours: Secondary schools and their effects on children.* Cambridge, MA: Harvard Univ. Press.

table success in nonacademic areas. Although children in these programs typically lag behind middle-class children in academic performance, they are less likely to become delinquents and are more likely to have permanent jobs. Furthermore, they are not as likely to be placed in special education classes (Lazar et al., 1982). In short, children who participate in these programs have a better chance of becoming productive, contributing members of the society.

We have shown that children who attend school learn to think about problems and approach problems in a different way than children who do not attend school. We have also seen that the effect of school is not limited to academic material. These positive assessments of schooling are not shared by everyone.

Herbert Ginsburg (1979) is one of an increasing number of psychologists and educators who feel that what children learn in school is irrelevant, limited, and trivial. None of these critics is proposing, however, that we abandon the idea of teaching children. They are suggesting that teaching be accomplished in some alternative, more effective fashion. John Holt, an author and educator, advocates teaching children within the home. Because children are so

## Learning at home
*Harvard Freshman*

Youth Learned It All at Home

BOONVILLE, Calif. (AP)—Grant Colfax, 18, will be a freshman this fall at Harvard University, where admissions officers say they found him "refreshing."

Not terribly unusual, one might think, except that 11 years ago, Colfax's parents, with approval from education officials, decided to keep their children out of school. Instead, Colfax stayed at home raising goats in rural Boonville, about 100 miles north of San Francisco.

He received lessons from his mother, a high school English teacher, and his father, a former sociology instructor at the University of Connecticut and at Washington University.

Although his family lives a mile from the nearest neighbor and does not own a television set, Colfax said that he never felt isolated and developed his social skills by showing his goats at fairs, participating in nuclear freeze activities, and joining a foreign film group.

But he had to convince Harvard that he could handle formal academic work. He made the point by getting straight A's in 18 units of classes in one semester at Santa Rosa Junior College.

Harvard admissions officer Robert Cashion, who interviewed Colfax for one of 2,200 freshman slots, said the young man struck him "as someone who really enjoyed the learning process. It was refreshing to see. It was really a remarkable thing."

"We talked about goat farming," he said. "We talked about construction. We talked about elec-

*The Associated Press*

tricity, about politics, living on a homestead, just about everything. He had a really different perspective on things, given his background."

"Most students come in with a very structured academic background. Here comes a kid who came completely self-taught."

Although his scores on the Harvard admissions tests were in the top 5 percent, Colfax said that they were not the decisive factor in his acceptance.

"They didn't take me because of my high scores on the tests," he said, "and they didn't take me because I may or may not be intelligent. They took me because I'm unique."

While his eight-year-old brother Garth is "still just having fun," Colfax's brother Drew recently built a telescope, and brother Reed is studying advanced geometry.

curious, Holt (1982) believes they will explore and master information better outside of the traditional school setting. In his view, schools submerge "curiosity, confidence, and the willingness to ask questions. It turns children into collectors of answers." Holt would rather see children investigate questions that they decide are interesting. Such questioning would develop their reasoning and problem solving capabilities (Mullen, 1983). As evidence for these beliefs, Holt cites case histories. One student, freed from the routines of school, memorized the constitution; another began extensive research into the history of the early West. Teaching children at home is an extreme alternative (see box). Another alternative is to change the structure of the school.

**Traditional and open classrooms**

Traditional and open classrooms present different classroom environments to students. Children learn well in both environments, but the two environments foster different styles of learning.

## THE STRUCTURE OF THE SCHOOL

Organization of the classroom, the teacher's approach to students, as well as the incentives that are used to motivate students are all factors that reflect the school's structure. Some classrooms are *open*; others are more *traditional*. Certain teachers give A's for effort, others give A's only when a student achieves a high level of performance. Do these structural differences affect what a child learns or how well a child learns? To answer this question, we will look first at traditional and open classrooms and then consider a more recent structural alternative—cooperative learning.

**The traditional and open classroom**

Jim's elementary school is regarded highly by parents. It stresses basic skills. In kindergarten, children begin to wind their way through a rigorous math and English curriculum. The math program proceeds in a step-by-step fashion beginning with counting and progressing to addition, subtraction, multiplication, and division. In the upper elementary grades, fractions, decimals, and word problems are taught in the same systematic fashion. The reading curriculum is similarly structured. Beginning with the sounds of letters, the curriculum works through primary readers and gradually introduces supplementary reading. The grammar and writing curriculum is integrated with reading. Each week children memorize a list of spelling words and a group of sentences that teach punctuation, capitalization, and writing skills.

Jennifer's school is also regarded as excellent. The emphasis in her school, however, is different. Jennifer's curriculum includes math and English, but she also has a daily opportunity to sign up for the cooking group. Each day this group of four students prepares a simple snack for the other students. Today is Jennifer's birthday and she is the student-of-the-week. She knows that the afternoon session will begin with each child in her class whispering something they like about her. The classroom has a puppet theatre, a book corner, and a science corner. At an open house in the spring, the children will enact *The Wizard of Oz*.

These two schools represent different philosophies of education. Jim's, the traditional approach, emphasizes basic skills. Supporters of this philosophy feel that academic knowledge is learned most efficiently if presented in a structured setting. Supporters of Jennifer's school, an open classroom, feel that children learn more and develop personally and socially when they are free to structure their learning experiences according to their own interests. Advocates of open education feel that a flexible setting and many different kinds of resources are necessary to foster optimum development (Giaconia & Hedges, 1982).

Both of these philosophical positions have been criticized. Critics of Jim's school regard his classroom as too restrictive and feel that it provides little opportunity for personal development or creativity. Critics of Jennifer's school feel that the basic skills are relegated to a secondary position in the curriculum.

Is one approach better than the other? Studies have compared the two educational approaches on several variables including test scores, self-esteem, adjustment, anxiety, attitudes toward school, creativity, curiosity, and cooperation (Horowitz, 1979). The results of over 200 studies comparing these two philosophies show that the children's academic skills do not differ. At times, students in open classrooms do better academically, while at other times students in traditional classrooms do better. In the majority of studies, the students do not differ. It seems that children learn in both settings.

Studies of anxiety and self-esteem were similarly mixed. In several studies, children in open classrooms were less anxious and had better self-concepts than children in traditional classrooms. Occasionally, children in traditional classrooms were less anxious and felt better about themselves. Most often, researchers found no difference in the students' anxiety levels or their self-concepts (Horowitz, 1979).

The traditional and open classrooms differed most on personal variables such as attitude toward teachers, adjustment to school, cooperativeness, and creativity. These differences favor the open classroom (Giaconia & Hedges, 1982). Children who learned in the less restrictive environment were more curious, had a more positive attitude toward school, were more autonomous, and had a more diverse circle of friends (Horowitz, 1979). Compared to children in traditional classrooms, they were more likely to think divergently and to come up with creative solutions to problems (Thomas & Berk, 1981).

If these studies were conclusive, then educators everywhere might use open classrooms. However, critics of these studies point out that the definitions of open and traditional classrooms are not explicit (Marshall, 1981). A child can have an open classroom, yet still have a very structured mathematics curriculum. Furthermore, children's achievement scores at the end of the year do not tell the entire story. Carr and Evans (1981) want researchers to evaluate what transpires between a teacher and a student. When they visited classrooms and observed first graders learning to read, they found that open and traditional classrooms do make a difference.

Children in traditional classrooms spent about 60 percent of their time doing activities that were outlined and supervised by the teacher—practicing phonetic drills or reading from a primer. Children in the open classes spent most of their time in tutorial sessions with the teacher or reading alone. Storytelling and imaginative play were favorite activities during the reading period. As one might expect, students in these classrooms showed better language skills, but students in the traditional classrooms were better readers (Carr & Evans, 1981).

The conclusion appears to be that children learn what they are taught (Minuchin & Shapiro, 1983). If they are taught to read by phonetically analyzing a word, they will use that strategy. If they are encouraged to tell stories and be imaginative, they will become facile with the language. Which strategy yields the best long-term results in terms of an informed, competent citizenry is not yet known.

Cooperation among students is an integral part of an open classroom, and this may be one of the reasons that children develop more sophisticated social skills. In recent years, a group of psychologists have introduced cooperative learning to the more traditional classroom.

## Cooperative and competitive learning

Since 1954, when the Supreme Court ruled that segregated schools were inherently unequal, social scientists have been searching for a satisfactory way to make educational resources equally available to all children. In the 1980s, almost all of our schools are racially mixed, but the interaction and cooperation between the races is often negligible (Stephan, 1978). Friendships rarely cross racial boundaries, and racial groupings are prominent at all grade levels. Although we have successfully desegregated most schools, the anticipated improvement in ethnic relations has not necessarily followed. In some communities, forced integration has heightened racial tension. The lesson we have learned is that "simply mixing children in the classroom and trusting to benign human nature" is not enough to defuse tension or foster interracial friendships (Gerard, 1983, p. 875).

Sports teams are the single exception to these disheartening data. Children who play on integrated teams are more likely to have friends outside their racial group than children who do not participate in sports (Slavin & Madden, 1979). Robert Slavin suggests that the cooperation necessary for team success builds friendships. He argues that schools should encourage this type of cooperation in the classroom. To achieve this goal, psychologists and educators have devised several strategies that teachers can use to encourage cooperative learning (Slavin, 1983).

Cooperative learning changes the structure of the classroom and alters the incentives so that students are encouraged to cooperate. In a typical cooperative

## MAGNET SCHOOLS

Magnet schools, as the name implies, attract students. The hope is that they will attract students from a variety of neighborhoods who otherwise would not attend that school. Typically, magnet schools are located in a school district that has a high percentage of minority students. By offering attractive and unique programs, magnet schools achieve racial balance without busing or redrawing school district lines. The concept of magnet schools, while initially limited to a few maverick schools, has grown to over 1,000 schools in more than 130 of the largest urban school districts.

To attract a heterogeneous student body, magnet schools must be innovative and maintain a reputation for excellence. Hence, magnet schools may offer a special program for gifted students, a tough, back-to-basics curriculum, or a laboratory science program. Magnet schools can often qualify for federal funds and can purchase computers or other equipment that will help attract students.

If magnet schools are successful, they could provide a model of painless desegregation. For this reason, the government is interested in how well magnet schools work. To determine how well they achieve their goals, we need to ask if magnet schools achieve racial balance in a school district. We need to ask whether children who attend these schools achieve at the same level as children who choose another school. Finally, we need to know how much magnet schools cost.

A report issued in 1984 begins to answer these questions. The Department of Education reports that magnet schools can help cities desegregate their schools, but the technique works best when it is combined with other methods of overcoming racial isolation. Certain cities, however, have relied exclusively on magnet schools to achieve a racial balance throughout their school district. Overall, the use of magnet schools has decreased the percentage of students in racially isolated schools from 60 percent to less than 30 percent. The answer to the first question, then, is that magnet schools can help desegregate schools.

The question of quality is perhaps more difficult to answer. In an attempt to assess quality, researchers visited schools across the United States and interviewed administrators, parents, and community representatives. They found that the most successful magnet schools had a coherent program that they were offering students. Both teachers and administrators were enthusiastic about the program and worked hard to make it successful. An innovative, entrepreneurial principal was usually behind a successful magnet school. Actual achievement results and comparisons between magnet schools and other schools have not been reported. Without this kind of information, no firm conclusions can be drawn, but the fact that parents continue to enroll their children suggests that the education is equal to the education they would receive elsewhere.

The cost of magnet schools has declined since the concept was first introduced. During the 1980–1981 school year, magnet schools cost an average of $200 more per pupil than other schools. But the next year, the cost declined to $59 per pupil. This extra cost must be balanced with the cost of busing large numbers of students.

All in all, the initial reports on magnet schools are encouraging. Magnet schools contribute to desegregation efforts. The programs offered are attractive to majority students and were given good marks for quality. One of the most optimistic notes is that the cost is not excessive.

Source: Lawry, J. H. & Associates. (1984). Survey of magnet schools: Analyzing a model for quality integrated education. Washington, DC: Department of Education.

scheme, students are divided into competing teams. The teacher sets up each team so that it contains both very able students and less able ones, girls and boys, and students from different racial backgrounds. The team can study together and help each other understand math, remember the presidents, or learn German grammar. When quizzes or tests are given, however, students perform independently. All of the team members contribute to the team's final score. Although the particulars of different cooperative schemes vary, the team concept is used in most cooperative classrooms.

**Effects of cooperative learning.** When cooperative learning techniques are used, student interaction increases. This interaction is the first step toward forming friendships. A second step occurs when individuals work together toward a common goal. Cooperative learning demands such effort. The third step occurs when individuals on the team help others to achieve their personal goals. This aspect of cooperative learning produces strong friendships. It is not surprising, then, that the effect of cooperative learning on interracial friendships is dramatic. Students from classrooms with a traditional curriculum seldom select friends from outside their ethnic group. Students in cooperative programs often have friends from other racial groups. The relationships that

**Cooperative classrooms**

*Spencer Kagan*

Cooperative classrooms are arranged so that there are four members on a team. Each team is carefully constructed so that boys and girls are equally dispersed and members of different races and different ability levels are included on each team.

are formed during cooperative learning experiences are long lasting and strong. Furthermore, the friendship is reciprocated (Slavin, 1983).

Cooperative learning also has beneficial effects on a child's self-esteem. Two of the most important components of self-esteem are the feeling that you are well liked by your peers and that you are doing well academically. In the cooperative learning scheme, students are needed and valued by their team-mates. Through a team effort, even the less capable students feel a sense of academic achievement.

Despite the social advantages in cooperative classrooms, few schools will adopt this strategy if the students are not learning. Therefore, it is critical to know how cooperative learning affects achievement. Cooperative learning methods that only use teams for study groups do not increase student achievement. But cooperative learning methods are effective if the team scores are based on how well each individual performs. Using cooperative techniques, elementary students gained over one year in math skills during the 24 weeks of the program. The control classes, using a highly regarded math curriculum, gained an average of seven months in their math skills (Slavin, Leavey, & Madden, 1984).

The makeup of the cooperative teams also has an effect on achievement in junior high math classes. If the groups are composed of two boys and two girls, the boys and girls achieve the same grades. Any imbalance in the number of boys and girls resulted in lower grades for the girls (Webb, 1984).

Another result is that the gap between black and white students' achievement seems to be narrowed by cooperative learning (Slavin & Oickle, 1981). This is particularly interesting because other longitudinal studies of traditional classrooms indicate a widening achievement gap between white and minority children as they move through the grades (Gerard, 1983). Perhaps group experiences that make minority students feel comfortable will help them achieve. Spencer Kagan supports this position and has compiled persuasive evidence that competitive environments provide a poor "match" for the needs of minority students (Kagan, Zahn, Widaman, Schwarzwald, & Tyrrell, 1984).

**Drawbacks of cooperative learning.**   Despite the enthusiasm cooperative learning has fostered, many psychologists are hesitant about the technique. Several critics have pointed out that cooperative learning emphasizes cooperation within a team, but it also encourages vigorous competition between teams. This competition may blunt the cooperative atmosphere. Another pitfall is that the least able member of teams could become the scapegoat when a team does not do well. Susan Crockenberg (1979) points out that cooperation may foster mutual exchange and group cohesiveness, but at the same time it could encourage high levels of conformity. Educators would be concerned if students conformed at the expense of their individual development. Cooperative learning offers an alternative to the tightly structured classroom in which students constantly compete for a limited number of high grades. The initial studies make cooperative learning a highly attractive alternative. In the next few years, more researchers will look at ways to implement cooperative learning strategies to achieve the best results.

## Competition

The cooperative learning studies hint that competition has a negative effect on children. The effect of both cooperation and competition was examined in the Robber's Cave experiments (Sherif, Harvey, White, Hood, & Sherif, 1961). This three-phase experiment was conducted by Muzafer Sherif and his colleagues at a boy scout summer camp adjacent to Robber's Cave State Park in Oklahoma. Initially, the 22 fifth-grade boys were divided into two groups that existed separately. The boys did not even know another group existed.

During the first phase of the experiment, the boys in each group hiked, made crafts, built hideouts, and organized games. Friendships between the boys began to appear. The experimenters watched for signs that a group was forming. To hasten the process, the counselors let the boys prepare their own dinner. The boys immediately divided up the labor and worked cooperatively. As they worked, certain boys emerged as leaders and others seemed comfortable in the role of follower. As the days passed, the boys agreed that their group should have a name. Selecting names, the Rattlers and the Eagles, was one of the milestones indicating that the boys saw themselves as a group.

Once groups were formed, the stage was set for intergroup rivalry. The counselors arranged for the Rattlers and the Eagles to meet. During the next five days, the two groups competed in baseball games, tent-pitching contests, touch football games, and a tug-of-war. The effect of this competition was startling. The group that lost was angry and disgusted. Their support for each other was eroded by internal friction and mutual recriminations. The best athletes threatened to harm the boys who did not try harder. During this phase, the groups lacked the harmony and cohesiveness they had before the competition. This lack of support was most obvious when two of the boys wrote letters asking to go home.

Having a competitor, however, ultimately tightened the ranks of both groups. The groups hardened into "we" and "they," and dissension within each group disappeared. Each group worked to win and make their opponents look foolish. The intense competition began to extend to camp raids and pranks such as burning the other group's flag. Name-calling was common, and each group wanted no involvement with any member of the other group. The second phase of the experiment had demonstrated that competition hardened the groups' boundaries. Every boy, whether a leader or a follower, expressed hostility toward the boys in the other group. As the competition escalated, the counselors intervened. During the final phase of the experiment, the counselors attempted to decrease hostility between the two groups. Bringing the groups together for fireworks and a picnic and minimizing competition between the groups did little to decrease the tension. The boys argued at the least excuse, and the arguments quickly turned into food fights, name-calling, and fist fights. Only when the boys were required to work together was harmony restored. Finding the cause of a break in a water pipe prodded cooperation between the two groups. Pooling their money to see a movie and working together when a truck developed engine trouble sharply reduced conflict and increased friendships across group lines. By the end of their time at camp, boys from both groups sat together at meals and at campfires. Their group solidarity was evident when, on the trip home, the Rattlers shared their prize money and bought soft drinks for everyone.

The lessons of the Robber's Cave experiment are clear. Competition promotes conflict between groups. But if two groups work cooperatively toward one goal, hostility will decrease and friendships will increase. These lessons from a free-flowing summer camp cannot be applied directly to the school setting. But we can use these lessons to guide investigations of the school environment. Competitive tournaments and competition for grades motivate many students. These students feel better about themselves, their school, and their classmates when they can compete and succeed. The same competitive tournaments have a negative effect on many minority students (Kagan et al., 1984). In contrast, cooperative techniques produce harmonious race relations and encourage prosocial development. They do not necessarily produce superior achievement or enhanced self-concepts.

Rather than promoting one classroom structure, it seems that we should include cooperative learning, competitive programs, and individualized instruction in the school. Cooperative techniques could be used when studying math, an individualized program could be instituted for reading, and a competitive classroom structure might be used for spelling. In this atmosphere, all of the students' needs would be met and students would learn how to compete, how to cooperate, and how to work individually. The burden for implementing these strategies and for blending techniques into useful classroom exercises falls on the teacher.

## TEACHERS

Teachers have direct daily contact with students and turn school policies into classroom practices. Accordingly, teachers should be expected to play an important part in student achievement. Good teachers should prod students to achieve, and poor teachers should have less success.

The evidence supporting these statements is mixed. Michael Rutter and his colleagues (1979) found that it was easier to be a good teacher in successful schools. Teachers as well as students benefited if the administration was supportive. The primary difference that he found among teachers was the ease with which experienced teachers managed the class. Inexperienced teachers were often befuddled by the day-to-day management problems regardless of whether they taught in a successful or an unsuccessful school. The more successful schools, however, provided the support that helped teachers overcome these problems quickly.

Rutter's survey demonstrates that teachers link the school environment and the student. However, Rutter's conclusions do not tell us how teachers influence students or how good teachers achieve their goals. To answer these questions, we have to visit the classroom and study the interaction between the teacher and the students. Such studies show that a single outstanding teacher can have a powerful impact on the child's basic skills. Eigil Pedersen and her colleagues describe one first-grade teacher whose students received high grades throughout elementary school. The work habits they established in first grade and the basic skills they learned gave them an edge over other students that persisted well beyond elementary school (Pedersen, Faucher, & Eaton, 1978).

The classrooms of outstanding teachers can be distinguished from other classrooms. These teachers focus on academic goals, have well-organized classes and presentations, and expect their students to perform well. This last factor has received a great deal of attention in the educational literature.

Teacher's expectations can function as *self-fulfilling prophecies*. If the teacher expects a student to receive an A, the student puts forth extra effort and achieves at a higher level. Conversely, if a teacher expects little from a particular student, that student can sense the hopelessness of the situation and gives up. Although expectations exert a clear effect in laboratory studies, it is not as clear that teachers' expectations have the same effect in the classroom (Brophy, 1983).

In 1968, Robert Rosenthal and Lenore Jacobson published a study which is now called the *Pygmalion* study. At the beginning of the school year, these researchers chose first- and second-grade students at random and told their respective teachers that these students were ready to "bloom." At the end of the school year, the identified students had gained an average of 40 points in their IQ. The other students had gained about 16 points. In the years following its publication, this study has been used to argue that teachers control the level of their students' achievement, influencing both success and failure. Researchers who jumped on the Pygmalion bandwagon seemed to believe that every low-achieving student would excel as soon as the teachers raised their expectatons. Other educators remained leery of the conclusions. After examining the study closely, they found that it had many deficiencies (West & Anderson, 1976).

A position between these two extremes represents the situation accurately. Teachers do have expectations, and these are likely to move the student's performance in the expected direction (Good, 1980). But students are also involved in this process. When psychologists are not providing false information, teachers form expectations on the basis of their interaction with the student (Cooper & Good, 1983). In other words, teachers respond to existing differences among students. In most cases, teachers' impressions are accurate and are based on the student's actual performance. Teachers' impressions are not irrevocable. They can be changed by differing behavior and attitudes (Brophy, 1983).

Teachers have always formed expectations about students. Difficulties occur when teachers treat students differently based on those expectations. For example, teachers are accused of encouraging high-ability students and discouraging less able ones. When high-ability students fail to answer a question correctly, teachers often provide clues or rephrase the question. When the less able students fail to answer correctly, teachers are less likely to provide these extra clues (Brophy, 1983). Teachers defend their behavior by arguing that a good student will often give an answer that is close to the correct answer. Rewording the question gives the student a chance to succeed. In contrast, the less able student's response is often so inaccurate that a clue or rewording is not likely to help. Asking another student to answer actually saves the less able student from repeated failure and continued embarrassment. In these situations, differential treatment, rather than being an expression of prejudice, can be the preferred educational strategy.

Jere Brophy (1983) supports this view when he argues that an instructional strategy designed for low achievers should differ from the instructional strategy used for high achievers. Low achievers learn more efficiently when the instruction is more structured and redundant. In reading, for example, low achievers may need frequent help from the teacher. Without this help, the students would flounder. The higher ability students can often proceed with little direction from the teacher. Other accusations such as "teachers give the best students longer assignments" also turn out to be true. Again, this differential treatment is designed to reduce frustration and failure and increase motivation and success. In short, teachers who systematically alter their instruction for low-achieving students are trying to maximize these students' achievement through appropriately individualized instruction (Brophy, 1983).

Any evaluation of the self-fulfilling prophecy notion should mention two facts that modify the effect. First, teachers' impressions are based upon student behavior. Second, teachers sometimes treat students differently for sound educational reasons. These facts, however, do not explain why randomly designated "bloomers" made conspicuous progress in the Rosenthal and Jacobson study. The Pygmalion effect does exist, and some teachers may be more swayed by expectations than others. In some classrooms, the less able students are not given as much time to answer questions, they are given inappropriate feedback or no feedback at all, they receive less of the teacher's attention, and they are criticized more often than high-achieving students (Brophy, 1983). All these small differences can act together to discourage less able students. Convinced that they cannot succeed, they do not try. However, only a few teachers fall into the expectations trap. Overall, the Pygmalion effect is not very strong (Raudenbush, 1984). By most assessments, the teacher's expectations alter a student's achievement by no more than 5 to 10 percent (Brophy, 1983).

The teacher links the school environment and the student. A school that has outstanding teachers on its staff will consistently produce well-educated students. Effective teachers pry high-quality work from their students, instill basic skills, and teach solid work habits. They do this by focusing on academic goals, providing a structured, organized environment, and demanding excellence.

## STUDENT DIVERSITY

A brief visit to any classroom is all it takes to see that students differ. The obvious physical differences are just the beginning. Some students are bright, curious, and interested. Others, just as intelligent, seem detached and hostile. One group of children solves problems quickly; another group finds the correct answers more slowly. Children who are social prefer to work in groups; others work better alone. Added to this diversity is a wide range of intellectual abilities. The school must try to adjust to all of these individual differences and provide a curriculum that optimizes each individual's development.

**Gifted children**

Children who have special gifts should be regarded as a national resource. If their talents are nurtured properly, they will be leaders in politics, in scientific innovation, and in solving the social problems that face the human race. But

**Student diversity**

"I'M USUALLY THREE DAYS AHEAD OF A REGULAR CLASS, ONE DAY AHEAD OF THE FAST LEARNERS, AND TWO DAYS BEHIND A CLASSFUL OF THEM."

©1984 by Sidney Harris

the educational fortunes of gifted students wax and wane depending on the political and economic climate of the society. In 1959, when Russian scientists were the first to launch a satellite, the country rallied behind the call for more scientists, and programs for gifted children sprouted everywhere. The same fervor was applied to economically disadvantaged groups in the 1960s. As a result, the gifted child's needs faded into the background. The 1970s were a time of economic cutbacks, and special funding for gifted programs was considered elitism. By the 1980s, we discovered that the students entering universities were unprepared to tackle a rigorous course of study. A national commission characterized the educational scene in the following terms: ". . . the educational foundations of our society are presently being eroded by a rising tide of mediocrity that threatens our very future as a Nation and a people" (Gardner, 1983, p. 5). This commission noted that we had squandered the gains in student achievement made in the wake of the Sputnik challenge and had dismantled the educational programs that nurtured those gains. The result is that the most able students are not prepared to meet the challenges of the 21st century.

The Scholastic Aptitude Test (SAT) taken by high school seniors provides another chronicle of the decline in skills among our nation's brightest students (see Figure 14–4). In 1973, 18 percent of the seniors who took the verbal portion of the SAT received scores over 550. By 1983, only 14 percent of the seniors scored over 550. In actual numbers, this means that 45,000 fewer students excelled on the test. The math scores of the brightest students have not declined as much. Still, there are 34,000 fewer students in these top categories (Admissions Testing Program, 1983).

**Mediocre education**

*Reprinted by permission: Tribune Company Syndicate, Inc.*

**Figure 14—4**                    SAT scores for gifted students

**National Aptitude analysis SAT—verbal 1973 to present**

| Score range | 1973 | 1974 | 1981 | 1982 |
|---|---|---|---|---|
| 750–800 | 1,793 | 2,305 | 2,041 | 1,479 |
| 700–749 | 10,744 | 12,372 | 8,221 | 6,761 |
| 650–699 | 27,242 | 28,716 | 19,633 | 20,996 |
| 600–649 | 58,477 | 55,373 | 39,717 | 41,212 |
| 550–599 | 86,810 | 86,364 | 68,307 | 69,932 |
| Total number and (percent) | 185,066(18) | 185,130(19) | 137,919(14) | 140,380(14) |

**National aptitude analysis SAT—math 1973 to present**

| Score | 1973 | 1974 | 1981 | 1982 |
|---|---|---|---|---|
| 750–800 | 8,780 | 9,871 | 6,570 | 8,351 |
| 700–749 | 22,808 | 26,371 | 20,358 | 21,177 |
| 650–699 | 54,535 | 54,029 | 43,379 | 42,388 |
| 600–649 | 82,906 | 79,573 | 73,259 | 78,906 |
| 550–599 | 133,072 | 120,281 | 114,566 | 117,118 |
| Total number and (percent) | 302,101(30) | 290,125(29) | 258,132(26) | 267,940(27) |
| Total number of students taking test | 1,014,853 | 985,239 | 994,046 | 998,270 |

In 1973, 185,000 students received verbal SAT scores above 550. In 1983, this number had dropped by almost 45,000 students despite little change in the number of students taking the test.

Source: Admissions Testing Program (1983). National Aptitude Analysis, 1973–1982. Educational Testing Service.

The conclusion that the talents of our gifted students are being squandered is inescapable. "Over half the population of gifted students do not match their tested ability with comparable achievement in school" (Gardner, 1983, p. 8). In the wake of this report and other data documenting the nation's educational slide, educators have begun to reexamine the development of the gifted student.

**Identifying the gifted student.** Traditionally, students who score in the top 1 or 2 percent on an IQ test have been identified as gifted. The Office of Education recognizes that not all gifted students will have high IQs or score well on achievement tests. Hence, they have expanded the definition of gifted to include outstanding abilities or high potential in (*a*) general intelligence, (*b*) specific academic ability, (*c*) creative or productive thinking, (*d*) leadership ability, (*e*) visual and performing arts, and (*f*) psychomotor ability. Even this expanded definition omits two critical factors that should be considered in identifying gifted students. Joseph Renzulli and James Delisle (1982) agree that above-average ability in some field is necessary. They would also like to see motivation and creativity considered. Students without superior ability who are especially motivated might well be candidates for a gifted program. Similarly, creative students might generate ideas that more gifted students would miss. Students who exhibit all three characteristics should obviously be included. Once identified, these students require a different set of educational opportunities than are normally provided (Stewart, 1981).

**Programs for the gifted.** Programs for the gifted student sometimes amount to nothing more than doubling the amount of math homework. This educational strategy is obviously misguided, because the gifted student grasps concepts quickly and needs less drill. Gifted students are actually penalized by this strategy. Although this strategy has been widely condemned, it still guides some programs.

A second strategy, enrichment, is designed to provide experiences that will broaden the gifted student's educational horizons. In enrichment programs, gifted students study topics such as biofeedback, the Chinese dynasties, and nutrition. The evaluation of these programs is mixed. Students are typically enthusiastic about enrichment programs, commenting that they enjoyed the additional subject material (Barbe, 1955). Most criticisms of enrichment programs are made by psychologists. They say that enrichment programs do not enhance the intellectual skills of gifted students (Stanley, 1967). Furthermore, psychologists propose that assembling all the gifted students in one school and taking them on trips to art galleries and museums is a form of elitism. As Ellis Page notes, "to be intellectually defensible, a program for the gifted must not be equally appropriate for the less gifted" (1979, p. 209).

The most acceptable educational strategy for gifted students is acceleration. Acceleration allows students to move through the regular curriculum at a faster rate. In endorsing acceleration, the United States Office of Education has noted that, "We are increasingly being stripped of the comfortable notion that a bright mind will make its own way. Intellectual and creative talent cannot survive educational neglect and apathy" (Office of Education, 1972, p. 1).

Acceleration takes a variety of forms. Students may be accelerated in an area of particular strength but remain in their regular classroom most of the day. This type of acceleration means that the teacher provides more advanced work. Another approach is to move the student to a higher level class to study a particular subject. In both of these alternatives, the gifted student stays with age-mates most of the day. A third alternative is to place all gifted students in one class and provide an accelerated curriculum for that class. This alternative provides academic acceleration without moving gifted children out of their age group. A final alternative is having gifted children skip a grade.

Once in high school, gifted students can be advised to take advanced English, math, and science classes. Early entrance into college, receiving college credit by examination, and part-time attendance in college are all ways to accelerate a gifted high school student.

How effective is acceleration? This educational strategy, especially when it involves skipping a grade, has not been highly regarded by teachers and administrators, but the evidence indicates that it is a very effective technique. Case histories of individuals who entered a university at 10, 11, and 13 years of age indicate that rather than being social outcasts who were bitter about their acceleration, these individuals thrived. The mathematician Gauss went to the university when he was 11, won fame in his studies, and lived a long life of intellectual accomplishment. Justice Bennett Van Syckel entered Princeton at 13, graduated at 16, and served 35 years as a Supreme Court Justice (George, Cohn, & Stanley, 1979). These success stories are not isolated occurrences.

Lewis Terman is regarded as the father of research with gifted students. He identified more than 1,500 school-age children with IQs above 140. He followed the development of these children for 50 years. To examine the effects of acceleration on the children's development, he divided his sample into two groups. One group graduated from high school before 16.5 years of age, and the other group graduated from high school after 16.5 years of age. He then looked at how successful the members of each group were as adults. It is important to note that not all of the brightest students were accelerated. Fifty men and 39 women with IQs between 150 and 190 graduated with their age-mates.

The accelerated students were more likely to graduate from college and attend graduate school. Almost half of the accelerated students chose professional or upper-level business occupations. Less than 20 percent of the second group were employed at this level. Were these accelerated students social misfits? The answer is no. "The influence of school acceleration in causing social maladjustment has been greatly exaggerated. There is no doubt that maladjustment does result in individual cases, but our data indicate that in a majority of subjects the maladjustment consists of a temporary feeling of inferiority which is later overcome" (Terman & Oden, 1947, p. 275). Academic success and vocational success came early and easily to the students who were accelerated. Social relationships were just as satisfactory in the two groups. Both groups reported a high proportion of happy marriages.

Julian Stanley's studies of mathematically advanced youth have reinforced Terman's conclusion. Of the 44 students who entered college early, all but one have made exciting academic progress and adjusted well. Even the one student who did not adjust quickly should not be counted a failure. By 15 years of age, he had graduated from high school and had earned a year of college credit (George et al., 1979). Nevertheless, this student underscores the point that not every student should be accelerated. The student must want to be accelerated and must be willing to tackle more advanced work. It is inevitable that a small proportion of these students will experience some adjustment problems. For most, these problems will be no more serious than the problems posed by changing schools. Given the low incidence of problems that Julian Stanley and Louis Terman have found, gifted and motivated students should be given the opportunity to attend college early.

Julian Stanley also warns that not accelerating a student may pose a different set of risks. Underachievement can result (Gardner, 1983). Further, gifted

## ACCELERATION OF GIFTED STUDENTS

Nina Teresa Morishige, the Japanese-American mathematical genius who, at age 18, is the youngest woman to win a Rhodes Scholarship, has worked her way through an impressive list of honors, academic and other, during her four undergraduate semesters here at Johns Hopkins University.

A student on full scholarship, she deals with such esoterica as the Yang-Mills field theory, the extraterrestrial lift of the quark, and particle physics, all of which have been focal interests during her advanced work, much of it at the graduate level.

On the basis of her record here and elsewhere, there seems little that the poised, fast-talking daughter of a professor of physics and a scholar in literature could not accomplish if she put her mind to it. She is to graduate in May with bachelor's and master's degrees—and a 4.0 grade point average, the maximum—in courses that range from real analysis (a quintessence of advanced algebra that she calls "memorable") to differential topology (a highly specialized geometry) and electromagnetic theory.

Morishige said that she was found to be a genius at age four with an IQ measured then at 171. Tervo Morishige, Nina's father, who teaches at Central State University in Edmond, carried home his college physics books and others borrowed from colleagues to encourage his daughter's education. Today, Morishige says, she has "pretty much passed" her father in conceptual mathematics.

Morishige has won other academic, musical, and sports honors. Before she was 16, she had won awards as an outstanding soloist on both flute and piano. One sports outlet that she enjoyed was softball, but her mother was afraid that she might break her fingers while playing. To allay her mother's fears, Morishige gave up baseball and started playing golf. She won first place in the PGA national junior girls' division during her seventh-, eighth- and ninth-grade years.

Nina Teresa Morishige is one example of a gifted child who is accelerated. She finished high school, her undergraduate degree, and a master's degree by age 18.

students can become bored, restless, and occasionally hostile when they are not challenged (Cunningham, 1984). Educators should balance these risks against the temporary difficulties that may result from acceleration.

In sum, acceleration for intellectually able youths provides academic and vocational benefits and poses minimal socioemotional problems. Acceleration has the additional advantage of not being an expensive educational strategy for the gifted. The student moves through the same curriculum, only at a faster pace.

**Academically handicapped students**

"I have a sickness about reading," was how a 10-year-old boy described his dyslexia (Mosse, 1982). Other children have problems attending, remembering the teacher's instructions, or thinking deductively. These academic handicaps worry parents and, in the past, have confounded educators.

Children with academic handicaps can succeed in school. Specialized help is now available for a variety of learning disabilities. The first step in the process involves testing the child to pinpoint the problems. Depending on the difficulty, children can be taught specific strategies to overcome their problem, or they can be taught a different approach to the same goal. To understand this process of diagnosis and remediation, let us examine one learning disability in some detail.

Dyslexia is a reading problem that afflicts people in all countries, at all levels of society, and without regard to emotional, cultural, or family circumstances. In the United States alone, millions of children and adults have trouble reading (Clarke, 1973). Among those millions there are statesmen, surgeons, writers, and even poets. Woodrow Wilson, Nelson Rockefeller, General George Patton, Hans Christian Anderson, and W. B. Yeats are a few eminent figures whose reading problems were well known (Clarke, 1973).

As in most learning disabilities, the causes for reading problems are only partially understood. We know that dyslexia runs in families, and one form of dyslexia is carried on the fifth chromosome (see Chapter 2). But dyslexia is really an umbrella term for many sorts of problems. The result of each of these problems is that the child has some difficulty reading or understanding printed material.

The child's problems may appear very early or very late in the multistep process of reading. At the simplest level, children have trouble seeing or hearing the difference between "b" and "p." Discriminating between letters involves low-level perceptual processes (Noell, 1983). Another child may be able to read fluently but not understand what the words mean. For this child, the problem is not in discriminating words or even reading them, but in understanding that the words have meaning. Children afflicted with this problem can pick up any book and read it in a mechanical monotone. After finishing,

**Remedial Smoke Reading**

"That settles it. You'll have to take remedial smoke reading."

*From* The Wall Street Journal, *with permission of Cartoon Features Syndicate*

# BILINGUAL EDUCATION

Even the words "bilingual education" touch a nerve among educators, parents, and students. Those who argue for bilingual education see it as a natural result of a pluralistic society. They feel that bilingual and bicultural education will meet the students' academic needs and, at the same time, recognize the value of their culture. Stripping minority students of their cultural ties is an affront that is unnecessary if bilingual programs are supported.

Critics of the bilingual programs suggest that the psychological well-being of the student and the need for cultural affirmation have been exaggerated. They point out that immersing the student in the new language is a quicker and more successful alternative than bilingual education. At their best, bilingual programs slow down the student's acculturation into the mainstream of society. At their worst, these programs guarantee that students never learn to speak the language and are relegated to a peripheral position in society.

Other alternatives exist (Ovando, 1983). A limited bilingual program, one that moves students into the new language after one or two years, has been suggested. Another suggestion is from individuals who want to maintain cultural ties but also want to see the child assimilated rapidly into the majority culture. They propose that the culture and the language be taught outside of school time. This alternative has been used successfully by Jewish communities to teach Hebrew and the history and traditions of Judaism.

Deciding among these alternatives means evaluating evidence about achievement, acculturation, and psychological well-being. Looking at the achievement literature first, we see that immersion programs are an effective, quick, and relatively painless way to learn a new language. In Canada, immersion students learning French achieved markedly higher levels of language proficiency than students in a French-English bilingual program (Genesee, 1983). In high school, immersion students performed as well as French-speaking students on science and math examinations. Genesee notes that the earlier the immersion expe-

rience, the more effective it was. This Canadian experiment demonstrates that immersion students do not suffer in other academic areas.

It should be noted that contemporary immersion programs do not endorse the "sink or swim" philosophy of earlier years. Rather than being thrown into a strange language community, students in immersion programs are offered highly structured introductions to the language. The first sessions may be no longer than 20 minutes and are gradually increased. The instruction is geared to the developmental level of the student and is designed to encourage the student to think and speak in a second language. At the same time, there is no denigration of the child's first language, and children are allowed to use their first language when talking among themselves (Genesee, 1983).

A final comment on the Canadian experiment, however, shows that it cannot be transplanted intact to the United States. Students enrolled in the immersion programs were primarily from the middle and upper social classes. They wanted to be proficient in both French and English. Their second language was never intended to replace their first. The students in the United States come primarily from the lower-middle and lower social classes. Furthermore, there is a tacit assumption that students will concentrate on English to the exclusion of their first language.

These cultural issues are as important in educational decisions as achievement scores. A task force examining bilingual education suggests that the students' cultural needs could be met in other ways (Ravitch, 1983). The members of the task force emphasized the need to learn English if children are to become an integral part of this culture. They found many students in bilingual programs who were not learning English. Often this was because the teacher switched between the two languages. Teaching in this manner becomes time consuming and tedious because every instruction has to be given in both languages. But most important, this approach is not conducive to the development of a second lan-

## BILINGUAL EDUCATION *Concluded*

guage (Ovando, 1983). Students ignore the teacher when he or she speaks the second language. They wait until the instructions are given in their primary language. Under this teaching strategy, some students have been in bilingual programs for several years and still cannot communicate, read, or write in English.

Instead of endorsing bilingual education, the task force made the following recommendations: (1) Bilingual programs should be structured to teach students to read, write, and speak English; (2) this must be the primary goal because without skill in English, the goal of equal opportunity will never be realized; (3) every public school student should have the opportunity to gain proficiency in a second language. If all students were learning two languages, the stigma of the second language would be removed and the culture of the minority group would be preserved.

Source: Ravitch, D. (1983, June 6). Bilingual instruction is an answer, but not the only one. *Los Angeles Times*, p. 22.

they have no idea what they have read. A third child may also be able to demonstrate the mechanics of reading but not be able to remember the words long enough to extract the meaning (Torgeson, 1980).

As children become fluent readers, they should form hypotheses about their reading and be able to predict what comes next. In the later elementary years, children are expected to combine more sophisticated reading strategies with the more elementary process of discriminating sounds. When children integrate these skills, they will be able to read fluidly, to remember what they read, and to make deductions based on their reading. From this short description, it is obvious that reading problems can evolve from problems in the areas of attention, perception, memory, symbolization, or conceptualization (Oakhill, 1982).

This point is underscored by cross-cultural studies of Chinese and Japanese children. In these cultures, children learn to read characters that represent an entire word. They do not have to master an alphabet and the phonemic sounds that accompany each letter. This cultural difference does not mean that Japanese and Chinese children do not have reading disabilities. Their reading problems stem from an inability to coordinate verbal memory and spatial representation (Stevenson, Stigler, Lucker, & Lee, 1982).

The first step in helping dyslexic children is to assess their reading skills. Initially, auditory discrimination is tested. Can the children hear the difference between "shack" and "sack"? Can they comprehend the meaning of words? To test for this, children are asked to explain what the word "trunk" means in the sentences: "The girls gave peanuts to the elephant. They put them in the trunk." Children's verbal memory is assessed by asking them to recall a list of words or sentences. Administering standardized reading tests and asking the child to read aloud provide other helpful clues about the child's reading skills.

Pinpointing the child's difficulty is the first step in solving the problem. Once we know that the child's problems are caused by the inability to hear the difference between "e" and "v" rather than the inability to remember what has been read, it is possible to design a strategy that will correct the problem.

Similar steps are used for a learning disability in mathematics. A child may have difficulty with mathematics and have no problems with any other subjects (Mosse, 1982). Ricardo, one of Mosse's patients, could not understand that numbers referred to a specific number of units. When fractions were being taught, Ricardo designed a unique solution. He used each of his classmates to designate one unit.

> I think about people . . . . If I am in class, I divide the boys and girls into one whole, the teacher into two wholes or into two and a half, because he is an adult. When math is hard, I take one third or one half out of each student. The halves I took away, I add them all, and I divide by the number I am dividing with. Then I see the result I get. It always comes out right. (Mosse, 1982, p. 234)

By using his classmates to indicate a unit, he was able to solve abstract math problems. Another child drew lines on paper to represent numbers. As shown in Figure 14–5, this strategy loses its usefulness when the numbers become very large.

Learning disabilities no longer mystify educators, physicians, and psychologists. This does not mean that all learning problems are solved quickly and easily. However, an understanding of the problem, an awareness that the child is not retarded, and some strategies for preventing the problem have helped many children feel confident that they can succeed in school and life.

**Figure 14–5**          **Academically handicapped students**

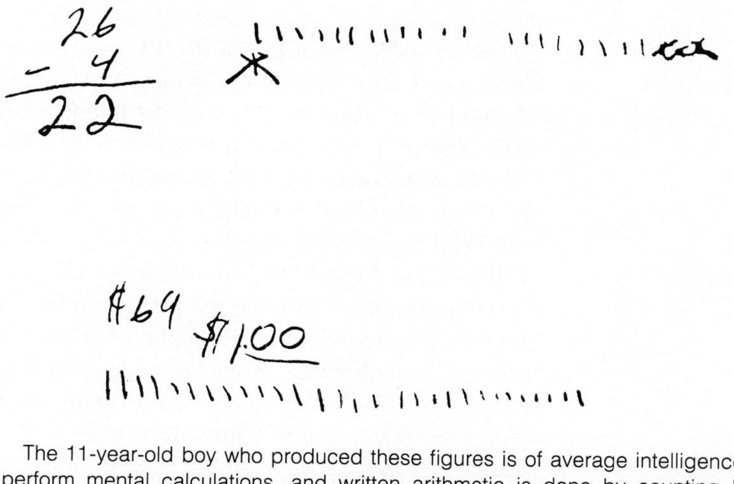

The 11-year-old boy who produced these figures is of average intelligence. He cannot perform mental calculations, and written arithmetic is done by counting lines that he draws. When too many lines are needed, as in the second example, the boy gives up.

Source: Mosse, H. L. (1982). *The complete handbook of children's reading disorders (p. 238)*. New York: Human Sciences Press.

**Differences in
conceptual style**

Intelligence is probably the area in which we see the most striking differences between children. How children use their intelligence also varies. Some children are reflective, weighing their answers before they act. Other children seem to leap at answers. Creative children use their intelligence to provide unique answers. These differences are described by the term *cognitive style*.

**Creativity.** Encouraging creative solutions to problems is one of the priorities of any society. In order to foster creative thought, we must first be explicit about the meaning of creativity. In recent years, creativity has been identified as fluency in thinking. A test of this fluency is to ask children to generate alternate uses for common objects such as a brick or a newspaper (Wallach & Kogan, 1965). Creative children generate a host of appropriate possibilities.

This fluency in thinking is more characteristic of some children than others. It can be isolated in children as early as three to four years of age (Harrington, Block, & Block, 1983). Children this young often expand on a single use for a brick ("you could use a brick to line a flower garden, a vegetable garden, a rose bush, etc"). Some children suggest several entirely different ways to use a brick or a newspaper. These responses are labeled "nonintended uses" and they are the best indicators of *divergent* thinking.

We can identify children who are divergent thinkers. Whether or not this trait is stable is a separate question. Harrington and his colleagues continued their study of four- and five-year-olds for seven years. When the children were in the sixth grade, their teachers were asked to identify children who were "creative in perception, thought, work, or play" (Harrington, Block, & Block, 1983). The teachers were more likely to select children who had excelled earlier on the tests of divergent thinking. Intelligence tests administered during the preschool years did not predict who was creative in sixth grade.

This study as well as studies of older children (Kogan & Pankove, 1972) tell us that assessments of divergent thinking tap a cognitive style variable that is somewhat stable. In other words, divergent thinking is not a transient characteristic. It is a continuing component of some children's cognitive repertoire. The trait is not, however, as stable as intelligence, suggesting that a supportive environment is necessary if this style is to be retained (Kogan, 1983).

**Field dependence and independence.** Another cognitive style variable relates to whether a child can separate parts of a field from the whole field. Children characterized as *field independent* can analyze pictures, such as the ones in Figure 14–2 into their distinct parts, while *field-dependent* children have trouble separating the parts from the whole. This dimension of cognitive style influences how the child approaches a variety of cognitive tasks—learning, remembering, problem solving, and spatial problems. In fact, the relevance of field independence to so many cognitive processes has prompted some researchers to ask if this measure is really just another form of IQ test (Kogan, 1983).

Field dependence, like divergent thinking, can be measured during preschool (Coates, 1972). A few children show high levels of field independence at three years of age. The early onset of this cognitive style has prompted some researchers to suggest that field independence is biologically determined (Thomas, 1982). The fact that children can be trained to score higher on tasks that measure field independence argues against a simple biological explanation.

On some of the assessments of field independence and field dependence, sex differences have emerged. Preschool girls, for example, are more field independent than preschool boys (Coates, 1974). This result is unexpected because boys generally have an advantage in any task that measures spatial skills (Maccoby & Jacklin, 1974). Nathan Kogan (1983) suggests that the girls' advantage in preschool reflects the girls' biological maturity. By adolescence, boys score higher than girls on this measure, and this advantage persists through adulthood (Witkin & Goodenough, 1981).

**Reflective versus impulsive children.** Psychologists are also intrigued by a third cognitive style variable—whether a child reflects on a task or approaches it impulsively (Cairns & Commock, 1981). In assessments of this variable, children examine a familiar object such as a bear or a leaf and find a second bear or leaf that matches the first (see Figure 14–6). In this task, psychologists are interested in how long the child takes to solve the problem and whether the answer is correct (Kagan, Rosman, Day, Albert, & Phillips, 1964). *Impulsive* children answer quickly and make many errors. Their approach relies on a global analysis of the figure. *Reflective* children take their time matching the figure. They make few errors, and their approach examines the component parts of the figure (Zelniker & Jeffrey, 1979). These styles, if used consistently in approaching cognitive tasks, could easily affect the child's classroom performance (Duryea & Glover, 1982).

**Figure 14–6**  **Cognitive styles**

The Matching Familiar Figures test has been used to assess whether children approach cognitive tasks in an impulsive or a reflective manner. Children are instructed to look at the initial picture and then find another picture that is an exact match.

Copyright 1964 by the American Psychological Association. Reprinted by permission of the author.

Some evidence that impulsive children approach all cognitive tasks similarly comes from a study by Janice Lawry and her co-workers. Lawry gave children a series of problems that became progressively more difficult. When the problems were easy, both the impulsive and the reflective children answered quickly and correctly. As the problems became more difficult, the reflective children took a longer amount of time and answered carefully. The impulsive children adhered to their fast, inaccurate strategy and began guessing wildly (Lawry, Welsh, & Jeffrey, 1983). This evidence suggests that the impulsive-reflective dimension is indeed a style that children use in approaching cognitive tasks.

The cognitive style of the reflective child leads to high levels of achievement in school. When required to attend to details or solve complex problems, reflective children perform admirably (Bush & Dweck, 1975). Impulsive children are usually placed at the lower end of the academic achievement scale (Kogan, 1983). Jack Block and his co-workers further characterize impulsive children as anxious, hypersensitive, and vulnerable (Block, Block, & Harrington, 1974). On the positive side, the impulsive child may have an advantage when problems of a global nature are being solved.

The reflective-impulsive style variable changes over time. All children become more reflective until about 10 years of age (Salkind & Nelson, 1980). As a result, by 7 to 10 years of age, psychologists report that both reflective and impulsive children can work independently and attend to the teacher (Moore, Haskins, & McKinney, 1980). Even if this dimension of individual differences is no longer obvious during classroom observations, it could still be a factor in cognitive tasks. In one short-term longitudinal study, reflective children were able to use concrete operational thinking skills by eight years of age. Their impulsive peers were not as advanced conceptually (Brodzinsky, 1982). In another longitudinal study, the reflective-impulsive dimension remained important until the teenage years (Messer & Brodzinsky, 1981). These investigators conclude that reflective and impulsive accurately describe two different styles that adolescents continue to use when they approach cognitive tasks.

These three cognitive style variables define a second area of student diversity which is important in school. Unlike differences in intelligence, these stylistic variables are affected by situational variables. The cognitive style research underscores another point. Intelligence is only one factor that affects a student's performance in school. Any comprehensive understanding of school achievement should include stylistic variables and motivational variables.

**Differences between the sexes**

In the early elementary years, girls are more obedient, cooperative, quiet, polite, and dependable. They are also likely to get better grades. Boys are more likely to have learning problems, reading difficulties, and exhibit problem behavior in the class (Strommen, McKinney, & Fitzgerald, 1983). By high school, women still have a verbal advantage. However, men now have an advantage in quantitative skills, visual spatial skills, and in field independence (Rosenthal & Rubin, 1982).

At the end of high school, men have an overwhelming advantage over women in the field of mathematics (Mullis, 1975). As a result of this advantage, men are channeled into fields that stress science and technology. Women are funneled into the humanities and social sciences. Ultimately, these sex differences in mathematics translate into limited career opportunities for women (Ernest, 1980).

The sex differences in math skills have attracted wide attention from educators, scientists, and women's groups. However, this difference is not always present. Girls excel at computation and hence have an advantage in the early years of school when computational skills are the mainstay of the math curriculum. During high school, the curriculum shifts to analysis, application, and reasoning. It is at this point that the differences in mathematics between males and females become obvious (Fox, Brody, & Tobin, 1980).

The fact that these differences exist during high school and college is undeniable. Julian Stanley and Camilla Benbow (1982) report that there are 17 males for every female who receives a score above 700 on the math section of the SAT. At least three suggestions for this difference have been offered. The first focuses on the fact that females take fewer math courses in high school (Ernest, 1980). If this is the problem, then women should be encouraged to study math in high school and college.

The second explanation focuses on differential treatment of boys and girls (Block, 1983). We know that a child's educational success is influenced by the parental expectations, support, and reinforcement (Seginer, 1983). Women have much less confidence about their mathematical skill than men. Some psychologists feel this lack of confidence begins during the elementary years because of low parental expectations for girls.

Doris Entwisle and David Baker (1983) found that even though boys and girls were in the same classes and were receiving the same grades in math, the boys expected to do well while the girls did not. When these investigators interviewed the parents, they found that the children's expectations mirrored their parents'— girls were expected to do poorly in math, and boys were expected to excel. Furthermore, parents felt that girls had to work harder in math classes than boys. They also did not believe their daughters needed advanced math classes (Parsons, Adler, & Kaczala, 1982). The possible consequences of these expectations are shown in Figure 14–7. Low expectations for females yield some success and some failure experiences. Because they expect to perform poorly, girls attribute their failures to a lack of ability. Their successes are attributed to luck. The expectancies are reversed for boys. Their failures are attributed to bad luck, and their successes become the index of their ability (Deaux, 1984). The result is that boys feel they can excel at math; girls are anxious and uncertain about their skills (Dew, Galassi, & Galassi, 1983).

A third explanation for the sex differences in mathematics is biological. This argument rests on the proposition that androgen leads to a particular pattern of human cognitive skills in which spatial skills are highly developed (see Hines, 1982). Consistent with this view is the fact that hormone levels are low in both sexes until 9 or 10 years of age. At this age, there is a gradual rise in androgen

**Figure 14–7**          **Expectations about success in math**

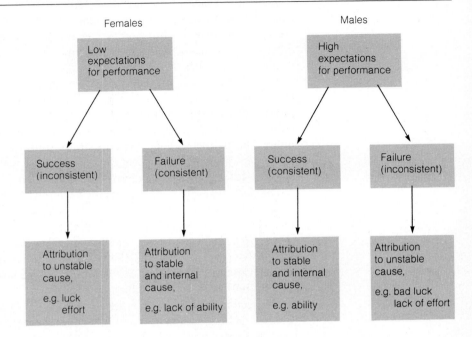

Females

| Low expectations for performance |

| Success (inconsistent) | | Failure (consistent) |

| Attribution to unstable cause, e.g. luck effort | | Attribution to stable and internal cause, e.g. lack of ability |

Males

| High expectations for performance |

| Success (consistent) | | Failure (inconsistent) |

| Attribution to stable and internal cause, e.g. ability | | Attribution to unstable cause, e.g. bad luck lack of effort |

Parental expectations may partially explain why females do not do as well as males in high school mathematics courses.

Copyright 1984 by the American Psychological Association. Reprinted by permission of the author.

secretion in males (Archer, 1976). Also, sex differences in cognitive skills are most apparent following puberty (Waber, 1979).

Despite these consistencies, it is dangerous to leap from biology to behavior when our knowledge of the effect of hormonal variables on behavior is scanty. We know that the development of the cortex follows a different path in male and female monkeys and that this difference is mediated by hormones (Goldman-Rakic, Isseroff, Schwartz, & Bugbee, 1983). This does not translate easily into information about math or reading skills in humans. We are left with some fascinating hypotheses that will undoubtedly guide future research. Robert Rosenthal and Donald Rubin point out, however, that the male superiority in math and in spatial skills has decreased in recent years. "Females appear to be gaining in cognitive skill . . . faster than the gene can travel!" (Rosenthal & Rubin, 1982, p. 711).

To summarize, males and females exhibit different patterns of cognitive skills which influence achievement in school. Girls in elementary school are more mature and better behaved. Their verbal advantage is evident throughout the elementary and high school years. After puberty, boys take the lead in mathematics and spatial skills. Differences in intellectual skill and cognitive

styles are also obvious in the classroom. The reasons for these student differences are as diverse as the students themselves. Certainly these differences stem
from biological variables, family variables, socialization practices, school variables, and cultural values. Various combinations of these factors can help
students excel or hinder their achievement in school.

## TELEVISION AS AN ADJUNCT TO THE SCHOOL

Television is an invention that has assumed incredible importance in our
culture. At the push of a button, a sound and light show appears that attracts
toddlers and preschoolers. This same invention offers comfort and companionship to elderly persons confined to their homes. For all others, television has
the potential to educate, entertain, and influence. In the last chapter, we
examined the impact of hours of viewing violent programs on children's behavior. In this chapter, we extend the discussion to include television's influence
on the child's cognitive processing, emotional functioning, imagination, and
socialization. By three years of age, children spend long hours watching television. Once children begin to attend school, there is a small decrease in
viewing time. As children stay awake longer, they join the rest of the family
watching television after school and after dinner. Teenagers seem to have
enough outside activities that their viewing time decreases. Young adults, especially parents with young children, often use the TV as a source of adult
conversation. For the elderly, television is a continuing and inexpensive source
of entertainment. Minority groups, women, and individuals from the lower
social strata watch more than the average amount of television each day. In
general, people who do not have much to do fill their days with television
(Pearl, Bouthilet, & Lazar, 1982).

Given the intrinsic interest in television and the position it has assumed in
our daily lives, it seems that we should be able to use it to teach children basic
skills, to educate the population about health and safety issues, and to enhance
social skills and social behavior. To date, these optimistic assessments of television's potential are yet to be realized (Wright & Huston, 1983). Instead, the
evaluations have been primarily negative.

**Television and
cognitive functioning**

In 1968, the Children's Television Workshop created a program designed
especially for children. The goal of this program, titled *Sesame Street*, was to
promote the intellectual and cultural growth of preschoolers, particularly disadvantaged preschoolers. *Sesame Street* combined animation, muppets, and
fast-paced music to teach children the letters of the alphabet and numbers.
Their regular cast of characters included individuals of all ages and races who
modeled tolerance, helping, sharing, and understanding.

Several evaluations of *Sesame Street* indicate that children who watched the
program were better prepared for kindergarten. They recognized letters and
numbers and could identify parts of the body. Children who watched the show

most often made the greatest gains in these skills. *Sesame Street* did not, however, narrow the gap between disadvantaged children and middle-class children. Perhaps middle-class children learned readily because their mothers also watched the show. At various times during the day, these mothers would bring up a scene or a lesson from *Sesame Street* (Cook, Appleton, Conner, Shaffer, Tabkin, & Weber, 1975).

The second program from the Children's Television Workshop, *The Electric Company*, was designed to teach reading. Although it has won several awards and is included in many second grade reading curricula, children who watch it at home and alone do not learn to read more effectively than children who do not watch this program. When adults are present to reinforce or extend the lessons, the lively animation is more effective. Used with no reinforcement or feedback, these programs are less likely to affect academic skills. Watching television is a passive experience compared to reading, playing dress up with a friend, or answering a mother's questions. Television requires no active response from the child and hence requires a minimum of mental effort, initiative, and imagination (Singer & Singer, 1983). It is no surprise, then, that watching hours of noneducational television during the preschool years predicts poor reading comprehension, ineffective use of language, lack of imaginative play, and poor school adjustment in second and third grade (Singer & Singer, 1983).

While television may not prepare a child for kindergarten or teach reading, it might teach children about language. Mabel Rice (1983) argues that some cartoons use very simple and redundant dialogue. This is the kind of speech that is suited to toddler's and preschooler's needs. Children may also learn more subtle information such as the social functions of language. Perhaps children will never learn adverbs or past participles from television, but Rice believes that television offers some relevant language experiences for young children.

**Television and prosocial behavior**

Television is more successful at teaching prosocial behavior. *Fat Albert and the Cosby Kids* and *Mr. Roger's Neighborhood* are two television shows that contain a moral or a message for children. After watching *Fat Albert*, over 90 percent of the children could state the main idea of the show, such as smoking is not healthy. Children who watched *Mr. Roger's Neighborhood* learned prosocial behaviors. After viewing this show, preschoolers spontaneously helped other children (Freidrich & Stein, 1975). These positive findings have encouraged researchers to show "prosocial" television to emotionally disturbed children. Over a period of one year, the television programming at a residential home was strictly controlled. During this period, altruism increased and aggression decreased (Sprafkin & Rubenstein, 1982). Robert Liebert, a veteran of television research, concludes that television can teach socialization when the programming is carefully and systematically designed.

These findings raise the question, "Do we want to use television in a planned program of socialization?" Should 30-second spots encouraging cooperation be part of the network's daily programming, or is such manipulation only a prelude to a complete Orwellian takeover? Watching television consumes more time in a child's life than any other activity except sleeping. What children watch can influence their values, beliefs, attitudes, and actions (Leibert, Sprafkin, & Davidson, 1982). To date, the networks have been controlling the children's programming and have labeled any attempt at outside regulation as censorship. But without any regulation, it is likely that the aggressive and violent programming of the last two decades will continue. One alternative is for parents to actively monitor the television programs their children watch. A slightly more aggressive stance is to petition advertisers not to buy commercial time on violent shows. It would be easy to convince advertisers not to buy commercial time on a violent program if no one watched that program. Similarly, more educational programming would exist if the audiences for these programs were larger.

**Attitudes and values learned from television**

Attitudes and values are other areas in which television has a marked impact on children. Attitudes toward people from other cultures are positively influenced by the children's show, *Big Blue Marble*. Attitudes can also be negatively influenced. Television often portrays characters in stereotypic roles. For example, women are submissive, senior citizens are often bumbling, and southern policemen are ignorant. The effect of a single program showing such stereotypes has influenced children's attitudes (Graves, 1980). Children who spend a lot of time watching television are more likely to believe such stereotypic notions as "girls should play with dolls" and "boys should play with trucks" (Frueh & McGhee, 1975).

Television does affect how the viewer perceives the real world. People who watch a great deal of television see the world as more menacing simply because so many antisocial and frightening incidents take place on television. Think of your own experiences over the last month. How many murders, robberies, and violent attacks have you personally encountered? Now consider the number that have taken place on the television programs you watch. It is easy to see how children can become frightened and concerned about events that really occur rather infrequently. Fortunately, parents can alleviate a child's concern by discussing frightening programs with the child.

**Providing information**

Television can be used to provide information. In fact, television has assumed the stance of sex educator. Children listed television as the second most important source of their sexual information. Television provided less sexual information than parents, but more than siblings, friends, books, or sex education programs at school (Roberts, 1982).

Antismoking messages, campaigns for the use of seat belts in cars, and pleas for complying with the speed limit can all be mounted on television. The advantage of these campaigns is that they reach millions of viewers in a short period of time. Of course, these messages may be contradicted when the leading character in a prime-time drama hops into the car without buckling his seat belt, lights up a cigarette, and races down the highway at 70 mph.

Even from this brief examination of the effects of television, we see that television is a two-edged sword. It can persuade, teach, create attitudes, and provide models. However, the effect can be either positive or negative. Television might persuade one person to try cocaine and another person to avoid it, simply by providing models of people either enjoying drugs or urging young people to abstain. Shows that teach academic skills may be used by some parents as an adjunct to their reading programs, and the children may profit enormously. The same television show, turned on to entertain the child and used in place of parental interaction, could have the opposite effect. By depicting people of several racial backgrounds working together, television may encourage racial harmony. Programming that promotes racial stereotypes can undermine those positive attitudes. Given the dual nature of television's influence, one can only urge parents to monitor the television programs their children watch. Parents can then interact with the child, reinforcing positive attitudes and values and overriding negative aspects and events. In this way, television can become a positive influence on a child's development.

## SUMMARY

Contemporary societies have given schools enormous responsibilities. The first is to educate children. As an extension of the culture, schools also have the responsibility for socializing children and promoting their development into competent, productive citizens. In this chapter, we have examined how well the schools have managed to fulfill these responsibilities.

School promotes the child's thinking skills. Children who attend school are able to classify information and think about events in a logical manner. They have learned how to organize information so that they can remember it. Schools also influence nonacademic skills. A child's self-esteem and many of the child's attitudes about life are nurtured in the classroom.

The classroom cannot be expected to equalize the tremendous individual differences between students. Very talented students will remain academically ahead of less able students. The fact that schools do not have the same success with all students does not mean that schools have no impact. Schools that focus on academics, have rigorous expectations, and involve the parents impel all children toward their optimal performance.

How to structure schools so that they have the greatest impact on all students remains an unsolved problem. Open classrooms reward student initiative and encourage independence. Children in these classroom settings are considered active agents who direct their own learning. More traditional classrooms place more burden on the teacher who guides the children toward specific curricular goals. Research on both types of classrooms reveals that, in general, children learn what they are taught. In an open classroom, they may learn to tell imaginative stories and hence improve their language skills. In a traditional classroom, they may learn phonics and hence become better readers.

Cooperative learning presents a third way of structuring the classroom. This strategy has been very successful in promoting interaction between students of different races, sexes, and abilities. In some of its applications, cooperative learning has also had a positive effect on student achievement. Psychologists studying the structure of classrooms believe that different structures facilitate different kinds of growth, and that optimal development may well be facilitated by a variety of structures used to accomplish different purposes. The classrooms of the future, then, may use cooperative strategies at one point during the day, encourage initiative and independence at other times, and have the teacher direct an assignment at a third time.

Teachers are the representatives of the culture and have been given the responsibility for helping students learn. Outstanding teachers have an impact on students that is felt for years. Less able teachers have trouble maintaining a learning environment, and their students suffer. The impact of the teacher has been studied thoroughly in the research on expectations. Teachers have been accused of discouraging student performance by having low expectations for a particular student. When this charge is investigated, it appears that in a small number of cases, it is true. But overall, teachers' expectations are formed through continuing interacting with the student, are subject to change, and have a limited impact on the student's achievement.

Differences among students challenge the teacher who often cannot meet the needs of all students simultaneously. Gifted children profit from fast-moving curricula that concentrate on concepts. They need to be accelerated to prevent boredom. Students with academic handicaps need to have their particular problem diagnosed. The teacher, in consultation with specialists, then designs an individual educational strategy.

Individual differences in ability have always been recognized by the school. Children also differ in the cognitive styles or strategies that they use to approach problems. A fluent, creative child may sit next to a quiet, reflective child. These cognitive styles are more subtle than intellectual differences, but may be no less important in devising an optimal educational program for the child.

Sex differences in achievement are another problem that educators face daily. In elementary school, girls excel academically while boys cause the majority of the behavioral problems. By junior high and high school, boys emerge as star students, especially in science and math. The reasons for these sex differences are not clear. Parental expectations, biology, and practice may all play a part.

Children spend as much time watching television as they do in any other activity, except sleeping. Hence, we can no longer ignore the impact that watching television has on the child's education. But listing television's effects is not easy. Television has the potential to be a powerful and a positive influence in the child's socialization. Under the proper circumstances, children can learn academic content from television. They can also learn prosocial behavior. They can acquire attitudes and values that build tolerance and understanding. Television can also have a powerful and negative influence on a child. What children learn from television depends on what they watch and how that experience meshes with their lives.

**Play**

Play as repetition and consolidation
Pretend play
Play as a precursor to innovation
The progression of play

**Invulnerable children**

Children born to psychotic parents
Children of poverty
Children of war

**Longitudinal studies of competence**

**Self-efficacy**

Factors that influence self-efficacy
Experiments on mastery and modeling

**Learned helplessness**

Effects of helplessness
Differences between competent and helpless children
Precursors of helplessness

**Sex differences in competence**

Parents' reactions to boys and girls
Sex differences that affect competence
Acquiring sex roles

**Summary**

# CHAPTER 15
## Competence

The family, the peer group, and the school all help mold the child. The child, however, is not a formless lump of clay to be fashioned by parents, peers, and teachers. The child is an active participant in the process of development. As psychologists have come to understand more about human development, they have seen that the child not only has a role but often directs the interaction. For example, if the infant smiles and coos, the mother is drawn into a playful interaction. If the infant begins to cry, turns away, or stares blankly, the mother is less likely to play.

Older children can also take the lead in parent-child interaction. In the Abecedarian project for example, the children had several strikes against them. Without some help, they seemed destined to fail in school. To prevent this, the Abecedarian project concentrated on building strong language skills. As an unexpected bonus, the children used their newly learned language skills to change their patterns of interacting with their mothers. By inviting their mothers to have a tea party and conversing over their imaginary cups of tea, these preschoolers minimized the mother's blunt, imperative communication style. Here again, the children directed the action (Ramey, MacPhee, & Yeates, 1982). As children develop, they have more conscious control over their own behavior. They also have a larger repertoire of skills they can use to influence their environments. They are not passive players on life's stage.

In this chapter, we will examine how children manage their environments. We especially want to look for the strengths of the child and the development of elusive traits such as competence, self-efficacy, and motivation. If we can understand how to help children acquire these qualities, we can help them surmount many of life's trials and optimize their potential.

Competence refers to a set of personal qualities. It includes, but is not limited to, cognitive competence (White, 1959). Broadly, *competence* is the "ability to generate and coordinate flexible, adaptive responses to demands and to generate and capitalize on opportunities in the environment" (Waters & Sroufe, 1983, p. 80). One example of the effect of competence on individuals is provided by a longitudinal study of gifted children which was begun in the 1920s by Lewis Terman. The children in Terman's study were identified as gifted while still in grade school. As a group, they scored in the top 1 percent of the entire population and had an average IQ of 151 (Terman & Oden,

1947). These individuals have now been studied for over 60 years, through adolescence, adulthood, and into retirement.

One part of this longitudinal study involved a comparison of men who had been very successful with those who had been less successful (Terman & Oden, 1947). The IQs of the two groups were almost identical. Sixty-eight percent of the successful group, called Group A, had professional occupations. Only 9 percent of the less successful group, called Group C, had professional occupations. The differences in formal education were equally significant. Ninety percent of the men in Group A graduated from college, but only 37 percent of Group C finished college. What caused these enormous differences in success?

Family factors provided part of the explanation. The successful men came from professional families and intact homes. The less successful men were likely to have grown up without a father, either because their father had died or because their parents had divorced. Personal variables also differentiated the two groups (see Figure 15–1). The professional men were given higher ratings on such qualities as perseverance, self-confidence, integration toward goals, appearance, attractiveness, alertness, poise, attentiveness, curiosity, and originality (Terman & Oden, 1947). These men had the social skills, the motivation, and the poise to obtain goals consistent with their intellectual skills. The men in Group C were more likely to have nervous symptoms and more than twice as likely to divorce than the men in Group A. As a group, they lacked the intangible qualities that insure success.

The Terman study offers a clear example of how personal factors influence the competence of adults. Trying to trace the development of these factors has

**Figure 15–1**                   **Competence**

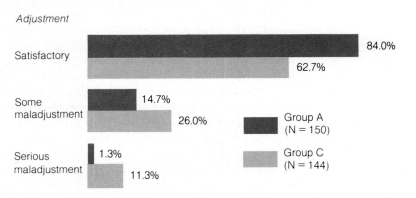

The gifted men in Terman's longitudinal study differed markedly on overall adjustment even though they had very similar IQs.

Source: Terman, L. M., & Oden, M. H. (1947). *The gifted child grows up.* Stanford, CA: Stanford University Press.

prompted psychologists to study many facets of a child's development. For example, psychologists have investigated children's play. They have asked how stress affects children. They have looked at children who have overcome poverty, illness, and unsupportive families, and seemed not only to survive, but to triumph. They have studied how children learn to be helpless in the hope that they would simultaneously learn how children become competent. Studying how children identify with members of their own sex may also help us understand how some children cope with environmental hardships while other children do not cope successfully. All of these areas of developmental psychology hold clues to how a child becomes a competent adult.

## PLAY

At first glance, the relationship between play and competence may seem obscure. Is it really important to study toddlers pushing a truck, preschoolers kneading Play Doh, or second graders playing hop-scotch, in order to understand competence? Developmental psychologists, taking their cue from the studies of other species, have come to think that play must have adaptive value or it would not be so common (Bruner, 1972). Play uses energy, makes the species more visible to predators, and can injure the young. If play did not serve some useful purpose, it would have disappeared during eons of evolution (Smith, 1982).

Jane Goodall's (1965) reports from the Gombe stream in Africa offered some clues to the importance of play. She described adult chimps who had developed a very skilled technique of catching termites. The chimps first put an appropriately sized twig into their mouths to moisten it. The twig was then dipped into the opening of a termite hole. After termites adhered to the twig, the chimps carefully removed their twig and gobbled up their catch.

Goodall relates the learning of this skill to the play behavior of young chimps. A young chimp, Merlin, lost his mother when he was three. His ability to catch termites lagged far behind that of his peers. The reason Goodall offered for this lapse is that chimps learn how to fish for termites by sitting by their mothers, playfully trying out the constituent acts of catching termites. Here, then, is one clue to the value of play. It informs the young about important behaviors in the culture. During play, the child has the opportunity to assemble and reassemble a variety of behavioral sequences that will become important in later years (Bruner, 1974).

Fighting is also learned through play. In order to signal that they are playing, baboons adopt a "play face" and a different, galumphing gait (Smith, 1982). If this signal is not interpreted correctly by the other baboons, a real fight breaks out. Once both baboons have signaled that this is play, they engage in the different posturing, teeth baring, and chasing that are components of fighting.

Jerome Bruner builds on these examples in his description of the importance of play. During play fighting and fishing for termites, there is no need to be successful. The young do not have to obtain food or defend their territory.

There are no consequences for success or failure. Play, then, allows one to learn in a less risky situation (Bruner, Jolly, & Sylva, 1976). Because there are no consequences, the young of a species do not have to be frustrated if they do not achieve a goal. The real goal is to practice and understand.

Understanding is another important aspect of play. Play offers the opportunity to become familiar with objects and learn about their characteristics. Becoming familiar with the characteristics of twigs is critical to later success at catching termites. In Bruner's view, play provides an opportunity to try combinations of behavior that would otherwise never be tried (Bruner et al., 1976).

These observations of other animals convinced developmental psychologists that play was important and gave new impetus to research on play in children. From the outset, however, psychologists realized that studying human children at play would yield different insights than studying other species. Children certainly learn adaptive skills through play, but they may also acquire problem solving skills and complex social skills (Christie & Johnsen, 1983). Given the long period in which humans are immature, it is likely that play has different forms. To understand the play of human children, then, we need to describe play and then look at its effects on competence.

**Play as repetition and consolidation**

Jean Piaget (1962) presents one of the most viable theories of play in humans. In his view, play is the starting point for the development of competence and symbolic skill. During infancy, play allows children to repeat and master a particular behavior. He gives the example of Laurent at seven months.

> After learning to remove an obstacle to gain his objective, Laurent began to enjoy this kind of exercise. When several times in succession I put my hand or a piece of cardboard between him and the toy he desired, he reached the stage of momentarily forgetting the toy and pushed aside the obstacle, bursting into laughter. What had been intelligent adaptation had thus become play, through transfer of interest to the action itself, regardless of its aim (Piaget, 1962, p. 92).

Notice that the repetition, or play, has nothing to do with the goal. The pleasure of this play came from the child's sense of control over himself and his environment. The skill Laurent acquired was exciting. Once infants master a problem, they can bask in the feeling of growing competence by doing it again (Rubin, Fein, & Vandenberg, 1983).

Piaget also points out that practice consolidates skills. At first, a new behavior is performed hesitantly. After practice, the skill is varied and generalized. Greta Fein (1982) gives the example of a child learning to go down a slide. Children's initial attempts are accompanied by parental hand holding, apprehension, and ignorance about the position of the body. As children practice this activity, they go down the slide sitting, lying, head first, or feet first. In Piaget's terms, the initial learning on the slide is adaptation, but the subsequent exercise is play. Going down the slide head first consolidates the initial learning. The old skill is incorporated into new variations, but the child is able to separate the essence—the sliding—from nonessential elaborations (Rubin, et al., 1983).

At any age, play may involve practicing and consolidating a new skill. Rolling a car back and forth and kneading Play Doh are examples of repetitive play for toddlers. Toddlers and preschoolers engage in the same kind of repetitive play as they learn language (Kuczaj II, 1982). Ruth Weir (1962) recorded her son, Anthony, playing with language. Every evening she left a tape recorder underneath her son's crib. When the lights were off and he was supposed to be going to sleep, he often began talking to himself. He formed negative sentences, asked questions correctly, and even reproved himself occasionally with an adult-like, 'Oh no, no.'

In the following sequence, he is playing with questions:

1. What color
2. What color blanket
3. What color mop
4. What color glass
(Weir, 1962, p. 109)

First, he establishes the frame for the question, then substitutes various objects. Anthony's language play fits Piaget's notions of practice and consolidation. It also demonstrates the beginning of representational play. Anthony is trying out sentences and is playing with symbols, not objects.

**Pretend play**

Toddlers and preschoolers often engage in symbolic play (Garvey, 1977). A piece of wood becomes a boat. A toy phone is used for an extended conversation. A white jacket symbolizes the doctor. By kindergarten, the toy phone and white jacket are no longer necessary during play. Children can hold an imaginary phone to their ear or announce with appropriate dignity, "Good morning, I'm Dr. Bones," and the make-believe session has begun. Developing the ability to pretend means that children can practice many scenarios. Unlike infants who actually drop rattles, bottles, and slices of orange to learn about dropping, preschool and kindergarten children can pretend to be fantasy heroes, mothers, or school principals. When they are finished pretending, they resume their normal identity. During pretend play, children interpret real activities and the meaning of those activities. At the same time, they practice their ability to represent the world (Pepler & Rubin, 1982). Pretend play thus becomes a powerful tool to understand the world. It has the potential to educate children about social roles at the same time that it prods the development of advanced cognitive skills.

Symbolic play initially appears toward the end of the first year and increases dramatically between 11 and 18 months of age (Zelazo & Kearsley, 1980). At these young ages, the representational component is isolated. For example, toddlers may pretend to go to sleep, curling up with a blanket and closing their

### Pretend play

*Jean-Claude Lejeune*

Pretend play prepares children for adult roles and prods cognitive and linguistic development.

eyes. In a few seconds, however, they will wake up and resume their real identity. By preschool, children's representational skills are more sophisticated. They are able to enact long, complex scenarios that revolve around family, school, or some imaginary theme (Rubin & Krasnor, 1980). By kindergarten, these pretend sketches may involve several cast members and be highly dramatized (Hetherington, Cox, & Cox, 1979).

In the last two decades, psychologists have come to believe that pretend play can have major effects on the child's development. One of the primary effects is on the child's ability to assume social roles. In hunting and gathering societies, children's pretend play is often a practice for future behaviors. The Yanomami children imitate the adults of their tribe by playing games that involve shooting arrows. The Himba, a pastoral people, watch their children pretend to herd cattle. The fact that the cattle are represented by large stones does not matter. The children still learn social roles and practice their herding skills (Eibl-Eiblesfeldt, 1982). Anthropologists have noticed that the pretend games that boys play often mirror their view of the adult male role in society. The same is true of girls. In contemporary Western cultures, boys relish fictional, superhero roles, while girls prefer to play a member of the family or to play school (Connally, 1980).

Not all pretend play prepares children for their adult roles. Pretend play is also thought to prod cognitive development. To investigate this hypothesis, psychologists have trained children in sociodrama and fantasy and then observed their cognitive skills (Smilansky, 1968). The sociodrama experiments typically have children enact common excursions, like going to the doctor or the grocery store. In the fantasy training, children enact a fairy tale such as

*The Three Billy Goats Gruff.* Both types of training have been found to increase scores on intelligence tests (Saltz & Brodie, 1982). In one of the longest studies of this kind, the children were studied for three years (Saltz, Dixon, & Johnson, 1977). Those children who were encouraged to pretend received IQ scores from three to nine points higher than children who had no training in pretend play (see Figure 15–2).

Results from similar training experiments indicate that pretend play improves language skills, creativity, and sequential memory (Rubin, Fein, & Vandenberg, 1983). Whether it is the pretend play that causes these gains has been questioned. It could be the verbal stimulation associated with play situations. It might be that children in these special groups became acquainted with the experimenters and were more at ease during the IQ tests.

Both of these alternative explanations have been answered by Eli Saltz and Jane Brodi (1982). They point out that during their three-year study, the experimenters interacted equally with all groups. They also discount the verbal stimulation theory. They point out that a third group of children answered questions about *The Three Billy Goats Gruff.* This group received as much verbal stimulation as children enacting the play. In the follow-up IQ testing, they did not differ from the control group (see Figure 15–2).

The literature indicates that imaginative play enhances development in a variety of areas (Rubin et al., 1983). Practicing for adult roles, learning new cognitive skills, and consolidating newly acquired behaviors occur naturally when children begin to pretend. It is not surprising, then, that educators have urged teachers to include structured play programs in the preschool and kindergarten curriculum. Teaching children to pretend is seen as an investment in later social and cognitive development.

| Figure 15–2 | Sociodrama and fantasy |
| --- | --- |

Means and standard deviations of IQ scores for 1973, 1974, and 1975 for each of the experimental conditions

| | Thematic-fantasy play (a) | | Sociodramatic play (b) | | Fantasy discussion (c) | | Control (d) | |
| --- | --- | --- | --- | --- | --- | --- | --- | --- |
| | Mean | SD | Mean | SD | Mean | SD | Mean | SD |
| 1973 | 103.9 | 14.9 | 98.5 | 21.2 | 96.3 | 13.6 | 91.7 | 15.0 |
| 1974 | 104.5 | 10.5 | 103.3 | 10.0 | 96.7 | 9.8 | 95.0 | 11.2 |
| 1975 | 97.5 | 22.9 | 97.3 | 18.5 | 94.7 | 15.5 | 92.7 | 17.4 |
| Grand mean | 101.6 | . . . | 98.9 | . . . | 95.7 | . . . | 92.6 | . . . |

© *The Society for Research in Child Development, Inc.*

Groups of nursery school children were given different opportunities to develop their ability to pretend. One group (*a*) acted out children's stories; a second group (*b*) acted out a trip to the doctor's; a third group (*c*) participated in a discussion of a children's story; a fourth group (*d*) received no special opportunities. The first two groups had higher IQ scores than the other groups and maintained their advantage over a three-year period.

**Play as a precursor to innovation**

Piaget hinted that repetition and play could have an impact on problem solving. Skills once mastered can be extended and generalized to new contexts. This view was discounted by many who thought play would be ineffective in solving problems. But Kathy Sylva and her colleagues decided to test the impact of play on problem solving. They presented preschool children with a problem called "Mr. Clamp." The desired object, a piece of colored chalk, was on a table in front of them, but out of their reach. The children were instructed to obtain the chalk, but they were required to stay in their chairs. This restriction prevented them from reaching for the chalk. On the table in front of the children were three sticks and two clamps (see Figure 15–3). None of the sticks was long enough to reach the chalk, but by clamping the three sticks together, the children could reach the chalk.

Children who were given this problem were initially divided into three groups. The first group, called the play group, was given time to play with a variety of sticks and clamps. In addition, they were shown how a clamp might fit on a stick. A second group, the demonstration group, saw an adult clamp

**Figure 15–3**          **Problem solving**

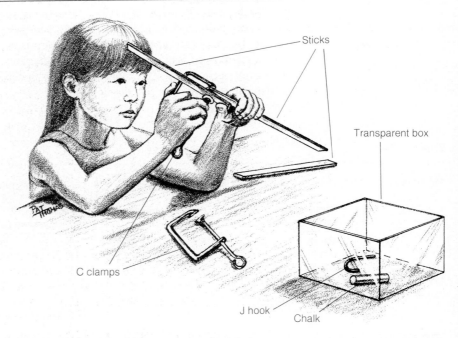

In this problem, children were asked to retrieve a piece of chalk beyond their reach. To do this, they had to figure out how to clamp the sticks together.

Source: Sylva, K., Bruner, J. S., & Genova, P. (1976). The relationship between play and problem solving in children three to five years old. In J. S. Bruner, A. Jolly, & K. Sylva (Eds.), *Play*. New York: Basic Books.

two sticks together. The third group was a control group which engaged in other activities. The 36 children who were allowed to play freely with the sticks and clamps were just as likely to solve the problem as the 36 children who had seen an adult demonstrate the solution. In the third group, only three of the 36 children could solve the problem.

It is impressive that simply playing with the materials led children to the solution. However, the number of children solving the problem is not the most important result of this experiment. The children who had an opportunity to play with the materials had a different approach to the problem. They did not become frustrated when they could not solve the problem. They continued to try new solutions to the problem. Furthermore, their solutions increased in complexity. The children who had observed an adult solve the problem did not adopt this play approach. If they could not clamp the sticks together immediately, they became discouraged. They were less likely to continue trying to solve the problem. Playing with the materials produced more than enthusiasm. The children in this group were productive and organized in their problem solving (Sylva, Bruner, & Genova, 1976; Sylva 1977).

An occasional study has reported that playing with materials is superior to receiving training to solve a problem (Smith & Dutton, 1979). These authors argue that training is inefficient because children lose interest and do not seem to remember what the adults have told them. In essence, motivation lags and attention wanders when someone tells children the solution (Smith & Dutton, 1979).

The attitudinal changes that accompany play are in some ways more important than whether problems can be solved through play. In attempting to analyze the development of this playful attitude, Corinne Hutt (1966) presented preschoolers with a toy which had levers, a buzzer, bells, and counters. When children first encountered the toy, they were curious, serious, and intent on exploration. Once the toy was inspected and understood, the child began playing with it. The child's interaction with the object now became much less serious. Children greeted the toy as a familiar friend and immediately began pushing the levers and watching the counters. These children had mastered the toy. A few children went beyond this level of play. They began to create new uses for the toy (Hutt & Bhavhani, 1976). What was earlier an interesting box with levers and counters was transformed into a spaceship making a scientific investigation of a distant planet. Each stage of play was accompanied by a change in attitude. While exploring, the child seemed to be asking, "What can this object do?" Curiosity and a serious demeanor dominated exploratory play. Mastery play was more relaxed and fun. The question asked by the children now became, "What can I do with this object?" Creative play had an air of exuberance about it (Hutt, 1984).

Even though several different laboratories have reported that playing with materials is as effective as being trained (Vandenburg, 1981), some questions remain (Rubin, et al., 1983). These experiments have been conducted primarily on preschoolers, and they have used very simple problems (Cheyne,

1982). Whether or not play would be as efficient with older children solving more complex problems has not been investigated.

Despite these criticisms, play does seem to motivate the child, encourage a sense of self-worth, and help preschool children organize information. These advantages have prodded psychologists to investigate play as a problem solving strategy. If you want children to learn to put together puzzles, should you let them play with the pieces or practice putting the pieces into a form board? Debra Pepler (1982) reports that children who work with the whole puzzle put it together readily, but their skill does not generalize to other puzzles or tasks.

When another group of children were given the puzzle pieces to use as blocks, the results were different. These children spent their time investigating the properties of the materials, playing symbolically with the materials, and grouping the materials. Later, when they were tested on assembling the pieces into a puzzle, they did not assemble it as fast as the first group. They did, however, develop a flexible set of ideas that generalized to other puzzles.

Pepler's conclusion is interesting. If you want children to solve one task, let them practice with the actual task. If you want them to learn a strategy that will apply to similar tasks, let them play with the components of those tasks. After such pretend play, children will react to problems with more flexibility, curiosity, spontaneity, and interest (Dansky, 1980). This kind of experiment has helped psychologists recognize that playful behavior generalizes broadly when it includes a representational quality or symbolic component. The pretend component encourages children to extend skills they have already mastered.

## The progression of play

The benefits from play are derived from a series of events. Initially, infants practice and consolidate simple behaviors. Their ability to recreate previous behaviors successfully provides a sense of competence. Repetition and consolidation can also be found in symbolic play. Pretend play opens new avenues of expression for the child. When preschoolers begin to play house or school, they are clearly practicing social roles. Pretend play also has cognitive benefits. It allows the child to move beyond the materials that are provided. With pretend play, the child can consider problems in a flexible, unrestricted manner. Two benefits of this mode of play are innovation and increased skill in problem solving.

Play at all ages and especially symbolic play instills an attitude that enhances competence. Exploring, then mastering a set of materials helps children understand the materials and gives them a sense of control. As Debra Pepler and Kenneth Rubin (1982) conclude, the sense of self-worth that comes from play may be the most important outcome of the play experience.

Play is one avenue that can be used to enhance competence. It is certainly an important avenue during the early years. However, play is only a small part of the child's total experience. Other environmental factors and family factors feed into the development of competence. The impact of these factors is seen clearly in children described as *invulnerable*.

## INVULNERABLE CHILDREN

Invulnerable children find ways to cope with severe financial, emotional, and social stress. Instead of buckling under the pressure, they retain mastery and control over their lives (Garmezy, 1976). An example of an invulnerable child is given by E. J. Anthony (1971).

> A woman suffering from schizophrenia of the paranoid type, insisted on eating at restaurants because she thought someone was poisoning the food at home. Her 12-year-old daughter adopted the same phobic attitude. Another daughter, 10, would eat at home when the father was there; he was normal. Otherwise she would go along to a restaurant. But a seven-year-old son always ate at home, and when the psychiatrist asked how he could do so, the boy simply shrugged and said, "Well, I'm not dead yet."
>
> The older girl eventually developed an illness like her mother's. The younger went to college and did reasonably well. The boy—the invulnerable—performed brilliantly all through school and afterward. His mother's illness apparently had given him both a tremendous need and a tremendous ability to overcome all sorts of problems. (Segal & Yahraes, 1978, p. 284)

Garmezy's early studies of invulnerable children proved that adversity can be overcome (Garmezy, 1983). Children who are institutionalized, hospitalized, separated from their parents, reared in poverty, or living in chaotic circumstances do not necessarily suffer long-term deficits in development. Instead, Garmezy saw the child as the sum of three sets of factors (see Figure 15–4). The first are factors that increase vulnerability. These include problems related to birth, temperament, and biogenetic problems. The second group of factors are events that trigger stress. Hospitalization, separation from parents, and war

**Figure 15–4**  **Table of risk factors**

| Protective factors | Factors that increase vulnerability | Events that trigger stress |
|---|---|---|
| Oldest child | Chronic poverty | Prolonged separation from primary caretaker |
| High activity level | Mother with little education | |
| Good-natured | Perinatal complications | Parental illness |
| Positive self-concept | Genetic abnormalities | Chronic family discord |
| Intelligent | Parental psychopathology | Divorce of parents |
| Autonomous | | Father absent |
| Structured household | | Change of schools |
| Support from additional adults | | Parental unemployment |
| | | Serious childhood illness |

The presence of several protective factors can help a child cope with environmental events that trigger stress.

Source: This was adapted from a table in Werner, E. E., & Smith, R. S. (1982). *Vulnerable but invincible.* New York: McGraw-Hill.

## Invulnerable children

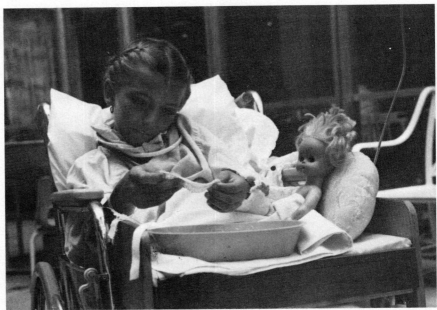

*Victor Dye*

Invulnerable children are capable of adjusting to stress and coping with their problems.

are some of the major events that trigger stress. Finally, there is a third set of factors that helps protect the child against stress. Garmezy's pioneering efforts prodded psychologists to describe these factors.

To isolate factors that protect children from stress, psychologists have studied children who were raised by schizophrenic mothers, black children raised in the ghetto, children of war, and children on the island of Kauai who were raised in poverty. Although children in these separate studies experienced very different kinds of stress, they developed similar ways of coping.

**Children born to psychotic parents**

Children who grow up in psychotic families and escape the effects of their environment seem to be protected by a number of factors (Garmezy, 1983). One of these is the child's temperament. Flexible children and those who are generally happy are able to cope with stress. A second variable is the sex of the child. Girls suffer less than boys. Finally, there are environmental factors that protect the child. A warm father or an encouraging school environment ameliorate the stress of living with a schizophrenic mother.

Despite their illness, some parents are able to sustain an emotional relationship with their children, expressing concern and interest. Children from these homes maintain their competence. If parents are unable to interact with their children or if their illness means that they are gone a great deal, the child's school performance and feelings of competence suffer (Baldwin, Cole, & Baldwin, 1983).

## Children of poverty

Black children who survive life in the inner-city ghetto develop remarkable social skills (Garmezy, 1983). They are typically well liked, sensitive, and socially responsive. These children also have a positive self-image and feel that they have control over their environment. Their homes are ordered and neat, in direct contrast to the disorganization of the inner city. At home, the mothers encourage their children to achieve in school. In this sample, too, personal factors combine with a supportive adult to provide a reasonable environment for growth.

The most extensive study of vulnerable children occurred on the island of Kauai, the "garden island" of the Hawaiian Islands. Emmy Werner and her colleagues enrolled all of the children born on the island during 1955 in their 30-year study. Almost 700 children were studied from infancy to adulthood. Extensive records were kept documenting birth complications, developmental problems, learning disorders, and adolescent rebellions. The longitudinal records also noted parental attitudes, home environments, social skills, and life goals (see Chapter 4).

When the subjects were 18, the investigators identified 42 girls and 30 boys who had each encountered four or more stress factors during their first two years of life. These children lived in chronic poverty. Many had constitutional difficulties. Chaotic family environments were very common. Nevertheless, not one of these children developed any serious learning or behavior problems during childhood or adolescence. Despite a less than optimal environment, these children became adults who managed their work, their families, and their social lives effectively. What helped these 72 children recover from their early difficulties and earned them the label *resilient*?

To answer this question, Emmy Werner and Ruth Smith (1982) compared the environments of three groups of adolescents. The first group of 72 adolescents were the resilient group. The second group of 90 adolescents had learning and behavior problems. A third group of 92 adolescents had a record of serious delinquency or mental health problems. All three of these groups were raised in poverty on Kauai and encountered at least three additional stressors in the form of constitutional or environmental problems during their formative years.

Even in infancy there were constitutional differences among these three groups of children. Temperamentally, the resilient children were characterized as good-natured and easy to deal with. Their mothers described them as "very active" and "cuddly and affectionate." Their easygoing temperaments were partly responsible for the fact that they were given a great deal of attention during the first year of life. Responsive, active infants have the potential for capturing even an initially unresponsive parent and drawing that parent into a cycle of effective interaction (Werner & Smith, 1982). Since the boys in the resilient group were more likely to be the firstborn, they had a further advantage in terms of securing attention.

As toddlers, the resilient children were socially at ease. They knew how to attract and use the support of adults. They actively tried to master their environment and showed a high degree of autonomy. The resilient children continued to have positive interactions with their mothers. The mothers of the other two groups were indifferent to their children, while the mothers of the resilient children were described as kind, temperate, and affectionate.

The resilient children often had an alternate caretaker—an older sibling, a grandmother, or another adult. The alternate caretaker helped the mother during the child's early years. By 10 years of age, the resilient children received higher scores on a test of mental abilities (The Primary Mental Abilities Test) than the children from the other two groups.

After age 10, the home environments of these resilient children began to differ for boys and girls. The girls seemed to be pushed toward greater autonomy, independence, and competence by events that might be considered stressful for boys. If their mother was employed and if the girls served as an alternate caretaker for a younger brother or sister, the girls were more competent. This was especially true if a grandmother or an older sibling provided emotional support for the girl. An employed mother also gave the girls an opportunity to see how an adult coped with financial stress.

The boys thrived if their home was structured, uncrowded, and harmonious. Boys did not fare as well as girls if their mothers were employed. The money the mother earned helped alleviate the family's economic stress. However, if the boys were not supervised while their mother was away from the home, they were more likely to get into trouble. Having a father was important for boys. The adolescents who had significant learning problems or got into trouble with authorities were from fatherless homes. All of the resilient boys had a father living in the home.

During adolescence, the resilient group began to differ from the other groups along other dimensions. They had learned to blend the qualities of masculinity and femininity. They were both assertive and yielding, instrumental and expressive, concerned about themselves and caring in their relationships. The resilient youth in the Kauai study, showed a healthy *androgyny*. The adolescents in the other two groups were more likely to be guided by societal stereotypes that define male and female roles.

Looking at the childhoods of all three groups, Werner and Smith found that the resilient children were subjected to fewer cumulative stresses than children from the other two groups. Resilient children were less likely to have serious illnesses. They came from families with no more than four children. The families of resilient children were stable and harmonious. The differences between the three groups led Werner and Smith to conclude that children can rebound from some difficulties, but as the problems accumulate, their ability to surmount them declines.

Michael Rutter (1979) found the same phenomenon among children from poverty-level neighborhoods in London. Children with just one risk factor were likely to overcome that stress, but as the stresses accumulated, so did their difficulties. A recent study of adolescents reaches similar conclusions (Garbarino, Sebes, & Schellenbach, 1984). Families described as high-risk have the most difficulty with their teenage children. Observers describe these families as chaotic. The parents are coercive and highly punitive. The special challenges of raising an adolescent place additional strain on this already unstable family system. Step families, which are often chaotic, are particularly likely to resort to abuse when adolescents become difficult. Families that are stable, harmonious, and supportive are better able to absorb the disruptive aspects of adolescence.

**Children of war**

In the middle-Eastern countries and Ireland, children have grown up surrounded by civil strife or wars.

> A Belfast working-class child . . . will mix, play, and be educated exclusively with his own religious group, and may never see a child of the 'other' group, except across a barricade. His home area is divided from other areas by armed sentries and steel barriers; he cannot leave this area, and to go out even in his own street after dusk is to court injury or death . . . His home is overcrowded, his father has a high chance of being unemployed, and poverty may be acute. (Fraser, 1974, p. 40–41)

Even when their daily lives are punctuated by gunfire and death, the majority of children seem to cope. The most salient protective factor in this type of setting is the behavior modeled by the adults in the child's life. Adults show the child how to maintain some control amid the chaos. Another protective factor is the emotional security that the child feels during periods of acute stress (Garmezy, 1983). Many children gain strength by identifying with the community and its goals. This understanding increases their courage. Even in war-torn environments, then, children summon strength from the adults and the community.

To summarize, children who are subjected to poverty, war, or psychotic parents are able to cope with stress if their environment includes sufficient protection. The protective factors are sometimes constitutional. Even as infants, these children are socially responsive and have an even temperament. As toddlers, such children are secure, unafraid, and display an independent spirit. Developing a loving, caring relationship with the mother during the first year provides additional protection against stress (Lewis, Feiring, McGuffog, & Jaskir, 1984). A caring teacher or loving grandmother who takes a personal interest in the child can help if the parents are absent or employed. A stable home seems to offer the most protection against stress. By adolescence, this stability is translated into a positive self-concept and a responsible, achievement-oriented attitude toward life.

The literature about invulnerable children provides another way of looking at competence. Children are likely to be competent if their list of stressful factors is short and balanced by a long list of protective factors. Some children will be competent despite the presence of several stressful factors. In this case, their environment offers enough support so that they can still cope with the stress. Children who live amid constant stress and have few constitutional or environmental supports are least likely to recover from the insults of the environment.

## LONGITUDINAL STUDIES OF COMPETENCE

The literature about invulnerable children underscores the power of a longitudinal design in studying the growth of competence. Studying children from infancy to adulthood allows objective coding of personal strengths, stressful

---

### AN INVULNERABLE CHILD

Ross's mother spent years in a mental institution. While she was away, he was reared by a heinous housekeeper who was hired to watch him and his two sisters. The housekeeper cared for nothing except her whiskey and her dog. Ross's alcoholic father went carousing almost every night. When both parents were home, they argued constantly; their verbal aggression turned into physical assault at least once a week . . . Sometimes they would throw furniture, glass figurines, and even knives at each other. Often these fights were held on the front porch and even the front yard where the neighbors could see. At other times the parents would yell and bloody each other's faces with their fists. Once, Ross's father ripped the telephone from the wall and threw it into the fire in the fireplace. There were also many incidents with weapons. One evening, for example, Ross's mother, wielding a butcher knife, threatened to end her life. Instead, she slashed her husband's face. Scenes like these usually ended with Ross's mother being held down, forced into a patrol car, and whisked back to the mental institution.

Ross was in the midst of it all. He would cry and beg his parents to stop and quietly settle their differences. Sometimes he would stand between them, but it was like trying to separate two fighting dogs. When Ross interfered, his parents

would strike wildly at him or push him away so they could get back to their battle. At other times, feeling humiliated, Ross busied himself closing curtains, windows, and doors to insulate the domestic war from onlooking neighbors. Whenever he sensed a fight coming on, Ross would hide dangerous weapons and fragile objects from his parents.

Eventually, Ross discovered that his best course of behavior was to withdraw altogether, so he spent hours alone in his room writing adventure stories. Daybreak was always a welcome sight. As morning finally broke and quiet fell over the house, Ross would breathe a sigh of relief because he knew his family had made it through another night.

Today Ross is a free-lance writer and college professor. He has a stable family life and long-term associations with others. His friends view him as likeable, intelligent, and helpful. The social worker in this case identified four characteristics that helped Ross cope. As a child he had good social skills and was able to maintain a high level of self-confidence. He was able to detach himself from the stressful sourroundings by retreating to his room to write stories. Finally, he had intellectual and creative skills that were not affected by the misfortunes at home.

---

From Bryan Robinson and Nell Fields © 1983. Casework with invulnerable children. *Social Work, 37*, 63–64.

environmental factors, and protective factors (Garmezy, Masten, & Tellegen, 1984). Other longitudinal studies, not concerned with invulnerable children, have contributed to our understanding of the development of competence.

Between 1929 and 1932, over 400 children living near Berkeley, California, were enrolled in longitudinal studies. The goal of these studies was to follow the development of children. Forty years later, Jack Block collected and analyzed the material about these individuals. His book, *Lives Through Time*, while essentially a study of personality development, alludes to the precursors of competence. Structured, supportive environments produced competent adults. Chaotic environments were more likely to produce insecure adults.

Competent adults came from families in which the father and mother had a positive relationship. The adults in the family adhered to typical sex roles. The father was effective in his job and respected. The mother was comfortable and competent in her role. As parents, they encouraged their children to develop a sense of responsibility and fair play. The mother and father were clear and consistent in discipline. They welcomed the child's participation in family discussions. They accepted and encouraged their child's growing independence. They were affectionate and available to their children (Block, 1971).

Families embroiled in continuing conflict lead to more pathological behavior among children. Some parents fought over sex, money, time, and child rearing. The interaction between parent and child was seldom satisfactory. Some of the parents were rejecting. Some were overinvolved. Some were unaffectionate. Some induced conflict. Some were neurotic. Some were absent. Some were suppressive. Some who meant well had to divide their efforts among many children. Children raised in these families had few social guidelines. Their place in the family was not respected. These children moved through life without the secure base that characterized children from more harmonious homes. As adults, these individuals were often alienated from their origins and yet trapped by them (Block, 1971).

This longitudinal study gave investigators confidence that early precursors to competence could be identified. Over an interval of 30 to 35 years, from the early teens to their mid-forties, individuals who were competent, poised, and resilient maintained those characteristics. Teenagers who were rebellious and hostile became men who lacked self-control and changed jobs frequently or women who were irresponsible and self-indulgent. Block (1981) notes that these are enduring and consequential personality structures.

The origin of these enduring traits was still a mystery. Hence, Jack Block and Jeanne Block began a longitudinal study of personality development. In 1968, they identified 130 nursery school children in Berkeley. These children were tested and observed at ages 3, 4, 5, 7, and 11. Now adolescents, they have provided a long-term look at the development of two aspects of personality, *ego-control* and *ego-resiliency*.

Among individuals, ego-control can range from no control, in which case the person is extremely impulsive, to overcontrol, in which case the person is extremely inhibited. The ideal is for people to maintain a moderate level of control over their actions. This level of control meshes with the individual's flexibility or resiliency. The ego-resilient person is characteristically described as competent, intelligent, and adaptive under stress. Children who are ego-resilient can choose among several strategies to solve a problem. They are resourceful when approaching a new situation and can maintain a high level of performance under stress. Children as young as three can be reliably assessed on this trait, which is an important component of both personality and cognitive tasks during the years from three to seven (Block & Block, 1980).

As part of their longitudinal study of personality, the Blocks also investigated the ability to delay gratification. Like ego-control and ego-resiliency, delay of gratification is an index of the control that children exercise over their lives. A common way of assessing a four-year-old's ability to delay gratification is to show him or her a desirable toy or gift. Before receiving the gift, however, the child must complete a task, such as putting a puzzle together. Children who can continue to focus on the puzzle are given high scores on delay of gratification. Typically these children are competent, attentive, and intelligent (Funder, Block, & Block, 1983).

The home environments of children able to delay gratification were similar to the environments of the competent adults that Jack Block described earlier. In general, the homes were ordered and peaceful. Also, children who could delay gratification often had several adults they could trust during their early years. Children who could not finish the puzzle before grabbing the gift were seen as very emotional. They were likely to have mothers who encouraged conflict and discouraged independence (Funder, et al., 1983). Their homes were chaotic and unstructured.

Delay of gratification was one measure of the control that four-year-olds could exercise. This ability predicted competence in several areas three and seven years later. Preschool girls who could delay gratification became competent, skilled seven-year-olds who could concentrate and plan ahead. The preschool boys became elementary school children who were described as reflective and planful.

The three threads of personality that the Blocks have traced over an eight-year period are part of the larger trait termed competence. From these studies we know that competence can be measured reliably. We also know that the precursors of competence can be identified early in a child's life. The results from these longitudinal studies reinforce the conclusions drawn from the studies of invulnerable children: Parents who provide an ordered, nurturing home environment in which the child feels a sense of control are likely to see their children grow into competent adults.

## SELF-EFFICACY

From the studies outlined in the preceding sections, we see that competence is associated with a particular constellation of home factors. Nevertheless, emphasizing longitudinal studies leaves the impression that competence is fixed by these early experiences. Even though a child's general approach to situations may be positively or negatively influenced by early experiences, building competence is a lifelong task. More experimentally oriented studies demonstrate that throughout life, events continue to affect a person's feeling of competence.

Children can exhibit competence in diverse areas—such as the cognitive, social, or physical area (Harter, 1982). Regardless of the area, being competent means being able to select and organize particular skills. If you are a competent student, you budget your time, read thoroughly, study effectively, and know how to take tests. As you proceed through college, you may have to acquire competence in writing, learning to do laboratory reports, and researching a topic in the library. Children and adults must be ready to develop competence in new areas. Whether or not they can approach new areas is determined partially by self-efficacy.

Self-efficacy depends on a positive self-perception. If people expect to succeed, they forge ahead. If they expect to fail, they might choose an alternate activity. Feelings of self-efficacy not only affect which activities we pursue, but they can also determine how much effort we put into different activities and how long we will persist if we encounter difficulties. Thus, drivers who distrust their skill in navigating twisting mountain roads will conjure up thoughts of wreckage and bodily injury. They may decide to stay home rather than attempt to reach a ski resort. Those who are confident of their driving capabilities will "anticipate sweeping vistas rather than tangled wreckage" (Bandura, 1983, p. 464). They will be the first on the slopes. *Perceived self-efficacy* refers to how successful people expect to be. If we perceive ourselves as successful, we can organize our cognitive and social skills to deal with everyday situations.

**Factors that influence self-efficacy**

Albert Bandura (1982a) outlined four different factors that determined a person's self-efficacy. The first is the experience a child has with mastering the environment. This is the most powerful factor in self-efficacy. Success heightens one's feelings of self-efficacy; repeated failures lower it. Vicarious experiences are a second factor. Seeing others who are competent encourages the observer to think, "I can do that too." Watching a competent model also teaches the observer how to deal with challenging or threatening situations. The third factor involves direct contact with other people. Parents and teachers can persuade children that they possess the capabilities for success. Remember that the invulnerable children often relied on adults to provide support, especially when the situation was stressful. The final factor that Bandura outlines in self-efficacy is a person's physiological state. Arousal during stressful situations may decrease a person's feelings of competence.

**Experiments on mastery and modeling**

Of these four factors, only the first two have been studied in children. Dale Schunk (1982) studied children's mastery of subtraction to see how self-efficacy developed. He first measured efficacy by having the children indicate "how sure you are that you could work problems like these and get the right answers" (Shunck, 1981, p. 95). The children's answers ranged from a score of 10, meaning that they were very uncertain, to a score of 100, meaning they were confident about their subtraction skills. Instruction in subtraction was then arranged for children who were not confident about their skills. One group of children reviewed their work periodically and recorded the number of pages they completed. As these children saw their progress during the training sessions, they developed a heightened sense of their ability to succeed in math. On the test following training, their self-efficacy had risen significantly. They had mastered the material.

Bandura's theory also predicts that observing a competent model will increase self-efficacy. To investigate this notion, Dale Schunk (1981) had an adult demonstrate the solutions to division problems. Children having difficulty with division problems watched. As the models worked on the problems, they explained the various strategies used to arrive at the correct solution. Another group of children studied the same pages independently. A third group received no help.

Observing a model increased the children's math skills as well as their confidence about solving division problems. Watching the model was more effective than the child working independently. But both of these groups of children had more success than the control group. The children in the control group were unable to solve the problems, and their interest lagged.

The early mastery experiments demonstrated that children's self-efficacy can be enhanced. According to the theory, such increases in self-efficacy should be accompanied by other positive attitudes. For example, the students should express more interest in math, they should perform better, and they should persist on difficult problems. Bandura and Schunk (1981) decided to see whether increased self-efficacy leads to attitudinal changes. They devised an experiment in which children could learn subtraction by mastering a series of subgoals. They reasoned that the subgoals would allow the children to master one skill at a time. This kind of step-by-step progression should enhance mastery and feelings of self-efficacy.

Their results documented the importance of mastery. The children who had mastered one goal at a time expressed more interest in mathematics. They persisted at difficult math problems. When given free time to pursue different activities, the children in the mastery group decided to solve more math problems! The investigators conclude that whether the area is math, English, or video games, a feeling of mastery breeds interest and involvement.

Children's perceptions of their skills have an important effect on their subsequent achievements. In fact, children's perceptions of efficacy can be used to predict later performance (Bandura, 1982b). Children who believe they are skilled in an area are able to sustain the effort needed for a truly outstanding performance (Salomon, 1982). A person plagued with self-doubts is much more likely to give up. It is not surprising, given these findings, that feelings of self-efficacy are important in selecting a career (Hackett & Betz, 1981). During mastery experiments, children begin to see that they control their performance in math. This feeling of control seems critical to the development of self-efficacy. In the experiments reviewed in this section, the feeling of control came from tangible progress. The longitudinal studies showed that a feeling of control came from the child's early environment. Chaotic, conflict-ridden environments will not foster children's beliefs that they control their environments. Structured environments in which the parents model competence seem much more likely to foster a feeling of control. The issue of control looms large in the development of competence (McKinney, 1980). One way of assessing how control affects competence is to look at the opposite of control—learned helplessness.

## LEARNED HELPLESSNESS

> Victor is a nine-year-old of unusual intelligence—at least his mother and his friends think so. His teacher disagrees. At home Victor is lively, quick to respond, highly verbal, and outgoing. With his playmates, he is the acknowledged leader, partly because of his charm and imagination. At school he is a problem.
>
> Victor was a slow starter when reading instruction began. He was eager, but just wasn't ready to make the connection between words on paper and speech. He tried hard at first, but made no progress. His answers were consistently wrong. The more he failed, the less he tried. In class, he remained silent most of the time. In the second grade he participated in music and art, but when reading began, he became sullen or aggressive. In an experimental summer program, Victor was taught to read Chinese characters. By the end of the summer he could read 150 characters. Despite this success, he still cannot read or write any English in the third grade. He is presenting more of a disciplinary problem, and his new teacher thinks he is mentally retarded. (Seligman, 1975)

Victor's plight offers an example of learned helplessness. Although he tried hard initially, Victor could not read. Despite his best efforts, he made no progress. His failure to read initiated a series of reactions that gradually affected his attitudes, his cognitive skills, and his emotional behavior in the classroom.

**Effects of helplessness**

Uncontrollable events undermine a child's motivation. Victor stopped trying. One year later, when he might have been ready to read, he had no desire to succeed. A loss of motivation is the first consequence of *learned helplessness*. A second consequence is emotional disturbance. Victor became sullen and aggressive. By third grade, his behavior was a continuing problem.

Feeling helpless also has major cognitive consequences. Once you believe that you do not control events, it is much more difficult to realize that you can control events. A classic example came from a series of experiments in which dogs received a painful but nondamaging shock (Seligman, 1975). Early in the experiment, the dogs could do nothing to stop the shocks. They learned to submit passively. In a later phase of the experiment, the dogs could jump

**Learned helplessness**

*George W. Gardner*

Learning that you are helpless to control events has far-reaching cognitive and emotional consequences.

over a barrier to escape the shock. Although they were free to move around and find the escape route, they never did. When the shock began, they lay down and whined. Naive dogs, those that had never experienced the first part of the experiment, learned to jump the barrier in a few trials. Victor's behavior is like the helpless dogs'. Although Victor might be able to read in third grade, his earlier failure has made it more difficult to learn.

Victor's case highlights some of the major points of Martin Seligman's theory of learned helplessness. The feeling that we have lost control of a situation and are helpless leads to a variety of intellectual, emotional, and social changes in behavior (Abrahamson, Seligman, & Teasdale, 1978). In essence, our feelings of mastery and self-efficacy are destroyed.

**Differences between competent and helpless children**

The early descriptions of learned helplessness caused a great deal of interest among psychologists. The theory indicated that motivational and attitudinal variables influenced performance, occasionally eclipsing the child's ability in an area. Furthermore, the theory predicted long-term consequences if the child adopted a helpless attitude. Carol Diener and Carol Dweck (1978) were

**Figure 15—5**        **Cards used in experiment on learned helplessness**

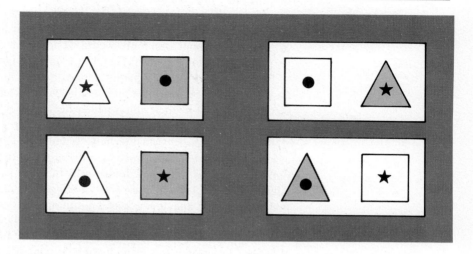

Four stimulus cards that allow children to assess which of several details on the card is "correct."

Source: Diener, C. I., & Dweck, C. S. (1978). An analysis of learned helplessness: Continuous changes in performance, strategy, and achievement cognitions following failure. *Journal of Personality and Social Psychology, 36,* 451–462.

among the first to examine the consequences of learned helplessness in children. Their first step was to divide a group of children into two groups. The first group saw themselves as helpless; the second saw themselves as competent. They then asked these two groups of children to identify which of six symbols on a deck of cards was "correct" (see Figure 15–5). The first child might point to the unshaded triangle with the star in the center. If the experimenter says "right," the child knows that the correct symbol is either the triangle, the star, or the unshaded figure. On the next guess, the child could point to the triangle with the dot in the center. In this way, the children could test a variety of hypotheses and identify the correct symbol for each deck of cards.

The two groups of children easily solved the eight training problems that were administered first. The next four problems were much more difficult. They were designed so that the children failed more often. When helpless children were asked why they thought they missed the testing problems, many said they were not smart enough to solve the problems. None of the children from the competent group attributed their failure to lack of intelligence. They were more likely to say that they did not try or it was just bad luck (see Figure 15–6).

As predicted by the theory, once helpless children failed, even their ability to think constructively about the problems deteriorated. By the fourth test problem, only 31 percent of the helpless children were trying useful strategies. In contrast, almost 85 percent of the competent children continued to try useful strategies. By their comments, many of these competent children indicated that they had not given up. One child mimicked the cliché, "When the going gets tough, the tough get going." Another child spontaneously said, "I love a challenge." The helpless children were likely to say, "This isn't fun anymore," or they talked about irrelevant events: "There is a talent show this weekend, and I am going to be Shirley Temple" (Diener & Dweck, 1978).

The competent children hardly noticed their failure. They concentrated on improving their performance and solving the problem. The helpless children seemed paralyzed by their failure. They decided they were powerless to change the outcome and spent little time looking for other solutions to the problem.

The differences between the helpless child and the competent child were exactly as predicted by learned helplessness theory. The children, although initially similar in skill, took dramatically different paths after they experienced failure. The helpless children were no longer motivated, they no longer tried useful strategies, and their success plummeted. The competent children ignored their failures and continued to try to solve their problems.

A helpless orientation can predispose a child to fail (Diener & Dweck, 1980). In a separate study using the same problems, the experimenters stopped after the training trials and asked the children how they thought they would perform if they were given 15 more problems. Even though both groups of children had been very successful on the training problems, the helpless children only expected to get 50 percent of the future problems right. The competent children expected to get 90 percent of the future problems right. Furthermore, the helpless children thought the rest of the children would do better. The competent children believed that other children would do worse.

In short, helpless children expect, predict, and remember failure. They underplay their successes and expect other children to outperform them. Even when they experience success, helpless children do not think that they will continue to be successful. A number of the helpless children were not even

**Figure 15—6**

**Helplessness and mastery**

|  | Group | |
| --- | --- | --- |
| **Attributional category** | **Helpless** | **Mastery-oriented** |
| Ability | 52  % | 0  % |
| Effort | 3.4 | 23.7 |
| Luck | 3.4 | 21.05 |
| Experimenter not fair | 6.8 | 23.7 |
| Task harder | 27.6 | 21.05 |
| No reason | 6.8 | 10.5 |

Children who are helpless attribute their failure to lack of ability. Children who feel a sense of mastery attribute their failure to luck or an unfair experimenter.

Source: Diener, C. I., & Dweck, C. S. (1978). An analysis of learned helplessness: Continuous changes in performance, strategy, and achievement cognitions following failure. *Journal of Personality and Social Psychology, 36,* 451–462.

sure that they could solve the simple training problems again (Diener & Dweck, 1980).

There are some hopeful notes in the area of learned helplessness. Children do not regard all situations as beyond their control even when they believe they are helpless in some situations (Dweck & Reppucci, 1973). Children may have a helpless orientation to math, yet feel confident of their ability in science. Another hopeful note is that learned helplessness can be alleviated. Carol Dweck (1975) selected 12 classroom failures as the targets for her rehabilitation experiment. These children were notorious for giving up and staring into space whenever they were presented with math problems. Six of these children were told that the reason for their failure was that they did not try hard enough. They were told that if they continued to try they would succeed. The other six were given such easy problems that they always succeeded. After the training, both groups were given new problems, some of which they could not solve. Failure devastated the group that had only solved easy problems. These children returned to staring into space. The children who had been urged to try harder did not become helpless when they failed. They continued to try and occasionally they succeeded. Every child experiences failure occasionally. Competent children have strategies that help them deal constructively with failure, while helpless children give up.

The effects of learned helplessness are similar whether the area being investigated is problem solving, mathematics, or reading (Butkowsky & Willow, 1980). Children who feel helpless have no persistence, anticipate failure, and attribute their failure to lack of skill. To supplant this helplessness with a feeling of mastery or competence, we must give children the feeling that they control their environments and the knowledge that they can succeed.

**Precursors of helplessness**

Many of the studies of learned helplessness begin by separating children into a helpless or a competent group and then assessing the groups' reaction to success or failure. It is important to ask how these children initially became helpless or competent. Certainly one suggestion is that a history of failure leads to learned helplessness (Johnson, 1981). This places a great deal of the responsibility for dealing with learned helplessness on educators. A second suggestion is that helplessness results when children have no control over their environments. Remember that competent children have orderly home environments (Block, 1973). It is possible that children who feel helpless are raised in unstructured environments in which they have little control.

Abused children are an extreme example of helplessness (see Chapter 12). They are guarded, passive, compliant, and anxious—the epitomy of helplessness. Their home environments are often chaotic, and their self-esteem is low. Because the violence in their homes is unpredictable, these children feel that they have little control over their lives. Parents who would never resort to physical abuse choose harsh ways to discipline their children. They threaten to punish the child or to take away some privilege: "If you are not back by 11 P.M., you will not be allowed to go out all next week." Children raised in homes like this obey because they feel coerced (Dix & Grusec, 1983). They

**Discipline using inductive reasoning and power assertion**

*Bohdan Hrynewych: Stock, Boston*

Parents who use reasoning as a disciplinary technique help their children. Parents who discipline by asserting their power convey the message that children have no control over their own lives.

do not feel that they are directing their own behavior. Compare the child who is abused or coerced with a child whose parents discipline through reasoning: "It's important not to hit other children. You could hurt them, and they won't want to play with you." When parents provide reasons for their discipline, the children gain a better understanding of the situation and can change their behavior accordingly (Hoffman, 1970). The disciplinary techniques used by parents are just one example of how parents might contribute to feelings of helplessness. Learned helplessness is probably an amalgam of personal attributes, stressful factors in the home environment, and protective factors. The home and the school can add to the stress or can provide protection from stress.

The learned helplessness research and the literature on self-efficacy make it clear that any assessment of competence must include motivational factors. Motivational factors affect attitudes toward learning, persistence, and even whether a child will explore a new area. These attitudes transfer into school achievement and career success. Children's expectations can determine whether they pursue and master new skills. Sometimes, the children's expectations bear little relation to the child's actual abilities. Children who are very skilled can become helpless. In fact, among females, the most competent can be most susceptible to motivational factors (Dweck & Elliott, 1983). For this reason, we need to turn our attention to sex differences in the development of competence.

## SEX DIFFERENCES IN COMPETENCE

Previous sections have described many of the factors that contribute to competence. Feelings of mastery, observing competent adults, being told you are competent, and coming from a structured and supportive home environment all enhance the development of competence. Combining these positive factors with optimum personal traits leads to a resilient child who can achieve competence even when faced with highly stressful events. This general description of the development of competence applies to both males and females. Each step on the path to achieving competence may be easier or more difficult, depending on the sex of the child. Many developmental psychologists believe that females are subtly directed toward helplessness while males are pushed toward mastery (Block, 1983).

Men tend to be individualistic, assertive, and expansive. Women are more likely to focus on the interpersonal harmony that exists within the group. Rather than insisting on mastery, women suppress their own interests in favor of the group's welfare. These differences between the sexes have generated considerable controversy in psychology. A major question concerns the origins of sex differences. A second issue is whether these differences affect competence.

Jeanne Block (1983) has argued that the sex differences we see in adults result from socialization practices. Young children of both sexes seek mastery. Because of their common strivings, sex differences during infancy and the preschool years are minimal (Maccoby & Jacklin, 1974, 1984). Block argues, however, that the school years bring differing socialization pressures. Referring to her own longitudinal study, she notes that at three years of age, boys and girls could be comfortably lumped together. By seven, they had taken somewhat different paths toward competence. As children approach adolescence, parents treat boys and girls differently. This differential treatment has important implications for the development of competence. To support her contention, Block outlines how parents react to the two sexes. She also chronicles the sex differences that are commonly accepted.

**Parents' reactions to boys and girls**

Parents respond to boys and girls differently even during infancy and the toddler period. Caroline Smith and Barbara Lloyd (1978) filmed mothers' responses to the same child when it was identified as a boy and when it was identified as a girl. When the adults were told the child was a female, they were likely to hand her a doll. When they believed the child was a male, they encouraged him to crawl or walk. If they handed him a toy, it was likely to be a hammer instead of a doll. Eleanor Maccoby and Carol Jacklin (1984) mention a similar difference in the way fathers treat boys and girls. Fathers were likely to offer sex-appropriate toys to their children and were more likely to roughhouse with their sons. Maccoby and Jacklin make the point, however, that parental treatment of boys and girls was not markedly different during the period from birth to six years of age.

During the school years, parental treatment of boys and girls diverges. Parents encourage their school-age sons to be independent, ambitious, self-reliant, and to assume responsibility (Hoffman, 1977). When fathers are teaching boys, they set high standards and encourage their sons to achieve (Block, Block, & Harrington, 1975). Girls, on the other hand, are encouraged to be nurturant, obedient, unselfish, kind, and well mannered. When fathers teach their daughters, they encourage them, joke with them, and protect them (Block, 1983). In short, parents act in more instrumental, mastery-oriented ways with their school-age sons and in more expressive, less achievement-oriented ways with their school-age daughters.

**Sex differences that affect competence**

It is not enough to know that parents treat boys and girls differently. We must know whether the parents' treatment affects behavior and, more specifically, how the parents' treatment affects the development of competence. In attempting to make this link, Block outlines the sex differences that are generally accepted. She then suggests how such sex differences could emerge from different parental treatment.

Sex differences in the domains of activity level, anxiety, achievement-related behavior, self-concept, and social relationships could all affect the development of competence. For example, a high activity level among boys might translate into higher levels of curiosity and exploratory behavior (Ginsburg & Miller, 1982). During the school years, boys describe themselves as more adventurous and daring than females. These same qualities may be translated into self-efficacy during the adult years.

The higher levels of anxiety that seem to characterize women can subtly affect competence in several ways. One direct offshoot of this anxiety is that females predict and expect to achieve less than their male peers. When they are successful, they attribute it to luck, not to ability (Deaux, 1984). The net result is a reduced sense of competence. This lack of competence is not limited to adolescence. During the years of young adulthood, the female's sense of competence declines while males see themselves as more competent (Nawas, 1971).

A second consequence of being anxious is that girls and women try to please others (Weisz & McGuire, 1980). Being cooperative helps females avoid anxiety, but it does not lead to feelings of power or control. When men describe themselves, they talk about their power and their feelings of efficacy and control. These adjectives reflect a self-concept in which potency and mastery are important components. Females describe themselves as generous and concerned about others. These adjectives are less concerned with competition and mastery (Block, 1983).

A final consequence of high levels of anxiety is a decrease in confidence. A lack of confidence means that women are less likely to be competitive and achievement-oriented (Spence & Helmreich, 1983). This is particularly true if the task is one which is perceived as masculine or if it is one in which women have little previous experience (Deaux, 1984).

In short, heightened anxiety in girls can be transformed into a pattern of learned helplessness (Dweck & Elliott, 1983). Girls do well until they encounter difficulty. Then their expectations drop, their performance deteriorates, and they express doubts about their ability to succeed. Girls may actually stop pursuing tasks they are capable of achieving because they lower their expectations.

Lower expectations can have a decided impact on achievement in specific

**Cross-sex activities**

Many cross-sex activities are enjoyed by adults. Children and adolescents are more reluctant to engage in activities seen as more appropriate for the opposite sex.

academic areas such as math or English. Children from 2d through 12th grade think verbal skills are more feminine than masculine. Adolescents clearly regard skill in mathematics as a masculine area (Kaczalak, 1981). Perceiving a field as masculine or feminine leads to expectations about performance in that field. Both sexes see themselves as more likely to fail on tasks that are not "sex-appropriate" (Huston, 1983). Girls think math is more difficult than boys and therefore think their likelihood of success is lower. Their expectations are different despite the fact that both sexes have received the same grades. Similarly, adolescent females expect success in English. Their male peers are more likely to expect failure. These kinds of stereotypes can influence children's motivation, their effort, their attraction to the task, and ultimately, their performance, particularly in areas that are thought of as "inappropriate" (Deaux, 1984).

It is interesting that women who see themselves as more masculine have a masculine attitude toward success and failure. If they succeed, they are pleased. They attribute their success to their effort and their skill. If they fail, they ignore it and continue trying (Welch, 1983). This reaction stands in marked contrast to the reaction of more feminine girls whose response to failure is to quit trying. Women who see themselves as masculine are also likely to have high levels of self-esteem (Whitely, 1983). Perhaps this is because they see themselves as assertive and powerful.

Althea Huston (1983) summarizes the sex difference literature by saying that girls expect less success, have lower aspirations, are more anxious about failure, and avoid risking failure. These cognitive sets can have a decided impact on feelings of competence and achievement. Perhaps the most distressing information is that intelligent girls are particularly likely to lack confidence (Licht & Dweck, 1980). These bright, high-achieving girls actually have lower expectations of success than girls who score at average levels (Stipek & Hoffman, 1980). Low expectations might prompt a female to make conservative choices. A single conservative choice in high school such as, "I don't need to take advanced algebra" is not particularly important. After all, the student can always take the course in college. However, a series of conservative choices made throughout the high school and college years could result in selecting a less challenging set of courses and a less challenging career (Parsons, 1983).

A closer look at the expectations of intelligent girls shows that they are more likely to be conservative when the situation is ambiguous or when they have no cues from their past performance as to how well they will do. If a situation is novel, girls are more likely to key on negative information. Boys look at the positive side when they predict how they will perform. It is important to note that intelligent girls are likely to be pursuing a course of study which is somewhat atypical for their sex. This means that from the outset they are likely to be less confident about their skills. At the first threat of difficulty, they think about sacrificing their goals and retreating to more comfortable arenas.

Block sums up her views and the literature in the following way: "Males and females grow up in psychological contexts that are importantly different, and

**Acquiring sex roles**

Jeanne Block's analysis of the development of competence places a great deal of importance on the socialization of males and females. Part of this socialization involves the sex roles that are endorsed by the culture. A brief description of how children acquire sex roles highlights the continuing effect that environmental contexts have on the development of competence.

The pressure to adopt a pattern of behavior that is congruent with your sex is dictated by the culture as well as the parents. In the first step of sex-role development, children come to realize that they are either boys or girls. This awareness, of belonging to one sex, is called *gender identity*. Although children reliably identify themselves as boys or girls by three years of age, it takes somewhat longer to realize that a person's sex is a constant trait. Boys and girls as old as five often believe that changing their hair or wearing different clothes will change their sex. Psychologists suspect that this insecurity causes preschoolers to seek out adult models of the same sex, friends of the same sex, and games appropriate for their sex. To cement their own gender identity, these young children often adhere to strict sex-role stereotypes. Many women professors have reported that their preschool daughters adopt a view that "women can't be doctors" despite the evidence in their own home that such a stereotype is not true.

In elementary school, these rigid stereotypes crumble. By eight years of age, children realize that gender is constant and that males and females can engage in activities typical of either sex (Ulian, 1976). But this awareness is compromised by the cultural depiction of sex roles. Children in elementary school learn that power and competence are typically associated with the male sex role. Their school books depict males as the central characters. The male heroes in these books are intelligent, resourceful, and solve most of the problems. Girls play supporting roles and are depicted as easily frightened and in need of protection (Gagnon, 1977). Television presents a similarly biased picture: men are aggressive and competent; women sell cleaning products or defer to men's wishes (Tavris & Offir, 1977).

Although girls realize that some women hold positions of power, they often lack the immediate models they need to offset the compliant, passive image of the female. Similarly, boys know that men can be sensitive, but if the adult males they know seldom express feelings, the boys are not likely to express such sensitivity.

During adolescence, sex roles undergo another change. Unsure of how they are perceived by the other sex and undecided about their goals in life, both males and females again adopt stereotypic sex roles. The traditional stereotype of the passive female that adolescent girls adopt can contribute to lower expectations for achievement as well as to decreased feelings of competence (Darly & Fazio, 1980).

Once the identity crisis of adolescence has passed, women replace stereo-

**Role models**

*Tom Harm: UPI*

A child's sex role is formed by seeing models of how men and women behave. Parents provide powerful models. Sex roles are also derived from books, television, movies, peers, and politicians.

typic sex roles with realistic assessments of how women should behave in different situations. Many adult women are forceful when they need to be and more compliant when that is appropriate. Evidence that sex-role stereotypes are not as compelling during adulthood comes from several sources. Men and women working in a steel factory have similar self-evaluations. The women do not see themselves as more helpless (Deaux & Ullman, 1983). Likewise, men and women in leadership positions hold similar views of their skills (Hollander, 1984). These studies reveal few differences between men and women who have similar responsibilities. Adults are also able to perform "inappropriate" roles with no loss to their self-esteem. For example, men do not regard their involvement with the housekeeping or their care of the children as incompatible with their masculine sex-role identity.

To summarize, sex-role identities vary depending on the age of the person and the sex roles that have been modeled by adults. Whether the culture encourages independence in females seems to be especially important to feelings of competence during the adolescent years. The different sex-role standards encountered by males and females during this period may foster different premises about the world, establish different competencies, and encourage the use of different strategies for dealing with new experiences (Block, 1983).

## SUMMARY

Competence does not spring into being at the touch of a developmental button. As much as any psychological trait discussed in this book, competence is an amalgam of factors. Some of these factors are personal and seem to have a biological base. The child's temperament, the child's good-natured and affectionate response to parents, and the integrity of the central nervous system are evidence of biological components that influence competence.

During play, children rely on these personal attributes as they begin to develop an attitude of mastery. Play offers the child a chance to understand the adult world and to practice organizing and consolidating skills that are needed to function competently. Preschoolers also use play to develop their problem solving skills. Manipulating and exploring materials facilitates solving problems that involve those materials. Symbolic play serves a somewhat different function. It opens the door to both cognitive and symbolic advances. By pretending to be the father of the household or the principal of the school, children try to understand the essence of different adult roles. The exploration, the cognitive skill, and the mastery that develop from playing during these early years establish a foundation of self-efficacy that can be converted into competence during later years.

The development of competence is enhanced by a stable home environment and transmitted by supportive parents. An orderly home with caring parents can foster competence even in the face of some biological disarray. Similarly, a chaotic home in which the child wrestles constantly with conflict or dissent fosters helplessness rather than competence. The force of the home environment in promoting competence has been well documented in studies of invulnerable children.

Children who have overcome extreme stress are offered substantial protection by their home environments. Children whose parents are psychotic, whose families live in poverty, or who live in a combat zone are all exposed to high levels of stress. Yet many of these children are able to cope with the stress and become competent adults. Factors that protect a child from stress can be listed with some confidence: (a) a home that is a haven in the storm; (b) parents who are suportive and caring; (c) parents who provide guidance; and (d) the presence of a caring adult who will support the child during difficult times.

By school age, many of the threads of competence are wound together into a factor that has been called self-efficacy, mastery, or ego-resiliency. Psychologists have found many competent children who feel that they control their environment, who envision success, and who strive toward mastery. More helpless children expect and remember failure. They give up when challenged and end up extending their helplessness, sometimes into areas in which they have considerable ability.

The components of competence are the same for males and females. Sex-role stereotypes and sex differences can, however, have the effect of lowering the expectations that women hold for themselves. To the extent that low expectations change the choices a woman makes, or alter her goals, they can influence achievement and competence.

# Glossary

**accommodation.** In Piaget's theory, the modification of current ways of thinking in order to better handle new events or objects.

**acetaldehyde.** A toxic chemical that results when alcohol is metabolized.

**activational function of hormones.** The capacity of hormones to turn on various processes from conception through the life cycle.

**adaptation.** In Piaget's theory, the functional principle by which individuals modify their thinking through accommodation and assimilation.

**amniotic fluid.** A watery liquid which protects the floating embryo from physical shocks and temperature changes.

**androgyny.** A blend of the more desirable stereotypic characteristics of masculinity and femininity.

**anoxia.** The lack of sufficient oxygen to the brain, often resulting in brain damage.

**anthropometric.** The study and techniques of measuring the human body for purposes of classification and comparison.

**aphasia.** The partial to total loss of the ability to articulate ideas of any kind.

**assimilation.** In Piaget's theory, the process of interpreting experiences according to current cognitive structures.

**attachment behavioral system.** The group of behaviors that protects the infant by initiating, maintaining, or eliciting proximity to the mother.

**attention deficit.** A disorder characterized by a short attention span, high distractibility, and impulsiveness.

**authoritarian.** A style of discipline in which the parents dominate the home and maintain rigid control over every aspect of their child's life. They are not particularly nurturing and do not consider the child's view.

**authoritative.** A style of discipline in which the parents direct their child's activities, but within a nurturing atmosphere. They consider the child's point of view and explain decisions.

**average evoked potential.** Electrodes placed on the surface of the brain record the electrical activity of the central nervous system. When a stimulus is presented, a particular waveform is evoked in response to that stimulation. The average evoked potential, or event-related potential as it is sometimes called, is currently being used to assess information processing and intelligence.

**axons.** The long, thin fibers which extend from the nerve cell body and conduct impulses away from it.

**basic drives.** Fundamental human needs, such as thirst and hunger, which must be regularly gratified or the individual will die.

**battered child syndrome.** A phrase coined in 1962 by Dr. Kempe to call attention to physical child abuse.

**behavior modification.** The use of reinforcement techniques to change behavior.

**behaviorists.** A school of psychology which studies only overt behavior and makes no reference to mental processes.

**Caesarean section.** A surgical procedure by which the fetus is removed through an incision made in the abdominal wall and uterus.

**category clustering.** A memory strategy in which related items are organized into groups.

**centromere.** The central area of a chromosome.

**cephalo-caudal development.** The progression of motor development from head to foot.

**cerebral cortex.** The outer layer of gray matter covering the brain.

**cerebral palsy.** A condition of impaired muscular coordination due to brain damage occurring at or before birth.

**chorion biopsy.** A prenatal test that can detect fetal defects during the first trimester of pregnancy.

**chromosome.** Rod-shaped structures in the nucleus of every cell. Genes are located along the length of the chromosome.

**chronometric analyses.** Measurement procedures that use time as a central variable, such as reaction time.

**chunking.** A memory strategy combining isolated bits of information into unrelated groups (chunks).

**circadian rhythm.** Any human process that exhibits a cycle of approximately 24 hours.

**classical conditioning.** A procedure in which a neutral stimulus such as a bell is paired with another stimulus such as food. After several pairings, the bell will evoke the same response as food.

**clinical method.** Piaget's interview procedure that varies the questions as a function of the child's answers.

**cognitive styles.** The different ways in which individuals process information. They consist of differing qualities in perception, thinking, and problem solving that contribute to the uniqueness of personality.

**competence.** A set of personal qualities that enable an individual to produce flexible and adaptive responses to demands and to capitalize upon opportunities.

**concrete operations.** Piaget's third stage of cognitive development. It is characterized by logical reasoning about concrete experiences and events, rather than abstract or hypothetical ones.

**constructivism.** A school of psychology which believes that the developing child actively constructs knowledge of the world through direct interaction with the environment.

**conventional moral reasoning.** Kohlberg's second stage of moral reasoning in which the individual is concerned about the good of society. Right and wrong are defined in terms of what will gain the approval of significant others and society.

**critical period.** A limited time interval during which certain experiences must occur if they are to be effective.

**cross-sectional study.** Studying different age groups at one point in time. One-, two-, and three-year-olds might all be studied in a cross-sectional study of attachment.

**cross-sequential study.** A method of studying children's development in which two or more short-term longitudinal studies are undertaken simultaneously. For example, one- and three-year-olds might each be followed for two years. The researchers would then be able to describe the changes in attachment behavior from one to five years of age.

**culture-free tests.** Intelligence tests that do not rely upon information about the culture.

**decenter.** In Piaget's theory, the ability to shift attention and thus simultaneously attend to more than one dimension of an object.

**defining issues test.** A modification of Kohlberg's original moral judgment interview. Instead of using a clinical interview, the author, James Rest, presents multiple choice questions at the end of the moral dilemmas.

**dendrites.** The short and branched extensions of a nerve cell that conduct impulses in the brain.

**de novo.** From Latin meaning new.

**deoxyribonucleic acid (DNA).** The complex chemical substance containing the genetic code.

**disequilibration.** In Piaget's theory, an imbalance between assimilation and accommodation that fosters cognitive growth.

**divergent thinking.** A style of thinking that moves away from common associations and solutions and generates ideas that are uncommon and novel.

**dominant gene.** The gene in a pair that will be expressed phenotypically over a recessive gene.

**duos.** The two-word sentences used early in the process of language acquisition.

**eidetic imagery.** An unusally good visual memory consisting of vivid images that are accurate representations of the environment.

**ego.** In Freud's theory, that province of the mind which is reality oriented and seeks to balance the opposing forces of the id and superego.

**egocentrism.** In Piaget's theory, the child's inability to recognize the differing perspectives held by others.

**ego-resiliency.** A blend of competence, intelligence, resourcefulness, and adaptability under stress.

**elaborated language code.** The type of enriched language modeled by middle-class parents consisting of long, complex, and abstract sentences.

**elaboration.** A memory strategy in which the individual creates images or phrases that link the items to be remembered.

**embryo.** The period of development in the human from two to eight weeks following conception during which basic body structures and organ systems are formed.

**empiricists.** Scientists who regard direct observation from experiments as more important than theory.

**en face.** A way of holding the human infant close so the adult and infant are looking directly into each other's eyes.

**engrossment.** The father's emotional reaction to his infant at birth.

**enzyme.** A variety of proteins which function as biochemical catalysts within the organism.

**epicanthic folds.** A fold of skin of the upper eyelid that tends to cover the inner corner of the eye.

**equilibration.** In Piaget's theory, the balanced state between assimilation and accommodation.

**event related brain potentials.** A technique used to study the cognitive processes of infants. Electrodes placed on the infant's scalp record the brain's response to stimulating events.

**exemplar model.** A strategy for organizing information in which children store every example of a concept.

**experimental strategy.** A scientific procedure in which the experimenter actually manipulates the variable of interest in several groups of subjects.

**facilitate (brain development).** The condition of adequate environmental stimulation that encourages normal brain development to occur.

**failure to thrive.** A term applied to infants who are not developing at a normal rate. Their delays are due to a lack of adequate emotional support from their parents.

**feature analysis.** One of three explanations as to how young children extract meaning from words. Presumably children extract a single feature or group of features that characterize an object and then apply the same label to other objects with the same feature.

**feature detectors.** The first and thus simplest level of perceptual experience. They are used heavily by infants as they respond to basic aspects of their environment such as straight lines, angles, or high notes.

**feral.** Human children who grow up without the benefit of human contact. They survive either on their own or are raised by other animals.

**field dependence.** A cognitive style reflecting an individual's inability to ignore misleading perceptual cues from the immediate environment.

**field independence.** A cognitive style reflecting an individual's ability to ignore misleading perceptual cues from the immediate environment.

**formal operations.** In Piaget's theory, the fourth stage of cognitive development in which abstract and hypothetical reasoning are present.

**gender identity.** The developing awareness in children that there are two different sexes and they belong to only one of them.

**gene.** A portion of DNA which transmits hereditary characteristics.

**genetic engineering.** Any conscious manipulation that affects the frequency or expression of genes.

**genotype.** The total set of inherited genes.

**goodness of fit.** The degree of harmony or matching between an individual and a particular setting.

**habituation.** A decrease in responsiveness as a result of repeated exposure to the same stimulus.

**hallucinations.** Visual or auditory experiences that are produced in the individual's mind in the absence of matching environmental stimuli.

**holophrases.** The one-word sentences first used by young children.

**hormone.** A complex and powerful chemical capable of sending messages to specially responsive cells.

**hyperactivity.** An unusually high activity level.

**id.** In Freud's theory, one of the three provinces of the mind. The id consists of primary drives which the infant tries to gratify.

**impulsive.** A cognitive style in which children respond quickly and make a large number of errors.

**imperative communication.** A style of instruction in which parents give children directions in terms of do's and don'ts without any explanation.

**imprinting.** An innate response in young birds to follow the first large moving object seen after birth. Since that object is usually the mother, an important bond is formed.

**induce (brain development).** Continued environmental stimulation that causes brain development to be more complex and advanced than normally would occur.

**information processing.** A description of the flow of information into and out of human memory.

**inner speech.** In Vygotsky's theory, the private speech which follows socialized speech. It becomes abbreviated and internalized and plays an important role in thinking.

**innoculation.** The notion that an appropriate intervention program early in life will protect a child from adverse outcomes for many years.

**instinctive drift.** The tendency of animals to return to innate behaviors that interfere with newly conditioned behaviors.

**instructive communications.** A style of instruction in which parents provide explanations with the directions they give their children.

**instrumental conditioning.** The basic learning process by which the frequency of a behavior increases or decreases as a function of reinforcement.

**intrauterine.** Within the human uterus.

**introspection.** A method of investigation that relies upon the individual describing subjective experiences.

**inversion.** Occurs during cell division when a segment of chromosomal material is turned around so that the normal sequence of the gene is changed.

**isolates.** Individuals who receive no nominations on a sociogram. This indicates that they were not sought out as friends by other members of their group.

**joint custody.** An arrangement following divorce in which both parents are involved in making decisions about the child's life. It does not always mean that the children live with each parent an equal amount of time.

**joint physical custody.** An arrangement following divorce in which both parents are involved in making decisions about the child's life and in which the child spends approximately equal amounts of time living with each parent.

**karotype.** A photograph of chromosomes obtained from a blood sample in which the cells have been cultured and stained.

**keyword technique.** A memory strategy in which the individual creates an image about the material to be remembered.

**language mapping.** A technique developed by Penfield in which language areas of the brain are detected by direct electrical stimulation of brain tissue.

**language universals.** Features of language development that are common across diverse cultures.

**learned helplessness.** An acquired but inaccurate belief that one is helpless regarding some aspect of functioning. This belief undermines motivation and often causes emotional disturbance.

**long-term memory.** That portion of human memory from which information is retrieved weeks or even months after it was stored.

**longitudinal study.** A research procedure in which the same individuals are studied over an extended period of time to determine how they change with increasing age.

**maintain (brain development).** A condition of adequate environmental stimulation that permits normal brain development.

**maturation.** The emergence of various skills as a result of a child's physical growth or neurological development, rather than learning.

**meiosis.** The process of cell division that produces sperm cells and egg cells, each with half the normal complement of chromosomes.

**metamemory.** The attempt to understand and think about the process of memory.

**mitosis.** The process of cell division in which new cells are produced.

**mnemonic.** Any action or plan undertaken to assist memory.

**morality of constraint.** Piaget's first stage of moral reasoning, in which children consider social rules to be as unchangeable as physical laws of nature. Right and wrong are understood largely in terms of punishments and rules are made by powerful others.

**morality of cooperation.** Piaget's second stage of moral reasoning, in which children recognize rules are social inventions that can be changed. Children at this stage show concern for equality and reciprocity.

**monozygotic twins.** Twins which develop from a single fertilized egg cell. These individuals are referred to as identical twins because they have exactly the same chromosomes.

**moro reflex.** A startle response infants make to a loud noise or loss of physical support. The arms are flung out to the side and then brought back toward each other.

**motherese.** The language parents use to speak to their infants. They speak slowly and distinctly, emphasize important words, and use short, redundant sentences.

**myelination.** The development of an insulating fatty sheath (myelin) around nerves, which speeds up the transmission of impulses by reducing interference between unrelated chemical messages.

**nature-nurture controversy.** A long-running and often heated argument in psychology as to the relative influence of heredity and the environment in determining various human characteristics.

**neural adaptability.** When subjects control the presentation of a stimulus, their brains respond to the stimulation quicker than when the experimenter controls the presentation of a stimulus. This is an index of neural adaptability.

**neuron.** A single cell that serves as the foundation of the body's nerves.

**neurotransmitters.** Chemicals that facilitate the transmission of nerve impulses.

**no-trial learning.** The ability to learn by watching another perform a behavior rather than having to try out or practice that behavior.

**nucleic acid.** The fluid that in combination with bits of protein forms chromosomes.

**object concept.** The infant's discovery that objects have a permanent existence independent of the infant's direct sensory or motor contact with the object.

**open classroom.** A flexible classroom atmosphere in which students are introduced to many areas of study. In open classrooms, students are allowed some freedom to choose what they learn.

**organization.** In Piaget's theory, the fundamental principle by which individuals combine and integrate perceptions and thoughts.

**organizational function of hormones.** The capacity of hormones to structure and arrange different systems in the body.

**overextend (overgeneralize).** The child's use of one word to refer to many similar objects.

**pedigrees.** Tracings of a trait or disorder through several generations of a family in order to study the influence of heredity.

**penetrance.** The extent to which the expression of a gene is limited by the operation of modifier genes or external environmental factors.

**perceived self-efficacy.** The degree to which individuals perceive themselves to be successful at various activities.

**perinatal period.** The time interval immediately before, during, and after birth.

**permissive.** A style of parenting in which the child is accepted in an almost unquestioning fashion. No standards are set by the parents, who are available as resources but exercise little control and do not communicate with the child.

**phenotype.** Those characteristics of the genes that are actually observable in the individual.

**phonology.** The study of the basic sounds that make up language.

**pleiotrophy.** The ability of one protein to have an effect on several traits or behaviors.

**polygenetic.** Those characteristics that are determined by not one but by many different genes.

**postconventional moral reasoning.** Kohlberg's third stage of moral reasoning, in which individuals differentiate between morality and laws. Moral decisions are made on the basis of the most good for the most people or upon other individually derived principles rather than simple conformity to some external authority.

**pragmatics.** The mechanics of language interaction, including using gestures and taking turns.

**preconventional moral reasoning.** Kohlberg's first stage of moral reasoning, in which the individuals are concerned about their own welfare. Individuals try to be obedient to avoid punishment and to meet their own hedonistic needs.

**prosocial behavior.** Positive actions directed toward another person without any expectation of reward or reinforcement. Examples include sharing, cooperation, and helping behaviors.

**prospective study.** A scientific investigation in which the data are obtained through the direct observation or measurement of individuals rather than having them report on events that happened in the past.

**prototype.** One of three explanations as to how children extract meaning from words. It involves children forming a model of what an object, such as dog, might be and then applying that label to anything remotely similar to their model.

**psychoanalytic theory.** A set of beliefs presented by Freud asserting that behavior is significantly influenced by mental processes, many of which are unconscious.

**psychosexual stages.** A series of five developmental periods presented by Freud.

**psychosocial retardation.** A form of retardation that is due to a lack of adequate environmental stimulation rather than organic brain damage.

**psychosocial stages.** A series of eight major life crises presented by Erikson.

**ptosis.** The drooping of the upper eyelid because of muscle failure.

**Pygmalion effect.** A term derived from studies of teachers' expectations. Researchers randomly picked students and then told teachers that these students were ready to "bloom." By the end of the school year, these students in fact evidenced substantial gains in IQ scores.

**rapid eye movements (REM).** A phase of sleep during which fast movements of the eye occur. Dreaming occurs during this phase of sleep.

**readiness.** The developmental level of a child which enables him or her to benefit from a particular environmental experience.

**recessive gene.** A gene which will not be expressed when paired with a dominant gene but will be expressed when paired with another recessive gene.

**reflective.** A cognitive style evidenced by individuals who take their time in solving problems and make few errors.

**reliability.** The repeatability of a test. On a reliable test, individuals will receive approximately the same scores on repeated administrations.

**resilient.** A term applied to children who are able to successfully cope with numerous stresses and still maintain control and mastery over their lives.

**restricted language code.** The relatively impoverished language used by lower-class parents, in which sentences are short and concrete.

**retrospective study.** A scientific investigation in which individuals are asked to recall and describe events that happened in the past.

**reversibility.** In Piaget's theory, the ability to mentally reverse the process of change and return it to its original state.

**Rh factor.** A blood component that is positive for the majority of individuals. For Rh-negative mothers, there can be an incompatibility with her Rh-positive fetus in which the mother's immunological system produces antibodies that cross the placental barrier and destroy the fetus's red blood cells.

**Rhogam.** A drug administered to Rh-negative mothers to prevent the complications of Rh incompatibility with their Rh-positive fetus.

**schemes.** In Piaget's theory, an organized set of actions characteristic of the sensory motor stage.

**self-fulfilling prophecy.** The process by which an expectation or prediction comes to influence events so that over time the expectation or prediction is confirmed.

**semantic memory.** The entire store of knowledge that individuals have retained in long-term memory.

**semantics.** The meaning of words.

**sensitive period.** A limited time interval during which a particular skill or behavior responds well to environmental stimulation. During later time intervals, this skill or behavior would not develop in the same optimal way. Language is a behavior that is often regarded as being best acquired during a sensitive period. This is a less restrictive concept than critical period.

**separation anxiety.** A set of behaviors reflecting upset by infants when they are separated from a primary caretaker.

**set point.** A particular point which is maintained by the body. In the case of weight, many adults maintain the same weight plus or minus a few pounds for many years. This weight would be the set point.

**short-term memory buffer.** A memory space used for current and new information. A new phone number will initially be stored in short-term memory. If you rehearse it or use it often, it is likely to become part of long-term memory.

**sign stimuli.** In ethological theory, a specific feature of the environment that releases a specific behavioral response in an animal.

**slow-wave sleep.** An EEG pattern characterized by waves from one to four cycles per second.

**social reinforcements.** A favorable response from a person to some behavior. Social reinforcements such as smiling, complimenting a person, or encouraging the person increase the likelihood of the behavior recurring.

**sociogram.** A technique for measuring various kinds of preferences and relationships within a group. The information is presented in the form of a diagram.

**sole custody.** An arrangement following divorce in which one parent makes most of the decisions regarding the child's life. The child lives with that parent and has limited contact with the other parent, typically alternate weekends.

**split custody.** An arrangement following divorce in which some of the children live with one parent and some with the other parent. Typically, boys live with fathers and girls with mothers.

**stability.** The extent to which a characteristic or behavior remains unchanged over time.

**stage.** A phase of development that is qualitatively different from other phases.

**standardization sample.** That group of individuals from which the interpretive norms for a test were derived.

**star.** An individual who receives a large number of nominations in a sociogram.

**strange situation.** An observational procedure used to study the quality of attachment between an infant and caretaker.

**stranger anxiety.** A set of distress behaviors exhibited by young infants when they encounter unfamiliar individuals. This usually begins around seven to nine months of age, after the infant has formed a specific attachment to a primary caretaker, and lasts into the second year of life.

**string measure.** An index obtained from evoked potentials by actually using a piece of string to measure the length of the graphically presented wave.

**structure.** In Piaget's theory, an organization of related items or concepts such as numbers or letters.

**superego.** In Freud's theory, that province of the mind which contains beliefs about right and wrong.

**synapse.** The small space between neurons over which chemical impulses travel.

**syntax.** The significance of word order in the meaning of language.

**tabula rasa.** The behaviorists' conception of the human infant as a "blank slate" which will be written upon by experience.

**teratogens.** External agents that cross the placental barrier and interfere with the normal development of the embryo or fetus.

**testosterone.** A male hormone.

**threshold phenomenon.** The recognition that there is little relationship between a measured skill and subsequent success once a minimal level of skill is achieved.

**traditional classroom.** A structured classroom setting which emphasizes learning the basics.

**translocation.** The exchange of genetic material that occurs when the tiny arms of chromosomes break off during cell division and reattach to a different chromosome.

**unconscious.** In Freud's theory, the belief that many important psychological processes take place outside the individual's conscious awareness.

**validity.** The extent to which a test actually measures what it claims to measure.

**zygote.** A female egg cell (ovum) that has been penetrated and fertilized by a sperm cell.

# Bibliography

A crane's life vowed for 6" chick. (1982). *Press Enterprise*, Section A–4.

Abel, E. L. (1980). Fetal alcohol syndrome: Behavioral teratology. *Pyschological Bulletin, 87*, 29–50.

Abramov, I., Gordon, J., Hendrickson, A., Hainline, L., Dobson, V., & La-Bossiere, E. (1982). The retina of the newborn human infant. *Science, 217*, 265–267.

Abramson, L. Y., Seligman, M. I. P., & Teasdale, J. D. (1978). Learned helplessness in humans: Critique and reformulation. *Journal of Abnormal Psychology, 87*, 49–74.

Ackerman, B. P. (1982). Contextual integration and utterance interpretation: The ability of children and adults to interpret sarcastic utterances. *Child Development, 53*, 1075–1083.

Adams-Tucker, C. (1982). Proximate effects of sexual abuse in childhood: A report on 28 children. *American Journal of Psychiatry, 139*, 1252–1256.

Admissions Testing Program. (1983). *National Aptitude Analysis, 1973–1982*. Princeton, NJ: Educational Testing Service.

Agren, G., & Meyerson, B. J. (1979). Long term effects of social deprivation during early adulthood in the Mongolian gerbil (Meriones unguiculatus). *Zeitschrift fur Tierpsychologie, 47*, 422–431. As cited by Immelmann, K., & Suomi, S. J. Sensitive phases in development. In K. Immelmann, G. W. Barlow, L. Petrinovich, & M. Main (Eds.) (1981). *Behavioral development: The Bielefeld Interdisciplinary Project*. New York: Cambridge University Press.

Ahrons, C. R. (1981). The continuing coparental relationship between divorced spouses. *American Journal of Orthopsychiatry, 51*, 415–428.

Ainsworth, M. D. S. (1973). The development of infant-mother attachment. In B. M. Caldwell & H. N. Ricciuti (Eds.), *Review of child development research*. (Vol. 3). Chicago: University of Chicago Press.

Ainsworth, M. D. S., & Wittig, B. A. (1969). Attachment and exploratory behavior of one-year-olds in a strange situation. In B. M. Foss (Ed.), *Determinants of infant behavior* (Vol. 4). London: Methuen.

Ainsworth, M. D. S., Blehar, M. C., Waters, E., & Wall, S. (1978). *Patterns of attachment*. Hillsdale, NJ: Lawrence Erlbaum.

Albee, G. W. (1982). The politics of nature and nurture. *American Journal of Community Psychology, 10*, 4–30.

Alexandrowicz, M. K., & Alexandrowicz, D. R. (1974). Obstetrical pain-relieving drugs as predictors of infant behavior variability. *Child Development, 45*, 934–945.

Allgaier, A. (1978). Alternative birth centers offer family-centered care. *Hospitals, 52*, 97–112.

Allik, J., & Valsiner, J. (1981). Visual development in ontogenesis: Some reevaluations. In H. W. Reese & L. P. Lipsitt (Eds.), *Advances in child development and behavior* (Vol. 15). New York: Academic Press.

Als, H., Tronick, E., Lester, B. M., & Brazelton, T. B. (1979). Specific neonatal measures: The Brazelton Neonatal Behavior Assesment Scale. In J. D. Osofsky (Ed.), *Handbook of infant development.* New York: John Wiley & Sons.

Amado, H., & Lustman, P. J. (1982). Attention deficit disorders persisting in adulthood: A review. *Comprehensive Psychiatry, 23*, 300–314.

Amato, J. C. (1977). Fetal monitoring in a community hospital: A statistical analysis. *Obstetrics and Gynecology, 50*, 269–274.

Ambulatory Pediatric Association. (1981). The WHO code of marketing of breastmilk substitutes. *Pediatrics, 68*, 432–434.

American Humane Association (1979). *National analysis of official child neglect and abuse reporting.* Englewood, CO: American Humane Association.

American Psychiatric Association. (1980). *Diagnostic and statistical manual of mental disorders (DSM III).* Washington, DC: American Psychiatric Association.

Anastasi, A. (1958a). Heredity, environment, and the question "How?" *Psychological Review, 65*, 197–208.

Anastasi, A. (1958b). *Differential psychology.* New York: Macmillan.

Anderson, C. W. (1980). Attachment in daily separations: Reconceptualizing day care and maternal employment issues. *Child Development, 51*, 242–245.

Anderson, R. C. (1975). Mnemotechnics in second-language learning. *American Psychologist, 30*, 821–828.

Anderson, R. C. (1981). Effects of prior knowledge on memory for new information. *Memory and Cognition, 9*, 237–246.

Anderson, R. C. (1982). Acquisition of cognitive skill. *Psychological Review, 89*, 369–406.

Andison, F. S. (1977). TV violence and viewer aggression: A cumulation of study results 1956–1976. *Public Opinion Quarterly, 41*, 314–331.

Anglin, J. M. (1977). *Word, object, and conceptual development.* New York: W. W. Norton.

Anisfeld, M., Masters, J. C., Jacobson, S. W., & Kagan, J. (1979). Interpreting "imitative" responses in early infancy. *Science, 205*, 214–219.

Anthony, B. J., & Graham, F. K. (1983). Evidence for sensory-selective set in young infants. *Science, 220*, 742–744.

Anthony, E. J. (1971). A clinical and experimental study of high risk children and their schizophrenic parents. In A. Kaplan (Ed.), *Genetic factors in schizophrenia.* Springfield, IL: Charles C Thomas.

Apgar, V. (1953). A proposal for a new method of evaluation of the newborn infant. *Anesthesia and Analgesia, 32*, 260–267.

Archer, J. (1976). Biological explanations of psychological sex differences. In B. B. Lloyd & J. Archer (Eds.), *Exploring sex differences.* New York: Academic Press.

Archer, J. (1981). Sex differences in maturation. In H. F. R. Prechtl & K. J. Connolly (Eds.), *Maturation and development: Biological and psychological perspectives.* Philadelphia: J. B. Lippincott.

Aries, P. (1962). *Centuries of childhood.* New York: Vintage Books.

Arnold, A. P. (1980). Sexual differences in the brain. *American Scientist, 68,* 165–173.

Asarnow, J. R., & Meichenbaum, D. (1979). Verbal rehearsal and serial recall: The mediational training of kindergarten children. *Child Development, 50,* 1173–1177.

Asher, S. R., & Renshaw, P. D. (1981). Children without friends: Social knowledge and social skill training. In S. R. Asher & J. M. Gottman (Eds.), *The development of children's friendships.* London: Cambridge University Press.

Ashley, M. J. (1981). Alcohol use during pregnancy: A challenge for the 80s. *Canadian Medical Association Journal, 125,* 141–143.

Ashmead, D. H., & Perlmutter, M. (1980). Infant memory in everyday life. In M. Perlmutter (Ed.), *Children's memory.* San Francisco: Jossey-Bass.

Associated Press. (1982, June 3). Health alert names industrial solvents. *Press Enterprise,* Section 1, p. 4.

Austin, V. D., Ruble, D. N., & Trabasso, T. (1977). Recall and order effects as factors in children's moral judgments. *Child Development, 48,* 470–474.

Avery, O. T., MacLeod, C. M., & McCarty, M. (1944). Studies on the chemical nature of the substance inducing transformation of pneumococcal types. *Journal of Experimental Medicine, 79,* 137–158.

Baher, E. (1976). *At risk: An account of the work of the battered child research department.* National Society for Prevention of Cruelty to Children. Boston: Routledge, & Kegan Paul.

Baker, L., DeFries, J. C., & Fulker, D. W. (1983). Longitudinal stability of cognitive ability in the Colorado Adoption Project. *Child Development, 54,* 290–297.

Baldwin, A. L. (1980). *Theories of child development.* New York: John Wiley & Sons.

Baldwin, A. L., Cole, R. E., & Baldwin, C. P. (1983). Parental pathology, family interaction, and the competence of the child in school. *Monographs of the Society for Research in Child Development, 47,* No. 197.

Baldwin, J. M. (1915). *Genetic theory of reality.* New York: G. P. Putnam's Sons.

Bandura, A. (1965). Vicarious processes. A case of no-trial learning. In L. Berkowitz (Ed.), *Advances in experimental social psychology* (Vol. 2). New York: Academic Press.

Bandura, A. (1977). *Social learning theory.* Englewood Cliffs, NJ: Prentice-Hall.

Bandura, A. (1982a). Self-efficacy mechanism in human agency. *American Psychologist, 37,* 122–147.

Bandura, A. (1982b). The assessment and predictive generality of self-percepts of efficacy. *Journal of Behavior Therapy and Experimental Psychiatry, 13,* 195–199.

Bandura, A. (1983). Self-efficacy determinants of anticipated fears and calamities. *Journal of Personality and Social Psychology, 45,* 464–469.

Bandura, A., & Schunk, D. H. (1981). Cultivating competence, self-efficacy, and intrinsic interest through proximal self-motivation. *Journal of Personality and Social Psychology, 41,* 586–598.

Bandura, A., & Walters, R. H. (1963). *Social learning and personality development.* New York: Holt, Rinehart & Winston.

Banks, M. (1980). The development of visual accommodation during early infancy. *Child Development, 51,* 646–666.

Barbe, W. B. (1955). Evaluation of special classes for gifted children. *Exceptional Children, 22,* 60–62.

Bardin, C. W., & Catterall J. F. (1981). Testosterone: A major determinant of extragenital sexual dimorphism. *Science, 211,* 1285–1294.

Barfield, A. (1976). Biological influences on sex differences in behavior. In M. S. Teitelbaum (Ed.), *Sex differences: Social and biological perspectives.* Garden City, NY: Doubleday Publishing.

Barlow, G. W. (1981). Genetics and development of behavior, with special reference to patterned motor output. In K. Immelmann, G. W. Barlow, L. Petrinovich, & M. Main (Eds.), *Behavioral development: The Bielefeld interdisciplinary project.* New York: Cambridge University Press.

Barnard, K. (1975). *A program of stimulation for infants born prematurely.* Seattle WA: University of Washington Press.

Barnett, C. R., Leiderman, P. H., Grobstein, R., & Klaus, M. H. (1970). Neonatal separation: The maternal side of interactional deprivation. *Pediatrics, 45,* 197–205.

Barrera, M. E., & Maurer, D. (1981). The perception of facial expressions by the three-month-old. *Child Development, 52,* 203–206.

Barrett, D. E., Radke-Yarrow, M., & Klein, R. E. (1982). Chronic malnutrition and child behavior: Effects of early calorie supplementation on social-emotional functioning at school age. *Developmental Psychology, 18,* 541–556.

Bartlett, K. (October 4, 1981). Twin study likely to open controversy. *Los Angeles Times,* Section I–B, pp. 5–7.

Barton, J. J., Rovner, S., Puls, K., & Read, P. A. (1980). Alternative birthing center: Experience in a teaching obstetric service. *American Journal of Obstetrics and Gynecology, 137,* 377–384.

Basser, L. S. (1962). Hemiplegia of early onset and the faculty of speech with special reference to the effects of hemispherectomy. *Brain, 85,* 427–460.

Bates, E., Bretherton, I., Beeghly-Smith, M., & McNew, S. (1982). Social bases of language development: A reassessment. In H. W. Reese & L. P. Lipsitt (Eds.), *Advances in child development and behavior* (Vol. 16). New York: Academic Press.

Bates, E., Carlson-Luden, V., & Bretherton, I. (1980). Perceptual aspects of tool using in infancy. *Infant Behavior and Development, 3,* 127–140.

Bates, J. E. (1980). The concept of difficult temperament. *Merrill Palmer Quarterly, 26,* 299–319.

Baumgarten, K. (1981). The advantages and risks of feto-maternal monitoring. *Journal of Perinatal Medicine, 9,* 257–274.

Baumrind, D. (1967). Child care practices anteceding three patterns of preschool behavior. *Genetic Psychological Monographs, 75.*

Baumrind, D. (1971). Current patterns of parental authority. *Developmental Psychology Monographs, 4,* (Part 2).

Baumrind, D. (1977) *Socialization determinants of personal agency.* Paper presented at the Society for Research in Child Development, New Orleans.

Baumrind, D. (1978). Reciprocal rights and responsibilities in parent-child relations. *Journal of Social Issues, 34,* 179–189.

Bayley, N. (1965). Comparisons of mental and motor test scores for ages 1–15 months by sex, birth order, race, geographical location and education of parents. *Child Development, 36,* 379–411.

Bayley, N. (1968). Behavioral correlates of mental growth: Birth to thirty. *American Psychologist, 23,* 1–17.

Bayley, N. (1969). *Manual for the Bayley scales of infant development.* New York: Psychological Corporation.

Bayley, N. (1970). Development of mental abilities. In P. H. Mussen (Ed.), *Carmichael's Manual of Child Psychology.* New York: John Wiley & Sons.

Bayley, N., & Schaefer, E. S. (1964). Correlations of maternal and child behaviors with the development of mental abilities: Data from the Berkeley growth study. *Monographs of the Society for Research in Child Development, 29,* No. 97.

Beckoff, M., & Byers, J. A. (1981). Mammalian social and locomotor play. In K. Immelmann, G. W. Barlow, L. Petrinovich, & M. Main (Eds.), *Behavioral development: The Bielefeld interdisciplinary project.* New York: Cambridge University Press.

Beilin, H. (1978). Inducing conservation through training. In G. Steiner (Ed.), *Psychology of the 20th century: Piaget and beyond* (Vol. 7). Zurich: Kindler Verlag.

Beilin, H. (1980). Piaget's theory: Refinement, revision, or rejection? In R. H. Kluwe & H. Spada (Eds.), *Developmental models of thinking.* New York: Academic Press.

Bejar, I. I. (1981). Does nutrition cause intelligence? Reanalysis of the Cali experiment. *Intelligence, 5,* 49–69.

Bell, C. S., Johnson, J. E., McGillicuddy-Delisi, A. V., & Sigel, I. E. (1981). The effects of family constellation and child gender on parental use of evaluative feedback. *Child Development, 52,* 701–704.

Bell, R. Q., & Harper, L. V. (1977). *Child effects on adults.* Hillsdale, NJ: Lawrence Erlbaum.

Bell, S. M., & Ainsworth, M. D. S. (1972). Infant crying and maternal responsiveness. *Child Development, 43,* 1171–1190.

Belsky, J., Steinberg, L. D., & Walker, A. (1982). The ecology of day care. In M. E. Lamb (Ed.), *Nontraditional families: Parenting and child development.* Hillsdale, NJ: Lawrence Erlbaum.

Benbow, C., & Stanley, J. C. (1980). Sex differences in mathematical ability: Fact or artifact. *Science, 210,* 1262– 1264.

Bennett, F. C., Sells, C. J., & Brand, C. (1979). Influences on measured intelligence in Down's Syndrome. *American Journal of Diseases of Children, 133,* 700–703.

Berg, K. (1979). *Genetic damage in man caused by environmental agents.* New York: Academic Press.

Berkowitz, L. (1983). Aversively stimulated aggression: Some parallels and differences in research with animals and humans. *American Psychologist, 38,* 1135–1144.

Berndt, T. J. (1981). Relations between social cognition, nonsocial cognition, and social behavior: The case of friendship. In J. H. Flavell & L. Ross (Eds.), *Social cognitive development*. Cambridge: Cambridge University Press.

Berndt, T. J. (1982). The features and effects of friendship in early adolescence. *Child Development, 53*, 1447–1460.

Bernstein, B. (1966). Elaborated and restricted codes. Their social origins and some consequences. In A. G. Smith (Ed.), *Communication and culture*. New York: Holt, Rinehart & Winston.

Berry, K. K. (1981). The male single parent. In I. R. Stuart & L. E. Abt. (Eds.), *Children of separation and divorce: Management and treatment*. New York: Van Nostrand Reinhold.

Bijou, S. W., & Baer, D. M. (1961). *Child Development* (Vol. 1). New York: Appleton-Century-Crofts.

Bijou, S. W., & Baer, D. M. (1965). *Child development: Universal stage of infancy* (Vol. 2). New York: Appleton-Century-Crofts.

Bijou, S. W., & Baer, D. M. (1967). *Child Development: Reading in experimental analysis*. New York: Appleton-Century-Crofts.

Bijou, S. W., Birnbrauer, J. S., Kidder, J. D., & Tague, C. (1966). Programmed instruction as an approach to teaching of reading, writing, and arithmetic to retarded children. *The Psychological Record, 16*, 505–522.

Binet, A. (1890). Perception d'enfants. *La Revue Philosophique, 30*, 582–611.

Birnholz, J. C., & Benacerraf, B. R. (1983). The development of human fetal hearing. *Science, 222*, 516–518.

Bjorklund, D. F., & Hock, H. S. (1982). Age differences in the temporal locus of memory organization in children's recall. *Journal of Experimental Child Psychology, 33*, 347–362.

Blanchard, R. W., & Biller, H. B. (1971). Father availability and academic performance among third-grade boys. *Developmental Psychology, 4*, 301–305.

Blasi, A. (1980). Bridging moral cognition and moral action: A critical review of the literature. *Psychological Bulletin, 88*, 1–45.

Blatt, M., & Kohlberg, L. (1975). The effects of classroom moral discussion upon children's level of moral judgment. *Journal of Moral Education, 4*, 129–161.

Blau, Z. S. (1981). *Black children/White children*. New York: Free Press.

Blinkhorn, S. F., & Hendrickson, D. E. (1982). Averaged evoked responses and psychometric intelligence. *Nature, 295*, 596–597.

Block, J. (1971). *Lives through time*. Berkeley, CA: Bancroft.

Block, J. (1981). Some enduring and consequential structures of personality. In A. I. Rabin, J. Aronoff, A. M. Barclay, & R. A. Zucker (Eds.), *Further explorations in personality*. New York: John Wiley & Sons.

Block, J. (1982). Assimilation, accommodation, and the dynamics of personality development. *Child Development, 53*, 281–295.

Block, J. H. (1973). Conceptions of sex role: Some cross-cultural and longitudinal perspectives. *American Psychologist, 28*, 512–526.

Block, J. H. (1976). Issues, problems, and pitfalls in assessing sex differences: A critical review of *The psychology of sex differences*. *Merrill Palmer Quarterly, 22*, 283–309.

Block, J. H. (1983). Differential premises arising from differential socialization of the sexes: Some conjectures. *Child Development, 54,* 1335–1354.

Block, J. H., & Block, J. (1980). The role of ego-control and ego-resiliency in the organization of behavior. In W. A. Collins (Ed.), *Development of cognition, affect, and social relations. The Minnesota Symposia on Child Psychology.* (Vol. 13). Hillsdale, NJ: Lawrence Erlbaum.

Block, J., Block, J. H., & Harrington, D. M. (1974). Some misgivings about the Matching Familiar Figures Test as a measure of reflection-impulsivity. *Developmental Psychology, 10,* 611–632.

Block, N. (1981). *Imagery.* Cambridge, MA: MIT Press.

Bloom, B. S. (1964). *Stability and change in human characteristics.* New York: John Wiley & Sons.

Bloom, L. (1973). *One word at a time: The use of single-word utterances before syntax.* The Hague: Mouton.

Bloom, L. (1981). Language development in relation to cognition. In R. E. Stark (Ed.), *Language behavior in infancy and early childhood.* NY: Elsevier-North Holland Publishing.

Bloom, L., & Lahey, M. (1978). *Language development and language disorders.* New York: John Wiley & Sons.

Bloom, L., Hood, L., & Lightbown, P. (1974). Imitation in language development: If, when, and why. *Cognitive Psychology, 6,* 380–420.

Bloom, L., Lifter, K., & Broughton, J. (1981). What children say and what they know: Exploring the relations between product and process in the development of early words and early concepts. In R. E. Stark (Ed.), *Language behavior in infancy and early childhood.* New York: Elsevier-North Holland Publishing.

Bloom, L., Merkin, S., & Wootten, J. (1982). *Wh* -questions: Linguistic factors that contribute to the sequence of acquisition. *Child Development, 53,* 1084–1092.

Blum, R. W., & Goldhagen, J. (1981). Teenage pregnancy in perspective. *Clinical Pediatrics, 20,* 335–340.

Blumberg, B. S., & Hesser, J. E. (1975). Anthropology and infectious disease. In A. Damon (Ed.), *Physiological anthropology.* New York: Oxford University Press.

Blurton-Jones, N., Ferriera, M., Farquhar-Brown, M., & McDonald, L. (1979). Aggression, crying and physical contact in one- to three-year-old children. *Aggressive Behavior, 5,* 121–133.

Blusztajn, J. K., & Wurtman, R. J. (1983). Choline and cholinergic neurons. *Science, 22,* 614–620.

Bodde, T. (1982, April). The body's answer to zero gravity. *Bioscience,* 249–251.

Boehm, F. H., Estes, W., Wright, P. F., & Growdon, J. F. (1981). Management of genital herpes simplex virus infection occurring during pregnancy. *American Journal of Obstetrics and Gynecology, 141,* 735–740.

Bonner, W. N. (1980). *Whales.* London: Blandford Press.

Bonvillian, J. D., Nelson, K. W., & Rhyne, J. M. (1981). Sign language and autism. *Journal of Autism and Developmental Disorders, 11,* 125–127.

Borges, S., & Lewis, P. D. (1981). Effects of alcohol on the developing nervous system. *Trends in Neurosciences, 4,* 13–15.

Börjeson, M. (1976). The aetiology of obesity in children. *Acta Paediatrica Scandinavia, 65,* 279–287.

Borke, H. (1975). Piaget's mountains revisited: Changes in the egocentric landscape. *Developmental Psychology, 11,* 240–243.

Borkowski, J. G. (in press). Signs of intelligence: Strategy generalization and metacognition. In S. R. Yussen (Ed.), *The growth of insight in children.* New York: Academic Press.

Boswell, D. A., & Green, H. F. (1982). The abstraction and recognition of prototypes by children and adults. *Child Development, 53,* 1028–1037.

Bouchard, T. J., & McGue, M. (1981). Familial studies of intelligence: A review. *Science, 212,* 1055–1059.

Boue, J., Boue, A., & Lazar, P. (1975). Retrospective and prospective epidemiological studies of 1500 karyotyped spontaneous human abortions. *Teratology, 12,* 11–26.

Boukydis, C. F. Z., & Burgess, R. L. (1982). Adult physiological response to infant cries: Effects of temperament of infant, parental status, and gender. *Child Development, 53,* 1291–1298.

Boveri, T. (1903). Uber die Konstitution der chromatischen Kernsubstanz. *Verh deutsch zool Ges. 13 Vers. Wurzburg,* 10–33. As cited by Dunn, L. C. (1965). *A short history of genetics.* New York: McGraw-Hill.

Bower, T. G. R. (1977). *A primer of infant development.* San Francisco: W. H. Freeman.

Bower, T. G. R. (1982). *Development in infancy* (2nd ed.). San Francisco: W. H. Freeman.

Bowerman, M. (1978a). The acquisition of word meaning: An investigation into some current conflicts. In N. Waterson & C. Snow (Eds.), *The development of communication.* New York: John Wiley & Sons.

Bowerman, M. (1978b). Systematizing semantic knowledge: Changes over time in the child's organization of word meaning. *Child Development, 49,* 977–987.

Bowes, W. A., Brackbill, Y., Conway, E., & Steinschneider, A. (1970). The effects of obstetrical medication on fetus and infant. *Monographs of the Society for Research in Child Development, 35,* No. 137.

Bowlby, J. (1969). *Attachment and loss: (Attachment)* (Vol. 1). New York: Basic Books.

Bowlby, J. (1973). *Attachment and loss: (Separation: Anxiety and anger)* (Vol. 2). New York: Basic Books.

Bowlby, J. (1980). *Attachment and loss: (Loss, sadness, and depression)* (Vol. 3). New York: Basic Books.

Brackbill, Y. (1976). Long-term effects of obstetrical anesthesia on infant autonomic function. *Developmental Psychobiology, 9,* 353–358.

Brackbill, Y. (1979). Obstetrical medication and infant behavior. In J. D. Osofsky (Ed.), *Handbook of infant development.* New York: John Wiley & Sons.

Bracken, M. R., & Holford, T. R. (1981). Exposure to prescribed drugs in pregnancy and association with congenital malformations. *Obstetrics and Gynecology, 58,* 336–344.

Braine, L. G., & Eder, R. A. (1983). Left-right memory in 2 year-old children: A new look at search tasks. *Developmental Psychology, 19,* 45–55.

Brainerd, C. J. (1977). *The origins of the number concept.* New York: Praeger Publishers.

Brainerd, C. J. (1978). *Piaget's theory of intelligence.* Englewood Cliffs, NJ: Prentice-Hall.

Breland, K., & Breland, M. (1961). The misbehavior of organisms. *American Psychologist, 16,* 681–684.

Bringuier, J. (1980). *Conversations with Jean Piaget.* Chicago: University of Chicago Press.

Broadbent, D. E. (1958). *Perception and communication.* Oxford: Pergamon Press.

Broadbent, D. E. (1977). The hidden preattentive processes. *American Psychologist, 32,* 109–119.

Brody, L. R. (1981). Visual short-term cued recall memory in infancy. *Child Development, 52,* 242–250.

Brodzinsky, D. M. (1982). Relationship between cognitive style and cognitive development: A 2 year longitudinal study. *Developmental Psychology, 18,* 503–508.

Brodzinsky, D. M., Messer, S. B., & Tew, J. D. (1979). Sex differences in children's expression and control of fantasy and overt aggression. *Child Development, 50,* 372–379.

Broman, S. H., Nichols, P. L., & Kennedy, W. A. (1975). *Preschool IQ: Parental and early developmental correlates.* Hillsdale, NJ: Lawrence Erlbaum.

Bronckart, J., & Ventouras-Spycher, M. (1979). The Piagetian concept of representation and the Soviet-inspired view of self-regulation. In G. Zivin (Ed.), *The development of self-regulation through private speech.* New York: John Wiley & Sons.

Bronfenbrenner, U. (1977). Ecological factors in human development in retrospect and prospect. In H. McGurk (Ed.), *Ecological factors in human development.* Amsterdam: North-Holland Scientific Publishers, Elsevier.

Bronfenbrenner, U. (1980). Ecology of childhood. *School Psychology Review, 9,* 294–297.

Bronson, W. C. (1981). Toddlers' Behaviors with Agemates: *Issues of interaction, cognition, and affect.* Norwood, NJ: Ablex.

Brookover, W., Beady, C., Flood, P., Schweitzer, J., & Wisenbaker, J. (1979). *School social systems and student achievement: Schools can make a difference.* New York: Praeger Publishers.

Brooks, P. H. (1978). Some speculations concerning deafness and learning to read. In L. S. Liben (Ed.), *Deaf children: Developmental perspectives.* New York: Academic Press.

Brophy, J. E. (1983). Research on the self-fulfilling prophecy and teacher expectations. *Journal of Educational Psychology, 75,* 631–661.

Brown, A. L. (1978). Knowing when, where, and how to remember: A problem of metacognition. In R. Glaser (Ed.), *Advances in instructional psychology* (Vol. 1). Hillsdale, NJ: Lawrence Erlbaum.

Brown, A. L., Bransford, J. D., Ferrara, R. A., & Campione, J. C. (1983). Learning, remembering, and understanding. In J. H. Flavell & E. M. Markman (Eds.), *The handbook of child psychology* (Vol. 3). New York: John Wiley & Sons.

Brown, A. L., & Campione, J. C. (1982). Modifying intelligence or modifying cognitive skills? More than a semantic quibble. In D. K. Detterman & R. J. Sternberg (Eds.), *How and how much can intelligence be increased?* Norwood, NJ: Ablex.

Brown, A. L., & DeLoache, J. S. (1978). Skills, plans, and self-regulation. In R. S. Siegler (Ed.), *Children's thinking: What develops?* Hillsdale, NJ: Lawrence Erlbaum.

Brown, A. L., & Palincsar, A. S. (1982). Inducing strategic learning from texts by means of informed, self-control training. *Topics in Learning and Learning Disabilities, 2,* 1–17.

Brown, B., & Rosenbaum, L, (1983, February). Stress and IQ. Paper presented at the American Association for the Advancement of Science, Detroit, MI.

Brown, F. (1979). The SOMPA: A system of measuring potential abilities. *School Psychology Digest, 8,* 37–46.

Brown, R. E. (1982). Breast-feeding and family planning: A review of the relationships between breast-feeding and family planning. *American Journal of Clinical Nutrition, 35,* 162–171.

Brown, R. W. (1973). *A first language: The early stages.* Cambridge, MA: Harvard Univ. Press.

Brown, R. W. (1980). The maintenance of conversation. In D. R. Olson (Ed.), *The social foundations of language and thought.* New York: W. W. Norton.

Brown, R. W., & Hanlon, C. (1970). Derivational complexity and order of acquisition in child speech. In J. R. Hayes (Ed.), *Cognition and the development of language.* New York: John Wiley & Sons.

Brown, R., & Kulik, J. (1982). Flashbulb memories. In U. Neisser (Ed.), *Memory Observed.* San Francisco: W. H. Freeman.

Brownell, K. D., & Stunkard, A. J. (1980). Physical activity in the development and control of obesity. In A. J. Stunkard (Ed.), *Obesity.* Philadelphia: W. B. Saunders.

Bruner, J. S. (1972). The nature and uses of immaturity. *American Psychologist, 27,* 687–701.

Bruner, J. S. (1974). Child's play. *New Scientist, 62,* 126–128.

Bruner, J. S. (1975). From communication to language—A psychological perspective. *Cognition, 3,* 255–287.

Bruner, J. S. (1976). *Play: Its role in development and evolution.* New York: Basic Books.

Bruner, J. S. (1976, December 17). Psychology and the image of man: Herbert Spencer lecture. *Times Literary Supplement.*

Bruner, J. S., Jolly, A., & Sylva, K. (1976). *Play—its role in development and evolution.* New York: Basic Books.

Bryant, P. E., & Trabasso, T. (1971). Transitive inferences and memory in young children. *Nature, 232,* 456–458.

Bullen, B. A., Reed, R. R., & Mayer, J. (1964). Physical activity of obese and nonobese adolescent girls appraised by motion picture sampling. *American Journal of Clinical Nutrition, 14,* 211–223.

Bullock, D., & Merrill, L. (1980). The impact of personal preference on consistency through time: The case of childhood aggression. *Child Development, 51,* 808–814.

Burnett, C. A., Jones, J. A., Rooks, J., Chen, C. H., Tyler, C. W., & Miller, C. A. (1980). Home delivery and neonatal mortality in North Carolina. *Journal of the American Medical Association, 244,* 2741–2745.

Bush, E. S., & Dweck, C. S. (1975). Reflections on conceptual tempo: Relationship between cognitive style and performance as a function of task characteristics. *Developmental Psychology, 11,* 567–574.

Butkowsky, I. S., & Willows, D. M. Cognitive-motivational characteristics of children varying in reading ability: Evidence for learned helplessness in poor readers. *Journal of Educational Psychology, 72,* 408–422.

Butler, N. R., & Goldstein, H. (1973). Smoking during pregnancy and the child's subsequent child development. *British Medical Journal, 4,* 573–575.

Byrne, J. M., & Horowitz, F. D. (1981). Rocking as a soothing intervention: The influence of direction and type of movement. *Infant Behavior and Development, 4,* 207–218.

Cabalsha, B., Duczynska, N., Borzymowska, J., Zorska, K., Koslaca-Folsa, A., & Bozkowa, K. (1977). Termination of dietary treatment in phenylketonuria. *European Journal of Pediatrics, 126,* 253–262.

Cairns, E., & Cammock, T. (1981). Development of a more reliable version of the Matching Familiar Figures Test. *Developmental Psychology, 11,* 555–560.

Cairns, R. B. (1979). *Social development.* San Francisco: W. H. Freeman.

Camara, K. A., Baker, O., & Dayton, C. (1980). Impact of separation and divorce on youths and families. In P. M. Insel (Ed.), *Environmental variables and the prevention of mental illness.* Lexington, MA: Lexington Books.

Cameron, J., Livson, N., & Bayley, N. (1967). Infant vocalizations and their relationship to mature intelligence. *Science, 157,* 331–333.

Campbell, S. (1979). Diagnosis of fetal abnormalities by ultrasound. In A. Milunsky (Ed.), *Genetic disorders and the fetus: Diagnosis, prevention, and treatment.* New York: Plenum Publishing.

Campione, J. C., & Brown, A. L. (1978). Toward a theory of intelligence: Contributions from research with retarded children. *Intelligence, 2,* 279–304.

Campos, J. J. (1976). Heart rate: A sensitive tool for the study of emotional development in the infant. In L. P. Lipsitt (Ed.), *Developmental psychobiology: The significance of infancy.* Hillsdale, NJ: Lawrence Erlbaum.

Cann, M. A. (1953). *An investigation of a component of parental behavior in humans.* Unpublished masters thesis, University of Chicago. As cited by E. H. Hess. (1970). Ethology and developmental psychology. In P. H. Mussen (Ed.), *Carmichael's Manual of Child Psychology.* New York: John Wiley & Sons.

Caplan, P. J., & Kinsbourne, M. (1976). Baby drops the rattle: Asymmetry of duration of grasp by infants. *Child Development, 47,* 532–534.

Caputo, D. V., Goldstein, K. M., & Taub, H. B. (1981). Neonatal compromise and later psychological development: A 10-year longitudinal study. In S. L. Friedman & M. Sigman (Eds.), *Preterm birth and psychological development.* New York: Academic Press.

Card, J. J., & Wise, L. L. (1978). Teenage mothers and teenage fathers: The impact of early childbearing on the parents' personal and professional lives. *Family Planning Perspectives, 10,* 199–205.

Carey, G., Goldsmith, H. H., Tellegren, A., & Gottesman, I. I. (1978). Genetics and personality inventories: The limits of replication with twin data. *Behavior Genetics, 8,* 299–313.

Carey, W. B., & McDevitt, S. C. (1978). Stability and change in individual temperament diagnoses from infancy to early childhood. *American Academy of Child Psychiatry, 17,* 331–337.

Carlson, D. B., & LaBarba, R. C. (1979). Maternal emotionality during pregnancy and reproductive outcome: A review of the literature. *International Journal of Behavioral Development, 2,* 343–376.

Carlson, J. S., & Jensen, C. M. (1982). Reaction time, movement time, and intelligence: A replication and extension. *Intelligence, 6,* 265–274.

Carlson, J. S., Jensen, C. M., & Widaman, K. (1983). Reaction time, intelligence, and attention. *Intelligence, 7,* 329–344.

Carlson, N. R. (1980). *Physiology of behavior.* (2d ed.). Boston: Allyn & Bacon.

Carpenter, G. (1974). Mother's face and the newborn. *New Scientist, 21,* 742–744.

Carr, T. C., & Evans, M. A. (1981, April). *Influence of learning conditions on patterns of cognitive skills in young children.* Paper presented at the Society for Research in Child Development, Boston, MA.

Case, R. (1978). Intellectual development from birth to adulthood: A neo-Piagetian interpretation. In R. S. Siegler (Ed.), *Children's thinking: What develops?* Hillsdale, NJ: Lawrence Erlbaum.

Case, R. (1980) The underlying mechanism of intellectual development. In J. R. Kirby and J. B. Biggs (Eds.), *Cognition, development, and instruction.* New York: Academic Press.

Case, R. (1981). Intellectual development: A systematic reinterpretation. In F. H. Farley & N. J. Gordon (Eds.), *Psychology and education: The state of the union.* Berkeley, CA: McCutchan Publishing.

Case, R., Kurland, D. M., & Goldberg, J. (1982). Operational efficiency and the growth of short-term memory span. *Journal of Experimental Child Psychology, 33,* 386–404.

Caspersson, T., Zech, L., & Johansson, C. (1970). Differential banding of alkylating fluorochromes in human chromosomes. *Experimental Cell Research, 60,* 315–319.

Cattell, R. B. (1982). *The inheritance of personality and ability: Research methods and findings.* New York: Academic Press.

Cavanaugh, J. C., & Borkowski, J. G. (1980). Searching for metamemory-memory connections: A developmental study. *Developmental Psychology, 16,* 441–453.

Cavanaugh, J. C., & Perlmutter, M. (1982). Metamemory: A critical examination. *Child Development, 53,* 11–28.

Cerami, A., & Washington, E. (1974). *Sickle cell anemia.* New York: The Third Press.

Chai, C. K. (1976). *Genetic evolution.* Chicago: University of Chicago Press.

Chalke, F. C. R., & Ertl, J. (1965). Evoked potentials and intelligence. *Life Sciences, 4,* 1319–1322.

Chance, M. R. A., & Jolly, C. (1970). *Social groups of monkeys, apes, and men.* New York: E. P. Dutton.

Chaney, M. S., Ross, M. L., & Witschi, J. C. (1979). *Nutrition*. Boston: Houghton Mifflin.

Chapman, M. (1983). Children's prosocial dispositions and behavior. In E. M. Hetherington (Ed.), *Handbook of Child Psychology* (Vol. 4). New York: John Wiley & Sons.

Chapman, M. (1977). Father absence, stepfathers, and the cognitive performance of college students. *Child Development, 48,* 1155–1158.

Chapman, R. S. (1981). Mother-Infant interaction in the second year of life. In R. L. Schiefelbusch & D. D. Bricker (Eds.), *Early language: Acquisition and intervention*. Baltimore: University Park Press.

Chechile, R. A., & Richman, C. L. (1982). The interaction of semantic memory with storage and retrieval processes. *Developmental Review, 2,* 237–250.

Cheek, D. B. (1979). *Fetal and postnatal cellular growth: Hormones and nutrition.* New York: John Wiley & Sons.

Chertok, L. (1972). Psychosomatic aspects of childbirth. In N. Morris (Ed.), *Psychosomatic medicine in obstetrics and gynecology.* New York: Karger.

Cheyne, J. A. (1982). Object play and problem-solving: Methodological problems and conceptual promise. In D. J. Pepler & K. H. Rubin (Eds.), *The play of children: Current theory and research.* London: Karger.

Chi, M. T. H. (1978). Knowledge structures and knowledge development. In R. S. Siegler (Ed.), *Children's thinking: What develops?* Hillsdale, NJ: Lawrence Erlbaum.

Chi, M. T. H., & Koeske, R. D. (1983). Network representation of a child's dinosaur knowledge. *Developmental Psychology, 19,* 29–40.

Chomsky, N. (1975). *Reflections on language.* New York: Pantheon Books.

Chomsky, N. (1978). On the biological basis of language capacities. In G. A. Miller & E. Lenneberg (Eds.), *Psychology and biology of language and thought.* New York: Academic Press.

Christie, J. F., & Johnsen, E. P. (1983). The role of play in social-intellectual development. *Review of Educational Research, 53,* 93–115.

Clark, E. (1977). Strategies and the mapping problem in first language acquisition. In J. MacNamara (Ed.), *Language learning and thought.* New York: Academic Press.

Clark, E. V. (1973). What's in a word? On the child's acquisition of semantics in his first language. In T. E. Moore (Ed.), *Cognitive development and the acquisition of language.* New York: Academic Press.

Clarke, A. (1980). Unbiased tests and biased people. *Behavioral and Brain Sciences, 3,* 337–338.

Clarke, A. M., & Clarke, A. D. B. (1976). *Early experience: Myth and evidence.* New York: Free Press.

Clarke, L. (1973). *Can't read, can't write, can't talk too good either.* New York: Walker & Co.

Clarke-Stewart, A., & Hevey, C. M. (1981). Longitudinal relations in repeated observations of mother-child interaction from 1 to 2½ years. *Developmental Psychology, 17,* 127–145.

Clarke-Stewart, K. A. (1973). Interactions between mothers and their young children:

Characteristics and consequences. *Monographs of the Society for Research in Child Development*, 38, No. 153.

Clarke-Stewart, K. A. (1978). And daddy makes three: The father's impact on mother and young child. *Child Development*, 49, 466–478.

Clarren, S. K., Alvord, E. C., Sumi, S. M., Streissguth, A. P., & Smith, D. W. (1978). Brain malformations related to prenatal exposure to ethanol. *Journal of Pediatrics*, 92, 64–67.

Clarren, S. K., & Smith, D. W. (1978). The fetal alcohol syndrome. *New England Journal of Medicine*, 298, 1063–1067.

Cleary, T. A., Humphreys, L. G., Kendrick, S. A., & Wesman, Q. (1975). Educational uses of tests with disadvantaged students. *American Psychologist*, 30, 115–124.

Clewell, W. H., Johnson, M. L., Meier, P. R., Newkirk, J. B., Zide, S. L., Hendee, R. W., Bowes, W. A., Hecht, F., O'Keefe, D., Henry, G. P., & Shikes, R. H. (1982). A surgical approach to the treatment of fetal hydrocephalus. *The New England Journal of Medicine*, 306, 1320–1325.

Clingempeel, W. G., & Reppucci, N. D. (1982). Joint custody after divorce: Major issues and goals for research. *Psychological Bulletin*, 91, 102–127.

Coates, S. (1974). Sex differences in field independence among preschool children. In R. C. Friedman, R. M. Richart, & R. L. Vandewiele (Eds.), *Sex differences in behavior*. New York: John Wiley & Sons.

Coates, S. W. (1972). *Preschool Embedded Figures Test Manual*. Palo Alto, CA: Consulting Psychologists Press.

Coates, T. J., & Thoresen, C. E. (1980). Obesity among children and adolescents. In A. E. Kazdin & B. Lahey (Eds.), *Advances in clinical child psychology*. New York: Plenum Publishing.

Cohen, E. L., & Wurtman, R. J. (1979). Nutrition and brain neurotransmitters. In M. Winick (Ed.), *Nutrition: Pre- and postnatal development*. New York: Publishing.

Cohen, L. B. (1979). Our developing knowledge of infant perception and cognition. *American Psychologist*, 34, 894–899.

Cohen, L. B., & Strauss, M. S. (1979). Concept acquisition in the human infant. *Child Development*, 50, 419–424.

Cohen, L. B., DeLoache, J. S., & Strauss, M. S. (1979). Infant visual perception. In J. D. Osofsky (Ed.), *Handbook of infant development*. New York: John Wiley & Sons.

Cohen, S. (1980). After effects of stress on human performance and social behavior: A review of research and theory. *Psychological Bulletin*, 88, 82–108.

Cohen, S. N., & Chang, A. C. Y. (1970). Recircularization and autonomous replication of a sheared R factor DNA segment in Escherichia-Coli transformants. *Proceedings of the National Academy of Science*, 70, 1293–1295.

Cohn, A. H., & Collignon, F. C. (1979). Evaluation of child abuse and neglect demonstration projects, 1974–1977 (Vols. I and II). NCHSR Research Report Series, DHEW Publication No. (PHS) 79-3217-1.

Colby, A., Kohlberg, L., Gibbs, J., & Lieberman, M. (1983). A longitudinal study of moral judgment. *Monographs of the Society for Research in Child Development*, 48, No. 200.

Cole, P. M., & Newcombe, N. (1983). Interference effects of verbal and imaginal strategies for resisting distraction on children's verbal and visual recognition memory. *Child Development, 54,* 42–50.

Coleman, J. S., Campbell, E. Q., Hobson, C. J., McPartland, J., Mood, A. M., Weinfeld, F. D., & York, R. L. (1966). *Equality of educational opportunity.* Washington, DC: U.S. Government Printing Office.

Coleman, W. T., & Selby, C. C. (1983). *Educating Americans for the 21st Century.* Washington, DC: National Science Foundation.

Coles, R. (1970). *Erik H. Erikson: The growth of his work.* Boston: Little, Brown.

College Entrance Examination Board. (1977). *On further examination: Report of the advisory panel on the scholastic aptitude test score decline.* Princeton: College Entrance Examination Board.

Colley, J. R. T., Holland, W. W., & Corkhill, R. T. (1974). Influence of passive smoking and parental phlegm on pneumonia and bronchitis in early childhood. *Lancet, 2,* 1031–1034.

Collins, J. T., & Hagen, J. W. (1979). A constructivist account of the development of perception, attention, and memory. In G. A. Hale & M. Lewis (Eds.), *Attention and cognitive development.* New York: Plenum Publishing.

Collins, R. C. (1983). Head Start: An update on program effects. *Society for Research in Child Development Newsletter.*

Collins, W. A., Wellman, H. M., Keniston, A., & Westby, S. D. (1978). Age-related aspects of comprehension and inference from a televised dramatic narrative. *Child Development, 49,* 389–399.

Collip, P. J. (1980). Obesity in childhood. In A. J. Stunkard (Ed.), *Obesity.* Philadelphia: W. B. Saunders.

Colombo, J. (1982). The critical period concept: Research, methodology and psychological issues. *Psychological Bulletin, 91,* 260–275.

Condon, W. S., & Sander, L. W. (1974). Neonate movement is synchronized with adult speech. *Science, 183,* 99–101.

Conel, J. L. (1939-1967). *The postnatal development of the human cortex* (Vols. 1–8). Cambridge, MA: Harvard Univ. Press.

Congenital anomalies and birth injuries among live births. (1976). United States, 1973–1974. U.S. Department of Health, Education, and Welfare. National Center for Health Statistics.

Connally, J. (1980). *The relationship between social pretend play and social competence in preschoolers: Correlational and experimental studies.* Unpublished doctoral dissertation, Concordia University, Montreal, Canada.

Connell, D. (1976). Individual differences in attachment related to habituation to a redundant stimulus (Doctoral dissertation, Syracuse University.) Cited by M. D. S. Ainsworth, M. C. Blehar, E. Waters, & S. Wall. (1978). *Patterns of attachment.* Hillsdale, NJ: Lawrence Erlbaum.

Connolly, B., & Russell, F. (1976). Interdisciplinary early intervention program. *Physical Therapy, 56,* 155–158.

Connolly, K. J. (1981). Maturation and the ontogeny of motor skills. In K. J. Connolly & H. F. R. Prechtl (Eds.), *Maturation and development: Biological and psychological perspectives.* Philadelphia: J. B. Lippincott.

Cook, T. D., Appleton, H., Conner, R. F., Shaffer, A., Tabkin, G., & Weber, J. S. (1975). *Sesame Street revisited*. New York: Russell Sage Foundation.

Cooper, H., & Good, T. (1983). *Pygmalion grows up: Studies in the expectation communication process*. New York: Longman.

Cooperman, P. (1978). *The literacy hoax*. New York: William Morrow.

Coopersmith, S. (1967). *The antecedents of self-esteem*. San Francisco: W. H. Freeman.

Cordes, C. (1983). Child advocates push for policy on infant leave. *APA Monitor, 8,* 19–21.

Corsale, K., & Ornstein, P. A. (1980). Developmental changes in children's use of semantic information in recall. *Journal of Experimental Child Psychology, 30,* 213–245.

Cottet-Emard, J. M., Peyrin, L., & Bonnod, J. (1980). Dietary induced changes in catecholamine metabolites in rat urine. *Journal of Neural Transmission, 48,* 189–201.

Courchesne, E. (1977). Event related brain potentials: A comparison between children and adults. *Science, 197,* 589–592.

Courchesne, E., Ganz, L., & Norcia, A. M. (1981). Event-related brain potentials to human faces in infants. *Child Development, 52,* 804–811.

Cowan, W. M. (1979). The development of the brain. *Scientific American, 241,* 112–133.

Cowan, C. P., Cowan, P. A., Coie, L. & Coie, J. B. (1978). Becoming a family: The impact of a first child's birth on the couple's relationship. In W. B. Miller (Ed.), *The first child and family formation*. Chapel Hill, NC: Carolina Population Center.

Cox, M. V. (1980). Visual perspective taking in children. In M. V. Cox (Ed.), *Are young children egocentric?* London: Billings & Son.

Crain, W. C. (1980). *Theories of development: Concepts and applications*. Englewood Cliffs, NJ: Prentice-Hall.

Cramer, P. (1981). Imagery and learning: Item recognition and associative recall. *Journal of Educational Psychology, 73,* 164–173.

Creasy, M. R., & Crolla, J. A. (1974). Prenatal mortality of trisomy 21 (Down's syndrome). *Lancet, 1,* 473–474.

Crockenberg, S. B. (1979). The effects of cooperative learning environments and interdependent goals on conformity in school-age children. *Merrill Palmer Quarterly, 25,* 121–132.

Crockenberg, S. B. (1981). Infant irritability, mother responsiveness, and social support influences on the security of infant-mother attachment. *Child Development, 52,* 857–865.

Cromer, R. F. (1981). Reconceptualizing language acquisition and cognitive development. In R. L. Schiefelbusch and D. D. Bricker (Eds.), *Early language: Acquisition and intervention*. Baltimore: University Park Press.

Cronbach, L. J. (1975). Five decades of public controversy over mental testing. *American Psychologist, 30,* 1–14.

Crook, W. G. (1980). Can what a child eats make him dull, stupid, or hyperactive? *Journal of Learning Disabilities, 13,* 53–57.

Crowe, R. R. (1974). An adoption study of antisocial personality. *Archives of General Psychiatry, 31,* 785–791.

Crystle, C. D., Kegel, E. E., France, L. W., Brady, G. M., & Olds, R. E. (1980). The Leboyer method of delivery: An assessment of risk. *Journal of Reproductive Medicine, 25,* 267–271.

Cummins, J. (1980). The construct of language proficiency in bilingual education. Paper presented at the Georgetown Round Table of Languages and Linguistics, Washington, DC.

Cunningham, S. (1984, February). Gifted battle myth to gain support for programs. *APA Monitor, 15,* 20–22.

Curtiss, S. (1977). *Genie: A psycholinguistic study of a modern-day "wild child."* New York: Academic Press.

Curtiss, S. (1982). *Genie: Language and cognition.* Unpublished paper, University of California, Los Angeles.

Czeisler, C. A., Moore-Ede, M. C., & Coleman, R. M. (1982). Rotating shift work schedules that disrupt sleep are improved by applying circadian principles. *Science, 217,* 460–462.

Damon, W. (1977). *The social world of the child.* San Francisco: Jossey-Bass.

Dansky, J. L. (1980). Cognitive consequences of sociodramatic play and exploration training for economically disadvantaged preschoolers. *Journal of Child Psychology and Psychiatry, 20,* 47–58.

Darley, J. M., & Fazio, R. H. (1980). Expectancy confirmation processes arising in the social interaction sequence. *American Psychologist, 35,* 867–881.

Darwin, C. (1877). A biographical sketch of an infant. *Mind, II,* 286–294. As reprinted in W. Kessen (1965). *The Child.* New York: John Wiley & Sons.

David, O. J., Grad, G., McGann, B., & Koltun, A. (1982). Mental retardation and "nontoxic" lead levels. *American Journal of Psychiatry, 139,* 806–809.

Davidson, E. H. (1976). *Gene activity in early development,* (2nd edition). New York: Academic Press.

Davies, D., Sperber, R. D., & McCauley, C. (1981). Intelligence-related differences in semantic processing speed. *Journal of Experimental Child Psychology, 31,* 387–402.

Davis, B. D. (1983). The two faces of genetic engineering in man. *Science, 219,* 1381.

de Castro, F., Rolfe, U. T., & Heppe, M. (1978). Child abuse: An operational longitudinal study. *Child Abuse and Neglect: The International Journal, 2,* 51–55.

Deaux, K. (1984). From individual differences to social categories. *American Psychologist, 39,* 105–116.

Deaux, K., & Ullman, J. C. (1983). *Women of steel.* New York: Praeger Publishers.

DeCasper, A. J., & Fifer, W. P. (1980). Of human bonding: Newborns prefer their mothers' voices. *Science, 208,* 1174–1176.

DeLoache, J. S. (1980). Naturalistic studies of memory for object location in very young children. In M. Perlmutter (Ed.), *Children's memory.* San Francisco: Jossey-Bass.

DeMause, L. (1980). Our forebears made childhood a nightmare. In G. J. Williams and J. Money (Eds.), *Traumatic abuse and neglect of children at home*. Baltimore: The Johns Hopkins Press.

Dempster, F. N. (1981). Memory Span: Source of individual and developmental differences. *Psychological Bulletin, 89*, 63–100.

Dennis, M., Sugar, J., & Whitaker, H. A. (1982). The acquisition of tag questions. *Child Development, 53*, 1254–1257.

Dennis, W. (1965). *The Hopi child*. New York: John Wiley & Sons.

Dennis, W. (1973). *Children of the creche*. New York: Appleton-Century-Crofts.

Deutsch, M. (1960). Minority group and class status as related to social and personality factors in scholastic achievement. *Monographs of Sociology and Applied Anthropology, 2*, 1–32.

Deutsch, M., & Brown, R. (1964). Social influences in Negro-white intelligence differences. *Journal of Social Issues, 20*, 24–35.

deVilliers, J. G., & deVilliers, P. A. (1973). A cross-sectional study of the acquisition of grammatical morphemes. *Journal of Psycholinguistic Research, 2*, 267–278.

deVilliers, J. G., & deVilliers, P. A. (1982). Language development. In R. Vasta (Ed.), *Strategies and techniques of child study*. New York: Academic Press.

deVilliers, P. A., & deVilliers, J. G. (1979). *Early Language*. Cambridge, MA: Harvard Univ. Press.

DeVries, R. (1980). The alternative birth center: Option or cooptation? Women and Health, 5, 47–60.

Dew, K. M. H., Galassi, J. P., & Galassi, M. D. (1983). Mathematics anxiety: Some basic issues. *Journal of Counseling Psychology, 30*, 443–446.

Diamond, E. L., Schmerler, H., & Lilienfeld, A. M. (1973). The relationship of intra-uterine radiation to subsequent mortality and development of leukemia in children. *American Journal of Epidemiology, 97*, 283–313.

Dick-Read, G. (1944). *Childbirth without fear*. London: Heinemann Educational Books.

Dickerson, J. W. T. (1981). Nutrition, brain growth and development. In H. F. R. Prechtl & K. J. Connolly (Eds.), *Maturation and development: Biological and psychological perspectives*. Philadelphia: J. B. Lippincott.

Diener, C. I., & Dweck, C. S. (1978). An analysis of learned helplessness: Continuous changes in performance, strategy, and achievement cognitions following failure. *Journal of Personality and Social Psychology, 36*, 451–462.

Diener, C. I., & Dweck, C. S. (1980). An analysis of learned helplessness: II. The processing of success. *Journal of Personality and Social Psychology, 39*, 940–952.

DiPietro, J. A. (1981). Rough and tumble play: A function of gender. *Developmental Psychology, 17*, 50–58.

Dirks, J. (1982). The effect of a commercial game on children's block design scores on the WISC-R IQ test. *Intelligence, 6*, 109–124.

Dix, T., & Grusec, J. E. Parental influence techniques: An attributional analysis. *Child Developmment, 54*, 645–652.

Dlugokinski, E., & Firestone, I. J. (1974). Other centeredness and susceptibility to charitable appeals: Effects of perceived discipline. *Developmental Psychology, 10*, 21–28.

Dobbing, J. (1976). Vulnerable periods in brain growth and somatic growth. In D. F. Roberts (Ed.), *The biology of the human fetus.* London: Taylor & Francis.

Dobbing, J., & Sands, J. (1973). Quantitative growth and development of human brain. Archives of Diseases in Childhood, 48, 757–767.

Dobbing, J., & Sands, J. (1979). Comparative aspects of the brain growth spurt. *Early Human Development, 3,* 79–83.

Dobzhansky, T. (1963). Anthropology and the natural sciences—the problem of human evolution. *Current Anthropology, 138,* 146–148.

Dodd, D. H., & White, R. M. (1980). *Cognition: Mental structures and processes.* Boston: Allyn & Bacon.

Dodge, K. A. (1982). Social information processing variables in the development of aggression and altruism in children. In C. Zahn-Waxler, M. Cummings, & M. Radke-Yarrow (Eds.), *The development of altruism and aggression: Social and sociobiological origins.* New York: Cambridge University Press.

Dodge, K. A., & Frame, C. L. (1982). Social cognitive biases and deficits in aggressive boys. *Child Development, 53,* 620–635.

Dodge, K. A., Coie, J. D., & Brakke, N. P. (1982). Behavior patterns of socially rejected and neglected preadolescents: The roles of social approach and aggression. *Journal of Abnormal Child Psychology, 10,* 389–409.

Doherty, W. J. (1983). Impact of divorce on locus of control orientation in adult women: A longitudinal study. *Journal of Personality and Social Psychology, 44,* 834–840.

Dollard, J., & Miller, N. E. (1950). *Personality and psychotherapy.* New York: McGraw-Hill.

Dollard, J., Dobb, L. W., Miller, N. E., Mowrer, O. H., & Sears, R. R. (1939). *Frustration and aggression.* New Haven, CT: Yale University Press.

Donovan, W. A., Leavitt, L. A., & Balling, J. D. (1978). Maternal physiological responses to infant signals. *Psychophysiology, 15,* 68–74.

Donders, F. C. (1969). On the speed of mental processes. *Acta Psycholgical, 30,* 412–431. (A reprinting and translation of the original article which appeared in 1868.)

Dorfman, D. D. (1980). What did Yale, Harvard, Rolls-Royce, and a black have in common in 1917? *The Behavioral and Brain Sciences, 3,* 339–340.

Douglas, V. I., & Peters, K. G. (1979). Clearer definition of attentional deficit. In G. A. Hale & M. Lewis (Eds.), *Attention and cognitive development.* New York: Plenum Publishing.

Drake, S. G. (1834). *Biography and history of the indians of North America.* Boston: O. L. Perkins & Hilliard, Gray & Co.

Dreher, J. J. (1966). Cetacean communication: Small group experiment. In K. S. Norris (Ed.), *Whales, Dolphins, and porpoises.* Berkeley, CA: University of California Press.

Dryden, R. (1978). *Before birth.* London: Heinemann Educational Books.

Dubowitz, L., & Dubowitz, V. (1981). *The neurological assessment of the preterm and full-term newborn infant.* Philadelphia: J. B. Lippincott.

Dunn, H. G., McBurney, A. K., Ingram, S., & Hunter, C. M. (1977). Maternal cigarette smoking during pregnancy and the child's subsequent development: II.

Neurological and intellectual maturation to the age of 6 years. *Canadian Journal of Public Health, 68,* 43–50.

Dunn, J. (1977). *Distress and comfort.* Cambridge, MA: Harvard Univ. Press.

Duryea, E. J., & Glover, J. A. (1982). A review of the research on reflection and impulsivity in children. *Genetic Psychology Monographs, 106,* 217–237.

Dweck, C. S. (1975). The role of expectations and attributions in the alleviation of learned helplessness. *Journal of Personality and Social Psychology, 31,* 674–685.

Dweck, C. S. (1981). Social-cognitive processes in children's friendships. In S. R. Asher & J. M. Gottman (Eds.), *The development of children's friendships.* London: Cambridge University Press.

Dweck, C. S., & Elliott, E. S. (1983). Achievement motivation. In E. M. Hetherington (Ed.), *Handbook of Child Psychology* (Vol. 4). New York: John Wiley & Sons.

Dweck, C. S., & Reppucci, N. D. (1973). Learned helplessness and reinforcement responsibility in children. *Journal of Personality and Social Psychology, 25,* 109–116.

Eaves, L. J., Last, K. A., Young, P. A., & Marten, N. Y. (1978). Model fitting approaches to the analysis of human behavior. *Heredity, 41,* 249–320.

Eckert, E. D., Heston, L. L., & Bouchard, T. J. (1981). MZ twins reared apart: Preliminary findings of psychiatric disturbances and traits. *Twin Research 3: Intelligence, personality, and development.* New York: Alan R. Liss.

Eckland, B. K. (1980). Competent teachers and competent students. *The Behavioral and Brain Sciences, 3,* 341–342.

Eckland, B. K. (1982). College entrance examination trends. In G. R. Austin & H. Garber. *The rise and fall of national test scores.* New York: Academic Press.

Economos, J. (1980). Bias cuts deeper than scores. *The Behavioral and Brain Sciences, 2,* 342–343.

Editorial. (1964). The drugged sperm. *British Medical Journal, 1,* 1063.

Eeg, O. O. (1980). Longitudinal developmental course of electrical activity. *Brain Development, 2,* 33–44.

Egeland, B., & Brunnquell, D. (1979). An at-risk approach to the study of child abuse: Some preliminary findings. *Journal of the American Academy of Child Psychiatry, 18,* 219–235.

Egeland, B., & Sroufe, L. A. (1981). Attachment and early maltreatment. *Child Development, 52,* 44–52.

Ehrhardt, A. A., & Meyer-Bahlburg, H. F. L. (1981). Effects of prenatal sex hormones on gender-related behavior. *Science, 211,* 1312–1318.

Ehrman, L., & Parsons, P. A. (1981). *Behavior genetics and evolution.* New York: McGraw-Hill.

Eibl-Eibesfeldt, I. (1979). Human ethology: concepts and implications for the sciences of man. *The Behavioral and Brain Sciences, 2,* 1–57.

Eibl-Eibesfeldt, I. (1982). The flexibility and affective autonomy of play. *The Brain and Behavioral Sciences, 5,* 160–162.

Eichorn, D., & Bayley, N. (1962). Growth in head circumference from birth through early adulthood. *Child Development, 33,* 257–271.

Einstein, E. (1982). *The stepfamily: Living, loving and learning.* New York: Macmillan.

Eisenberg-Berg, N. (1979). Development of children's prosocial moral judgment. *Developmental Psychology, 15*, 128–137.

Eisenberg-Berg, N., & Neal, C. (1979). Children's moral reasoning about their own spontaneous prosocial behavior. *Developmental Psychology, 37*, 1097–1126.

Elias, M. (1981, April 26). Retarded children learn to read. *Los Angeles Times*, Section 6, p. 1.

Emde, R. N. (1980). Emotional availability: A reciprocal reward system for infants and parents with implications for prevention of psychosocial disorders. In P. M. Taylor (Ed.), *Parent-infant relationships*. New York: Grune & Stratton.

Emery, A. E. (1979). *Elements of medical genetics* (5th ed.). Edinburgh: Churchill Livingstone.

Emery, R. E. (1982). Interparental conflict and the children of discord and divorce. *Psychological Bulletin, 92*, 310–330.

Emler, N., Renwick, S., & Malone, B. (1983). The relationship between moral reasoning and political orientation. *Journal of Personality and Social Psychology, 45*, 1073–1080.

Emmerich, W. (1977). Structure and development of person-social behaviors in economically disadvantaged preschool children. *Genetic Psychology, 95*, 191–245.

Ennis, R. H. (1978). Conceptualization of children's logical competence: Piagets, propositional logic and an alternative proposal. In L. S. Siegel & C. J. Brainerd (Eds.), *Alternatives to Piaget: Critical essays on the theory*. New York: Academic Press.

Entwisle, D. R., & Baker, D. P. (1983). Gender and young children's expectations for performance in arithmetic. *Developmental Psychology, 19*, 200–209.

Epstein, A. S. (1980). *Assessing the child development information needed by adolescent parents with very young children* (Final Report). Ypsilanti, MI: High/Scope Educational Research Foundation.

Epstein, H. T. (1978). Growth spurts during brain development: Implications for educational policy and practice. In J. S. Chall & A. F. Mirsky (Eds.), *Education and the Brain*. Chicago: University of Chicago Press.

Epstein, H. T. (1979). Correlated brain and intelligence development in humans. In M. E. Hahn, C. Jensen, & B. C. Dudek (Eds.), *Development and evolution of brain size*. New York: Academic Press.

Epstein, J., Breslow, J. L., Fitzimmons, M. J., & Vayo, M. M. (1978). Pleiotropic drug resistance in cystic fibrosis fibroblasts: Increased resistance to cyclic AMP. *Somatic Cell Genetics, 4*, 451–464.

Ericsson, K. A., Chase, W. G., & Faloon, S. (1980). Acquisition of a memory skill. *Science, 208*, 1181–1182.

Erikson, E. H. (1963). *Childhood and Society* (2d ed.). New York: W. W. Norton.

Ernest, J. (1980). Is mathematics a sexist discipline? In L. H. Fox, L. Brody, & D. Tobin (Eds.). *Women and the mathematical mystique*. Baltimore: The Johns Hopkins Press.

Eron, L. D. (1982). Parent-child interaction, television violence, and aggression of children. *American Psychologist, 37*, 197–211.

Eron, L. D., Walder, L. O., Huesmann, L. R., & Lefkowitz, M. M. (1978). The convergence of laboratory and field studies. In W. W. Hartup & J. DeWitt (Eds.), *Origins of Aggression*. The Hague: Mouton.

Estes, W. K. (1978). The information processing approach to cognition: A confluence of metaphors and method. In W. K. Estes (Ed.), *Handbook of learning and cognitive processes* (Vol. 5). Hillsdale, NJ: Lawrence Erlbaum.

Eysenck, H. J. (1983). Revolution in the theory and measurement of intelligence. *Revue Canadienne de Psycho-education, 12,* 3–17.

Fabricius, W. V., & Wellman, H. M. (1983). Children's understanding of retrieval cue utilization. *Developmental Psychology, 19,* 15–21.

Fagan, J. F. (1973). Infants' delayed recognition memory and forgetting. *Journal of Experimental Child Psychology, 16,* 424–450.

Fagan, J. F. (1977a). An attention model of infant recognition. *Child Development, 48,* 345–349.

Fagan, J. F. (1977b). Infant recognition memory: Studies in forgetting. *Child Development, 47,* 68–78.

Fantz, R. L. (1964). Visual experience in infants: Decreased attention to familiar patterns relative to novel ones. *Science, 147,* 668–670.

Farah, M. J., & Kosslyn, S. M. (1982). Concept development. In H. W. Reese and L. P. Lipsitt (Eds.), *Advances in child development and behavior* (Vol. 16). New York: Academic Press.

Farber, S. (1980). *Identical twins reared apart: A reanalysis.* New York: Basic Books.

Farran, D. C. (1982). Mother-child interaction, language development, and the school performance of poverty children. In L. Feagans & D. C. Farran (Eds.), *The language of children reared in poverty.* New York: Academic Press.

Farrington, D. P. (1982). Longitudinal analyses of criminal violence. In M. E. Wolfgang & N. A. Weiner (Eds.), *Criminal violence.* Beverly Hills, CA: Sage Publications.

Fein, G. G. (1982). Skill and intelligence: The functions of play. *The Brain and Behavioral Sciences, 5,* 163–164.

Feingold, B. F. (1975). *Why your child is hyperactive.* New York: Random House.

Feldman, C. F., & Toulmin, S. (1975). Logic and the theory of mind. In J. K. Cole & W. J. Arnold (Eds.), *Nebraska Symposium on Motivation, 23,* 409–476.

Feldman, H. (1981). A comparison of intentional parents and intentionally childless couples. *Journal of Marriage and the Family, 43,* 593–600.

Feshbach, N. D., & Feshbach, S. (1982). Empathy training and the regulation of aggression: Potentialities and limitation. *Academic Psychology Bulletin, 4,* 399–413.

Feshbach, S. (1970). Aggression. In P. H. Mussen (Ed.), *Carmichael's manual of child psychology* (Vol. 2). New York: John Wiley & Sons.

Field, T. (1982). Infant arousal, attention and affect during early interactions. In L. Lipsett (Ed.), *Advances in infant behavior and development.* Hillsdale, NJ: Lawrence Erlbaum.

Field, T. M., Woodson, R., Greenberg, R., & Cohen, D. (1982). Discrimination and imitation of facial expressions by neonates. *Science, 218,* 179–181

Findley, P. (1933). *The story of childbirth.* Garden City, NY: Doubleday Publishing.

Fine, M. A., Moreland, J. R., & Schwebel, A. I. (1983). Long-term effects of divorce on parent-child relationsips. *Developmental Psychology, 19,* 703–713.

Finke, R. A. (1980). Levels of equivalence in imagery and perception. *Psychological Review, 87,* 113–132.

Finkelstein, N. W., & Ramey, C. T. (1977). Learning to control the environment in infancy. *Child Development, 48,* 806–819.

Fischman, S. E. (1979). Psychological Issues in the genetic counseling of cystic fibrosis. In S. Kessler (Ed.), *Genetic counseling: Psychological dimensions.* New York: Academic Press.

Flapan, D. (1968). *Children's understanding of social interaction.* New York: Teachers College Press.

Flavell, J. H. (1971). What is memory development the development of? *Human Development, 14,* 272–278.

Flavell, J. H. (1977). *Cognitive development.* Englewood Cliffs, NJ: Prentice-Hall.

Flavell, J. H. (1981). Cognitive monitoring. In W. P. Dickson (Ed.), *Children's oral communication skills.* New York: Academic Press.

Flavell, J. H., & Wellman, H. M. (1977). Metamemory. In R. V. Kail, Jr., & J. W. Hagen (Eds.), *Perspectives on the development of memory and cognition.* Hillsdale, NJ: Lawrence Erlbaum.

Flavell, J. H., Everett, B. A., Croft, K., & Flavell, E. R. (1981). Young children's knowledge about visual perception: Further evidence for the Level 1-Level 2 distinction. *Developmental Psychology, 17,* 99–103.

Flavell, J. H., Speer, J. R., Green, R. L., & August, D. L. (1981). The development of comprehension monitoring and knowledge about communication. *Monographs of the Society for Research in Child Development, 46,* No. 192.

Floderus-Myrhed, B., Pedersen, N., & Rasmuson, I. (1978). Assessment of heritability for personality, based on a short-form of the Eysenck Personality Inventory: A study of 12,898 twin pairs. *Behavior Genetics, 10,* 153–162.

Foch, T. T., & McClearn, G. E. (1980). Genetics, body weight, and obesity. In A. J. Stunkard (Ed.), *Obesity.* Philadelphia: W. B. Saunders.

Forbes, G. B. (1982). Nutrition and hyperactivity. *Journal of the American Medical Association, 248,* 355–356.

Foreyt, J. P., & Goodrick, G. K. (1981). Childhood obesity. In E. J. Mash & L. G. Terdal (Eds.), *Behavioral assessment of childhood disorders.* New York: Guilford Press.

Forrest, D. W. (1974). *Francis Galton: The life and work of a Victorian genius.* New York: Taplinger Publishing.

Fossey, D. (1983). *Gorillas in the mist.* Boston: Houghton Mifflin.

Foster, H., & Freed, D. (June, 1980). Joint custody. *Trial,* pp. 22–27.

Fouts, R. S. (1974). Capacities for languages in great apes. *Proceedings of the 18th international congress of anthropological and ethnological sciences.* The Hague: Mouton.

Fouts, R. S. (1982, April 22). Chimpanzees, communication and controversy. Invited address given at California State University, San Bernardino.

Fouts, R. S., & Budd, R. L. (1979). Artificial and human language acquisition in the chimpanzee. In D. A. Hamburg & E. R. McCown (Eds.), *The great apes.* Menlo Park, CA: Benjamin/Cummings Publishing.

Fowles, J. (1977). *The magus: A revised edition.* Boston: Little Brown.

Fox, L. H., Brody, L., & Tobin, D. (1980). *Women and the mathematical mystique.* Baltimore: The Johns Hopkins Press.

Fox, N., Kagan, J., & Weiskopf, S. (1979). The growth of memory during infancy. *Genetic Psychology Monographs, 99,* 91–139.

Fraiberg, S. (1974). Blind infants and their mothers: An examination of the sign system. In M. Lewis & L. A. Rosenblum (Eds.), *The effect of the infant on its caregiver.* New York: John Wiley & Sons.

Frankel, M. T., & Rollins, H. A. (1983). Does mother know best? Mothers and fathers interaction with preschool sons and daughters. *Developmental Psychology, 19,* 694–702.

Frankenburg, W. K., & Dodds, J. B. (1967). The Denver developmental screening test. *Journal of Pediatrics, 71,* 181–185.

Franklin, A. W. (1977). *The challenge of child abuse.* New York: Academic Press.

Franklin, B. A. (1982, March 3). Rhodes scholar intent on pushing herself beyond what seems possible. *Press Enterprise,* p. 1.

Frazer, M. (1974). *Children in conflict.* New York: Penguin Books.

Freedman, D. G. (1974). *Human infancy: An evolutionary perspective.* Hillsdale, NJ: Lawrence Erlbaum.

Freedman, D. G. (1979). *Human sociobiology.* New York: Free Press.

Freud, A., & Dann, S. (1951). An experiment in group up-bringing. In R. S. Eisler, A. Freud, H. Hartmann, & E. Kris (Eds.), *The Psychoanalytic Study of the Child* (Vol. 6). New York: International Universities Press.

Freud, S. (1964). *An outline of psycho-analysis.* (Vol. 23). Translated by J. Strachey. London: Hogarth Press.

Freud, S. (1965). *New introductory lectures on Pschoanalysis.* New York: W. W. Norton.

Freud, S. (1971). The case of the Wolf-Man. In M. Gardiner (Ed.), *The Wolf-Man.* New York: Basic Books.

Fribourg, S. (1982). Cigarette smoke and sudden infant death syndrome. *American Journal of Obstetrics and Gynecology, 142,* 934.

Friedhoff, A. J. (1972). Biochemical aspects of schizophrenia. In A. R. Kaplan (Ed.), *Genetic factors in schizophrenia.* Springfield, IL: Charles C Thomas.

Friedman, S. L., & Sigman, M. (1981). *Preterm birth and psychological development.* New York: Academic Press.

Friedrich, L. K., & Stein, A. H. (1975). Prosocial television and young children: The effects of verbal labeling and role playing on learning and behavior. *Child Development, 46,* 27–38.

Friedrich, W. N., & Wheeler, K. K. (1982). The abusing parent revisited: A decade of psychological research. *The Journal of Nervous and Mental Disease, 170,* 577–587.

Frodi, A. M., & Lamb, M. E. (1978). Fathers' and mothers' responses to the faces and cries of normal and premature infants. *Developmental Psychology, 14,* 490–498.

Frodi, A. M., & Lamb, M. E. (1980). Infants at risk for child abuse. *Infant Mental Health Journal, 1,* 240–247.

Frueh, T., & McGhee, P. E. (1975). Traditional sex role development and amount of time spent watching television. *Developmental Psychology, 11,* 109.

Fujiwara, M. (1978). Problem of obesity in Japan. In J. C. Somogyi (Ed.), *Nutritional, psychological and social aspects of obesity.* New York: Karger.

Funder, D. C., Block, J. H., & Block, J. (1983). Delay of gratification: Some longitudinal personality correlates. *Journal of Personality and Social Psychology, 44,* 1198–1213.

Furman, W., & Bierman, K. L. (1983). Developmental changes in young children's conceptions of friendship. *Child Development, 54,* 549–557.

Furstenberg, F. F. (1981). Remarriage and intergenerational relations. In R. W. Fogel, E. Hatfield, S. B. Kiesler, & T. Shanes (Eds.), *Stability and change in the family.* New York: Academic Press.

Furth, H. G. (1969). *Piaget and knowledge: Theoretical foundations.* Englewood Cliffs, NJ: Prentice-Hall.

Furth, H. G. (1971). Linguistic deficiency and thinking: Research with deaf subjects. 1964–1969. *Psychological Bulletin, 76,* 58–72.

Furth, H. G., & Wachs, H. (1974). *Thinking goes to school.* New York: Oxford University Press.

Furth, H. G., & Youniss, J. (1971). Thinking in deaf adolescents: Formal operations and language: A comparison of deaf and hearing adolescents. *International Journal of Psychology, 6,* 49–64.

Gagnon, J. H. (1977). *Human sexualities.* Glenview, IL: Scott, Foresman.

Gaiter, J. L., & Johnson, A. A. (1981, April). Father-infant interaction in an intensive care nursery. Paper presented at Society for Research in Child Development, Boston, MA.

Galaburda, A. M., & Kemper, T. L. (1979). Cytoarchitectonic abnormalities in developmental dyslexia: A case study. *Annals of Neurology, 6,* 94–100.

Galton, F. (1869). *Hereditary genius: An inquiry into its laws and consequences.* London: Macmillan Publishers.

Galton, F. (1883). *Inquiries into human faculty and its development.* London: Macmillan Publishers.

Galton, F. (1885). On the anthropometric laboratory at the late International Health Exhibition. *Journal of the Anthropological Institute, 14,* 206–211.

Garbarino, J. (1980). Preventing child maltreatment. In R. H. Price, R. F. Ketterer, B. C. Bader, & J. Monahan (Eds.), *Prevention in mental health.* Beverly Hills, CA: Sage Publications.

Garbarino, J. (1982). *Children and families in the social environment.* Hawthorne, NY: Aldine Publishing.

Garbarino, J., & Crouter, A. (1978). Defining the community context of parent-child relationships: The correlates of child maltreatment. *Child Development, 49,* 604–616.

Garbarino, J., & Stocking, S. H. (1981). *Protecting children from abuse and neglect.* San Francisco: Jossey-Bass.

Garbarino, J., Seber, J., & Schellenbach, C. (1984). Families at risk for destructive parent-child relations in adolescence. *Child Development, 55,* 184–194.

Garber, H., & Heber, F. R. (1977). The Milwaukee project: Indications of the effectiveness of early intervention in preventing mental retardation. In P. Mittler (Ed.), *Research to practice in mental retardation* (Vol. 1). Baltimore: University Park Press.

Garcia, G. D. (1983, April 25). Hope stirs in the ghetto. *Time*, p. 95.

Gardiner, M. (1971). *The Wolf-Man*. New York: Basic Books.

Gardner, B. T., & Gardner, R. A. (1979). Two comparative psychologists look at language acquisition. In K. E. Nelson (Ed.), *Children's language* (Vol. 2). New York: Halsted Press.

Gardner, D. P. (1983). A *nation at risk*. Washington, DC: U.S. Department of Education.

Gardner, H., & Winner, E. (1982). First intimations of artistry. In S. Strauss (Ed.), *U-shaped behavioral growth*. New York: Academic Press.

Gardner, J., & Gardner, H. A. (1970). A note on selective imitation by a six-week-old infant. *Child Development, 41*, 1209–1213.

Gardner, L. I. (1972). Deprivation Dwarfism. *Scientific American, 227*, 76–82.

Gardner, R. A. (1982). *Family evaluation in child custody litigation*. Cresskill, NJ: Creative Therapeutics.

Gardner, R. A., & Gardner, B. T. (1980). Comparative psychology and language acquisition. In T. A. Sebeok & J. Umiker-Sebeok (Eds.), *Speaking of apes*. New York: Plenum Publishing.

Garmezy, N. (1976). Vulnerable and invulnerable children: Theory, research, and intervention. *Catalog of Selected Documents in Psychology, 6*, 1–96.

Garmezy, N. (1982). Commentary. *Monographs of the Society for Research in Child Development*, No. 199.

Garmezy, N. (1983). Stressors of childhood. In N. Garmezy & M. Rutter (Eds.), *Stress, coping, and development in children*. New York: McGraw-Hill.

Garmezy, N., Masten, A. S., & Tellegen, A. (1984). The study of stress and competence in children: A building block for developmental psychopathology. *Child Development, 55*, 97–111.

Garn, S. M., Johnston, M., Ridella, S. A., & Petzold, A. D. (1981). Effect of maternal cigarette smoking on Apgar scores. *American Journal of Diseases in Children, 135*, 503–506.

Garron, D. (1977). Intelligence among persons with Turner's syndrome. *Behavior Genetics, 7*, 105–127.

Garvey, C. (1977a). *Play*. Cambridge, MA: Harvard Univ. Press.

Garvey, C. (1977b). Play with language and speech. In S. Ervin-Tripp & C. Mitchell-Kernan (Eds.), *Child Discourse*. New York: Academic Press.

Garvey, W. P., & Hegrenes, J. R. (1966). Desensitization techniques in the treatment of school phobia. *American Journal of Orthopsychiatry, 36*, 147–152.

Gathorne-Hardy, J. (1972). *The rise and fall of the British nanny*. London: Dial Press.

Geber, M., & Dean, R. F. A. (1967). Precocious development in newborn African infants. In Y. Brackbill & G. Thompson (Eds.) *Behavior in infancy and early childhood*. New York: Free Press.

Gelman, R. (1972). Logical capacity of very young children: Number invariance rules. *Child Development, 43*, 75–90.

Gelman, R. (1979). Preschool thought. *American Psychologist, 34,* 900–905.

Gelman, R. (1982) Accessing one-to-one correspondence: Still another paper about conservation. *British Journal of Psychology, 73,* 209–220.

Genesee, F. (1983). Bilingual education of majority-language children: The immersion experiments in review. *Applied Psycholinguistics, 4,* 1–46.

George, C., & Main, M. (1979). Social interactions of young abused children: Approach, avoidance, and aggression. *Child Development, 50,* 306–318.

George, C., & Main, M. (1979). Social interactions of young abused children: Approach, avoidance, and aggression. *Child Development, 50,* 306–318.

George, W. C., Cohn, S. J., & Stanley, J. C. (1979). *Educating the gifted: Acceleration and enrichment.* Baltimore: The Johns Hopkins Press.

Gerard, H. B. (1983). School desegregation: The social science role. *American Psychologist, 38,* 869–877.

Gerbner, G., & Gross, L. (1980). The violent face of television and its lessons. In E. L. Palmer & A. Dorr (Eds.), *Children and the faces of television.* New York: Academic Press.

Geschwind, N. (1979). Specializations of the human brain. *Scientific American, 241,* 180–197.

Gesell, A., & Ilg, F. L. (1943). *Infant and child in the culture of today.* New York: Harper & Row.

Gesell, A., & Thompson, H. (1929). Learning and growth in identical infant twins: An experimental study by the method of co-twin control. *Genetic Psychology Monographs, 6,* 1–124.

Giaconia, R. M., & Hedges, L. V. (1982). Identifying features of effective open education. *Review of Educational Research, 52,* 579–602.

Gibbs, J. C., Widaman, K. F., & Colby, A. (1982). Construction and validation of a simplified, group-administerable equivalent to the Moral Judgment Interview. *Child Development, 53,* 895–910.

Gibson, E. J., & Walk, R. R. (1960). The "visual cliff." *Scientific American, 202,* 2–9.

Gill, W. B., Schumacher, G. F., Bibbo, M., Strausm F. H., & Schoenbe, H. W. (1979). Association of diethylstilbestrol exposure in utero with cryptochidism, testicular hypoplasia or semen abnormalities. *Journal of Urology, 122,* 36–39.

Ginsburg, H. J., & Miller, S. M. (1982). Sex differences in children's risk-taking behavior. *Child Development, 53,* 426–428.

Ginsburg, H., & Opper, S. (1979). *Piaget's theory of intellectual development.* Englewood Cliffs, NJ: Prentice-Hall.

Gintzler, A. R. (1980). Endorphin-mediated increases in pain threshold during pregnancy. *Science, 210,* 193–194.

Gleason, J. B. (1967). Do children imitate? *Proceedings of the international conference on oral education of the deaf, 2,* 1441–1448.

Glick, P. C. (1979). Children of divorced parents in demographic perspective. *Journal of Social Issues, 35,* 170–182.

Golbus, M. S., Harrison, M. R., Filly, R. A., Callen, P. W., & Katz, M. (1982). In utero treatment of urinary tract obstruction. *American Journal of Obstetrics and Gynecology, 142,* 383–386.

Gold, D., & Andres, D. (1978a). Comparisons of adolescent children with employed and unemployed mothers. *Merrill Palmer Quarterly, 24,* 243–254.

Gold, D., & Andres, D. (1978b). Developmental comparisons between ten-year-old children with employed and unemployed mothers. *Child Development, 49,* 75–84.

Gold, D., & Andres, D. (1978c). Relations between maternal employment and development of nursery-school children. *Canadian Journal of Behavioral Science, 10,* 116–129.

Gold, D., Andres, D., & Glorieux, J. (1979). The development of Francophone nursery-school children with employed and nonemployed mothers. *Canadian Journal of Behavioral Science, 11,* 169–173.

Goldberg, S. (1972). Infant care and growth in urban Zambia. *Human Development, 15,* 77–89.

Golding, W. (1977). *Lord of the flies.* New York: G. P. Putnam's Sons.

Goldman, A. S. (1980). Critical periods of prenatal toxic insults. *Drugs and chemical risks to the fetus and newborn.* New York: Alan R. Liss.

Goldman-Rakic, P. S., Isseroff, A., Schwartz, M. L., & Bugbee, N. M. (1983). The neurobiology of cognitive development. In J. J. Campos & M. M. Haith (Eds.), *Handbook of child psychology* (Vol. 2.) New York: John Wiley & Sons.

Goldstein, K. M., Caputo, D. V., & Taub, H. B. (1976). The effects of prenatal and perinatal complications on development at 1 year of age. *Child Development, 47,* 613–621.

Goldstein, M. (1982, May). The fight agains SIDS. *Parents,* pp. 83–86.

Gollin, E. S. (1981). Development and plasticity. In E. S. Gollin (Ed.), *Developmental plasticity: Behavioral and biological aspects of variations in development.* New York: Academic Press.

Good, T. (1980). Classroom expectations: Teacher-pupil interactions. In J. McMillan (Ed.), *The social psychology of school learning.* New York: Academic Press.

Goodall, J. (1965). Chimpanzees of the Gombe Stream Reserve. In I. DeVore (Ed.), *Primate behavior: Field studies of monkeys and apes.* New York: Holt, Rinehart & Winston.

Goodwin, D. W., Schulsinger, L., Harmanson, L., Guze, S. B., & Winokur, G. A. (1973). Alcohol problems in adoptees raised apart from alcoholic biological parents. *Archives of General Psychiatry, 28,* 238–243.

Gordon, I. J. (1975). *The infant experience.* Columbus, OH: Charles E. Merrill Publishing.

Goren, C. C., Sarty, M., & Wu, P. (1975). Visual following and pattern discrimination of face-like stimuli by newborn infants. *Pediatrics, 56,* 544–549.

Gottesman, I. I. (1975). Possible directions for developmental human behavior genetics. In K. W. Schaie, V. E. Anderson, G. E. McClearn, & J. Money (Eds.), *Developmental human behavior genetics.* Lexington, MA: D. C. Heath.

Gottesman, I. I., & Shields, J. (1972). *Schizophrenia and genetics: A twin study vantage point.* New York: Academic Press.

Gottfried, A., Wallace, L. P., Sherman, B. S., King, J., Coen, C., & Hodgman, J. E. (1981). Physical and social environment of newborn infants in special care units. *Science, 214,* 672–675.

Gottlieb, B. H. (1981). The role of individual and social support in preventing child maltreatment. In J. Garbarino & S. H. Stocking (Eds.), *Protecting children from abuse and neglect*. San Francisco: Jossey-Bass.

Gottlieb, G. (1976). The roles of experience in the development of behavior and the nervous system. In G. Gottlieb (Ed.), *Neural and behavioral specificity: Studies on the development of behavior and the nervous system* (Vol 3). New York: Academic Press.

Gottlieb, J., & Leyser, Y. (1981). Friendship between mentally retarded and nonretarded children. In S. R. Asher & J. M. Gottman (Eds.), *The development of children's friendships*. New York: Cambridge University Press.

Gottman, J. M. (1977). Toward a definition of social isolation in children. *Child Development, 48*, 513–517.

Gottman, J. M. (1983). How children become friends. *Monographs of the Society for Research in Child Development, 48*, No. 201.

Gove, F., Arend, R., & Sroufe, L. A. (1979). Competence in preschool and kindergarten predicted from infancy. Unpublished manuscript, University of Minnesota, Minneapolis.

Grad, R., Bash, D., Guyer, R. Acevedo, Z. Trause, M. A., & Rekauf, D. (1981). *The father book: Pregnancy and beyond*. Washington, DC: Acropolis Books.

Graham, D. (1981). The obstetric and neonatal consequences of adolescent pregnancy. In E. R. McAnarney & G. Stickle (Eds.), *Pregnancy and childbearing during adolescence: Research priorities for the 80s*. New York: Alan R. Liss.

Granzberg, G., & Steinbring, J. (1980). *Television and the Canadian Indian*. (Techical Report). Manitoba, Canada: University of Winnipeg, Department of Anthropology.

Gratch, G. (1972). A study of the relative dominance of vision and touch in six-month-old infants. *Child Development, 43*, 615–623.

Gratch, G. (1979). The development of thought and language in infancy. In J. D. Osofsky (Ed.), *Handbook of infant development*. New York: John Wiley & Sons.

Graves, S. B. (1980). Psychological effects of black portrayals on television. In S. B. Withy & R. P. Abeles (Eds.), *Television and social behavior*. Hillsdale, NJ: Lawrence Erlbaum.

Gray, J. A., & Drewett, R. F. (1977). The genetics and development of sex differences. In R. B. Cattell & R. M. Dreger (Eds.), *Handbook of modern personality theory*. New York: Halsted Press.

Green, A. H. (1980). *Child maltreatment*. New York: Jason Aronson.

Greenberg, J., & Kuczaj, S. A. II (1982). Towards a theory of substantive word-meaning acquisition. In S. A. Kuczaj II (Ed.), *Language development: Syntax and semantics* (Vol. 1). Hillsdale, NJ: Lawrence Erlbaum.

Greenberg, M., & Morris, N. (1974). Engrossment: The newborn's impact upon the father. *American Journal of Orthopsychiatry, 44*, 520–531.

Greenfield, P. M., & Smith, J. H. (1976). *The structure of communication in early language development*. New York: Academic Press.

Grinder, R. E. (1978). *Adolescence*. New York: John Wiley & Sons.

Grinker, J. (1981). Behavioral and metabolic factors in childhood obesity. In M. Lewis & L. A. Rosenblum (Eds.), *The uncommon child*. New York: Plenum Publishing.

Grobstein, R. (1979). Amniocentesis counseling. In S. Kessler (Ed.), *Genetic counseling: Psychological dimensions*. New York: Academic Press.

Grossmann, K., & Grossmann, K. (1981). Parent-infant attachment relationships in Bielefeld: A research note. In K. Immelmann, G. W. Barlow, L. Petrinovich, & M. Main (Eds.), *Behavioral Development: The Bielefeld interdisciplinary project*. London: Cambridge University Press.

Grusec, J. E., Kuczynski, L., Rushton, J. P., & Simutis, Z. M. (1978). Modeling, direct instruction, and attributions: Effects on altruism. *Developmental Psychology, 14*, 51–57.

Gummerman, K., & Gray, C. R. (1971). Recall of visually presented material: An unwonted case and a bibliography for eidetic imagery. *Psychonomic Monograph Supplements, 4*, 189–195.

Gurucharri, C., & Selman, R. L. (1982). The development of interpersonal understanding during childhood, preadolescence, and adolescence: A longitudinal follow-up study. *Child Development, 53*, 924–927.

Guth, L., & Clements, C. D. (1975). Growth and regeneration in the central nervous system. *Experimental Neurology, 48*, 251–257.

Haavik, S., Altman, K., & Woelk, C. (1979). Effects of the Feingold diet on seizures and hyperactivity: A single-subject analysis. *Journal of Behavioral Medicine, 2*, 365–374.

Haber, R. N. (1980a). Eidetic images are not just imaginary. *Psychology Today, 14*, 72–83.

Haber, R. N. (1980b). Twenty years of haunting eidetic imagery: Where's the ghost? *The Behavioral and Brain Sciences, 2*, 583–629.

Hackett, G., & Betz, N. E. (1981). A self-efficacy approach to the career development of women. *Journal of Vocational Behavior, 18*, 326–339.

Haith, M. M. (1980). *Rules that babies look by: The organization of newborn visual activity*. Hillsdale, NJ: Lawrence Erlbaum.

Haith, M. M., & Goodman, G. S. (1982). Eye movement control in newborns in darkness and unstructured light. *Child Development, 53*, 974–977.

Hakuta, K. (1975). Learning to speak a second language: What exactly does the child learn? In D. P. Dato (Ed.) *Georgetown University roundtable of languages and linguistics*. Washington DC: Georgetown University Press.

Hale, G. A. Development of Children's attention to stimulus components. In G. A. Hale & M. Lewis (Eds.) (1979), *Attention and cognitive development*. New York: Plenum Publishing.

Hamerton, J. L., Canning, N., Ray, M., & Smith, S. (1975). A cytogenetic survey of 14,069 newborn infants: Incidence of chromosome abnormalities. *Clinical Genetics, 8*, 223–243.

Hammer, M. (1972). Schizophrenia: Some questions on definition in cultural perspective. In A. R. Kaplan (Ed.) *Genetic factors in schizophrenia*. Springfield, IL: Charles C Thomas.

Hampson, R. B. (1979, April). Peers, pathology, and helping: Some kids are more helpful than others. Paper presented at Society for Research in Child Development, San Francisco.

Hansen, H. (1978). Decline of Down's Syndrome after abortion reform in New York State. *American Journal of Mental Deficiency, 83*, 185–188.

Hanson, J. W., Streissguth, A. P., & Smith, S. W. (1978). The effects of moderate alcohol consumption during pregnancy on fetal growth and morphogenesis. *Journal of Pediatrics, 92,* 457–460.

Hardy, J. B., & Mellits, E. D. (1972). Does maternal smoking during pregnancy have a long-term effect on the child? *Lancet, 2,* 1332–1336.

Harlow, H. F. (1958). The nature of love. *American Psychologist, 13,* 673–685.

Harlow, H. F., & Harlow, M. K. (1962). Social deprivation in monkeys. *Scientific American, 207,* 62–67.

Harlow, H. F., & Harlow, M. K. (1969). Effects of various mother-infant relationships on rhesus monkey behaviors. In B. M. Foss (Ed.), *Determinants of infant behavior.* (Vol. 4). London: Methuen.

Harlow, H. F., & Zimmerman, R. R. (1959). Affectional responses in the infant monkey. *Science, 130,* 421–432.

Harrington, D. M., Block, J. H., & Block, J. (1978). Intolerance of ambiguity in preschool children: Psychometric considerations, behavioral manifestations, and parental correlates. *Developmental Psychology, 14,* 242–256.

Harrington, D. M., Block, J. H., & Block, J. (1983). Predicting creativity in preadolescence from divergent thinking in early childhood. *Journal of Personality and Social Psychology, 45,* 609–623.

Harris, B. (1979). Whatever happened to Little Albert? *American Psychologist, 34,* 151–160.

Harris, F. R., Wolf, M. M., & Baer, D. M. (1964). Effects of adult social reinforcement on child behavior. *Young Children, 20,* 1–6.

Harrison, M. R., Golbus, M. S., Filly, R. A., Callen, P. W., Katz, M., Lorimier, A. A., Rosen, M., & Jonsen, A. R. (1982). Fetal surgery for congenital hydronephrosis. *New England Journal of Medicine, 306,* 591–593.

Harter, S. (1982). The perceived competence scale for children. *Child Development, 53,* 87–97.

Hartley, S. E., & Sainsbury, C. (1981). Acute leukaemia and the same chromosome abnormality in monozygotic twins. *Human Genetics, 58,* 408–410.

Hartup, W. W. (1983). Peer relations. In E. M. Hetherington (Ed.), *Handbook of child psychology.* (Vol. 4). New York: John Wiley & Sons.

Harvald, B., & Hauge, M. (1965). Hereditary factors elucidated in twin studies. In J. V. Neewl, M. W. Shaw, & W. J. Schull (Eds.), *Genetics and the epidemiology of chronic diseases.* Washington, DC: U.S. Department of Health, Education, and Welfare.

Hay, D. F., Nash, A., & Pedersen, J. (1983). Interaction between six-month-old peers. *Child Development, 54,* 557–562.

Hayes, C. (1951). *The ape in our house.* New York: Harper & Row.

Hayes, L. A., & Watson, J. S. (1981). Neonatal imitation: Fact or artifact. *Developmental Psychology, 17,* 655–660.

Hazen, N. L., & Durrett, M. E. (1982). Relationship of security of attachment to exploration and cognitive mapping abilities in 2-year-olds. *Developmental Psychology, 18,* 751–759.

Headings, V. E. (1979). Psychological issues in sickle cell counseling. In S. Kessler (Ed.), *Genetic counseling: Psychological dimensions.* New York: Academic Press.

Hearold, S. L. (1979). Meta-analysis of the effects of television on social behavior. Doctoral dissertation, University of Colorado. As cited by R. D. Parke & R. G. Slaby. (1983). The development of aggression. In E. M. Hetherington (Ed.), *Handbook of child psychology* (Vol. 4). New York: John Wiley & Sons.

Hebb, D. O. (1976). Physiological learning theory. *Journal of Abnormal Child Psychology, 4,* 309–314.

Heilbrun, A. B. (1982). Cognitive models of criminal violence based upon intelligence and psychopathy levels. *Journal of Consulting and Clinical Psychology, 50,* 546–557.

Hein, A., Vital-Durand, F., Salinger, W., & Diamond, R. (1979). Eye movements initiate visual-motor development in the cat. *Science, 204,* 1321–1322.

Henderson, R. W. (1981). Home environment and intellectual performance. In R. W. Henderson (Ed.), *Parent-child interaction: Theory, research and prospects.* New York: Academic Press.

Hendin, D., & Marks, J. (1978). *The genetic connection.* New York: William Morrow.

Hendrickson, D. E. (1982). The biological basis of intelligence, Part II: Measurement. In H. J. Eysenck (Ed.), *A model for intelligence.* New York: Springer-Verlag.

Henig, R. M. (1981, March 22). The child savers. *The New York Times,* Section 6, p. 34–36.

Henry, R. M. (1980). A theoretical and empirical analysis of 'reasoning' in the socialization of young children. *Human Development, 23,* 105–125.

Herbst, A. L. (1981a). The current status of the DES exposed population. *Obstetrics and Gynecology Annual, 10,* 267–278.

Herbst, A. L. (1981b). Diethylstilbestrol and other sex hormones during pregnancy. *Obstetrics and Gynecology, 58,* 35s–40s.

Herbst, A. L., Ulfelder, H., & Poskanzer, D. S. (1971). Adenocarcinoma of the vagina. Association of maternal stilbestrol therapy with tumor appearance in young women. *New England Journal of Medicine, 11,* 284.

Herman, J. F., Roth, S. F., Miranda, C., & Getz, M. (1982). Children's memory for spatial locations: The influence of recall perspective and type of environment. *Journal of Experimental Child Psychology, 34,* 257–273.

Herman, L. M. (1980). Cognitive characteristics of dolphins. In L. M. Herman (Ed.), *Cetacean behavior: Mechanisms and functions.* New York: John Wiley & Sons.

Herrnstein, R. J. (1982). IQ testing and the media. *The Atlantic Monthly, 250,* (2), 68–74.

Herschel, M. (1978). Dyslexia revisited. *Human Genetics, 40,* 115–134.

Herzog, E., & Sudia, C. E. (1973). Children in fatherless families. In B. M. Caldwell & H. M. Ricciuti (Eds.), *Review of child development research* (Vol. 3). Chicago: University of Chicago Press.

Hess, R. D., & Camara, K. A. (1979). Post-divorce family relationships as mediating factors in the consequences of divorce for children. *The Journal of Social Issues, 35,* 79–96.

Hess, E. H. (1970). Ethology and developmental psychology. In P. H. Mussen (Ed.), *Carmichael's manual of child psychology.* New York: John Wiley & Sons.

Hess, E. H. (1972). Imprinting in a natural laboratory. *Scientific American, 227,* 24–32.

Hess, E. H. (1973). *Imprinting: Early experience and the developmental psychobiology of attachment.* New York: Van Nostrand Reinhold.

Heston, L. L. (1970). The genetics of schizophrenic and schizoid disease. *Science, 167,* 249–256.

Hetherington, E. M. (1981). Children and divorce. In R. W. Henderson (Ed.), *Parent-child interaction.* New York: Academic Press.

Hetherington, E. M., Camara, K. A., & Featherman, D. L. (1983). Achievement and intellectual functioning of children in one-parent households. In J. T. Spence (Ed.), *Achievement and achievement motives.* San Francisco: W. H. Freeman.

Hetherington, E. M., Cox, M., & Cox, R. (1978). The aftermath of divorce. In J. H. Stevens, Jr., & Matthews, M. (Eds.), *Mother-child, father-child relations.* Washington, DC: National Association for the Education of Young Children.

Hetherington, E. M., Cox, M., & Cox, R. (1979). Play and social interaction in children following divorce. *Journal of Social Issues, 35,* 26–49.

Hetherington, E. M., Cox, M., & Cox, R. (1982). Effects of divorce on parents and children. In M. E. Lamb (Ed.), *Nontraditional Families: Parenting and child development.* Hillsdale, NJ: Lawrence Erlbaum.

Hewitt, J. K., & Broadhurst, P. L. (1983). Genetic architecture and the evolution of aggressive behavior. In E. C. Simmel, M. E. Hahn & J. K. Walters (Eds.), *Aggressive behavior: Genetic and neural approaches.* Hillsdale, NJ: Lawrence Erlbaum.

Hicks, S. P., & D'Amato, C. J. (1980). Effects of radiation on development, especially of the nervous system. *American Journal of Forensic Medicine and Pathology, 1,* 309–317.

Hier, D. B., & Crowley, W. F. (1982). Spatial ability in androgen-deficient men. *New England Journal of Medicine, 306,* 1202–1205.

Hilgard, E. R. (1981). Imagery and imagination in American psychology. *Journal of Mental Imagery, 5,* 5–66.

Hines, M. (1982). Prenatal gonadal hormones and sex differences in human behavior. *Psychological Bulletin, 92,* 56–80.

Hirschi, T., & Hindelang, M. J. (1977). Intelligence and delinquency: A revisionist review. *American Sociological Review, 42,* 571–587.

Hock, E. (1980). Working and nonworking mothers and their infants: A comparative study of maternal caregiving characteristics and infant social behavior. *Merrill Palmer Quarterly, 26,* 79–101.

Hock, E., Coady, S., & Cordero, L. (1973, March). Patterns of attachment to mothers of one-year-old infants: A comparative study of full-term infants and prematurely born infants who were hospitalized throughout the neonatal period. Paper presented at the biennial meeting of the Society for Research in Child Development, Philadelphia.

Hofer, M. A. (1981). *The roots of human behavior: An introduction to the psychobiology of early development.* San Francisco: W. H. Freeman.

Hoff-Ginsberg, E., & Shatz, M. (1982). Linguistic input and the child's acquisition of language. *Psychological Bulletin, 92,* 3–26.

Hoffman, L. W. (1977). Changes in family roles, socialization, and sex differences. *American Psychologist, 32,* 644–657.

Hoffman, L. W. (1980). The effects of maternal employment on the academic attitudes, and performance of school-aged children. *School Psychology Review, 9,* 319–335.

Hoffman, L. W. (1983). Increased fathering: Effects on the mother. In M. E. Lamb & A. Sagi (Eds.), *Fatherhood and family policy.* Hillsdale, NJ: Lawrence Erlbaum.

Hoffman, M. L. (1970). Moral development. In P. H. Mussen (Ed.), *Carmichael's manual of child psychology* (Vol. 2). New York: John Wiley & Sons.

Hoffman, R. F. (1978). Developmental changes in human infant visual-evoked potentials to patterned stimuli recorded at different scalp locations. *Child Development, 49,* 110–118.

Hoffman, S. (1977). Marital instability and the economic status of women. *Demography, 14,* 67–77.

Hofmann, M. J., Salapatek, P., & Kuskowski, M. (1981). Evidence for visual memory in the averaged and single evoked potentials of human infants. *Infant Behavior and Development, 4,* 401–421.

Hogan, R., & Weiss, D. S. (1976). Personality correlates of superior achievement. *Journal of Counseling Psychology, 21,* 144–149.

Holden, C. (1980). Identical twins reared apart. *Science, 207,* 1323–1328.

Holford, R. M. (1975). The relation between juvenile cancer and obstetric radiography. *Health Physician, 28,* 153–156.

Hollander, E. P. (1984). Leadership and power. In G. Lindzey & E. Aronson (Eds.), *Handbook of social psychology* (3d ed.). Reading, MA: Addison-Wesley Publishing.

Holt, J. (1982). *Teach your own: New and hopeful paths for parents and educators.* New York: Dell Publishing.

Holtzman, W. H., Diaz-Guerro, R., & Swartz, J. D. (1975). *Personality development in two cultures.* Austin, TX: University of Texas Press.

Honzik, M. P., MacFarlane, J., & Allen, L. (1948). The stability of mental test performance between two and eighteen years. *Journal of Experimental Education, 4,* 309–324.

Hood, L., & Bloom, L. (1979). What, when, and how about why: A longitudinal study of early expressions of causality. *Monographs of the Society for Research in Child Development, 44,* No. 181.

Hooke, C. J. (1981). Coffee in pregnancy. *Lancet, 1,* 554.

Horgan, D. (1980). Nouns: Love 'Em or Leave 'Em. *Annals of the New York Academy of Sciences, 345,* 5–26.

Horn, J. M., Loehlin, J. C., & Willerman, L. (1979). Intellectual resemblance among adoptive and biological relatives: The Texas Adoption Project. *Behavior Genetics, 9,* 177–207.

Horn, J., Plomin, R., & Rosenman, R. (1976). Heritability of personality traits in adult male twins. *Behavior Genetics, 6,* 17–30.

Horowitz, F. D., & Sullivan, J. W. (1981). Mother-child interaction issues. In R. L. Schiefelbusch & D. D. Bricker (Eds.), *Early language: Acquisition and intervention.* Baltimore: University Park Press.

Horowitz, R. (1979). Psychological effects of the "open classroom." *Review of Educational Research, 49,* 71–86.

Howes, C. (1983). Patterns of friendship. *Child Development, 54,* 1041–1051.

Hsia, D. Y. (1970). Phenylketonuria and its variants. In A. G. Steinberg & A. G. Bearn (Eds.), *Progress in medical genetics.* (Vol. 7). New York: Grune & Stratton.

Hsu, C., Soong, W., Stigler, J. W., Hong, C., & Liang, C. (1981). The temperamental characteristics of Chinese babies. *Child Development, 52,* 1337–1340.

Hsu, T. C. (1979). *Human and mammalian cytogenetics: An historical perspective.* New York: Springer-Verlag.

Hubel, D. H., & Wiesel, T. N. (1979). Brain mechanisms of vision. *Scientific American, 241,* 150–162.

Huff, H. A., & Halton, A. (1978). Is there directed reaching in the human neonate? *Developmental Psychology, 14,* 425–426.

Humphrey, G., & Humphrey, M. (1932). *The wild boy of Aveyron.* New York: Appleton-Century-Crofts.

Hunkapiller, T., Huang, H., Hood, L., & Campbell, J. H. (1982). The impact of modern genetics on evolutionary theory. In R. Milkman (Ed.), *Perspectives on evolution.* Sunderland, MA: Sinauer Associates.

Hunt, E. (1982). Towards new ways of assessing intelligence. *Intelligence, 6,* 231–240.

Hunt, E., & Love, T. (1982). The second mnemonist. In U. Neisser (Ed.), *Memory observed.* San Francisco: W. H. Freeman.

Hunt, J. (1981). Predicting intellectual disorders in childhood for preterm infants with birthweights below 1501 gm. In S. L. Friedman & M. Sigman (Eds.), *Preterm birth and psychological development.* New York: Academic Press.

Hunt, J. McV. (1961). *Intelligence and experience.* New York: Ronald Press.

Hunter, R. S., Kilstrom, N., Kraybill, E. N., & Luda, F. (1978). Antecedents of child abuse and neglect in premature infants: A prospective study in a newborn intensive care unit. *Pediatrics, 161,* 629–635.

Hurley, L. S. (1980). *Developmental nutrition.* Englewood Cliffs, NJ: Prentice-Hall.

Huston, A. C. (1983). Sex-typing. In E. M. Hetherington (Ed.), *Handbook of Child Psychology* (Vol. 4). New York: John Wiley & Sons.

Hutt, C. (1966). Exploration and play in children. *Symposium of the Zoological Society of London, 18,* 61–81.

Hutt, C. (1984). Towards a taxonomy and conceptual model of play. In S. J. Hutt, D. A. Rogers, & C. Hutt (Eds.), *Developmental processes in early childhood.* London: Routledge & Kegan Paul.

Hutt, C., & Bhavnani, R. (1976). Predictions from play. In J. S. Bruner, A. Jolly, & K. Sylva (Eds.), *Play.* New York: Basic Books.

Hyman, C. (1981). Families who injure their children. In N. Frude (Ed.), *Psychological approaches to child abuse.* Totowa, NJ: Rowman & Littlefield.

Ilfeld, F. W., Ilfeld, H. S., & Alexander, J. R. (1982). Does joint custody work? A first look at outcome data on relitigation. *American Journal of Psychiatry, 39,* 2–66.

Immelman, K., & Suomi, S. J. (1981). Sensitive phases in development. In K. Immelmann, G. W. Barlow, L. Petrinovich, & M. Main (Eds.), *Behavioral development: The Bielefeld Interdisciplinary Project.* New York: Cambridge University Press.

Ingram, D. (1981). The transition from early symbols to syntax. In R. L. Schiefelbusch & D. D. Bricker (Eds.), *Early language: Acquisition and intervention*. Baltimore: University Park Press.

Inhelder, B. (1962). Some aspects of Piaget's genetic approach to cognition. In W. Kessen & C. Kuhlman (Eds.), Thought in the young child. *Monographs of the Society for Research in Child Development, 27*, No. 2.

Inhelder, B., & Piaget, J. (1958). *The growth of logical thinking from childhood to adolescence*. New York: Basic Books.

Inhelder, B., & Piaget, J. (1964). *The early growth of logic in the child*. New York: W. W. Norton.

Inhelder, B., & Piaget, J. (1979). Procedures et structures. *Archives de Psychologie, 47*, 165-176. Cited in R. Vuyk (1981). *Overview and critique of Piaget's genetic epistemology, 1965–1980*. New York: Academic Press.

Inhelder, B., Sinclair, H., & Bovet, M. (1974). *Learning and the development of cognition*. Cambridge, MA: Harvard Univ. Press.

Iosub, S., Fuchs, M., Bingol, N., Stone, R. K., & Gromisch, D. S. (1981). Long-term follow-up of three siblings with fetal alcohol syndrome. *Alcoholism: Clinical and Experimental Research, 5*, 523–527.

Isaacs, C. D. (1982). Treatment of child abuse: A review of the behavioral intervention. *Journal of Applied Behavior Analysis, 15*, 273–294.

Jacky, P. B., Beek, B., & Sutherland, G. R. (1983). Fragile sites in chromosomes: Possible model for the study of spontaneous chromosome breakage. *Science, 220*, 69–70.

Jacobs, J. W. (1982). The effect of divorce on fathers: An overview of the literature. *American Journal of Psychiatry, 139*, 1235–1241.

Jacobson, C. D., & Gorski, R. A. (1981). Neurogenesis of the sexually dimorphic nucleus of the preoptic area in the rat. *Journal of Comparative Neurology, 196*, 519–529.

Jacobson, H. N. (1981). Nutritional risks of pregnancy during adolescence. In E. R. McAnarney & G. Stickle (Eds.), *Pregnancy and childbearing during adolescence: Research priorities for the 1980s*. New York: Alan R. Liss.

Jacobson, S. W. (1979). Matching behavior in the young infant. *Child Development, 50*, 425–430.

James, W. P. T., & Sahakian, B. J. (1981). Overgrowth: Energetic significance in relation to obesity. *Progress in Clinical and Biological Research, 61*, 25–53.

Jarvik, L. F., Klodin, V., & Matsuyama, S. S. (1973). Human aggression and the extra Y chromosome. *American Psychologist, 28*, 674–683.

Jeans, P. C., Smith, M. B., & Stearns, G. (1955). Incidence of prematurity in relation to maternal nutrition. *Journal of the American Dietary Association, 31*, 576–581.

Jeffery, R. W. (1976). The influence of symbolic and motor rehearsal on observational learning. *Journal of Research in Personality, 10*, 116–127.

Jeffrey, W. E. (1980). The developing brain and child development. In M. C. Wittrock (Ed.), *The brain and psychology*. New York: Academic Press.

Jelliffe, D. B., & Jelliffe, E. F. P. (1979). Early infant nutrition: breast feeding. In M. Winick (Ed.), *Nutrition: Pre and Postnatal development*. New York: Plenum Publishing.

Jencks, C., Smith, M., Acland, H., Bane, M. J., Cohen, D., Gintin, H., Heyns, B., & Michelson, S. (1972). *Inequality: A reassessment of the effect of family and schooling in America.* New York: Harper & Row.

Jensen, A. R. (1972). *Genetics and education.* New York: Harper & Row.

Jensen, A. R. (1980). *Bias in Mental Testing.* New York: Free Press.

Jensen, A. R. (1981a). *Straight talk about mental tests.* New York: Free Press.

Jensen, A. R. (1981b). Reaction time and intelligence. In M. Friedman, J. P. Das, & N. O'Connor (Eds.), *Intelligence and learning.* New York: Plenum Publishing.

Jensen, A. R. (1982). Bias in mental testing: A final word. *The Behavioral and Brain Sciences, 5,*337–338.

Jensen, A. R., & Munro, E. (1979). Reaction time, movement time, and intelligence. *Intelligence, 3,* 121–126.

Jensen, A. R., & Reynolds, C. R. (1983). Sex difference on the WISC-R. *Personality and Individual Differences, 4,* 223–226.

Jensen, A. R., Schafer, E. W. P., & Crinella, F. M. (1981). Reaction time, evoked brain potentials and psychometric *g* in the severely retarded. *Intelligence, 5,* 179–197.

Joffe, J. M. (1979). Influence of drug exposure of the father on perinatal outcome. *Clinics in Perinatology, 6,* 21– 36.

Johanson, D. C., & Edey, M. (1981). *Lucy: The beginnings of humankind.* New York: Simon & Schuster.

Johnson, C. (1977). *Two community protective service systems: Nature and effectiveness of service intervention.* Athens GA: Regional Institute of Social Welfare Research.

Johnson, D. S. (1981). Naturally acquired learned helplessness: The relationship of school failure to achievement behavior, attributions and self-concept. *Journal of Educational Psychology, 73,* 174–180.

Johnson-Laird, P. N., & Wason, P. C. (1977). *Thinking: Readings in cognitive science.* Cambridge: Cambridge University Press.

Jones, K. L., & Smith, D. W. (1973). Recognition of the fetal alcohol syndrome in early infancy. *Lancet, 2,* 999–1001.

Jones, K. L., Smith, D. W., Streissguth, A. P., & Myrianthopoulos, N. C. (1974). Outcome in offspring of chronic alcoholic women. *Lancet, 1,* 1076–1078.

Joslyn, W. D. (1973). Androgen-induced social dominance in infant female rhesus monkeys. *Journal of Child Psychology and Psychiatry, 14,* 137–145.

Kaback, M. M. (1977). *Tay-Sachs disease: Screening and prevention.* New York: Alan R. Liss.

Kaczalak, C. M. (1981, April). *Sex-role identity, stereotypes and their relationships to achievement attitudes.* Paper presented at Society for Research in Child Development, Boston, MA.

Kadushin, A., & Martin, J. A. (1981). *Child abuse: An interactional event.* New York: Columbia University Press.

Kagan, J. (1969). Inadequate evidence and illogical conclusions. *Harvard Educational Review, 39,* 274–277.

Kagan, J. (1970). The determinant of attention in infancy. *American Scientist, 58,* 298–306.

Kagan, J. (1971). *Change and continuity in infancy.* New York: John Wiley & Sons.

Kagan, J. (1979a). The form of early development: Continuity and discontinuity and emergent competences. *Archives of General Psychiatry, 36,* 1047–1054.

Kagan, J. (1979b). Reflections on infancy. *Young Children, 34,* 4–10.

Kagan, J. (1981). *The second year.* Cambridge, MA: Harvard Univ. Press.

Kagan, J., & Lewis, M. (1965). Studies of attention in the human infant. *Merrill-Palmer Quarterly, 11,* 95–127.

Kagan, J., Kearsley, R. B., & Zelazo, P. R. (1978). *Infancy: Its place in human development.* Cambridge, MA: Harvard Univ. Press.

Kagan, J., Klein, R. E., Finley, G. E., & Rogoff, B. (1977). A study in cognitive development. *Annals of the New York Academy of Science, 285,* 374–388.

Kagan, J., Rosman, B. L., Day, D., Albert, J., & Philips, W. (1964). Information processing in the child. *Psychological Monographs, 78,* No. 578.

Kagan, S., Zahn, G. L., Widaman, K., Schwarzwald, J., & Tyrrell, G. (1984). Classroom structural bias. In R. Slavin, S. Sharan, S. Kagan, R. Hertz-Lazarowitz, C. Webb, & R. Schmuck (Eds.), *Learning to cooperate, cooperating to learn.* New York: Plenum Publishing.

Kaij, L. (1957). Drinking habits in twins. *Acta Genetic et Statistica Medica, 7,* 437–441.

Kail, R., & Bisanz, J. (1982). Cognitive development: An information-processing perspective. In R. Vasta (Ed.), *Strategies and techniques of child study.* New York: Academic Press.

Kamii, C. (1981). Application of Piaget's theory of education: The preoperational level. In I. E. Sigel, D. M. Brodzinsky, & R. M. Golinkoff (Eds.), *New Directions in Piagetian theory and practice.* Hillsdale, NJ: Lawrence Erlbaum.

Kamii, C., & DeVries, R. (1978). *Physical knowledge in preschool education.* Englewood Cliffs, NJ: Prentice-Hall.

Kan, Y. W., Golbus, M. S., & Trecartin, R. (1976). Prenatal diagnosis of sickle cell anemia. *New England Journal of Medicine, 294,* 1039–1040.

Kandel, D. B. (1978). Homophily, selection, and socialization in adolescent friendships. *American Journal of Sociology, 36,* 306–312.

Kaplan, S. J., & Pelcovitz, D. (1982). Child abuse and neglect and sexual abuse. *Psychiatric Clinics of North America, 5,* 321–332.

Karenyi, T. D., & Chitkara, U. (1981). Selective birth in twin pregnancy with discordancy for Down's syndrome. *New England Journal of Medicine, 304,* 1525–1527.

Kato, H. (1971). Mortality in children exposed to the A-bombs while in utero. *American Journal of Epidemiology, 93,* 435–442.

Katz, A. J. (1979). Lone fathers: Perspectives and implications for family policy. *The Family Coordinator, 28,* 521–528.

Kavanaugh, R. D., & Jirkovsky, A. M. (1982). Parental speech to young children: A longitudinal analysis. *Merrill Palmer Quarterly, 28,* 287–311.

Kaye, K. (1982). *The mental and social life of babies.* Chicago: University of Chicago Press.

Kaye, K., & Charney, R. (1980). How mothers maintain "Dialogue" with two-year-olds. In D. R. Olson (Ed.), *The social foundations of language and thought.* New York: W. W. Norton.

Kaye, K., & Marcus, J. (1981). Infant imitation: The sensory motor agenda. *Developmental Psychology*, *17*, 258–265.

Keasey, C. B. (1971). Social participation as a factor in the moral development of preadolescents. *Developmental Psychology*, *5*, 216–220.

Keating, D. P. (1979). Adolescent thinking. In J. Adelson (Ed.), *Handbook of Adolescence*. New York: John Wiley & Sons.

Keating, D. P., & Bobbitt, B. (1978). Individual and developmental differences in cognitive processing components of mental ability. *Child Development*, *49*, 155–169.

Kee, D. W., Bell, T. S., & Davis, B. R. (1981). Developmental changes in the effects of presentation mode on the storage and retrieval of noun pairs in children's recognition memory. *Child Development*, *52*, 268–279.

Keller, F. S., & Schoenfeld, W. N. (1950). *Principles of psychology*. New York: Appleton-Century-Crofts.

Kempe, C. H. (1978). Sexual abuse, another hidden pediatric problem: The 1977 C. Anderson Aldrich lecture. *Pediatrics*, *62*, 382–389.

Kempe, R. S., & Kempe, C. H. (1978). *Child abuse*. Cambridge MA: Harvard Univ. Press.

Kempthorne, O., & Wolins, L. (1982). Testing reveals a big social problem. *The Behavioral and Brain Sciences*, *5*, 327–336.

Kendall, C. R., Borkowski, J. G., & Cavanaugh, J. C. (1980). Metamemory and the transfer of an interrogative strategy by EMR children. *Intelligence*, *4*, 255–270.

Kessen, W. (1965). *The child*. New York: John Wiley & Sons.

Kessler, D. B., & Newberger, E. H. (1981). At risk: The developing infant. *Children Today*, *10*, 10–14.

Kessler, S. (1979). The psychological foundations of genetic counseling. In S. Kessler (Ed.), *Genetic Counseling: Psychological dimensions*. New York: Academic Press.

Killen, M., & Uzgiris, I. C. (1981). Imitation of actions with objects: The role of social meaning. *Journal of Genetic Psychology*, *138*, 219–23.

Kimble, D. P. (1977). *Psychology as a biological science* (2d ed.). Santa Monica, CA: Goodyear Publishing.

Kitzinger, S. (1981). *The complete book of pregnancy and childbirth*. New York: Alfred A. Knopf.

Klahr, D. (1980). Information processing models of intellectual development. In R. H. Kluwe & H. Spada (Eds.), *Developmental models of thinking*. New York: Academic Press.

Klaus, M. H., & Kennell, J. H. (1976). *Maternal-infant bonding: The impact of early separation or loss on family development*. St. Louis: C. V. Mosby.

Klaus, M. H., & Kennell, J. H. (1982). *Parent-infant bonding*. St. Louis: C. V. Mosby.

Klineberg, O. (1952). Racial and national differences in mental traits. In W. Monroe (Ed.), *Encyclopaedia of educational research. (rev. ed.). New York: Macmillan.*

*Knight, E. W. (1940). Twenty centuries of education*. Lexington, MA: Ginn.

Koch, R., Azen, C. G., Friedman, E. G., & Williamson, M. L. (1982). Preliminary report on the effects of diet discontinuation in PKU. *Journal of Pediatrics*, *100*, 870–875.

Kochupillai, N., Verma, I. C., Grewal, M. S., & Ramalingaswami, V. (1976). Down's syndrome and related abnormalities in an area of high background radiation in coastal Kerala. *Nature, 262,* 60–61.

Kofsky, E. (1966). A scalogram study of classificatory development. *Child Development, 37,* 191–204.

Kogan, N. (1983). Stylistic variation in childhood and adolescence: Creativity, metaphor, and cognitive styles. In J. H. Flavell & E. M. Markman (Eds.), *Handbook of Child Psychology* (Vol. 4). New York: John Wiley & Sons.

Kogan, N., & Pangrove, E. (1972). Creative ability over a five-year span. *Child Development, 43,* 427–442.

Kohlberg, L. (1958). *The development of modes of moral thinking and choice in the years 10 to 16.* Unpublished doctoral dissertation, University of Chicago.

Kohlberg, L. (1976). Moral stages and moralization: The cognitive-developmental approach. In T. Lickona (Ed.), *Moral development and behavior: Theory, research, and social issues.* New York: Holt, Rinehart & Winston.

Kohlberg, L. (1981). *The philosophy of moral development.* New York: Harper & Row.

Kolata, G. (1983). Huntington's disease gene located. *Science, 222,* 913–015.

Komrower, G. M., Sardharwalla, I. B., Coutts, J. M., & Ingham, D. (1979). Management of maternal phenylketonuria: An emerging clinical problem. *British Medical Journal, 1,* 1383–1387.

Korbin, J. E. (1981). *Child abuse and neglect: Cross-cultural perspectives.* Berkeley CA: University of California Press.

Korner, A. F. (1974). Methodological considerations in studying sex differences in the behavioral functioning of newborns. In R. C. Friedman (Ed.), *Sex differences in behavior.* New York: John Wiley & Sons.

Kossan, N. (1981). Developmental differences in concept acquisition strategies. *Child Development, 52,* 290–298.

Kotelchuck, M. (1976). The infant's relationship to the father: Experimental evidence. In M. E. Lamb (Ed.), *The role of the father in child development.* New York: John Wiley & Sons.

Kovisto, M., Herva, R., & Linna, S. (1981). Serial duplication of 10 (q21-q22) in a mentally retarded boy with congenital malformations. *Human Genetics, 57,* 224–225.

Krashen, S. D. (1975). The critical period for language acquisition and its possible bases. *Annals of the New York Academy of Sciences, 263,* 211–224.

Krauss, R. M., & Glucksberg, F. (1977). Social and nonsocial speech. *Scientific American, 236,* 100–105.

Krebs, E. G. (1969). *The Wechsler Preschool and Primary Scale of Intelligence and prediction of reading achievement in first grade.* Doctoral dissertation, Rutgers, The State University.

*Kreutzer, M. A., Leonard, C., & Flavell, J. H. (1975). An interview study of children's knowledge about memory. Monographs of the Society for Research in Child Development, No. 159.*

Kringlen, E. (1966). Schizophrenia in twins, an epidemiological-clinical study. *Psychiatry, 29,* 172–184.

Krous, H. F., Campbell, G. A., Fowler, M. W., Catron, A. C., & Farber, J. P.

(1981). Maternal nicotine administration and fetal brain stem disease: A model with implications for sudden infant death syndrome. *American Journal of Obstetrics and Gynecology, 140,* 743–746.

Kuczaj, S. A., II (1983). Language play and language acquisition. In H. W. Reese (Ed.), *Advances in child development and behavior* (Vol. 17) New York: Academic Press.

Kuczaj, S. A., II (1982). *Language development: Syntax and semantics* (Vol. 1). Hillsdale, NJ: Lawrence Erlbaum.

Kuhn, D. (1972). Mechanisms of change in the development of cognitive structures. *Child Development, 43,* 833–844.

Kuhn, D. (1976). Short-term longitudinal evidence for the sequentiality of Kohlberg's early stages of moral development. *Developmental Psychology, 12,* 162–166.

Kuhn, D. (1977). Conditional reasoning in children. *Developmental Psychology, 13,* 342–353.

Kuhn, D. (1981). The role of self-directed activity in cognitive development. In I. E. Sigel, D. M. Brodzinsky, & R. M. Golinkoff (Eds.), *New directions in Piagetian theory and practice.* Hillsdale, NJ: Lawrence Erlbaum.

Kuhn, D., & Angelev, J. (1976). An experimental study of the development of formal operational thought. *Child Development, 47,* 697–706.

Kuhn, D., & Ho, V. (1980). Self-directed activity and cognitive development. *Journal of Applied Developmental Psychology, 1,* 119–133.

Kuhn, D., & Phelps, K. (1984). Microgenetic studies of scientific reasoning. In H. W. Reese & L. P. Lipsitt (Eds.), *Advances in child development and behavior* (Vol. 18). New York: Academic Press.

Kurdek, L. A., Blisk, D., & Siesky, A. E. (1981). Correlates of children's long-term adjustment to their parents' divorce. *Developmental Psychology, 17,* 565–579.

Kurtz, B. E., Reid, M. K., Borkowski, J. G., & Cavanaugh, J. C. (1982). On the reliability and validity of children's metamemory. *Bulletin of the Psychonomic Society, 19,* 137–140.

LaBarba, R. C. (1981). *Foundations of developmental psychology.* New York: Academic Press.

Ladd, G. W. (1981). Effectiveness of a social learning method for enhancing children's social interaction and peer acceptance. *Child Development, 52,* 171–178.

Lagerspetz, K. M. J., & Lagertspetz, K. Y. H. (1983). Genes and aggression. In E. C. Simmel, M. E. Hahn, & J. K. Walters (Eds.), *Aggressive behavior: Genetic and neural approaches.* Hillsdale, NJ: Lawrence Erlbaum.

Laidler, K. (1980). *The talking ape.* New York: Stein & Day Publishers.

Lamaze, F. (1958). *Painless childbirth, psychoprophylactic method.* Chicago: Henry Regnery.

Lamb, M. E. (1978). Qualitative aspects of mother- and father-infant attachments. *Infant Behavior and Development, 1,* 265–275.

Lamb, M. E. (1981). *The role of the father in child development* (rev. ed.). New York: John Wiley & Sons.

Lamb, M. E. (1982a). Parental behavior and child development in nontraditional families: An introduction. In M. E. Lamb (Ed.), *Nontraditional Families.* Hillsdale, NJ: Lawrence Erlbaum.

Lamb, M. E. (1982b). Maternal employment and child development: A review. In M. E. Lamb (Ed.), *Nontraditional Families*. Hillsdale, NJ: Lawrence Erlbaum.

Lamb, M. E. (1982c). Early contact and maternal-infant bonding; One decade later. *Pediatrics, 70,* 763–768.

Lamb, M. F. (1982d). Paternal influences on early socio-emotional development. *Journal of Child Psychology and Psychiatry and Allied Disciplines, 23,* 185–190.

Lamb, M. E., & Bronson, S. K. (1980). Fathers in the context of family influences: Past, present, and future. *School Psychology Review, 9,* 336–353.

Lamb, M. E., & Levine, J. A. (1983). The Swedish parental insurance policy: An experiment in social engineering. In M. E. Lamb & A. Sagi (Eds.), *Fatherhood and family policy*. Hillsdale, NJ: Lawrence Erlbaum.

Lamb, M. E., Frodi, A. M., Hwang, C., & Frodi, M. (1982). Varying degrees of paternal involvement in infant care: Attitudinal and behavioral correlates. In M. E. Lamb (Ed.), *Nontraditional families: Parenting and child development*. Hillsdale, NJ: Lawrence Erlbaum.

Lamb, M. E., Frodi, A. M., Hwang, C., Frodi, M., & Steinberg, J. (1982). Mother- and father-infant interaction involving play and holding in traditional and nontraditional Swedish families. *Developmental Psychology, 18,* 215–221.

Lambert, N. M. (1981). Psychological evidence in Larry P. v. Wilson Riles: An evaluation by a witness for the defense. *American Psychologist, 36,* 937–952.

Lambert, W. E. (1981). Bilingualism and language acquisition. *Annals of the New York Academy of Sciences, 379,* 9–22.

Lane, H. (1976). *The wild boy of Aveyron*. Cambridge, MA: Harvard Univ. Press.

Lange, G. (1978). Organization-related processes in children's recall. In P. A. Ornstein (Ed.), *Memory development in children*. Hillsdale, NJ: Lawrence Erlbaum.

Langer, J. (1969). *Theories of development*. New York: Holt, Rinehart & Winston.

Langer, J. (1980). *The origins of logic: Six to 12 months*. New York: Academic Press.

Langlois, J. H., & Downs, A. C. (1980). Mothers, fathers, and peers as socialization agents of sex-typed play behaviors in young children. *Child Development, 51,* 1217–1247.

Langlois, J. H., & Stephan, C. (1977). The effects of physical attractiveness and ethnicity on children's behavioral attributions and peer preferences. *Child Development, 48,* 1694–1698.

Larry P. v. Wilson Riles. (1972). U.S. District Court for the Northern District of California, No. C-71-2270RFP.

Larsen, G. Y. (1977). Methodology in developmental psychology: An examination of research on Piagetian theory. *Child Development, 48,* 1160–1166.

Latham, M. C. (1978). Nutrition and culture. In B. Winikoff (Ed.), *Nutrition and national policy*. Cambridge, MA: MIT Press.

Lawrence, V. W., Kee, D. W., & Hellige, J. B. (1980). Developmental differences in visual backward masking. *Child Development, 51,* 1081–1089.

Lawry, J. A., Welsh, M. C., & Jeffrey, W. E. (1983). Cognitive tempo and complex problem solving. *Child Development, 54,* 912–920.

Lawson, M. J. (1980). Metamemory: Making decisions about strategies. In J. R. Kirby & J. B. Biggs (Eds.), *Cognition, development and instruction*. New York: Academic Press.

Lazar, I., & Darlington, R. (1982). Lasting effects of early education: A report from the consortium for longitudinal studies. *Monographs of the Society for Research in Child Development, 47*, No. 195.

Lazarus, A. A. (1971). *Behavior therapy and beyond.* New York: McGraw-Hill.

Leahy, R. L. (1981). Parental practices and the development of moral judgment and self-image disparity during adolescence. *Developmental Psychology, 17*, 580–594.

Leask, J., Haber, R. N., & Haber, R. B. (1969). Eidetic imagery in children: II. Longitudinal and experimental results. *Psychonomic Monograph Supplements, 3*, 25–48.

Leboyer, F. (1975). *Birth without violence.* New York: Alfred A. Knopf.

Lee, C. L. (1981, April). Perceived difficult temperament and mother-toddler interaction sequences. Paper presented at the Society for Research in Child Development, Boston, MA.

Lefkowitz, M. M. (1981). Smoking during pregnancy: Long-term effects on offspring. *Developmental Psychology, 17*, 192–194.

Lehrke, R. G. (1978). Sex linkage: A biological basis for greater male variability. In R. T. Osborne, C. E. Noble, & N. Weyl (Eds.), *Human variation: The biopsychology of age, race, and sex.* New York: Academic Press.

Leib, S. A., Benfield, D. G., & Guidubaldi, J. (1980). Effects of early intervention and stimulation on the preterm infant. *Pediatrics, 66*, 83–90.

Leiderman, P. H. (1981). Human mother-infant social bonding: Is there a sensitive phase? In K. Immelmann, G. W. Barlow, L. Petrinovich, & M. Main (Eds.), *Behavioral development: The Bielefeld interdisciplinary project.* New York: Cambridge University Press.

Lemoine, P., Harousseau, H., Borteyru, J. P., & Menuet, J. C. (1968). Les enfants de parent alcooliques: Anomalies observees a propos de 127 cas. *Quest Medical, 25*, 452–458.

Lempers, J. D., Flavell, E. R., & Flavell, J. H. (1977). The development in very young children of tacit knowledge concerning visual perception. *Genetic Psychology Monographs, 95*, 3–53.

Lenneberg, E. (1967). *Biological foundations of language.* New York: John Wiley & Sons.

Leopold, W. F. (1939). *Speech development of a bilingual child: A linguist's record: Vocabulary growth in the first two years* (Vol. 1). Evanston, IL: Northwestern University Press.

Leung, E. H. L., & Rheingold, H. L. (1981). Development of pointing as a social gesture. *Developmental Psychology, 17*, 215–220.

LeVay, S., Hubel, D. H., & Wiesel, T. N. (1980). The development of ocular dominance columns in normal and deprived monkeys. *Journal of Comparative Neurology, 191*, 1–51.

Levine, L. (1980). *Biology of the gene.* St. Louis: C. V. Mosby.

Levy, H. L., Kaplan, G. N., & Erickson, A. M. (1982). Comparison of treated and untreated pregnancies in a mother with phenylketonuria. *Journal of Pediatrics, 100*, 876–880.

Levy-Shiff, R. (1982). The effects of father absence on young children in mother-headed families. *Child Development, 53*, 1400–1408.

Lewin, J. (October, 1981). How you can help prevent child molesting. *Parade Magazine*.

Lewis, M. (1982). The social network systems model: Toward a theory of social development. In T. M. Field, A. Huston, H. C. Quay, L. Troll, & G. E. Finley (Eds.), *Review of Human Development*. New York: John Wiley & Sons.

Lewis, M., & Brooks-Gunn, J. (1981). Visual attention at three months as a predictor of functioning at two years of age. *Intelligence, 5,* 131–140.

Lewis, M., Feiring, C., McGuffog, C., & Jaskir, J. (1984). Predicting psychopathology in six-year-olds from early social relations. *Child Development, 55,* 123–136.

Liben, L. S. (1978). The development of deaf children: An overview of issues. In L. S. Liben (Ed.), *Deaf children: Developmental perspectives*. New York: Academic Press.

Liberman, A. M. (1974). Language processing: State-of-the-art report. In R. Stark (Ed.), *Sensory Capabilities of Hearing Impaired Children*, Baltimore: University Park Press.

Liberman, A. M. (1980). On finding that speech is special. *American Psychologist, 37,* 148–167.

Licht, B. G., & Dweck, C. S. (1984). Sex differences in achievement orientations: Consequences for academic choices and attainments. In M. Marland (Ed.), *Sex differentiation and schooling*. London: Heinemann Educational Books.

Lieberman, J. J. (1976). Childbirth practices: From darkness into light. *Journal of Obstetric, Gynecologic and Neonatal Nursing, 8,* 41–45.

Liebert, R. M., Sprafkin, J. N., & Davidson, E. S. (1982). *The early window: Effects of television on children and youth*. Elmsford, NY: Pergamon Press.

Liederman, J., & Coryell, J. (1981). Right-hand preference facilitated by rightward turning biases during infancy. *Developmental Psychobiology, 14,* 439–450.

Lightcap, J. L., Kurland, J. A., & Burgess, R. L. (1982). Child abuse: A test of some predictions from evolutionary theory. *Ethology and Sociobiology, 3,* 61–67.

Lindsay, P. H., & Norman, D. A. (1977). *Human information processing*. New York: Academic Press.

Linehan, E. J. (1979). The trouble with dolphins. *National Geographic, 155,* 506–539.

Lipsitt, L. P., & Werner, J. S. (1981). The infancy of human learning processes. In E. S. Gollin (Ed.), *Developmental plasticity: Behavioral and biological aspects of variations in development*. New York: Academic Press.

Loeber, R., Weissman, W., & Reid, J. B. (1983). Family interactions of assaultive adolescents, stealers, and nondelinquents. *Journal of Abnormal Child Psychology, 11,* 1–14.

Loehlin, J. C., & Nichols, R. C. (1976). *Heredity, environment and personality: A study of 850 sets of twins*. Austin, TX: University of Texas Press.

Loevinger, J. (1976). *Ego development*. San Francisco: Jossey-Bass.

Londerville, S., & Main, M. (1981). Security of attachment, compliance and maternal training methods in the second year of life. *Developmental Psychology, 17,* 289–299.

London, P. (1970). The rescuers: Motivational hypotheses about Christians who saved

Jews from the Nazis. In J. Macaulay and L. Berkowitz (Eds.), *Altruism and help-ing behavior*. New York: Academic Press.

Longstreth, L. E. (1981). Revisiting Skeels' final study: A critique. *Developmental Psychology, 17*, 620–625.

Lorenz, K. Z. (1943). Die angeborenen formen moglicher erfahrung. *Zeitschrift für Tierpsychologie, 5*, 235–409.

Lorenz, K. Z. (1965). *Evolution and modification of behavior*. Chicago: University of Chicago Press.

Lorenz, K. Z. (1966). *On aggression*. New York: Harcourt, Brace & World.

Lovaas, O. I. (1961). Effect of exposure to symbolic aggression on aggressive behavior. *Child Development, 32*, 37–44.

Lovaas, O. I., Freitag, G., Gold, V. J., & Kassorla, I. C. (1965). Experimental studies in childhood schizophrenia: Analysis of self-destructive behavior. *Journal of Experimental Child Psychology, 2*, 67–84.

Lowenstein, J. S., & Koopman, E. J. (1978). A comparison of the self-esteem between boys living with single-parent mothers and single-parent fathers. *Journal of Divorce, 2* 195–208.

Lowenstein, L. F. (1982). Effects of lead poisoning. *British Journal of Clinical and Social Psychiatry, 1*, 13–15.

Lowry, J. H., & Associates. (1984). *Survey of magnet schools: Analyzing a model for quality integrated education*. Washington, DC: U.S. Department of Education.

Luepnitz, D. A. (1982). *Child Custody*. Lexington, MA: Lexington Books.

Lumsden, C. J., & Wilson, E. O. (1981). *Genes, mind, and culture: The coevolutionary process*. Cambridge, MA: Harvard Univ. Press.

Lund, R. D. (1978). *Development and plasticity of the brain*. New York: Oxford University Press.

Luria, A. R. (1968). *The mind of a mnemonist*. New York: Basic Books.

Luria, A. R. (1976). *Cognitive development: Its cultural and social foundations*. Cambridge, MA: Harvard Univ. Press.

Lynch, M. A., & Roberts, J. (1982). *Consequences of child abuse*. New York: Academic Press.

Lynn, R. (1982). IQ in Japan and the United States shows a growing disparity. *Nature, 297*, 222–223.

Lytton, H. (1980). *Parent-child interaction*. New York: Plenum Publishing.

MacCarthy, D. (1977). Deprivation dwarfish viewed as a form of child abuse. In A. W. Franklin (Ed.), *The challenge of child abuse*. New York: Academic Press.

Maccoby, E. E., & Jacklin, C. N. (1974). *The psychology of sex differences*. Stanford, CA: Stanford University Press.

Maccoby, E. E., & Jacklin, C. N. (1980). Sex differences in aggression: A rejoinder and reprise. *Child Development, 51*, 964–980.

Maccoby, E. E., & Jacklin, C. N. (1984, April). As cited by C. Turklington. Parents found to ignore sex stereotypes. *APA Monitor, 15*,12.

Maccoby, E. E., Kahn, A. J., & Everett, B. A. (1983). The role of psychological research in the formation of policies affecting children. *American Psychologist, 38*, 80–85.

MacKinnon, C. E., Brody, G. H., & Stoneman, Z. (1982). The effects of divorce and maternal employment on the home environments of preschool children. *Child Development*, *53*, 1392–1399.

MacLusky, N. J., & Naftolin, F. (1981). Sexual differentiation of the central nervous system. *Science*, *211*, 1294–1302.

Madigan, E. C. (1957). Are sex mortality differentials biologically caused? *Milbank Memorial Fund Quarterly*, *35*, 202–223.

Madsen, M. C., & Shapira, A. (1977). Cooperation and challenge in four cultures. *Journal of Social Psychology*, *102*, 189–195.

Magenis, R. E., Overton, K. M., Chamberlin, J., Brady, T., & Lovrien, E. (1977). Parental origin of the extra chromosome in Down's syndrome. *Human Genetics*, *37*, 7–16.

Mahler, M. S., Pine, F., & Bergman, A. (1975). *The psychological birth of the human infant: Symbiosis and individuation*. New York: Basic Books.

Main, M. (1981a). Abusive and rejective infants. In N. Frude (Ed.), *Psychological approaches to child abuse*. Totowa, NJ: Rowman & Littlefield.

Main, M. (1981b). Avoidance in the service of attachment. In K. Immelmann, G. W. Barlow, L. Petrinovich, & M. Main (Eds.), *Behavioral development: The Bielefeld Interdisciplinary Project*. London: Cambridge University Press.

Main, M., & Weston, D. R. (1981). The quality of the toddler's relationship to mothers and to fathers: Related conflict behavior and the readiness to establish new relationships. *Child Development*, *52*, 932–940.

Marek, G. R. (1982). Toscanini's memory. In U. Neisser (Ed.), *Memory observed*. San Francisco: W. H. Freeman.

Markman, E. M. (1981). Two different principles of conceptual organization. In M. E. Lamb & A. L. Brown (Eds.), *Advances in developmental psychology* (Vol. 1). Hillsdale, NJ: Lawrence Erlbaum.

Marshall, H. H. (1981). Open classrooms: Has the term outlived its usefulness? *Review of Educational Research*, *51*, 181–192.

Martin, H. P., & Beezley, P. (1976a). Therapy for abusive parents: Its effects on the child. In H. P. Martin (Ed.), *The abused child: A multidisciplinary approach to developmental issues and treatment*. Cambridge, MA: Ballinger Publishing.

Martin, H. P., & Beezley, P. (1976b). Personality of abused children. In H. P. Martin (Ed.), *The Abused child: A multidisciplinary approach to developmental issues and treatment*. Cambridge, MA: Ballinger Publishing.

Martin, P. P., & Wachs, T. D. (1981, April). A longitudinal study of temperament and its correlates in the first year of life. Paper presented at the Society for Research in Child Development, Boston, MA.

Massie, R. & Massie, S. (1975). *The journey*. New York: Alfred A. Knopf.

Matarazzo, J. D. (1972). *Wechsler's measurement and appraisal of adult intelligence* (5th ed.). Baltimore: Williams & Wilkins.

Matas, L., Arend, R. A., & Sroufe, L. A. (1978). Continuity of adaptation in the second year: The relationship between quality of attachment and later competence. *Child Development*, *49*, 547–556.

Maternity ward nightmare. (1978). *Time, 112*, (9), p. 42.

Mattsson, A., Schalling, D., Olweus, D., Low, H., & Svensson, J. (1980). Plasma testosterone, aggressive behavior and personality dimensions in young male delinquents. *Journal of American Academy of Child Psychiatry, 19,* 476–490.

Maugh, T. H. (1981a). A new understanding of sickle cell emerges. *Science, 211,* 265–267.

Maugh, T. H. (1981b). Sickle cell (II): Many agents near trials. *Science, 211,* 468–470.

Maurer, D., & Barrera, M. (1981). Infants' perception of natural and distorted arrangements of a schematic face. *Child Development, 52,* 196–202.

Maurer, D., & Salapatek, P. (1976). Developmental changes in the scanning of faces by young infants. *Child Development, 47,* 523–527.

Mayer, M. D., Harris, W., & Wimpfheimer, S. (1936). Therapeutic abortion by means of X-ray. *American Journal of Obstetrics and Gynecology, 18,* 179–183.

McBroom, P. (1980). *Behavioral genetics.* Washington, DC: U.S. Department of Health, Education, and Welfare.

McCall, R. B. (1977). Childhood IQs as predictors of adult educational and occupational status. *Science, 197,* 484–485.

McCall, R. B. (1981). Early predictors of later IQ: The search continues. *Intelligence, 5,* 141–148.

McCall, R. B., & Kennedy, C. B. (1980). Subjective uncertainty, variability of experience, and the infant's response to discrepancies. *Child Development, 51,* 285–287.

McCall, R. B., & McGhee, P. E. (1977). The discrepancy hypothesis of attention and affect in human infants. In I. C. Uzgiris & F. Weizmann (Eds.), *The structuring of experience.* New York: Plenum Publishing.

McCall, R. B., Eichorn, D. H., & Hogarty, P. S. (1977). Transitions in early mental development. *Monographs of the Society for Research in Child Development, 42,* No. 3.

McCall, R. B., Kennedy, C. B., & Appelbaum, M. I. (1977). Magnitude of discrepancy and the distribution of attention in infants. *Child Development, 48,* 772–786.

McCarthy, E. D., Laugner, T. S., Gersten, J. C., Eisenberg, J. G., & Orzeck, L. (1975). Violence and behavior disorders. *Journal of Communication, 25,* 71–85.

McCarthy, J. (1981). Social consequences of childbearing during adolescence. In E. R. McAnarney & G. Stickle (Eds.), *Pregnancy and childbearing during adolescence.* New York: Alan R. Liss.

McClearn, G. E., & DeFries, J. C. (1973). *Introduction to behavioral genetics.* San Francisco: W. H. Freeman.

McCord, J. (1979). Some child-rearing antecedents of criminal behavior in adult men. *Journal of Personality and Social Psychology, 37,* 1477–1486.

McDonald, J. (1980). A day at a time: Living with sickle cell. *Essence, 11,* 50–55.

McFadden R. D. (1979, March 10). EPA, citing miscarriages, restricts 2 herbicides. *The New York Times,* Section 2, p. 10.

McFarlane, A. (1977). *The psychology of childbirth.* Cambridge, MA: Harvard Univ. Press.

McGhee, P. E. (1979). *Humor: Its origin and development.* San Francisco: W. H. Freeman.

McGrath, E. (1983, March 18). Confucian work ethic. *Time, 121*, 52.

McGraw, M. B., & Breeze, K. W. (1941). Quantitative studies in the development of erect locomotion. *Child Development, 12*, 267–303.

McGrew, W. C. (1972). *An ethological study of children's behavior.* New York: Academic Press.

McKay, H., Sinisterra, L., McKay, A., Gomez, H. S., & Lloreda, P. (1978). Cognitive growth in Columbian malnourished children. *Science, 200*, 270–278.

McKinney, J. P. (1980). Engagement style (agent vs. patient) in childhood and adolescence. *Human Development, 23*, 192–209.

McLaughlin, B. (1980). Differences and similarities between first- and second-language learning. *Annals of the New York Academy of Sciences, 379*, 23–32.

McNeil, D. G. (1978, August 1). Upstate waste site may endanger lives. *New York Times*, Section 1, p. 1.

McQuarrie, H. G. (1980). Home delivery controversy. *Journal of the American Medical Association, 243*, 1747–1748.

Meadow, K. P. (1975). The development of deaf children. In E. M. Hetherington (Ed.), *Review of Child Development Research* (Vol. 5). Chicago: University of Chicago Press.

Mehler, J. (1982). Studies in the development of cognitive processes. In S. Strauss, (Ed.), *U-shaped behavioral growth.* New York: Academic Press.

Meichenbaum, D. (1977). *Cognitive-behavior modification.* New York: Plenum Publishing.

Meltzoff, A. N., & Moore, M. K. (1977). Imitation of facial and manual gestures by human neonates. *Science, 198*, 75–78.

Melyn, M. A., & White, D. T. (1973). Mental and developmental milestones of noninsitutionalized Down's syndrome children. *Pediatrics, 52*, 542–545.

Mendel, G. J. (1866). Versuche uber Pflanzen-Hybriden. *Verhandlunger des Naturforschunden Vereines in Bruenn, 4*, 3–47.

Mendels, J. (1974). Biological aspects of affective illness. In S. Arieti & E. B. Brody (Eds.), *Adult clinical psychiatry, Vol III of American handbook of psychiatry* (2d ed.). New York: Basic Books.

Mercer, J. R. (1977). Implications of current assessment procedures for Mexican-American children. *Bilingual Education.* California State University, Los Angeles: National Dissemination and Assessment Center.

Mercer, J. R. (1979). In defense of racially and culturally non-discriminatory assessment. *School Psychology Digest, 8*, 89–115.

Messer, S. B., & Brodinsky, D. M. (1981). Three-year stability of reflection-impulsivity in young adolescents. *Developmental Psychology, 17*, 848–850.

Meyer, M. B., & Tonascia, J. (1981). Long-term effects of prenatal X-ray of human females. *American Journal of Epidemiology, 114*, 327–335.

Michener, J. (1959). *Hawaii.* New York: Random House.

Mikkelsen, M., Fischer, G., Stene, J., Stene, E., & Petersen, R. (1976). Incidence study of Down's syndrome in Copenhagen, 1960–1971, with chromosome investigation. *Annals of Human Genetics, 40*, 177–182.

Milavsky, J. R., Kessler, R., Stipp, H., & Rubens, W. S. (1982). Television and aggression: Results of a panel study. In D. Pearl, L. Bouthilet, & J. Lazar (Eds.),

*Television and behavior: Ten years of scientific progress and implications for the eighties* (Vol. 2). Washington, DC: U.S. Government Printing Office.

Milich, R., Landau, S., Kilby, G., & Whitten, P. (1982). Preschool peer perceptions of the behavior of hyperactive and aggressive children. *Journal of Abnormal Child Psychology, 10,* 497–510.

Miller, N., & Maruyama, G. (1976). Ordinal position and peer popularity. *Journal of Personality and Social Psychology, 33,* 123–131.

Miller, P. H. (1983). *Theories of Developmental Psychology.* San Francisco: W. H. Freeman.

Miller, P. H., & Zalenski, R. (1982). Preschoolers' knowledge about attention. *Developmental Psychology, 18,* 871–875.

Miller, R. W., & Blot, W. J. (1972). Small head size after in-utero exposure to atomic radiation. *Lancet, 2,* 784–787.

Milunsky, A. (1979). The prenatal diagnosis of chromosomal disorders. In A. Milunsky (Ed.), *Genetic disorders and the fetus: Diagnosis, prevention, and treatment.* New York: Plenum Publishing.

Minturn, L., & Lambert, W. W. (1964). *Mothers in six cultures.* New York: John Wiley & Sons.

Minuchin, P. P., & Shapiro, E. K. (1983). The school as a context for social development. In E. M. Hetherington (Ed.), *Handbook of Child Psychology* (Vol. 4). New York: John Wiley & Sons.

Mischel, W., & Baker, N. (1975). Cognitive transformations of reward objects through instructions. *Journal of Personality and Social Psychology, 31,* 254–261.

Mischel, W., Ebbesen, E., & Zeiss, A. (1972). Cognitive and attentional mechanisms in delay of gratification. *Journal of Personality and Social Psychology, 21,* 204–218.

Modgil, S., & Modgil, C. (1976). *Piagetian research: Cross-cultural studies* (Vol. 8). Windsor: NFER Publishing, Test Div.

Moely, B. E. (1977). Organization factors in the development of memory. In R. V. Kail, Jr., & J. W. Hagen (Eds.), *Perspectives on the development of memory and cognition.* Hillsdale, NJ: Lawrence Erlbaum.

Moen, P. (1982). The two-provider family: Problems and potentials. In M. E. Lamb (Ed.), *Nontraditional Families.* Hillsdale, NJ: Lawrence Erlbaum.

Moghe, M., Patel, Z. M., Peter, J. J., & Ambani, L. M. (1981). Cytogenetic studies in a selected group of mentally retarded children. *Human Genetics, 58,* 184–187.

Mohs, M. (1982). IQ. *Discover, 3,* 18–25.

Molfese, D. L. (1977). Infant cerebral asymmetry. In S. J. Segalowitz & F. A. Gruber (Eds.), *Language development and neurological theory.* New York: Academic Press.

Money, J., & Ehrhardt, A. A. (1972). *Man and woman, boy and girl.* Baltimore: The Johns Hopkins Press.

Money, J., Klein, A., & Beck, J. (1979). Applied behavioral genetics: Counseling and psychotherapy in sex-chromosomal disorders. In S. Kessler (Ed.), *Genetic counseling: Psychological dimensions.* New York: Academic Press.

Moore, K. (1979, March). Symposium on object permanence. Society for the Research in Child Development, San Francisco.

Moore, M. G., Haskins, R., & McKinney, J. D. (1980). Classroom behavior of reflective and impulsive children. *Journal of Applied Developmental Psychology, 1*, 59–75.

Moore, T. (1968). Language and intelligence: A longitudinal study of the first eight years, Part II: Environmental correlates of mental growth. *Human Development, 11*, 1–18.

Morgan, T. H. (1905). Sex limited inheritance in Drosophila. *Science, 32*, 120–122.

Morishima, H. O., Yeh, M. N., & James, L. S. (1979). Reduced uterine blood flow and fetal hypoxemia with acute internal stress: Experimental observation in the pregnant baboon. *American Journal of Obstetrics and Gynecolocy, 134*, 270–275.

Morrison, F. J., & Manis, F. R. (1982). Cognitive processes and reading disability: A critique and proposal. In C. J. Brainerd & M. Pressley (Eds.), *Verbal processes in children*. New York: Springer-Verlag New York.

Morrow, J. F., Cohen, S. N., Chang, A. C. Y., Bayer, H. W., Goodman, H. M., Helling, R. B. (1974). Replication and transcription of eukaryotic DNA in Escherichia-coli. *Proceedings of the National Academy of Science, 71*, 1743–1747.

Moshman, D. (1979). Development of formal hypothesis-testing ability. *Developmental Psychology, 15*, 104–112.

Moskowitz, B. A. (1978). The acquisition of language. *Scientific American, 239*, 92–110.

Mosse, H. L. (1982). *The complete handbook of children's reading disorders*. New York: Human Sciences Press.

Mueller, E., & Brenner, J. (1977). The origins of social skills and interaction among playgroup toddlers. *Child Development, 48*, 854–861.

Mullen, N. (1983, June 15). Taking kids out of school to learn. *Los Angeles Times*, Section V, p. 22–23.

Muller, P. F., Campbell, H. E., Graham, W. E., Brittain, H., Fitzgerald, J. A., Hogan, M. A., Muller, V. H., & Rittenhouse, A. H. (1971). Perinatal factors and their relationship to mental retardation and other parameters of development. *American Journal of Obstetrics and Gynecology, 109*, 1205–1210.

Mullis, I. V. S. (1975). *Educational achievement and sex discrimination*. Denver: National Assessment of Educational Progress.

Mulvihill, J. J., Klimas, J. T., Stokes, D. C., & Risemberg, H. M. (1976). Fetal alcohol syndrome: Seven new cases. *American Journal of Obstetrics and Gynecology, 125*, 937–941.

Murakami, R. Nakamura, H. Mizojiri, T., Aida, M., & Matsuo, T. (1981). A study of brain development in low-birth-weight infants using computerized tomography. *Neuropediatrics, 12*, 132–142.

Murphy, L. B. (1937). *Social behavior and child personality*. New York: Columbia University Press.

Murray, A. D., Dolby, R. M., Nation, R. L., & Thomas, D. B. (1981). Effects of epidural anesthesia on newborns and their mothers. *Child Development, 52*, 71–82.

Mussen, P. H., & Eisenberg-Berg, N. (1977). *Roots of caring, sharing, and helping*. San Francisco: W. H. Freeman.

Mussen, P. H., Honzik, M. P., & Eichorn, D. H. (1982). Early adult antecedents of life satisfaction at age 70. *Journal of Gerontology, 37,* 316–322.

Naeye, R. L., Blanc, W., Leblanc, W., & Khatamee, M. A. (1973). Fetal complications of maternal heroin addiction: Abnormal growth, infections, and episodes of stress. *Journal of Pediatrics, 83,* 1055–1061.

Nagle, J. J. (1979). *Heredity and human affairs.* St. Louis: C. V. Mosby Co.

Nawas, M. M. (1971). Change in efficiency of ego functioning and complexity from adolescence to young adulthood. *Developmental Psychology, 4,412–415.*

Neimark, E. D. (1975). Intellectual development during adolescence. In F. D. Horowitz (Ed.), *Review of child development research* (Vol. 4). Chicago: University of Chicago Press.

Neimark, E. D. (1976). The natural history of spontaneous mnemonic activities under conditions of minimal experimental constraint. In A. D. Pick (Ed.), *Minnesota symposium on child psychology* (Vol. 10). Minneapolis MN: University of Minnesota Press.

Neimark, E. D. (1981). Confounding with cognitive style factors: An artifact explanation for the apparent nonuniversal incidence of formal operations. In I. E. Sigel, D. M. Brodzinsky, & R. M. Golinkoff (Eds.), *New directions in Piagetian theory and practice.* Hillsdale, NJ: Lawrence Erlbaum.

Neisser, U. (1967). *Cognitive Psychology.* New York: Appleton-Century-Crofts.

Neisser, U. (1976). *Cognition and reality.* San Francisco: W. H. Freeman.

Neisser, U. (1982). *Memory observed.* San Francisco: W. H. Freeman.

Nelson, K. (1973). Structure and strategy in learning to talk. *Monographs of the Society for Research in Child Development, 38,* No. 149.

Nelson, K. (1979). Explorations in the development of a functional semantic system. In W. Collins (Ed.), *The Minnesota symposia on child psychology: Children's language and communication* (Vol. 12). Hillsdale, NJ· Lawrence Erlbaum.

Nelson, K. (1981). Individual differences in language development: Implications for development and language. *Developmental Psychology, 17,* 170–187.

Nelson, K. B., & Ellenberg, J. H. (1981). Apgar scores as predictors of chronic neurologic disability. *Pediatrics, 68,* 36–44.

Nelson, K. E. (1980). Theories of the child's acqisition of syntax: A look at rare events and at necessary, catalytic, and irrelevant components of mother-child conversation. *Annals of the New York Academy of Sciences, 345,* 45–68.

Nelson, K., & Ross, G. (1980). The generalities and specifics of long-term memory in infants and young children. *Children's memory.* San Francisco: Jossey-Bass.

Nelson, L., Ingelman-Sundberg, A., & Wirsen, C. (1965). *A child is born.* New York: Delacorte Press.

Nelson, N. M., Enkin, M. W., Saigal, S., Bennett, K. J., Milner, R., & Sackett, D. L. (1980). A randomized clinical trial of the Leboyer approach to childbirth. *New England Journal of Medicine, 302,* 655–660.

Nesselroade, J. R., & Baltes, P. B. (1974). Adolescent personality development and historical change: 1970–1972. *Monographs of the Society for Research in Child Development, 39,* No. 154.

Nichols, R. C. (1966). The resemblance of twins in personality and interests. *National Merit Scholarship Corporation Research Reports, 2,* 1–23.

Ninio, A., & Bruner, J. (1978). The achievement and antecedents of labeling. *Journal of Child Language*, 5, 1–16.

Nisan, M., & Kohlberg, L. (1982). Universality and variation in moral judgment: A longitudinal and cross-sectional study in Turkey. *Child Development*, 53, 865–876.

Noell, E. A. (1983). Reading. In C. T. Wren (Ed.), *Language learning disabilities*. Rockville, MD: Aspen Systems.

Northway, M. L., & Weld, L. (1957). *Sociometric testing: A guide for teachers*. Toronto: University of Toronto Press.

O'Banion, D., Armstrong, B., Cummings, R. A., & Stange, J. (1981). Disruptive behavior: A dietary approach. *Journal of Autism and Childhood Schizophrenia*, 8, 325–337.

O'Connor, S. Vietze, P. M., Sherrod, K. B., Sandler, H. M., & Altemeier, W. A. (1980). Reduced incidence of parenting inadequacy following rooming-in. *Pediatrics*, 66, 176–182.

O'Driscoll, K., & Stronge, J. M. (1975). The active management of labour. *Clinics in Obstetrics and Gynecology*, 2, 3–17.

O'Leary, K. D., & Pelham, W. E. (1977). Behavior therapy and withdrawal of stimulant medication with hyperactive children. *Pediatrics*, 60, 101–115.

Oakhill, J. (1982). Constructive processes in skilled and less skilled comprehenders' memory for sentences. *British Journal of Psychology*, 73, 13–20.

Oden, M. H. (1968). The fullfillment of promise: 40-year follow-up of the Terman gifted group. *Genetic Psychology Monographs*, 77, 3–93.

Oden, S., & Asher, S. R. (1977). Coaching children in social skills for friendship making. *Child Development*, 48, 495–506.

Ogra, P. L., & Greene, H. L. (1982). Human milk and breast feeding: An update on the state of the art. *Pediatrics Research*, 16, 266–271.

Oliver, C. M., & Oliver, G. M. (1978). Gentle birth: Its safety and its effect on neonatal behavior. *Journal of Obstetric and Gynecological Nursing*, 4, 35–40.

Olson, G. M. (1979). Infant recognition memory for briefly presented visual stimuli. *Infant Behavior and Development*, 2, 123–134.

Oltman, P. K., Raskin, E., & Witkin, H. A. (1971). *Group Embedded Figures Test*. Palo Alto, CA: Consulting Psychologists Press.

Olweus, D. (1979). Stability of aggression. *Psychological Bulletin*, 86, 852–875.

Olweus, D. (1980). Familial and temperamental determinants of aggressive behavior in adolescent boys: A causal analysis. *Developmental Psychology*, 16, 644–666.

Olweus, D. (1982). Development of stable aggressive reaction patterns in males. In R. Blanchard and C. Blanchard (Eds.), *Advances in the study of aggression* (Vol. 1). New York: Academic Press.

Olweus, D., Mattsson, A., Schalling, D., & Low, H. (1980). Testosterone, aggression, physical and personality dimensions on normal adolescent males. *Psychosomatic Medicine*, 42, 253–269.

Ovanda, C. J. (1983). Bilingual/Bicultural education: Its legacy and its future. *Phi Delta Kappan*, 64, 564–568.

Packer, M., & Rosenblatt, D. (1979). Issues in the study of social behavior in the first week of life. In D. Schaffer and J. Dunn (Eds.), *Psychological and medication implications of early experience*. New York: John Wiley & Sons.

Page, E. B. (1979). Acceleration vs. enrichment: Theoretical perspectives. In W. C. George, S. J. Cohn, & J. C. Stanley (Eds.), *Educating the gifted: Acceleration and enrichment*. Baltimore: The Johns Hopkins Press.

Paivio, A. (1971). *Imagery and verbal processes*. New York: Holt, Rinehart, & Winston.

Parachini, A. (1980, May 1). Testicle cancer on the increase. *Los Angeles Times*, Section 5, p. 1.

Paraskevopoulos, J., & Hunt, J. McV. (1971). Object construction and imitation under differing conditions of rearing. *Journal of Genetic Psychology, 119*, 301–321.

Parke, R. D. (1977). Punishment in children: Effects, side effects and alternative control strategies. In H. Hom and P. Robinson (Eds.), *Early childhood education: A psychological perspective*. New York: Academic Press.

Parke, R. D. (1979). Perspectives on father-infant interaction. In J. D. Osofsky (Ed.), *Handbook of infant behavior*. New York: John Wiley & Sons.

Parke, R. D. (1981). *Fathers*. Cambridge, MA: Harvard Univ. Press.

Parke, R. D., & Lewis, N. G. (1981). The family in context: A multilevel interactional analysis of child abuse. In R. W. Henderson (Ed.), *Parent-Child Interaction*. New York: Academic Press.

Parke, R. D., & O'Leary, S. E. (1976). Father-mother-infant interaction in the newborn period: Some findings, some observations and some unresolved issues. In K. Riegel and J. Meacham (Eds.), *The developing individual in a changing world: Social and Environmental Issues* (Vol. 2). The Hague: Mouton.

Parke, R. D., & Sawin, D. B. (1976). The father's role in infancy: A re-evaluation. *The Family Coordinator, 25*, 365–371.

Parke, R. D., & Slaby, R. G. (1983). The development of aggression. In E. M. Hetherington (Ed.), *Handbook of child psychology* (Vol. 4). New York: John Wiley & Sons.

Parke, R. D., & Suomi, S. J. (1981). Adult male-infant relationships: Human and nonhuman primate evidence. In K. Immelmann, G. W. Barlow, L. Petrinovich, & M. Main (Eds.), *Behavioral development: The Bielefeld interdisciplinary project*. London: Cambridge University Press.

Parke, R. D., Hymel, S., Power, T. G., & Tinsley, B. R. (1980). Fathers and risk: hospital-based model of intervention. In D. B. Sawin, R. C. Hawkins, L. O. Walker, & J. H. Penticuff (Eds.), *Psychsocial risk in infant-environmental transactions*. New York: Bruner/Mazel.

Parker, S. T., & Gibson, K. R. (1977). Object manipulation, tool use and sensorimotor intelligence as feeding adaptations in cebus monkeys and great apes. *Journal of Human Evolution, 6*, 623–641.

Parmelee, A. H., & Sigman, M. (1976). Development of visual behavior and neurological organization in pre-term and full-term infants. In A. Pick (Ed.), *Minnesota symposia on child psychology* (Vol. 10). Minneapolis, MN: University of Minnesota.

Parsons, J. E. (1983). Expectancies, values, and academic behaviors. In J. T. Spence (Ed.), *Achievement and achievement motives*. San Francisco: W. H. Freeman.

Parsons, J. E., Adler, T. F., & Kaczala, C. M. (1982). Socialization of achievement attitudes and beliefs: Parental influences. *Child Development*, 53, 310–321.

Parten, M. B. (1932). Social participation among preschool children. *Journal of Abnormal and Social Psychology*, 27, 243–269.

Pascual-Leone, J. (1980). Constructive problems for constructive theories: The current relevance of Piaget's work and a critique of information-processing simulation psychology. In R. H. Kluwe & H. Spada (Eds.), *Developmental models of thinking*. New York: Academic Press.

Pascual-Leone, J., & de Ribaupierre, A. (1979). Formal operations and *M* power: A neo-Piagetian investigation. *New Directions for Child Development*, 5, 1–43.

Passman, R. H., & Longeway, K. P. (1982). The role of vision in maternal attachment: Giving 2-year-olds a photograph of their mother during separation. *Developmental Psychology*, 18, 530–533.

Passman, R. H., & Weisberg, P. (1975). Exploratory and play behavior of young children in an unfamiliar environment: The effects of maternal and nonsocial "security" objects. *Developmental Psychology*, 11, 170–177.

Pastor, D. L. (1981). The quality of mother-infant attachment and its relationship to toddlers' initial sociability with peers. *Developmental Psychology*, 17, 326–335.

Patterson, F. G. (1978). The gestures of a gorilla: Language acquisition in another Pongid. *Brain and Language*, 5, 72–97.

Patterson, F. G., & Linden, E. (1981). *The education of Koko*. New York: Holt Rinehart & Winston.

Patterson, G. R. (1980). Mothers: The unacknowledged victims. *Monographs of the Society for Research in Child Development*, 45, No. 186.

Patterson, G. R. (1982). *Coercive family processes*. Eugene, OR: Castalia Publishing.

Patterson, K. A., & Peterson, V. L. (1980). The alternative birth center movement in the San Francisco and Bay area. *Journal of Nurse-Midwifery*, 3, 23–27.

Pea, R. D. (1980). The development of negation in early child language. In D. R. Olson (Ed.), *The social foundations of language and thought*. New York: W. W. Norton.

Peal, E., & Lambert, W. E. (1962). The relation of bilingualism to intelligence. *Psychological Monographs*, 76, 1–23.

Pearl, D., Bouthilet, L., & Lazar, J. B. (1982). *Television and behavior: Ten years of scientific progress and implications for the eighties* (Vol. 2). Washington, DC: U.S. Government Printing Office.

Pedersen, E., Faucher, T. A., & Eaton, W. W. (1978). A new perspective on the effects of first grade teachers on children's subsequent adult status. *Harvard Educational Review*, 48, 1–31.

Pedersen, F. A. (1980). *The father-infant relationship: Observational studies in a family*. New York: Praeger Publishers.

Pedersen, F. A. (1981). Father influences viewed in a family context. In M. E. Lamb (Ed.), *The role of the father in child development*. New York: John Wiley & Sons.

Pedersen, F. A., Cain, R. L., Zaslow, M. J., & Anderson, B. J. (1982). Variation in infant experience associated with alternative family roles. In L. Laosa & I. Sigel (Eds.), *Families as learning environments for children*. New York: Plenum Publishers.

Pedersen, F. A., Rubenstein, J., & Yarrow, L. J. (1979). Infant development in father-absent families. *Journal of Genetic Psychology, 135,* 51–61.

Penfield, W., & Roberts, L. (1959). *Speech and brain mechanisms.* Princeton, NJ: Princeton University Press.

Pepler, D. J. (1982). Play and divergent thinking. In D. J. Pepler & K. H. Rubin (Eds.), *The play of children: Current theory and research.* Basel, Switzerland: S. Karger.

Pepler, D. J., & Rubin, K. H. (1982). *The play of children: Current theory and research.* Basel, Switzerland: S. Karger.

Perlmutter, L. H., Engel, T., & Sager, C. J. (1982). The incest taboo: Loosened sexual boundaries in remarried families. *Journal of Sex and Marital Therapy, 8,* 83–96.

Perlmutter, M. (1980). *Children's memory.* San Francsico: Jossey-Bass.

Perriss, B. W. (1981). Analgesia and Anaesthesia. *Clinics in Obstetrics and Gynaecology, 8,* 475–506.

Persson-Blennow, I., & McNeil, T. F. (1982). Factor analysis of temperamental characteristics in children at 6 months, 1 year, and 2 years of age. *British Journal of Educational Psychology, 52,* 51–57.

Pezdek, K., & Chen, H. (1982). Developmental differences in the role of detail in picture recognition memory. *Journal of Experimental Child Psychology, 33,* 207–215.

Phipps-Yonas, S. (1979). Teenage pregnancy and motherhood: A review of the literature. *American Journal of Orthopsychiatry, 50,* 403–431.

Piaget, J. (1926). *The language and thought of the child.* London: Routledge & Kegan Paul.

Piaget, J. (1948). *The moral judgment of the child.* New York: Free Press.

Piaget, J. (1952). *The origins of intelligence in children.* New York: International Universities Press.

Piaget, J. (1954). *The construction of reality in the child.* New York: Ballantine Books.

Piaget, J. (1962). *Plays, dreams, and imitation in childhood.* New York: W. W. Norton.

Piaget, J. (1964). Development and learning. In R. E. Ripple & V. N. Rockcastle (Eds.), *Piaget rediscovered.* Ithaca, NY: Cornell University.

Piaget, J. (1969). *The child's conception of the world.* Totowa, NJ: Littlefield, Adams.

Piaget, J. (1970a). Piaget's theory. In P. H. Mussen (Ed.), *Carmichael's handbook of child psychology* (Vol. 1). New York: John Wiley & Sons.

Piaget, J. (1970b). *Science of education and the psychology of the child.* New York: Orion Press.

Piaget, J. (1971). *Biology and knowledge.* Chicago: University of Chicago Press.

Piaget, J. (1977). *The development of thought: Equilibration of cognitive structures.* New York: Viking Press.

Piaget, J., & Inhelder, B. (1956). *The child's conception of space.* London: Routledge & Kegan Paul.

Piaget, J., & Inhelder, B. (1972). *Mental imagery in the child.* New York: Basic Books.

Piaget, J., & Inhelder, B. (1973). *Memory and intelligence.* New York: Basic Books.

Pick, H. L., Jr., & Rieser, J. J. (1982). Children's cognitive mapping. In M. Potegal (Ed.), *Spatial abilities*. New York: Academic Press.

Pihl, R. O., & Niaura, R. (1982). Learning disability: An inability to sustain attention. *Journal of Clinical Psychology, 38,* 632–648.

Piotrkowski, C. S., & Katz, M. H. (1982). Indirect socialization of children: The effects of mothers' jobs on academic behavior. *Child Development, 53,* 1520–1529.

Pisacano, J. C., Lichter, H., Ritter, J., & Siegal, A. P. (1978). An attempt at prevention of obesity in infancy. *Pediatrics, 61,* 360–364.

Plomin, R. (1981). Ethological behavioral genetics and development. In K. Immelmann, G. W. Barlow, L. Petrinovich, & M. Main (Eds.), *Behavioral development: The Bielefeld interdisciplinary project*. New York: Cambridge University Press.

Plomin, R. (1983). Developmental behavioral genetics. *Child Development, 54,* 253–259.

Poindron, P., & LeNeindre, P. (1980). Endocrine and sensory regulation of maternal behavior in the eye. In J. S. Rosenblatt, R. A. Hinde, C. Beer, & M. C. Busnel (Eds.), *Advances in the study of behavior* (Vol. 11). New York: Academic Press.

Pollitt, E., & Leibel, R. L. (1976). Iron deficiency and behavior. *Journal of Pediatrics, 88,* 372–381.

Posner, M. I. (1978). *Chronometric explorations of the mind*. Hillsdale, NJ: Lawrence Erlbaum.

Posner, M. I., & Boies, S. J. (1971). Components of attention. *Psychological Review, 78,* 391–408.

Posner, M. I., Pea, R., & Volpe, B. (1982). Cognitive-neuroscience: Developments toward a science of synthesis. In J. Mehler, E. C. T. Walker, & M. Garrett (Eds.), *Perspectives on mental representation*. Hillsdale, NJ: Lawrence Erlbaum.

Power, T. G., & Parke, R. D. (1981). Play as a context for early learning: Lab and home analyses. In I. E. Siegel & L. M. Laosa (Eds.), *The family as a learning environment*. New York: Plenum Publishing.

Prescott, J. H. (1981). Clever Hans: Training the trainers, or the potential for misinterpreting the results of dolphin research. *Annals of the New York Academy of Science, 364,* 130–137.

Pressley, M. (1982). Elaboration and memory development, *Child Development, 53,* 296–309.

Pressley, M., Heisel, B. E., McCormick, C. B., & Nakamura, G. V. (1982). Memory strategy instruction with children. In C. J. Brainerd & M. Pressley (Eds.), *Verbal Processes in Children*. New York: Springer-Verlag.

Pressley, M., Levin, J. R., & Delaney, H. D. (1982). The mnemonic keyword method. *Review of Educational Research, 52,* 61–91.

Provence, S., & Lipton, R. C. (1962). *Infants in Institution*. New York: W. W. Norton.

Purpura, D. P. (1974). Dendritic spine "dysgenesis" and mental retardation. *Science, 186,* 1126–1128.

Pylyshyn, Z. W. (1973). What the mind's eye tells the mind's brain: A critique of mental imagery. *Psychological Review, 80,* 1–24.

Quinn, L. (1981). Reading skills of hearing and congenitally deaf children. *Journal of Experimental Child Psychology, 32,* 139–161.

Radin, N. (1981). The role of the father in cognitive, academic, and intellectual development. In M. Lamb (Ed.), *The role of the father in child development* (2d Ed.) New York: John Wiley & Sons.

Radin, N., & Russell, G. (1983). Increased father participation and child development outcomes. In M. E. Lamb & A. Sagi (Eds.), *Fatherhood and family policy.* Hillsdale, NJ: Lawrence Erlbaum.

Radke-Yarrow, M., Zahn-Waxler, C., & Chapman, M. (1983). Children's prosocial dispositions and behavior. In E. M. Hetherington (Ed.), *Handbook of child psychology* (Vol. 4). New York: John Wiley & Sons.

Ragozin, A. S. (1980). Attachment behavior of day care children: Naturalistic and laboratory observations. *Child Development, 51,* 409–415.

Ragozin, A. S., Basham, R. B., Crnic, K. A., Greenberg, M. T., & Robinson, N. M. (1982). Effects of maternal age on parenting role. *Developmental Psychology, 18,* 627–634.

Ramey, C. T., & Haskins, R. (1981). The modification of intelligence through early experience. *Intelligence, 5,* 5–19.

Ramey, C. T., MacPhee, D., & Yeates, K. O. (1982). Preventing developmental retardation: A general systems model. In D. K. Detterman & R. J. Sternberg (Eds.), *How and how much can intelligence be increased?* Norwood, NJ: Ablex.

Rantakallio, P. (1978). Relationship of maternal smoking to morbidity and mortality of the child up to the age of five. *Acta Paediatrica Scandinavica, 67,* 621–631.

Rasmussen, T., & Milner, B. (1977). The role of early left-brain injury in determining lateralization of cerebral speech functions. In S. Dimond & D. Blizzard (Eds.), *Evolution and lateralization of the brain.* New York: New York Academy of Sciences.

Raudenbusch, S. W. (1984). Magnitude of teacher expectancy effects on pupil IQ as a function of the credibility of expectancy induction: A synthesis of findings from 18 experiments. *Journal of Experimental Psychology, 76,* 85–97.

Raven, J. C, (1938). *Standard Progressive Matrices.* London: H. K. Lewis.

Ravitch, D. (1983, June 6). Bilingual instruction is an answer, but not the only one. *Los Angeles Times,* p. 20.

Rebelsky, F., & Black, R. (1972). Crying in infancy. *Journal of Genetic Psychology, 121,* 49–57.

Reid, J. B., Taplin, P. S., & Lorber, R. (1981). A social interactional approach to the treatment of abusive families. In R. Stuart (Ed.), *Violent behavior: Social learning approaches to prediction, management, and treatment.* New York: Bruner/Mazel.

Reinisch, J. M. (1981). Prenatal exposure to synthetic progestins increases potential for aggression in humans. *Science, 211,* 1171–1173.

Reinisch, J. M. (1984, March 28). The Kinsey report. *Press Enterprise,* Section E, p. 3.

Reinisch, J. M., & Haskett, R. F. (1981). Postnatal gonadal steroid effects on human behavior. *Science, 211,* 1318–1325.

Reis, M., & Gold, D. (1977). Relation of paternal availability to problem-solving and sex-role orientation in young boys. *Psychological Reports, 40,* 823–829.

Renzulli, J. S., & Delisle, J. R. (1982). Gifted Persons. In H. E. Mitzel (Ed.), *Encylopedia of educational research* (5th ed.). New York: Free Press.

Report to the Nutrition Foundation. (1980). New York: National Advisory Committee on Hyperkinesis and Food Additives.

Reschly, D. J. (1981). Evaluation of the effects of SOMPA measures on classification of students as mildly mentally retarded. *American Journal of Mental Deficiency*, 86, 16–20.

Reschly, D. J., & Sabers, D. L. (1979). An examination of bias in predicting MAT scores from WISC-R scores for four ethnic-racial groups. *Journal of Educational Measurement*, 16, 1–9.

Resnick, D. P., & Resnick, L. B. (1977). The nature of literacy: An historical exploration. *Harvard Educational Review*, 47, 370–385.

Resnick, L. B. (1980). The role of invention in the development of mathematical competence. In R. H. Kluwe & H. Spada (Eds.), *Develomental models of thinking*. New York: Academic Press.

Rest, J. R. (1979a). *Development in judging moral issues*. Minneapolis, MN: University of Minnesota Press.

Rest, J. R. (1979b). *Revised manual for the Defining Issues Test*. Minneapolis, MN: Minnesota Moral Research Projects.

Rest, J. R. (1983). Morality. In J. H. Flavell & Ellen M. Markham (Eds.), *Handbook of Child Psychology* (Vol. 3). New York: John Wiley & Sons.

Reynolds, C. R., & Jensen, A. R. (1983). WISC-R subscale patterns of abilities of blacks and whites matched on full scale IQ. *Journal of Educational Psychology*, 75, 207–214.

Rheingold, H. L., & Eckerman, C. O. (1971). Departures from the mother. In H. R. Schaffer (Ed.), *The origins of human social relations*. London: Academic Press.

Rice, M. The role of television in language acquisition. *Developmental Review*, 3, 211–224.

Richardson, S. A., Goodman, N., Hastorf, A. H., & Dornbusch, S. M. (1961). Cultural uniformity in reaction to physical disabilities. *American Sociological Review*, 26, 241–247.

Rickard, K. M., Forehand, R., Atkeson, B. M., & Lopez, C. (1982). An examination of the relationship of marital satisfaction and divorce with parent-child interactions. *Journal of Clinical Child Psychology*, 11, 61–65.

Riekehof, L. (1963). *Talk to the deaf*. Springfield, MO: Gospel Publishing House.

Riesen, A. H. (1982). Effects of environments on development in sensory systems. In W. D. Neff (Ed.), *Contributions to sensory physiology* (Vol. 6). New York: Academic Press.

Rimsza, M. E., & Niggemann, E. H. (1982). Medical evaluation of sexually abused children: A review of 311 cases. *Pediatrics*, 69, 8–14.

Ringler, N. M., Trause, M. A., Klaus, M. H., & Kennell, J. H. (1978). The effects of extra postpartum contact and maternal speech patterns on children's IQs, speech and language comprehension at five. *Child Development*, 49, 862–865.

Ristau, C. A., & Robbins, D. (1982). Language in the great apes. In J. S. Rosenblatt, R. A. Hinde, C. Beer, & M. Busnel (Eds.), *Advances in the study of behavior*. New York: Academic Press.

Roberts, E. J. (1982). Children's sexual learning. *Dissertation Abstracts International*, *43*, (5-A), 1400–1401.

Robins, L. N. (1978). Aetiological implications in studies of childhood histories relating to antisocial personality. In R. D. Hare & D. Schalling (Eds.), *Psychopathic behavior*. New York: John Wiley & Sons.

Robinson, B. E., & Fields, N. H. (1983). Casework with invulnerable children. *Social Work*, *28*, 63–65.

Roche, A. F. (1981). The adipocyte-number hypothesis. *Child Development*, *52*, 31–43.

Rode, S. S., Chang P., Fisch, R. O., & Sroufe, L. A. (1981). Attachment patterns of infants separated at birth. *Developmental Psychology*, *17*, 188–192.

Rodeck, C. H., & Morsman, J. M. (1983). First trimester chorion biopsy. *British Medical Bulletin*, *39*, 338–42.

Rodeheffer, M., & Martin, H. P. (1976). Special problems in developmental assessment of abused children. In H. P. Martin (Ed.), *The abused child: A multidisciplinary approach to developmental issues and treatment*. Cambridge, MA: Ballinger Publishing.

Rogoff, B. (1981). Schooling and the development of cognitive skills. In H. C. Triandis & A. Heron (Eds.), *Handbook of cross-cultural psychology: Developmental Psychology* (Vol. 4). Boston: Allyn & Bacon.

Rohwer, W. D. (1980). An Elaborative conception of learner differences. In R. E. Snow, P. A. Federico, & W. E. Montague (Eds.), *Aptitude, Learning and instruction* (Vol. 2.). Hillsdale, NJ: Lawrence Earlbaum.

Ronning, R. R. (1977). Modeling effects and developmental changes in dealing with a formal operations task. *American Education Research Journal*, *14*, 213–223.

Rose, R. M., Gordon, T. P., & Bernstein, I. S. (1972). Plasma testosterone levels in the male rhesus: Influences of sexual and social stimuli. *Science*, *187*, 643–645.

Rose, S. A. (1981). Developmental changes in infants' retention of visual stimuli. *Child Development*, *52*, 227–233.

Rose, S. A., Gottfried, A. W., Melloy-Carminar, P., & Bridger, W. H. (1982). Familiarity and novelty preferences in infant recognition memory: Implications for information processing. *Developmental Psychology*, *18*, 704–713.

Rosenberg, L., Mitchell, A. A., Shapiro, S., & Slone, D. (1982). Selected birth defects in relation to caffeine-containing beverages. *Journal of the American Medical Association*, *247*, 1429–1432.

Rosenblatt, J. S., & Siegel, H. I. (1975). Hysterectomy-induced maternal behavior during pregnancy in the rat. *Journal of Comparative and Physiological Psychology*, *89*, 685–700.

Rosensweig, M. R., Krech, D., Bennett, E. L., & Diamond, M. C. (1962). Effects of environmental complexity and training on brain chemistry and anatomy: A replication and extension. *Journal of Comparative and Physiological Psychology*, *55*, 429–437.

Rosenthal, D. (1963). *The Genain Quadruplets*. New York: Basic Books.

Rosenthal, R., & Jacobson, L. (1968). *Pygmalion in the classroom: Teacher expectation and pupils' intellectual development*. New York: Holt, Rinehart & Winston.

Rosenthal, R., & Rubin, D. B. (1982). Further meta-analytic procedures for assessing cognitive gender differencers. *Journal of Educational Psychology, 74,* 708–712.

Rosenzweig, M. R., & Bennett, E. L. (1978). Experiential influences on brain anatomy and brain chemistry. In G. Gottlieb (Ed.), *Early influences: Studies on the development of behavior and the nervous system* (Vol. 4). New York: Academic Press.

Rosett, H. L., Snyder, P., Sander, L. W., Lee, A., Cook, P., Weiner, L., & Gould, J. (1979). Effects of maternal drinking on neonate state regulation. *Developmental Medicine and Child Neurology, 21,* 464–473.

Rousseau, J. J. (1762). *Emile, or Education.* As translated by B. Foxley (1948). London: J. M. Dent & Sons.

Rovee-Collier, C. K., & Capatides, J. B. (1979). Positive behavioral contrast in 3 month-old infants on multiple conjugate reinforcement schedules. *Journal of the Experimental Analysis of Behavior, 32,* 15–27.

Rovee-Collier, C. K., & Sullivan, M. W. (1980). Organization of infant memory. *Journal of Experimental Psychology: Human Learning and Memory, 6,* 798–807.

Rovee-Collier, C. K., Sullivan, M., Enright, M., Lucas, D., & Fagen, J. W. (1980). Reactivation of infant memory. *Science, 208,* 1159–1161.

Rovet, J., & Netley, C. (1981). Turner Syndrome in a pair of dizygotic twins: A single case study. *Behavior Genetics, 11,* 65–72.

Rozovski, S. J., & Winick, M. (1979). Nutrition and cellular growth. In M. Winick (Ed.), *Nutrition: Pre- and postnatal development.* New York: Plenum Publishing.

Rubenstein, J., & Howes, C. (1976). The effects of peers on toddler interaction with mothers and toys. *Child Development, 47,* 597–605.

Rubin, K. H., & Krasnor, L. R. (1980). Changes in the play behaviors of preschoolers: A short-term longitudinal investigation. *Canadian Journal of Behavioral Science, 12,* 278–282.

Rubin, K. H., Fein, G. G., & Vandenberg, B. (1983). Play. In E. M. Hetherington (Ed.), *Handbook of child psychology* (Vol. 4). New York: John Wiley & Sons.

Rubin, Z. (1980). *Children's friendships.* Cambridge, MA: Harvard Univ. Press.

Rubinstein, E. A. (1983). Television and behavior: Research conclusions of the 1982 NIMH report and their policy implications. *American Psychologist, 38,* 820–826.

Rumack, C. M., Guggenheim, M. A., Rumack, B. H., Peterson, R. C., Johnson, M. L., & Braithwaite, W. R. (1981). Neonatal intracranial hemorrhage and maternal use of aspirin. *Obstetrics and Gynecology, 58,* 52s–57s.

Ruppenthal, G. C., Arling, G. L., Harlow, H. F., Sackett, G. P., & Suomi, S. J. (1976). A ten-year perspective on motherless-mother monkey behavior. *Journal of Abnormal Psychology, 85,* 341–349.

Russell, K. P. (1980). The course and conduct of normal labor and delivery. In R. C. Benson (Ed.), *Current obstetric and gynecologic diagnosis and treatment,* (3d ed.) Los Altos, CA: Lange Medical Publications.

Rutter, M. (1979a). Protective factors in children's responses to stress and disadvantage. In M. W. Kent & J. E. Rolf (Eds.), *Primary prevention of psychopathology: Social competence in children* (Vol. 3). Hanover, NH: University Press of New England.

Rutter, M. (1979b). Maternal deprivation, 1972–1978: New findings, new concepts, new approaches. *Child Development, 50,* 283–305.

Rutter, M. (1981). Psychological sequelae of brain damage in children. *American Journal of Psychiatry*, *138*, 1533–1544.

Rutter, M. (1982). Temperament: Concepts, issues, and problems. In *Temperamental differences in infants and young children*. CIBA Foundation Symposium. London: Pitman Publishing.

Rutter, M. (1983). School effects on pupil progress: Research findings and policy implications. *Child Development*, *54*, 1–29.

Rutter, M., Korn, S., & Birch, H. (1963). Genetic and environmental factors in the development of "primary reaction patterns." *British Journal of Social and Clinical Psychology*, *2*, 161–173.

Rutter, M., Maughan, B., Mortimore, P., & Ouston, J. (1979). *Fifteen thousand hours*. London: Open Books.

Ryan, E. D., & Simons, J. (1982). Efficacy of mental imagery in enhancing mental rehearsal of motor skills. *Journal of Sport Psychology*, *4*, 41–51.


Sackett, C. P., Porter, M., & Holmes, H. (1965). Choice behavior in rhesus monkeys: Effect of stimulation during the first month of life. *Science*, *147*, 304–306.

Saigal, S., Nelson, N. M., Bennett, K. J., & Enkin, M. W. (1981). Observations on the behavioral state of newborn infants during the first hour of life. *American Journal of Obstetrics and Gynecology*, *139*, 715–719.

Salatas, H., & Flavell, J. H. (1976). Retrieval of recently learned information: Development of strategies and control skills. *Child Development*, *47*, 941–948.

Salk, L. (1973). The role of the heartbeat in the relationship between mother and infant. *Scientific American*, *228*, 73–77.

Salkind, N. J., & Nelson, C. F. (1980). A note on the developmental nature of reflection-impulsivity. *Developmental Psychology*, *3*, 237–238.

Sallade, J. A. (1973). Comparison of the psychological adjustment of obese vs. nonobese children. *Journal of Psychosomatic Research*, *17*, 89–96.

Salomon, G. (in press). Television is "easy" and print is "tough": The differential investment of mental effort in learning as a function of perceptions and attributions. *Journal of Educational Psychology*. As cited by Bandura, A. (1982). The assessment and predictive generality of self-percepts of efficacy. *Behavior Therapy and Experimental Psychiatry*, *13*, 195–199.

Saltz, E., & Brodie, J. (1982). Pretend-play training in childhood: A review and critique. In D. J. Pepler & K. H. Rubin (Eds.), *The play of children: Current theory and research*. Basel, Switzerland: S. Karger.

Saltz, E., & Dixon, D. (1982). Let's pretend: The role of motoric imagery in memory for sentences and words. *Journal of Experimental Child Psychology*, *34*, 77–92.

Saltz, E., Dixon, D., & Johnson, J. (1977). Training disadvantaged preschoolers on various fantasy activities: Effects on cognitive functioning and impulse control. *Child Development*, *48*, 367–380.

Salzinger, S., Kaplan, S., & Artemyeff, C. (1983). Mothers' personal social networks and child maltreatment. *Journal of Abnormal Psychology*, *92*, 68–76.

Samelson, F. (1980). J. B. Watson's Little Albert, Cyril Burt's twins, and the need for a critical science. *American Psychologist*, *35*, 619–625.

Sameroff, A. J. (1981). Longitudinal studies of preterm infants: A review of chapters

17–20. In S. L. Friedman & M. Sigman (Eds.), *Preterm birth and psychological development*. New York: Academic Press.

Sameroff, A. J., & Cavanaugh, P. J. (1979). Learning in infancy: A developmental perspective. In J. D. Osofsky (Ed.), *Handbook of infant development*. New York: John Wiley & Sons.

Sameroff, A. J., Seifer, R., & Zax, M. (1982). Early development of children at risk for emotional disorder. *Monographs of the Society for Research in Child Development*. No. 199.

Sameroff, A. J., & Seifer, R. (1983). Familial risk and child competence. *Child Development, 54*, 1254–1268.

Sanders, R. J., & Bever, T. G. (1979). Can an ape create a sentence? *Science, 211*, 87–88.

Santrock, J. W. (1972). The relation of type and onset of father absence to cognitive development. *Child Development, 43*, 455–469.

Santrock, J. W., & Warshak, R. A. (1979). Father custody and social development in boys and girls. *Journal of Social Issues, 35*, 112–125.

Santrock, J. W., Warshak, R., Lindbergh, C., & Meadows, L. (1982). Children's and parent's observed social behavior in stepfamilies. *Child Development, 53*, 472–480.

Sattler, J. M. (1982). *Assessment of children's intelligence and special abilities*. Boston: Allyn & Bacon.

Sattler, J. M., & Gwynne, J. (1982). White examiners generally do not impede the intelligence performance of black children: To debunk a myth. *Journal of Consulting and Clinical Psychology, 50,*196–208.

Savage-Rumbaugh, E. S., Rumbaugh, D., & Boysen, S. (1980). Do apes use language? *American Scientist, 68*, 49–61.

Savin-Williams, R. C. (1979). Dominance hierarchies in groups of early adolescents. *Child Development, 50*, 923–935.

Savin-Williams, R. C. (1980). Social interactions of adolescent females in natural groups. In H. C. Foot, A. J. Chapman, & J. R. Smith (Eds.), *Friendship and social relations in children*. New York: John Wiley & Sons.

Scarisbrick, J. J. (1970). *Henry VIII*. Berkeley, CA: University of California Press.

Scarr, S. (1981). Genetic differences in "g" and real life. In M. P. Friedman, J. P. Das, & N. O'Connor (Eds.), *Intelligence and learning*. New York: Plenum Publishing.

Scarr, S., & Weinberg, R. A. (1976). IQ test performance of black children adopted by white families. *American Psychologist, 31*, 726–739.

Scarr, S., & Weinberg, R. A. (1978). The influence of "family background" on intellectual attainment. *American Sociological Review, 43*, 674–692.

Scarr, S., & Weinberg, R. A. (1983). The Minnesota adoption studies: Genetic differences and malleability. *Child Development, 54*, 260–267.

Scarr-Salapatek, S., & Williams, M. L. (1973). The effects of early stimulation on low birth-weight infants. *Child Development, 44*, 94–101.

Schacter, F. F. (1979). *Everyday mother talk to toddlers: Early intervention*. New York: Academic Press.

Schaefer, G., & Zisowitz, M. L. (1964). *The expectant father*. New York: Simon & Schuster.

Schafer, E. W. P. (1979). Cognitive neural adaptability: A biological basis for individual differences in intelligence. *Psychophysiology, 16,* 199.

Schafer, E. W. P., & Marcus, M. M. (1973). Self-stimulation alters human sensory brain responses. *Science, 181,* 175–177.

Schafer, E. W. P., & Peeke, H. V. S. (1982). Down syndrome individuals fail to habituate cortical evoked potentials. *American Journal of Mental Deficiency, 87,* 332–337.

Schaffer, H. R., & Emerson, P. E. (1964). The development of social attachments in infancy. *Monographs of the Society for Research in Child Development, 29,* No. 94.

Schiff, M., Duyme, M., Dumaret, A., Stewart, J., Tomkiewicz, S., & Feingold, J. (1978). Intellectual status of working-class children adopted early into upper-middle-class families. *Science, 200,* 1503–1504.

Schlesinger, I. M., & Namir, L. (1978). *Sign language of the deaf*. New York: Academic Press.

Schneider, W. (1982). *Developmental trends in the metamemory-memory behavior relationship: An integrative review*. Unpublished manuscript. Stanford, CA: Stanford University.

Schofield, J. W. (1981). Complementary and conflicting identities: Images and interaction in an interracial school. In S. R. Asher & J. M. Gottman (Eds.), *The development of children's friendships*. London: Cambridge University Press.

Schuckit, M. D., Goodwin, W., & Winokur, G. A. (1972). A study of alcoholicm in half-siblings. *American Journal of Psychiatry, 128,* 1132–1136.

Schull, W. J., Otake, M., & Neel, J. V. (1981). Genetic effects of the atomic bomb: A reappraisal. *Science, 213,* 1220–1227.

Schunk, D. H. (1981). Modeling and attributional effects on children's achievement: A self-efficacy analysis. *Journal of Educational Psychology, 73,* 93–105.

Schunk, D. H. (1982). Progress self-monitoring: Effects on children's self-efficacy and achievement. *Journal of Experimental Education, 51,* 89–93.

Schwartz, B., & Lacey, H. (1982). *Behaviorism, science, and human nature*. New York: W. W. Norton.

Schwartz, D., & Mayaux, M. J. (1982). Female fecundity as a function of age: results of artificial insemination in nulliparous women with azoospermic husbands. *New England Journal of Medicine, 306,* 404–406.

Schwartz, P. (1983). Length of day-care attendance and attachment behavior in eighteen-month-old infants. *Child Development, 54,* 1073–1078.

Schwarz, R. H. & Yaffe, S. J. (1980). *Drug and chemical risks to the fetus and newborn*. New York: Alan R. Liss.

Schwebel, A. I. (1983). Long-term effects of divorce on parent-child relationships. *Developmental Psychology, 19,* 703–713.

Scott, J. P. (1983). A systems approach to research on aggressive behavior. In E. C. Simmel, M. E. Hahn, & J. K. Walters (Eds.), *Aggressive behavior: Genetic and neural approaches*. Hillsdale, NJ: Lawrence Erlbaum.

Seabright, M. (1971). A rapid banding technique for human chromosomes. *Lancet*, 2, 971–972.

Sears, R. R. (1970). Relation of early socialization experiences to self-concept and gender role in middle childhood. *Child Development, 41*, 267–289.

Sears, R. R., Rau, L., & Alpert, R. (1965). *Identification and Child rearing*. Stanford, CA: Stanford University Press.

Segal, J., & Yahraes, H. (1979). *A child's journey*. New York: McGraw-Hill.

Seginer, R. (1983). Parents' educational expectations and children's academic achievements: A literature review. *Merrill Palmer Quarterly, 29*, 1–23.

Seligman, M. E. P. (1975). *Helplessness*. San Francisco: W. H. Freeman.

Selman, R. L. (1981). The child as a friendship philospher. In S. R. Asher & J. M. Gottman (Eds.), *The development of children's friendships*. London: Cambridge University Press.

Seltzer, V. C. (1982). *Adolescent social development: Dynamic functional interaction*. Lexington, MA: D. C. Heath.

Selye, H. (1979). The stress concept and some of its implications. In V. Hamilton & D. M. Warburton (Eds.), *Human stress and cognition*. New York: John Wiley & Sons.

Serbin, L. A., Tonick, I. J., & Sternglanz, S. H. (1977). Shaping cooperative cross-sex play. *Child Development, 48*, 924–929.

Serunian, S. A., & Broman, S. H. (1975). Relationship of Apgar scores and Bayley Mental and Motor Scores. *Child Development, 46*, 696–700.

Seshadri, S., Hirode, K., Naik, P., & Malhotra, S. (1982). Behavioral responses of young anaemic Indian children to iron-folic acid supplements. *British Journal of Nutrition, 48*, 233.

Severo, R. (1981, February 4). Air Academy to drop its ban on applicants with sickle cell gene. *New York Times*, Section 1, p. 1.

Seward, J. P., & Seward, G. H. (1980). *Sex differences: Mental and temperamental*. Lexington, MA: D. C. Heath.

Seyfarth, R. M., Cheney, D. L., & Marler, P. (1980). Monkey responses to three different alarm calls: Evidence of predator classification and semantic communication. *Science, 210*, 801–803.

Shannon, D. C., & Kelly, D. H. (1982a). SIDS and near-SIDS. *New England Journal of Medicine, 306*, 959–964.

Shannon, D. C., & Kelly, D. H. (1982b). SIDS and near-SIDS. *New England Journal of Medicine, 306*, 1022–1028.

Shantz, C. U. (1983). Social Cognition. In J. H. Flavell & E. M. Markman (Eds.), *Handbook of child psychology* (Vol. 3). New York: John Wiley & Sons.

Shapiro, S., Schlesinger, E. R., & Nesbitt, R. E. (1968). *Infant, perinatal, maternal, and childhood mortality in the United States*. Cambridge, MA: Harvard Univ. Press.

Shatz, M. (1982). On mechanisms of language acquistion: Can features of the communicative environment account for development? In L. Gleitman & E. Wanner (Eds.), *Language acquisition: The state of the art*. New York: Cambridge University Press.

Shatz, M., & Gelman, R. (1973) The development of communication skills: Modifications in the speech of young children as a function of listener. *Monographs of the Society for Research in Child Development, 38,* No. 152.

Shaywitz, S. E., Cohen, D. J., & Shaywitz, B. A. (1980). Behavior and learning difficulties in children of normal intelligence born to alcoholic mothers. *Journal of Pediatrics, 96,* 978–982.

Shekim, W. O., Davis, L. G., Bylund, D. B., Brunngraber, E., Fikes, L., & Lanham, J. (1982). Platelet MAO in children with attention deficit disorder and hyperactivity: A pilot study. *American Journal of Psychiatry, 139,* 936–938.

Shepard, R. N. (1982). Perceptual and analogical bases of cognition. In J. Mehler, E. C. T. Walker, & M. Garrett (Eds.), *Perspectives on mental representation.* Hillsdale, NJ: Lawrence Erlbaum.

Sherif, M., Harvey, O. J., White, B. J., Hood, W. R., & Sherif, C. W. (1961). *Inter-group conflict and cooperation: The Robber's Cave Experiment.* Norman, OK: University of Oklahoma Press.

Sherrod, L. R. (1979). Social cognition in infants: Attention to the human face. *Infant Behavior and Development, 2,* 279–294.

Shields, J. (1962). *Monozygotic twins brought up apart and brought up together.* London: Oxford University Press.

Shipe, D., Vandenberg, S., & Williams, R. D. B. (1968). Neonatal Apgar ratings as related to intelligence and behavior in preschool children. *Child Development, 39,* 861–866.

Shirley, M. M. (1931). *The first two years, a study of twenty-five babies. Postural and locomotor development* (Vol. 1). Minneapolis, MN: University of Minnesota Press.

Shriberg, L. K., Kevin, J. R., McCormick, C. B., & Pressley, M. (1982). Learning about "famous" people via the keyword method. *Journal of Educational Psychology, 74,* 238–247.

Shultz, T. R., & Horibe, F. (1974). Development of the appreciation of verbal jokes. *Developmental Psychology, 10,* 13–20.

Shy, K. K., Frost, F., and Ullom, J. (1980). Out-of-hospital delivery in Washington state, 1975 to 1977. *American Journal of Obstetrics and Gynecology, 137,* 547–552.

Siegel, E., Bauman, K. E., Schaefer, E. S., Saunders, M. M., & Ingram, D. D. (1980). Hospital and home support during infancy: Impact on maternal attachment, child abuse and neglect, and health care utilization. *Pediatrics, 66,* 183–190.

Siegel, L. S., & Hodkin, B. (1982). The garden path to understanding of cognitive development: Has Piaget led us into the poison ivy? In S. Modgil & C. Modgil (Eds.), *Jean Piaget: Consensus and controversy.* New York: Holt, Rinehart & Winston.

Siegler, R. S. (1977). The twenty questions game as a form of problem solving. *Child Development, 48,* 395–403.

Siegler, R. S. (1978). The origins of scientific reasoning. In R. S. Siegler (Ed.), *Children's thinking: What develops?* Hillsdale, NJ: Lawrence Erlbaum.

Siegler, R. S. (1983). Five generalizations about cognitive development. *American Psychologist, 38,* 263–277.

Simeonsson, R. J., Cooper, D. H., & Scheiner, A. P. (1982). A review and analysis of the effectiveness of early intervention programs. *Pediatrics, 69,* 635–641.

Simmel, E. C., Hahn, M. E., & Walters, J. K. (1983). *Aggressive behavior: Genetic and neural approaches.* Hillsdale, NJ: Lawrence Erlbaum.

Simoneau, K., & Decarie, T. (1979). Cognition and perception in the object concept. *Canadian Journal of Psychology, 33,* 382–395.

Simpson, G. B., & Lorsbach, T. C. (1983). The development of automatic and conscious components of contextual facilitation. *Child Development, 54,* 760–772.

Sinclair, H. (1975). The role of cognitive structures in language acquisition. In E. H. Lenneberg & L. Lenneberg (Eds.), *Foundations of language development, I.* New York: Academic Press.

Singer, D. G. (1983). A time to reexamine the role of television in our lives. *American Psychologist, 38,* 815–817.

Singer, J. L., & Singer, D. G. (1983). Psychologists look at television: Cognitive, developmental, personality, and social policy implications. *American Psychologist, 38,* 826–834.

Siniscallo, M. (1979). Human gene mapping and cancer biology. In CIBA Foundation Symposium 66, *Human Genetics: Possibilities and realities.* New York: Excerpta Medica.

Sjöström, L. (1980). Fat cells and body weight. In A. J. Stunkard (Ed.), *Obesity.* Philadelphia: W. B. Saunders.

Skells, H. (1966). Adult status of children with contrasting early experiences. *Monographs of the Society for Research in Child Development, 31,* No. 3.

Skinner, B. F. (1948). *Walden II,* New York: Macmillan.

Slavin, R. E. (1983). *Cooperative Learning.* New York: Longman.

Slavin, R. E., & Madden, N. A. (1979). School practices that improve race relations. *American Educational Research Journal, 16,* 169–180.

Slavin, R. E., & Oickle, E. (1981). Effects of cooperative learning teams on student achievement and race relations: Treatment by race interactions. *Sociology of Education, 54,* 174–180.

Slavin, R. E., Leavey, M., & Madden, N. A. (1984). Effects of Team Assisted Individualization on the mathematics achievement of academically handicapped and non-handicapped students. *Journal of Educational Psychology, 76,* 244–253.

Sloan, D., Shapiro, S., & Mitchell, A. A. (1980). Strategies for studying the effects of the antenatal chemical environment on the fetus. In R. H. Schwarz & S. J. Yaffe (Eds.), *Drug and chemical risks to the fetus and newborn.* New York: Alan R. Liss.

Slobin, D. I. (1966). The acquisition of Russian as a native language. In F. Smith & G. A. Miller (Eds.), *The ontogenesis of language.* Cambridge, MA: MIT Press.

Slobin, D. I. (1971). *Psycholinguistics.* Glenview, IL: Scott, Foresman.

Slobin, D. I. (1973). Cognitive prerequisites for the development of grammar. In C. A. Ferguson & D. I. Slobin (Eds.), *Studies of child language development.* New York: Holt, Rinehart & Winston.

Slobin, D. I. (1978, May 19). Universal and particular in the acquisition of language. Paper presented at the University of Pennsylvania.

Slobin, D. I., & Welsh, C. A. (1973). Elicited imitation as a research tool in developmental psycholinguistics. In C. A. Ferguson & D. I. Slobin (Eds.), *Studies of child language development.* New York: Holt, Rinehart & Winston.

Smilansky, S. (1968). *The effects of sociodramatic play on disadvantaged preschool children.* New York: John Wiley & Sons.

Smith, C., & Lloyd, B. (1978). Maternal behavior and perceived sex of infant: Revisited. *Child Development, 49,* 1263–1265.

Smith, C. A. (1947). The effect of wartime starvation in Holland upon pregnancy and its product. *American Journal of Obstetrics and Gynecology, 53,* 599–606.

Smith, E. J. (1981). The working mother: A critique of the research. *Journal of Vocational Behavior, 19,* 191–211.

Smith, G. F., & Berg, J. (1976). *Down's anomaly* (2d ed.). New York: Churchill Livingstone.

Smith, P. K. (1982). Does play matter? Functional and evolutionary aspects of animal and human play. *The Behavioral and Brain Sciences, 5,* 139–184.

Smith, P. K., & Dutton, S. (1979). Play and training in direct and innovative problem solving. *Child Development, 50,* 830–836.

Smith, S. D., Kimberling, W. J., Pennington, B. F., & Lubs, H. A. (1983). Specific reading disability: Identification of an inherited form through linkage analysis. *Science, 219,* 1345–1347.

Snow, C. E. (1972). Mothers' speech to children learning language. *Child Development, 43,* 549–567.

Snow, C. E. (1977). The development of conversation between mothers and babies. *Journal of Child Language, 4,*1–22.

Snow, C. E., & Hoefnagel-Hohle, M. (1978). The critical period for language acquisition: Evidence from second language learning. *Child Development, 49,* 1114–1128.

Snow, C. E., Dubber, C., & deBlauw, A. (1982). Routines in mother-child interaction. In L. Feagans & D. C. Farran (Eds.), *The language of children reared in poverty.* New York: Academic Press.

Snow, J. (1853). On the administration of chloroform during parturition. *Association Medical Journal,* p. 500. As cited in Brackbill, Y. Obstetrical medication and infant behavior. In J. D. Osofsky (1979), *Handbook of infant development.* New York: John Wiley & Sons.

Sokol, R. J., Zabor, I., & Rosen, M. G. (1976). Slowing of active labor associated with internal fetal monitoring. *American Journal of Obstetrics and Gynecology, 124,* 764–765.

Solomons, G., & Solomons, H. C. (1975). Motor development in Yucatecan infants. *Developmental Medicine and Child Neurology, 35,* 1283–1295.

Sophian, C. (1980). Habituation is not enough: Novelty preferences, search, and memory in infancy. *Merrill Palmer Quarterly, 26,* 239–257.

Sophian, C. (1982). Selectivity and strategy in early search. *Journal of Experimental Child Psychology, 34,* 342–349.

Sorce, J. F., & Emde, R. N. (1981). Mother's presence is not enough: Effect of emotional availability on infant exploration. *Developmental Psychology, 17,* 737–745.

Sosa, R., Kennell, J., Klaus, M., Robertson, S., & Urrutia, J. (1980). The effect of a supportive companion on perinatal problems, length of labor and mother-infant interaction. *New England Journal of Medicine, 303,* 597–600.

Sosa, R., Klaus, M. H., Kennell, J. H., & Urrutia, J. J. (1976). The effect of early mother-infant contact on breastfeeding, infection and growth. In *Breastfeeding and the mother.* CIBA Foundation symposium 45, Amsterdam: Elsevier Publishing.

Sostek, A. M., & Anders, T. F. (1981). The biosocial importance and environmental sensitivity of infant sleep-wake behaviors. In K. Bloom (Ed.), *Prospective issues in infancy research.* Hillsdale, NJ: Lawrence Erlbaum.

Soyka, L. F., & Joffe, J. M. (1980). Male mediated drug effects on offspring. In R. H. Schwarz & S. J. Yaffe (Eds.), *Drug and chemical risks to the fetus and newborn.* New York: Alan R. Liss.

Spearman, C. (1927). *The abilities of man.* New York: Macmillan.

Spence, J. T., & Helmreich, R. L. (1983). Achievement-related motives and behaviors. In J. T. Spence (Ed.), *Achievement and achievement motives.* San Francisco: W. H. Freeman.

Spiro, M. (1963). Education in a communal village in Israel. In G. Spindler (Ed.), *Education and Culture.* New York: Holt, Rinehart & Winston.

Sprafkin, C., Serbin, L. A., & Elman, M. (1982). Sex typing of play and psychological adjustment in young children: An empirical investigation. *Journal of Abnormal Child Psychology, 10,* 559–568.

Sprafkin, J. N., & Rubinstein, E. A. (1982). Using television to improve the social behavior of institutionalized children. *Prevention in Human Services.* Cited by R. M. Liebert, J. N. Sprafkin, & E. S. Davidson (Eds.), *The early window.* Elmsford, NY: Pergamon Press.

Springer, S. P., & Deutsch, G. (1981). Left brain, right brain. San Francisco: W. H. Freeman.

Sroufe, L. A. (1979). The coherence of individual development: Early care, attachment, and subsequent developmental issues. *American Psychologist, 34,* 834–841.

Stanley, J. C, (1979). Identifying and nurturing the intellectually gifted. In W. C. George, S. J. Cohn, & J. C. Stanley (Eds.), *Educating the gifted: Acceleration and enrichment.* Baltimore: The Johns Hopkins Press.

Stanley, J. C. (1976). Identifying and nurturing the intellectually gifted. *Phi Delta Kappan, 58,* 234–237.

Stanley, J. C., & Benbow, C. P. (1982). Huge sex ratios at upper end. *American Psychologist, 37,* 972.

Stare, F. J., Whelan, E. M., & Sheridan, M. (1980). Diet and hyperactivity: Is there a relationship? *Pediatrics, 66,* 521–525.

Stark, R. E. (1981). *Language behavior in infancy and early childhood.* NY: Elsevier-North Holland Publishing.

Starkey, D. (1981). The origins of concept formation: Object sorting and object preference in early infancy. *Child Development, 52,* 489–497.

Starr, R. H., Jr. (1979). Child abuse. *American Psychologist, 34,* 872–879.

Staub, E., & Jancaterion, W. (1975). Teaching others, participation in prosocial action and prosocial induction as a means of children learning to be helpful. Cited in D. J. DePalma & J. M. Foley (Eds.), *Moral development, current theory and research.* Hillsdale, NJ: Lawrence Erlbaum.

Steele, M. W., & Berg, W. R. (1966). Choromosome analysis of human amniotic-fluid cells. *Lancet, 1*, 383–384.

Steinberg, L. D. (1981). Transformations in family relations at puberty. *Developmental Psychology, 17*, 833–840.

Steiner, J. E. (1979). Human facial expressions in response to taste and smell stimulation. In H. W. Reese & L. P. Lipsitt (Eds.), *Advances in child development and behavior* (Vol. 13). New York: Academic Press.

Steinman, S. (1981). The experience of children in a joint-custody arrangement: A report of a study. *American Journal of Orthopsychiatry, 51*, 403–414.

Stene, J. Fischer, G., Stene, E., Mikkelsen, M., & Petersen, E. (1977). Paternal age effect in Down's syndrome. *Annals of Human Genetics, 40*, 299–306.

Stephan, W. G. (1978). School desegregation: An evaluation of predictions made in Brown vs. Board of Education. *Psychological Bulletin, 85*, 217–235.

Sterman, M. B. (1972). The basic rest-activity cycle and sleep. In C. B. Clemente, D. P. Purpura, & F. E. Mayer (Eds.), *Sleep and the maturing nervous system.* New York: Academic Press.

Sterman, M. B. (1979). Ontogeny of sleep: Implications for function. In R. Drucker-Colin, M. Shkurovich, & M. B. Sterman (Eds.), *The functions of sleep.* New York: Academic Press.

Stern, C. (1973). *Principles of human genetics.* San Francisco: W. H. Freeman.

Stern, D. N. (1974). Mother and infant at play: The dyadic interaction involving facial, vocal, and gaze behaviors. In M. Lewis & L. A. Rosenblum (Eds), *The effect of the infant on its caregiver.* New York: John Wiley & Sons.

Stern, D. N. (1977). *The first relationship: Infant and mother.* Cambridge, MA: Harvard Univ. Press.

Stern, D. N. (1981). The development of biologically determined signals of readiness to communicate, which are language "resistant." In R. E. Stark (Ed.), *Language behavior in infancy and early childhood.* NY: Elsevier-North Holland Publishing.

Stern, L. (1981). In vivo assessment of the teratogenic potential of drugs in humans. *Obstetrics and Gynecology, 58*, 3s–8s.

Sternberg, R. J., Guyote, M. J., & Turner, M. E. (1980). Deductive Reasoning. In R. E. Snow, P. Federico, & W. E. Montague (Eds.), *Aptitude, learning and instruction: Cognitive process analyses of aptitude* (Vol. 1). Hillsdale, NJ: Lawrence Erlbaum.

Sternberg, S, (1966). High-speed scanning in human memory. *Science, 153*, 652–654.

Stevenson, H. W. (1970). Learning in children. In P. H. Mussen (Ed.), *Carmichael's manual of child psychology.* New York: John Wiley & Sons.

Stevenson, H. W., Parker, T., Wilkinson, A., Bonnevaux, B., & Gonzalez, M. (1978). Schooling, environment, and cognitive development: A cross-cultural study. *Monographs of the Society for Research in Child Development, 43*, No. 175.

Stevenson, H. W., Stigler, J. W., Lucker, G. W., & Lee, S. (1982). Reading disabilities: The case of Chinese, Japanese, and English. *Child Development, 53*, 1164–1181.

Stevenson, R. E. (1977). *The fetus and newly born infant.* St. Louis: C. V. Mosby.

Stewart, A., & Kneale, G. W. (1970). Radiation dose effects in relation to obstetric X-rays and childhood cancers. *Lancet, 1*, 1185–1188.

Stewart, E. D. (1981). Learning styles among gifted/talented students: Instructional technique preferences. *Exceptional Children, 48,* 134–138.

Stickle, G. (1981). Overview of incidence, risks and consequences of adolescent pregnancy and childbearing. In E. R. McAnarney & G. Stickle (Eds.), *Pregnancy and childbearing during adolescence.* New York: Alan R. Liss.

Stipek, D. J., & Hoffman, J. M. (1980). Children's achievement related expectancies as a function of academic performance histories and sex. *Journal of Educational Psychology, 72,* 861–865.

Stoll, C. (1981). Cytogenetic findings in 122 couples with recurrent abortions. *Human Genetics, 57,* 101–103.

Stott, D. H. (1971). The child's hazards in utero. In J. G. Howells (Ed.), *Modern perspectives in international child psychiatry.* New York: Bruner/Mazel.

Strauss, M. A., Gelles, R., & Steinmetz, S. (1980). *Behind closed doors.* Garden City, NY: Doubleday Publishing.

Streissguth, A. P., Herman, C. S., & Smith, D. W. (1978a). Intelligence, behavior, and dysmorphogenesis in the fetal alcohol syndrome: A report on 20 clinical cases. *Journal of Pediatrics, 92,* 363–367.

Streissguth, A. P., Herman, C. S., & Smith, D. W. (1978b). Stability of intelligence in the fetal alcohol syndrome: A preliminary report. *Alcoholism, 2,* 165–170.

Streissguth, A. P., Landesman-Dwyer, S., Martin, J. C., & Smith, D. W. (1980). Teratogenic effects of alcohol in humans and laboratory animals. *Science, 209,* 353–361.

Stromeyer, C. F. (1982). An adult eidetiker. In U. Neisser (Ed.), *Memory observed.* San Francisco: W. H. Freeman.

Strommen, E. A., McKinney, J. P., & Fitzgerald, H. E. (1983). *Developmental psychology: The school-aged child.* Homewood, IL: Dorsey Press.

Sudia, C. E. (1981). What services do abusive and neglecting families need? In L. H. Pelton (Ed.), *The social context of child abuse and neglect.* New York: Human Sciences Press.

Sumner, P. E., & Phillips, C. R. (1981). *Birthing Rooms: Concept and reality.* St. Louis: C. V. Mosby.

Suomi, S. J. (1977). Adult male-infant interactions among monkeys living in nuclear families. *Child Development, 48,* 1255–1271.

Suomi, S. J., & Harlow, H. F. (1977). Early separation and behavioral maturation. In A. Oliverio (Ed.), *Genetics, environment, and intelligence.* Amsterdam: North-Holland, Scientific Publishers, Elsevier.

Sutherland, G. R., & Hinton, L. (1981). Heritable fragile sites on human chromosomes. *Human Genetics, 57,* 217–219.

Sutton, W. S. (1903). The chromosomes in heredity. *Biological Bulletin, 4,* 24–39.

Svanum, S., Bringle, R. G., & McLaughlin, J. E, (1982). Father absence and cognitive performance in a large sample of six to eleven year-old children. *Child Development, 53,* 136–143.

Svare, B. (1983). Psychobiological determinants of maternal aggressive behavior. In E. C. Simmel, M. E. Hahn, & J. K. Walters (Eds.), *Aggressive behavior: Genetic and neural approaches.* Hillsdale, NJ: Lawrence Erlbaum.

Svejda, M. J., Campos, J. J., & Emde, K. N. (1980). Mother-infant "bonding": Failure to generalize. *Child Development, 51*, 775–779.

Swanson, J. M., & Kinsbourne, M, (1980). Food dyes impair performance of hyperactive children on a laboratory learning test. *Science, 207*, 1485–1487.

Sylva, K. (1977). Play and learning. In B. Tizard & D. Harvey (Eds.), *The biology of play*. Philadelphia: J. B. Lippincott.

Sylva, K., Bruner, J. S., & Genova, P. (1976). The relationship between play and problem solving in children three to five years old. In J. S. Bruner, A. Jolly, & K. Sylva (Eds.), *Play*. New York: Basic Books.

Symons, D. (1978). *Play and aggression: A study of rhesus monkeys*. New York: Columbia University press.

Takashima, S., & Asakura, T. (1983). Desickling of sickled erythrocytes by pulsed radio-frequency field. *Science, 220*, 411–413.

Tanner, J. M. (1978). *Fetus into man: Physical growth from conception to maturity*. Cambridge, MA: Harvard Univ. Press.

Tavris, C., & Offir, C. (1977). *The longest war: Sex differences in perspective*. New York: Harcourt Brace Jovanovich.

Teberg, A. J., Wu, P. Y., Hodgman, J. E., Mich, C., Garfinkle, J., Azen, S., & Wingert, W. A. (1982). Infants with birth weights under 1500 grams: Physical, neurological, and developmental outcome. *Critical Care Medicine, 10*, 10–14.

Terman, L. M, (1925). *Genetic studies of genius* (Vol. 1). Stanford, CA: Stanford University Press.

Terman, L. M., & Merrill, M. A, (1972). *Stanford-Binet Intelligence Scale*. Boston: Houghton Mifflin.

Terman, L. M., & Oden, M. H. (1947). *Genetic studies of genius: The gifted child grows up* (Vol. 4). Stanford, CA: Stanford University Press.

Terman, L. M., & Oden, M. H. (1959). *Genetic Studies of Genius: The gifted group at mid-life* (Vol. 5). Stanford, CA: Stanford University Press.

Terrace, H. S. (1979). *Nim*. New York: Alfred A. Knopf.

Terrace, H. S. (1981). A report to an academy. *Annals of the New York Academy of Sciences, 364*, 94–114.

Test-tube baby: It's a girl. (1978, August 7). *Time*, p. 68.

Tetzlaff, J. M. (1982, June 20). An album of proud fathers. *Press Enterprise*, Section 3, p. 1.

Thelen, E. (1981). Rhythmical behavior in infancy: An ethological perspective. *Developmental Psychology, 17*, 237–257.

Therman, E. (1980). *Human chromosomes: Structure, behavior, effects*. New York: Springer-Verlag New York.

Thoman, E. B. (1981). Affective communication as the prelude and context for language learning. In R. L. Schiefelbusch & D. D. Bricker (Eds.), *Early language: Acquisition and intervention*. Baltimore: University Park Press.

Thomas, A., & Chess, S. (1977). *Temperament and development*. New York: Bruner/Mazel.

Thomas, A., & Chess, S. (1980). *The dynamics of psychological development*. New York: Bruner/Mazel.

Thomas, A., & Chess, S. (1981). The role of temperament in the contributions of individuals to their development. In R. M. Lerner & N. A. Busch-Rossnagel (Eds.), *Individuals as producers of their development*. New York: Academic Press.

Thomas, A., & Chess, S. (1984). *Origins and evolution of behavior disorders*. New York: Bruner/Mazel.

Thomas, A., Chess, S. Birch, H. G., Hartzig, M. E., & Korn, S. (1963). *Behavioral individuality in early childhood*. New York: New York University Press.

Thomas, A., Chess, S., & Korn, S. J. (1982). The reality of difficult temperament. *Merrill Palmer Quarterly, 28*, 1–20.

Thomas, A., Chess, S., Sillen, J., & Mendez, O. (1974). Cross-cultural study of behavior in children with special vulnerabilities to stress. In D. Ricks, A. Thomas, & M. Roff (Eds.), *Life history research in psychopathology* (Vol. 3). Minneapolis, MN: University of Minnesota Press.

Thomas, H. (1982). A strong developmental theory of field dependence-independence. *Journal of Mathematical Psychology, 26*, 169–178.

Thomas, N. G., & Berk, L. E. (1981). Effects of school environments on the development of young children's creativity. *Child Development, 52*, 1153–1162.

Thompson, J. S., & Thompson, M. W. (1980). *Genetics in medicine*. Philadelphia: J. B. Saunders.

Thompson, R. A. (1983). The father's case in child custody disputes: The contributions of psychological research. In M. E. Lamb & A. Sagi (Eds.), *Fatherhood and family policy*. Hillsdale, NJ: Lawrence Erlbaum.

Thompson, R. A., Lamb, M. E., & Estes, D. (1982). Stability of infant-mother attachment and its relationship to changing life circumstances in an unselected middle-class sample. *Child Development, 53*, 144–148.

Thompson, R. J. (1979). Effects of maternal alcohol consumption on offspring: Review, critical assessment, and future directions. *Journal of Pediatric Psychology, 4*, 265–277.

Thomson, M. E., Hartsock, T. G., & Larson, C. (1979). The importance of immediate postnatal contact: Its effect on breastfeeding. *Canadian Family Physician, 15*, 1374–1378.

Thornton, R. R. (1981). Home delivery: How safe? *South Dakota Journal of Medicine, 34*, 17–18.

Tieger, T. (1980). On the biological basis of sex differences in aggression. *Child development, 51*, 943–963.

Tinbergen, N. (1951). *The study of instinct*. London: Oxford University Press.

Tinbergen, N. (1963). *Animal behavior*. Alexandria, VA.: Time-Life Books.

Tipton, R. H., & Lewis, B. W. (1975). Induction of labour and perinatal mortality. *British Medical Journal, 1*, 391.

Tjio, J. H., & Levan, A. (1965). The chromosome number of man. *Hereditas, 42*, 1–6.

Todd, C. M., & Perlmutter, M. (1980). Reality recalled by preschool children. In M. Perlmutter (Ed.), *Children's memory*. San Francisco: Jossey-Bass.

Tomlinson-Keasey, C. (1982). Structures, functions and stages: A trio of unresolved issues in formal operations. In S. Modgil & C. Modgil (Eds.), *Jean Piaget: Consensus and Controversy*. New York: Holt, Rinehart & Winston.

Tomlinson-Keasey, C., & Smith-Winberry, C. (1983, April). An integration deficit in deaf children. Paper presented at Society for Research In Child Development, Detroit, MI.

Tomlinson-Keasey, C., Eisert, D., Kahle, L., Hardy-Brown, K., & Keasey, C. B. (1979). The structure of concrete operational thought. *Child Development, 50,* 1058–1068.

Torgeson, J. (1980). Implications of the LD child's use of efficient task strategies. *Journal of Learning Disabilities, 13,* 364–371.

Townes, P. L., Ziegler, N. A., & Lenhard, L. W. (1965). A patient with 48 chromosomes (XYYY). *Lancet, 1,* 1041–1043.

Traxel, W. L, (1982). Hyperactivity and the Feingold diet. *Archives of General Psychiatry, 39,* 624.

Tsubaki, T., & Irukayama, K. (1976). *Minamata disease.* New York: Elsevier-North-Holland Publishing.

Tulkin, S. R., & Konner, M. J. (1973). Alternative conceptions of intellectual functioning. *Human Development, 16,* 33–52.

Tumulty, K. (1984, February 25). Insufficient evidence cited on Agent Orange. *Los Angeles Times,* Section 1, p. 1.

Turiel, J. (1981). The doctors I can't forgive. *Redbook, 156,* 44–50.

Turkewitz, G. (1977). The development of lateral differentiation in the human infant. *Annals of the New York Academy of Science, 299,* 309–317.

Turnbull, C. M. (1972). *The mountain people.* New York: Simon & Schuster.

Turner, W. (1979, March 9). Conflict over forest spray and childbirth. *The New York Times,* Section 1, p. 16.

Twentyman, C. T., & Plotkin, R. C. (1982). Unrealistic expectations of parents who maltreat their children: An educational deficit that pertains to child development. *Journal of Clinical Psychology, 38,* 497–503.

U.S. Department of Health and Human Services. (1981). *The health consequences of smoking: The changing cigarette: A report of the Surgeon General.* Washington, DC: U.S. Government Printing Office.

U.S. Department of Health Education and Welfare. (1979). *Facts of life and Death.* DHEW Publication No. 79–122. Washington, DC: U.S. Government Printing Office.

U.S. Department of Health Education and Welfare. (1979). *Prenatal development of the human with special reference to cranial facial structures: An atlas.* DHEW publication No (NIH) 77–946. Washington, DC: U.S. Government Printing Office.

U.S. Office of Education. (1972). *Education of the gifted and talented: Report to the congress.* Washington, DC: U.S. Government Printing Office.

Uchida, I. A. (1979). Radiation-induced nondisjunction. *Environmental Health Perspectives, 31,* 13–17.

Uchida, I. A., & Curtis, E. J. (1961). A possible association between maternal radiation and mongolism. *Lancet, 2,* 848–850.

Ulian, D. Z. (1976). The development of conceptions of masculinity and femininity. In B. Lloyd & J. Archer (Eds.), *Exploring sex differences.* London: Academic Press.

Underwood, B. J. (1982). False recognition produced by implicit verbal responses. In B. J. Underwood (Ed.), *Studies in learning and memory.* New York: Praeger Publishers.

United Press International. (1982). Homicides affecting children under 14. National center for disease control.

Urrutia, J. J., Sosa, R., Kennell, J. H., & Klaus, M. H. (1980). Prevalence of maternal and neonatal infections in a developing country: Possible low-cost preventive measures. *CIBA Foundation Symposium 77.* Amsterdam: Exerpta Medica.

Uzgiris, I. C. (1976). Organization of sensorimotor intelligence. In M. Lewis (Eds.), *Origins of intelligence.* New York: Plenum Publishing.

Valenti, C. Shutta, E. F., & Kehaty, T. (1969). Cytogenetic diagnosis of Down's syndrome in utero. *Journal of American Medical Association, 207,* 1513–1514.

van den Berg, B. J. (1977). Epidemiologic observations of prematurity: Effects of tobacco, coffee, and alcohol. In D. M. Reed & F. J. Stanley (Eds.), *Epidemiology of Prematurity* (pp. 157–176). Baltimore: Urban and Schwarzenberg.

van Lawick-Goodall, J. (1973). Cultural elements in a chimpanzee community. In E. W. Menzel (Ed.), *Precultural primate behavior.* Basel, Switzerland: S. Karger.

Vandell, D. L., Wilson, K. S., & Buchanan, N. R. (1980). Peer interaction in the first year of life: An examination of its structure, content, and sensitivity to toys. *Child Development, 51,* 481–488.

Vandenberg, B. (1981). The role of play in the development of insightful tool-using strategies. *Merrill Palmer Quarterly, 27,* 97–109.

Vaughan, R. (1981). Coffee in pregnancy. *Lancet, 1,* 554.

Vaughn, B. E., & Waters, E. (1981). Attention structure, sociometric status, and dominance: Interrelations, behavioral correlates, and relationships to social competence. *Developmental Psychology, 17,* 275–288.

Vaughn, B. E., Gove, S., & Egeland, B. (1980). The relationship between out-of-home care and the quality of infant-mother attachment in an economically disadvantaged population. *Child Development, 51,* 1203–1214.

Veridiano, N. P., Delke, I., Rogers, J., & Tancer, M. L. (1981). Reproductive performance of DES-exposed female progeny. *Obstetrics and Gynecology, 58,* 58–61.

Vernon, P. A, (1981). Reaction time and intelligence in the mentally retarded. *Intelligence, 3,* 345–355.

Vietze, P., Falsey, S., Sandler, H., O'Connor, S., & Altemeier, W. A. (1980). Transactional approach to prediction of child maltreatment. *Infant Mental Health Journal, 1,* 248–261.

Visher, E. B., & Visher, J. S. (1979). *Stepfamilies: A guide to working with stepparents and stepchildren.* New York: Bruner/Mazel.

von Senden, M. (1960). *Space and sight.* Translated by P. Heath. New York: Free Press.

Voyat, G. E. (1982). *Piaget systematized.* Hillsdale, NJ: Lawrence Erlbaum.

Vygotsky, L. S. (1962). *Thought and Language.* Cambridge, MA: MIT Press.

Waber, D. P. (1979a). The ontogeny of higher cortical functions: Implications for sex differences in cognition. In M. A. Wittig & A. C. Petersen (Eds.), *Sex-related differences in cognitive functioning.* New York: Academic Press.

Waber, D. P. (1979b). Cognitive abilities and sex related variations in the maturation of cerebral cortical functions. In M. A. Wittig & A. C. Petersen (Eds.), *Sex-related differences in cognitive functioning.* New York: Academic press.

Wachs, T. D., & Hubert, N. C. (1981). Changes in the structure of cognitive-intellectual performance during the second year of life. *Infant Behavior and Development, 4*, 151–161.

Wada, J. A., Clarke, R., & Hamm, A. (1975). Cerebral hemispheric asymmetry in humans. *Archives of Neurology, 32*, 239–246.

Waddington, C. H. (1962). *New patterns in genetics and development.* New York: Columbia University Press.

Wahler, R. G. (1980). The insular mother: Her problems in parent-child treatment. *Journal of Applied Behavior Analysis, 13*, 207–219.

Walden, T. A., & Ramey, C. T., (1983). Locus of control and academic achievement: Results from a preschool intervention program. *Journal of Educational Psychology, 75*, 347–358.

Waldvogel, S. (1982). Childhood memories. In U. Neisser (Ed.), *Memory observed.* San Francisco: W. H. Freeman.

Wallach, M. A., & Kogan, N. (1965). *Modes of thinking in young children.* New York: Holt, Rinehart & Winston.

Wallerstein, J. S. (1983, November 6). Divorce trauma found to be lasting on child. *Press Enterprise*, Section A-3.

Wallerstein, J. S., & Kelly, J. B. (1980). *Surviving the breakup: How children and parents cope with divorce.* New York: Basic Books.

Walter, T., Kovalskys, J., & Stekel, A, (1983). Effects of mild iron deficiency on infant mental development scores. *The Journal of Pediatrics, 102*, 519–522.

Warner, R., & Rosett, H. (1975). The effects of drinking on offspring: An historical survey of the American and British literature. *Journal of Studies on Alcohol, 36*, 1395–1420.

Warren, D. I. (1981). Support systems in different types of neighborhoods. In J. Garbarino & S. H. Stocking (Eds.), *Protecting children from abuse and neglect.* San Francisco: Jossey-Bass.

Warren, N. (1972). African infant precocity. *Psychological Bulletin, 78*, 353–367.

Warshak, R. A., & Santrock, J. W. (1983). Children of divorce: Impact of custody disposition on social development. *Life-span developmental psychology: Nonnormative life events.* New York: Academic Press.

Wasz-Hoechert, O., Lind, J., Vuorenoski, T., Partanen, T., & Valanne, E. (1968). *The infant cry.* London: Heinemann Educational Books.

Waters, E. (1978). The reliability and stability of individual differences in infant-mother attachment. *Child Development, 49*, 483–494.

Waters, E., & Sroufe, L. A. (1983). Social competence as a developmental construct. *Developmental Review, 3*, 79–97.

Waters, E., Vaughn, B. E., & Egeland, B. R. (1980). Individual differences in infant-mother attachment relationships at age one: Antecedents in neonatal behavior in an urban, economically disadvantaged sample. *Child Development, 51*, 208–216.

Waters, H. S. (1982). Memory development in adolescence: Relationships between metamemory, strategy use, and performance. *Journal of Experimental Child Psychology, 33,* 183–195.

Watson, J. B. (1928). *Psychological care of infant and child.* New York: W. W. Norton.

Watson, J. B., & Rayner, R. (1920). Conditioned emotional reactions. *Journal of Experimental Psychology, 3,* 1–14.

Watson, J. D. (1968). *The double helix.* New York: Signet.

Watson, J. D., & Crick, F. H. (1953). Molecular structure of nucleic acids: A structure for deoxyribose nucleic acid. *Nature, 171,* 737–738.

Watson, J. S. (1971). Cognitive-perceptual development in infancy: Setting for the seventies. *Merrill Palmer Quarterly, 17,* 139–152.

Watson, J. S. (1972). Smiling, cooing, and "the game." *Merrill Palmer Quarterly, 18,* 323–341.

Watson, J. S. (1982). Memory in infancy. In J. Piaget, J. P. Bronkart, & P. Mounoud (Eds.), *Encyclopedia de la pleidade: La psychologie.* Paris: Gallimard.

Watson, J. S., & Ramey, C. T. (1972). Reactions to response-contingent stimulation in early infancy. *Merrill Palmer Quarterly, 18,* 219–228.

Weatherall, D. J., Higgs, D. R., Bunch, C., Old, J. M., Hunt, D. M., Pressley, L., Clegg, J. B., Bethlenfalvay, N. C., Sjolin, S., Koler, R. D., Magenis, E., Francis, J. L., & Bebbington, D. (1981). Hemoglobin-H disease and mental retardation: A new syndrome or a remarkable coincidence. *New England Journal of Medicine, 305,* 607–612.

Weathersbee, P. S., Olsen, L. K., & Lodge, T. R. (1977). Caffeine and pregnancy. *Postgraduate Medicine, 62,* 64–69.

Webb, N. M. (1984). Sex differences in interaction and achievement in cooperative small groups. *Journal of Educational Psychology, 76,* 33–44.

Weiner, P. C., Hogg, M. I. J., & Rosen, M. (1977). Effects of naloxone on pethidine induced neonatal depression. Part II—Intramuscular naloxone. *British Medical Journal, 11,* 229–231.

Weiner, P. C., Hogg, M. I. J., & Rosen, M. (1979). Neonatal respiration feeding and neurobehavioral state. Effects of intrapartum bupivacaine pethidine and pethidine reversed by naloxone. *Anaesthesia, 34,* 996–1004.

Weir, R. (1962). *Language in the crib.* The Hague: Mouton.

Weisenberg, M. (1977). Pain and pain control. *Psychological Bulletin, 84,* 1008–1044.

Weiss, R. S. (1979). Growing up a little faster: The experience of growing up in a single-parent household. *The Journal of Social Issues, 35,* 97–111.

Weissbluth, M. (1981). Sleep duration and infant temperament. *Journal of Pediatrics, 99,* 817–819.

Weisz, J. R., & McGuire, M. (1980). *Sex differences in the relation between attributions and learned helplessness in children.* Unpublished manuscript. University of North Carolina, Chapel Hill.

Weitkamp, L. R., Stancer, H. C., Persad, E., Flood, C., & Guttorms, S. (1981). Depressive disorders and HLA-A gene on chromosome 6 that can affect behavior. *New England Journal of Medicine, 305,* 1301–1306.

Welch, R. L. (1983). The effects of perceived "task gender" and induced success/failure upon subsequent task performance of psychologically androgynous and highly feminine women. *Dissertation Abstracts International, 43,* (12-b), p. 4166.

Wellman, H. M., Ritter, R., & Flavell, J. H. (1975). Deliberate memory behavior in the delayed reactions of very young children. *Developmental Psychology, 48,* 780–787.

Werner, E. E., & Smith, R. S. (1977). *Kauai's children come of age.* Honolulu: University of Hawaii Press.

Werner, E. E., & Smith, R. S. (1979). An epidemiologic perspective on some antecedents and consequences of childhood mental health problems and learning disabilities. *Journal of the American Academy of Child Psychiatry, 18,* 292–306.

Werner, E. E., & Smith, R. S. (1982). *Vulnerable but invincible.* New York: McGraw-Hill.

Werner, H. (1948). *Comparative psychology of mental development.* New York: International Universities Press.

Werner, J. S., & Perlmutter, M. (1979). Development of visual memory in infants. In H. W. Reese & L. P. Lipsitt (Eds.), *Advances in child development* (Vol. 13). New York: Academic Press.

West, C., & Anderson, T. (1976). The question of preponderant causation in teacher expectancy research. *Review of Educational Research, 46,* 613–630.

Whitaker, H. A., Bub, D., & Leventer, S. (1981). Neurolinguistic aspects of language acquisition and bilingualism. *Annals of the New York Academy of Sciences, 379,* 59–74.

White, B. L. (1971). *Human infants: Experience and psychological development.* Englewood Cliffs, NJ: Prentice-Hall.

White, B. L. (1978). *Experience and environment* (Vol. 2). Englewood Cliffs, NJ: Prentice-Hall.

White, B. L., & Watts, J. (1973). *Experience and environment* (Vol. 1). Englewood Cliffs, NJ: Prentice-Hall.

White, K. D., Ashton, R., & Lewis, S. (1979). Learning a complex skill: Effects of mental practice, physical practice, and imagery ability. *International Journal of Sport Psychology, 10,* 71–78.

White, K. R. (1982). The relation between socioeconomic status and academic achievement. *Psychological Bulletin, 91,* 461–481.

White, R. (1959). Motivation reconsidered: The concept of competence. *Psychological Review, 66,* 297–333.

Whiteley, J. H. (1981). Canadian research on infant development. *Canadian Psychology, 22,* 55–68.

Whiting, B. B., & Edwards, C. P. (1973). A cross-cultural analysis of the behavior of children aged 3-11. *Journal of Social Psychology, 91,* 171–188.

Whiting, B., & Whiting, J. W. M. (1975). *Children of six cultures.* Cambridge, MA: Harvard Univ. Press.

Whitley, B. E. (1983). Sex role orientation and self-esteem: A critical meta-analytic review. *Journal of Personality and Social Psychology, 44,* 765–778.

Whitley, R. J., Nahmias, A. J., Soong, S. Galasso, G. G., Fleming, C. L., & Alford, C. A. (1980). Vidarabine therapy of neonatal herpes simplex virus infection. *Pediatrics, 66,* 495–501.

Widdowson, E. M. (1951). Mental contentment and physical growth. *Lancet, 1,* 1316–1318.

Wiesenfeld, A. R., Malatesta, C. A., & DeLoach, L. L. (1981). Differential parental response to familiar and unfamiliar infant distress signals. *Infant Behavior and Development, 4,* 281–295.

Wiggins, R. C. (1982). Myelin development and nutritional insufficiency. *Brain Research Reviews, 4,* 151–175.

Wilkie, J. R. (1981). The trend toward delayed parenthood. *Journal of Marriage and the Family, 43,* 584–591.

Willcourt, R., & Queenan, J. T. (1981). Fetal scalp blood sampling and trascutaneous PO2. *Clinics in Perinatology, 8,* 87–99.

Willerman, L. (1979). Effects of families on intellectual development. *American Psychologist, 34,* 923–929.

Willerman, L., & Fiedler, M. F, (1977). Intellectually precocious preschool children: Early development and later intellectual accomplishments. *Journal of Genetic Psychology, 131,* 13–20.

Williams, C. D. (1959). The elimination of tantrum behavior by extinction procedures. *Journal of Abnormal and Social Psychology, 59,* 269–274.

Williams, G. J. (1980a). Child abuse and neglect: Problems of definition and incidence. In G. J. Williams & J. Money (Eds.), *Traumatic abuse and neglect of children at home.* Baltimore: The Johns Hopkins Press.

Williams, G. J. (1980b). Cruelty and kindness to children: Documentary of a century, 1874–1974. In G. J. Williams & J. Money (Eds.), *Traumatic abuse and neglect of children at home.* Baltimore: The Johns Hopkins Press.

Wilson, E. O. (1975). *Sociobiology: The new synthesis.* Cambridge, MA: Harvard Univ. Press.

Wilson, G. S., Desmond, M. M., & Verniaud, W. M. (1973). Early development of infants of heroin-addicted mothers. *American Journal of Diseases in Children, 126,* 457–462.

Wilson, H. (1980). Parental supervision: A neglected aspect of delinquency. *British Journal of Criminology, 20,* 203–235.

Wilson, R. S. (1976). Concordance in physical growth for monozygotic and dizygotic twins. *Annals of Human Biology, 3,* 1–10.

Wilson, R. S. (1983). The Louisville twin study: Developmental synchronies in behavior. *Child Development, 54,* 298–316.

Winchester, A. M. (1971). *Human genetics,* Columbus, OH: Charles E. Merrill Publishing.

Winick, M. (1979). Malnutrition and mental development. In M. Winick (Ed.), *Nutrition: Pre- and postnatal development.* New York: Plenum Press.

Winick, M. (1980). *Nutrition in health and disease.* New York: John Wiley & Sons.

Winick, M., & Rosso, P. (1969). The effects of severe early malnutrition on cellular growth of human brain. *Pediatric Research, 3,* 181–185.

Winick, M., & Rosso, P. (1975). Malnutrition and central nervous system development. In J. W. Prescott, M. S. Read, & D. B. Coursin (Eds.), *Brain function and malnutrition: Neuropsychological methods of assessment.* New York: John Wiley & Sons.

Winick, M., Meyer, K. K., & Harris, R. C. (1975). Malnutrition and environmental enrichment by early adoption. *Science, 190,* 1173–1175.

Witkin, H. A., & Goodenough, D. R. (1981). *Cognitive styles: Essence and origins.* New York: International Universities Press.

Witkin, H. A., Mednick. S. A., Schulsinger, F., Bakkestrom, E., Christiansen, K. O., Goodenough, D. R., Hirschhorn, K., Lundsteen, C., Owen, D. R., Philip, J., Rubin, D. B., & Stocking, M. (1976). Criminality in XYY and XXY men. *Science, 193,* 547–555.

Witter, F., & King, T. M. (1980). Cigarettes and pregnancy. In R. H. Schwarz & S. J. Yaffe (Eds.), *Drug and chemical risks to the fetus and the newborn.* New York: Alan R. Liss.

Wittrock, M. C. (1980). Learning and the Brain. In M. C. Wittrock (Ed.), *The brain and Psychology.* New York: Academic Press.

Wohlwill, J. F. (1973). *The study of behavioral development.* New York: Academic Press.

Wolf, D., & Gardner, H. (1981). On the structure of early symbolization. In R. L. Schiefelbusch & D. D. Bricker (Eds.), *Early language: Acquisition and intervention.* Baltimore: University Park Press.

Wolfe, D. A., & Sandler, J. (1981). Training abusive parents in effective child management. *Behavior Modification, 5,* 320–335.

Wolff, P. H. (1969). The natural history of crying and other vocalizations in infancy. In B. M. Foss (Ed.), *Determinants of infant behavior* (Vol. 4). London: Methuen.

Wolff, P. H. (1981). Normal variation in human maturation. In H. F. R. Prechtl & K. J. Connolly (Eds.), *Maturation and development: Biological and psychological perspectives.* Philadelphia: J. B. Lippincott.

Wolff, P., Levin, J. R., & Longobardi, E. T. (1974). Activity and children's learning. *Child Development, 45,* 221–223.

Wolff, P. & Levin, J. R. (1972). The role of overt activity in children's imagery production. *Child Development, 43,* 537–547.

Wood, S., Moriarty, K. M., Gardner, B. T., & Gardner, R. A. (1980). Object permanence in child and chimpanzee. *Animal Learning and Behavior, 8,* 3–9.

Woolridge, P., Hall, L., Hughes, L., Rauch, T., Stewart, G., & Richman, C. L. (1982). *Bulletin of the Psychonomic Society, 20,* 249–252.

World Health Organization. (1951). Expert Committee on Mental Health, Report of the Second Session, Technical Report Series No. 31 WHO Monograph, Geneva.

Worthington, E. L., & Martin, G. A. (1980). A laboratory analysis of response to pain after training in three Lamaze techniques. *Journal of Psychosomatic Research, 24,* 109–116.

Wright, J. C., & Huston, A. C. (1983). A matter of form: Potentials of television for young viewers. *American Psychologist, 38,* 835–843.

Wurtman, R. J., & Wurtman, J. J. (1977). *Nutrition and the brain: Determinants of the availability of nutrients to the brain* (Vol. 1). New York: Raven Press.

Yakovlev, P. I., & LeCours, A. (1967). The myelogenetic cycles of regional maturation of the brain. In A. Minkowski (Ed.), *Regional development of the brain in early life.* Philadelphia: F. A. Davis.

Yarrow, M. R., Scott, P., & Waxler, C. Z. (1973). Learning concern for others. *Developmental Psychology, 8,* 240–260.

Yogman, M. W., Dixon, S., Tronick. E., Als, H., & Brazelton, T. B. (1979,

March). The goals and structure of face-to-face interaction between infants and fathers. Paper presented to the Society for Research in Child Development, New Orleans, LA.

Yonge, G. D, (1982). Some concerns about the estimation of learning potential from the system of multicultural pluralistic assessment. *Psychology in the Schools, 19,* 482–486.

Yoonessi, M., Mariniello, D. A., Wieckowska, W. S., Angtuaco, M. G., & Diesfeld, P. (1981). DES Story, *New York State Journal of Medicine, 81,* 195–198.

Youth learned it all at home. (1983, August 30). *Los Angeles Times,* Section 3, p. 3.

Yule, W., Gold, R. D., & Busch, C, (1982). Long-term predictive validity of the WPPSI: An 11-year follow-up study. *Personality and Individual Differences, 3,* 65–71.

Yunis, J. J., & Prakash, O. (1982). The origin of man: A chromosomal pictorial legacy. *Science, 215,* 1525–1530.

Zabel, R. H., & Zabel, M. K. (1982). Ethological approaches with autistic and other abnormalities. *Journal of Autism and Developmental Disorders, 12,* 71–83.

Zahavi, S. L., & Asher, S. R. (1978). The effect of verbal instructions on preschool children's aggressive behavior. *Journal of School Psychology, 16,* 146–153.

Zahn-Waxler, C., Friedman, S. L., & Cummings, E. M. (1983). Children's emotions and behaviors in response to infants' cries. *Child Development, 54,* 1522–1528.

Zahn-Waxler, C., Radke-Yarrow, M., & King, R. A. (1979). Child rearing and children's prosocial initiations toward victims of distress. *Child Development, 50,* 319–330.

Zajonc, R., & Markus, G. B, (1976). Birth order and intellectual development. *Psychological Review, 82,* 74–88.

Zamenhof, S., & Van Marthens, E. (1978). Nutritional influences on prenatal brain development. In G. Gottlieb (Ed.), *Early influences: Studies on the development of behavior and the nervous system.* New York: Academic Press.

Zeigler, E., & Berman, W. (1983). Discerning the future of early childhood intervention. *American Psychologist, 38,* 894–906.

Zeigler, M. E, (1979). The father's influence on his school-age child's academic performance and cognitive development (Doctoral dissertation, University of Michigan).

Zelazo, P. R. (1976). From reflexive to instrumental behavior. In L. P. Lipsett (Ed.), *Developmental psychobiology.* Hillsdale, NJ: Lawrence Erlbaum.

Zelazo, P. R., & Kearsley, R. B. (1980). The emergence of functional play in infants: Evidence for a major cognitive transition. *Journal of Applied Developmental Psychology, 2,* 85–117.

Zelazo, P. R., Zelazo, N. A., & Kolb, S. (1972). "Walking" in the newborn. *Science, 176,* 314–315.

Zellweger, H., & Simpson, J. (1977). *Chromosomes of man.* London: William Heinemann, Medical Books.

Zelnik, M. (1981). Sexual activity among adolescents. In E. R. McAnarney & G. Stickle (Eds.), *Pregnancy and childbearing during adolescence.* New York: Alan R. Liss.

Zelniker, T., & Jeffrey, W. E. (1979). Attention and cognitive style in children. In G. A. Hale & M. Lewis (Eds.), *Attention and cognitive development.* New York: Plenum Publishing.

Zeskind, P. S. (1980). Adult responses to cries of low and high risk infants. *Infant Behavior and Development, 3,* 167–177.

Zigler, E. (1975, January 18). Letter to the editor. *New York Times Magazine.*

Zivin, G. (1979). Removing common confusions about egocentric speech, private speech, and self-regulation. *The development of self-regulation through private speech.* New York: John Wiley & Sons.

# Name Index

# Subject Index

*This book has been set by Linotron 202, in 10 point
Avanta, leaded 2 points. Chapter numbers are 16
point Spectra Extra Bold and chapter titles are 18
point Spectra. Part numbers are 16 point Spectra
Extra Bold and part titles are 18 point Spectra. The
size of the type page is 37 by 48 picas.*